D0077795

Global Strategic Management

Global Strategic Management

Gerardo R. Ungson and Yim-Yu Wong

M.E.Sharpe
Armonk, New York
London, England

HD
30.28
.U535
2008

7084406

Copyright © 2008 by M.E. Sharpe, Inc.

All rights reserved. No part of this book may be reproduced in any form
without written permission from the publisher, M.E. Sharpe, Inc.,
80 Business Park Drive, Armonk, New York 10504.

Library of Congress Cataloging-in-Publication Data

Ungson, Gerardo R.
  Global strategic management / by Gerardo R. Ungson and Yim-Yu Wong.
    p. cm.
  Includes bibliographical references and index.
  ISBN 978-0-7656-1688-3 (pbk. : alk. paper)
  1. Strategic planning. 2. Globalization—Economic aspects. I. Wong, Yim-Yu. II. Title.

HD30.28.U535 2007
658.4'012—dc22   2006024565

Printed in the United States of America

The paper used in this publication meets the minimum requirements of
American National Standard for Information Sciences
Permanence of Paper for Printed Library Materials,
ANSI Z 39.48-1984.

BM (p)   10   9   8   7   6   5   4   3   2   1

To Gerardo's grandparents:
Dr. Victoriano Ungson, Sr., and Ma. Corazon de Castro Ungson
Casiano Rivera, Sr., and Marina Bañez Rivera

To Yim-Yu's parents:
Bak Wai Wong and Shuk Ching Lui

Contents

Preface and Acknowledgments   xiii

Part I. The Global Context

1. Global Strategic Management: An Overview   3
   Two Global Scenarios   3
   The Changing Competitive Landscape   5
   Key Challenges Facing Managers   7
   Defining Globalization   9
   The Dark Side of Globalization   9
   Globalization in a Historical Context   13
   A Synthesis of Globalization: Implications for Management   26
   The Global Imperative   28
   A Framework for Global Strategic Management   30
   Summary   35
   Key Terms   36
   Discussion Questions   37
   Action Item 1.1. A Thought Experiment   37
   Case-in-Point. Starbucks in Shanghai: Examining the
     Dynamics of Global Expansion   37

Part II. External/Internal Analysis

2. Analyzing the External Environment   47
   Nanotechnology: A New Industrial Frontier?   47
   The Changing External Environment   49
   Macroenvironmental Analysis   50

Industry Analysis: Five Forces of Competition   56
The Role of Complementors   67
Analyzing an Industry's Globalization Potential   71
Antitrust: A Cautionary Note   80
Implications   81
Summary   82
Key Terms   83
Discussion Questions   84
Action Item 2.1. PEST Analysis   84
Action Item 2.2. Understanding Industry Dynamics   85
Case-in-Point. The Semiconductor Industry: Historical Origins and
   Competition in the 1990s   87

3. Formulating Strategy and Developing a Business Model   94
Kodak and the Demise of Camera Film   94
Strategy and Business Models   97
Components of a Business Model   98
Representing Value Propositions   103
Understanding the Sources of Competitive Advantage   115
Refining the Business Model: Competitive Dynamics   119
Extending the Structure of the Game   126
Summary   128
Key Terms   130
Discussion Questions   130
Action Item 3.1. Developing Your Business Model   130
Case-in-Point. Disney Around the World   132

Part III. Strategic Choice and Positioning

4. Positioning Strategic Choices in a Global Context   143
Asia's New Customized Dolls   143
Why Strategic Positioning Is Important   144
Foreign Direct Investment: A Historical Perspective   146
Global and Multidomestic Industries   153
A Framework for Global Strategy   155
Positioning Strategic Choices in a Global Context   158
Summary   174
Key Terms   176
Discussion Questions   176
Action Item 4.1. Strategic Choice Positioning for Three
   Industries   177
Case-in-Point. Store Wars: Wal-Mart Takes on Japan   177

Part IV. Leveraging Competitive Advantage

5. Leveraging Competitive Advantage Through Global Marketing 185
    Microsoft's Cultural Missteps 185
    The Need for Global Marketing 186
    Developing a Global Marketing Orientation 187
    Developing the Global Marketing Strategy: Targeting What
        Markets to Enter 188
    Developing the Global Marketing Strategy: How to Enter
        Target Markets 194
    Developing the Global Marketing Strategy: When to Enter
        Target Markets 198
    Putting the Global Marketing Strategy Together: An Analytical
        Framework 208
    Summary 217
    Key Terms 218
    Discussion Questions 218
    Action Item 5.1. Entry Strategy Selection 219
    Case-in-Point. Unilever Raises Its India Game 220

6. Leveraging Competitive Advantage Through Global Sourcing 225
    IKEA: From Retailer to a Cult Brand 226
    Why Global Sourcing? 227
    From Domestic Purchasing to Global Sourcing 228
    Types of Global Sourcing 229
    Global Sourcing: Five Levels of Development 233
    Locating Global Sourcing Partners 235
    Key Success Factors for Global Sourcing 236
    Guidelines for Implementing Global Sourcing 241
    The Benefits of Global Sourcing 242
    From Sourcing to Outsourcing: Emerging Patterns 245
    Outsourcing from "Make-or-Buy" to Strategic Transformation 246
    A Framework for Examining Outsourcing Decisions 252
    Summary 260
    Key Terms 262
    Discussion Questions 262
    Action Item 6.1. Role Playing 263
    Case-in-Point. Huawei's Generation—The Next Global Supplier? 263

7. Leveraging Competitive Advantage Through Strategic Alliances 271
    Which of the Two Scenarios Will Prevail? 271
    Strategic Alliances: Lessons about Partnerships 272
    Why Strategic Partnerships? 273

Defining Strategic Alliances 273
Benefits of Strategic Alliances 276
Alliances in the New Competitive Landscape 277
The Risks of Strategic Alliances 280
The Causes of Alliance Failure 281
Managing Strategic Alliances 286
Emerging Global Alliances and Partnerships 299
Summary 300
Key Terms 302
Discussion Questions 302
Action Item 7.1. Recommendation for a Joint Venture 302
Case-in-Point. Alliance Dynamics Within NUMMI 303

8. Leveraging Competitive Advantage Through Innovation 312
Apple Computers: Championing Strategic Innovation 313
Why Innovation? 314
The Emergence of a Knowledge-based, Digital Economy 316
Key Drivers of a Knowledge-based, Digital Economy 317
How the Knowledge-based, Digital Economy Will Affect Business 324
Types of Innovation: Product, Process, and Service 327
The Emerging Context of Innovation and Creativity in a
    Knowledge-based, Digital Economy 331
Toward Strategic Innovation: The New Innovative Context 338
Summary 348
Key Terms 350
Discussion Questions 350
Action Item 8.1. Mini-Cases 351
Case-in-Point. The Seoul of Design 351

Part V. Implementing the Strategic Plan

9. Implementing Strategy Using Structures and Processes 363
Nokia's Revitalization Initiatives 364
Why Strategic Implementation? 365
Why Is Implementation Crucial? 367
Fundamental Principles of Implementation 368
The Basic Design Variables 369
The First Design Principle: Congruency 376
The Second Design Principle: Stage-of-Growth 380
Organizing Framework 382
Designing the Global Organization 384
Human Resource Management (HRM): Its Role in Strategic
    Implementation 390
Conclusions 398

Summary   400
Key Terms   402
Discussion Questions   402
Action Item 9.1. Applying Congruency Analysis to Your
    Organization   403
Case-in-Point. Transforming IWDS's Business in Asia: The
    Role of Global HRM   404
Case-in-Point. Can Philips Learn to Walk the Talk?   410

10. Implementing Strategy by Cultivating a Global Mindset   416
    Geography of Thought   417
    A Global Mindset and Strategic Implementation   417
    Culture and Managerial Behavior   419
    Synthesizing the Frameworks   427
    The Global Mindset   429
    Ethnocentrism   436
    A Learning Program for Addressing Ethnocentrism and
    Developing Cross-Cultural Skills   439
    An Assessment Methodology   444
    Summary   447
    Key Terms   448
    Discussion Questions   448
    Action Item 10.1. Testing for Ethnocentrism   449
    Case-in-Point. MindTree and Cultural Diversity   450

11. Implementing Strategy Using Financial Performance Measures   459
    Cooking the Books at Woolworth   460
    The Role of Financial Analyses in Strategic Implementation   461
    The Financial Statements: Accounting Conventions   464
    Strategic Objectives and Performance Measures   471
    Assessing Financial Health Through Financial Ratios   472
    Analysis by Disaggregation: The DuPont Formula   479
    Using Marketing Ratios   481
    Revisiting the Value Problem: ROE versus EVA   482
    Economic Value Added (EVA) and Market Value Added (MVA)   484
    Testing the Sustainability of a Business Strategy   485
    Relating Valuation to Strategy   490
    Toward a Balanced Scorecard   494
    Financial Reporting in the Context of International Operations   496
    Summary   497
    Key Terms   499
    Discussion Questions   500
    Case-in-Point. Benchmarking to Economic Value Added:
        The Case of Airways Corporation of New Zealand Limited   501

Part VI. Integration

12. Integration and Emerging Issues in Global Strategic Management   521
         Objectives   521
         A Case Study: Can Strategy Save Argosis?   522
         Reviewing the Global Strategic Management (GSM) Framework   533
         Exploring Future Trends and Directions   538
         Summary   553
         Key Terms   554
         Discussion Questions   555

Name Index   559
Subject Index   565
About the Authors   579

Preface and Acknowledgments

We are borrowing from the future . . . what we teach the next generation is a reflection of ourselves . . .
—Tommy Benjamin from Old Crow, at the 1999 Summit in Mt. Village, Alaska

One key task of any instructor in international business is to maintain a good balance between concepts, context, and skills. Having collectively taught courses on strategy, management, and international business for over twenty years, our experience is that some texts are good at one, maybe two, but not all three of these, although it is generally accepted that the three are closely interrelated. Most knowledgeable, thoughtful people acknowledge the difficulty in keeping concepts and context current given that the world is constantly in flux. However, if there is an area that has received a short shrift, it is that of skills—this could mean the capabilities that prospective employers expect newly minted graduates to possess upon embarking on a career in international business, or the capabilities expected of business managers assigned to international operations. Thus, the first goal of *Global Strategic Management* is to provide intellectual and practical guidelines with which students can *execute* goals and strategies that lead to meaningful and productive *results*. This book is packed with frameworks, cases, anchoring exercises, techniques, and tools to help students and managers emerge with a completed business plan after the last chapter. Most, if not all, of the above have been used not only in the our own classrooms, but have been tested in numerous classrooms and management programs around the world.

With the growing popularity of international business, the business school curriculum has begun to offer multiple courses in international business as well as in business strategy. A typical international business course covers long-established theories that have become standard over the years: political economy, culture, theories of international trade and foreign direct investment, the global monetary system, the multinational firm, modes of entry, and business operations (export/import, manufacturing, human resource management, accounting). While most textbooks do a credible job of covering these topics, the focus is not on the *strategic choices* faced by international managers. Consequently, there is a lack of strategic orientation requiring the integration of international business topics and analytical skills into a larger view of sustainable competitive advantage. While business strategy books do well when it comes to providing a strategic orientation, they lack a comprehensive treatment of international topics and applied international contexts (strategic alliances, worldwide supply chains, global strategic positioning) that meet the requirements of managers operating internationally. As such, the second goal of *Global Strategic Management* is to focus on strategy and how firms build competitive presence and advantages in a global context. A learning objective is to have students and managers *understand* and *evaluate* the major issues involved in strategy formulation and implementation in a global context.

Global Strategic Management represents a platform of shared ideas born out of our individual teaching, research, and consulting experience. The practice of international business and research in this field have been undergoing continuous transformation as multinational firms and comparative management evolve in a changing global economy. A close reading of the research on firms that have conducted business abroad, supplemented by our own observations and field research, indicates that many firms fall short of their goals and objectives, despite good intentions. As discussed in this book, these experiences are manifest in empirical studies of joint venture failures, outsourcing, and international sourcing activities. Thus, the third goal of *Global Strategic Management* is to provide an accessible framework that will help guide students and managers in making strategic decisions that are sound and effective. Therefore, this book offers a *unifying process* that demarcates the necessary steps in analyzing the readiness of a firm with respect to doing business abroad. We argue that essential for doing business abroad is a well-developed ability to think strategically.

The organizing logic of this process, one that unfolds in the book, is that leaders in an international firm need to thoroughly understand three key factors, or antecedents: the firm's strategy and business model, the globalization potential of its industry, and the firm's reasons for going global. Thereafter, strategic positioning is contingent on how these three antecedents cohere and interrelate. Depending on their ability to exploit international opportunities, firms can leverage their competitive position in four areas: international marketing, worldwide sourcing and supply-chain management, innovation, and strategic partnerships. Our chapters on implementation go beyond standard treatises on structures and processes, and include the development and cultivation of a global mindset, and financial analytics that directly relate financial logic and performance measures to strategy.

This book is written with two audiences in mind. First, it is aimed at students who have had an introductory class in international business. Therefore, it is not intended to be an exhaustive survey of the international business terrain (already done quite ably by existing international business books), but a work focused on essential *strategic* concepts and practices. In contrast to other texts, we have emphasized the impact of three major trends: globalization, technology, and knowledge-based services. Far from being fads, these trends have influenced the basic logic and direction of international business. This book can complement undergraduate and graduate capstone business policy courses, possibly as a second reference book, should the instructors in these courses opt for a better coverage of international business topics and context. Second, the applied focus of this book is directed at business managers, and it aims specifically to help them understand the emerging global competitive landscape and apply the frameworks and analytical tools in the context of their real-world experiences.

Our ideas about global strategy were influenced by the intellectual legacy built by George Yip, Michael Porter, and Gary Hamel. Their ideas about strategy and business models are pivotal to our framework. Our students have benefited from Roger Best's (University of Oregon) grounded approach to strategic management and his analytical frameworks. His work is reflected in several parts of this book. In writing this book, we benefited from the advice, suggestions, criticisms, and counsel of our students, friends, business contacts, and academic colleagues. Thomas E. Maher (Professor Emeritus, California State University–Fullerton) diligently read most of the chapters and returned them to us filled with red markings detailing his edits, questions, concerns, criticisms, and suggestions. Professor Manuel Serapio (University of Colorado at Denver) not only provided feedback on earlier chapters but also contributed an original case co-authored with Annmarie Neal (Chapter 8). Professors Jay Jayaram (University of South Carolina), Scott Marshall (Portland State University), John O'Shaughnessy, Joe Messina, Roblyn Simeon, and Yuli Su (all from San Francisco State University, or SFSU) provided detailed feedback on selected chapters in their area of expertise. Professor Richard Steers (University of Oregon) offered encouragement and specific advice in early phases of the book's writing. We are grateful to Charles Snow (Pennsylvania State University) and Rosalie Tung (Simon Fraser University) for their encouragement. We acknowledge the assistance of Professor Daniel Braunstein (Emeritus, Oakland University) in collecting some data for the book. Professor Horacio "Junbo" Borromeo (Asian Institute of Management) was instrumental in linking us with MindTree Corporation. We appreciate the time provided by Chris Larson (E-LOAN, Chapter 4), Patis and Tito Tesoro (Asia's Customized Dolls, Chapter 4), and Rafael de la Rosa (Jollibee, Chapter 4) for on-site interviews in preparing their cases. We are particularly grateful to Geoffrey Moore and Pat Granger (TCG Advisors), Bruce Greenwald (Columbia University), Daniel Collins (University of Iowa), W. Bruce Johnson (University of Iowa), Robert Ingram (University of Alabama), Bruce Baldwin (Arizona State University), and Richard Mason (Southern Methodist University), for their kind assistance in our adoption of their works. We are grateful to Chang Yung-Fa, Chairman of the Evergreen Group, and to Joel Nicholson, Department of International Business (SFSU), Tony Chan, Tricia Tran, and the College of Business (SFSU) for providing the necessary support and resources for this project. Pat Cierra, Sandy Lee, and Dorothy Platell, the staff members at the Department of International Business, SFSU, have consistently offered assistance throughout the time of writing.

Several of our students at SFSU, notably Hon Pui Lam, Greggory Cates, Baver Mersin, Bonnie Lee, Jennifer Lew, and Wietse Bloemzaad, provided us with suggestions to make the book more "reader-friendly." While we have used some materials in the undergraduate, MBA, and EMBA programs at San Francisco State University, we were fortunate to test and try out some ideas and chapters in venues outside of SFSU, notably at the MBA program at the Rotterdam School of Management, Netherlands; the Executive Management Program at the Hanoi Business School; the MM Program at the Asian Institute of Management in the Philippines; and the MBA Program at St. Georges' University at Grenada, Grenada.

The editorial team at M.E. Sharpe, truly delightful partners, offered support throughout the process. We owe special thanks to Harry Briggs, executive editor, who guided us through the editorial process. Elizabeth Granda was most helpful in providing feedback about our numerous tables, exhibits, and graphs, not to mention our queries about copywriting. We are grateful to Stacey Victor, production editor, Nancy Connick, typesetter and designer, and Angela Piliouras, managing editor, for providing comments, advice, and suggestions during the copyediting and production phases of the book. Susanna Sharpe was helpful in clarifying particular passages of the book. Even so, we take responsibility for any errors.

Written acknowledgments have a special way of reframing memories. Our greatest debt is to our families for their love, patience, and support. Yim-Yu dedicates this book to her parents. Their discipline, guidance, and patience, particularly during her early childhood, laid the foundation for her personal development and professional growth. She also wishes to acknowledge her sister and brothers, Yim Ying Wong, Kim Man Wong, and Kim Ping Wong, who have been a constant source of support throughout her academic career. Gerardo is grateful to his family—Suki, Melissa, Carlo, and Rainelle—for their support. He dedicates this book to his grandparents who never failed to take pride in what then appeared to be "little" accomplishments. The unwavering support of his parents, Trinidad and Luz, is also noteworthy. He hopes to continue the practice of acknowledging "little" accomplishments with his granddaughter, Tegan Martin, a fast-growing, two-and-a-half-year-old at the time of this writing, who has used recycled draft copies of this manuscript to practice her drawing skills.

Gerardo R. Ungson
Yim-Yu Wong

PART I: THE GLOBAL CONTEXT

1. Global Strategic Management: An Overview

PART II: EXTERNAL / INTERNAL ANALYSIS

2. Analyzing the External Environment
3. Formulating Strategy and Development a Business Model

PART III: STRATEGIC CHOICE AND POSITIONING

4. Positioning Strategic Choices in a Global Context

PART IV: LEVERAGING COMPETITIVE ADVANTAGE

5. Leveraging Advantage Through Global Marketing
6. Leveraging Advantage Through Global Sourcing
7. Leveraging Advantage Through Strategic Alliances
8. Leveraging Advantage Through Innovation

PART V: IMPLEMENTING THE STRATEGIC PLAN

9. Implementing Strategy Using Structures and Processes
10. Implementing Strategy by Cultivating a Global Mindset
11. Implementing Strategy Using Financial Performance Measures

PART VI: INTEGRATION

12. Integration and Emerging Issues in Global Strategic Management

1 Global Strategic Management: An Overview

The future does not begin tomorrow . . . it began yesterday.
—Anonymous

The best way to predict the future is to invent it.
—Alan Kay

CHAPTER OUTLINE

- Two Global Scenarios
- The Changing Competitive Landscape
- Key Challenges Facing Managers
- Defining Globalization
- The Dark Side of Globalization
- Globalization in a Historical Context
- A Synthesis of Globalization: Implications for Management
- The Global Imperative
- A Framework for Global Strategic Management

LEARNING OBJECTIVES

- Understand the challenges faced by the contemporary manager.
- Understand what globalization is.
- Know the benefits and costs of globalization.
- Understand the three phases of globalization in historical perspective.
- See how globalization specifically affects management.
- Understand the reasons why a firm should go global.
- Understand and follow the framework for global strategic management.

TWO GLOBAL SCENARIOS

Imagine yourself as a manager in the near future. You have been asked to identify and understand the key drivers that will shape the global future. The exercise will be useful for you and your associates in terms of anticipating change, understanding the dynamics that create such change, and positioning a future strategy that capitalizes on the opportunities presented by these future scenarios. Compiled below are two global scenarios based on numerous analyses and extrapolations. Which scenario might become the basis of your future assessment?

SCENARIO 1: 2025—FAVORABLE

Globalization—the growing interconnectedness reflected in expanded trade, information, capital, goods, services, and people—has become a ubiquitous force in society and the economy. The collaboration between governments, corporations, the scientific sector, and communities has produced relative prosperity, global peace, and security; in particular, gaps in income distribution, poverty, hunger, and communicable diseases have been radically reduced. Technological advances, particularly molecular manufacturing (nanotechnology), have lowered the impact of a world population approaching 10 billion. Vaccines and genetic engineering have virtually eliminated most acquired and inherited diseases.[1] China and India have emerged as key economic players, and even the poorest countries have been able to leverage cheap technologies to work, albeit a slower rate, to their advantage. To the surprise of the world's environmentalists, China reversed its previously poor record of cleaning its natural environment. At this time, just enough steel, coal, oil, and railroads have developed to link township and village enterprises (*xiangzhen qiye*) all over the country.[2] More firms have become global, more diverse, both in size and origin, and have actively promoted and diffused technologies that have, in turn, further integrated the world economy and promoted progress in the developing world. The wave of democratization, particularly among the states of the former Soviet Union and Southeast Asia, has gained ground. The previously volatile Middle East region has stabilized with political Islam creating an authority transcending national boundaries. Such stability has muted terrorism, which, while existent, is now a much smaller force than at its pinnacle on 9/11.[3]

SCENARIO 2: 2025—PESSIMISTIC

Globalization, once considered an irreversible force, has slowed, as a result of catastrophic regional wars, calamitous weather systems, natural disasters, and a global depression. The failure of global communities to resolve many major flashpoints all over the world has created a power vacuum, with cultural "silos" (walled-off nations and regions) emerging after increases in global conflicts.[4] New technology has significantly enriched the already rich nations and enterprises, but has also accelerated the gap between the worlds' very rich and very poor, exacerbating the fear and tension that have smoldered for years. Excluded from the benefits of capitalism and ignored by developed countries, the developing world resents the rise of China and India, seemingly the only beneficiaries of globalization.[5] But even a different China has emerged, one that has collapsed into a morass of decadence, corruption, and greed. As feared by critics some decades earlier, China's environment has become a sewer of damage and waste. With China's insatiable demand for oil and other energy sources, major disruptions of oil supplies have sharply increased the price of oil and gasoline.[6] The disregard for the Kyoto Protocols by the United States, Australia, and a growing host of countries has exacerbated global warming, leading to calamitous weather patterns and natural disasters. Global terrorism has reached new heights with newly organized military cells in the Middle East and Asia, fueled by the rise of poverty throughout the world.[7]

THE CHANGING COMPETITIVE LANDSCAPE

Managerial actions comprise decisions about the future. It is thus widely acknowledged that the methodology of scenario forecasting, along the lines presented in the opening example, will grow in importance. Scenarios not only project images of the future, but also engage individuals in the process of examining their underlying assumptions about how decisions and events might lead to one outcome or another. This process lends itself to purposeful thinking about resources and capabilities and the extent to which they are suited for possible actions in some future state. Scenarios are intriguing not so much because of their projections, but because they represent a microcosm of managerial challenges that reflect the possibility of deep change and transformation in the future. Thinking critically and purposefully about change, transformation, and future states involves a systematic process—one that is further developed in this book. It is little wonder that the renowned poet Charles Kittering once said: "I'm interested in the future because I will be spending the rest of my life there." In a different light, the futurist Peter Bishop remarked: "The present is but a temporary condition."

For a perspective on changes and transformations, let us go back for a moment to the 1980s.[8] Some readers will remember this period vividly, while others who were growing up at the time might have to ask their parents about it. In 1980, the United States was in an economic shambles, with the "misery index" (inflation plus unemployment) at its height in 1980. The inflation rate stood at 14 percent, the unemployment rate at over 10 percent, and the interest rate at 21 percent. In the area of technology, the prototype music compact disk (CD) was introduced at the end of the 1970s. There were no high-speed fax machines. The VCR was still in its infancy. The very earliest cable television stations, like HBO, catered to small audiences, and CNN had just been launched. Mobile music, such as Sony's Walkman, was hardly in existence. But perhaps more conspicuously, the use of personal computers was limited and rudimentary, and certainly there were no wireless cell phones. The economic hegemony of the United States was threatened by an Asian superpower, Japan. Best-selling books at the time extolled the virtues of the Japanese economy and impelled U.S. firms to emulate Japanese management philosophies, management practices, and work methods.[9] With an eye toward the new millennium, the twenty-first century was dubbed as the "Asian century," but this was in reference to Japan, not China or India.

Not surprisingly, in numerous conferences over the years, the question posed to business leaders has been: "What key trends will have the most impact on the future survival and success of your organization?" Most, if not all, respond: "*Change, discontinuity, uncertainty.*" While the changes foreseen are consistent with the experiences faced by business managers for several decades, they seem to be more intense at present. Consider some representative responses:

- *About competition:* "Competitors are much more varied than before; they come from different parts of the world; they bring in very different business models. Because competition is much more intense, it's hard to maintain and sustain the competitive advantage. The weathered rules about cost efficiency or having better quality don't seem to hold. More nimble competitors have trumped many established market leaders. And this is assuming managers can identify their competitors; on some occasions, they cannot. . . ."
- *About customers:* "They have become more knowledgeable and certainly much more demanding. Because of their direct access to the Internet, they usually check on comparative prices before they even visit the store. The new technology has afforded them so many choices. As a result, they are less loyal; if they are not satisfied with a single incidence of less-than-expected service, they will not hesitate to leave."
- *About change and technology:* "It is true that firms can exploit new technological advances. Yet, because of continuous improvement in cost and delivery, there is that constant uncertainty that can impair even the best-laid strategic plans. Managers have to keep tracking developments, both inside and outside the industry. They have to develop resilient responses to technologies that they have not imagined or anticipated. They have to learn to live with uncertainty."

Collectively, these changes are hardly incidental or unconnected, nor do they occur by chance, but stem from fundamental transformations in the world that have defined the competitive landscape over the years. Even so, change is not confined to business organizations. Some twenty-five years ago, classroom instruction in our field consisted primarily of lectures and some business cases. Instructors would occasionally use transparencies to guide them through the lecture, in addition to writing key points on blackboards or on white sheets attached to multiple easels. Students considered any lecture handouts that might be provided by the instructor as a benefit, almost a gift, something that mitigated the necessity of copious note-taking. In dramatic contrast, today's students are likely to see a whole array of pedagogical tools, including laptops used by both professors and students during class; PowerPoint slides that are available before or after each lecture through online websites; audio-conferencing sessions beamed to multiple audiences online; and virtual blackboards on which assignments, readings, textbook passages, and even instructor notes are posted.

Students and managers seek to understand how changes and transformations in the world economy affect the way they approach the future. They want to know how specific changes in competition, customers, and technology across the world might affect their activities. They want to capitalize on this knowledge to build an advantage for themselves and their organizations. They wish to develop a plan of action to deal effectively with these changes. The plan of action developed in this book is organized as a process called *global strategic management.* Adopting global strategic management does not occur by mere intentions; it involves a meticulous process of understanding globalization and its impact on the organization; the selection of specific strategies and tactics that meet the objectives of foreign market entry, while retaining the strongest aspects of the organization's business model; the development of organizational competencies in ways that leverage advantage through a commitment to worldwide customers; selective partnership and alliances; creative use of sourcing and supply chains; and the restructuring of an organizational culture by way of responsive structures, processes, and human resource policies. Fundamentally, it entails the cultivation of a global mindset and a commitment to continual strategic and organizational transformation as well as procedures for tracking performance.

The development of this process is anchored in a *strategic* perspective. This book seeks to understand how firms build and sustain competitive advantage in their quest for global presence and domination. By adopting a strategic perspective, the focus is on how these advantages can be translated into superior performance, not only in financial terms, but also in terms of satisfying customer needs and meeting higher demands of community and society. Nevertheless, the strategic perspective does not imply that this book belongs in the realm of high-level policy decisions intended exclusively for top management. While corporate strategy involves a process of appraisal and action that may be ultimately legitimized and validated by top management, every individual has a role in strategy, either by having direct input in its formulation or by being a participant in its implementation. Therefore, the goal is to provide intellectual and practical guidelines for students and managers to *establish* and *execute* goals and strategies that lead to meaningful and productive *results*.

KEY CHALLENGES FACING MANAGERS

In the last quarter of the twentieth century, international business was shaken by a revolution in global competition that continues to blur industry boundaries, disrupt the rules of competition, and shift the location and balance of economic wealth around the world. The first such transformation is that of globalization, the subject of this chapter. The topic of innumerable academic and practitioner publications, **globalization,** defined broadly, is the deepening interconnection between individuals, organizations, and nations, and one of the most pervasive concepts advanced in the past few decades. Few would disagree that the twenty-first century is the new age of globalization. Because globalization conjures conflicting images of progress and repression, it is also not well understood,[10] prompting the need for firms to have a clear understanding of globalization and its impact on the firm. Globalization is a rich context for diagnosing change in the relevant external environment and the impact on a firm's business model. The adoption of a strategic perspective—defining goals and strategy, crafting a complete business model, appraising the firm's capabilities, understanding the external environment, and effective implementation—is hence placed in the context of a globalizing world.

Historically, globalization was accelerated by technological advances, notably in transportation and communications. Currently, the pace of globalization is determined by digitally based technologies, particularly in the convergence of the computing, communications, and data-storage sectors that define a digitally based economy. Broadly defined, **digitally based technologies** are new product applications in which information is stored and supplied in the form of binary digits. This concept is developed further in this chapter, as well as in Chapter 8. Within this digitally based economy, wealth is created by knowledge and by the ability to manipulate and transform it at electronic speed.[11] Technological advances, particularly the introduction of the facsimile (fax) machine and personal computers, have revolutionized the potential for small and large organizations to operate over vast geographical distances. Within a matter of years, communications were enhanced with another even more revolutionary development—the Internet. With a PC and a telephone line, anyone can link up to a global communications network, with access to almost everyone else, for purposes of sheer personal communication, or for virtual and instantaneous shopping. This level of connectivity facilitates more transactions by enhancing both the breadth and depth of information, and by pacing globalization. Such developments have created new products (search engines, iPod's Podcast), while destroying others (camera film, print-based encyclopedias). Accordingly, more so than ever, firms have to be adaptive, innovative, and competitive to keep abreast of the influx of new technologies. Because of its linkage with globalization, the theme of new technologies permeates this entire book, with a separate chapter devoted to implications for strategy and managerial practice.[12]

Related to this second trend, but perhaps much less pronounced than globalization and technology, is the emergence of **knowledge-based services**, a term referring to both the fast-growing service sector within industrialized economies and the relative importance of the service component in a product offering. In the United States alone, the service sector makes up approximately two-thirds of gross domestic product.[13] Focus on the knowledge component of a service sector upholds the power of information over physical factors such as land, labor, and capital.[14] Because knowledge is continuously transmitted, its value does not depreciate; in fact, it increases over time. Correspondingly, attention has shifted from the mere processing of information to its transmission and transformation into new knowledge. In management, this has led to knowledge-based workers who are an essential part of an organization's intellectual capital. Within a product offering, the relative importance of knowledge-based services has increased as well. In marketing, opportunities for new products and services that involve customer input and participation are now possible; customized Nike apparel and Levi Strauss jeans are but two examples. Multiple offerings for consumers have become the norm, reflecting the increased knowledge, experience, and discretion of consumers. Not many years ago, consumers had two or three choices for personal computers; today, they have close to thirty.[15]

The collective forces of globalization, digital-based technologies, and knowledge-based services have forged an emerging economy that is *global, intensely interconnected,* and *constantly changing.* The goal of global strategic management is to make *explicit* the inextricable link between these three forces and to illuminate how they have affected the process of formulating and implementing strategies. In the current environment, missing the next opportunity can be difficult to overcome, if not disastrous, particularly in international business. For example, leading American manufacturers of consumer electronics ignored the global market and have since been nonplayers in an industry dominated by the Japanese and Europeans.[16] Few market leaders made successful transitions from vacuum tubes to transistors or from transistors to integrated circuits.[17] Disruption of the status quo has become commonplace.[18] Taken in tandem with political upheavals all over the world, heightened concerns about world terrorism, the degradation of the natural environment, and the surge of skepticism and cynicism about the immoral practices of some well-established multinational firms, we are indeed in a period of discontinuity and change.

These challenges become even more amplified in a global context in which companies around the world are constantly jockeying for competitive positions, whether it be for new features in cell phones, new ways to download videos or notable items from the Internet to cell phones and iPods, new standards that define DVD players in a high-definition television (HDTV) context, or for biotechnological breakthroughs leading to newer and bolder therapies. These challenges are particularly relevant for U.S. firms, many of which have previously approached the global market—gingerly if not reluctantly.[19] In the Chinese language, "crisis" is expressed in two characters— "danger" and "opportunity." These two characters aptly describe the environment in which globalization, technological discontinuity and uncertainty, and strong service imperatives are facts of economic life and competition. In this context, there are priceless opportunities for those who *understand* these challenges, who *position* themselves correctly, and who *implement* strategies effectively by designing appropriate structures and processes.

DEFINING GLOBALIZATION

While globalization is a recognized term in the populist vernacular, attempts to define it have been elusive, if not contentious. According to Hilary French, director of Worldwatch Institute's Global Governance Project and author of *Vanishing Borders*, "The term means vastly different things to different people. To some, globalization is synonymous with the growth of global corporations whose far-flung operations transcend national borders and allegiances. To others, it signals a broader cultural and social integration, spurred by mass communications and the Internet. The term can also refer to the growing permeability of international borders to pollution, microbes, refugees and other forces."[20] In Exhibit 1.1, we provide a sampling of the evolving conceptualizations of the term that have far-reaching implications for business and society. Exhibit 1.2 provides some statistics in support of globalization. Because a globalizing world affects corporations and customers (see Exhibit 1.2), it behooves everyone to understand its full implications. Some will be introduced later in this chapter, and others are developed more fully throughout this book.

THE DARK SIDE OF GLOBALIZATION

Despite the benefits of globalization, the case against it has strengthened as well.[21] The antiglobalization movement is demanding human rights and the reduction of income inequality, as well as opposing child labor, low occupational safety and environmental standards, poverty, and global exploitation (e.g., sweatshops in Indonesia, China, India, Africa, and the Caribbean). Its goal is to impede the growth of international trade by curbing the power of multinational firms, specifically the

Exhibit 1.1

Seven Evolving Definitions of Globalization

1	Interconnections between overlapping interests of business and society	This view sees the globalized world in terms of a convergence between business and society. While these two are not always harmoniously integrated, interests and priorities become convergent over time.
2	Shifts in traditional patterns of international production, investment, and trade.	This view interprets shifts and trends in the world economy, some of which are pulling previously distinct domestic economies, but with others creating their own regional identities.
3	Absence of borders and barriers to trade between nations	This view is that of a society without borders and spatial boundaries. Territoriality disappears as the organizing principle, and will be replaced by powerful multinational firms that are linked across the triadic economies.
4	Functional integration of internationally dispersed activities; more a process than an end-state	Rather than an end-state, this view emphasizes the evolutionary nature of a global world. Moreover, as international trade intensifies, there will be more integration of finance, technology, and production.
5	World integration of finance, nation-states, and technologies within a free market enterprise	This view emphasizes the drivers of globalization (technology, finance, and information) with the inevitable consequence of moving into a world with free trade as the predominant ideology.
6	Movement in the direction of greater integration, as both natural and man-made barriers to international economic exchange continue to fall	This view emphasizes the economic phenomenon of increased integration of markets occasioned by markets, technology, and diminishing government-imposed barriers to international trade and capital flows.
7	Increased permeability of traditional boundaries of almost any kind, including physical borders such as space and time, nation-states and economies, industries and organizations, and less tangible borders such as cultural norms	This rather broad view goes beyond the physical border of nation-states and the functional borders of business enterprises to more intangible boundaries of cultural norms and values. While it is not clear that the globalized world will have a single culture and society, it is stated that borders and boundaries of any kind will have fewer consequences for society and business practice.

Sources: Definitions of globalization correspond to the following sources: (1) Juanita Brown, "Corporation as Community: A New Image for a New Era," in J. Rensch, ed., *New Traditions in Business* (San Francisco: Berrett-Koehler, 1992), 123–139; (2) Peter Dicken, *Global Shift* (New York: Guilford Press, 1998); (3) Kenichi Ohmae, *The Borderless World: Power and Strategy in the Interlinked Economy* (New York: Harper Row, 1999); (4) Peter Dicken, *Global Shift: Reshaping the Global Economic Map in the 21st Century* (New York: Guilford, 2003); (5) Thomas L. Friedman, *The Lexus and the Olive Tree* (New York: Anchor Books, 2000); (6) Martin Wolf, *Why Globalization Works* (New Haven, CT: Yale University Press, 2004); (7) Barbara Parker, *Globalization and Business Practice: Managing Across Borders* (London: Sage Publications, 1998).

diffusion of policies and practices that harm local communities and the natural environment. It also opposes global agreements and has targeted companies and economic institutions that regulate and assess global trade practices, such as the World Trade Organization (WTO), the World Bank, the Organization of American States, the North American Free Trade Agreement (NAFTA), and the International Monetary Fund (IMF).

The cause of antiglobalization was dramatized by activists at the November 1999 meeting of the WTO held in Seattle. What was supposed to be a routine meeting to develop an agenda for the next round of world trade negotiations turned violent, with

Exhibit 1.2

Evidence of a Global Economy

The following reams of facts are used to support claims that globalization is not only pervasive but irreversible as well.

- The *National Post* reports that more than US$1.5 trillion moves around the world every day in foreign exchange markets.
- By 2030 it is estimated that 80 percent of the world's GDP will be produced and consumed in global markets. Worldwide, globally addressable GDP is expected to reach as much as $73 trillion, which is 12 times what it is today.
- Between 1970 and 1998, foreign direct investments grew twice as fast as trade, and the number of transnational corporations grew from 7,000 to over 50,000. U.S. investments tripled between 1982 and 1986.
- International joint ventures have grown 25 percent in the last five years alone.
- In 1955, 75 of the 100 largest industrial businesses in the world were American; by 1996, that number had dropped to 24. Only 8 U.S. industrials are likely to be in the top 100 by the year 2037, according to the *Harvard Business Review.*
- For the largest U.S.-based corporations, such as ExxonMobil, Gillette, Bank of Boston, Coca-Cola, and Citicorp, sales outside the United States were 77, 68, 67, 67, and 65 percent of total sales, respectively. Colgate, Digital Equipment, Avon, IBM, Hewlett-Packard, Warner-Lambert, JP Morgan, Procter and Gamble, DuPont, Intel, and Salomon are 50 percent or higher.
- *Time* magazine reports that three-quarters of the world's mail is currently written in English, as is 80 percent of e-mail.

Sources: Robert Rosen, *Global Literacies: Lessons on Business Leadership and National Cultures* (New York: Simon and Schuster, 2000); Lowell Bryan, Jane Foster, Jeremy Oppenhiem, and William Rall, *Race for the World: Strategies to Build a Great Global Firm* (Boston: Harvard Business School Press, 1998); Jeffrey A. Rosensweig, *Winning the Global Game: A Strategy for Linking People and Profits* (New York: Free Press, 1998); Joseph Boyett and Jimmie Boyett, *The Guru Guide to the Knowledge Economy* (New York: John Wiley, 2000).

an estimated fifty thousand protesters clashing with police, blocking access to the meeting grounds, and creating chaos on the streets of Seattle.

Nor is the antiglobalization cause confined to public demonstrations. It has permeated basic assumptions about cultural hegemony. Some countries, notably France, have resisted aspects of globalization that are identified closely with American interests. In France, Jose Bove, a sheep farmer, vandalized a McDonald's store in the southwestern part of France in the summer of 1999 to protest against U.S. trade sanctions on Roquefort cheese, reflecting a concern that globalization might affect France's cultural and linguistic traditions.

The spillover of this continuing debate becomes even more acute when policymakers are faced with the challenge of introducing a totally isolated culture to the modern influences of globalization. One case, that of the Nukak-Makú, is featured in Box 1.1 (also see the end-of-the-chapter action item).

Antiglobalists also argue that the unimpeded flow of capital, enabled by a financial infrastructure that facilitates quick and rapid withdrawal, can result in the hasty withdrawal of money from the region, leading to adverse dislocations.[22] Consider the case of South Korea in the Asian financial crisis of 1997. South Korea's liberaliza-

Box 1.1

Discovering the Future: The Nukak-Makú Experience

New discoveries have a way of reframing histories. For as long as they existed, the Nukak-Makú have lived a Stone Age life. They roamed across hundreds of miles of isolated parts of the pristine Amazon jungle, unmindful of the outside world. A good part of their existence consisted of hunting monkeys (a delicacy) with blowguns and eating berries from the forest floor. The world of the Nukak-Makú was shattered when they decided to wander out of the forest, declaring that they were ready to join the modern world.

    While there is avid speculation as to why they decided to do this, it is a foregone conclusion that they are woefully unprepared for the modern world. Reflecting the depth of isolation, they have no concept of money, property, the role of government, or even the existence of the country in which they live, Colombia.

    What is emerging likewise is the uncertainty on the part of the modern world regarding how to incorporate the Nukak-Makú into modern civilization. In the past, the little contact the Nukak-Makú had with the outside world left them vulnerable to Western diseases, such as influenza and the common cold, for which they had no natural immunity. Even with aid comes the concern that it would only lead to dependency, thus reducing the group's chances of integrating successfully into the new world.

    The conundrum of how to integrate the Nukak-Makú was captured poignantly by Belisario, the only one among them who had been to the outside world before and spoke some Spanish. When asked about the group's future, he simply said, "The future . . . what's that?"

    Source: Adapted from Juan Forero, "Leaving the Wild, and Rather Liking the Change," *New York Times,* May 11, 2006, A–1.

tion initiatives came along with its aspirations to join the Organization for Economic Cooperation and Development (OECD). While Korea had long contended that it had to manage the pace of liberalization in ways that did not create macroeconomic or societal imbalances, it faced significant challenges, both domestically and internationally, which were exposed in the wake of the financial crisis. Prior to the crisis, the advanced countries in the Western world preferred a quicker pace of market liberalization in Asia, while Asian countries had preferred a slower one. This had long been a topic of dispute between the United States and Japan, as well as recently between the United States and both Korea and China. Nevertheless, in its aspiration to join the OECD, Korea initiated the process of liberalizing its domestic market, relaxing its investment inflows, and accelerating the globalization of its multinationals, the *chaebol*s. In opening the country's capital account (encourage the inflow of foreign capital), Korea effectively provided guarantees to nonresidents that they could withdraw their investments from the country at will.[23] Korea's crisis was precipitated by the loss of confidence on the part of these foreign creditors and investors as the structural weaknesses of Korea's financial system became more evident in the course of democratization and globalization.[24] While not directly a result of globalization, it is nevertheless argued that this crisis might not have occurred had Korea been more realistic in its expectations of investors' joining its globalization (*Segwehwah*) initiatives.[25] In effect, Korea adopted market liberalization policies *prematurely* in order to join the ranks of the OECD, only to realize that it did not have the infrastructure to support these policies.[26]

    Opponents of globalization do not restrict their objections to free trade alone, but

Exhibit 1.3

The Dark Side of Globalization

As indicated, globalization is a contentious and complicated issue. Globalization, through free trade, is celebrated for improving the physical and economic well-being of people worldwide. Nevertheless, there are detractors who argue that people's overall welfare has deteriorated with globalization. Specific arguments are listed below.

- The vast majority of trade and investment takes place between industrial nations, dominated by global corporations that control 33 percent of exports.
- Of the 100 largest economies in the world, 51 are corporations.
- Eighty percent of foreign direct investment went to twenty countries, notably China, which is the largest recipient of FDI.
- The assets of the 200 richest people in the world are greater than the combined income of the 20 billion-plus people at the bottom of the pyramid.
- Only 33 countries managed to sustain 3 percent annual growth per capita between 1980 and 1996. In 59 countries, per capita GDP decreased. Eighty countries have lower per capita income today [2000] they did a decade ago.
- The World Bank reports that 200 million more people are living in absolute poverty (less than $1 per day) than in 1987—remarkable considering China's economic progress.
- The earnings of the average CEO in the United States are 416 times the earnings of the average worker.

Source: Data excerpted from Jay Mazur, "Labor's New Internationalism," *Foreign Affairs* 79 (January/February 2000): 115–141.

point out globalization's negative effects on the social and cultural milieu as well. Some specific negative effects are listed in Exhibit 1.3. The debate between proponents and opponents of globalization is continuing and will likely extend into the future.[27] While a detailed treatise is beyond the scope of this book, we offer a few pointers on where the two sides differ in order to provide a wider context to this debate (see Exhibit 1.4). These arguments notwithstanding, globalization has been shaped by a number of fundamental economic transformations over several centuries. To develop a better appreciation of these fundamental transformations, we present a historical account of three phases of globalization. For students and managers, the implication is that globalization is here to stay and that the important thing is to understand its processes and consequences.

GLOBALIZATION IN A HISTORICAL CONTEXT

While many people think that globalization is a phenomenon of the twentieth century, there have been indications that globalization occurred before then. Professors Karl Moore and David Lewis, a strategy academician/consultant and an economic historian respectively, traced the evolution of commerce over 5,000 years and have proposed three phases of globalization: the first occurred during the golden years of merchant voyages in the 1440s to the 1880s; the second ushered in the *Pax Britannica,* from 1880 to 1931; and the third, the age of *Pax Americana*, spanned from 1931 to 2000.[28] In our discussion of the third phase, we draw on *New York Times* syndicated columnist Thomas Friedman, who has depicted this emerging phase of globalization as a "flat world."[29] To appreciate the extent of previous economic transformations that have

Exhibit 1.4

The Globalization Debate: Point and Counterpoint

Issues	Antiglobalization	Proglobalization
Trade	Despite the purported benefits of free trade, these are elusive in the context of the United States (and the rest of the world). The system of laissez-faire has been destructive and has led to problems related to the federal deficit, the reliance on foreign imports, widespread downsizing, environmental destruction.[1]	Historical evidence proves the antiglobalization argument to be erroneous: increased trade has, in fact, led to economic growth and prosperity around the world. Even so, international economic integration is more limited than otherwise claimed: the high-income countries are open to trade and capital flows, but protect labor-intensive and agricultural products, while many developing countries remain closed to trade, capital movements, and immigration flows. It is necessary to distinguish between market failures and ill-advised politics and poorly implemented policies.[2]
Culture and environment	The emergent global economy is threatening the environment and cultural diversity, not only by disregarding environmental issues, local tastes, and cultural differences, but by imposing a form of social control over attitudes, expectations, and behavior of people all over the world.[3]	Income increases that result from globalization do not necessarily lead to environmental harm. Increasing incomes, in fact, reduce pollution, but not without an appropriate environmental policy.[4] The imposition of social control with the attendant loss of cultural autonomy does not hold up against facts and emerging local/regional activism.[5]
Inequality	Current globalization policies have plunged the great majority of U.S. workers into a great worldwide "race to the bottom," creating impoverished segments in a no-win scramble for work. On a worldwide basis, this has also led to income inequality, with the rich becoming richer while the poor, excluded from accruing the benefits of globalization, end up in even worse shape.[6]	While the ratio of average incomes in the richest countries versus the poorest has risen, as has the absolute gap in living standards between them, global inequality between individuals has fallen since the 1970s. Income inequality has not risen in most developing countries that have integrated with the world economy, with the exception of China. Meanwhile, the welfare of humanity, judged by life expectancies, infant mortality, literacy, hunger, fertility, and the incidence of child labor, has improved enormously.[7]
Power of multinationals	Using the banner of free trade, corporations have managed to impose autocratic governance over modestly democratic countries, displacing local businesses and solidifying control over their natural resources.[8]	Despite some isolated cases, corporations are not as powerful as countries, nor do they dominate the world through their brands. Many of those who protest the conditions of workers do so in comparison to their own happy state, not in comparison with the actual alternatives for those workers. There is, however, an undesirable race to the top through subsidies. While the power of corporations can make one uncomfortable, it should not be exaggerated.[9]

| Capital flows | Capital flows are a salient feature of globalization. Unimpeded or uncontrolled capital flows, however, wreak worldwide havoc in that they undermine the ability of a country to control its economy, leading to the financial crises that have occurred over the past decades.[10] | The IMF has abandoned its traditional excessive preoccupation with free capital mobility; it has learned that some form of some capital tax might be needed in special circumstances, and it has become more cognizant about the role of institutions and safeguards.[11] |
| Institutions | There are limits to economic globalization. Global trade requires global government management. Absent these, liberalization and privatization cannot occur too quickly because they will cause too much pain, poverty, and unemployment.[12] | Reflecting on past financial crises, proglobalization economists acknowledge that globalization requires management. They recommend the strengthening of a country's system of rules and regulations, banking institutions, the role of foreign financial institutions, deposit insurance, bankruptcy regimes, and exchange-rate policies.[13] |

[1]Ravi Batra, *The Myth of Free Trade: The Pooring of America* (New York: Touchtone, 1993), pp. 5–21.
[2]Martin Wolf, *Why Globalization Works* (New Haven: Yale University Press, 2004), p. 143.
[3]William Greider, Ralph Nader (eds.); *The Case Against Free Trade: GATT, NAFTA, and the Globalization of Corporate Power* (San Francisco: An Earth Island Press Book, 1993), p. 47.
[4]Jagdish Bhagwati, *In Defense of Globalization* (New York: Oxford University Press, 2004).
[5]Bhagwati, *In Defense of Globalization*, pp. 106–122.
[6]Alan Tonelson, *The Race to the Bottom: Why a Worldwide Worker Surplus and Uncontrolled Free Trade Are Sinking American Living Standards* (Boulder, CO: Westview Press, 2002).
[7]Wolf, *Why Globalization Works*, pp. 138–172.
[8]John Cavanagh and Jerry Mander, "Design for Corporate Rule," In John Cavanagh and Jerry Mander (eds.), *Alternatives to Economic Globalization: A Better World is Possible* (San Francisco: Berrett-Koehler Publishers, 2004), pp. 32–54; David C. Korten, *When Corporations Rule the World* (West Hartford, CT: Kumarian Press; San Francisco: Berrett-Koehler Publishers, 1996), pp. 25–36.
[9]Wolf, *Why Globalization Works*, pp. 220–248; Bhagwati, *In Defense of Globalization*, pp. 162–195.
[10]George Soros, *George Soros On Globalization* (New York: Public Affairs/Perseus Book Group, 2002), pp. 1–7.
[11]Bhagwati, *In Defense of Globalization*, pp. 199–207.
[12]Joseph E. Stiglitz, *Globalization and Its Discontents* (New York: W.W. Norton and Co., 2003), pp. 15–21.
[13]Wolf, *Why Globalization Works*, pp. 278–304; Bhagwati, *In Defense of Globalization*, pp. 228–239.

shaped our current conceptions of globalization, we provide a brief historical review of international business (see Exhibit 1.5).[30]

EARLY ORIGINS OF TRADE

Economic historians date the origin of trade to the Sumerians (3500 B.C.E.), who resided in southern Mesopotamia in the area of modern-day Iraq. Based on records as far back as 2500 B.C.E., Sumerian merchants would travel to Syria and the Asian Minor to exchange textiles and crops for stones, timber, metals, and other items.[31] The Sumerians' economic centers were their temples which functioned as repositories of wealth (mostly grain) and as distribution centers. The Sumerians were eventually conquered and united under Babylonian rule in 1730 B.C.E. The absence of clear historical records, however, prompted other researchers to question whether market trading did occur, at least in the modern context in which we understand trading as the exchange of goods based on some pricing mechanism.[32] This revisionist interpretation depicts traders in this early period not as merchants who were motivated by profit, but as functionaries vested by status based on descent or training. Prices were not determined by supply and demand, but by "equivalencies" decreed by authority and custom.[33]

Prior to the invention of coinage, early trade was primitive and transacted largely in the form of barter, or goods exchanged for goods.[34] Historical evidence discloses a thriving trade commerce in Elba (now northern Syria and Lebanon) that was supported by a fixed system of prices based on gold and silver and by the world's first legal framework for international commerce.[35] When Elba was later dethroned by Assyria, the new ruler, Sargon, forged trade relations with Egypt that already had a sea trade with neighboring partners. At around 715 B.C.E., the earliest coins were made in Lydia and Ionia (or the western part of what we now call Turkey) from electrum, an alloy of gold and silver. Each coin had its own predetermined weight and a government guarantee for its use. The development of coinage facilitated the rapid expansion of trade and commerce, especially among the Greeks and eventually the Romans. By the fifth and sixth centuries B.C.E., considered to be the height of prosperity in Athens and the Age of Pericles, rudimentary forms of foreign exchange markets had developed. The rise of the Roman Empire and *Pax Romana* led to the first single monetary economy that could be favorably described as the "first European Union."[36]

FIRST PHASE OF GLOBALIZATION (1450–1880)

International trade and exchange continued through the years but suffered a setback during the Dark Ages, which commenced with the fall of Rome circa C.E. 400 and ended around the eleventh century. Despite the decline of trade in Europe, this period is also known for the Golden Age of Islam and China's market revolution under the Tang Empire.[37] Trade in Europe was revived in the Middle Ages with the rise in population and the introduction of new farming techniques that stimulated innovations.[38] With the inception of the European voyages of discovery during the fifteenth century, a new age of managed trade began, highlighted by Portuguese Vasco de Gama's famous journey in 1497 when he discovered the sea route to India by way of the southern cape of Africa.

Exhibit 1.5

Three Phases of Globalization at a Glance

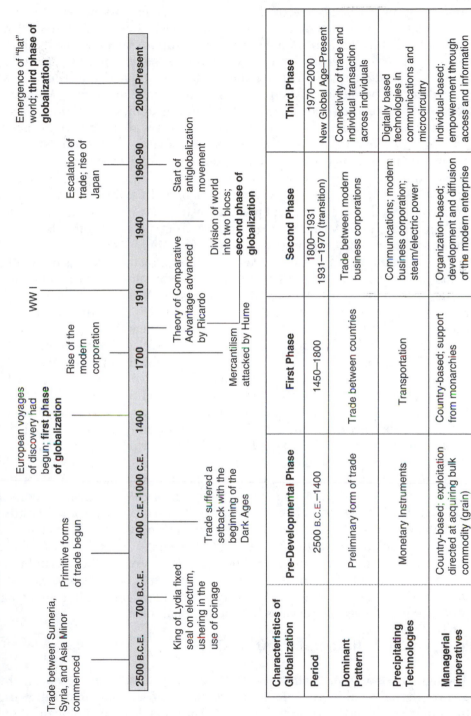

Timeline labels:

- Trade between Sumeria, Syria, and Asia Minor commenced
- King of Lydia fixed seal on electrum, ushering in the use of coinage
- Primitive forms of trade begun
- Trade suffered a setback with the beginning of the Dark Ages
- European voyages of discovery had begun; **first phase of globalization**
- Rise of the modern corporation
- Theory of Comparative Advantage advanced by Ricardo
- Mercantilism attacked by Hume
- Division of world into two blocs; **second phase of globalization**
- WW I
- Escalation of trade; rise of Japan
- Start of antiglobalization movement
- Emergence of "flat" world; **third phase of globalization**

Timeline: 2500 B.C.E. | 700 B.C.E. | 400 C.E.–1000 C.E. | 1400 | 1700 | 1910 | 1940 | 1960-90 | 2000-Present

Characteristics of Globalization	Pre-Developmental Phase	First Phase	Second Phase	Third Phase
Period	2500 B.C.E.–1400	1450–1800	1800–1931 1931–1970 (transition)	1970–2000 New Global Age–Present
Dominant Pattern	Preliminary form of trade	Trade between countries	Trade between modern business corporations	Connectivity of trade and individual transaction across individuals
Precipitating Technologies	Monetary Instruments	Transportation	Communications; modern business corporation; steam/electric power	Digitally based technologies in communications and microcircuitry
Managerial Imperatives	Country-based; exploitation directed at acquiring bulk commodity (grain)	Country-based; support from monarchies	Organization-based; development and diffusion of the modern enterprise	Individual-based; empowerment through access and information

Source: Karl Moore and David Lewis, *Foundations of Corporate Empire: Is History Repeating Itself?* (Upper Saddle River, NJ: Financial Times Prentice-Hall, 2000); Peter Dicken, *Global Shift* (New York: Guilford Press, 2003); Thomas Friedman, *The Lexus and the Olive Tree* (New York: Anchor Books, 2000); Thomas Friedman, *The World Is Flat: A Brief History of the 21st Century* (New York: Anchor Books, 2004).

During this period, trade between countries was intensive and spanned the entire world, prompting some scholars to term this as the **first phase of globalization**.[39]

While the roots of international trade theory were sown in this first phase of globalization, it was the **joint-stock chartered company** that became the institutional vehicle for fostering economic expansion during this first phase.[40] Portugal, Spain, and Holland adopted their own versions of naval enterprise to circumvent what was considered to be monopolistic practices by the Venetian Empire. Moreover, these countries also favored trade to be managed by monarchies, not partnerships.[41] Naval expeditions were largely financed by the joint-stock chartered companies that had proven very effective in raising huge amounts of capital. This joint-stock chartered company operated on capital or shares contributed by its members who also shared in its profits as well as the risks.[42] Moreover, with adequate capital and factories, the joint-stock chartered company was so efficient and flexible that it served as a parent for many other economic and political institutions.[43] The East India Company is perhaps the best-known example of a joint stock company. Another later entrant was the Dutch East India Company, which dominated Indonesia.

The prevailing doctrine that guided such endeavors at the time was **mercantilism**—a belief that the economic wealth of a country was measured by the amount of precious metal, specifically gold and silver, that it possessed. Mercantilist doctrines supported the belief in strong naval fleets that were considered at the time to be essential in acquiring and protecting these precious metals. Mercantilist doctrines also favored a strong interventionist nation-state. Scottish philosopher David Hume (1711–1776) eventually attacked this belief, arguing that it was the quantity and value of imports that a nation's exports could purchase, not the value of precious metals, which ultimately determined a country's economic welfare and prosperity. Hume also argued that amassing gold would simply raise its domestic price, discourage exports, create trade imbalances, and ultimately reduce the country's stock of gold.[44] Another Scotsman, Adam Smith (1723–1790) extolled the virtues of specialization, arguing that nations with an absolute advantage in the production of particular goods should concentrate on these goods, and that such specialization be the basis for trade with other nations.[45] It was not until 1817, however, that the English economist David Ricardo (1772–1823) introduced the world to the **theory of comparative advantage**. This theory postulated that one country's advantage over another is based on land, labor, and capital, and that nations should produce those goods for which they have the greatest relative advantage.[46] While the premises of the theory tend to be crude and oversimplified, it is still the centerpiece of every course on the theory of international trade. It is the basis for estimating a country's competitive advantage in the production of goods and services for international trade.

Second Phase of Globalization (1880–1931)

The first phase of globalization (1450–1880) has generally been associated with the growth in trade and investment across countries, specifically under the auspices of the joint-stock, chartered trading company. The second phase of globalization (1880–1931) set the stage for the modern multinational corporation in that coordination of the firm's activities across borders became possible primarily because of technological advances. Specifically, technological advances in telecommunication and transportation facilitated this coordination of activities by multinational firms.[47] The telegraph was invented in 1844, and the years 1880 to 1930 were shaped by the spread of electric power, broadcast, telephones, and mass production. In the mid-nineteenth century, sailing packets took twenty-one days to cross the Atlantic; by the 1880s, passenger steamships took five to six days. Heretofore, long-distance communication was tied to transportation; the first transatlantic cable, which was laid in 1886, forever broke the tie. Later advances in electricity, mass production, radio technology, and air travel further reduced communication time.

Post-1750 heralded an epoch in the world's commercial history: the advent of the **First Industrial Revolution**. The diffusion of technological inventions, coupled with the growth of factories, provided the infrastructure for industrialization.[48] Huge social, economic, and technological transformations changed Europe from an agricultural to an industrial society. Capitalism trumped feudalism. London had already become the world's foremost financial market, with the Bank of England having issued its first bank notes (1694), and the East India Company and the Bank of England having been the leading joint stock monopoly since the 1600s.[49] With England freed from big government and land wars, and with its flourishing physical infrastructure of canals, rivers, and ports, it was clearly a period of British dominance and a fitting setting for the First Industrial Revolution.[50] In the nineteenth century, large numbers of people and large quantities of capital circulated between continents without restriction. Britain led the world in manufacturing, trade, naval power, and economic hegemony. As world trade continued to grow between 1800 and 1930, it is estimated that over 60 percent of it was European and heavily British. Moreover, British multinationals ruled the world, with British American Tobacco, Courtaulds, Dunlop, Lever Brothers, Pilkington, Royal Dutch Shell, among others, in their economic heyday.[51]

The economic prophet at this time was Adam Smith, who legitimized free-market ideology. Smith published *The Wealth of Nations* in 1776, a book that would radically reverse economic thinking in its advocacy of unbridled capitalism.[52] For Smith, real wealth did not lie in land and capital as much as it did in productive labor. **Liberalism**, according to Smith, was based on self-interest, or the uninterrupted effort of any individual to better his condition; hence, it was the basis for economic growth. According to Smith, while acting out of self-interest, individuals are led by an "invisible hand" to promote the public good as well. This doctrine has evolved into the dominant paradigm that continues to influence management thinking and business practice up to this day.

Around the end of World War I, the economic hegemony of the British was showing signs of decline. Many overseas investments had been liquidated, and many free-standing companies had been sold. Free-market economies, representing the dominant economic belief, had become much less popular during economic contraction, and the image of the country gentleman and dweller, with its attendant values, trumped that of the business hustler. While there are many established theories about the decline of the British Empire, much outside the scope of this book, it is appropriate to add that the British had failed to capitalize on newer technologies.[53] With their preference for investment in coal and steam, they were slow in adapting to electricity and petroleum. In the 1870s, the United Kingdom produced 30 percent of the world's total industrial output, compared to the United States with 25 percent and Germany with 13 percent. In contrast, by 1913 the United Kingdom's share of world output had declined to 14 percent, while the United States had increased its proportion to 36 percent.[54] In contrast to the first phase of globalization that highlighted the role of the joint-stock chartered companies, the **second phase of globalization** featured intense trade between large modern corporations that reached its peak during the dominance of Great Britain (*Pax Britannica*) and continued until the beginning of the Great Depression in 1929. The next period of globalization would be defined by the United States (*Pax Americana*).

THIRD PHASE OF GLOBALIZATION (1931–2000)

The rise of United States began with its rapid economic progress in the latter half of the nineteenth century. The nation had emerged from the Civil War with almost double the number of business establishments as had existed in the 1850s. Following the construction of railways and the discovery of oil, business activity grew rapidly after 1865, with the United States soon becoming the richest and most powerful nation in the world. What spurred this growth was its own industrial revolution, prompted by the continuous diffusion of technologies, the rapid growth of its cities, the growing competitiveness of its industries, its widening array of railways and transportation, and its flurry of individual entrepreneurship.

The roots of the **third phase of globalization** can be traced to the post–World War II period, specifically with mass production that reached its peak during the 1930s. This period from 1931–1970 is considered to be a transitory period leading to the next phase. Two later developments shaped and defined this third phase of globalization: international trade escalated in the 1970s and the advances in miniaturization that led to the diffusion of the microchip and computers in the 1970s. A distinctive part of this third phase is what some scholars have called the "new global age" or the "flat world" that is discussed in the next section. In a 1911 publication entitled *The Principles of Scientific Management*, Frederick Taylor, a mechanical engineer and founder of "systems engineering," used time and motion studies to break up a task into several sub-elements in an effort to make production less costly and more efficient.[55] His goal was to remove all extraneous elements of the job that led to inefficiency. The specialization of work alone produced remarkable results. Task specialization built on earlier notions of division of labor espoused by Adam Smith.[56] In his now-classic case of a pin manufacturing plant, Smith observed that one worker in charge of the entire assembly could manufacture only 20 pins a day. When the task was broken down into parts, with workers specializing on only one component, a workgroup of 10 individuals produced as many as 48,000 pins per day, a 240-fold increase in productivity. In the twentieth century, the United States was dominated by hierarchical firms, highlighted by the prominence of standardization and mass production, particularly in the automobile industry, where Ford's famous "one color, one car" dictum was immortalized.

There was a tremendous escalation of international trade and competition during the second half of the twentieth century. During the 1970s, despite oil shocks and

Exhibit 1.6

World Exports of Merchandise and Commercial Services, 1990–2001

Year	Value (US$ billions) 2001	Annual percent change		
		1999	2000	2001
Merchandise	5,984	4.0	13.0	−4.5
Commercial Services	1,458	3.0	6.0	−0.5

Source: World Trade Organization, "World Trade Developments in 2001 and Prospects for 2002," in *International Trade Statistics 2002* (Geneva: World Trade Organization, 2002), p. 3.

Exhibit 1.7

Growth in the Volume of World Merchandise Trade by Selected Region, 1990–2001
(Annual percentage change)

Exports				Imports		
1990–2001	2000	2001		1990–2001	2000	2001
5.5	11.0	−1.5	World	6.0	11.5	−1.5
6.0	9.5	−5.0	North America	7.5	11.5	−3.5
8.0	8.5	2.0	Latin America[a]	10.0	12.5	−1.0
4.5	9.0	−1.0	Western Europe	4.0	8.0	−3.0
4.5	9.5	−1.5	European Union (15)	4.0	8.0	−2.5
5.5	17.0	8.0	Central and Eastern Europe/ Baltic States/CIS[b]	5.0	16.0	14.0
7.0	16.0	−3.5	Asia	7.0	16.0	−1.5
1.5	9.5	−10.0	Japan	4.5	11.0	−1.5
9.0	16.5	−5.5	Six East Asian traders[c]	6.5	16.5	−9.0

Source: World Trade Organization, "World Trade Developments in 2001 and Prospects for 2002," in *International Trade Statistics 2002* (Geneva: World Trade Organization, 2002), p. 23.

[a] Mexico not included in this report.
[b] CIS = Commonwealth of Independent States.
[c] Hong Kong, South Korea, Malaysia, Singapore, Taiwan and Thailand.

stagflation, world trade grew nearly 20 percent faster per annum than world output (4.0 percent versus 3.4 percent respectively). The disparity intensified sharply in the 1980s and the early 1990s, during which period international trade grew roughly 60 percent faster per annum than world output (4.9 percent versus 3.0 percent).[57] Another indication, noted by economic geographer Peter Dicken, was the shift in geopolitical and economic centers of production.[58] In 1960s, American firms manufactured nearly half of the world's motor vehicles, compared to 2 percent by Japanese firms. By the late 1970s, the Japanese firms had drawn even. In 1967, Japan accounted for slightly over 1 percent of the world stock of outward foreign direct investment; by 1990 its share had risen to nearly 20 percent. Over the same period, the U.S. share dropped from 50 percent to 26 percent.[59] While the United States has maintained its level of competitiveness, it is widely acknowledged that the rest of the world has caught up, with the European Community, notably Germany, and East Asia, specifically Japan, becoming household

Exhibit 1.8

Growth in the Value of World Merchandise Trade by Region, 2001

Exports					Imports			
Value (US$ billions)	Annual percentage change				Value (US$ billions)	Annual percentage change		
2001	1990–2001	2000	2001		2001	1990–2001	2000	2001
5,984	5	13	−4	World	6,270	5	13	−4
991	6	14	−6	North America	1,408	7	18	−6
347	8	20	−3	Latin America[a]	380	11	16	−2
2,485	4	4	−1	Western Europe	2,524	4	6	−3
2,291	4	3	−1	European Union (15)	2,334	4	6	−3
286	7	26	5	Central and Eastern Europe/Baltic States/ CIS[b]	267	6	14	11
129	8	14	12	Central and Eastern Europe	159	10	12	9
103	—	39	−2	Russian Federation	54	—	13	20
141.2	3	27	−5	Africa	136	3	4	2
237	5	42	−9	Middle East	180	5	13	4
1,497	7	18	−9	Asia	1,375	6	23	−7
403	3	14	−16	Japan	349	4	22	−8
266	14	28	7	China	244	15	36	8
568	7	19	−12	Six East Asian traders[c]	532	6	26	−13

Source: World Trade Organization, "World Trade Developments in 2001 and Prospects for 2002," in *International Trade Statistics 2002* (Geneva: World Trade Organization, 2002), p. 24.

[a] Mexico not included in this report.

[b] CIS = Commonwealth of Independent States.

[c] Hong Kong, South Korea, Malaysia, Singapore, Taiwan and Thailand.

names among the world's growing economic elites. Recent figures that indicate the pattern of trade distribution by economic regions are provided in Exhibits 1.6 to 1.9.

With the escalation of trade and foreign direct investment, many industrialized countries have prospered through the years, spurring more competition and advancing globalization in its second phase. Even so, globalization also called attention to the disparities between those who benefited from it and those excluded from these benefits, sowing the first seeds of discontent among fledgling antiglobalization movements.[60] First, there was a shift in the world's focus that went beyond a country's economic growth to a concern for the social, economic, health, and psychological problems of the less developed or developing nations. Second, the economic differences between countries classified as "haves" and "have-nots" became more pronounced. The haves were represented by the three political-economic blocs, the so-called triad, consisting of the European Union, the Pacific Rim, and North America. The have-nots were the rest of the world. Eastern Europe and the former Soviet Union were considered the "future haves" as they strengthened their economic ties with the West.

This view of the world disclosed a phenomenon of imbalance.[61] It was apparent that economic growth was stronger in the private than in the public sector, that there

Exhibit 1.9

Growth in the Value of World Trade in Commercial Services by Region, 2001

Exports					Imports			
Value (US$ billions)	Annual percentage change				Value (US$ billions)	Annual percentage change		
2001	1990–2001	2000	2001		2001	1990–2001	2000	2001
1,460	6	6	0	World	1,445	5	7	−1
299	6	9	−3	North America	229	6	14	−6
58	6	11	−3	Latin America[a]	71	7	12	0
679	5	2	1	Western Europe	647	5	2	1
612	5	1	1	European Union (15)	605	5	2	2
56	—	11	11	Central and Eastern Europe/Baltic States/CIS[b]	59	—	19	13
31	5	0	0	Africa	37	3	7	−3
33	—	16	−7	Middle East	45	—	8	−7
303	8	12	−1	Asia	355	6	8	−3
33	17	15	9	China	39	23	16	9
64	4	13	−7	Japan	107	2	1	−7
146	9	12	0	Six East Asian traders[c]	133	8	13	−3

Source: World Trade Organization, "World Trade Developments in 2001 and Prospects for 2002," in *International Trade Statistics 2002* (Geneva: World Trade Organization), p. 24.

[a] Mexico is not included in this report.

[b] CIS = Commonwealth of Independent States.

[c] Hong Kong, South Korea, Malaysia, Singapore, Taiwan and Thailand.

was a subsequent weakening in regulatory power in government, and that there was no supranational control in terms of policy or regulations on corporate behavior, nor a value system for social responsibility.[62] To participate in economic growth, governments needed to work closely with business leaders. Political scientists, economists, and business analysts played a critical role in the new world order.[63]

Although not a new trend, cooperative actions, that is, strategic alliances among the "haves" nations, were undertaken to protect and preserve their prosperity and stability, which might be upset by the discontented have-not nations.[64] Such strategic alliances, which evolved into government networks with the aid of technology, became key vehicles for commerce during this period. Moreover, established institutions, notably the United Nations, became the forum for world leaders to discuss their policies and differences, while others, such as the World Bank and the General Agreement on Trade and Tariffs (GATT), became instruments for accelerating international trade. These supranational developments offered the world the foundation for the configuration of the new world of the twenty-first century known as transgovernmentalism.[65]

2000s AND THE NEW GLOBAL AGE

A distinctive part of this third phase of globalization differs from the first two phases in that it involves the globalization of individuals in what Friedman describes as a "flat world." Friedman emphatically states: "When the world is flat . . . you can innovate without having to immigrate."[66] While this phase is inextricably related to escalating patterns of international trade and the mass production of goods and services, Friedman identified a number of trends that precipitate the third phase of globalization: There was the end of the Cold War, specifically the 1989 fall of the Berlin Wall, which allowed us to think of the entire world as a seamless whole. In 1995, Netscape connected a new digital world with Web-based software applications that led to entirely new business methods and businesses, such as eBay, Amazon, and Google. And the introduction of the "open-source movement" led to new opportunities for online collaboration among programmers that disrupted traditional business models that were based primarily on internal innovations.

Taken collectively, these trends (called "flatteners") are transforming the way individuals and corporations are empowered, specifically in three points of convergence suggested by Friedman. First, advances in information technology have created a global Web-virtual playing field that encourages and facilitates multiple forms of collaboration regardless of time, geography, and distance. For Google, Amazon, and Yahoo users in particular, Friedman sees a trend that he labels "in-forming," meaning the use of the Web to build and deploy one's own supply of information, entertainment, and knowledge. The next generation of Web activities will highlight new forms of mass collaboration and business opportunities as individuals continue to customize, personalize, and publish their blogs as potential business activities. Second, new business skills and practices have developed to a point where firms can capitalize on emerging collaborative forms as part of their corporate strategies. For example, England-based WPP, the second-largest advertising-marketing-communications consortium in the world, created customized collaborative teams, changed its office architecture, and even dismantled its office floors to allow a vast pool of specialists to be organized on short notice to work with a specialized project. Third, as globalization intensifies, more individuals will have access to the tools of collaboration and will be joining the global economic labor force at a faster pace than before. One such pattern is the outsourcing of intellectual and clerical work from industrialized countries to low-wage, highly educated workers in India and China (Chapter 6). Reflecting this development, close to 400 out of Forbes 500 companies have invested in more than 2,000 projects located in various parts of mainland China.

What defines this third phase is the intensity of **spatial connectedness**, meaning the emergence of individual networks or larger clusters involving the continuous flow of goods, capital, labor, and services.[67] Compared to previous times, these new networks are much more dense, interconnected, and far more consequential in terms of their activities. These networks have encouraged widespread knowledge as well as the clustering of specific knowledge. International businesses maximize location economies by matching their needs to the locations/regions. Hence, "global webs" have been created, and knowledge and technology transfers occur frequently as part of globalization.[68] In the mid-1990s, John Dunning, a professor of international business at Rutgers University, suggested that "the nationality of a firm's ownership will become less relevant to the location of its wealth-creating activities and to its impact on national economic welfare."[69] Modern corporations have a wide global network

---

Box 1.2

When Technology Matters: Catapulting Africa into the Twenty-First Century

She lives in the Congo River, unable to write her last name. She has no freezer, let alone electricity. Yet she has a business. When orders for fish come, she simply retrieves them out of a river where fish are tethered live on a string. How does she manage this business?

With her cell phone.

Cell phones have transformed rural Africa. It has an average of just one landline for every thirty-three persons, but it is the world's fastest-growing cell phone market. Consider the statistics: from 1999 to 2004, mobile phone subscribers in Africa have increased from 7.5 million to 76.8 million, a staggering average annual increase of 58 percent. One in eleven Africans is a mobile subscriber. It is reported that South Africa, the wealthiest country on the continent, accounted for one-fifth of the growth. In contrast, Asia, the second fastest expanding market, grew by an annual average of just 34 percent during the same period.

A number of factors have paced the explosive growth in cell phone use: the privatization of telephone monopolies in the 1990s, the emergence of fierce competitors, and cheaper units (a used handset sells for $50 or less in South Africa).

Charging a mobile phone in parts of Africa combines high- and low-tech modalities. A popular method is by using a car battery owned by someone who might not even own a car. Others use a gas station. Some simply charge the phones of others for a modest fee, creating a business for themselves in the process.

Globalization is paced by technological advances and innovations. While globalization remains a distant portal, the African experience with cell phones provides graphic testimony that technology, notably the cell phone, is enabling the transition from land-line telephone to twenty-first-century instant messaging.

Source: Adapted from Sharon LaFraniere, "Cellphones Catapult Rural Africa to 21st Century," *New York Times,* August 25, 2005, A–1.

---

of suppliers. For example, the parts for the Dell notebook computer Friedman used while writing his book came from more than 30 major suppliers, with more than 400 subcontractors from more than 50 countries.[70] This third phase of globalization is also characterized by the blurring of traditional industry boundaries and the breakdown of conventional competitive strategies (more will be said about this in Chapters 3 and 12).[71] Horizontal control models, such as network and virtual communities, have taken over the traditional hierarchy (also see Chapter 10).[72] Managers who previously worked in big companies found that "virtual companies" became good options for career moves.[73] All in all, globalization offers a mixed bag of benefits and risks to individuals and business managers. The manner in which they respond will determine eventual winners and losers. (An interesting account of how technology has facilitated the growth of cell phones in Africa is provided in Box 1.2.)

The increased access to information among the world's citizens has greatly highlighted disparities in wealth, environmental degradation, and the social consequences of international trade. Outgrowths of this greater awareness are indicated by the Global Compact (a voluntary initiative for businesses to align their operations to universally accepted principles relating to human rights, the environment, and labor), the UN Millennium Developmental Goals (a program aimed to reducing world poverty by 50 percent in 2015, along with reductions in HIV/AIDS and advances in education), and a variety of market-based certification schemes with environmental and/or social performance criteria.

A SYNTHESIS OF GLOBALIZATION: IMPLICATIONS FOR MANAGEMENT

Our review of globalization in a historical context suggests four themes. The first emphasizes the intensification of trade, the international mobility of capital and other factors of production, and the transfer of foreign direct investment. As a whole, these pertain to the *economic* side of globalization. A second theme emphasizes the integration of noneconomic factors, such as emerging cultural homogeneity and the permeability of cultural norms. We refer to these collectively as the *cultural* side of globalization. Cultural homogeneity results from the declining role of distance, geography, and territoriality, and the prominent role of media in diffusing cultural values. A third theme emphasizes the role of governments in reducing trade tariffs and restrictions through bilateral and multilateral agreements. This is the *political* side of globalization. The fourth focuses on how technology has accelerated globalization by reducing distance and territoriality, enhancing deregulation, and facilitating the emergence of new, strong international competitors.[74] We refer to this as the *technological* side of globalization. Taking into account the different perspectives of globalization can clarify what appear to be confusing and contradictory statements. For example, a person can agree on the merits of the technological factors that have accelerated globalization, but might not like the resulting cultural homogeneity that can result.[75] It is hence important to define which side of globalization one is concerned about, and then proceed accordingly.

The four themes have two characteristics that are common and reinforce one another. The first is **connectivity**. This refers to the increased economic linkages between individuals in the expansion of trade and investment. Everyone operating in the global economy seems to be interconnected. The economic actions of a company or a country affect and are affected by economic, political, social, and cultural events in other societies—more than ever before. From a business standpoint, closer economic linkages have made it possible to do business, or almost anything else, instantaneously with billions of other people in the world. While many firms focused primarily on marketing abroad for many years, they now have to integrate their marketing, production, supply line, and financial activities on a worldwide basis, without sacrificing their strong regional focus, to take advantage of globalization. The second characteristic is the speed, or **pace** of globalization. The interconnectedness between individuals is occurring more quickly than ever before. For many, not only is the pace of globalization a fast one, it might also be an irreversible one.[76] For corporations, the pace of globalization matters. Not only do these firms have to build advantages on a global scale, they need to do it as fast, if not faster, than their erstwhile competitors. Moreover, firms have to be attentive to how globalization can adversely affect them. For example, financial crises are not new, but as illustrated by the 1997 Asian financial meltdown and others that immediately followed it, their magnitude and speed are qualitatively different, creating a greater sense of economic vulnerability and insecurity.[77] Despite such adverse effects, however, proponents of globalization argue that economic connectedness and intensified trade have created wealth and prosperity on a worldwide basis, and in so doing, have alleviated poverty, income inequality, and social ills.

Another distinguishing characteristic of the current globalization is the degree to which governments have intervened to reduce obstacles to the flow of goods, services, and capital worldwide, that is, the political side of globalization.[78] This underscores the argument that governments can accelerate globalization, but can also reduce it. Therefore, there is a need to distinguish between globalization that is accelerated by technological and market forces from globalization that results from government politics and policies.[79] Some scholars contend that the biggest obstacles to economic globalization are not failures in the market but ill-advised governmental politics and policies.[80]

Our short and cursory review of globalization leads to two important conclusions and implications that we have adapted in developing the core arguments in this book: First, the debate over whether the world is "global" or not, and whether globalization is temporary or irreversible, tends to obscure what we think is its critical implication for business practice: *globalization is a dynamic process that is still unfolding.* Hence, while there are globalizing forces at work, we have not reached a fully global world as envisioned by those who argue that nation-states are no longer relevant, and that the role of global corporations without any allegiance to place or community is to provide standardized products and services to homogeneous customers all over the world. In a provocative book, *The End of Globalization,* Alan Rugman, a professor of international business at Indiana University, reports that most globalization activity is limited and confined within a triad of Europe, Japan, and the United States, based on a study of 441 multinationals of the Fortune 500.[81] What matters then, in our view, is to understand the *drivers* of globalization, and to determine how the *pace* of industry globalization affects the strategies and operations of organizations. Second, in contrast to the belief that globalization is creating a monolithic, homogeneous world, we argue that globalization impels the need for *both* standardization and integration, *and* local adaptation and responsiveness. The two are not mutually exclusive; in fact, they are inextricably related. This is well stated by Wharton management professor Mauro Guillen who, in his book, *Limits to Convergence,* argues against the accepted wisdom that homogeneity results from globalization:

> Globalization actually encourages diversity in economic, social and organizational form, rather than convergence. It intensifies our consciousness of the world as a whole, making us more aware of each other, and perhaps more prone to be influenced by one another without necessarily making us more like each other. But it is precisely because globalization enhances mutual awareness in the world that *diversity* in organizational form is *expected* as countries and firms seek to *differentiate* themselves in the global economy.[82] (Emphasis added.)

In summary, two core arguments support our view about globalization, and these provide the basis of our ensuing discussion and analysis:

- Globalization is a process that continues to unfold up to this day. Thus, it is essential that managers understand the drivers of globalization, and how the pace of globalization is affecting their industry and company operations.
- Globalization is not solely the provision of standardized products and services to a "borderless," worldwide society. While there are undoubtedly many

benefits from standardization, particularly in a fast-globalizing industry, such homogenizing forces also beget diversity, for which the need for local adaptation becomes paramount.

THE GLOBAL IMPERATIVE

Going global has become a way of conducting business for some U.S. firms, while others have been operating predominantly as domestic firms. Thus, one of most pressing questions asked of managers is whether their firms should extend beyond their national borders and go global: "Is this really an issue for all firms, or for only some firms? "Is it for me?" In recent years, access to foreign markets has been made possible as worldwide economic development has progressed and domestic markets have opened their doors to foreign firms. As more companies go global, the dynamics of globalization gradually change the business environment.

It is not clear whether globalization is an external issue of the business environment, which causes organizations to react, or a strategic issue of the firm, which motivates organizations to initiate action. Most likely it is a combination of proactive and reactive approaches, where some companies choose to globalize and others do so in response to the pressure brought about by companies that have already gone global. To a large extent, this depends on an understanding of the individual firm's capabilities and the manner in which globalization is assumed, or expected, to influence the firm's competitive position. In the 1950s, E.J. Kingston-McCloughry (1896–1972), former Air Vice-Marshal, Royal Air Force, used the term *global strategy* in his book of the same title.[83] Until the early 1980s, terms like *global* and *multinational* were used widely and interchangeably. It was at that time that scholars began differentiating between the two. The late Harvard Business School professor Theodore Levitt is said to be the first to offer a distinction between them,[84] with other scholars offering comparable views.[85] In general, multinational corporations operate in multiple countries and exploit differences among multiple international consumer groups. Global corporations market a minimum number of products to a maximum number of countries by exploiting similarities in international consumer groups. Because each product covers a wide range of geographic locations, the company becomes "global." Some examples include Matsushita and Hitachi. While the multinational company seeks differentiation as the primary means to build competitive advantage, the global company aims for the integration of scale and scope to achieve a cost leadership position. Harvard University professor Christopher Bartlett and the late INSEAD professor Sumatra Ghoshal have introduced the concept of a **transnational corporation**, which recognizes that each of the above two approaches is partial, but in order to manage efficiency and innovation simultaneously, exploits each and every combination, including learning, as leverage in building advantage.[86]

All in all, competing in overseas markets provides opportunities for companies to earn corresponding returns in ways that exploit their core competencies, while allowing further growth opportunities through local learning. For most firms, going global becomes a critical link to long-term success. Some believe that going global is inevitable if a company is to retain its ability to compete against traditional rivals. And some management practitioners and researchers are convinced that a company's long-term success and survival are not simply based on its global presence but on its ability to achieve global dominance.[87] In their book *The Quest for Global Dominance,* Vijay Govindarajan, professor of international business at Dartmouth College, and Anil K. Gupta, professor of strategy at the University of Maryland, have presented five reasons why companies should consider going global.[88] In acquainting themselves with these imperatives, managers can also assess whether going global is right for a particular company.

The Growth Imperative

The **growth imperative** refers to the urgency and need to grow beyond the current market. Because markets for most industries in developed countries are becoming mature, firms have to look elsewhere to market their goods and services. Assuming that the demand for their products is significant, then the logical path for growth is through international markets. Such is the path being taken by Wal-Mart, Starbucks, IKEA, and other leading firms. Scholars believe that the international market is huge and growing, estimated conservatively at about $6 trillion in 2001 and projected to be about $73 trillion within thirty years.[89] With diminishing regulatory and technological barriers to trade, the potential is enormous for any company that can capitalize on it. Thus, Govindarajan and Gupta's first reason is straightforward: for a company to continue its trajectory of growth, it has to sell overseas.

The Efficiency Imperative

For many companies, the amount of production that results from the most efficient plant exceeds the market demand feasible within this country. The **efficiency imperative** refers to the fact that, for the sake of efficiency, a firm will have to sell overseas in order to justify the volume of production needed to support investment in research and development, production, marketing, and so on. For example, Mercedes cannot afford to simply sell in Europe, let alone Germany, because its production volume far exceeds the demand in these countries. By selling 20 percent in the United States, Mercedes is able to spread its operating costs over a large base and thus become more efficient.[90]

The Knowledge Imperative

After World War II, when U.S. firms were dominant in the world economy, they did not have to look beyond the national border for sales. In addition, much of the know-how for manufacturing goods and services was in the United States. This is no longer true. Other countries have excelled in particular products: Japan in photolithography, Brazil in cosmetics and plastic surgery; Bulgaria in laser eye surgery; China in textiles and shoes; Taiwan in PC motherboard technology. Termed "lead countries," such places are also hotbeds of innovation.[91] The **knowledge imperative** suggests that firms who seek to keep abreast of these new developments need to go where the knowledge is. Moreover, it is widely acknowledged that firms gain know-how as they adapt their products and services to the local environment. When General Electric started selling

CT scanners in India, it had to adapt these to local use, making them simpler, more transportable, and much cheaper.[92]

THE GLOBALIZATION OF CUSTOMERS

Another reason for going global is that most firms' customers are already there. The **globalization of customers** means that as a consequence of globalization, customers have become more homogeneous in terms of their demand. Around the world, you are likely to see others like you having similar tastes for jeans, Nike shoes, Apple iPods, Perrier bottled mineral water, and so on. If customers have a craving for Coke or Pepsi, for example, then Coca-Cola and Pepsi will lose opportunities by simply not being there. And when these companies start marketing in Vietnam, for example, it is only a matter of time before their ancillary suppliers, specifically advertising agencies, need to get there to capitalize on their own market opportunities. A popular advertisement is American Express' "Don't leave home without it." How many people would want to carry this card around the world if it was only honored in the United States?[93]

THE GLOBALIZATION OF COMPETITORS

Finally, Govindarajan and Gupta remind us that "globalization is no longer an option but a strategic imperative for all but the smallest firms."[94] The **globalization of competitors** occurs because one's own competitors are already operating globally. Thus, not having a presence abroad can be dysfunctional, in that a firm surrenders potential sales to its competitors, almost by default. For some executives, this is the distinguishing characteristic of a global business, that is, an industry becomes global when its key competitors become global players.

Reflecting on the experiences of U.S. multinationals in 1985, Gary Hamel (a strategy professor at the London Business School and founder of the consulting firm *Strategos*), and C.K. Prahalad (a professor of strategy at the University of Michigan), said that corporate response to the threat of foreign competition is often misdirected and ill timed—in part because many executives do not fully understand what global competition is.[95] Since then, as indicated earlier in this chapter, global competition has intensified and now poses a more central strategic challenge for leading businesses. Not only has global competition become even more pronounced, but many do not see the full implications of changes brought about by globalization and technology. While our knowledge has grown, responding to these challenges has not gotten any easier. The key questions are, therefore: *How do firms succeed in this global economy? What new strategic templates are needed for firms to effectively play the game?*

A FRAMEWORK FOR GLOBAL STRATEGIC MANAGEMENT

In this book, we present a framework for thinking about these questions, and templates for developing global strategic processes in this competitive landscape. Imperatives for developing global strategic management could not be greater. John H. Dunning of Rutgers University has suggested that "firms need to maximize location, internationalization, and ownership advantages on a global scale in order to compete successfully,

Exhibit 1.10

Global Strategic Management Framework

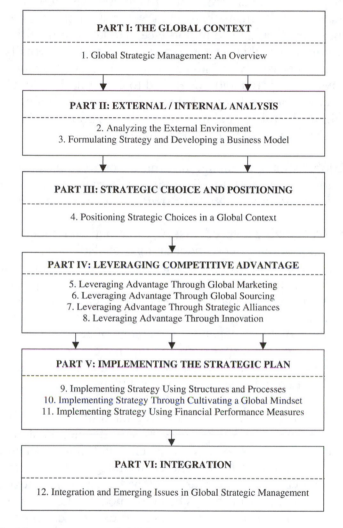

and the globalization process and the free movement of labor and capital has helped to make this become more achievable."[96]

In 1990, Edwin Artzt, former chairman and CEO of Procter & Gamble, expressed a similar sentiment:

> Globalization means doing a better job than your competitors at satisfying consumers' needs and their demand for quality, no matter where they live. It means creating the network and infrastructure to efficiently compete in the increasingly homogeneous worldwide marketplace. Globalization has special meaning with Procter & Gamble. It means that we will continue to change from a United States–based business that sells some of its products in international markets into a truly world company. A company that thinks of everything it does—including the development of products—in terms of the entire world.[97]

While firms have generally extended their core strategies to international markets, they have to examine all sources of value-added activities on an integrated, worldwide basis, while maintaining a strong regional focus. The global imperative applies to managers at all levels, from the CEO to line managers and middle and lower levels of management. It affects the way in which strategies are developed and implemented. Going global has gained importance in today's competitive environment and is more of a requirement than a choice. A company that is internally driven to go international on a limited basis will inevitably go global. A company that is not so driven must always be prepared and positioned to confront the global challenge at any time. In this section, we outline a schematic framework to analyze and develop strategies that are driven by this global imperative. As the book unfolds, each of the components of the framework will be explained in greater detail.

Global strategic management builds on five phases of planning and analysis that provide a framework for deploying resources and a plan of action: *recognizing antecedents; analysis; choice of strategy; process;* and *implementation/integration.*

- Recognizing antecedents: Any international undertaking poses risks, as well as opportunities. Such undertakings are also expensive and can engender competitive reactions. For these reasons, it is important to recognize the *antecedents* of any strategic planning process at the advent of the process.
- Analysis: Multinational corporations encounter diverse competitors in greater numbers as they move from the domestic to the global arena. The competitive scope of a firm depends on its range of activities. The breadth of product coverage, location, expansion, and the like define the range for which competition is anticipated. The *analysis* of the external and internal environments becomes the second requirement in building a plan of action.
- Choice of strategy: Analysis leads to the *choice of strategy* that is central in the planning effort of any firm. Included in this appraisal of the forces that drive competition and its key players is the development of a business plan that defines the firm's strategy, resources, customer interface, and value partnerships.
- Process: Following the choice of strategy, it becomes essential to understand how competitive advantage is developed in a global context. This entails a close examination of how the firm's business model matches up against the pace of industry globalization. Four competitive contexts prescribing a firm's growth trajectory are presented. Because a proper analysis of these competitive contexts is the core of the global strategic management, the discussion is organized in terms of a *process* of building advantage and enhancing the firm's ability to exploit international opportunities. The four core areas of this process include international marketing, sourcing and outsourcing strategies, strategic alliances and partnerships, and the enhancement of the firm's innovative capabilities. These four areas also provide options for managers to improve and strengthen their business models as these reflect their ability to exploit international opportunities.
- Implementation and integration: Finally, organizations succeed or fail to the extent that they select appropriate strategies and then design organizational

structures *and* processes to support and accommodate the requirements of these strategies. Therefore, the selection of a good strategy by itself does not guarantee success—to be effective, strategies have to be *implemented* and *integrated* properly. Implementation entails the design of appropriate structures, processes, and human resource management programs. It also involves the cultivation of a global mindset and the close monitoring of company financial performance. Integration is the synthesis of each part of strategic planning into a coherent whole. This is typically represented by a firm's business plan.

Following the logic and arguments advanced in this introductory chapter, the book is organized as follows: Chapter 1 has discussed the key challenges facing the contemporary business manager. We reviewed the history of globalization, specifically its three phases, to underscore that globalization is an evolving process with specific implications for managers. The chapter also discussed different viewpoints on globalization and how it affects the strategies and operations of any firm. The chapter's key point is that globalization, paced by technology and a service imperative, sets the mandate and agenda for the international manager.

Chapter 2 is concerned with the appraisal of the external environment. The starting point of any strategic effort is to appraise the external environment and to analyze the profit potential of the industry. We review significant developments in the economic, technological, cultural, and demographic environment, as well as key frameworks that have been researched extensively and validated in practice. The main argument is that without a careful and deliberate analysis of the external environment, firms risk entering markets prematurely, or not entering them at all, leading to vulnerabilities for the firm itself and priceless opportunities for competitors.

Chapter 3 deals with the assessment of the internal environment, specifically a firm's capabilities, through a business model. A business model involves the analysis of a firm's strategy, resources, customer interfaces, and value partnerships. It can determine whether its scope and direction as related to its international goals are warranted. Appraising the external environment and analyzing the firm's business model set the stage for determining the choice of a strategy to capitalize on international market opportunities.

Chapter 4 provides specific guidelines for a diagnostic framework to aid in analyzing the choice of a strategy. Two determinants impel the choice of strategy: the pace of industry globalization, and the ability of a firm to exploit international markets, as discerned from its business model. The juxtaposition of these two determinants leads to four generic strategies: a *pure global* strategy, a *pure local* or *multidomestic* strategy, a *core formula* strategy, and an *incremental* strategy. The key point is that determining a strategy is not arbitrary, but the result of purposeful and careful analysis.

Chapter 5 covers international marketing. Having decided on a core strategy, a firm is left with three interlocking decisions: (1) what markets to enter, (2) how to enter, and (3) when to enter. Traditionally, large and unserved markets were considered attractive. The chapter also discusses the advantages and disadvantages of different modes of entry. The feasibility of exporting, licensing, joint ventures, and wholly owned subsidiaries is based on risk, degree of control, and the extent of resource commitments. The main point is that international marketing needs to be carefully thought out in advance; many missed opportunities result from risky and ill-conceived marketing programs.

Chapter 6 discusses sourcing opportunities, an area that has become increasingly important for multinational firms in recent years. Competitive advantages derive from a firm's ability to build and exploit supply chains that transcend national boundaries. The chapter also details important patterns in offshore outsourcing. The chapter's main argument is that, in the current international environment that is increasingly connected and dense, it is critical for any firm to build advantages through creative sourcing outlets and supply chains.

Chapter 7 covers strategic alliances and collaborative partnership. As an extension of a firm's business model, strategic partnerships have now become an important weapon in a firm's strategic arsenal. The chapter builds on previous research to discuss why some alliances fail, and how to improve on their management. The chapter also discusses the advantages and disadvantages of strategic alliances based on available published research. In the current environment, it is hardly possible for any one firm to cover all its bases, thus making partnerships a compelling alternative.

Chapter 8 is devoted to the topic of innovation in the context of the knowledge-based digital economy. Traditional and contemporary theories about innovation are discussed, with a focus on how they impact global strategies. The chapter reviews the transition from the Machine Age to the Information Age and its far-reaching implications for how business is transacted and practiced. It also addresses how innovative capabilities are built and enhanced in this context. The key point is that a good understanding of innovation and technology can facilitate the transformation of organizations and lead to new competencies in today's global, technological environment.

Chapter 9 discusses how firms can use structures and processes to facilitate the execution of their strategies. Today, many companies are struggling to develop organizations that retain the capability for global reach balanced by local adaptation. We focus on leading-edge applications that emphasize the systemic interrelationships between four design variables—organizational structure, management processes, people, and culture—adjusting all four to achieve coordinated patterns in the global environment. Without the support and commitment of key people, most strategies are bound to fail. The chapter discusses several approaches to human resource management, with some extensions to management in Asia. The main point is that without adequate structures and processes, even a well-formulated strategic plan is bound to fail.

Chapter 10 builds on prior chapters with a discussion of culture, examining how an understanding of cultural differences leads to a global mindset. Many believe that this understanding is the most important requisite for sustaining any global strategy. The twenty-first century changed the paradigm of competence. To accommodate new requirements, new imperatives for a global mindset are needed. The manager with a global mindset has the capability to see across markets, through multiple territories, and to develop a keener consciousness about both commonalities and differences. In sum, developing and cultivating a global mindset is now a necessary part of implementation, no longer a luxury for international managers.

Chapter 11 discusses various financial performance measures that can be used to evaluate the sustainability of a business model. It illustrates how to use certain financial ratios and how to gauge performance from financial statements. It also presents new ways of evaluating the use of resources in the context of global strategies. The key point is that strategies cannot be evaluated and implemented outside the context of financial performance measures.

Chapter 12 presents a fictional case based on a synthesis of selected real-world events ("Can Strategy Save Argosis?"). The case is designed to integrate the analytical frameworks presented throughout the book. It is an opportunity for readers to integrate the entire book and use this case as a basis for anchoring or applying global strategic management in organizations. The last part of the chapter discusses emerging trends in international business as these relate to global strategic management. The key objective of the chapter is for readers to integrate the various frameworks in the book into a coherent whole—to learn by application and have fun.

SUMMARY

1. This chapter examines the concept of globalization and the challenges it has created for the international business manager. Globalization, paced by technology and a service imperative, sets the mandate and agenda for managers.

2. Strategic global management is both a perspective and a process of understanding how firms build and sustain competitive advantage in international operations. It is concerned with how competitive advantages are translated into superior performance. It involves every person in the firm, not just top management.

3. Three specific forces have stirred a revolution in international business and have characterized the new competitive landscape: globalization, digitally based technological advances, and the emergence of a knowledge-based service economy. The goal of this book is make explicit the interconnections between these three forces.

4. Defining globalization has been elusive. Globalization has both its supporters and its critics, each with their own logic, perspective, and statistics. Proponents emphasize the benefits of increased international trade and how this has created growth and prosperity. Opponents argue that globalization has led to greater division between the rich and the poor, a lack of concern for human rights, child labor, an abusive labor environment, the exploitation of local communities, and the like, with negative spillover to the social and cultural environments. Every manager should understand how globalization can facilitate or impede their strategies and activities.

5. A historical review suggests three phases of globalization. The first phase occurred during the merchant voyages in the 1400s to the 1880s; the second, which ushered in the *Pax Britannica*, occurred from 1880 to 1931; and the

third, the age of *Pax Americana,* spanned from 1931 to the present.

6. Based on this historical review, four themes of globalization are salient: economic, cultural, technological, and political. What is common across these themes are two tendencies: connectivity and pervasiveness. It is also noted that governmental politics and policies distinguish the current globalization from previous ones.

7. Two core arguments are forwarded: first, globalization is a process that continues to unfold; second, it is not about the provision of products and services in a "borderless" world, but an attention to and concern for standardization and local adaptation.

8. Globalization has been a phenomenon in the U.S. business community for several decades and has gained a lot of attention in international management and the world economy. In the 1980s, terms like *global* and *multinational* were used widely and interchangeably. Global corporations market a minimum number of products to a maximum number of countries by exploiting similarities in international consumer groups. Going global is a decision that should be carefully considered and not taken blindly. There are risks as well as opportunities. Five imperatives should be reviewed and assessed before a firm decides to go global: growth, efficiency, knowledge, customers, and competitors.

9. Global strategic management builds on five phases of planning and analysis that provide a framework for deploying resources and a plan of action: recognizing antecedents, analysis, choice of strategy, process, and implementation/integration.

10. This book presents a framework for thinking about two questions: How do firms succeed in this global economy? What strategic templates are needed for firms to effectively compete in the international arena?

KEY TERMS

Globalization	Third phase of globalization
Digitally based technologies	Spatial connectedness
Knowledge-based services	Connectivity
First phase of globalization	Pace (of globalization)
Mercantilism	Transnational corporation
Theory of Comparative Advantage	Growth imperative
Joint-stock chartered company	Efficiency imperative
First Industrial Revolution	Knowledge imperative
Liberalism	Globalization of customers
Second phase of globalization	Globalization of competitors

DISCUSSION QUESTIONS

1. What are the key trends of the global environment that affect the contemporary business manager? How is the manager affected by them? Please be specific with your answers.
2. "Going global is imperative." Discuss the validity of this view with ample evidence.
3. Analyze the definitions of globalization and identify the key concepts found in these definitions. Have the definitions changed over time? In light of current developments in globalization, do these definitions fully represent globalization? If yes, how so? If not, why not, and how would you define the current stage of globalization?
4. What are the arguments against globalization? Do you agree/disagree? Please defend your position.
5. What is meant by global shift? It is said that the global environment has shifted several times over the past centuries and culminated in today's globalization. Please discuss this development and provide your predictions for the next stage of globalization.
6. A lot of credit has been given to the invention of the modern business corporation in the early stage of globalization. What role do corporations play in today's globalization?
7. Compare and contrast the three phases of globalization in the twentieth and twenty-first centuries. Based on this trend, what will the next level of globalization entail and when this will be apparent to us?

ACTION ITEM 1.1. A THOUGHT EXPERIMENT

Consider a case put forward by John Meyer and his associates:[98] In breaking news, it was announced by CNN today that an island, previously unknown and inaccessible to the rest of the world, had been discovered, with inhabitants and ample resources. In small groups, discuss your views and responses to the following question: *How would a newly discovered island be incorporated into world society?*

CASE-IN-POINT. STARBUCKS IN SHANGHAI: EXAMINING THE DYNAMICS OF GLOBAL EXPANSION

To say that Starbucks Corporation "stirred" up the habitual coffee cup would be an understatement.[99] Founded in Seattle, Washington in 1971, the company takes its name from the coffee-loving first mate in Herman Melville's classic, *Moby Dick.* In 1987, the company had sales of only $10 million. By 2006, it was a chain with over $7.8 billion a year, boasting 7,500 company-owned outlets nationwide in more than 35 countries, with 2 to 5 new stores opening literally every day—clearly the world's number one specialty coffee retailer.[100]

In the early 1980s, Howard Schultz took a week-long coffee-buying trip to Milan, Italy. At the time, he was a coffee buyer for Starbucks Coffee Co., which sold fresh, whole coffee beans in five specialty stores in Seattle. What he saw in Italy fascinated him and left a lasting impression. Crowds of city dwellers began each day with a stop at a coffee bar. The *baristas* performed their chore of making coffee drinks with exotic names like *latte macchiato* and *espresso con panna* with unbridled passion. Cafés were bustling, boisterous, and filled with the rich aroma of coffee.[101]

In the United States, a coffee price war had been raging for many years. Maxwell House (owned by General Foods) and Folgers (owned by Procter & Gamble) were engaged in a fierce battle over coffees that were not only considered bland and similar, but were used as "loss leaders" to lure shoppers into supermarkets, where coffee was generally sold. Nevertheless, the two brands commanded more than 60 percent of the coffee market. Competition among Maxwell House, Folgers, and Nescafé (owned by Nestlé), was based on price and thus their products were considered commodities. To reduce costs, coffee sold by the majors was made from inexpensive Robusta beans that were sold in cans. With the market shrinking (Americans were drinking less coffee), the majors fought hard advertising battles to maintain share. "Just a fad, this whole-bean coffee thing . . ." the executives concluded.[102]

Undaunted by the pattern of coffee sales, Schultz petitioned his bosses to let him start a café. They refused, citing that they wanted to be in the coffee bean business, not the restaurant business. Schultz quit in order to try the idea on his own. He pursued 242 investors for more than a year. He was rejected 217 times. Finally, he raised $1.7 million—some of it from his own former bosses. In April 1986, Schultz opened his first café in Pike's Market in downtown Seattle. The coffee he served was Starbucks.[103]

In less than a year, Schultz had opened up two more cafés. He bought out his former bosses for $4 million. By August 1987, Schultz had the Starbucks name on his three cafés, but was ignored by the majors that were still engaged in a competitive struggle. By the end of 1988, Folgers was winning the war on the grocery store front. Maxwell House had slipped to a 26.4 percent market share, and its parent company, General Foods, responded with a higher proportion of cheap, bitter, Robusta beans in its blends.[104]

Meanwhile, Starbucks had become a phenomenon in Seattle and was positioning itself to spread to the rest of the United States. A new business plan was developing that went counter to many of the industry's established practices. The firm hired experienced executives from corporations like Pepsi to manage finances and human resources. They named their servers *baristas,* Italian for bartenders. This signaled a change in the culture of the staff Starbucks hired. Each new *barista* was given twenty-five hours of classes on coffee history and lore, quality, drink preparation, and brewing the perfect cup at home. Using this training, the *baristas* educated customers on the romance and sophistication of coffee drinking.[105]

In a move that was contrary to industry practice, in 1991, Schultz introduced Bean Stock, a stock option plan for employees. All of Starbucks' employees, including part-timers, received equity in the company in the form of stock options and a comprehensive health care plan. This approach was so novel that Schultz was invited by President Clinton to talk about it. Reflecting back, Schultz asked: "If the fate of your business is in the hands of a twenty-year old, part-time worker who goes to college or pursues acting on the side, can you afford to treat him or her as expendable?"[106] Turnover of counter help was less than 60 percent, very low for the food-service industry. The cafés had created a culture and a strong, loyal customer base.

Changes in consumer preferences became more aligned with the Starbucks business model. During the period of declining industry sales, people had been consuming soft drinks. Starbucks' strategy had created a new market niche: consumers who liked the taste of coffee made from higher quality beans and who enjoyed the café ambience. More important, this status-conscious segment could also afford the higher price for a premium cup of coffee. For these reasons, coffee drinkers were enjoying the first major expansion in years. Although gourmet coffee was priced 80 to 100 percent higher than traditional coffee, people bought it. Even at $6 per pound, the pleasure worked out to only 10 cents per cup. Once considered a commodity, coffee had now become a differentiated product, or what some have described as an "affordable luxury." Specifically, when ordinary people bought a frothy latte, they were buying something as good as any CEO, movie star, or wealthy entrepreneur could buy. They might not be able to afford an expensive car or a luxurious vacation home, but they could treat themselves to a latte for $4.95 that was prepared to order.[107]

By 1990, Starbucks, along with a growing number of gourmet coffee companies, had $717 million in sales, a 13.5 percent share of the $5.3 billion coffee market. Profit margins were as high as 25 percent. By 1991, the coffee gourmet segment sales had increased to $800 million, while industry-wide sales had dropped to $4.5 billion, led by declines at the majors. At the same time, the café had begun to reach critical mass in a few select cities. Seattle, already dubbed "Latteland" by local columnists, led the way with 150 cafés. By 1992, Chicago had 40; Vancouver was close behind. Meanwhile, Starbucks became one of the fastest-growing brands and the darling of Wall Street and business school pundits.[108]

At the present, some wonder how long this coffee gourmet run will last. Already, Starbucks is facing saturation in the United States, with the addition of almost 2 to 5 new café outlets every day. In Seattle, there is one Starbucks outlet for every 13,340 residents.[109] While Starbucks' rise has been meteoric, surpassing investors' expectations, its rapid growth has tarnished the early entrepreneurial image: Starbucks is becoming more known as a "corporatist" firm. The crowding of new cafés became a joke when the *Onion,* a satirical publication, featured the headline: "New Starbucks Opens in Restroom of Existing Starbucks."[110] To continue at this staggering growth rate, Starbucks has no choice except to open up and expand cafés abroad.

But where?

In 2003, *Wall Street Journal* staff reporter Geoffrey Fowler reported that Nanjing Lu, the main shopping center in Shanghai, China, appeared to be Starbucks' first choice for its next China foray.[111] Researchers adopted a practice initiated by Starbucks' founder, Howard Schultz, during the founding of the first Seattle café at Pike's Street Market, and begun to stake out potential cafés in Shanghai with hand-held counting devices, tallying the number of likely customers.

Even so, Starbucks' strategy for expanded China operations in Shanghai raised numerous questions and concerns.[112] First, China's tradition is steeped in tea, not coffee. Second, the price tag of 20 yuan, or $2.65, for a medium-sized latte accounted for a significant portion of the monthly disposable income; specifically, the average

Chinese three-person household in Shanghai was about $143 in April 2003. Third, Starbucks' corporate status as a large U.S. multinational could arouse some degree of anti-Americanism among China's activists. After Starbucks opened its store in Beijing's hallowed Forbidden City in December 2000, 70 percent of people surveyed opposed this American icon in the center of this Chinese historical landmark.

Starbucks' strategy was designed to lure more affluent consumers who are part of China's middle class into high-traffic café locations. Moreover, the new Starbucks' low-budget marketing would involve no big advertising budgets, no television or mass circulation, and that Starbucks would create a café ambience that appealed to the Chinese customer.[113]

Thus far, Starbucks' activities in China have been quite favorable. In Beijing, Starbucks has reported an annual sales growth of more than 30 percent in recent years. In Shanghai, Starbucks' net profit reached 32 million yuan ($4 million) in less than two years after operations started. Schultz sees China as becoming the company's largest market outside of Northern America.[114]

Even so, such growth has not occurred without growing pains. Currently, Starbucks faces more intense challenges in its China operations. The company prevailed in its lawsuit against the Shanghai Xing Ba Ke Coffee Shop, which had infringed on Starbucks' trademark rights by using a variation of the green Starbucks logo and the name Xing Ba Ke (i.e., a transliteration of Starbucks in Chinese characters is *xing*—pronounced "shing"—meaning star, and *ba ke* that sounds like bucks).[115] Moreover, there is some talk of having Chinese officials formally requesting Starbucks to leave Beijing's Forbidden City as part of an overall major face-lift, although this action is still pending and remains a subject for extensive blogging.[116]

CASE DISCUSSION QUESTIONS

1. Describe the strategies employed by the coffee majors and by Starbucks. Describe main differences in their assumptions, mission, product/market scope, and sources of differentiation.
2. Discuss how globalization has facilitated and hindered Starbucks' strategy.
3. You are among the many firms competing against Starbucks. What's your next move? What can you do to reverse the tide? How do you take advantage of the renewed interest in coffee? How do you compete against a Starbucks?
4. How might you characterize Starbucks' quest for global presence according to Govindarajan and Gupta's five imperatives?
5. Regarding Starbucks' entry into China, what should be the next move? How can Starbucks maximize the power of its business design? Will Starbucks be vulnerable by moving too quickly? What could go wrong, and what can be done about it?

NOTES FOR CHAPTER 1

1. James Canton, "Future Compass: Three Global Scenarios for 2010," Institute for Global Futures, www.futureguru.com/article31.php; the Millennium Project scenarios: Global Normative Scenario, http://www.millennium-project.org/millennium/normscen.html.

2. James Ogilvy and Peter Schwartz, with Joe Flower, *China's Futures: Scenarios for the World's Fastest Growing Economy, Ecology, and Society* (San Francisco: Jossey Bass, 2000).

3. *Mapping the Global Future: Report of the National Intelligence Council's 2020 Project*, available at www.dni.gov/nic/NIC_2020_project.html.

4. Adapted from Canton, "Future Compass."

5. *Mapping the Global Future.*

6. Ogilvy and Schwartz, *China's Futures.*

7. *Mapping the Global Future.*

8. This depiction of the 1980s is adapted from Peter Schwartz, Peter Leyden, and Joel Hyatt, *The Long Boom: A Vision for the Coming Age of Prosperity* (Reading, MA: Perseus Books, 1999), pp. 14–15. Cited from Joseph H. Boyett and Jimmie Boyett, *The Guru Guide to the Knowledge Economy* (New York: John Wiley & Sons, 2001), pp. 3–4.

9. Among the best-sellers at the time include: Ezra Vogel, *Japan as Number One* (Cambridge: Harvard University Press, 1979); William Ouchi, *Theory Z: How American Business Can Meet the Japanese Challenge* (Reading, MA: Addison-Wesley, 1981); Richard Pascale and Anthony Athos, *The Art of Japanese Management* (New York: Simon & Schuster, 1981); Chalmers Johnson, *MITI and the Japanese Miracle* (Stanford, CA: Stanford University Press, 1982); James Abegglen and George Stalk, Jr., *Kaisha: The Japanese Corporation* (New York: Basic Books, 1985).

10. See Martin Wolf, *Why Globalization Works* (New Haven: Yale University, 2004): 13–19; and Jagdish Bhagwati, *In Defense of Globalization* (New York: Oxford University Press, 2004): 10–13. Both critique antiglobalists who equate sales with GDP in assessing the power of corporations. Wolf argues that antiglobalists have confused gross sales with GDP. Because GDP accounting computes the value added of each company (the difference between sales and the cost of inputs), GDP is different from the value of gross sales. Therefore, with this correction, the value added of General Motors, for example, would only be $42 billion, not the $185 billion that antiglobalists have used to construct their argument (see pp. 221–222).

11. In view of the importance of new technology, we introduce the core themes here, but develop them further separately in chapter 8.

12. See chapter 8.

13. See Robert E. Yuskavage and Erich H. Strassner, "Gross Domestic Product by Industry for 2002," *Survey of Current Business* (May 2003). Available at www.findarticles.com/p/articles/mi_3sur/is_5_83/ai_102841589.

14. Similarly, our discussion of how knowledge-services have led to individual empowerment is discussed fully in chapter 8.

15. Regis McKenna, "Marketing Is Everything," *Harvard Business Review* (January 1, 1991), Reprint Number 91108.

16. A very good discussion is Michael Borrus, James Millstein, and John Zysman, *Responses to the Japanese Challenge in High Technology* (Berkeley, CA: Berkeley Roundtable on the International Economy, 1983).

17. See Clayton M. Christensen, *The Innovator's Dilemma: When New Technologies Cause Great Firms to Fail* (Boston: Harvard Business School Press, 1997).

18. Richard D'Aveni, *Hypercompetition: Managing the Dynamics of Strategic Maneuvering* (New York: Free Press, 1994).

19. Vern Terpstra and Ravi Sarathy, *International Marketing* (New York: Dryden Press, 2005).

20. Hilary French, *Vanishing Borders: Protecting the Planet in the Age of Globalization* (New York: W.W. Norton, 2000), p. 1.

21. For a perspective on antiglobalization, see David Henderson, *Anti-Liberalism 2000: The Rise of New Millennium Collectivism* (London: Institute for Economic Affairs, 2001).

22. See Gerardo Ungson, "When Interpretations Collide: The Case of Asia's Financial Crisis," *Journal of Management Inquiry* 7, no. 3 (December 1998): 321–341.

23. Manuel F. Montes, *Currency Crisis in Southeast Asia* (Singapore: Institute for Southeast Asian Studies, 1998), p. 11.

24. Duck-Woo Nam, "The Financial Crisis in Korea," *Korea Economic Update,* 9, no. 1 (January 1998).

25. Gerardo R. Ungson, R. Steers, and Seung Ho Park, "Reappraising Korea: The Crisis, Aftermath, and Future Challenges," in a special issue, "Tamed Tigers: Restructuring, Liberalization and Changing Business Systems in the East Asian Economies," ed. Oded Shenkar and Manuel Serapio, Jr., *International Management Review* 39 (1999): 51–83.

26. Ibid.

27. See two books in particular: John Ralston Saul, *The Collapse of Globalism and the Reinvention of the World* (New York: Overlook Press, 2005), in which the author dissects claims that globalism (or economic globalization) has delivered on its promises; instead, he argues that it is failing as "positive nationalism," evidenced by the policy turnaround in New Zealand that has become part of the landscape and an antidote to globalization. Seattle University professor Barbara Parker also provides an extensive treatise about globalization in *Globalization and Business Practice* (London: Sage Publications, 1998, 2005).

28. Karl Moore and David Lewis, *Foundations of Corporate Empire: Is History Repeating Itself?* (London: FT Prentice Hall, 2000).

29. Thomas L. Friedman, *The World Is Flat: A Brief History of the Twenty-First Century* (New York: Farrar, Straus, and Giroux, 2005).

30. Moore and Lewis (cited in note 28) take issue with Friedman's earlier assertion that only two stages of globalization have occurred. See Thomas L. Friedman, *The Lexus and the Olive Tree* (New York: Anchor Books, 2000). In fact, Friedman revised his thesis in positing three stages (see Thomas Friedman, "Globalization 3.0 Has Shrunk the World to Size Tiny," *Yale Global Online,* April 7, 2004, http://yaleglobal. yale.edu). In view of such disagreements, we have adopted Moore and Lewis's three stages, but also place Friedman's description of the current globalization as a detailed part of the third phase.

31. See Samuel Noah Kramer, *The Sumerians—Their History, Culture and Character* (Chicago: University of Chicago, 1963); Nicole Postgate, *Early Mesopotamia: Society and Economy at the Dawn of History* (New York: Routledge, 1994).

32. Economic anthropologist Karl Polanyi cites the absence of the purported market/trading system in the writings of Herodotus, who had visited Babylon between 470 and 460 BCE; an examination of the legal character of economic transactions from the Old Babylonian period; the lack of reference from reliable archaeological records on the walled towns of Palestine; and the ensuing work of A.L. Oppenheim. See Karl Polanyi, "Marketless Trading in Hammurabi's Time," in *Trade and Markets in the Early Empires*, Karl Polanyi, Conrad M. Arensberg, and Harry Pearson (eds.) (Glencoe, Illinois: the Free Press and The Falcon Wing Press, 1957): 12–25.

33. Ibid., pp. 19–20.

34. This account is based on Edward J. Waddle, "A Brief History of Ancient Coins," *Hands-On History* (Frederick, MD: Online Version, 1999), http://www.ancienthistory.com/history.shtml. Also see Moore and Lewis, *Foundations of Corporate Empire*, p. 62. Even so, transactions were also characterized in terms of gift giving, redistribution, and reciprocity. See Karl Polanyi, "Marketless Trading in Hammurabi's Time," p. 18.

35. Moore and Lewis, *Foundations of Corporate Empire*, p. 19.

36. Ibid., pp. 100–01.

37. Ibid., p. 120.

38. Ibid., p. 142.

39. Ibid., pp. 184–85.

40. Ibid., p. 193.

41. Ibid., pp. 187 and 194.

42. Ibid., pp. 195–96.

43. Ibid., p. 196.

44. See David Hume, *Essays, Moral, Political, and Literary* (New York: Cosimo Press, 2006) (Vol. I first published 1742) (*Political Discourses*, Vol. II, first published 1752).

45. Adam Smith, *An Inquiry into the Nature and Causes of the Wealth of Nations*, Edwin Cannan (ed.) (London, U.K.: Methuen & Company, 1904, First published in 1776).

46. David Ricardo, Principles of Political Taxation and Economy, reprinted in J.R. McCulloch, *The Works of David Ricardo* (London: John Murray, 1888).

47. Information for this section is drawn from the following sources: The Commercial Cable Company, as told by the President and others, http://www.cial.org.uk/cable13.htm; Dave and Patricia Kustra, Their Journey to America, http://www.akvhs.org/their_journey_to_america.htm; and Daniel Headrick, British Imperial Postal Network, Paper to the International Economic History, Helsinky, August 2006, http://www.helsinki.fi/iehc2006/papers3/Headrick.pdf.

48. The technological inventions included the spinning machine, the mechanical loom, the puddling process for steelmaking, the steamship, and the threshing and reaping machine. See Note 49.

49. *National Geographic Visual History of the World* (Washington, DC: National Geographic Society, 2005), p. 430.

50. Moore and Lewis, *Foundations of Corporate Empire*, pp. 16–17.

51. Ibid., p. 214.

52. Adam Smith, *An Inquiry into the Nature and Causes of the Wealth of Nations* (Oxford: Clarendon, 1776; repr. 1869).

53. Moore and Lewis, *Foundations of Corporate Empire*, pp. 220–221.

54. Peter Dicken, *Global Shift: Reshaping the Global Economic Map in the 21st Century* (New York: Guilford, 2003), p. 32.

55. Frederick W. Taylor, *Principles of Scientific Management* (New York: Harper Brothers, 1911).

56. Lawrence Hrebiniak and William F. Joyce, *Implementing Strategy* (New York: MacMillan, 1984), pp. 135–136.

57. Dicken, *Global Shift*, p. 19.

58. Ibid., p. 32.

59. Ibid.

60. Paul Ekins, *A New World Order: Grassroots Movements for Global Change* (London: Routledge, 1992).

61. Marvin Cetron and Owen Davies, *The Haves and Have-Nots of the New World Order* (New York: St. Martin's Press, 1991).

62. See detailed accounts by Richard Barnet and John Cavanagh, *Global Dreams: Imperial Corporations and the New World* (New York: Touchstone, 1994); John Dunning, *Multinational Enterprises and the Global Economy* (Reading, MA: Addison-Wesley, 1994); Noam Chomsky, *World Orders, Old and New* (New York: Columbia University Press, 1994); and Anne-Marie Slaughter, "The Real New World Order," *Foreign Affairs* 76, no. 5 (1997): 183–197.

63. Dunning, *Multinational Enterprises and the Global Economy*.

64. Given the importance of strategic alliance, we develop the topic as a separate chapter (Chapter 6). Also see: Cetron and Davies, *The Haves and Have-Nots of the New World Order,* and Dunning, *Multinational Enterprises and the Global Economy*.

65. Slaughter, "The Real New World Order," 183–197.

66. Friedman, *The World Is Flat*. Transcript, http://www.imf.org/external/np/tr/2005.

67. See Dicken, *Global Shift*. We also discuss networks as new forms of organizational structures in chapter 7.

68. Chong Ju Choi, "Global Competitiveness and National Attractiveness," *International Studies of Management and Organization* 29, no. 1 (1999): 3–13.

69. Dunning, *Multinational Enterprises and the Global Economy*, p. 42.

70. Friedman, *The World Is Flat*, pp. 416–419.

71. This is discussed in detail in chapter 3 (p. 119) and 12 (pp. 544–545).

72. Peter Senge, *The Fifth Discipline: The Art and Practice of the Learning Organization* (New York: Doubleday Currency, 1990).

73. M.J. Xavier and John C. Henderson, "Real Strategies for Virtual Organizing," *Sloan Management Review* 40, no. 1 (1998): 33–48.

74. M.A. Hitt, B.W. Keats, and S.M. DeMarie, "Navigating in the New Competitive Landscape: Building Strategic Flexibility and Competitive Advantage in the 21st Century," *The Academy of Management Executives* 12, no. 4 (1998): 22–42.

75. Barbara Parker, *Globalization and Business Practice,* pp. 12–20. Also see Martin Wolf, *Why Globalization Works*, p. 18.

76. Perhaps the most prominent among the hyperglobalists is Japanese management consultant Kenichi Ohmae, who has advocated a "borderless" world. See Kenichi Ohmae, *The Borderless World: Power and Strategy in the Interlinked Economy* (New York: Harper Business, 1999).

77. Jagdish Bhagwati, *In Defense of Globalization* (New York: Oxford University Press, 2004), p. 12.

78. Ibid., p. 11.

79. Ibid., p. 11.

80. Ibid. Also see Martin Wolf, *Why Globalization Works* (New Haven, CT: Yale University Press, 2004).

81. Alan Rugman, *The End of Globalization: Why Global Strategy Is a Myth and How to Profit from the Realities of Regional Markets* (New York: AMACOM, 2001).

82. Mauro Guillen, *Limits of Convergence: Globalization and Organizational Change in Argentina,*

South Korea, and Spain (New Jersey: Princeton University Press, 2001), p. 70.

83. E.J. Kingston-McCloughry, *Global Strategy* (New York: Frederick A. Praeger, 1957).

84. Theodore Levitt, "The Globalization of Markets," *Harvard Business Review* 61, no. 3 (May/June 1983): 92–102.

85. See R.J. Allio, "Formulating Global Strategy," *Planning Review* (March/April 1989): 22–27; and Richard Hodgetts and Fred Luthans, *International Management* (New York: McGraw-Hill, 1994).

86. Christopher A. Bartlett and Sumantra Ghoshal, *Managing Across Borders: The Transnational Solution* (Boston: Harvard Business School Press, 1998). This view is developed further in chapter 4.

87. Vijay Govindarajan and Anil Gupta, *The Quest for Global Dominance: Transforming Global Presence into Global Competitive Advantage* (San Francisco: Jossey-Bass, 2001).

88. Ibid., pp. 2–23.

89. Lowell L. Bryan and Jane N. Fraser, "Getting to Global," *McKinsey Quarterly* 4 (1999): 68–81.

90. Example cited from Joseph H. Boyett and Jimmie T. Boyett, *The Guru Guide to the Knowledge Economy* (New York: John Wiley, 2001), p. 271.

91. Lead countries have innovative competitors, demanding customers, or both. See George S. Yip, *Total Global Strategy* (New York: Prentice Hall, 2003), pp. 42–44.

92. Boyett and Boyett, *The Guru Guide to the Knowledge Economy*, pp. 271–272.

93. Ibid., p. 272.

94. Govindarajan and Gupta, *The Quest for Global Dominance*, p. 2.

95. Gary Hamel and C.K. Prahalad, "Do You Really Have a Global Strategy?" *Harvard Business Review* 63(4): 139–148.

96. Dunning, *Multinational Enterprises and the Global Economy*.

97. Ed Artzt, "Strategies for Global Growth." Speech delivered at a meeting for leading financial analysts at Procter & Gamble (Cincinnati, Ohio, May 21, 1990): p. 1.

98. Adapted from John Meyer, John Boli, George Thomas, and Francisco Ramirez, "World Society and the Nation-State," *American Journal of Sociology* 103 (1): 144–181.

99. Starbucks Case, Basic Marketing Module by Gene Johnson, Management Development Resource Group (MDRG), New Jersey, 1999.

100. Richard Boulton, Barry Libert, and Steve Samek, *Cracking the Value Code* (New York: HarperCollins, 2000), pp. 37–38.

101. Howard Schultz, *Pour Your Heart Into It: How Starbucks Built a Company One Step at a Time* (New York: Hyperion Publishing, 1997), pp. 50–53.

102. Adrian Slywotsky, *Value Migration: How to Think Several Steps Ahead of Competition* (Boston, MA: Harvard Business School Press, 1996), pp. 159–160.

103. Ibid., pp. 164–165.

104. Ibid., p. 161.

105. Ibid., p. 165.

106. Schultz, *Pour Your Heart Into It*, p. 125.

107. Philip Bernosky, "Mantra," *Applied Marketing* (July 12, 2006), www.bernosky.com/index.php?option=com_content&task=view&id=23&Itemid=9.

108. Slywotsky, *Value Migration*, pp. 171–173.

109. "Maximum Starbucks Density," January 24, 2005, http://www.kottke.org/05/01/maximum-starbucks-density.

110. "New Restroom Opens in an Existing Starbucks," *The Onion*, 33, no. 20, June 27, 1998, http://www.theonion.com/content/node/29030.

111. The section about Starbucks' expansion into China is drawn from Geoffrey Fowler, "Starbucks' Road to China," *Wall Street Journal*, July 14, 2003; "Coffee Wars Heat Up: New Strategies to Jolt the Caffeine-Conscious Consumer," *Marketing Wharton Reports*, available at http://knowledge.wharton.upenn.edu/index.cfm?fa+printArticle $ID.

112. Geoffrey Fowler, "Starbucks' Road to China," *Wall Street Journal*, July 14, 2003.

113. Ibid.

114. "Starbucks Soars in China," *Asia Times Online,* June 15, 2006, http://www.atimes.com/atimes/China_Business/HF15Cb06.html.

115. Geoffrey Fowler, "Starbucks Wins China Court Case Over Landmark," *CorpWatch*, January 3, 2006, http://www.corpwatch.org/article.php?id=13005.

116. Geoffrey Fowler, "How Blogging Can Galvanize China," *China Digital Times*, October 2, 2007, http://chinadigitaltimes.net/2007/01/how_blogging_can_galvanize_china_geoffrey_a_fowler.php.

PART I: THE GLOBAL CONTEXT

1. Global Strategic Management: An Overview

PART II: EXTERNAL / INTERNAL ANALYSIS

2. Analyzing the External Environment
3. Formulating Strategy and Developing a Business Model

PART III: STRATEGIC CHOICE AND POSITIONING

4. Positioning Strategic Choices in a Global Context

PART IV: LEVERAGING COMPETITIVE ADVANTAGE

5. Leveraging Advantage Through Global Marketing
6. Leveraging Advantage Through Global Sourcing
7. Leveraging Advantage Through Strategic Alliances
8. Leveraging Advantage Through Innovation

PART V: IMPLEMENTING THE STRATEGIC PLAN

9. Implementing Strategy Using Structures and Processes
10. Implementing Strategy by Cultivating a Global Mindset
11. Implementing Strategy Using Financial Performance Measures

PART VI: INTEGRATION

12. Integration and Emerging Issues in Global Strategic Management

2 Analyzing the External Environment

Ready, Fire, Aim.
—Staffers' alleged motto for former President Jimmy Carter

Those who ignore their environment do so at their peril because consequences that affect
them will likely be defined by others.
—Anonymous

CHAPTER OUTLINE

- Nanotechnology: A New Industrial Frontier?
- The Changing External Environment
- Macroenvironmental Analysis
- Industry Analysis: Five Forces of Competition
- The Role of Complementors
- Analyzing an Industry's Globalization Potential
- Antitrust: A Cautionary Note
- Implications

LEARNING OBJECTIVES

- Become acquainted with some important frameworks for assessing the external environment.
- Understand the overall picture using macroenvironmental analysis.
- Understand the five forces that determine the profit potential of any industry.
- Augment this analysis by understanding the role of complementors.
- Extend the analysis to a global context through industry globalization drivers.

NANOTECHNOLOGY: A NEW INDUSTRIAL FRONTIER?

It is widely acknowledged among business strategists that the starting point of any strategic planning effort consists of analyzing the profit potential of the industry. It is an appropriate beginning in that, whether the industry's potential is good or poor, it behooves all to understand how to compete within it. Because some industries are relatively mature, they tend to be easier to analyze than others. But new or embryonic industries are among the most promising in terms of growth and development, both in domestic and international markets. Whatever an industry's stage of growth, it is important to understand its underlying dynamics. In our opening case, we focus on nanotechnology, perhaps the most anticipated as the "next" generation of products and services that can reinvigorate technological advances already sown by communications technology, the personal computer, and the Internet.

Nanotechnology is likely to change the way in which almost everything—including medicine, computers, and cars—is designed and constructed. "Nano" is a prefix indicating a factor of 10^{-9}, such as nanoseconds or nanometers. Placed in perspective, one nanometer, or a billionth of one meter, is 1/75,000th the width of a human hair. Nanotechnology refers to the general field of applied science and technology that involves the precise measurement and manipulation of matter that consists of less than 100 nanometers.[1] The excitement over nanotechnology is that, at this very small size, scientists can potentially produce new materials that are smaller, stronger, and tougher for applications in a wide range of industries.

For example, nanomachines can be linked together to make artificial muscle fibers to change physical properties and make products lighter, stronger, cleaner, less expensive, and more precise. Even though nanotechnology is still five to fifteen years down the road, its potential effects in artificial muscle fibers have been considered cautiously.[2]

Applied to the computer industry, nanotechnology can be used to make a molecular computer capable of storing trillions of bytes of data in an objects the size of dice. Professor Donald Fitzmaurice of University College, Dublin, is researching the use of DNA to direct the assembly of nano-scale electronic components. That technology will require a whole new generation of computer components to go with it.[3]

Nanotechnology as applied to the medical field in the near future defies the imagination. Nanotechnological microbiology allows doctors to inject nanosurgeons into the thigh or buttock. Assisted by nanonurses, they can move anywhere as needed and perform delicate internal operations. The nanosurgeons can be very sharp and precise. Because of their tiny size, they can operate without leaving scars on the skin. Pre-programmed nanorobots can be absorbed along with fluid into the human body to attack bad cells wherever they are and rebuild the molecular structure of cancer cells and viruses, rendering them harmless. Taken even further, nanotechnological advances will facilitate facial surgery and could reverse the outward signs of aging.[4]

Nanotechnology can also be applied to environmental protection. The nano-bio revolution may very well offer changes in agricultural productivity. Airborne nanorobots have the potential ability to reconstruct the ozone layer. Water can be purified and oil spills cleaned up by nanoparticles. Industrial waste and pollution can also be reduced by using nanotechnology. Nanomachines can move objects bigger than themselves and cause a chemical reaction that will change the properties of materials. The technology could be used to re-create or renew materials and turn waste into resources or food, changing the world's battle with famine. The implications of its impact on the planet are immeasurable. The world may not need to deforest, drill for oil, or mine for coal.[5]

Despite the benefits, there are significant concerns about nanotechnology. Researchers implore us to be mindful of the impact of nanoparticles that travel freely through the environment and the human body.[6] They are so miniscule and fine that they can slip into the blood vessel wall. Once they are in the blood, they can move uninhibitedly and can even enter the fetus. Moreover, they can create chemical reactions that could destroy the immune system, alter enzyme exchanges, generate allergic reactions, or intervene with cell communications. For example, some products containing nanoparticles, such as sunscreen and baby lotions, prompt intense concerns. As for the environment, nanoparticles can penetrate plant roots and affect our food source, and not necessarily for the better. Accordingly, measures have been proposed to monitor how and where nanoparticles should be stored and distributed.

Despite the concerns about nanotechnology, it is regarded one of the most significant technological developments, one that will profoundly affect society. Fitzmaurice offered a provocative idea when he said: "This grand convergence of biotechnology and nanotechnology is going to blur the distinction between the animate and inanimate worlds, which could cause problems because the way we organize our society is based on a well-defined distinction between living and non-living. There could be ethical issues over the rights we assign to synthetic materials that are alive and at the same time not alive."[7]

THE CHANGING EXTERNAL ENVIRONMENT

In Chapter 1 we introduced the third phase of globalization as the new world order faced by the contemporary business manager, and one that is increasingly shaped by digital technology. The complexity of this new, globalized world order is due largely to new global competitors and new technologies. Our opening example illustrates how embryonic industries, such as nanotechnology, have the potential to shape patterns of competition in years to come. While the analysis of an industry is central to any appraisal of the external environment, the global environment faced by contemporary managers is a multifaceted one that has become even more complex as the number of markets served by the firm continues to increase.

Rapid technological changes have occurred, with far-reaching implications for worldwide trade and investment. All firms conduct business in the context of the external environment. Thus, a key requirement of management is to assess the external environment facing the firm. This can be overwhelming, as information overload can quickly tax cognitive limits and resources. Because managers are prompted to focus on vital trends, some not-too-auspicious but important ones can be overlooked. Assessing the external environment is the first step needed in determining a firm's competitive position (see Figure 2.1).

In this chapter, a number of important frameworks for assessing the external envi-

Figure 2.1 **Analyzing the Environment and Strategic Choice and Positioning: The External Environment**

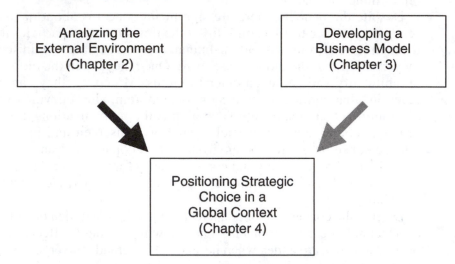

ronment are introduced: (1) macroenvironmental analysis/PEST; (2) industry analysis and competitive behavior; (3) value net; and (4) globalization potential of an industry. These frameworks are designed to help managers assess the industry environment from both a broad, macro perspective and a specific, narrow one. As part of the larger goal of positioning a firm's strategy in a global context, this chapter includes a discussion of the effects of globalization on an industry. These frameworks, along with an examination of the firm's business model, which is the topic of the next chapter, provide the basis for readying a firm for global competition.

MACROENVIRONMENTAL ANALYSIS

Because the macroenvironment can change quickly, we do not suggest that existing trends are necessarily permanent, but that they have relevance to managers at the time of this writing. The expectation is that managers will rigorously monitor and update their knowledge of these trends on a regular basis.[8] The following important trends are regularly cited as leading to the emergence of a global digital economy unprecedented in economic development:[9]

- As of late 2007, the foreign exchange market—the largest and most liquid market in the global economy—approximates $1.5 trillion per day. While this market has enabled almost instant transmission of funds for transactions around the world, the unrestricted flow of significantly high volume has also raised concerns about its potential for creating a global crisis, particularly for the less developed economies.
- The collapse of communism as an economic system and the diffusion of the market economy have opened up the world, notably emerging economies, to market-based international business activities.
- Major trading nations and regions, such as Latin America, China, and Southeast

Asia, are gaining economic clout and have become significant competitors in the business landscape.

- Regional integration blocs, notably the European Union and NAFTA (North American Free Trade Agreement) signatories, have reduced and removed the barriers to trade between their members. Since their inception, trade within the EU and NAFTA has increased substantially, although more work is needed to make economic integration more effective.

- From 2004 onward, Latin America and the Caribbean economies have surged forward, with Brazil and Mexico as the powerhouses of the region. Brazil has emerged as one of the world's leading producers of ethanol, a sugarcane alternative to gasoline fuel. In 2006, Mexico was the fourteenth largest economy in the world and the only Latin America member for the Organization for Economic Co-operation and Development (OECD).

- Technological developments such as IT (information technology) have led to cost and logistical efficiencies for organizations, notably United Parcel Service (UPS) and DHL in logistics and Wal-Mart in retailing.

- The Internet also holds the prospect of dramatically expanding the potential for international business transactions by providing low-cost means of searching for and buying products across national frontiers.

- Heightened awareness about global warming and environmental degradation has led to new imperatives for firms to develop or change their business models through clean technology.

- Microfinancing (or "small loans") is fast becoming the preferred source of funds for individuals in impoverished parts of the world, prompting several financial institutions to incorporate it as part of their product offerings. Though microfinancing is not regarded as a solution to eradicating world poverty, it is widely acknowledged as alleviating the plight of the poor and creating new entrepreneurs.

Macroenvironmental analysis can be segmented into major trends in political/legal, economic, demographic, technological, and sociocultural terms in order to pinpoint specific opportunities and pressure points.

The **political/legal environment** includes laws, government agencies, and pressure groups that can potentially influence a firm's goals and operations. The following examples illustrate the impact of political/legal trends on certain industry groups:[10]

- Mandatory recycling laws have given the recycling industry a major impetus in innovating new products and recycling processes.

- Recent pending regulations would require many food labels to carry more information. In addition, the rise of "low-carb" foods appears to correspond to both consumer and governmental pressures for healthier food to combat obesity and poor health.

- In response to an awareness of "political correctness," various firms have been labeling their products as "Fair Trade Certified." Kraft recently introduced coffee that is "Certified Sustainable," and Procter & Gamble also introduced its coffee brand as "Rainforest Alliance Certified."

- Possible regulations relating to the taxation of e-mail messages and other Internet applications will have significant impact on Internet service providers and customers at large.

- The enactment of the Patriot Act in the wake of the September 11, 2001, tragedy has led to limitations on privacy, individual rights, and freedom. Heightened vigilance at airports and other points of departure has also spurred the development of security devices, encryption codes, and so forth.
- The activation of the Critical Infrastructure Information Act by the U.S. Department of Homeland Security will force companies to share information on their weaknesses in everything from power plants to computer networks while protecting proprietary data and addressing potential legal liabilities.
- The passage of the 2002 Sabarnes-Oxley Act will influence organizations to enact better corporate governance, accountability, and ethical codes of behavior. A survey of 321 companies in 2004 indicated that businesses with more than $5 billion in revenue expect to spend an average of $4.7 million each year implementing the new Act, in addition to $1.5 million each year to upgrade new software and designing systems.[11]

Economic trends include not only broad "megatrends"—some of which have been mentioned above—but also include specific changes in income distribution. Nations vary in their level of income and distribution channels. Marketers often distinguish countries using five different income distribution patterns: (1) very low incomes; (2) mostly low incomes; (3) very low and very high incomes; (4) low, medium, and high incomes; and (5) mostly medium incomes. In the market for luxury cars that cost $100,000 or more, for example, the market would be very small in type 1 and 2 countries, but large in type 3. In fact, one of the largest markets for Lamborghinis is Portugal (income pattern 3), which is one of the lower income countries in Western Europe, but one with enough very wealthy families to afford such luxury.[12] An example of how income distribution patterns are used in strategic planning is that of Kenya Airlines (see Box 2.1). While there are numerous trends, the following list illustrates the impact of economic events in our changing world:

- Urbanization in India and China will escalate. From 1998 to 2007, about 170 million have moved from the countryside to urban cities in China. In India, about 31 villagers migrate from rural to cities every minute. Over the projected next 43 years, migration will create a level of 700 million. Collectively, these patterns will define a new phenomenon: the earth will be more urban than rural for the first time in our history.[13]
- GDP growth rate differentials from 2003 to 2007 for the following countries were as follows: Australia (2.8 to 3.6%); Brazil (0.1 to 5.1%); Mexico (1.0 to 4.5%); China (8 to 10.5%); India (4.3 to 8.5%); France (0.1 to 2.3%); Germany (–0.1 to 2.2%); and the United States (2.45 to 4.4%).[14]
- In the 2007–08 *Global Competitiveness Index*, the top ranked competitive countries are: (1) United States, (2) Switzerland, (3) Denmark, (4) Sweden, and (5) Germany. The lower ranked competitive countries are: (127) Timor-Leste, (128) Mozambique, (129) Zimbabwe, (130) Burundi, and (131) Chad.[15]

Box 2.1

Kenya Airways and the Growing Middle Class

President Mwai Kibaki of Kenya continues to push social and economic reforms even though his efforts were weakened by corruption allegations against top government officials. The country follows IMF's guidance on poverty reduction and growth facility.

Kenya's economic growth heavily depends on its landscape and wildlife tourism, which grew from 2003 to 2004 by 18.7 percent, from 1.1 million to 1.4 million people, while earnings from tourism rose by 51.9 percent, from approximately US$358 million to US$544 million. Kenya, now a dominant economy in East Africa, enjoyed a 4–5 percent real GDP growth rate per year from 2001 to 2005.

With a population of 34 million, Kenya has a small but fast-growing urban middle class that makes up the target market for high-end products. Together with the rest of African's growing middle class, Kenya's urban middle class has a huge appetite for better goods and services. African entrepreneurs look to import from China and India, as both countries have built reputations for quality and more competitive prices.

Kenya Airways capitalizes on this opportunity and targets the rapidly rising number of travelers between Africa and countries such as Thailand, Mumbai, India, China, Turkey, and others. China seems to be particularly important in air traffic. One need only see how many Chinese products are on Kenya's store shelves to know what is filling Kenya Airways' cargo carriage. Kenya Airways CEO Titus Naikuni estimated that cargo carriage returning to Africa from these countries would grow at 20 percent per year. He also said, "Passengers don't go and buy feathers, they like weighty things." Located on the eastern edge of Africa, Kenya Airways also serves passengers who fly into the African continent, where the general economy is also growing.

The traffic goes both ways. Kenya Airways already has direct flights to Dubai and Guanghzhou. Titus Naikuni states that the volume of passengers going to Kenya from China is estimated to grow about 10 percent per year. To ensure that both inbound and outbound flights are served well, the company also has a Chinese website for passenger convenience.

Sources: Intelligence Brief: Kenya, Power and Interest News Report, December 6, 2005, www.pinr.com/report.php?ac=view_printable&report_id=407&language_id=1, retrieved on March 9, 2006; "Kenya Leaders: Voting out Corruption," *The Economist*, January 28, 2006, p. 14; "Kenya Benefiting from Increased Inflow of Chinese Tourists," *Xinhua*, February 1, 2006, 20:27:39, http://english.sina.com/life/1/2006/0201/64061.html; Kenya: Country Outlook, EIU ViewsWire, February 21, 2006; Kenya: Economic Structure, EIU ViewsWire, New York, February 8, 2006; Chris Williams, "Setting the Context: Kenya," *Housing Finance International*, September 2005, pp. 20–26. "Kenya Sees China as a Shopping Mall," Reuters via Yahoo!, December 20, 2005.

- In 2007, South Korea was ranked the largest in the world in terms of the usage and the applications of the Internet. In 2006, there were more than 23.9 million landlines with more than 40.2 million mobile cell phones. Moreover, Koreans are among the world's top bloggers, with one out of three Koreans writing a post about companies and products at least once a week.[16]

Demographics includes the size and growth rate of populations in different cities, regions, and nations; age distribution and ethnic mix; educational levels; household patterns; and the regional characteristics and movements of people around the world. Demographics is the central focus of marketing management, but it should also be a serious consideration for global strategists. Analysts are keenly interested in key demographic indicators that affect the ongoing activities of firms:[17]

- The world's population is exploding, with over 6.5 billion people, and growing at the rate of 1.14 percent per annum.
- The highest population, measured as a percentage of world population, resides in China (20 percent) and India (17.2 percent), but the highest growth rates are occurring in the Middle East and in Africa.
- About 80 percent of the world's population resides in less developed countries. The U.S. Bureau of Census projects that about 95 percent of the world's population will occur in this sector by 2020; in contrast, those living in more developed countries will fall from 20 percent to about 16 percent.
- National populations also vary in terms of age mix. Based on the percentage of people who are 65 years or older, Italy, Greece, Sweden, Belgium, and Japan rank among the world's oldest populations; in contrast, the developing countries in Africa and western and southwest Asia rank among the world's youngest based on the percentage of people who are 15 years or younger.

The **technological environment** refers to product, process, and services improvement. An assessment of this environment is made based on the advancement of the field. It is perhaps the most volatile in terms of new trends. It has released such wonders as space travel, stem cell research, and nanotechnology, but also such horrors as nuclear accidents, computer viruses, and weapons of mass destruction. While there are numerous trends, the following ones illustrate the future impact of technology in our changing world:[18]

- "Smart dust," or networks of cheap, low-power computerized sensors will start monitoring the food, workplaces, and the welfare of nations.
- There will be increased convergence among core technologies, with PCs, TVs, and entertainment becoming more integrated.
- Open source, the free software movement that was started by Linux, will become the norm for future innovation.
- Virtual auctioning and new methods of pricing will emerge on the Internet.
- The proliferation of wireless broadband products and services will increase connectivity and spur globalization.
- Neurotechnology, defined as the application of tools, drugs, and diagnostics for influencing the human nervous system, especially the brain, will have a far-reaching impact on treating mental illness, such as Alzheimer's disease and schizophrenia, as well as bolstering the immune system, and eventually one's longevity.
- Mesh networks, or connections between nodes that are self-healing or are enabled to hop from node to node, will accelerate broadband connectivity that will, in turn, create radically new business models and transform patterns of work and recreation.

The **sociocultural environment** relates to values, beliefs, and norms that are shaped by societies. Exhibit 2.1 summarizes findings reported by the *Far Eastern Economic Review* regarding Asian lifestyles, as one example of the sociocultural environment.

A popular method of integrating and summarizing the factors with a significant influ-

Exhibit 2.1 **Asian Lifestyles**

The following charts present survey results on the values, beliefs, and norms of respondents in selected Asian countries.

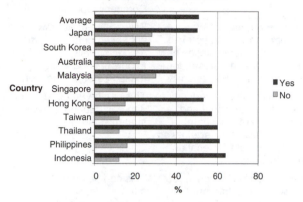

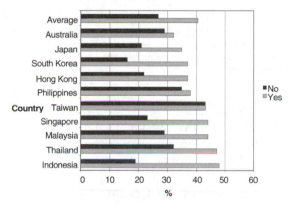

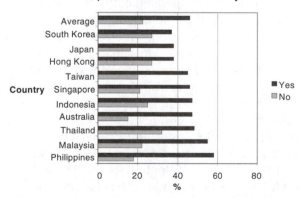

Sources: "Hitting the Road," *Far Eastern Economic Review,* September 2, 2004, p. 47; "Streamlined Lives," *Far Eastern Economic Review,* September 2, 2004, p. 46.

Exhibit 2.2

A PEST (Political-Economic-Societal-Technological) Example

Key Trends	Potential Impact on Company Operations	Possible Company Responses
Political: The emergence of post–September 11 measures to enhance national security places new restrictions on customers' desire for privacy and individual expression.	Will require more privacy enhancements on existing products, while conforming to new national security measures on the horizon.	Work with New Product Development on consumer options, privacy codes, and encryption procedures.
Economic: As a result of deregulation, boundaries between national and local telecom carriers have been blurred, with significant uncertainty as to which party should offer local and long-distance service.	This can be an opportunity or a threat, depending on what strategies are enacted.	Focus on political activities to get a head start on regulatory changes; conduct sensitivity analysis on various pricing schemes for local and long-distance services.
Technological: New advances in communications using Internet technologies provide an effective substitute for existing products and services.	This can be an opportunity or a threat, depending on what strategies are enacted.	Conduct a study to determine best consolidated option, whether to hedge or to consolidate broadband IT technologies.
Socio-cultural: Customers have become more demanding as a result of better education, more awareness of industry issues, and a greater feeling of empowerment.	With new expectations, more responsiveness to customers is needed throughout the organization.	Have Marketing Department develop new studies on customer responsiveness indices.

ence on a firm's operations is through **PEST** (political-economic-societal-technological) analysis. PEST was first developed by General Electric to engender awareness of such trends and their impact on the company's operations. Exhibit 2.2 contains a sample PEST for a hypothetical firm to recognize, define, and exploit emerging trends.

INDUSTRY ANALYSIS: FIVE FORCES OF COMPETITION

Macroenvironmental analysis can identify the issues that will have broad-scale impact on a company and help the company anticipate key changes and contingencies in the future. It also limits tunnel vision, which can lead to misplaced strategies on the part of the firm. Even so, there is a need to step in closer to examine more direct influences on firm profitability. Harvard University professor and strategy guru Michael Porter sees a thorough understanding of an industry as the starting point of any strategic endeavor.

Michael Porter changed the way strategy had been taught with his publication of the Five Forces model of competition. Previously, trends in the external environment were analyzed for opportunities and threats that impacted the strategies of firms. In the Five Forces model, selected forces within an industry are assessed to determine its overall profit potential. Robert M. Grant, a management professor from Georgetown University, provides a basic overview.[19] What will affect the level of firm profitability? If the firm is to realize profits, the price that customers are willing to pay should exceed its total costs. However, with stronger competition, the firm is

Exhibit 2.3

Industry Profitability (Total Return to Shareholders)

Rank	Industries (1989–99)	Annual Rate %	Industries (1992–2002)	Annual Rate %	Industries (1996–2006)	Annual Rate %
1	Computer peripherals	57.7	Entertainment	21.8	Homebuilders	24.6
2	Securities	28.6	Automotive retailing and services	20.0	Health care: Pharmacy, other services	20.6
3	Computer and data services	24.3	Securities	19.5	Securities	18.6
4	Computers, office equipment	22.8	Semiconductors	19.0	Petroleum refining	16.8
5	Diversified financials	22.6	Medical products and equipment	17.5	General merchandisers	15.9
6	Soaps, cosmetics	21.4	Household and personal products	15.4	Specialty retailers	15.4
7	Pharmaceuticals	20.6	Beverages	15.2	Metals	14.1
8	Pipelines	20.5	Pharmaceuticals	15.1	Oil and gas equipment, services	14.0
9	Specialty retailers	20.5	Diversified Financials	15.0	Pipelines	13.4
10	Insurance: Life, health (stock)	20.1	Publishing, printing	15.0	Energy	13.4
11	Commercial banks	19.5	Industrial and farm equipment	14.8	Hotels, casinos, resorts	13.4
12	Telecommunications	18.2	Network and communications	14.4	Mining, crude-oil production	13.1
13	Food services	17.6	Food services	13.9	Medical products and equipment	12.8
14	Publishing, printing	16.5	Homebuilders	13.0	Health care: Insurance, mngd. care	12.7
15	Aerospace	16.0	Commercial banks	12.7	Industrial and farm equipment	12.0
16	Beverages	16.0	Insurance	12.7	Telecommunications	11.7
17	Chemicals	15.0	Hotels, casinos, resorts	12.5	Wholesalers: Diversified	11.6
18	Industrial and farm equipment	14.6	Wholesalers: Health care	11.6	Commercial banks	11.5
19	Electronics, electrical equipment	13.6	Health care	10.6	Beverages	11.5
20	Entertainment	12.8	Computers, office equipment	10.5	Insurance: P&C (stock)	11.3
21	Mail, package, freight delivery	12.2	Computers, data services	10.2	Diversified financials	11.2
22	Scientific, photo, control equip.	11.9	Engineering and construction	10.2	Wholesalers: Health care	11.0
23	Food	11.4	Electronics	10.1	Household and personal products	10.9
24	Insurance: P&C (stock)	11.3	Specialty retailers	9.6	Electronics, electrical equipment	10.8
25	General merchandisers	11.3	Aerospace and defense	9.2	Utilities: Gas and electric	10.8
26	Metal products	11.0	Insurance: Life, health (stock)	9.0	Food and drug stores	10.1
27	Forest and paper products	10.7	Chemicals	8.5	Network, other communications equipment	9.4
28	Food and drug stores	10.2	Mail, package, freight delivery	7.9	Food production	9.2
29	Wholesalers	9.7	Petroleum refinery	7.9	Computers, office equipment	9.2
30	Engineering, construction	9.4	Mining: Crude and distribution	7.2	Chemicals	9.1

(continued)

Exhibit 2.3 *(continued)*

Rank	Industries	1989–99 Annual Rate %	Industries	1992–2002 Annual Rate %	Industries	1996–2006 Annual Rate %
31	Motor vehicles and parts	9.4	Utilities: Gas and electric	7.1	Food consumer products	9.0
32	Metals	9.4	Wholesalers: Diversified	7.1	Apparel	7.9
33	Petroleum refining	9.3	Telecommunications	7.0	Pharmaceuticals	7.8
34	Airlines	8.7	Food: consumer products	7.0	Railroads	7.5
35	Railroads	8.4	Apparel	5.7	Aerospace and defense	7.0
36	Utilities: Gas and electric	8.2	Railroads	4.5	Entertainment	6.6
37	Health care	6.5	Packaging, containers	3.8	Publishing, printing	6.1
38	Automotive retailing, services	5.8	General merchandisers	3.8	Airlines	3.9
39	Temporary help	3.0	Forest and paper products	3.8	Packaging, containers	3.8
40	Building materials, glass	2.2	Food and drug stores	3.2	Semiconductors, other	2.7
41	Hotels, casinos, resorts	2.0	Trucking, truck leasing	1.7	Wholesalesrs: Electronics and office equipment	2.5
42			Energy	1.3	Information technology services	2.1
43			Metals	0.0	Motor vehicles and parts	-0.2
44			Food production	-0.5		
45			Wholesalers: Food and grocery	-0.7		
46			Wholesalers: Electronics, office equipment	-1.1		
47			Motor vehicles and parts	-1.4		
48			Airlines	-8.3		
	The 500 median	12.8		9.1		11.0

Source: Adapted from multiple issues of "How the Industries Stack Up," *Fortune*, April 17, 2000, F–29; April 14, 2003, F–27; April 30, 2007, F–33.

Exhibit 2.4   **Porter's Five Forces Model**

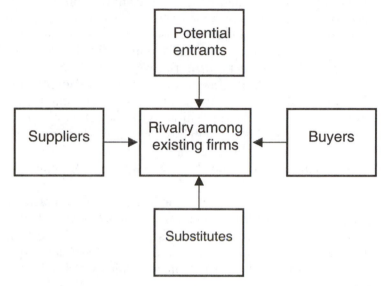

Rivalry:	How intense is the rivalry/competition among firms in the industry?
Buyers:	How much power do buyers have? What can be done to neutralize their power?
New Entrants:	How easy or difficult is it to enter the industry? How can entry barriers be erected?
Suppliers:	How much power do suppliers have? What accounts for their power? What can be done to neutralize their power?
Substitutes:	Are there substitute products or services? What effect do these substitutes have?

Source: Adapted from Michael E. Porter, *Industry Analysis and Competitive Behavior* (New York: Free Press, 1980), p. 4.

limited in terms of raising prices because customers can shop for what they consider to be the best price for value. The firm's buyers exert pressure on the company to produce goods and services that meet their requirements. Moreover, substitute products, for example, in the case of steel and aluminum, matter in that they (aluminum manufacturers) set a price ceiling for whatever price a firm (steel firm) can charge. Profits are also determined by the firm's cost structure. The surplus of price over cost needs to be distributed to a number of parties, specifically employees who have the first rights to compensation. Suppliers who have provided goods and services also have to be paid. All in all, every firm belongs to an industry group with its own set of competitive dynamics. Intuitively, more competition leads to lower profits. In fact, left unabated, these collective pressures from buyers, suppliers, and competitors can bring down the level of profitability to the industry floor rate of return with conditions akin to perfect competition. Exhibit 2.3 shows that industries vary significantly in their levels of profitability.

Even a cursory observation indicates that patterns of industry profitability endure over time. Examining the data from 1989 to 2005, some industries (securities, pharmaceuticals, diversified financials) were more stable in terms of profitability than others (airlines, motor vehicles and parts). The basic argument is that the level of industry profitability is neither random nor the result of arbitrary firm's actions, but is determined to some extent by *industry structure*. Industry structure determines competition and profitability across industries. Porter explains the pattern of industry performance as a result of basic forces as formalized in the **five forces model**. This model consists of *intensity of rivalry, new entrants, producers of substitute products, suppliers,* and *buyers* (see Exhibit 2.4).[20] Taken collectively, these forces can bring down the level of industry profitability. The silver lining is that a firm can achieve higher-than-average performance if it is able to position itself correctly even in an unattractive industry. We will expand on this in Chapter 3, but raise it here to provide perspective on how strategy is linked to industry competitive dynamics. In short, in using the five forces model, a manager should be able to answer the following questions:[21]

- Is this an attractive (profitable) industry? Which characteristics support high profitability and which diminish profit potential? How will attractiveness change in the future? What are the critical uncertainties? What is the primary or dominant force?
- What can be done to enhance future industry attractiveness? Are there more interesting markets or segments on which we should focus?

INTENSITY OF RIVALRY

Intensity of rivalry refers to the competition among rivals within a particular industry. In some industries, firms compete aggressively, sometimes pushing prices so low that competition within the industry becomes self-destructive. The airline industry, with its constant price wars, is one example of this. In other industries, competition is less severe and more benign. Within the pharmaceutical industry, for example, price is not the limiting factor inasmuch as there are other avenues, such as advertising or doctor's referrals, in which to push sales. Because the oil industry is also able to pass along cost increases to customers, competition between oil firms is more benign. However, rivalry becomes intense as firms within an industry jockey for better strategic position, as we are beginning to see in the pharmaceutical and biotechnology industries. The level of intensity within the industry indicates the severity of competition. The more severe the competition is, the less attractive the industry is. From the firm's point of view, the lower the level of competitive intensity, the more attractive the industry. The following is a set of factors that affect the intensity of rivalry.

- Rivalry intensifies as the number of competitors increases and as competitors become more equal in size and capability. When competitors are fairly equal in the resources they possess, each can combat the others' strategic moves without overly exhausting themselves. A market dominated by a single firm (Microsoft in PC operating systems) can exercise considerable control. In contrast, commodity markets tend to be price competitive because no single firm can control or influence prices. In markets dominated by two suppliers—Visa and Mastercard in electronic credit cards, Airbus and Boeing in commercial aircraft, Gillette and Schick in razor blades—prices tend to be set at similar levels.[22]

- Rivalry is usually stronger when demand for the product is growing slowly. This can happen when a product is moving toward maturity or is declining in its life cycle. Examples are products in low-growth industries, such as mining, nonferrous metal, iron, and steel. At the maturity stage of the product life cycle, when new growth opportunity is very low, or when there is a slow economy, price competition is the most viable way to draw customers. Firms tend to use price cuts or other discounting weapons to boost unit volume. In contrast, growth industries, such as electronic art products or herbal heath products, are less vulnerable to price competition.

- Rivalry is stronger when the switching cost to customers is low. The **switching cost** refers to the one-time cost involved in switching from one brand to another or to substitutes. This includes searching for a different brand or substitute, the time incurred in learning about the new product, and the cost of training personnel. Switching costs might explain why individuals do not switch computer, accounting systems, or telephone systems on a whim. When the risk of investment is small for customers, they are more inclined to try new products or different brands. In contrast, buyers of General Electric medical scanning technologies might be less willing to switch to new competitor products because of the anticipated costs of retraining personnel.

- Rivalry is more intense when fixed costs as a percentage of total costs are high. Because of a higher breakeven point, pressure to use capacity, which encourages industries to overproduce, leads to lower prices. Overinvestment led to periodic excess capacity in personal computers (1984–85), in memory chips on a cyclical basis, and in telecommunications during the first half of 2000.[23]

- Rivalry is more intense when there is a lack of product differentiation, or when products become commodities. In this situation, price is the chief weapon in competition. Dobson et al., note that with significant product differentiation (e.g., cars, cigarettes, fashion), less aggressive forms of competition are used (e.g., advertising, research and development, non-price differentiation).

- Rivalry increases in proportion to the size of the payoff when a strategic move is successful. When a particular strategic move is worth the effort, firms are tempted to keep repeating it at a level at which returns can be realized. Indirectly, when industries are designated as "strategic," as in the case of semiconductors, then firms are expected to stay within the industry and not yield to international competitors.

- Rivalry tends to be more vigorous when it costs more to get out of a business than to stay in it and compete. If noncompetitive firms have to struggle just to break even, they are highly motivated to try every tactic or strategy available to maintain or expand their market share. If, in contrast, noncompetitive firms can easily close their businesses and leave the industry, there will be fewer competitors and more room for the remaining firms to expand their market share.

- Rivalry becomes more volatile and unpredictable the more diverse the competitors are in terms of vision, strategic intent, objectives, strategy, resources, and country of origin. This implies that when a group of competitors is homogeneous, a single strategy might be sufficient to compete. Competitors that think alike and have shared experiences tend to stabilize the "rules of competition." The emergence of diverse competitors, such as the Japanese, Koreans, and Chinese, can disrupt these "rules" and create intense competition. Rivalry is stronger when one or more competitors are dissatisfied with their market position and launch moves at the expense of their rivals. This can create a vicious competitive cycle that exhausts the firms involved.

- Rivalry increases when strong companies outside the industry acquire weak firms in the industry and launch aggressive, well-funded moves to transform their newly acquired competitors into major market contenders. This triggers drastic changes in the industry to which current firms must react strongly.

THREAT OF NEW ENTRANTS

Threat of new entrants refers to the competitive threat from the newcomers. An industry that earns a return on invested capital in excess of its cost of capital will attract entrants. This is particularly true at the growth stage of its life cycle. The downside is that the more players in the market, the more severe the competition. New entry into the industry invariably reduces the existing firms' profitability by adding capacity and introducing new methods of competition. Therefore, incumbent firms should be concerned with any lack of entry barriers because high barriers generally preserve the industry's competitive balance. Whenever possible, firms should monitor new entry. In general, the higher the barriers of entry in an industry, the lower the threat to firms already in the industry and the more attractive the industry becomes. The threat of new entrants is affected by the following:

Economies of Scale

The concept of **economies of scale** suggests that the more units produced, the lower the average cost of production. The existence of economies of scale discourages entry because new entrants must enter on a large scale or else suffer from a cost-disadvantaged position. In large jet engines, the importance of scale economies in research and development and manufacturing has resulted in only three viable firms (General Electric, Pratt and Whitney, and Rolls-Royce).[24] The need for scale economies was a motivating factor in the acquisition of smaller manufacturers such as Ford's acquisition of Jaguar in 1989, General Motors's acquisition of Svenska Aeroplan AB (SAAB) in 1989, and Volkswagen's acquisition of *Sociedad Española de Automóviles de Turismo* (SEAT) in 1986.

Cost Disadvantages Independent of Size

Incumbent firms have (absolute) cost advantages over a new entrant, due, for example, to the learning (experience) curve, proprietary inputs, or patented know-how, which are all independent of size. Pepsi took advantage of Coca-Cola's absence in Vietnam (access initially denied to Coca-Cola) to learn about the country's culture, customers, and distribution systems. Dell Computers has an advantage in terms of its experience with the "direct marketing" model in the United States. Oil companies have historical reach in the Middle East and Africa. Honda's experience with the internal combustion engine, honed by years of car racing, is hard to duplicate.

Learning (Labor) and Experience (Process) Effects

The **learning and experience effects** refer to the cumulative cost benefits from repetitive activity. In some businesses, such as aerospace, shipbuilding, and semiconductors, learning and experience can provide significant cost advantages. The greater the cost advantage of incumbent firms, the more difficult it is for newcomers to enter and to catch up. In cases where entrants are not able to match the experience and specialized know-how of incumbent firms, they will be deterred from entry. If incumbent firms have the technology that is proprietary and specialized, new entrants will find it difficult to compete unless they can offer something unique, or find ways of significantly revamping their production processes at a cost lower than incumbent firms. Historically, Japanese semiconductor firms were able to leapfrog past any cost advantages enjoyed by their American counterparts by developing more efficient manufacturing methods, receiving government support, and capitalizing on other cost advantages arising from their *keiretsu* structure (see Case-in-Point case). A similar pattern occurred when the Korean semiconductor firms were able to overtake the Japanese some time later.

High Switching Costs

Entry is also difficult in cases where switching costs are high. Are buyers and/or suppliers contracted to dealing with incumbent firms? Are there significant costs if they decide to switch? Consider the costs of switching medical technology equipment (imaging machines) if firms currently use machines manufactured by General Electric. There are costs of retraining, displacement, manuals, initial errors, consumer acceptance, warranty considerations, and disposal of old units. Currently, consumers might be hesitant in purchasing a high-end VCR machine because of the incertainty between two competing designs: Blue Ray and HDTV. Because the two systems are not compatible, enormous costs can be incurred if a consumer had to switch from one to another.

High Capital Requirements for Entry

The higher the capital requirements to start up a business, the smaller the number of new firms that are able to enter the industry and trigger more competition. The lower the capital requirements, the easier for newcomers to enter. In 2007, the start-up costs for Subway was between $75–$223 thousand, and for McDonald's, it was between $655 thousand to $1.3 million. Other top franchises were Dunkin' Donuts, with a start-up cost of between $179 thousand–1.6 million, and Domino's Pizza with a figure between $141.4–415.1 thousand.[25]

Limited Channels of Distribution

Channels of distribution become limited when distributors have little confidence in new firms, in which case access to distribution is blocked. Dobson, Starkey, and Richards see this in vertically integrated industries, such as petroleum and brewing. Robert Grant suggests that "in the United States and Britain, food and drink manufacturers are increasingly required to make lump-sum payments to the leading supermarket chains in order to gain shelf space for a new product. In one study, it was reported that late entrants into consumer goods incurred an additional advertising and promotional expense amounting to 2.12 percent of sales revenue."[26]

Differentiation

Differentiation becomes an entry barrier when firms within an industry can offer products with attractive features or functions, resulting in high brand loyalty. When brand preferences and customer loyalty have been built up, and when current firms have secured their market share, entry is difficult. New entrants have to be more creative, more diligent, and willing to spend a lot of money to entice customers to switch to their own products and services. Typically, brand loyalty varies across different industries. The percentage of U.S. consumers loyal to a single brand varies from under 30 percent in batteries, canned vegetables, and garbage bags, to 61 percent in toothpaste, 65 percent in mayonnaise, and 71 percent in cigarettes.[27] In industries with high brand loyalty, new entrants will have a more difficult time unless they can provide products and services that consumers consider to be superior to existing offerings.

Aggressive Retaliation on the Part of Existing Firms

A firm contemplating entry might be discouraged if it excepts incumbent firms would react with a price war. For example, Procter & Gamble, Nintendo, Microsoft, and Sony are considered to react aggressively to competitors' strategies that threaten their market share. In this regard, firms monitor business periodicals, such as the *Wall Street Journal*, to assess competitors' intentions and activities. It is not unusual for firms to signal their intentions, possible retaliation, through popular business outlets. While price wars can benefit the consumer, it is generally not good for companies involved as this can lower margins and even lead to bankruptcy. Thus, even the threat of potential retaliation can be an entry barrier.

Regulatory Policies

Government regulations, standards, and administrative procedures can heighten or lower entry possibilities for prospective newcomers. Host governments often put up trade restrictions, such as tariffs and quotas, in order to protect domestic producers and deter foreign businesses. For a prolonged period of time, it was difficult to enter the Japanese domestic market because government regulations favored local procurement and Japanese customers stayed with their regular (Japanese) suppliers. In many cities in the United States, city governments limit the entry of new taxicab services. In such a case, government regulations act as an entry barrier.

THREAT OF SUBSTITUTES

Threat of substitutes comes from indirect competitors who offer products that can serve similar purposes. The potential for profit in any industry is determined by the maximum price that a customer is willing to pay. Pressure on an industry will be stronger when there are more close substitutes (i.e., demand related). In a hypothetical situation involving transportation if the only service available is through an airline, then prices can be sky high. However, if railway services also become available, then this will limit the price that can be charged for airline travel. Grant argues that with "few substitutes, such as is the case with cigarettes and gasoline, then consumers will tend to be indifferent to price—that is, the demand is inelastic with respect to price." In considering the influence of substitutes, the strategist needs to examine their price/cost, quality, and disruptive potential. The threat of substitutes usually comes about in several ways:

- Buyers' switching costs are low (i.e., it is easy to change one's choice of product). In contrast, if the substitute creates high switching costs to buyers, the threat is low because switching would appear too costly to them. To illustrate how switching costs operate, one should consider the cost of product services relative to one's utility.[28]
- If the performance and quality of the substitute does not fulfill customer expectations, the threat is correspondingly low. For example, efforts to reduce traffic through the promotion of BART (Bay Area Rapid Transit) in the San Francisco Bay Area have proven to be ineffective because people view it as a poor substitute for driving their own vehicles.

The threat of substitute is strong if the following conditions are present:

- Firms producing substitutes are reducing costs (e.g., investing in new machinery can result in faster turnaround and fewer defects, thus reducing costs). Take, for example, the comparative cost of steel and plastic. When the price of steel spiraled, buyer-firms using steel switched to lower cost substitutes (e.g., plastics and aluminum.) However, with firms using electric arc furnaces to melt steel ("mini-mills"), there is the potential of costs and prices being reduced. Depending on how low steel prices go, there is a strong possibility that buyer-firms will switch back to steel.
- Substitute producers are increasing value for their products by enhancing quality. Continued advances in telecommunications can lower its price/cost ratio, threatening airlines further. With the advent of SARS in Asia in 2003, business customers resorted to increased video-conferencing and other telecommunications that had developed new and updated features.
- There is intense competition between the substitute producers (leading to low prices and/or favorable price-performance characteristics).

BARGAINING POWER OF SUPPLIERS

An industry's relationship with its supplying industry directly affects a firm's cost position. The **bargaining power of suppliers** explains the influence the upstream industries have on the downstream industry. The higher the bargaining power the suppliers have, the weaker the firms of the buying industry. Dobson et al. cite the case of "supplies" (labor) organized into a trade union. Where an industry has a high percentage of labor unions, its profitability is reduced. Firms with no unions generally have an return on investment of 25 percent; that is reduced to 19 percent when unionization is over 75 percent.[29]

- If the supplier industry is filled with numerous suppliers, thus providing the buying industry with various alternatives, the bargaining power of the suppliers is low. If there are only a few suppliers, this could give them the power to dictate prices, quality, and terms of trade. Such was the case with oil-producing countries in the 1970s that led to the formation of OPEC.
- If there are substitutes (e.g., synthetic fiber) competing with supplier industries (e.g., natural fiber), the bargaining power of suppliers is low. Suppliers of natural fiber have to sell at large volumes to garment manufacturers to offset the power of the suppliers of synthetic fiber. In this case, the cost relative to total purchases becomes the critical deciding factor.
- If the industry as a whole, or the better part of it, is the major customer of the supplying industry, the bargaining power of the suppliers is low and the survival of the supplying industry largely depends on that one industry.
- If members of an industry can perform backward integration (e.g., automobile firms), which means that they make supplies instead of buying them from the supplying industry, it weakens the bargaining power of suppliers (e.g., automobile parts manufacturers).

BARGAINING POWER OF BUYERS

Bargaining power of buyers refers to the ability of buyers to negotiate and create favorable terms for themselves. A particular industry becomes more attractive if its buyers have low bargaining power. In general, an industry prefers that the bargaining power of its buyers be low. There are various factors that contribute to the bargaining power of buyers.

- If switching costs are high for buyers shifting from brand to brand or to substitutes, they will be reluctant to change frequently. Because they are loyal to a particular brand, the buyers' bargaining power is low across the industry. With low switching costs, however, buyers are more discriminating, and this enhances their bargaining power. In the case of airline travel, buyers on a tight budget might go for the lowest cost provider (e.g., Southwest Airlines), even if they might prefer others (e.g., Jet Blue).
- If the number of buyers is small and their purchases are not important to a supplier industry, they do not significantly affect the supplier industry's profit and loss. There are plenty of substitute products, particularly in industries producing flashlights, fastening materials, paper clips, and so forth. If there are only a few buyers, each of whom buys in large volume, the situation changes.
- If buyers are not well informed about the sellers' products, prices, and costs, it gives sellers a chance to manipulate prices and the bargaining power of buyers is low. On the contrary, if buyers have abundant information about sellers, they

can negotiate better results. But the power of buyers is increasing because the Internet is disclosing prices to customers who buy books, records, and CDs.

- If it is not feasible for buyers to pursue backward integration, and their only choice is to buy from particular sellers, they are not a threat to those sellers. Hence, the bargaining power of the buyers is low. But some buyers pose the threat of integrating backward. GM, Ford, and Chrysler have reduced their dependence on automobile suppliers by manufacturing a portion of their own (tapered integration) i.e., part of their supplies are from internal production while the rest is from outside suppliers. Backward integration implies total integration, that is, a buyer resorts to totally producing internally what they previously sourced from others.
- If buyers have discretion as to whether and when they make purchases, they tend to have more bargaining power. Buyers are particularly sensitive to price: take, for example, consumers, or buyers for whom the product purchase constitutes a large portion of their total costs. Those firms that purchase in bulk or large quantities (i.e., Wal-Mart) drive for a higher bargain, thereby depressing prices and occasionally the profits of supplying industries.
- Buyers' profits are marginal and they therefore want to reduce costs.
- Buyers have selling influence, that is, retailers and wholesalers have the power to influence consumers by promoting a company's products.

The strength of these five forces will vary between industries, as will the dominant force, and levels of industry profitability. As Porter puts it, "the collective strength of these forces determines the ultimate profit potential in the industry. The forces range from intense in industries like tires, paper, and steel—where no firms earn spectacular returns—to relatively mild in industries like oil-field equipment and services, cosmetics, and toiletries—where high returns are quite common." An example of a completed industry analysis is provided in Exhibit 2.5.

THE ROLE OF COMPLEMENTORS

The five forces analysis is based on the logic that each force has the power to expropriate some if not all of a firm's profits. Left unchecked, each force can undermine the industry's profit potential. As such, this analysis provides an excellent context for analyzing the relevant issues facing the firm as it formulates its strategy. Yet if the objective is to understand the profit potential of an industry, the five forces analysis leaves out the critical role of complementors, or the providers of complementary products and services. **Complementors** are companies that offer products that add value to the products sold by another company. For example, physicians function as complementors for the pharmaceutical industry in that they do not buy pharmaceutical drugs, but prescribe and dispense them for their patients. More often than not, providers of complementary products (i.e., demand of these products is positively related) will be complementors as well. Some examples include the manufacturers of razors and blades, DVDs and movies, and coffee and coffee products. A third example of complementors is the relationship between Microsoft and Intel. The success of Microsoft Windows platform is due, in large part, to its partnership with Intel, and vice-versa. Intel microprocessors can embed new Microsoft operating systems that

Exhibit 2.5

Example of Industry Analysis: Business Plan Software

Competitive Forces	Relative Importance	Competitive Impact (1–5)*	Assessment of the Five Forces: Summary
Competitive rivalry	25%	4	Favorable (The basis of competition is through differentiation services, not price)
Competitor entry	20%	3	Medium threat (Well-known consulting firms have the potential to enter the market with their own branded software)
Substitutes	30%	2	Real threat (There are many substitutes for business plan software, including on-site consulting services, business school courses, extended learning, and certificate programs)
Supplier power	10%	5	Favorable (There are abundant sources of suppliers in a competitive market)
Buyer power	15%	3	Medium threat (Despite strategies to enhance differentiation by industry incumbents, buyers have hardly any switching costs, i.e., they can switch between programs with relative ease.)

Competitive Attractiveness Index = 2.65 (weighted average).

*Competitive impact is scored from 1 = Highly unfavorable or unattractive in terms of undermining the industry profit potential, to 5 = Highly favorable or attractive in terms of enhancing industry profit potential.

Primary force: Substitute products are the biggest threat because of their numbers and potential ability to lower prices.

Key Points:
- Currently, there are few firms offering the exact same service. Two competitors dominate the business plan software market with a 60 percent share. This has discouraged severe price wars within the industry. The basis of competition is through differentiated product offerings and services.
- Capital requirements and fixed costs are relatively low (about 7 percent of operating costs), thus allowing for easy competitor entry. A threat would be large software companies such as Microsoft, Oracle, or IBM, which have large discretionary cash and face few hurdles entering the industry. However, it is unlikely that they will enter this relatively small market.
- Substitutes are the primary force within this industry because they are plentiful and available. These include traditional management consultants, academicians, MBA students, even general purpose management consultants. The switching costs are extremely low. Therefore, customers' willingness to switch depends on competitive services and price.
- Buyer power (mostly consumers) is strong because of consumers' expectations for service and value pricing. Switching costs barely exist. Buyers are less likely to be brand loyal. Official research indicates that demand is inelastic.
- Suppliers such as software development and manufacturing companies have relatively low impact on the profitability of the industry because it is relatively easy to develop and manufacture CD-ROMs.

Strategy Implications

The profit potential of this business plan software industry is slightly unfavorable. While the basis of rivalry is not price, but differentiated products, the ease of entry and plentiful substitutes limit industry profitability. In order to overcome these threats, firms need to continuously differentiate and add value to product offerings and services.

Source: The format that highlights three categories (analysis, key points, and strategic implications) is adapted from Roger J. Best, Lecture Notes for BA 453, University of Oregon, Eugene, Oregon, Fall 2000. The industry example, figures, and analysis have all been revised from a supervised student project.

Box 2.2

"Wintel" and the Rise of Complementors

Among many complementors in the business world, perhaps the most visible is the partnership between Microsoft and Intel. Because of this interdependency between Microsoft's operating environment and Intel's microprocessors, the term "Wintelism" has become popular, although its usage can carry pejorative meanings in the broad computing establishment. The term is a concatenation of Windows (Microsoft's operating environment) and Intel (the largest manufacturer of central processing units [CPUs] and the originator of the x86 processor architecture used in many of today's PC-compatible computers).

At about the end of the 1980s and the beginning of the 1990s, IBM suffered a serious setback in the wake of the PS/2 disaster, and Microsoft's Windows operating environment emerged as the de facto standard. Intel, the leading manufacturer of microprocessors, supplied the chips that made Microsoft's Windows environment work. Intel's ability to sell a new microprocessor depended critically on Microsoft's ability to optimize its operating system for Microsoft's new products.

Despite the visibility of the Wintel partnership, there was very little interaction between the two firms. Initially, meetings were ad hoc, in the form of dinners between Bill Gates and Andy Grove. By 1995, the two companies moved to more formalized approaches whereby the dinners involved a small number of full-time Intel engineers onsite at the Microsoft location. Moreover, both Microsoft and Intel appointed a person in their company to act as the official liaison.

Once the closest of partners, the two firms have operated at an uneasy distance from one another ever since their first major dispute. Intel's investment in Native Signal Processing (NSP), a specialized software technology with application program capabilities, was considered by Microsoft to have transgressed into its territory. Intel had also developed NSP as an extension to Windows 3.1 when Microsoft was ready to release Windows 95. In many of the skirmishes, Microsoft had the upper hand. In fact, both firms continue to flirt with one another's competitors from time to time, most notable in Microsoft's close relationship with Advanced Micro Devices (AMD).

Although there are many alternatives to Wintel, most have only a tiny market share. The two leading alternatives to Wintel on the desktop and small server are Linux and other free Unix-like operating systems, and Apple Computer's Macintosh computers with PowerPC processors. Even so, the threat is a small one, considering Microsoft's own investment in Linux. While the jury is still out regarding the future of Wintelism, it has been an example of two firms working as complementors, and meeting their individual goals.

Sources: Adapted from David Yoffie, Ramon Casadesus Masanell, and Sasha Mattu, "Wintel (A): Cooperation or Conflict?" Harvard Business School Case 704419, August 20, 2003.

can leverage their joint products into numerous personal computer applications. It is no wonder that this budding partnership is dubbed the Age of Wintelism (see Box 2.2). While complementors do not fit within the five forces analysis in that they do not expropriate profits, they nonetheless are significant in determining the success of an industry and thereby increasing its profit potential.[30]

To account for the role of complementors, New York University professor Adam Brandenburger and Yale professor Barry Nalebuff have proposed the value net as a reformulation of the five forces analysis (see Exhibit 2.6).[31] The **value net** casts competitors, sellers of substitutes, and potential entrants as "competitors." Following Porter's logic, all restrain prices and reduce the profit potential of firms in the industry. However, suppliers and customers, along with complementors, are represented as separate entities.

Exhibit 2.6

The Value Net

The value net highlights the critical role that "complementors" can play in influencing business success or failure.

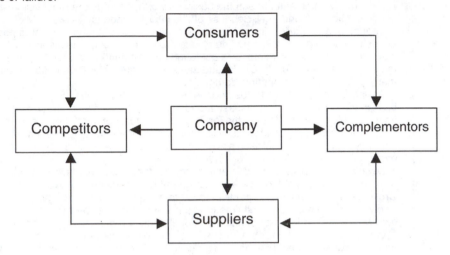

Company: Focal firm that is the object of the analysis.
Competitors: Firms that offer competing products and services, including new potential entrants and substitutes.
Consumers: Buyers of products and services.
Complementors: Firms from which customers buy complementary products, or to which suppliers sell complementary resources.
Suppliers: Suppliers of inputs to firms in the industry.

Source: Adapted from Adam Brandenburger and Barry Nalebuff, *Co-opetition* (New York: Doubleday, 1996), p. 17.

While suppliers can exert pressure on costs and quality, they can also enhance the value of a firm. In the case of Dell computers, suppliers play a critical role in quality assurance and delivery, not to mention controlling costs. Because of their role, Dell president Michael Dell considers suppliers as "partners," more than mere providers of supplies. Similarly, consumers can add to the value of transactions with their proposals for improving products and services and their suggestions for new products. Because of the attention to all parties involved in determining profit potential, the use of the value net, along with the five forces framework, provides a good structure for analyzing an industry. As Brandenburger and Nalebuff phrase it, "Thinking [about] complements is a different way of thinking about business. It's about finding ways to make the pie bigger rather than fighting with competitors over a fixed pie. To benefit from this insight, think about how to expand the pie by developing new complements or making existing complements more affordable."[32]

Exhibit 2.7

Industry Globalization Drivers

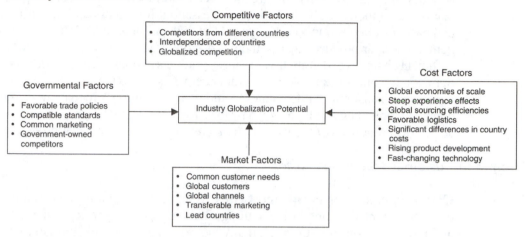

Source: Adapted from George S. Yip, *Total Global Strategy* (Upper Saddle River, NJ: Prentice Hall, 2003), pp. 28–63.

ANALYZING AN INDUSTRY'S GLOBALIZATION POTENTIAL

While it is tempting to simply extend the context of the five forces framework or the value net to international operations, it does not work seamlessly or effectively to do so. This is because managers faced with developing global strategies need to ask different questions. Industry analysts ask: What determines the relative profitability or attractiveness of a given industry? In contrast, international managers need to augment this analysis with another question: *What is the globalization potential of my industry?*

George S. Yip proposed a set of industry conditions that create the potential for global strategies.[33] In his work, not all industries present the same environments for global strategy. Some industries (semiconductors, consumer electronics, television) have a higher level of globalization potential than others (book publishing, health care, high-definition television [HDTV] standards). Managers have to recognize when industry conditions provide opportunities to pursue global strategies, or as we develop more fully in Chapter 4, develop alternative strategies. While Professor Yip developed his framework in the context of diagnosing globalization potential, we can use it to assess the pace of globalization as well. In Chapter 1, we argued that managers should not only know what factors drive globalization, but also should be aware of how the pace of globalization can affect their business. For us, globalization potential is inextricably related to the pace of globalization, that is, the higher the globalization potential, the faster is the pace of industry globalization. Yip's framework is grouped into four categories: *market, cost, governmental,* and *competitive.* They are called **industry globalization drivers**. Taken altogether, these drivers can accelerate the pace of industry globalization. The framework is illustrated in Exhibit 2.7.

MARKET GLOBALIZATION DRIVERS

Market globalization drivers are the forces and factors that affect the pace of globalization of an industry. Market drivers are essential for understanding customer demand and patterns of consumption. The pace of globalization is accelerated if more customers demand similar products, that is, there is a "convergence" in demand, as when there are sufficient channels of distribution to supply products and services to worldwide customers. Semiconductors, for example, have similar demands across the world—a PC manufacturer in Europe, Asia, or the United States would seek a common 1-megabyte memory chip. In contrast, publishing is still governed by local regulations and has less of a uniform demand across different parts of the world. There are five market globalization drivers.

Common Customer Needs and Tastes

Common customer needs and tastes "represent the extent to which customers in different countries want the same things in the product or service category that defines an industry."[34] Because there are many factors, such as culture, climate, infrastructure, and the like that affect the tastes and preferences of consumers, the higher the level of commonalities among consumer groups, the more likely that highly standardized products will be accepted by them. Marketers such as Stanford University professor Theodore Leavitt see the demand for many goods converging in most countries.[35] Today, teenagers all over the world wear Nike athletic shoes and Levi's jeans. In contrast to thirty years ago, bottled water is now consumed around the world, no longer a luxury item confined to the most exclusive cafes in Paris. As consumer needs converge or become more common, the pace of globalization will be much faster.

Global Customers

Global customers are typically companies that purchase certain items in large quantities on behalf of an entire organization and distribute them to subsidiaries. They generate a demand for large batches of standardized products. Consider Wal-Mart and furniture retailer IKEA.[36] When these firms source items, they purchase in large lots. In doing so, they are also able to secure cost economies that they can then leverage into low prices. It is now acknowledged that at least 70 percent of items sold in Wal-Mart's stores (not including the food products) have a Chinese component.[37] This reflects Wal-Mart's role as a global consumer. The presence of global consumers such as Wal-Mart in an industry tends to accelerate the pace of globalization.

Global Channels

Global channels denotes the distribution of particular types of products on a large scale or in a somewhat universal way. This reduces the cost of handling various distribution requirements. Supply chains have been carefully crafted around the world to take advantage of sourcing opportunities and to open up channels of distribution. IKEA once found channels to be closed to them—a form of retaliation from the traditional furniture retailers. IKEA has since opened up these channels to become the world's leading low-cost furniture retailer.[38] To the extent that global channels are developed and employed, the faster the pace of industry globalization.

Transferable Marketing

Transferable marketing refers to the degree of adaptation that has to be made for brands that are to be transferred to overseas markets. If the marketing schemes, models, or strategies can be transferred from country to country with very little adjustment, the application of global strategies will be easier and the faster the pace of globalization. A good example is Procter & Gamble, the leading world supplier of laundry detergents. P&G is able to use marketing developed in Europe in its Asian markets, thus saving on the cost of redesigning their promotional and advertising schemes.[39] To the extent that marketing strategies and practices can be transferred and diffused, the faster the pace of industry globalization.

Lead Countries

The more infrequent the transfer, the less global the industry is. When innovation is concentrated in a few countries that are leading the development of new products and processes, these are called **lead countries**. Non-lead-country consumers tend to look to lead countries for trends. The existence of lead countries allows companies to promote products in other countries by using their reputation in lead countries. The popularity of the United States reflects its lead-country status in many industries, notably financial services, entertainment, information technology, biotechnology, and nanotechnology. Japan's strengths are in optic design and materials management, while Korea's Samsung is beginning to excel in photo-plasma technology.[40] As more lead countries emerge, and as more firms participate in these lead countries to be exposed to sources of innovation, the faster the pace of industry globalization.

COST GLOBALIZATION DRIVERS

Cost globalization drivers are the cost factors and forces that can change the pace of globalization. When costs are reduced to the point that products become affordable, the pace of globalization is enhanced. A major benefit of global strategy is cost reduction resulting from scale and scope economies. Cost globalization drivers are factors that help cost reduction. Thus, semiconductors and VCRs have quickly become global industries, primarily because their cost of production have sharply decreased over a short time. Meanwhile, with the high process and differing standards for HDTV, its pace of globalization is relatively slower. There are seven cost globalization drivers.

Global Scale Economies

Economies of scale (cost efficiencies that are realized when the volume of an activity is increased) are important for cost reduction. Global strategy requires economies of scale at the global level to achieve cost benefits that merit global strategies. This occurs when a single market is not large enough for competitors to optimize economies of scale, at which case the use of multiple markets becomes necessary. In some cases, economies of scope (cost efficiencies that are realized by spreading activities across different product lines and multiple plants), which allow a firm to sell multiple products in multiple countries, becomes an important component of a global strategy aimed at reducing costs. Firms within industries with large fixed costs, such as chemicals, steel, petroleum, and automobiles tend to utilize expansion strategies in which economies of scale and scope can be realized. In fact, world markets for steel and consumer electronics have resulted from cost reductions emanating from scale. In the case of automobiles, multinational firms have benefited from efficiencies in scope arising from multiple plants and locations.

Steep Experience Effects

An experience (learning) curve represents the cost efficiencies gained by repetitively performing an activity. In a series of studies of many products including bottle caps, refrigerators, and long-distance calls, conducted by the BCG (Boston Consulting Group), researchers observed a remarkable regularity in which costs (and prices) were reduced with cumulative production. Doubling of cumulative production typically reduced unit costs by 20 to 30 percent (defined now as 80 percent and 70 percent experience curves, respectfully). The greater the reduction in unit costs with increased production, the steeper the experience curve.[41] In the case of global strategy, this means that experience effects should be applicable to many locations and that experience effects gained from one place can be applied and utilized in other locations to enhance the overall global-level effects. In the case of semiconductors, for example, the cost per unit over time reduces by 30 percent whenever experience is doubled.[42]

Global Sourcing Efficiencies

This is similar to economies of scale, but from the supply side. In order to achieve global sourcing efficiencies, a firm has to be able to purchase inputs on a large scale at low cost via well-established coordination among suppliers worldwide. Again, we revert to our example of Wal-Mart, which excels in worldwide sourcing efficiencies, particularly in China.[43] McDonald's also benefits from its global sourcing, specifically using local supplies for its basic food ingredients.

Favorable Logistics

This refers to the economies in transporting products versus the value of the products. When products are low in value but have high transportation costs, the use of standardized products across multiple consumer groups is discouraged. A favorable situation occurs when cost benefits and logistical convenience are not only available in a small number of countries or only regionally, but exist in many countries globally. With a ramped-up supply chain, Cisco can move quickly around the world in search of its best source of supplies. The ability of Starbucks to secure vital partnerships with suppliers in Latin America and Africa has facilitated its global strategy.[44]

Differences in Country Costs

Global firms tend to seek the lowest-cost suppliers, designers, or skilled labor. To achieve that goal, different cost levels in different countries must exist in order for global strategy to be successfully implemented. There will be minimal or no cost benefits if there are no differences or if the differences are insignificant. Vietnam, India, and China have become desirable because of their lower labor costs.[45] A good number of North American publishers have started to produce software in India where they are able to pay programmers a much lower wage but with comparable quality in the products.[46]

High Product Development Costs

High product development costs relative to the size of the national market can be a driver of globalization, but two considerations apply. On one hand, to reduce total costs when the costs of product development are high, firms are motivated to promote more products in various markets in order to reduce the average cost of development per unit. On the other hand, high product development costs discourage some less resourceful firms to participate in the competition. Semiconductor costs are significant, with a new plant costing over $1.5 billion. This has led to various consortia, SEMATECH being one example, that share developmental costs across competitors.[47]

Fast-Changing Technology

For products that rely on fast-changing technology, firms have to spread out the cost of the product via multiple, large markets before the product becomes obsolete and before imitations appear. Thus, industries characterized by fast-changing technologies (e.g., semiconductors) tend to have a greater globalization potential and a faster pace of globalization. Because new semiconductor plants are expensive and have a three-to-five-year lifespan, Samsung and Hyundai must rely on large markets to meet their returns on investment, which, in turn, accelerates the pace of semiconductor globalization.[48]

GOVERNMENT GLOBALIZATION DRIVERS

As discussed in Chapter 1, government policies can enhance or impair the pace of globalization. Such policies are referred to as **government globalization drivers.** If policies favor free trade and relatively open access, then globalization is enhanced. To the extent that policies deter market entry, then the pace of globalization is much slower. These policies' existence depends on the overall friendly or unfriendly environment that governments provide to business. There are five government globalization drivers.

Favorable Trade Polices

Favorable trade policies include trade liberalization for foreign investment and user-friendly business polices, which create possibilities for global firms. Lower tariff rates for the semiconductor industry have enhanced its globalization pace, for example. In contrast, the worldwide market for agrarian products would be much more developed if tariffs were reduced. Average tariff rates have fallen significantly since 1950, and under the Uruguay Agreement, tariffs reached 3.9 percent (falling from between 9 and 26 percent) in 2000. The lowering of rates will facilitate the globalization of production.[49]

Compatible Technical Standards

As countries adopt different technical standards for products, sometimes for the sake of protecting home markets and consumers, it will be difficult to transfer and standardize products. Compatible technical standards among countries provide a platform for facilitating product transfer and product standardization. For example, differing standards prevent HDTV from being widely adopted around the world. In contrast, when DVD standards were openly adopted, DVD sales soared and DVDs become a global product.

Common Marketing Regulations

Common marketing regulations refer to the uniformity of the marketing environment in different countries. The more uniform they are, the easier it is for standardized products to be marketed across multiple consumer groups. Consider the current dispute between the United States and the European Union regarding genetically modified food and vegetables. With the EU disputing the safety of such items, the pace of globalization for the products has been slow.[50]

Government-Owned Competitors and Customers

Government-owned competitors tend to be more aggressive in entering foreign markets, particularly if they have the support from their governments. This is particularly applicable to some Chinese firms. They are more capable of pursuing foreign markets. The opposite is true in the case of government-owned customers, with their preference for buying from local suppliers. In this specific case, government-owned customers become a barrier to globalization. The preference on the part of European customers to source from local suppliers, instead of buying much cheaper semiconductors with comparable quality from Japan, impeded the development of the European PC industry. Even so, government-owned corporations are not necessarily successful in their global activities. One source of controversy is China's hold on its SOEs (state-owned enterprises), which comprise about 60 percent of China's GDP. Since SOEs tend to be the primary source of employment, they are encouraged by the Chinese government despite their poor performance.[51]

Host Government Concerns

Some aspects of a foreign firm's global strategies cause legitimate concerns that discourage host governments from being open-minded toward it. Some of these issues include tax avoidance by the firm and the possibility that the firm may frequently relocate its subsidiaries from country to country.

COMPETITIVE GLOBALIZATION DRIVERS

Competitive globalization drivers are the competitive forces that can change the pace of globalization. Competition spurs the pace of globalization by bringing in different rivals, products and services, and sources of competitive advantage. There are five competitive globalization drivers.

High Exports and Imports

A high volume in the export and import of certain goods is an indication that potential standardized products exist. Manufacturing the products near their markets will make sense for transportation cost reduction. Essentially, more trade between countries spurs the pace of globalization. Between 1980 to 1994, total output grew by about 40 percent, but this was outpaced by world trade, which grew by more than 70 percent.[52]

Competitors from Different Continents

When rivals in a particular industry come from various backgrounds, competition tends to be more severe. Hence it is important for firms to pursue global strategies to combat competition. The entry of the Chinese and the Vietnamese into telecommunications signals different strategies that will only intensify competition and increase the pace of globalization. Reflecting on the entry strategies used by Japanese firms in the 1970s and 1980s, it is not unusual for new competitors from different countries to introduce new strategies, thereby changing the rules of competition.

Interdependence of Countries

Interdependence among foreign subsidiaries allows firms to compensate for one subsidiary's weaknesses by sharing resources among all subsidiaries. It also spurs competitors to pursue similar strategies to offset rivals. With interdependent countries, firms can subsidize attacks on competitors in other countries. Komatsu's success against Caterpillar in the United States stemmed in part from Komatsu's success in Eastern Europe, which allowed the company to drive down costs through experience.[53] Without having to compete directly with Caterpillar in Eastern Europe, Komatsu was able to prepare itself when it battled Caterpillar in the United States.

Globalized Competition

When globalized competitors actively engage in global activities, the competitive factor is changed and other firms are pressured to become global firms as well. Consequently, more firms become global and the industry itself is gradually transformed into one that is global. As banks become more multinational in their operations, they tend to heighten competition as well. This was the case with Citibank, which found competition in Asia to be quite intense with the established presence of Chase Manhattan, J.P. Morgan, and HSBC.

Transferable Competitive Advantage

If a firm's competitive advantage, the basis for its success in competition, can be transferred from market to market, it is inspired to keep going abroad and to duplicate its success from country to country. The successful application of its Direct System by Dell Computers in London and China will certainly leverage its entry into new markets that are receptive to this system. The same holds for Starbucks, which has successfully penetrated Latin America, Asia, and parts of Europe using its strategy of creating a superior coffee experience for targeted customers.

In summary, all four globalization drivers dictate the globalization potential of an industry, or its pace of globalization. What are the implications for further firm positioning? Intuitively, if the pace of globalization is high, it behooves firms in that industry to quickly develop global strategies. As the globalization of the competitive landscape intensifies, there is growing pressure for companies to develop an international market presence. Nevertheless, having a global presence does not ensure that a firm will sustain its competitive advantage. Its ability to learn quickly from experiences and develop dynamic capabilities become important considerations in forging a successful endgame. This can be contrasted with an industry that is slower in its pace of globalization, where firms can develop capabilities at a slower rate, or can afford to learn from the experiences of the pioneers or "first movers" (see Chapter 5). Exhibit 2.8 illustrates the different drivers underlying the globalization potential of the semiconductor memory segment.

FURTHER APPLICATIONS OF THE GLOBALIZATION FRAMEWORK: SERVICES

In an updated version of his framework, Yip includes services and the Internet among industry globalization drivers. He distinguishes between three kinds of services: people processing, possession processing, and information processing.[54] People processing services involve the consumer's participation as part of the production process. For example, in Dell's Direct System, consumers are encouraged to customize their personal computers to fit their needs. Possession processing services do not require customer participation in the production process itself, but that services are enhanced at the point of delivery. For example, automobile service shops can offer to pick up customers at designated places and times. Information-based services involve the collecting, manipulating, interpreting, and transmitting data and information on behalf of targeted customers. For example, Charles Schwab offers its customers a wide array of financial information for them to be more informed in their financial decisions.

Depending on the type of service involved, the pace of industry globalization will vary. For example, for market globalization drivers, the less the customer is involved, the easier it is to standardize service-offerings. The extent to which the Dell Direct System can apply across parts of the world will depend on the firm's ability to balance its customers'

Exhibit 2.8

Assessing Industry Globalization Potential

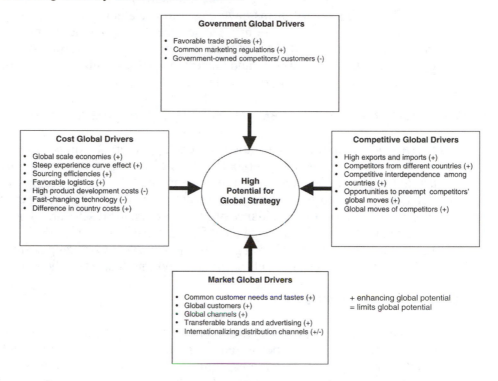

Source: Application of the Semiconductor Memory Segment is based on the globalization driver model from George S. Yip, *Global Strategy II* (Upper Saddle River, NJ: Prentice Hall, 2003), pp. 32–56.

customization needs against its sourcing and manufacturing capabilities. Because customization is a core part of Dell's strategy and one of its distinctive competencies, it is very likely that Dell will be able to implement customization on a global scale. This is different for Nike, however, with its recent offering to have customers design and customize their own athletic shoes using the Web. While this can work on a relatively limited scale, it has the potential of overtaxing the company's use of manufacturing subcontractors if carried on a global scale. To the extent that fixed costs are low, possession-based services are able to extend services across multiple locations (PC service centers).

All in all, while some providers limit their choice of services and have focused on standardization over customization, others have extended their services successfully in multiple locations worldwide. The decision to do this depends on the cost and level of customer adaptation. Typically, services that require little adaptation facilitate the transfer of marketing schemes around the world. This often happens in major countries like the United States in the restaurant and hotel business. The Ritz-Carlton, for example, can enact its five-star services around the world. The same can be argued for McDonald's and Kentucky Fried Chicken. In contrast, accounting services are much more difficult to transfer. Specifically, the higher status of British accountants compared to their counterparts in the

United States limits the potential communality of clients' expectations, and thus limits the transferability of U.S. accountancy services to the United Kingdom.[55]

With globalization, there is additional pressure on firms to extend services around the world. In this regard, firms have began to use electronic channels and powerful databases to deliver information-based services, for example, from a central hub to multiple locations worldwide, as part of their strategy. Enterprising firms, such as FedEx, UPS, Charles Schwab, and General Electric Capital have resorted to use information processing to improve and to successfully extend their services abroad.

FURTHER APPLICATIONS OF THE GLOBALIZATION FRAMEWORK: THE INTERNET

In terms of marketing globalization drivers, the Internet brings customers together, and communication via the Internet enhances efficiency in distributing information to customers. The efficiencies and communication that the Internet brings to global firms reduce the overall costs of operation. The Internet provides a favorable environment for globalization through the avoidance of trade barriers, the disclosure of nonstandardized marketing regulations, and the demand for technical standards among countries. Thus, the Internet can accelerate market globalization drivers by bringing customers together, and by making it more efficient for firms to communicate with their customers.

ANTITRUST: A CAUTIONARY NOTE

When analyzing the external environment, particularly within the five forces analysis, a continuing question has been regarding the role of government in determining an industry's profit potential. Porter has long maintained that government is not a separate force, but that government actions and regulations influence the context of each force. Thus, there are myriad governmental regulations related to entry, supplier quality, pricing, and consumer protection, many of which are beyond the scope of this book. Even so, a discussion of external environmental analysis is not complete without some reference to antitrust, an area that perhaps directly impacts entry and pricing.

At a general level, antitrust laws prohibit firms from coordinating their actions through collusion and other agreements that would reduce competition.[56] Antitrust laws are enforced by two agencies: the Antitrust Division of the U.S. Department of Justice and the Federal Trade Commission (FTC). The Department of Justice (DOJ) oversees the enforcement of antitrust laws using the **Sherman Act** (1890), which has two general provisions: first, it stipulates that any contract or conspiracy that restrains trade among several states within the United States, or with foreign nations, is illegal; and second, the monopolization or conspiracy to monopolize any part of trade by any unit is deemed a felony. Both provisions have associated penalties. The Department of Justice is also charged with enforcing the **Clayton Act** (1914, amended in 1936), which adds more detail to the Sherman Act and generally prohibits price discrimination that would lessen competition. The Federal Trade Commission Act in 1914 created the FTC with a mandate to prevent unfair methods of competition and deceptive practices. The FTC and DOJ have since extended their jurisdiction to cover the anticompetitive effects of mergers.

Even with this brief overview, it is apparent that any industry analysis can be affected by various interpretations of antitrust laws and application. The breakup of AT&T into the "Baby Bells" in 1980, as well as the continued troubles of Microsoft both in the United States and abroad, provides testimony to the power of antitrust and public perception of monopoly power. What are other implications for managers engaged in the analysis of their external environments? California State of Technology economist R. Preston McAfee adds three specific reasons why managers need to know about antitrust regulations: first, antitrust laws have the effect of restricting the set of legal actions available to the firm, thus restricting profitable strategies on occasion; second, private antitrust suits are often used to harass a competitor, which means that a firm can be unduly inconvenienced even if it does not engage in uncooperative behavior; and third, managers can be charged with significant fines and prison sentences of three years or more for violating antitrust laws. As the adage goes, "ignorance is no excuse." We recognize that some of the conditions and strategies described earlier can fall within the rubric of antitrust laws. While a full treatise about antitrust is beyond the scope of this book, antitrust provides a cautionary note in any analysis of competition.

IMPLICATIONS

A belief that is gaining popularity and acceptance is that the starting point of any analysis is the industry. This is important in identifying the critical determinants of industry profitability. Even so, we start our analysis with a macroscopic view because this context influences industry profitability at a broader level and serves as a signal for top management on important current and future trends that influence a firm's operations. A PEST (political-economic-societal-technological) analysis accommodates this requirement. It also helps managers understand how value is created and transferred to potentially different sectors of the environment. It is critical to understanding the impact of particular trends and the effectiveness of a firm's current position. Central to any strategic analysis is industry analysis, in which structural forces that bear on industry profitability are examined for their relative impact. A good industry analysis suggests that management attention is directed at the most significant force. The value net incorporates the crucial role of complementors. While it might be tempting to simply extend the five forces model to cover international operations, this is not sufficient. It is perhaps more appropriate to pose a different type of question: what is the globalization potential of a given industry as gauged by its pace? The globalization potential, or pace of globalization, sets the competitive context in which proper firm positioning should then take place.

External environmental analysis is the starting point of a good analysis but cannot be the sole determinant of a firm's strategy. As a context for strategy, external analysis serves the following purposes: (1) it identifies relevant issues facing the firm; without such analysis, a firm faces the danger of ignoring an issue altogether, or developing a very narrow perspective of its ensuing strategy; (2) it helps focus attention on the most critical issue. Through focus, a firm achieves some efficiency. Otherwise, it stands the risk of attending to too many issues and depleting its resources in the process, and (3) it is helpful in co-aligning a firm's internal strengths and resources against critical external issues. The assessment of a firm's internal capabilities from the standpoint of its business model is the subject of the next chapter. Taken in tandem with external analysis, internal analysis sets the stage for a firm to formulate strategy.

SUMMARY

1. This chapter introduces four important frameworks: (1) macroenvironmental analysis; (2) industry analysis and competitive behavior; (3) the value net; and (4) globalization potential of an industry. Because the macroenvironment can change rapidly, trends are not necessarily permanent and require rigorous monitoring and updating on a regular basis.

2. Macro-environmental analysis can also be segmented into several major areas: political/legal, economic, demographic, technological, and sociocultural. Political/legal trends concern political events, changes of laws and the like. Economic trends can cover both broad and specific changes in income distribution. Demographics provides the central focus of marketing management and should also be a serious consideration for global strategies. The technological environment is perhaps the most volatile of all. The sociocultural environment relates to values, beliefs, and norms that are shaped by societies. Political-economic-societal-technological (PEST) analysis is a popular method of integrating and summarizing the factors that affect a firm's operations.

3. Michael Porter's five forces model is used to conduct industry analysis in terms of attractiveness, which is influenced by profitability. Intensity of rivalry refers to the competition among rivals within a particular industry. The more severe the competition is, the less attractive the industry is.

4. Regarding the threat of new entrants, new entry into the industry invariably reduces the existing firms' profitability by adding capacity and introducing new methods of competition. As for threat of substitutes, pressure on an industry will be stronger when there are more close substitutes for products (i.e., demand related). The higher the bargaining power of suppliers, the weaker the firms of the buying industry. As for the bargaining power of buyers, a particular industry becomes more attractive if its buyers have low bargaining power. The strength of the five forces varies between industries, and consequently so do levels of industry profitability.

4. The value net adds to this analysis by incorporating the role of complementors. These are units that enhance the value of an industry through the provision of complementary products and services.

5. George S. Yip proposed a set of industry conditions that create the potential for global strategies. These conditions are grouped into four categories: market, cost, governmental, and competitive. Market globalization drivers analyze the pace of globalization. The pace is accelerated if more customers demand similar products, resulting in a worldwide market. Cost globalization drivers analyze the costs of production. To the extent that costs are reduced to the point that products become affordable, then the pace of globalization is enhanced. Government globalization drivers analyze to what extent government policies

favor free trade and relatively open access. Competitive globalization drivers analyze how different rivals, products and services, and sources of competitive advantage spur the pace of globalization.

6. There are three kinds of services: people-processing, possession-processing, and information-processing. The more processing functions can be automated for the standardization of production, the more possible it is for globalization to occur. The Internet provides a favorable environment for globalization through the avoidance of trade barriers, the disclosure of non-standardized marketing regulations, and the demand for technical standards among countries.

7. As a cautionary note, antitrust laws restrict the strategies of the firm in the interest of upholding competition. Firms are also limited in terms of legal action they can take; firms can be harassed by antitrust claims; and firms can be fined significantly if they are found to violate antitrust laws.

8. As a context for strategy, external analysis serves the following purposes: (1) It identifies relevant issues facing the firm; without such analysis, a firm faces the danger of ignoring an issue altogether, or developing a very narrow perspective of its ensuing strategy. (2) It helps focus attention on the most critical issue, and through focus, a firm achieves some efficiency. Otherwise, it stands the risk of attending to too many issues and depleting its resources in the process. (3) it is helpful in co-aligning a firm's internal strengths and resources against critical external issues.

KEY TERMS

Macroenvironmental analysis	Bargaining power of buyers
Political/legal environment	Complementors
Economic trends	Value net
Demographics	Industry globalization drivers
Technological environment	Market globalization drivers
Sociocultural environment	Common customer needs and tastes
PEST	Global customers
Five forces model	Global channels
Intensity of rivalry	Transferable marketing
Switching cost	Lead countries
Threat of new entrants	Cost globalization drivers
Economies of scale	Government globalization drivers
Learning and experience effects	Competitive globalization drivers
Differentiation	Sherman Act
Threat of substitutes	Clayton Act
Bargaining power of suppliers	

DISCUSSION QUESTIONS

1. What are the purposes of performing environmental analysis? What is meant by "levels" of environment and how should they be analyzed?
2. What are the macro-environment trends that dominate the current global environment? Please cite and discuss their implications.
3. How can the macro-environment be segmented? Please identify the latest development in each segment and provide a complete analysis of the current macro-environment using these segments.
4. Discuss the basic principles of Porter's five forces of competition model and how this model helps managers in performing global strategic management.
5. What is meant by the terms *intensity of rivalry*, *threat of new entrants*, *threat of substitutes*, *bargaining power of buyers*, and *bargaining power of suppliers*, and how does each of them affect the attractiveness of an industry? Please select three industries and thoroughly examine them using the five forces.
6. Discuss the basic principles of Yip's industry globalization drivers and explain how this model helps managers in performing global strategic management.
7. What is meant by *market globalization drivers*, *cost globalization drivers*, *government globalization drivers*, and *competitive globalization drivers*? Please select three industries and thoroughly examine them using these four drivers.
8. Use three cases to illustrate how overlooking the macro, industry, and global potential environments can be detrimental to companies.

ACTION ITEM 2.1. PEST ANALYSIS (GENERAL ELECTRIC)

This exercise is designed for you individually, or in groups, to conduct a PEST Analysis, as illustrated in Exhibit 2.5. You are also encouraged to re-read the pertinent section of this chapter before embarking on this exercise.

- Agree on twelve major trends (political-economic-societal-technological) that you believe will be instrumental in shaping values and patterns in your company environment for the next ten years.
- Determine twenty major complaints or needs that your major customers have expressed about your product/service at present.
- Rate each of the twelve trends you identified for its convergence with your customers' complaints or needs. A rating of 10 indicates high convergence and a rating of 1 indicates no convergence.
- Rate the degree of pressure emanating from key customer groups regarding each complaint or need. A rating of 10 indicates high pressure and a rating of 1 indicates low pressure.
- Summarize each complaint and trend in terms of two dimensions: the degree of convergence and relative pressure. If possible, develop contingency plans for those identified within the high convergence–high pressure category.

ACTION ITEM 2.2. UNDERSTANDING INDUSTRY DYNAMICS

Understanding the structure of an industry and how the forces within it operate can aid performance if the organization can take action to influence these forces and avoid those that are negative. The task is to determine which of these forces is of the greatest importance to your organization. The following forces, based on Michael Porter's model, can potentially impact the operations and performance of your organization.

INSTRUCTIONS: Please fill out this worksheet using the attached supplement for additional details on each question (if necessary). You will have an opportunity to discuss your responses in your group, as well as in class.

1. Potential Rate of Growth of Industry:

____ 0–3%   ____ 9–12%   ____ 16–21%
____ 3–6%   ____ 12–15%   ____ > 21%
____ 6–9%   ____ 15–16%

2. What are the major firms in your industry (domestic and international)?

_____

_____

_____

_____

_____

3. Who are your direct competitors?

_____

_____

_____

_____

_____

4. What is the basis of competition (price, service, technology)?

_____

_____

_____

_____

_____

5. Extent of Fixed Costs:

Low   ____   ____   ____   ____   ____   High
         1   2   3   4   5

6. Extent of Product Differentiation:

Low   ____   ____   ____   ____   ____   High
         1   2   3   4   5

7. Intensity of Competition Among Firms:

Extremely   ____   ____   ____   ____   ____   No competition
competitive   1   2   3   4   5

8. Ease of Entry of New Firms in the Industry:

No barriers   ____   ____   ____   ____   ____   Virtually impos-
            1   2   3   4   5   sible to enter

9. Degree of Product Substitutability:

Low   ____   ____   ____   ____   ____   High
         1   2   3   4   5

10. Degree of Bargaining Power Buyers and Customers Possess:

Buyers   ____   ____   ____   ____   ____   Selling firms
dictate terms   1   2   3   4   5   dictate

11. Degree of Bargaining Power Suppliers and Vendors Possess:

Suppliers   ____   ____   ____   ____   ____   Purchasing
dictate terms   1   2   3   4   5   firms dictate

12. General Level of Management Capability:

Many capable managers   ___ 1   ___ 2   ___ 3   ___ 4   ___ 5   Very few capable managers

Additional Comments: _____

_____

_____

Source: Alan J. Rowe, Richard O. Mason, Karl Dickel, Robert Mann, Robert Mockler, *Strategic Management* 4th ed. (New York: Addition-Westley Publishing Company, 1994), p. 124. Used with permission.

CASE-IN-POINT. THE SEMICONDUCTOR INDUSTRY: HISTORICAL ORIGINS AND COMPETITION IN THE 1990s

If there is a landmark industry that underpins the third phase of globalization, it would be semiconductors.[57] Semiconductors are materials, notably silicon, that function as conductors, permitting electrical current to flow, or as insulators that cut off the flow under particular circumstances. Semiconductors, when used to control the input of electric power, can transmit coded signals for particular uses (i.e., computer, satellite, and consumer appliances).

The invention of the semiconductor is traced to the work of two men: Jack Kilby and Robert Noyce. Acting independently, they invented the integrated circuit. On September 12, 1958, a group of Texas Instruments executives gathered in Kilby's residence to see if this tiny oscillator-on-a-chip, half an inch long and narrower than a toothpick, was finally ready. The integrated circuit had provided the answer to the problem of the "tyranny of numbers," or engineers' previous inability to increase computing power because of the limitations of complex wiring. The men in the room looked at the sine wave again. Then everyone broke into broad smiles. A new era of electronics had been born.[58]

At about the same time, Robert Noyce worked out the idea, dubbed the "Monolithic Idea," in words quite similar to those Jack Kilby had entered in his notebook six months before. Noyce wrote, "it would be desirable to make multiple devices on a single piece of silicon, in order to be able to make interconnections between devices as part of the manufacturing process, and thus reduce size, weight, etc. as well as cost per active element."[59]

At the time, neither likely anticipated the full impact of what they had invented: in the integrated circuit, they had ushered in the era of microelectronics and the basis for what we presently refer to as the high-tech industry. What is particularly striking about the invention of the integrated circuit, in contrast with other previous inventions, is the pervasiveness of its effects in a relatively short period of time. As semiconductor technology developed, the miniaturization of electronics created new markets and revolutionized applications data computing, communications, test and measurements, and industrial equipment.

New consumer products such as the personal computer, digital watches, sophisticated alarms and sensor devices, programmable sewing machines, and automotive controls have come to fruition with the new technology. As the miniaturization of electronics continues, industries like the automated office, financial services, transportation, and artificial intelligence will become stronger components of our industry. It is no wonder that one high-tech executive once referred to the chip as "the crude oil of the 1990s."

The world semiconductor industry was once completely dominated by U.S. firms. Earlier inventions of the integrated circuit and subsequent improvements were based on a massive influx of defense dollars, notably the Minuteman II missile program. Antitrust regulations at the time excluded American Telephone and Telegraph (i.e., Western Electric, the manufacturing arm of AT&T) and International Business Machines (IBM) from entering the industry, creating opportunities for smaller merchant firms for which a number of major innovations and process modifications originated. Even with the subsequent entry of IBM and AT&T as major captive producers, the structure of the semiconductor industry was a viable one, with small-scale producers serving "niche" markets that were not as successfully serviced by the larger merchant firms.[60]

Since the discovery of the transistor in 1949, the United States has enjoyed economic and scientific supremacy in high technology, with modest competition from Great Britain. The success of U.S. firms as innovators in the field was facilitated by early Pentagon funding in semiconductors. The climate for innovation was enhanced by the unique structure of a "Silicon Valley" that combined the benefits of venture capital funding, university research, and a cluster of budding entrepreneurs into one area. Moreover, the implosion of growth markets (computers, software, CAM/CAD, etc.) arising from new innovations in microelectronics was easily accommodated by the large size of the U.S. domestic market, paving the way for even more innovations.

In the past, Japan had relied on both the United States and Europe for key innovations, which they secured through licensing and cross-licensing agreements. Through superior production techniques, ingenious "reverse engineering" capabilities, and institutional support from the Japanese government and ministries, Japanese firms have excelled in driving down the costs of these products for commercial consumption. Videocassette recorders and compact discs provide graphic testimony to these accomplishments. Securing licenses from Philips and other companies, the Japanese firms have been able to drive down the costs of these products to a price acceptable to consumers—a feat that had eluded the products' inventors.[61]

Playing a "catch-up" role, European firms are examining how to work within the constraints imposed by the European Economic Community to become competitive in high technology. While a number of European firms, notably Philips and A.G. Siemens, are not lacking in innovation (as represented by their invention of the videorecorder and the compact disc), they have not been able to diffuse these products at a competitive level. The limited size of individual European markets, a preference to compete in the U.S. market instead of their own, and myopic managerial strategies developed through the years account for such failures.[62]

Understanding the dynamics of growth in this industry reminds us what generates growth and development. The growth of semiconductors has been nothing less than spectacular. Gordon Moore, former chairman of Intel Corporation, once predicted that the number of transistors per chip would double approximately every two years. Viewed at the time as a fairly optimistic estimate, this has now been dubbed "Moore's Law" because of its uncanny degree of accuracy (also see chapter 8). Since the early 1960s, the rate of growth in the complexity of integrated circuits has increased nearly 100 percent every two-and-a-half years. The growth of semiconductors results from frequent innovations in the base product that are quickly diffused to other high-technology sectors. Innovations comprise new product innovations (e.g., transistors to integrated circuits) and process modifications (e.g., CMOS-NMOS-BIPOLAR).

An important feature of semiconductors is their centrality in the electronic information industries. The structure of this overall industry has been likened to an inverted pyramid: at the "upstream" are producers of advanced materials and manufacturing equipment; the "midstream" consists of semiconductor producers; and the "downstream" are numerous end-users of semiconductors.[63] The intensity of the interdependence between these industries distinguishes them from traditional capital-intensive industries. Innovations in semiconductors create an implosion of applications for the computer, instrumentation, telecommunications, and consumer-related markets.

Diffusion is accelerated by the declining costs of semiconductor devices that accompany better process improvements and production automation.[64] It is also true, however, that advances in semiconductors resulted from developments in one end-user, that is, computer-aided design and computer-aided engineering. This degree of synergy between manufacturers and end-users is what creates opportunities for many high-tech sectors. From this context, the weakening of one or more sectors in the pyramid can result in an erosion for the entire spectrum of industries.

Prior to 1977, competitive success in semiconductors was based on four factors: consumer acceptance of product design, availability of second-source suppliers, aggressive pricing, and credible delivery acceptance.[65] At the early stage of the product life cycle, competition focused on product development as several firms would compete to have their product design accepted as the industry standard. Mostek's design of the 16k DRAM is one example of a clear favorite. Once a favorite was selected, other firms typically entered the race as second-source producers and competed on the basis of price, marketing and distribution, quality, and reliability. Since funds obtained from a mature product were typically invested in a new product, it was important for firms to maintain the cycle of investment and reinvestment.[66]

The Japanese entry into the 64k DRAM market in the late 1970s and early 1980s changed the competitive rules in the industry. Japanese firms utilized their strengths as low-cost manufacturers of the product to aggressively attack the U.S. market and exploit the financial constraints experienced by U.S. firms during recessionary periods. The success of Japanese semiconductor firms derives from their ability to exploit vulnerabilities of their rivals in managing the economic cycle that is generic to semiconductor manufacturing.[67] The pattern is depicted using the 64k DRAM as a representative example.

The commodity-like status of the 64k DRAM in tandem with lower costs allows the semiconductor firm to hence recoup some of its investment in the early growth stages. As with any product, funds from internal sources are critical to financing new products. In this case, forces for innovation arise from large markets for nonstandardized applications (i.e., EPROM and EEPROM) made possible by the design capabilities of VLSI (very large scale integration). Such applications of advanced circuitry include computer peripherals, analytical testing instruments, laser testing applications, and other software products.[68]

CASE DISCUSSION QUESTIONS

1. What economic, technological, and cultural factors facilitated the emergence of the semiconductor industry?
2. What factors account for the early success of U.S. semiconductor firms?
3. What actions and strategies propelled Japanese firms to seriously challenge the hegemony of U.S. firms?
4. What factors limited the effectiveness of European firms in this regard?
5. Use Internet sources to get an update on the semiconductor industry. What has changed? Who are the leaders? Based on your new information, use Porter's five forces analysis to assess the attractiveness of the industry. Use Yip's industry globalization drivers to assess the pace of globalization in this industry.

NOTES FOR CHAPTER 2

1. Nano 101: An Insider's Guide to the World of Nanotechnology, 2002 Forbes/Wolfe Nanotech Report, www.forbesnanotech.com, p. 2.

2. Kevin Bonsor, "How Nanotechnology Will Work," http://science.howstuffworks.com/nano-technology.htm/printable, retrieved on March 9, 2006; "Nanotechnology Will Bring Total Change in Human Life," *The Hindu,* March 7, 2006, p. 1; "Science and Technology: Tiny Pieces of the World With Power to Change Planet," *The Scotsman,* September 17, 2005, p. 38.

3. "Nanotechnology Will Bring Total Change in Human Life"; "Science and Technology."

4. Jimmy Lee Shreeve, "Technology: Big Trouble in the Mini-Revolution? Nanotechnology Could Treat Cancer or Create Clean Energy. But What Happens If Nano-particles Enter Our Bodies?" *The Independent,* December 7, 2005, p. 44.

5. Clive Cookson, "'Nanomachines' Represent Huge Stride in Technology," *Financial Times,* September 8, 2005, p. 6.

6. Shreeve, "Technology: Big Trouble in the Mini-Revolution?"

7. "Small Motor, Huge Power," *Times* (London), September 8, 2005, p. 3; "University of Michigan: New Nanotech Drug Delivery Systems Under Study for Cancer Therapy," *Healthcare Mergers, Acquisition & Ventures Week,* March 18, 2006, p. 155.

8. Among the core sources of trend-spotting and analysis, see John Naisbitt, *Megatrends: Ten Directions Transforming Our Lives* (New York: Touchstone Books, 1996, 1997); also see Patricia

Aburdene, *Megatrends 2010: The Rise of the Conscious Capitalism* (Charlottesville, VA: Hampton Roads, 2005).

9. This section was synthesized from the following sources: (a) Frank McDonald and Fred Burton, International Business (London: Thomson, 2002), p. 1. We adopted the second and the fourth trend that were also updated; (b) For trend 1, we used data from Sam W. Cross, "The Foreign Exchange Market in the United States" (Chapter 3), Monograph published by the Federal Reserve Bank of New York, EconPapers, http://econpapers.repec.org/bookchap/fipfednmo/1998aatfemitu.htm. Readers are advised to read George Soros, *George Soros on Globalization* (New York: Perseus Books, 2002) and Joseph E. Stiglitz, *Globalization and Its Discontents* (New York: W.W. Norton & Company, 2003) for a full treatment about the problems of an unimpeded capital flow; (c) Information about Mexico and Brazil are drawn from "Global Prospects: Latin America and the Caribbean: 2007 Report, Published by the World Bank, http://siteresources.worldbank.org/INTGEP2007/Resources/LAC_Regional_Prospects.pdf and from "Brazil," LatinFocus: The Leading Source for Latin American Economies, http://www.latin-focus.com/; (d) For global warming and clean tech, we recommend Ron Pernick and Clint Wilde, *The Clean Tech Revolution* (New York: HarperCollins Publishers, 2007); and (e) For microfinancing, see Muhammad Yanus, *Banker for the Poor: Micro-lending and the Battle Against World Poverty* (New York: Perseus Books, 2003).

10. The first trend is drawn from Kotler, *Marketing Management* (Upper Saddle River, NJ: Prentice Hall, 2003), p. 161; the second trend is from http://www.healthpolitics.org/program_transcript5qs.asp?p=childhood_obesity; and the third trend is from http://www.rainforest-alliance.org/news.cfm?id=yuban.

11. Deborah Solomon and Cassell Bryan-Low, "Companies Complain About Cost of Corporate-Governance Rules," *Wall Street Journal,* February 10, 2004.

12. Kotler, *Marketing Management*, p. 156.

13. Anand Giridharadas, "Rumbling Across India Toward a New Life in the City," *The New York Times*, November 25, 2007, pp. 1, 3; Jenalia Moreno, "China's Urbanization Creates Challenges," *Houston Chronicle*, April 21, 2007, p. 3.

14. http://www.theodora.com/wfb2003/rankings/gdp_real_growth_rate_1.html; http://www.immigration-usa.com/wfb2004/rankings/economy/gdp_real_growth_rate_2004_1.html; http://www.photius.com/rankings/economy/gdp_real_growth_rate_2005_1.html; http://www.photius.com/rankings/economy/gdp_real_growth_rate_2006_1.html; and http://www.photius.com/rankings/economy/gdp_real_growth_rate_2007_1.html.

15. Michael E. Porter, Jennifer Blanke, Thierry Geiger, Xavier Sala-i-Martin, and Irene Mia, *The Global Competitiveness Report 2007–2008: 2007 World Economic Forum* (New York: Palgrave-Macmillan, 2007).

16. See National Internet Development Agency of Korea. Internet Statistics Information System March 2007, http://isis.nida.or.kr.index_unssl.jsp; and Edelman-Korea, *PR Study of Korean Bloggers* (2007). Seoul, Korea. Both studies are discussed extensively in Sang-Myung Lee and Gerardo R. Ungson, "Towards a Theory of Synchronous Technological Assimilation: The Case of Korea's Internet Economy." *Journal of World Business* (forthcoming).

17. These trends are synthesized from the following sources: Kotler, *Marketing Management*, pp. 151–54; "World Population at a Glance: 1996 and Beyond." U.S. Department of Commerce, Economics and Statistics, Bureau of Census, September 1996; and "http://medicine.jrank.org/pages/1376/Population-Aging-World-s-oldest-youngest-populations.html">Population Aging—World's Oldest And Youngest Populations.

18. Synthesized from the following: Fred Vogelstein, "10 Tech Trends to Bet On," *Fortune*, February 23, 2004, pp. 74–91; James Canton, *The Extreme Future: The Top Trends That Will Reshape the World for the Next 5, 10, and 20 Years* (New York: Penguin Group Inc., 2006); and "The Transformational Potential of Mesh Networks," Trends eMagazine, July 2007, pp. 22–26.

19. Adopted from Robert Grant, *Contemporary Strategy Analysis* (Malden, MA: Blackwell, 2002), pp. 66–67.

20. Michael E. Porter, "How Competitive Factors Shape Strategy," *Harvard Business Review* (March 1, 1979), reprint no. 79208. In addition to Porter, the section draws largely from Grant, *Contemporary Stategy Analysis*, pp. 59–70, and from Paul Dobson, Kenneth Starkey, and John Richards, *Stategic Management* (Malden, MA: Blackwell Publishing, 2004), quotes from pp. 27–29, including the Porter quotation on p. 67.

21. Suggested by Gene Johnson, MDRG Training, 1999.

22. These examples are updated from Grant, *Contemporary Strategy Analysis*, p. 78.

23. Grant, *Contemporary Strategy Analysis* (Malden, MA: Blackwell, 1995), p. 67.

24. Ibid., p. 62.

25. "2007 Franchise 500 Ranking." *Entrepreneur*, http://www.entrepreneur.com/franchise/franchise 500/.

26. Grant (note 23), pp. 63–64; original source from Buzzell and Farris, "Marketing . . ." 1977: 128.

27. "Brand loyalty is rarely blind loyalty," *Wall Street Journal* (October 19, 1989), B1, quoted by Grant, *Contemporary Strategy Analysis*, p. 63.

28. Grant, pp. 60–61.

29. Ibid. p. 70.

30. See Pankaj Ghemawat, *Strategy and the Business Landscape* (Upper Saddle River, NJ: Prentice Hall, 2001).

31. Adam Bradenburger and Barry Nalebuff, *Co-opetition* (New York: Currency Doubleday, 1996), p. 17.

32. Ibid, pp. 14–15.

33. George Yip, *Global Strategy II* (Upper Saddle River, NJ: Prentice Hall, 2003).

34. Ibid, pp. 32–33.

35. Theodore Levitt, "The Globalization of Markets," *Harvard Business Review* (May/June 1983): 92–102.

36. The case of IKEA is discussed fully in chapter 8 (Sourcing).

37. Ted C. Fishman, *China Inc: How the Rise of the Next Superpower Challenges America and the World* (New York: Scribner, 2006).

38. Christopher Bartlett and Ashish Nanda, "Ingvar Kaprad and IKEA," *Harvard Business School Case* (May 1990), product no. 390132.

39. Christopher Bartlett, "Procter & Gamble: The Vizir Launch," *Harvard Business School Case* (November 1983), product no. 384139.

40. Bruce Einhorn, Moon Ihlwan, William C. Symonds, and Andrew Park, "Your Next TV," *Business Week,* April 4, 2005, p. 32.

41. Louis Telle, "The Learning Curve: Historical Review and Comprehensive Survey," *Decision Sciences* 10 (1979): 302–328.

42. David Yoffie and Alvint Wint, "Global Semiconductor Case—1987," *Harvard Business School Case* (November 1987), product no. 388052.

43. Pankaj Ghemawat, Steven Bradley, and Ken Mark, "Wal-Mart Stores in 2003," *Harvard Business School Case* (September 2003), product no. 704430.

44. Nancy Koehn, "Howard Schultz and Starbucks Coffee Company," *Harvard Business School Case* (February 2001), product no. 801361.

45. "China and India: A Special Report," *Business Week,* August 22–29, 2005, pp. 49–134.

46. Stephen Haag, Maeve Cummings, and Amy Phillips, *Management Information Systems for the Information Age* (New York: McGraw-Hill, 2005).

47. George Lodge, "SEMATECH," *Harvard Business School Case* (March 1989), product no. 889514.

48. Gerardo R. Ungson, Richard Steers, and Seung Ho Park, *The New Korean Enterprise* (Boston: Harvard Business School Press, 1999).

49. Charles W. Hill, *International Business: Competing in the Global Marketplace* (New York: McGraw-Hill, 2001).

50. See "Down the Forest, Something Stirs," *Economist,* January 6, 2005.

51. Ted Fishman, *China Inc.: How the Rise of the Next Superpower Challenges America and the World* (New York: Scribners, 2005).

52. Peter Dicken, *Global Shift: Reshaping the Global Economic Map* (New York: Guilford, 2003), p. 25.

53. Christopher Bartlett and Susan Ehrlich, "Caterpillar," *Harvard Business School Case* (September 1989), product no. 390036; Christopher Bartlett and U. Srinivasa Rangan, "Komatsu Ltd." *Harvard Business School Case* (February 1985), product no. 385277.

54. This entire section is based on R. Preston McAfee, *Competitive Solutions* (Princeton, NJ: Princeton University Press, 2002), pp. 204–224; see page 204 for reasons why managers need to know about antitrust.

55. Yip, *Global Strategy II,* pp. 30–31.

56. Ibid., p. 35.

57. This case was revised from an earlier version by Gerardo R. Ungson and John D. Trudel, *Engines of Prosperity: Templates for the Information Age* (London: Imperial College Press, 1998), pp. 207–211. Used with permission.

58. T.T. Reid, *The Chip* (New York: Simon & Schuster, 1984), pp. 66–67.

59. Ibid, p. 13.

60. A more detailed history of the evolving industry structure is presented in the following sources: *The Semiconductor Industry: Trade Related Issues* (Paris: The Organization for Economic Cooperation and Development, 1985); *The Competitive Status of the U.S. Electronics Industry* (Washington, DC: National Academy Press, 1984); Daniel I. Okimoto, Takuo Sugano, and Franklin B. Weinstein, *Competitive Edge: The Semiconductor Industry in the U.S. and Japan* (Stanford, CA: Stanford University Press, 1984).

61. James G. Abegglen and George Stalk, *Kaisha: The Japanese Corporation* (New York: Basic Books; 1985); Chalmers Johnson, "The Institutional Foundations of Industrial Policy, " *California Management Review* 27 (1985): 58–69.

62. Ian Mackintosh, *Sunrise Europe: The Dynamics of Information Technology* (Oxford, UK: Basil Blackwell, 1986).

63. Thomas Howell, William Noellert, Janet MacLaughlin, and Alan Wolff, *The Microelectronics Race: The Impact of Government Policy on International Competition* (Boulder, CO: Westview Press, 1987), pp. 4–6.

64. W. Finan and A. LaMond. "Sustaining U.S. Competitiveness in Microelectronics: The Challenge to U.S. Policy," in *U.S. Competitiveness in the World Economy, Boston, Massachusetts*, ed. Bruce R. Scott and George C. Lodge (Boston: Harvard Business School Press, 1985), p. 174.

65. Ibid.

66. Regis McKenna, S. Cohen, and M. Borrus "International Competition in High Technology," *California Management Review* 2 (1985): 15–32.

67. Ibid.

68. Ibid.

3 Formulating Strategy and Developing a Business Model

Behold the turtle, he makes progress only when he sticks his neck out.
—Bruce Levin

Nothing is more terrible than activity without insight.
—Thomas Carlyle

CHAPTER OUTLINE

- Kodak and the Demise of Camera Film
- Strategy and Business Models
- Components of a Business Model
- Representing Value Propositions
- Understanding the Sources of Competitive Advantage
- Refining the Business Model: Competitive Dynamics
- Extending the Structure of the Game

LEARNING OBJECTIVES

- Learn the differences between a strategy and a business model.
- Understand the different components of a business model and how they enhance value.
- Operationalize a business model through value propositions.
- Understand different generic strategies, both traditional and contemporary.
- Learn to assess a business model using financial information.

KODAK AND THE DEMISE OF CAMERA FILM

Once the dominant player in both film and film processing, Eastman Kodak Co. will stop selling reloadable film-based consumer cameras in the United States, Canada and Europe. Viewed as a painful concession to the emergence of filmless digital photography, this decision also reflects how a previously successful strategy can act as a blinder when a firm fails to capitalize on a new technology that renders existing ones obsolete.[1]

In 1888, founder George Eastman launched the first camera that boasted great ease of use (i.e., "You press the button; we do the rest"). In 1900, Kodak introduced the Brownie camera, which cost the consumer just one dollar. It was an instant success. The company introduced the first pocket camera in the 1960s, and the even smaller 110mm film camera in the 1970s. Kodak maintained its position as industry leader for over a century, with numerous product innovations and high sales.[2] In 2001, Kodak had 75 percent of the market for all films, and processed 40 percent of all film in the United States. But the emergence of digital photography, which does not require film, sounded an ominous note for Kodak's traditional areas of dominance.

In the late 1990s, when the emergence of digital cameras and digital technologies began, Kodak decided to defend its traditional camera and film business with an innovation of its own: the Advanced Photo System (APS) that was introduced in 1996. The brainchild of five major companies in the photography industry, including Kodak, Canon Inc., and Fuji Photo Film Co., APS looked like an early winner. It was considered to be the biggest innovation since the introduction of the 35mm camera. The film-and-camera combination not only provided more benefits than traditional 35mm, but it was also less expensive than digital cameras at that time. It offered multiple shots and prints (panoramic and regular) from one exposure, the ability to change film mid-roll, lighting improvement, and an indicator for flash errors. The APS film also had a magnetic coating that ensured better quality and a foolproof cartridge for easy loading. It was seen as a bridge between traditional and digital photography, and had the potential to displace traditional 35mm film as the primary photography format.[3]

Kodak became the leader in APS with its introduction of the Advantix Preview Camera in 2000. While Advantix combined digital imaging features, it was still a traditional film-loadable camera—a feature that the company thought to be attractive to its current consumers. It allowed users to preview photos on a 1.8-inch color LCD screen and decide if they liked the photos; hence, the name "Preview." It also offered the option of ordering multiple prints through a high-end imprinting technology. Kodak seemed to have found the formula for successfully integrating popular features of digital imaging into a traditional film camera.[4]

Despite the Advantix Preview's simplicity and versatility, it was not too long before Kodak's competitors came up with their own models. Konica's Revio was a brightly-colored, small palm-sized APS camera that provided a self-portrait system. Canon's limited edition ELPH brand APS "Shades" cameras combined new bright colors and shapes appeal. Olympus introduced the I-Zoom 3000, a small, lightweight camera with "James Bond" appeal. The Olympus Camedia CS211 incorporated the instant film and print technology from Polaroid so that users could take a digital image and print the photos on the spot. The latter was a hit among "prosumers" such as real estate agents, police officers, and others who wanted these functions and features for professional reasons.[5]

Together, Minolta, Nikon, Fuji, Kodak, and Canon poured over $1 billion into promoting and perfecting the APS format. The APS also received a boost from a very popular U.S. daytime television talk show, *The Oprah Winfrey Show*, when various APS camera models were featured on the program as "high-tech breakthroughs." In 1997,

Kodak launched a benefit-driven $100 million promotional campaign to "relaunch" APS products. All together, Kodak spent over $1 billion on the APS. But despite the amount of money funneled into the APS, the system barely created a market for itself. Consumers did not find the advantages sufficient to justify the additional 15 percent in the price of the film. Even at its peak in 2000, the highest market share the APS camera ever achieved was about 20 percent of sales of all film-based cameras. It was downhill from there, with market share decreasing by over 40 percent in the following year. In 2003, Kodak sold only half of the 2.5 million units produced. Nikon and Pentax left the APS market in the United States. Minolta, Olympus and Konica all postponed the introduction of new models. Only Canon found its ELPH brand APS camera profitable, and captured the rest of the market share.[6]

As one of the biggest investors in the APS, a new technology in a sunset business, Kodak in particular had been hurt in two ways. First, Kodak had engaged in a price war with Fuji Photo Film Co. that cost it both market share and profits at the same time the company was struggling to explore digital technology. Second, although Kodak claimed to have developed the first digital camera in 1996, underestimating the potential of the digital camera made Kodak a late entrant into the market. As the company set digital technology aside, the technology continued to advance rapidly without Kodak. The enhanced functions and features of digital cameras and falling selling prices created obstacles for latecomers to the market. Aggressive contenders such as Sony had already successfully made the transition from video technology to still digital photography. Computer maker Hewlett-Packard also entered the digital photography market. Kodak found the margin in the crowded digital camera very thin.[7]

Changes in technology eventually led to changes in consumer preference. Film-less photography took over the industry in the United States. Industrywide, sales of reloadable film-based cameras fell by 15 percent in 2003. Kodak saw the need for radical transformation. After a century of domination in the camera film business in the United States, Kodak experienced falling revenue for four consecutive years, along with the plummeting of its stock price. Kodak then made a monumental announcement on January 13, 2004: the company would abandon the production of reloadable film-based consumer cameras in the United States, Europe, and Canada by the end of the year. Mark A. Schneider, a vice-president at Kodak said, "We recognize the format won't achieve some of the goals we had originally hoped for." Many observers felt that the company would have to radically refocus and reconceptualize its strategy. Shifting away from the film market appeared to go against Kodak's 120-year foundation and competency in paper, chemical, and film technology. But not to make the shift would be even more risky.[8]

Kodak's new strategy can be described as a "hybrid": its core business will be digitally related, but it will still retain key activities related to increasing the sales of its traditional 35mm film market segment in selected parts of the world. Within a digitally related core business, Kodak intends to invest in the relevant technologies of the digital camera, such as inkjet printers and papers for consumers and high-end digital printing for "prosumers." If successful, Kodak will offer the complete digital photography process, from capturing the image to producing prints.

Within the traditional 35mm film market, Kodak will continue to produce disposable single-use film cameras for the global market, but specifically for emerging markets, such as India and China. The growth rate of traditional film business in these two countries is estimated to be at 6-8 percent and 7-9 percent respectively. A promising development was that APS was well received in some overseas markets even with the emergence of digital photography. For example, in Japan, the APS cameras accounted for 40 percent of the reloadable-film based camera market. Accordingly, Kodak plans to introduce new, premium lines of 35mm and Advantix films for existing APS users. There is some question whether Kodak can succeed in implementing this hybrid strategy. For the present, however, observers hope that Kodak has learned from its past failures and that it will not underestimate the power of new technology in upstaging the competitive parameters of any industry.

STRATEGY AND BUSINESS MODELS

After an extensive appraisal of the external environment, the next logical step in formulating a business model involves understanding a firm's strategy, its internal resources, and its source of competitive advantage. Yet, as Kodak's experiences illustrate, formulating a new strategy with far-reaching consequential effects is not for the faint of heart. Kodak was the first to introduce the reloadable camera and it attained a formidable advantage in camera film, perhaps best reflected when consumers simply associated film with Kodak. In recent years, however, the company began to lose ground to filmless, digital technology, prompting its momentous decision to drop its traditional product line.

In a different case, Toyota Motor Corp., one of the world's largest automobile manufacturers, already plans to stop the production of pure gasoline engines in the future. In 2002, the company announced plans to use gasoline-electric hybrid engines in all vehicles by 2012 to increase fuel efficiency and reduce tailpipe emissions.[9] While hybrid engines are more appropriate for small-size cars, by 2004 Toyota had already enhanced its hybrid engine technology to fit into a luxury, larger vehicle—the Lexus sport utility vehicle. The jury is still out on whether Kodak's move into digital photography will usher back its historical dominance, or whether Toyota will successfully lead automobile manufacturing into a new era in the hybrid engine design. What is certain is that both firms are bound to face more formidable competition in the future.

The rationale for competitive business strategy is based on two interrelated concepts: *competition* and *uncertainty*.[10] Competition is directed at understanding industry conditions and one's competitors. Without competition, it is difficult to talk about strategy (although it still makes sense to plan). Competition is also rooted in the lack of resources for the parties involved. When critical resources are scarce, competition intensifies. Uncertainty is another reason for developing strategy, and the reason for most plans. When one cannot predict the future with certainty and confidence, strategies are needed in anticipation of opportunities and threats that might affect the company. For Kodak and Toyota, the uncertainty of their technologies and the

Figure 3.1   **Analyzing the Environment and Strategic Choice and Positioning:
Developing a Business Model**

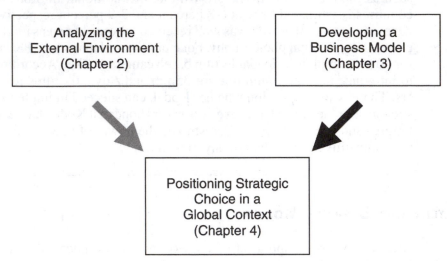

emergence of strong competitors provide the impetus for change and the rationale for a new strategy.

With the growing popularity of strategy, however, the nomenclature has become more complex. It is difficult to distinguish between "strategy" and a "business model."[11] Worse, the terms mean different things to different people. For some, strategy means the manner in which the firm makes money. For others, it is a formal representation of goals and processes oriented to securing operational funds. Others might not be even able to articulate what a business model is. Gary Hamel asserts that, "strategy" and "business model" are two different concepts. **Strategy** gives a firm the conceptual base of action—it is the essence of competing. A **business model** articulates and interprets strategy with action; it is the operational aspect of strategy. Thus, while strategy is a critical part of any business model, it does *not* comprise it. In other words, a business model can be more comprehensive in its description of how a strategy can be sustained over time. All in all, understanding strategy and business models is a key antecedent in deciding whether or not to go global (see Figure 3.1). This chapter presents a framework for linking the different facets of strategy and business models.

COMPONENTS OF A BUSINESS MODEL

Consider the current competition between Amazon.com and Barnes & Noble. Amazon, the premier online retailer, offers a boutique of services through the Internet. Capitalizing on its success in pioneering online transaction and sales for books, it disrupted the traditional "bricks-and-mortar" method of book retailing. For many observers, Amazon rendered this tradition obsolete. Barnes & Noble, a traditional book retailer, attempted to match Amazon's online services, but failed. Competition of their online activities went beyond books to include shopping services. In 1999, Amazon sued

Barnes & Noble for infringing their one-step check-out technology. Although the case was settled in 2002, the competition between firms in this industry is reflected in different business models.[12] Currently, Barnes and Noble is banking on its prime retail locations to deliver value to its customers. A visit to one of its stores will reveal a setting sprinkled with comfy sofas, overstuffed chairs, built-in coffee bars, and cozy tables with paramour lighting. Barnes & Noble hopes to match Amazon.com with a new experience for its customers. In recent years, the built-in café model has also been adopted by another bookstore, Borders. And Fry's, primarily an electronic equipment and home appliance store, now offers a book and magazine section.

All in all, "models" are mental representations of the physical world. A business model is no different, except that it emphasizes elements within a firm that create wealth or value. It also suggests how any one firm is different from another. Management consultant and professor Gary Hamel offers four components of any business model: *strategy*, *resources*, *consumer interfaces*, and *value partnerships*.[13]

STRATEGY: THE ESSENCE OF COMPETING

Strategy is a commonly used word. *Webster's New Dictionary* defines it as "the science of planning and directing large-scale operations, specifically of maneuvering forces into the most advantageous position prior to actual engagement."[14] The term originates in the military, specifically from the Greek *strategos,* meaning "general." As wars became costlier and more complex, it became obvious that victory depended on factors other than size, bravery, and prowess. Sir Liddell Hart, an English military historian, states that "the true aim of strategy is not to battle but to achieve such an advantageous position that, if it does not of itself bring the enemy to surrender, would produce a sure victory in the battlefield."[15] Hart condenses military strategy to a single word: *concentration* ("concentration of strength against weaknesses"). Certainly, wartime military strategies have provided useful insights about positioning and concentration. Even so, while military strategy has direct implications on business strategy, there are a few important differences:[16]

- Competition among businesses does not necessarily mean the destruction of the enemy. In fact, competition can improve efficiency and effectiveness.
- Segmentation and positioning in business strategy facilitate the use of an indirect approach, as it is possible to find and target a specific segment of the market. Both also make defense difficult. While the use of the indirect approach has been employed in military battles, its use in business strategy opens up possibilities for cooperation and co-existence, as opposed to simply obliterating the enemy.[17]

While many scholars generally acknowledge the military origin of strategy, others argue that current concepts of strategy are based on a strong Western perspective, particularly assumptions about the purposes and consequences of strategy. For a taste of this debate, see Box 3.1. When speaking of "strategy," the tendency is to couch it in terms of top-management decisions. After all, Kodak executives were responsible for making choices about the company's product lines. Even so, we maintain that

Box 3.1

Metaschools of Strategy

Henry Mintzberg, McGill University's strategy professor and a noted expert in this field, contends that "Human nature insists on a definition for every concept. The field of strategic management cannot afford to rely on a single definition." In a provocative book, *What Is Strategy and Does It Matter?* Oxford University professor Richard Whittington draws on various definitions, suggesting that strategy can be distinguished by "process" (deliberate versus emergent) and "outcomes" (unitary "profit maximization" vs. pluralistic goals, such as growth, employee satisfaction, or social welfare). Accordingly, Whittington defines four schools of strategy: rational/classical, evolutionary, processual, and institutional.

Rational/Classical School of Strategy

The rational/classical school, represented by the work of Harvard strategy guru Michael Porter and his associates, is characterized by deliberate planning and a belief in the primacy of markets as clearing mechanisms that lead to efficient transactions. This school views managers as deliberately rational, if not purposeful, decision makers. Firms are seen as acting to maximize profits, and it is assumed that relatively efficient markets emerge over time in a free market economy. Rational analysis and objective decisions make a key difference in determining the long-term success or failure of the firm. Organizations are seen as monolithic entities, led by able executive visionaries. Formulating strategic choices is the critical task. Strategic implementation is conceived as co-aligning strategic opportunities and requirements with appropriate structures, processes, and corporate cultures. For many, this represents mainstream thinking and it continues to influence the development of thought and practice to the present time.

The Evolutionary School of Strategy

The evolutionary school, represented in the works of population ecologists Glenn Carroll, Michael Hannah, and John Freeman, is characterized by an uncontested belief in the superior power of market forces. Because the external environment is seen as too unpredictable, too implacable to predict, its dynamism cannot be anticipated, much less accounted for in full. Accordingly, the assessment of the external environment, as recommended by the rational/classical school of strategy, is not only unworkable, but also irrelevant. Competitive pressures weed out marginal, unprofitable firms, much in the tradition of Herbert Spencer and Charles Darwin's "survival of the fittest." Successful strategies evolve only after natural selection. Thus, managers need to be aware of their costs and efficient in their activities. Moreover, they should develop lean organizational structures over time. Efficiency is the favored strategy when they cannot control events in their environments. Managers need to be less concerned about the consequences of their own actions: in the long run, it is the market that dictates the types of firms that survive.

The Processual School of Strategy

The processual school of strategy, represented by Dartmouth professor James Brian Quinn and McGill professor Henry Mintzberg, regards formal planning as important, but only as one of many analytical and political events that combine to determine overall strategy. They agree with the evolutionary school that strategies rarely result as originally conceived or intended. Plans may go unrealized, while patterns may appear without preconceptions. The process used to arrive at a total strategy is usually fragmented, evolutionary, and largely intuitive. However, unlike the evolutionary school, the processual school sees a proactive role for managers. Top managers rarely design their overall strategy in a formal planning cycle, but instead use a series of incremental processes, such as pieces of formal strategic analysis, that contribute to the final strategy. The eventual strategy evolves as internal decisions and external events come together

(continued)

Box 3.1 *(continued)*

in the minds of managers. The success of incrementalism depends on top management's ability to create the awareness, broaden the understanding, legitimize the acceptance, and secure the commitment needed to implement strategies effectively.

The Systemic School of Strategy

For systemic thinkers, strategy matters, but not in the sense that the rational/classicist theorists think. Strategies depend on the particular social settings in which they are embedded, that is, the extent to which actions can be interpreted. Strategists deviate from rational thinking, not because they are stupid or even disagree with rational thinking, but because, in their cultures, the rules underlying rational thinking make little sense. Specifically, firms are not all profit maximizers as depicted in rational/classic and evolutionary schools. While the systemic school acknowledges managers to be limited by cognitive processing and political compromise, these managers are not confined to developing processes alone in their quest for strategy. For the systemic school, norms derive not so much from cognitive bounds but from the cultural rules of society. It is not at all surprising to systemic thinkers that the Japanese, for example, devote little attention to strategy. It is more likely for the Japanese to attribute strategy as a product of relational activities between politicians, government bureaucracies (such as the Ministry of Trade and Industry), and business firms. The keiretsu-like groupings, so unlike those in the Western world, provide incentives (i.e., bank financing, interfirm sharing of directors and funds, contractor–subcontractor relations) that compel Japanese to act in certain ways that Western-ers find difficult to understand (why invest resources during recessionary periods?), or controversial (why sacrifice profitability for market share?).

Source: Adapted from Richard Whittington, *What Is Strategy and Does It Matter?* (London: Routledge, 1993), pp. 10–41; Henry Mintzberg, "The Strategy Concept I: Five Ps for Strategy," *California Management Review* (Fall 1987), vol. 30, no. 1, pp. 11–24; James B. Quinn, *Strategies for Change* (Homewood, IL: Richard D. Irwin, Inc., 1980).

"strategy" is an element grounded in everyday experiences. For example, strategy is popular in sports competition (i.e., how do managers defeat an opposing team, or compensate for a weak left-handed tennis return?). Readers are familiar with the concept of having a job-hunting "strategy." Others simply understand strategy as actions to be undertaken in the future.

In these everyday contexts, "strategy" is interchangeable with a *plan of action* that is oriented toward the realization of some goal.[18] While goals might not always be explicit, and at times are even elusive, thoughts and actions are purposeful, that is, they are deliberate and goal-oriented. An individual might not have a specific firm in mind as the first choice when looking for a job, but might be attracted to the firm that provides the quickest trajectory for career advancement. Yet formalizing goals into actionable plans is essential for evaluating progress and validating one's actions. George Schaefer, ex-CEO of Caterpillar, said: "An explicit strategy is absolutely necessary. Implicit is not good enough in the competitive environment in which we operate."[19] This is why firms go through a formal strategic planning process that culminates in a formal and written business plan.

A related way of thinking about "strategy" is that it is a *process* for achieving a goal, that is, a set of activities or routines that leads managers from the current state to a desired state. When the great hockey player Wayne Gretzky once was asked why he was so good, he simply replied: "It's because I skate to where the puck is going, not where it has been."[20] As a strategist, Gretsky anticipates and visualizes the desired state and enacts the necessary maneuvers to get there; he simply is not content to skating to where the puck is. Thinking of strategy as a process also means examining patterns of decisions over time. Anheuser-Busch Companies, Inc., the market leader in the beer industry, staked its position in terms of a continuous stream of production that emphasized the "purity" of ingredients that were attractive to traditional segments of the beer-drinking population. Miller Brewing Company, its major competitor, pursued a different path in introducing new products, new sizes, and low-calorie beer (Miller Lite), which catered to a different and younger market segment.

A popular representation of "strategy" is that of a *position* relative to a comparison group. Marketing people define positioning as the firm's image in the minds of its consumers.[21] To this end, marketers have spent significant amounts on advertising to position firms in the minds of primary consumers.[22] Nike might not want to be known as a manufacturer of athletic shoes but as "the world's premier sports company." Starbucks will probably eschew the label "high-quality coffee café," preferring to be known as the "provider of the ultimate coffee experience." Tata Motors Ltd., one of India's foremost automobile companies, has positioned its first indigenously designed car—the $6,600 Indica—as the prelude to a targeted $2,200 car in the future. For Chairman Ratan Tata, this represents "a way to change the rules of the game . . . to change the way business is done."[23] Yet positioning is hardly an exact science. Mercedes-Benz flanked Cadillac by selling more expensive cars, but it continues to undermine its own high-end position by selling cheaper versions of its luxury cars, such as its A-class and C-class vehicles.[24]

Another way of defining strategy, although much less pronounced than the first three, has to do with *perspective,* or a basic *philosophy.*[25] This captures the deep beliefs and values of the firm, perhaps originating with the owner. At the inception of Matsushita some three hundred years ago, it was decreed that the company "offer products to benefit mankind and that it would be a truly global organization."[26] Such a statement was made even before globalization had entered the popular language. Strategies as perspectives are also reflected in various decisional rules such as that of former General Electric chairman Jack Welch, who mandated that, unless a product category was number 1 or number 2 in its segment, it would be discarded.[27]

Taken collectively, these different perspectives suggest that *strategy is a series of interlocking decisions oriented at achieving a sustainable competitive advantage.* This definition has a number of implications. First, strategy is an individual *choice,* or results from decisions among individuals. Wal-Mart's strategy represents the vision and actions taken by Wal-Mart's founder, Sam Walton, that have been continually reaffirmed by generations of Wal-Mart managers. Thus, strategy is not preordained by the environment or by some powerful force. Second, decisions are *interlocked* or *intertwined.* There is a degree of purposefulness that underlies patterns in a stream of decisions. In the case of Wal-Mart, this pattern relates to "everyday low prices" offered to customers. Third, strategies are *relative* to one's competitive position. That is, a strategy can be defensive if one's position is attacked by competitors, and it can also be offensive when it takes a proactive approach in anticipation of competitors' actions. In either case, strategy is formulated relative to a competitor. Finally, the goal of strategy is to create a *sustainable gap* from a firm's competitors. Typically this involves a significant investment of resources. In Wal-Mart's case, sustainable competitive advantages arise from attracting new customers and retaining current ones, reducing operational costs, enhancing product and service quality, exploring and maintaining business networks, innovating and experimenting with new technologies, reconceptualizing business practices, and developing management know-how.

The key to a successful strategy is for the firm to do what it takes to successfully differentiate itself from its competitors. In fundamental ways, strategies define what a firm is all about. Strategies provide consistency and cohesion to a firm's actions and behaviors.[28] Strategies also define what makes a particular firm different or unique from others. In short, strategies tell managers where they should go and how to get there. One mistake, however, is to confuse strategy with a mission statement, or an overarching set of goals and values. This can be exacerbated when firms assume that they already have a strategy simply by having a mission statement. Unfortunately, mission statements, while important in formalizing a firm's purposes and visions of the future, have two weaknesses. First, some are so broad, universal, pompous, and pretentious that it is difficult to discern how the firm is really different from others. As an aside, how many times have managers encountered an establishment purporting to provide the *best* product in the *world*? Second, some mission statements read more like tactical objectives, which are narrow and simplistic (e.g., our mission is to obtain a 12 percent return on investment). At a minimum, the mission statement should state the firm's strategy and philosophy in terms that leave little question as to how it is different and unique from others.[29]

Another indication of firm strategies is gleaned from the ever-rising popularity of "bumper mission statements." Every business should be able to summarize its direction, purpose, and strategy, preferably in a few words (also called the "bumper sticker") that capture how the company wants to position itself in the minds of its customers. In some cases, the ability to define the mission in terms of a bumper sticker enables the company to define the "driving force" that characterizes a particular company.[30] Exhibit 3.1 provides some examples.

REPRESENTING VALUE PROPOSITIONS

Strategy can also be represented as a firm's **value proposition**. In essence, this is an explicit statement of a company's value and advantage relative to its core competitors.[31] While there are different ways of doing this, our preferred format is presented in Exhibit 3.2, as formulated by Roger Best, marketing professor at the University of Oregon. As a diagnostic tool, viewing value propositions in this light can reveal the distinctive strengths and weaknesses of each firm. In this example, value propositions are formulated for three hypothetical competitors. The first step is to define customer satisfaction requirements, that is, what core dimensions do consumers look for when deciding on a product. In this example, these include high quality, up time, service, responsiveness, pricing, and ease of use. The second step is to evaluate the relative importance of each requirement. Each is ranked on a scale from 1 (poor) to 10

Exhibit 3.1

Representative Bumper Stickers

Company	Bumper Sticker Strategy
Dow	Living. Improved daily.
Verizon	We never stop working for you.
McGraw-Hill Construction	Recover. Rebuild. Rebound.
FedEx	Relax, it's FedEx.
Panasonic	Ideas for life.
Fujitsu	The possibilities are infinite.
Honda	The power of dreams.
Samsonite	Life's a journey.
Toshiba	Don't copy. Lead.
Accenture	High performance. Delivered.
Toyota	Moving forward.
Cingular	Raising the bar.
Prudential Financial	Growing and protecting your wealth.
Microsoft	Your potential. Our passion.
T. Rowe Price	Invest with confidence.
Oracle	The best companies run Oracle.
Principal Financial Group	We'll give you an edge.
Hitachi	Inspire the next.
HP	Solutions for the adaptive enterprise.
BMW	The ultimate driving machine.
The Smile Train	Changing the world one smile at a time.
American Red Cross	Together, we can save a life.
Samsung	Samsung. Inside and out.
Canon	Image Anyware.
Hendrick's	A most unusual gin.
Hyundai	Drive your way.
Ebel	The architects of time.
Breitling	Instruments for professionals.
Pitney Bowes	Engineering the flow of communication.
Ford	Innovation is our mission.
Mercedes-Benz	Unlike any other.
Kyocera	The new value frontier.
Coca-Cola	Make every drop count.
Lufthansa	There is no better way to fly.
Emcor	Build it. Power it. Service it.
AT&T	Your world. Delivered.
UBS	You and Us.
Princess Cruises	Escape completely.
Royal Caribbean	Get out there.
Avis	We try harder.
Epson	Exceed your vision.
Nokia	Connecting people.
Bose	Better sound through research.
Chrysler	Inspiration comes standard.
Best Buy	Thousands of possibilities. Get yours.
Volkswagen	Drivers wanted.
Caesar's Palace	Live famously.
Mitsubishi Motors	Driven to thrill.
Timberland	Make it better.
Aramis	The impact never fades.
Citigroup	Live richly.
Movado	The art of time.
Levi's	The original.

Source: Obtained from company websites.

Exhibit 3.2

Defining a Value Proposition

Customer Satisfaction Requirements	Importance of Requirement[a]	Competitors' Performance[b]		
		Competitor A	Competitor B	Competitor C
Functional quality/effectiveness	9	8	5	7
Ease of use	9	6	9	6
Technical support	8	8	4	7
Affordability	8	6	10	7
After-sales service	8	6	7	6
Regulatory support	8	5	8	4
Research database availability	7	9	7	8
Consumer referrals and feedback	7	7	9	5
Consumer Satisfaction Index (CSI)[c]		**68**	**73**	**62.5**

CSI (Competitor A) = 68
CSI (Competitor B) = 73
CSI (Competitor C) = 62.5

Notes:

[a] Importance of Requirements rated from 1 (very unimportant) to 10 (very important). Typically this is obtained from interviewing a targeted consumer group or an expert panel.

[b] Competitor Performance rated from 0 (disastrous) to 10 (outstanding). Typically this is obtained from interviewing a targeted consumer group or an expert panel.

[c] To compute this, first multiply the importance rating with the competitor rating for each customer satisfaction requirements. For example in the case of Competitor A, this would be functional quality/effectiveness (9 x 8 = 72), ease of use (9 x 6 = 54), technical support (8 x 8 = 64), affordability (8 x 6 = 48), after-sales service (8 x 6 = 48), regulatory support (8 x 5 = 40), research database availability (7 x 9 = 63), consumer referrals and feedback (7 x 7 = 49). The sum equals 438. Second, compute the "perfect" score, that is, if every factor is assigned a rating of 10, i.e., (9 x 10) + (9 x 10) + (8 x 10) + (8 x 10) + (8 x 10) + (8 x 10) + (7 x 10) + (7 x 10), which sum will equal 640 (also, by simply multiplying 64 by 10). Thus, 640 = maximum score; a performance rating of 10 on each factor. The maximum score will vary with the number of factors and the importance assigned to each performance factor. The CSI is obtained by dividing (438/640) x 100 = 68.

Source: Adapted from Roger J. Best, *Market-Based Management* (Upper Saddle River, NJ: Prentice Hall, 1977), p. 12. Customer satisfaction requirements and numbers have been changed from the original.

(excellent). The third step is to have consumers—both current and prospective—rank three companies. These calculations lead to a consumer satisfaction index (CSI), or the weighted sum of customer requirements and customer ratings of these requirements. The CSI scores for competitor A (68), competitor B (73), and competitor C (62.5) are determined accordingly.

The use of this analysis provides clues and guidelines on how each company can improve its value proposition. For example, competitor A should consider a strategy that focuses on improving its service staff, being more responsive to customer problems, and delivering more value that is consistent with its pricing and terms. Competitor B appears to suffer from consumer perceptions of lower quality and service, and should improve on these areas. For competitor C, quality of service and problem responsiveness should be improved. Thus, in addition to identifying points of distinction, this method suggests areas where managerial attention is needed.

Box 3.2

The Resource-based Theory of the Firm

In contrast to market-based positioning, which takes the environment as a starting point, the resource-based theory of the firm maintains that a firm's resources and capabilities provide the principal basis for its strategy and the primary source of its competitive advantage. In highly volatile environments, external adaptation might not necessarily provide stability and constancy for a firm's strategy because it already has a bundle of resources and competencies with which to define its business and identity.

    Refinements to this resource-based approach were introduced as part of an integrated theory. By emphasizing the uniqueness of each company, core competency became the basis for competitive advantage. That is, a firm can distinguish itself from others in terms of its under-lying different or relatively unique set of resources and competencies. C.K. Prahalad, strategy professor at the University of Michigan, and Gary Hamel, strategy professor at the London Business School and founder of the consulting firm *Strategos,* define core competencies as "the collective learning in the organization, especially how to co-ordinate diverse production skills and integrate multiple streams of technology." Ohio State management professor Jay Barney goes a further step in relating resource-based approaches to sustainable competitive advantage, suggesting that core resources and activities should be rare, durable, and difficult to imitate. Resources and capabilities are imitable if they are transferable and/or replicable. The more rare, durable, and difficult to imitate a resource is, the stronger the firm's competitive advantage will be and the longer it can last.

    Sources: J.B. Barney, "Firm Resources and Sustained Competitive Advantage," *Journal of Management* 17 (1991): 99–120; J. Mahoney and J.R. Pandian, "The Resource-based View Within the Conversation of Strategic Management," *Strategic Management Journal* 13 (1992): 363–380; M.A. Peterlaf, "The Cornerstones of Competitive Advantage: A Resource-based View," *Strategic Management Journal* 14 (1993): 179–192; C.K. Prahalad and Gary Hamel, "The Core Competencies of the Corporation," *Harvard Business Review* (May–June 1990): 79–91; David Collins and Cynthia Montgomery, "Competing on Resources: Strategy in the 1990s," *Harvard Business Review* (July–August 1995): 119–28. Robert M. Grant, *Contemporary Strategy Analysis*, 2002, p. 133.

CORE AND DISTINCTIVE COMPETENCIES: WHAT A COMPANY OWNS

A key element in a strategy is the development of competencies within an organization. **Competencies** are capabilities that a company possesses, and they are central to the resource-based theory of the firm (see Box 3.2). They can be assessed using an internal environment analysis. From an internal environment analysis, strengths and weaknesses of the company are identified. The strengths that a company possesses can be further developed into **capabilities**, things that the company is particularly good at relative to its other strengths and capabilities. For example, these capabilities can be the company's mastery of logistics or the special touch it offers in after-sales services. At this point, these capabilities are still being compared with other capabilities within the company. The strongest ones that emerge out of a pool of capabilities are known as "competencies of the company."

Typically, academicians have distinguished between a basic competence, a core competence, and a distinctive competence. A basic competence (or strength) is an internal activity that a company performs better than other internal activities. This can be a physical activity (project management), or something less tangible (know-how). A **core competence** is a well-performed internal activity that is central, not peripheral, to a company's strategy, competitiveness, and profitability. Great teaching can be a core competence in a university where teaching skills are central to the basic mission. A **distinctive competence** is a competitively valuable activity that a company performs better than its rivals, and it is important for three reasons: it represents something that rivals do not have; it has the potential for being a cornerstone of strategy; and it can provide a competitive edge in the marketplace.

Among its many competencies, Sony is known for miniaturizing electronic products, such as audio-tape players and/or recorders, CD players, and so forth. One such Sony product, the Walkman, was originally a miniaturized audiotape player and recorder. Recently, however, Sony's competency has been undermined by South Korea's Samsung, which has developed and advanced the process of miniaturization even further with key breakthroughs in digital cameras, home audio systems, audio components, televisions, camcorders, DVD, MP3 players, and cell phone features. While a core competence underpins a firm's strategy, it is *not* necessarily a distinctive competence and it can be vulnerable to competitive pressures.

In the area of entertainment, Walt Disney is known for making animated and imaginative movies and creating theme parks (see the "Case-In-Point" at the of this chapter). Raised in a harsh family by his father, a stern disciplinarian with a violent temper, Walt Disney passed idle hours creating imaginary friends with pen and paper. "Fantasy," he used to say, "that is, good acceptable fantasy, is really only fact with a whimsical twist." Not surprisingly, the Walt Disney Company's distinctive competencies are creating for children, teenagers, and adults the illusion and imagination of a forever happy, perfect, and unreal world. Once a firm has identified its core and distinctive competencies, it can take advantage of them and build its business around them. These competencies become the basis of the firm's policy regarding product development and business approach.

In the area of telecommunications, traditional standards were nationally configured, such that a cellular customer in Finland could not use the phone in most parts of the world. However, the adoption of new standards, specifically the Global System for Mobile Communication (GSM) pioneered by European telephone carriers, altered traditional usage, permitting customers to use their phones wherever they traveled. Ericsson and Nokia capitalized on this new standard, creating core competencies that have since led the world in this development, although competitors are emerging. Other examples of distinctive competences are provided in Exhibit 3.3.

A popular way to assess where competencies are is to undertake a **SWOT** (strengths-weaknesses-opportunities-threats) analysis. The "strengths" part of the internal environment analysis is where organizational competencies can be identified. While other formulations exist (i.e., TOWS threats-opportunities-weaknesses-strengths), the essential logic of SWOT is to expound on all four dimensions with the end-in-view of matching analyzing strengths and weaknesses against external opportunities and threats. In this way, core and distinctive strengths in an organization are revealed. A representative example of a SWOT analysis is depicted in Exhibit 3.4.

Exhibit 3.3

Examples of Distinctive Competences

Companies	Distinctive Competencies
Sharp Corporation	Expertise in flat-panel display technology
Toyota, Honda, Nissan	Low-cost, high-quality manufacturing capability and short design-to-market cycles
Intel	Ability to design and manufacture ever more powerful microprocessors for PCs
Motorola	Defect-free manufacture (six-sigma quality) of cell phones
Google, Yahoo	Deep expertise in search engines
Nokia, Ericsson	Expertise in GSP (global satellite positioning) applications, e.g., GSM

Exhibit 3.4

A SWOT Example

Strengths	Weaknesses	Opportunities	Threats
Advanced technology	Lack key skills/ competencies	Alliances or joint ventures to extend customer coverage	Demographic changes that disagree with the current strategies
Creative advertising	Excess debt, cash shortage	Acquiring rivals	Changes in buyer needs for product
Alliances or joint ventures	Problematic internal operation	Good timing to exploit new technologies	Stagnant market growth rate
Product innovation speed	Inferior marketing skills	Transferring competences to new products	Falling sales due to substitutes
Strong strategy	Lack strategic direction	Enlarging customer coverage	Growing leverage of customers or suppliers
Above average cost advantages	Obsolete R&D	Good timing to extend brand name/image	Vulnerability to business cycle
Advanced product quality	Outmoded facilities	Promoting to new geographic areas	Higher operating cost due to new regulations
Market leader	Below average profits	Taking over market shares from rivals	Unfavorable trade policies
Superior customer service	Decrease in product line	Vertical integration	New competitors entering the market
Abundant financial resources	Above average costs of production	Increasing product line	
Widely recognized brand name image/ reputation			

CUSTOMER INTERFACES: VALUE ADDED BY CUSTOMERS

Customer interfaces refer to the active interaction and exchange between producers and customers. **Value added** refers to any additional benefit integrated into products and services during the course of production. Distinctive competencies and core competencies provide the basis for success but do not guarantee it unless the company delivers the right value through its products and services. However, the connection between providers and customers is often overlooked. In many cases, marketing research is carried out during the earlier part of product development and new market expansion. Once a new market group or location is established, the connection between the company and its customers becomes secondary to the company's operation. Companies should have a built-in interface with customers so that open communication will take place on a continuing basis.

Retaining consumers can redound to the company's competitive advantage. One can imagine the expense involved in losing customers that translates to lost revenue and diminished market share. One can also imagine the benefits of highly satisfied consumers who are able, by word of mouth and endorsements, to function as ambassadors of the company to which they are loyal. Much to the chagrin of afflicted companies, dissatisfied customers do not often complain, but they talk and spread the bad news. Well-documented studies indicate that out of 100 dissatisfied customers, only 4 will complain.[32] Of the 96 dissatisfied customers who do not complain, 91 will exit the business as customers. Even worse, each dissatisfied customer will tell eight to ten other people of his or her dissatisfaction. The market impact of dissatisfied customers can be enormous. A summary of studies of consumer retention provides remarkable testimony to these observations.

- Sixty-five percent of the average company's business comes from its present, satisfied customers.[33]
- Anecdotal and case evidence indicates that it costs 5–10 times as much to acquire a new customer as it does to retain an existing customer.[34]
- Large-sample academic studies indicate that retaining customers lowers operational costs and also reduces strategic and operational risks of the firm.[35]

Technological advances, notably those in communications, have ushered in the age of consumer-centric power. Digitalization, biotechnology, and smart materials have created opportunities for new products and services that, with shorter life cycles, portend continuous offerings for consumers. In contrast to previous eras, consumers are smarter, more discriminating, and harder to satisfy. Nevertheless, a compelling finding from market research is that product variety has not necessarily resulted in better consumer experiences.[36] In this day and age, consumers have acquired increased importance, and their role has gone from acceptance of products as they are to leading product improvement. The next section examines this shift based on the work of Professors C.K. Prahalad and Venkat Ramaswamy, both from the University of Michigan business school.[37]

Greater Information Access

As discussed in Chapter 1, the **Information Age** is the period from the 1980s onward during which information began to move at a fast rate due to technological advancement. During the inception of the Information Age, at a time when access to information was becoming widespread on account of the personal computer, the U.S. Navy restricted the flow of information. In retrospect, this might be understandable in that privileged information was believed to be only for those involved in a decision. For many of the "command-and-control" economies, such as the former Soviet Union and China, information meant state power, and public access to information could potentially liberate people and curtail this power.

This is no longer true today in most parts of the world. With unprecedented access, consumers can gather information and make informed decisions. Take the case of the health care industry. No longer are patients passive people who simply react to authoritative directions from physicians. Today, health care consumers are proactive in learning about diseases and treatments; tracking the records of doctors, hospitals, and clinics; the latest clinical drug trials; related cases and databases. Taken collectively, these practices have given rise to a $1 trillion health care industry in which consumers participate more fully in their own treatment and preventative care.[38]

Broader Global Perspective

Global perspective refers to the global view of the world. People today have far more access to greater amounts of information than at any other time in world history. With a flick of a switch, we can see what is happening in other countries. This ability to transmit information instantly has multiplied business opportunities, exposed risks, and intensified reactions to managerial decisions. According to Kenichi Ohmae, Japan's most respected management theorist and author of the book *The End of the Nation State,* information technology has had three accelerating effects on globalization that are excepted below:

- At a macroeconomic level, information technology has made it possible for capital to be shifted instantaneously anywhere in the world. As a consequence, the speed of cross-border financial transactions has been radically increased. The productivity of certain industries, such as telecommunications, has been greatly enhanced.
- At the market level, information technology has changed what customers everywhere can know about the way other people live, about the products and services available to them, and about the relative value such offerings provide.
- At the company level, information technology has changed what managers can know in real time about their markets, products, and organizational processes.[39]

Networking

Networking refers to taking advantage of the connections between people via technological instruments such as the Internet. People have a natural tendency to coalesce around common interests, needs, and experience. With advances in the Internet, specifically messaging and digital-based telephone services, virtual communities have emerged and have sustained themselves. Perhaps the most notable of these is eBay, the world's premier online marketplace. Founded in 1995 by a French-Iranian immigrant, Pierre Omidyar, this company has evolved into a sophisticated virtual marketplace that has set the standards for person-to-person online trading in nearly 18,000 categories, ranging from a broken laser pointer (eBay's first product) to a corporate jet (eBay's most expensive trade). eBay has led in the development of ratings for both buyers and sellers, payment processing ("Pay Pal"), bidding regulations and practices (Half.com, "Buy-It-Now"), and discussion forums (eBay Park). In 2006, eBay had a global presence in 37 markets, including the United States; about 233 million registered users worldwide. In the first quarter of 2007, eBay net revenues totaled $1.25 billion with 49 percent from U.S. operations and 51 percent from international business operations.[40]

Lurking in the background, however, is Alibaba.com., based in Hangzou, and the world's leader in B2B (business-to-business online trading). It is backed by Yahoo! and Cisco Systems. In 2007, Alibaba accounted for more than two-thirds of the B2B online trade activities in China. Its strategy is to source goods from around the world for a growing list of small and mid-sized businesses in China.[41] Given the size of China's market, it's no understatement that the potential for Alibaba's growth is meteoric. After the company's successful IPO offering in November 2007, its stock price more than doubled in less than a week.

For those engaged in blogging, Cyworld, introduced in 1999 by SK Telecommunications in South Korea, has created a truly shared virtual community founded on an innovative social networking system (SNS). This new system departs from the traditional view of blogging as a personalized, fragmented, and extremely focused activity. Cyworld boasts one-third of total Internet users in South Korea as members (estimated as 34 million in 2006) and a blog site with more than 11,000,000 homepages in 2007. Visitors log in more than 700 page views on average monthly, including 80 percent of university students who have a personal homepage on it. What makes Cyworld different is that it brings together individuals with shared and common interests in a grand scale. The name Cyworld is a combination of "Cyber" and "World" and is interpreted as "cyber world for good relationship" in Korean. Cyworld can be compared to "MySpace" or "Facebook" in the United States. Because Koreans rank among the world's top bloggers, it's likely that SNS will become more pervasive as blogging is adopted by a wider constituency.[42]

Experimentation and Activism

More than anything else, consumers are now oriented at fashioning their own experiences through constant *experimentation*. While Napster has been accused of engaging in piracy by which the intellectual property rights of artists were violated, a different interpretation suggests that consumers demand more say on how their music should be packaged and delivered to them. In contrast to the company-centric attitude of giving consumers "packaged" music, regardless of whether consumers like some songs or not, the Napster case highlights the emerging trend imperative that consumers want personalized packages to suit their tastes.

Activism is also reflected in greater demands by consumers and action groups for better corporate governance and social responsibility. Take the case of CalPers, which

Exhibit 3.5

An Example of a Customer Action Plan for a Hypothetical Firm

Critical Initiatives	Action Items
Know and anticipate customer	• Refine and update segmentation models and rules of engagement
	• Conduct research, analyze results, and respond
	• Develop research profiles that depict changing customer expectations and future market trends
	• Increase consumer responsiveness through direct and indirect interface with customers and sales channels to obtain first-hand input
Know and anticipate competitive actions	• Conduct competitor research, analyze results, and develop competitive responses
	• Conduct research on previous competitor actions
	• Develop scenarios about competitors' actions
	• Create contingency plans to address anticipated competitive threats
Build the proper products and services for customers	• Plan and develop new products and services in a timely and quality manner
	• Develop and offer pricing opportunities that create awareness
	• Examine existing products to determine how possible extensions can improve the firm's value proposition
	• Explore new features and technologies to better meet customer demand and generate new revenue streams

Source: Adapted from MDRG Training, 1999–2002.

in 1991 embarked on a new strategy of targeting specific companies as a way of influencing its portfolio. American Express agreed to establish an independent compensation committee; Salomon Brothers adopted a formal policy requiring that a majority of its directors come from outside the company; and ITT adjusted its pay scheme. The role of the board of directors, whose activities had been shrouded in secrecy, increasingly shifted to responsibility for the oversight of their companies. Recently, CalPers has taken this strategy to target its constituent holdings in Japan.[43]

Rising Expectations

Consumers are not only discriminating, they also have higher expectations. They are less loyal to companies whose service is mediocre. At Southwestern Bell Corporation, now the new AT&T, the consideration of churn rates (customer turnover) has prompted managers to monitor the problem and to determine how to retain consumers. As indicated earlier, a well-known statistic is that it costs corporations five times more to recruit new customers than it does to keep loyal ones within their fold.[44]

The generational gap is reflected in a story of the late Malaysian tycoon Tai Chik Sen, whose family controls the big Soon Seng Group, and who maintained a humble lifestyle even after accumulating tremendous wealth. When local reporters asked about his modest lifestyle in contrast to his sons, who were driving around Kuala Lumpur in flashy BMWs, he said: "My sons have a rich father. I don't."

One method of assessing value creation by customers is through a Customer Initiatives Action Plan, as illustrated in Exhibit 3.5. Born out of numerous studies on customer satisfaction, this plan segments the firm's different market segments, with able contingency options on how to deal with each segment to ensure that the companies to retain them.

Value Partnership: Appropriating the Returns from Successful Partners

Traditional concepts of the buyer–supplier relationships force the parties into adversarial roles, necessitating constant vigilance and control of their mutual actions and activities. While occasionally necessary, this has led to enormous coordination problems, frustration, and opportunity costs. In response, some companies have looked for alternatives. The "Big Three" in the U.S. automobile industry, for example, pioneered a practice called "tapered integration." As an example, Ford would produce internally some of its most critical components as leverage in cases when suppliers might opportunistically raise prices, or should quality decline.[45] Yet there are a number of ways in which partners can play key roles in enhancing a firm's business model. **Value partnership** is the incorporation of buyer–supplier relationship into the value creation process.

Facilitating Integration

Firms that are able to work efficiently with their partners—suppliers and buyers—can reap advantages that can, in turn, strengthen their business models. One classic example is Cisco. It has been observed that more than 50 percent of Cisco's products are never even touched by a Cisco factory or employee. Very recently, some reports have that number up to 100 percent.[46] They are just magically assembled and shipped by Cisco's able suppliers. Customers are not even aware that Cisco never touched the products. Like Cisco, Nokia is using its supplier networks to dramatically reduce working capital and increase flexibility.[47]

Another example of excellent buyer–supplier relations is Dell Computers. Dell's strategy is to provide consumers with computers that are almost tailor-made. This is inspired by the fact that most computers available in stores are made in cookie-cutter fashion and cannot completely satisfy the ever-changing needs and preferences of consumers. After all, computers are fairly big-ticket items, and consumers like them to be as close to their specifications as possible.

Conventional thinking suggests that tailor-made merchandise should be more expensive than standardized or prefabricated merchandise, but Dell's business model broke this rule. Although Dell's business model on the outside reflects the image of "build-to-order," the essence of its model is the ability to source, assemble, and distribute at low cost. Dell builds the computers when orders are placed so there is no waste of time in making merchandise that will have to be kept as inventory. That Dell is able to deliver on its mission to provide a superior customer experience through direct and comprehensive customer service is no accident. In order to achieve this at relatively low costs, it is essential for Dell to work almost seamlessly with its suppliers and buyers.

Take Dell's relationship with Sony, one of its prime suppliers. Dell essentially avoided carrying any inventory of monitors by committing to buy a fixed number of monitors every month, but picking as many as needed every day. Thus, Airborne Express or United Parcel Service comes to Austin, Texas, every day to pick up 10,000 computers for delivery to the Sony factory in Mexico. Then, while everyone was asleep in Austin, the factory would match up computers and monitors that would then be delivered to customers the following day.[48]

Such seamless integration extends to buyers as well. When Dell loads software onto Eastman Chemical's PCs, it distinguishes between the analyst workstation, sales, personnel, and other parts of the organization. This saves Eastman the needless hassle of loading the software themselves. More importantly, Dell already delivers pre-programmed machines that meet the exact specifications of the buyers.

Another important source of added value will come from an emerging type of business intermediary that is replacing the traditional middleman: the "infomediary." Introduced by John Hagel III and Marc Singer, both consultants at McKinsey and Company, infomediaries are companies that collect and manage access to consumer information.[49] This service involves the collection, dissemination, and control of a variety of types of information. It can also include any person or organization that facilitates the exchange of information between other parties. Infomediaries have become a crucial element in a firm's business model because of the linking services they provide on behalf of host firms. The Internet, for example, will not function without the services of search engines and portals such as Yahoo! and Excite.

In *Mastering the Digital Marketplace,* Douglas Aldrich, managing director of A.T. Kearney, lists the following operations offered by the merging infomediaries: integration of informational services and needs (Add-a-Photo); aggregating services and needs (Freight forwarders); creating a floating price system based on supply and demand (eBay); managing the flow of products from initial suppliers to final buyers (FastParts Trading Exchange); managing the ever-changing electronic affinity group (GE Trading Process Network); saving time for valued network members (Travelocity); managing operational functions (Gateway); and developing new customers (Telia Telecommunications).[50] As networks continue to evolve and as traditional intermediaries fade away, the roles and functions of infomediaries will only grow in greater proportion. Their structure and value-added will be distinctive characteristics of the new economy.

The Pixar-Disney partnership, albeit a short-lived one, was one of Hollywood's most lucrative. It generated $2.6 billion in revenues since 1995 from a string of animated, computer-generated, and critically acclaimed features such as *Toy Story*, *Monsters, Inc.*, *A Bug's Life*, and *Finding Nemo*. In that partnership, Pixar created the movies while Disney marketed them.

Facilitating Partners in Value Creation

Value creation is often considered to be a company's task, but it should be the outcome of a partnership between customers and the company.[51] Value creation fails when companies incorrectly identify what customers perceive as value. Proper communication between the company and the customer is required. Pauliina Hivornen and Nina Helander, both marketing professors at the University of Oulu in Finland, suggest that value creation in service industries is a process, and that customers have their own value-creation process.[52] They developed a three-phase model. At the first phase, the customer's value-creation process can be identified by the services provider. At the second phase, the services provider should have an understanding of customer relations when pursuing the process of creating values for the customer company. At the last phase, the service should occur only when value creation stems from the supplier's core competencies. Hence, a long-term, constructive relationship is critical in value creation.

Exhibit 3.6   **An Example of Value Partnership: Nike Corporation**

Nike's partners	Value-added contributions
Subcontractors	Pay higher than average with necessary amenities
Host governments	Provide community support
College/high school athletes	Limited to support to athletic teams
Coaches	Limited to extensive support for athletic teams
Professional athletes	Extensive support and endorsements
Research and development	Focused on athlete's welfare and performance
On-site field visits	Personal support

Source: Constructed from Nike presentations, University of Oregon, 1999–2001.

Although this model was originated for business customers in service industries, it is also applicable to individual consumers and manufacturing industries. Business and individual customers are alike because when making purchase decisions, they constantly evaluate whether values should be created for their businesses or their daily lives. To minimize the waste of resources for both the company and the customer, the company should go beyond mere constant communication with customers, however beneficial that might be. Companies should seek active partnership with customers in value creation. A partnership implies a commitment from all parties in order to achieve common goals. In an ideal partnership, both parties are honest and open with each other so that a "win-win" result can be obtained. Customers should feel free to discuss their needs, and companies should welcome suggestions. An example of value partnership is presented in Exhibit 3.6 using Nike Corporation as an example. Note that Nike Corporation has a strategy for each critical partner that adds value to its business plan.

UNDERSTANDING THE SOURCES OF COMPETITIVE ADVANTAGE

Perhaps the most difficult question to answer in the preparation of business plan is: *What makes this firm different, or truly distinctive from others?* It is important, therefore, to probe deeper into the sources of competitive advantage. While much of this material has been introduced in business strategy classes, it is reviewed here to provide better context to the above question.[53]

TRADITIONAL SOURCES OF ADVANTAGE

Competitive advantage is an advantage that a firm has in relation to other competitors. Robert Grant's formulation is as follows: a firm gains a competitive edge (i.e., earn a higher rate of return against its rivals) in one of two ways: either it can supply an identical product or service at a lower cost, or it can supply a product or

Exhibit 3.7

Examples of Cost Leadership

Strategic Approach	Examples
Company works hard to achieve the lowest costs of production and distribution so that it can price its products or services lower than its competitors and win a large market share.	• Texas Instruments • Emerson Electric • Southwest Airlines • Dell Computer • Wal-Mart • Dollar Tree Stores

Exhibit 3.8

Examples of Differentiation

Strategic Differentiator	Examples
Consulting	McKinsey: Well-known and validated methods and tools for management/executive development
Procurement	Peet's Coffee: Pays careful attention to quality and purity of ingredients
Product development	Leapfrog: Interactive toys to teach children skills
Technology development	Apple Computers: Unique product design and development in PCs and consumer-related applications (iPod)
Outbound logistics	Federal Express: Integrated logistics system with Memphis hub for reliable delivery
Sales channels	Salesforce.com: Strong leader in on-demand customer relationship management
Outsourcing	Infosys: Deep experience as an outsourcing vendor
Sales force	IBM: No one was ever fired for buying from IBM
Supply chain	Solectron, Toyota: Uncanny ability to forge extensive supply connections
Market research	Procter & Gamble: Constantly monitors its customers, assessing new market needs
Promotion	Purdue: "It takes a tough man to make a tender chicken."

service that is differentiated in such a way that the customer is willing to pay a price premium beyond the additional costs of differentiation. In the former case, the firm is considered to have a **cost advantage**. To the extent that it is lowest-cost provider, then it has a strong position within the marketplace. In the latter case, the firm enjoys a **differentiation advantage**, or provides something unique that is valuable to the buyer beyond a low price.[54]

While the two are related in terms of providing value to the firm, they are distinct in their underlying objectives and philosophies. Exhibits 3.7 and 3.8 provide some principal features of cost and differentiation strategies.

By combining these two types of advantage with the firm's choice of scope, a firm can either service a full range of market segments with different products and services (broad scope), or it can develop a focus strategy that is aimed at servicing a narrow niche (narrow scope). Harvard professor and strategy guru Michael Porter has been

Exhibit 3.9

Four Generic Strategies

Strategy	Description
Cost Leadership	• Characterized by rigorous cost control • Objective is to be lowest cost in the industry • Enables company to earn returns even after competitors compete away their profits • Products/services generally priced below industry average
Differentiation	• Objective is to create a unique product/service • Uniqueness must be valued by customer • Customers pay higher prices for uniqueness they value
Broad Focus	• Company attempts to serve many markets with a wide range of products and services
Narrow Focus	• Company concentrates on serving a few market segments well rather than going after the whole market

Source: Adapted from Michael E. Porter, *Industry Analysis and Competitive Behavior* (New York: The Free Press, 1980), pp. 35–41.

credited for defining these four distinct generic strategies, each with its own focus, philosophy, and set of capabilities. **Generic strategies** are the general strategies popularly adopted by business entities during competition. Exhibit 3.9 summarizes these basic approaches to developing advantage. In previous decades, the use of broad cost and differentiation strategies was popular. In the current competitive environment, however, going head-to-head against larger competitors may not be the manner in which to build advantage. In *Blue Ocean Strategy,* W. Chan Kim and Renee Mauborgne, professors of strategy at INSEAD, studied 150 strategic moves that spanned more than a hundred years and thirty industries. Their conclusion: tomorrow's leaders will succeed not by battling rivals head-to-head (red ocean), but by locating uncontested market space or niches (blue ocean).[55] Box 3.3 features special cases of firms that have successfully positioned their strategies for targeted market niches.

CONTEMPORARY SOURCES OF ADVANTAGE

Contemporary sources of advantage are the advantages developed to suit the current global competitive environment and long-term success. While cost leadership, differentiation, and focus remain popular, new sources for building advantage have been proposed. In fact, in a provocative book, *Hypercompetition,* Dartmouth management professor Richard D'Aveni argues that traditional sources of advantage (i.e., the traditional generic strategies) no longer provide long-term security.[56] International Business Machines (IBM) and General Motors (GM), household names in computers and automobiles, were once viewed as unassailable in global competition. Both companies had economies of scale, massive advertising budgets, excellent distribution systems, cutting-edge R&D, deep cash pockets, and power over buyers and suppliers. Yet, both IBM and GM appeared inertial, unable to exploit major opportunities, and fell prey to new and smaller competitors. Former Hewlett-Packard (HP) CEO Lewis Platt remarked that, "The only mistake they [IBM and GM] made is, they did whatever it was that made them leaders a little too long." Platt's words were prophetic; it was not long before an "outside" CEO, one who completely lacked ties to HP's past practices, replaced him.[57]

Box 3.3

Finding That Elusive Market Niche: Cases of Strategic Focus

If a market niche is found and secured, a firm does not need to go head-to-head against an already established incumbent or market leader. Consider the following cases.

Online Micro-financing

While serving the world's poor has been a popular cause throughout history, this segment has been largely ignored until recently. The revival of micro-financing by the Muhammad Yunus and the Grameen Bank brought renewed attention to the growing importance of this market segment. In 2005, two Stanford graduates founded kiva.org, a San Francisco-based, online service that brings together aspiring everyday lenders with micro-financing institutions to serve the world's poor with interest rates lower than the worldwide average for micro-financing loans. The average amount of a loan is $70. The service includes photos of loan recipients and stories about them, enabling lenders some discretion in selecting aspiring small-business owners. While there is concern about scam artists taking advantage of this service, this organization has already touched many of the the lives of this growing segment.

Nutraceutical Products

"Nutraceuticals" generally refer to natural and organic foods and dietary supplements that are believed to lead to a superior health value. The concern for good preventative healthcare, a distrust of pharmaceutical drugs, the acceptance of alternative healthcare practices, and younger and more health conscious consumers are the principal drivers behind what is considered to be the most dynamic segment within the food industry. The global market for this segment was projected at $74.7 billion by 2007.

Mobile ESPN

ESPN now offers a personalized, sports-focused alternative to traditional sources of sports information. This feature will enable customers to watch SportsCenter, follow a fantasy football player, videos, sports clips, and get live updates of NFL games on their specially designed cell phones. In partnership with Verizon Wireless, Mobile ESPN is part of a new breed of cell phone carriers called mobile virtual network operators, which purchase wholesale minutes and data from large cell phone carriers in order to sell cell phones and service to a niche audience.

Cirque du Soleil

Cirque du Soleil, created in 1984 by a group of street performers, is now among Canada's largest cultural exports. In less than twenty years, Cirque du Soleil achieved a level of public awareness that took Ringling Brothers and Barnum & Bailey—the market leaders—more than a hundred years to achieve. It offers a theatric show that combines the arts of the circus and the street, and features original music, lighting effects, and costumes. Unlike the traditional circus, there are no animals in the shows. The focus is on creating a new experience based on different themes. Cirque du Soleil has realized that in order to beat the competition, it has to stop trying to beat it.

Sources: Sonia Narang, "Web-based Microfinancing," *New York Times*, December 10, 2006; "An Introduction to the U.S. Nutraceuticals Industry," Food Policy Institute, http://www.foodpolicyinstitute.org/docs/facts/nutraceuticals.pdf.; "Global nutraceuticals market to reach $74.7 billion by 2007," Research Studies (Business Communications, Inc.), March, 2003; Ryan Kim, "Battle Rages for the Luxury Phone Market," *San Francisco Chronicle* (January 2, 2006), C1; W. Chan Kim and Renee Mauborgne, *Blue Ocean Strategy* (Boston: Harvard Business School Press, 2005), pp. 3–5; "ESPN and Verizon Wireless Announce Exclusive Multi-Year Licensing Agreement for Award-Winning ESPN Sports Content," http://mobile.espn.go.com/; Cirque du Soleil, http://www.cirquedusoleil.com.

D'Aveni has challenged the traditional premise held by Porter and his colleagues that the pursuit of a strategy is a sustainable competitive advantage. For D'Aveni, strategy is also the creative destruction of the opponents' advantage. **Hypercompetition** is the result of a series of competitive countermoves—"dynamic strategic interactions"—that lead to the erosion, destruction, and neutralization of each firm's competitive advantages. Competitive moves are so ferocious that traditional sources of competitive advantage can no longer be sustained. He views hypercompetition as particularly pervasive, extending from high-technology industries to more mundane ones like hot sauce and cat food.

D'Aveni's research suggests that the escalation of competition can occur *within* or *across* specific arenas. Specifically, "firms escalate competition by increasing the level of quality or lowering the price of their goods. They also escalate efforts to develop new know-how, move faster, invade or create new strongholds, and build deep pockets. Competition continues until firms exhaust the advantages of that arena. Then, they move on to know-how in the second arena, until the benefits of these advantages become too expensive. A third possible step is to attempt to create strongholds to limit competition, until these too are finally breached. This leads to the use of deep pockets until the time when firms deplete their resources or make alliances to balance off the resources of competing alliances." While such a progression ultimately finds resolution in a "perfectly competitive" world (at least, theoretically), this state is purposefully avoided by corporations seeking profit. In one sense, a paradox occurs: while firms act in ways oriented toward achieving perfect competition, they must attempt to avoid it in order to attain abnormal profits, thus leaving them to hibernate in a hypercompetitive world.

Another imperative for sustaining advantage is through strategic learning. **Strategic learning** refers to the ability to learn fast and to develop a system for learning. In fact, Ray Stata, chairman of Analog Devices, echoed a sentiment expressed earlier by Arie P. de Gues, head of planning at Royal Dutch/Shell, that, "the ability to learn faster than competitors may be the only sustainable competitive advantage."[58] To this end, organizations have to develop institutional forms of learning. In the case of the Shell planning group, this was achieved through scenario planning with the aid of computers. Another group of authors, John Redding and Ralph Catalanello, suggest that broad-based learning can be achieved through a learning cycle characterized by continuous planning, improvised implementation, and deep reflection.[59]

Whether the focus is on the traditional or contemporary treatments of competitive advantage, the goal is to define what makes a firm truly distinctive. In doing so, one can determine the whether the firm's strategy is, in fact, sustainable. Exhibit 3.10 summarizes contemporary treatments on competitive advantage.

REFINING THE BUSINESS MODEL: COMPETITIVE DYNAMICS

In D'Aveni's discussion of hypercompetition, competitive situations arise when the evaluation of a course of action depends not only on the choices a manager makes, but also on the choices made by others. Such a context applies to strategic decisions in which a manager is contemplating whether or not to acquire another firm or enter a new market, or how to respond to a rival seeking to enter the incumbent's market. **Competitive dynamics** refers to a series of offensive and defensive actions taken by rivals.

Exhibit 3.10

Contemporary Treatments on Competitive Advantage

Contemporary Sources of Advantage	Description
Speed	• Objective is to be the pioneer and to reap first-mover advantages
	• Since time represents opportunities, being first to market will yield competitive advantages
	Examples: Intel Corporation; FedEx
Know-how	• Objective is to develop proprietary knowledge
	• Know-how, such as patent or intellectual property rights, can forestall later competitive attacks
	Examples: Genentech; Chiron
Learning	• Objective is to develop a culture of learning and renewal that will enable quick identification of opportunities and threats
	Example: Shell Planning Group

In situations like these, the best course of action requires a manager to think through his or her opponents' options, their strategic intent, and predict the way they will act or react. This is called "thinking forward and reasoning backward."[60] This ability to look forward and reason backward provides valuable insights for strategists. An initial action can provoke a response that is either aggressive or accommodating. A price war typically results when a response to an initial action (price cut) is aggressive (matching the price cut), if not downright hostile (an even lower price cut). One example of an aggressive action was when New York Air, a 1980 start-up airline that was owned by Texas Air Corporation and headed by Frank Lorenzo, aggressively cut its introductory flights to Washington and New York to a measly $0.29 in response to a price cut by its competitor, Eastern Air Lines. When a company builds a facility, its profitability will often depend on whether or not competitors add capacity as well. Because excess capacity cannot be as easily sold, higher inventory costs will result and this situation can impel competitors to cut their prices. In fact, in oligopoly markets, such strategic decisions are influenced by the retaliatory countermoves that are made in response to initial decisions.[61] Much like chess masters, the best business strategists must be skilled at predicting future rounds of competitive moves and countermoves.

Historically, the application of game theory has provided a structured process that can help managers make better strategic decisions when faced with the uncertainty of competitive conduct (see Box 3.4). In general, games can be structured in two basic ways: *sequentially* and *simultaneously*. In many real-world situations, sequential actions are the norm. A chess player makes the first move before any response can follow. The same is true in a tennis game (one person serving), or in a baseball game (the pitcher initiates, the batter responds). In a business setting, sequential moves are typical in price actions, product introductions, capacity expansions, and market entry. The structure of a typical game that describes a sequential competitive situation is that one party initiates an action that is followed by way of a response by another.

Another structure in game theory is the simultaneous move, where participants act at

Box 3.4

Game Theory: A Historical Overview

In 1921, French mathematician Emile Borel published the first set of papers on the theory of games. Since his interest was poker, his goal was to find the "best" strategy for playing a game that involved bluffing and second-guessing. Because he did not develop these ideas further, however, the honor and credit of developing and popularizing game theory was bestowed on John Von Neumann, a Hungarian mathematician and Princeton academic icon, who became renowned for his intelligence, brilliance, and personality quirks.

In his 1928 paper "The Theory of Parlor Games," Von Neumann first approached the topic of game theory and proved the famous Minimax Theorem. He teamed up with Oskar Morgenstein, an Austrian economist at Princeton, to develop the theory in the book *Theory of Games and Economic Behavior* (1944), which revolutionized the field of economics. While intended for economists, applications of game theory have been extended to warfare, political science, psychology, sociology, recreational games, and, recently, business strategy.

What compels scholars from different fields to apply game theory is its paradoxical view of cooperation and competition, as represented by the Prisoner's Dilemma Game. Consider the following examples:

- During a drought, a person has to decide whether to act in his own self-interest and water his garden, or to exercise restraint and conserve water. It is not necessary for one person to exercise restraint if most others in the community are doing so. However, if most individuals in the community are watering their gardens, it is futile for one individual to exercise restraint since he/she has little impact on the entire water supply.
- Suppose six farmers, each with one cow weighing 1,000 lbs., share a plot of grazing land that can only sustain six cows without deterioration from overgrazing. For every additional cow added, the weight of each animal decreases by 100 lbs. Thus, if each farmer has the opportunity to add one cow, he gains by having two cows weighing 900 lbs., instead of one weighing 1,000 lbs. But if all six farmers add a cow, they are worse off because their two cows will weigh 400 lbs. each (1,000 less 600), instead of one cow weighing 1,000 lbs. (called the "tragedy of the commons" in the book by the same name, this described the plight of small farmers in England during the period of enclosures in the eighteenth century).

Many interactions in the business world can be modeled using game theory. Adam Brandenburger, Barry Nalebuff, Avinash Dixit, Penkaj Ghemawat, and Robert Axelrod are among those who have extended game theory to business strategy applications. In 1994, game theory received serious accolades with the Nobel Prize awarded to Americans John Harsanyi, John Nash (featured in the movie, *A Beautiful Mind*), and German Reinhard Selten for their application of game theory to international trade. In 2005, game theory reached another watershed with the Nobel Prize awarded to Hebrew University professor Robert Aumann and University of Maryland professor Thomas Schilling for defining applications to the arms races and price wars.

Sources: Adapted from the historical narratives of William Poundstone, *Prisoner's Dilemma* (New York: Anchor Books, 1993); Anatol Rapoport and Albert M. Chammath, *Prisoner's Dilemma: A Study in Conflict and Cooperation* (Ann Arbor: University of Michigan Press, 1965); Von Neumann and Game Theory, http://cse.stanford.edu/class/sophomore-college/projects-98/gametheory/html. Examples are excerpted from "Applications of Game Theory," http://cse.stanford.edu/class/sophomore-college/projects-98/game-theory/applications.html; and "N-Person Prisoners' Dilemma," http://cse.stanford.edu/class/sophomore-college/projects-98/game-theory/npd.html.

the same time. Picture a game of "rock, paper, scissors." A pair of scissors trumps paper (by cutting it), but a rock trumps this pair of scissors (by breaking it), and a paper trumps a rock (by covering it). This game cannot be structured as a sequential moves. If it were, the first move automatically loses by being exposed and becoming vulnerable to a dominant response. Thus, it has to be played simultaneously. The same is true in business with simultaneous bidding, or in cases where the first move is not disclosed and remains unknown.

Exhibit 3.11   **To Enter or Not? Komatsu vs. Caterpillar**

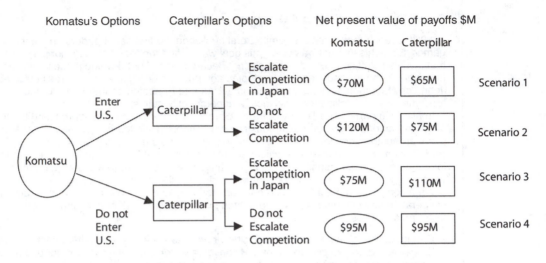

Source: Adapted from H. Courtney, "Games Managers Should Play," *McKinsey Quarterly*, 2000 Strategy Anthology, p. 48. Firm names and NPV payoffs have been changed.

ILLUSTRATING A SEQUENTIAL GAME: KOMATSU VERSUS CATERPILLAR

In a **sequential game**, the players are allowed to make a move in a particular order. In this way, the players are able to see what previous moves have been made and can respond in a way that reflects this limited knowledge. It is imperative that the players get as much information about the other player's actions, background, and motivations. University of Maryland professor Hugh Courtney specifies such information: "A thorough economic analysis of the industry—including market research and estimates of competitors' costs and capacity—is usually needed to estimate the payoffs of different strategies for different players, given their strategic objectives."[62]

For example, in the 1990s, a competitive battle raged between Caterpillar and Komatsu. Capitalizing on its success outside the United States, Komatsu, a Japanese upstart, was contemplating entry into Caterpillar's home market, the United States. In order to illustrate the use of a sequential game, the example stylizes the terms of a hypothetical competition based on our modification of an earlier example by Courtney.

> Caterpillar's dominance in earth-moving equipment has been challenged by a Japanese upstart—Komatsu. Among its many options, Komatsu was looking into a long-range strategy of entering Caterpillar's primary market (the United States). Anticipating the arrival of a challenger, Caterpillar considered its reactions, including whether to retaliate by escalating competition in Komatsu's home turf in Japan. What should both firms do?

This stylized competition is based on a market entry case in which two competitors are each deciding on their strategies and their consequences thereafter. The hypothetical payoff diagram (Exhibit 3.11) presents the two players (Caterpillar and Komatsu), an assumption that Komatsu moves first, the possible sequence of moves and countermoves, and payoffs (represented here as net present values). The dynamics can be illustrated in four possible scenarios:

- *Scenario 1: Komatsu enters the United States; Caterpillar retaliates by escalating activity in Japan.* Komatsu earns a NPV of $70 million, while Caterpillar earns $65 million.
- *Scenario 2: Komatsu enters the United States; Caterpillar does not retaliate.* Komatsu earns a NPV of $120 million, while Caterpillar earns $75 million.
- *Scenario 3: Komatsu does not enter the United States; Caterpillar escalates activity in Japan.* Komatsu earns a NPV of $75 million, while Caterpillar earns $110 million.
- *Scenario 4: Komatsu does not enter the United States; Caterpillar does not escalate activity in Japan.* Komatsu and Caterpillar both earn a NPV of $95 million.

In analyzing this exercise, four points should be taken into account. First, the payoffs are hypothetical and used principally for establishing learning points for this application of sequential games. While Komatsu did enter the United States in 1996, and Caterpillar responded by escalating competition in Japan, these decisions were not based on the above payoffs. Second, perfect information is not required for this application. What is essential is for Caterpillar to observe Komatsu's initial decision; that would be the basis for its own future action. Third, the payoffs favor aggressive decisions, that is, Caterpillar stands to lose more by escalating competition in Japan, perhaps reflecting intense local competition and more stretched resources, than if it accommodated Komatsu's entry into the United States. Similarly, the payoffs suggest that any lack of a response by Komatsu to Caterpillar's escalation of activity in Japan will favor the latter. Fourth, the payoffs are relatively favorable if both Komatsu and Caterpillar refrain from any aggressive action. This situation is developed further in our discussion of the Prisoner's Dilemma (next section).

University of Maryland management professor Hugh Courtney offers three specific insights that were made from a similar exercise from which our stylized case was based.[63] First, it illustrates the first-mover advantage in the game. Specifically, Komatsu's action to commit to a new plant in the United States can influence Caterpillar's incentives to stay in the United States, and not to escalate activity in Japan. Without this first move by Komatsu, Caterpillar can peremptorily escalate competitive activity in Japan, a situation that can lead to severe competition and the lowest payoffs for both firms. Second, it demonstrates the symmetry of the first-mover advantage. Specifically, Caterpillar can move first and, in turn, influence Komatsu's response. Thus, it is important for Komatsu to credibly commit itself as soon as possible. Third, Komatsu and Caterpillar need to understand the limited prospects for growth. Without such an understanding, wrong decisions are likely to be made. In general, while it is profitable for one new plant to be built in the industry, new capacity can lead to excess

Exhibit 3.12   **Prisoner's Dilemma**

		Prisoner 1's options	
		Cooperate/confess	**Defect/remain silent**
Prisoner 2's options	**Cooperate/confess**	Early parole for both (1 year)	Long sentence for P2 (10 years), P1 let go
	Defect/remain silent	Long sentence for P1 (10 years), P2 let go	Token warning for both (Let go)

capacity, that can result in turn, to deep price discounting by firms, and eventually to lower profits. Examining assumptions by "looking forward and reasoning backward" is also helpful in this regard. The specific nature of these payoffs can be analyzed in a simultaneous game, specifically the case of the Prisoner's Dilemma, discussed in greater length in the next section.

ILLUSTRATING A SIMULTANEOUS GAME: STARBUCKS VERSUS PEET'S COFFEE

A **simultaneous game** is one in which all rivals make competitive moves without prior knowledge of each other's strategy. In price competition, the sequence of moves is not significant.

Simultaneous games are also used to describe a common form of competitive interactions. One of the most celebrated of cases analyzed in game theory by means of a non-zero-sum game is the Prisoner's Dilemma.[64] The game presents situations in which there are large joint benefits from cooperation but strong individual incentives to deviate. The game got its name from a hypothetical situation confronting a shrewd prosecutor who detains two individuals but cannot conclusively prove their guilt. He makes the following offer to each: "You may choose to confess or remain silent. If you confess and your accomplice remains silent I will drop all charges against you and use your testimony to ensure that your accomplice does serious time. Likewise, if your accomplice confesses while you remain silent, he will go free while you do the time. If you both confess I get two convictions, but I'll see to it that you both get early parole. If you both remain silent, I'll have to settle for token sentences on firearms possession charges. If you wish to confess, you must leave a note with the jailer before my return tomorrow morning."[65]

Exhibit 3.13   **Starbucks vs. Peet's Coffee**

PEET'S COFFEE

		Discount	No Discount
Discount		A LOW PROFITS $100,000 *Low Profits* *$100,000*	B VERY LOW PROFITS $50,000 *High Profits* *$300,000*
No Discount		C HIGH PROFITS $300,000 *Very Low Profits* *$50,000*	D MEDIUM PROFITS $175,000 *Medium Profits* *$175,000*

Starbucks (label on left vertical axis)

Source: Adapted from Bruce Greenwald and Judd Kahn, *Competition Demystified* (New York: Penguin, 2005), p. 165. Example and figures have been changed.

Notes: Outcomes and payoffs for Starbucks are italicized, while those for Peet's Coffee are not. Payoffs are hypothetical estimates of profits per day.

The situation is that each prisoner has a choice between only two options, i.e., to confess or to remain silent, but cannot make a good decision without knowing what the other one will do. The "dilemma" faced by the prisoners here is that, whatever the other does, each is better off confessing than remaining silent. However, if both confess, the outcome would be a jail term of one year for both of them, a worse fate than if both had remained silent ("let go"). The dilemma is that each prisoner gains when both cooperate, but if only one of them cooperates or confesses, the other one, who defects or who remains silent, will gain more. If both defect or remain silent, both lose (or gain very little), but not as much as the prisoner who cooperates or confesses. The whole game situation and its different outcomes can be summarized in Exhibit 3.12. An informal assessment is that 80 to 90 percent of competitive interactions fit within this scope or model.[66]

To illustrate the use of a simultaneous game (and the Prisoner's Dilemma), a hypothetical case between Starbucks and Peet's Coffee is described.[67]

> Two leading competitors—Starbucks and Peet's Coffee—are contemplating how to compete in a new location for which market demand and customer preferences have yet to be established. For simplicity, let's say both cafés are scheduled to open simultaneously, on April 1. In addition, prices are the same for both cafés. Both firms have the same options: keep the same high prices they offer in other locations, or offer discounted prices for designated popular coffee drinks for an undisclosed time period. Because a reduced price is anticipated to be regarded as positive for customers, the company that does this is bound to earn more profits, resulting from increased market share, while the one that does not will have less volume and thus will earn much less. However, if both companies reduce prices, this can result in a price war that would only be unfavorable for both firms. What should both companies do?

The choices for both firms are represented in Exhibit 3.13. A number of key points here illustrate the simultaneous game. Although each firm can earn medium profits ($175,000), by charging similarly high prices, there are powerful incentives for each firm to deviate from this arrangement because reducing prices will lead to additional volume and increase profits significantly ($300,000). For this simultaneous game, that is, the Prisoner's Dilemma, to be operative, however, the following assumptions need to be present. First, both firms have to move at the same time (this explains the assumption of a common April 1 opening). Second, the two firms are purely self-interested (they are not concerned about educating customers in ways that improve overall coffee sales). Third, they only care about profits (i.e., payout), not about reputation or their community standing. Fourth, they cannot meet to consult each other on their decisions (tipping or implicit signaling is not allowed).[68] How is the dilemma solved? Since the case requires that Starbucks and Peet's play this game for an indefinite time period, learning from one's adversary is facilitated. University of Michigan political scientist Robert Axelrod argued that the *tit-for-tat* rule (a variation of "an eye for an eye") works well in this situation.[69] Along this line of reasoning, the firms can start out by cooperating, that is, charging high prices, or deviating, that is, reducing prices, during the first period, but from then on one firm mimics the others' action from each preceding period. Thus, if Starbucks offers a discount, so should Peet's Coffee. Similarly, if Starbucks decides not to offer the discount, neither should Peet's Coffee. Consumers will presumably still buy coffee drinks, even without any discount (although they will benefit from reduced prices if the firms proceed in this direction). This does not mean that either firm cannot offer a discount. It can, but it should be aware of the consequences.

EXTENDING THE STRUCTURE OF THE GAME

Knowing the basics of sequential and simultaneous games, managers can organize the information into a framework that allows them to analyze the competitive situation in a systematic and comprehensive manner:[70]

DEFINE THE STRATEGIC ISSUE.

What is the strategic issue? Is it a pricing, capacity, or market entry decision? Because these decisions entail different levels of commitment, it's important to identify the issue at the outset. Pricing decisions (e.g., price cuts) are easier to reverse than entry decisions involving new plants and/or additions to existing capacity.[71] Pricing and entry decisions require a deep understanding of the strategies, motivations, and capabilities of the players involved.

DETERMINE THE RELEVANT PLAYERS.

Who are the relevant players? Which players will have the greatest impact on the success of a particular strategy? While basic game theory depicts the competitive actions of two players or competitors, it is reasonable to expect that suppliers, distributors, and providers of complementary goods can impact the game as well. Understanding how different players can impact the game will provide valuable insights into future interactions between them.

IDENTIFY EACH PLAYER'S STRATEGIC OBJECTIVES.

What are the objectives of each player? What is the pattern of their previous decisions? While basic game theory assumes that rational players compete to maximize profits, this is not necessarily the case in real life. In the short run, they often base decisions on market share or growth. The inability to recognize strategic objectives can lead to adverse, unexpected consequences. For example, the entry of the Holland Sweetener Company (HSC) to challenge Nutrasweets' markets after the patent expired resulted in a vicious rivalry between them. Far from benefiting these two companies, however, the resulting dynamics only served their buyers, Coca-Cola and Pepsi, who were able to renegotiate better prices with Nutrasweet.[72]

IDENTIFY THE POTENTIAL ACTIONS FOR EACH PLAYER.

What are the options and potential actions for each player? Again, the use of looking forward and reasoning backward might prove useful here. Moreover, patterns of previous decisions should be carefully examined. On occasion, using competitive role-playing exercises can provide insights as well.

It is generally assumed that tactics in game theory are based on perceptions of what others do. Much like the game of poker, however, revealing only part of the game with discrete disguises becomes part of the strategy. Other tactics include overt actions such as guarantees and warrantees. After all, what is a better way to signal one's seriousness and confidence than a money-back guarantee to all customers?[73]

This is exactly what happened to Japanese game-making company Nintendo. The company anticipated huge Christmas sales, but with a chip shortage underway, it could not satisfy the demand of toy stores. Instead of panicking or explaining to nervous shoppers that they lacked inventory, Nintendo ended up selling one game to many parties with promises to deliver a second after January 1. The potential of a shortage and a marketing fiasco turned into a public relations coup.[74]

DETERMINE THE LIKELY STRUCTURE OF THE GAME.

Will decisions be made sequentially? Simultaneously? Who is likely to take the lead? Who is likely to follow? Will the game be repeated? Most business games hardly resemble the one-shot decision, but are repeated over and over in most markets.

While there are no rules for the games businesses play for which all parties agree on and abide by, it behooves managers to have their own rules that they follow and enforce. This rich subject is treated elsewhere under the rubric of promises, assurances, and brinkmanship.[75]

Understanding the game one is playing is part of a much larger, more complex setting. Game theorists recognize this complexity with more advanced treatments of the subject. Even so, even with this brief introduction, applications of game theory should avoid common errors and traps that include: (a) seeing only part of the game, (b) assuming that the game will not change, (c) failing to think about changing the game methodically, (d) thinking that one has to be unique, and (e) believing that success must come at the others' expense.[76]

This chapter covers the core of strategy, specifically the need for firms to build competitive advantages to differentiate themselves from their rivals. It is important to distinguish between strategy, that is, the essence of competing, and a business model, that is, one that articulates and interprets strategy with action. In Chapter 2 we presented various frameworks for assessing the external environment. In this chapter, the next step of formulating a strategy focuses attention on how a firm should position itself against this environment in ways that makes any advantages explicit and enduring. Traditional sources of competitive advantages include cost and quality differentiation. More contemporary treatments emphasize learning, disruption, and competitive dynamics. Advanced treatments of the subject involve applications of complex game theory models. Another recent approach is to simplify the dynamics of competition emphasizing the need to build or maintain entry barriers and the need for captive loyalty through quality differentiation.[77] While business practitioners are generally receptive to the analytical frameworks discussed in this chapter, they also emphasize the role of luck in sustaining advantage in addition to visionary risk-taking.[78] Our emphasis on the basics of strategy and business models, however, provides a point of departure in further understanding how these concepts can be extended to an international context, the subject of the chapters to follow.

SUMMARY

1. The rationale for strategy is based on two interrelated concepts: competition and uncertainty. Competition is directed at understanding industry conditions and one's industry rivals. Uncertainty means one cannot predict the future with confidence and certainty.

2. Strategy and a business model, while interrelated, have been confused. Strategy gives the firm the conceptual base of action—it is the essence of competition. A business model articulates and interprets strategy with action.

3. Strategy has its roots in the Greek word, *strategos* (the art of the general), and thus has military antecedents. Even so, military and business competition are different in that business competition does not mean the destruction of the enemy, and it can impel the use of an indirect approach through segmentation and positioning.

4. Strategy can be represented as follows: a plan (formal explication goals and activities); a process (a pattern in a stream of past decisions); a position (the firm's image in the minds of consumers); and a philosophy (deep beliefs and values).

5. Strategy is a series of interlocking decisions aimed at achieving a sustainable competitive advantage. It is a purposeful choice; decisions are intertwined and interrelated; it is relative to a rival or competitor; and its goal is to create a sustainable performance gap.

6. Strategy should not be confused with a firm's mission. A mission states a firm's reason for being, inclusive of its purpose, philosophy, and distinctive-

ness. A strategy builds on the mission in delineating ways by which a firm distinguishes itself from others. For simplicity and focus, firms also employ "mission bumper stickers."

7. A firm's value proposition is an explicit statement of its value and advantage relative to its principal competitors.

8. A basic competence is an internal activity that a firm performs better than any other internal activity. A core competence is a well-performed internal activity that is central to the firm's strategy. A distinctive competence is a competitively valued activity that a firm performs better than its rivals.

9. Retaining customers can redound to a firm's advantage. It is more costly to acquire customers than it is to retain them.

10. Consumers have become important for the following reasons: unprecedented information access using new technology; broader awareness through a global perspective; more experimentation and activism; and rising customer expectations.

11. Value partnerships emphasize cooperative rather than adversarial transactions. This can be achieved through integration, the use of complementors and infomediaries, and co-creation.

12. Traditional sources of advantage consist of cost leadership (supply side advantages); differentiation (demand side advantages); and focus (segmentation using either cost or differentiation).

13. Contemporary sources of advantage include competitive dynamics (hypercompetition), strategic learning, and disruption.

14. Some final considerations include answers to the following questions: Is the business model valued in the marketplace? Is it sustainable against competitive imitation?

15. The application of game theory provides a structured process that can help managers make better strategic decisions when faced with the uncertainty of competitive conduct.

16. In basic game theory, two types of structures are typically analyzed: Simultaneous games where the two players need to make decisions at about the same time. Price discounting and closed simultaneous bidding are examples of this game. The Prisoner's Dilemma game is a special case of a simultaneous game. The second type is the sequential game, where the action of the first player is followed by that of another player, presumably where the second action is influenced by the first. Entry decisions, capacity building, and new product introduction are examples of this second type.

17. The subject of strategy encompasses all sources of competitive advantages. Traditional treatments focus on cost and quality differentials; contemporary treatments emphasize competitive dynamics and game theory. Business practitioners suggest that serendipitous events, luck, and risk taking are also factors that affect the sustainability of a firm's strategy.

KEY TERMS

Strategy	Networking
Business model	Value partnership
Value proposition	Competitive advantage
Competencies	Cost advantage
Capabilities	Differentiation advantage
Core competence	Generic strategies
Distinctive competence	Contemporary sources of advantage
SWOT	Hypercompetition
Customer interfaces	Strategic learning
Value added	Competitive dynamics
Information Age	Sequential game
Global perspective	Simultaneous game

DISCUSSION QUESTIONS

1. Discuss the key differences between a strategy and a business model.
2. How might you recommend a mission statement be formulated?
3. Is it possible for a company to follow a cost leadership and a differentiation strategy simultaneously?
4. Three generic strategies have been discussed: overall cost leadership, product differentiation, and focus. Briefly define these strategies. Discuss the differences between each of these strategies in terms of their underlying objectives. Discuss the circumstances under which each of these strategies would have the greatest likelihood of success. Discuss the risks associated with each strategy.
5. In framing his four generic strategies, what assumption does Michael Porter make about the underlying relationship between firm profitability and market share? In view of this relationship, why does he then argue that firms that are stuck in the middle face a precarious position when compared to cost leaders and differentiators?
6. A local business person said, "I do not understand how resources can really add value to any firm's business model because they are fixed and static." How would you respond to this comment based on your understanding of the interrelationship between competitive advantage, strategic resources, and core processes?
7. George Yip observes: "Managers should beware, though, of the usual danger in pursuing experience curve strategies—overaggressive pricing that destroys not just the competition but the market also." Please explain this statement with particular attention to how misguided pricing destroys both competition and the market.

ACTION ITEM 3.1. DEVELOPING YOUR BUSINESS MODEL

In order to successfully develop your business model, it is important to address its four principal components.

STRATEGY

Do you have a strategy? To make this assessment, take the time to answer the following key questions below.

- What do you do differently from your competitors?
- Do previous investments support/enhance your difference?
- What is your value proposition to customers that they cannot get elsewhere?
- What are your key sources of competitive advantage?
- Which are the 20 percent of your products on which you make 80 percent of your profits?
- Who are your most profitable customers?
- Who is your most serious competitor?
- How would key customers compare your most profitable products against those of your main competitors?
- Who are the two or three possibly new or minor competitors that you are concerned about? Why?

After this assessment, embark on an exercise that demarcates your value proposition. Using Exhibit 3.2 as a guide, do the following:

- Identify the key expectations and requirements of your principal consumer segments.
- Rank each requirement in terms of importance (1 = not important, 9 = very important).
- Identify two to three key competitors.
- Select a representative sample of customers and noncustomers. Have them rank your firm and others in terms of the customer requirements.
- Using Exhibit 3.2 as a guide, calculate your value proposition scores. How do you compare against your competitors? Is the pattern of your firm consistent with your company's "bumper sticker"?

RESOURCES

Using Exhibit 3.4 as a guide, develop a SWOT of your company. Try to identify reasons why you classified items accordingly.

External Analysis

Use the following questions to guide your deliberation.
- What are the major environmental factors and trends affecting your business and marketing position?
- What opportunities/threats do environmental factors and trends present to your position?
- What information will be needed to confirm the trends and to aid in determining courses of action?

- What are the short-term (one year) and longer-term (two to five years) impacts of these trends on the business?
- How certain are you of these factors and trends?

Internal Analysis

Use the following questions to guide your deliberation.

- What positions do you occupy in the minds of the customers, suppliers, buying influences, competitors, employees, and other relevant people?
- What are the critical factors that differentiate you from your competitors?
- What factors will affect your ability to respond to opportunities and threats?
- What are the elements of your Achilles' heel?
- What can you do to increase your strengths and minimize your weaknesses?

Customer Interfaces

Please answer the following questions:

- Who are your key customer groups?
- How do you currently reach them?
- What information do you provide on their behalf?
- In your interactions with them, do they create value for your products and services? Why or why not?

Use Exhibit 3.5 to prepare a customer action plan as a supplement to your business plan.

Value Partnerships

Please answer the following.

- Please identify your partners, suppliers, and network (if you have one).
- How do you add value to your interactions with them?
- How do they add value to your products and services?

Prepare an Action Plan for each of your partners, suppliers, and network.

Source: Questions are drawn from Richard J. Koch and Richard Koch, *Smart Things to Know about Strategy* (Oxford, U.K.: Capstone Publishing Ltd., 1999), pp. 10–11 ; Michel Roberts, *Strategy Pure & Simple II: How Winning Companies Dominate Their Competitors* (New York: McGraw-Hill, 1998), p. 3.

Case-In-Point: Disney Around the World

While Walt Disney, the founder of Walt Disney Studios, did not invent the amusement park, he is well-known for having *reinvented* it. Disney found that most such parks were largely designed for children, but he felt that there should also be a park that parents and children could enjoy together. Inspired by the cartoon and movie characters created by the Walt Disney Studios, Disney created a type of amusement park that came to be known as the "theme park."

Even though all signs pointed to success when Disneyland first opened, Walt Disney said that Disneyland would never be finished as long as there is imagination still alive. In accordance with these words, Disneyland continues to introduce new attractions and stretches the imagination of their engineers, also know as the "imagineers." Creativity and individuality are encouraged to raise employees' sense of importance and interest in their jobs.

Walt Disney Company maintains stringent training standards for its front-line theme park employees, whom they call cast members. Their training puts a heavy emphasis on human relations skills. Janitorial cast members are particularly important because they are often the first ones to have contact with the visitors. They are taught to carry out their responsibility with the goal of creating a pleasant atmosphere for visitors. Park employees are cross-trained and trained by peers. In addition, new employees receive periodic evaluations by their peers. Discussion and feedback sessions are also undertaken regularly. Peer pressure, instead of complex policies, works as the primary control factor. In the early days, theme park management already had very clear-cut priorities, and these priorities served as decision guidelines. For example, safety, courtesy, appearance, and efficiency were the guiding elements.[79] As long as the employees felt that their actions fit expectations based on these elements, they were empowered to make decisions on the spot.

Disney theme parks are complemented by Disney television programs, motion pictures, and merchandise. All of these off-site experiences come together in the theme park tour, during which one can revisit familiar characters.

DISNEYLAND IN ANAHEIM, CALIFORNIA, 1955

Disneyland was opened on July 17, 1955.[80] It was the most publicized amusement park in history. The $8 million investment was promoted as a "kiddieland for adults" and attracted 40,000 visitors the first summer it opened. During the first year of operation, the park averaged 10,000 visitors per day, which was more than the company needed to break even.[81] Typically, the expenses for admission, rides, food, and amusements in Disneyland were about twice as much as other amusement parks. Visitors also said that Disneyland was so large that it was impossible to see the whole park in one day. This was a boon to Disneyland management because it meant the visitors would then return to see the rest of the park. In addition, there were enough exhibits, shows, scenic wonders, and activities that were free of charge to warrant a second visit. Adults appeared to have as much fun in the park as children. They accounted for 75 percent of the rides taken, or about 7.7 rides per visit, while children accounted for 4.4 rides.[82] Disneyland found that many visitors were young adults and couples on a low budget and on a brief vacation. Common complaints concerned long lines waiting for rides because each ride took too few people, excessive commercialism, and sore feet from walking and standing. Even though these complaints persisted, Disneyland remained the most attended amusement park in California. It recorded attendance of 13,360,000 in 2004.[83]

Operating a theme park was a new venture to Walt Disney Studios. Disneyland was an imaginative world where happiness and excitement were delivered and were the only feelings management wanted their visitors to experience. The theme park offers an illusory world to its visitors, and they are willing to pay to live in an artificial environment for a short time.

With its original features and attractions based on Disney Studios productions, Disneyland is an American original. Disney found the formula for success in the theme park business.

World Disney Resort, Orlando, Florida, 1971, 1982, 1989, and 1998

The success of Disneyland in Anaheim was the model for Disney's eastern movement to Florida for the World Disney Resort. The resort was completed in stages: the Magic Kingdom in 1971; the Experimental Prototype Community of Tomorrow, a.k.a. EPCOT, in 1982; the Disney-MGM Studio in 1989; and the Animal Kingdom in 1998. This time, Disney had the space that Anaheim could not offer. It took advantage of the vast land of 28,000 acres near Orlando to expand its tourist services.[84] In addition to the attractions, it offers hotels, golf courses, campgrounds, and shopping villages.

The core competence that Disney developed in the theme park business it developed between 1955 and 1970 was a successful domestic regional transfer from the West Coast to the East. The Magic Kingdom is a replica of Disneyland in California. In Florida, Disney took it one step further and expanded into the hotel and merchandise retailing businesses.

Tokyo Disneyland, 1983, and Tokyo DisneySea, 2001

The first Disney theme park built outside of the United States was Tokyo Disneyland, located on the shores of Tokyo Bay. Tokyo Disneyland has been a success from the beginning. It draws up to 17 million visitors annually. It attracted 300 million visitors in the nineteen years and 208 days after its inauguration, a record that took thirty-four years for Disneyland in California.[85] More significantly, it survived the recession in Japan during which all theme parks suffered losses.

Tokyo Disneyland offers seven themed "lands" and a total of forty-six attractions.[86] Conceptually, it is not different from the theme parks in the United States. Its officials have suggested two factors in this success. First, it is located in an area with a residential population of 30 million. Second, it contains the crucial American culture that appeals to the Asians. The American flavor is what the park visitors go to Tokyo Disneyland for. The Tokyo Disneyland was designed to be a close replica of Disney theme parks in the United States. It is critical to the park's success that the visitors have all-around and complete American experiences when they are in Tokyo Disneyland. Hence, signs, shows, and food are Westernized. Visitors are given as close to authentic an exposure to American culture as possible. Many other theme parks built in Japan by foreign companies naturally adapted to Japanese culture over time. They lost their American personality and hence their attractiveness to Japanese. In contrast, according to Koji Mitzutani, spokesperson for Tokyo Disneyland, "The park was created to bring Disneyland into Japan as intact as possible."[85] Adaptations were made to a very limited degree.

One cannot deny that the Disney theme, cartoon and movie characters, and the know-how of running a theme park all contribute to the park's success. Tokyo Disneyland was a natural and almost effortless transfer of core competence from a domestic to foreign market. Up to that point, Disney was fairly lucky in the challenging international marketplace.

The success of Tokyo Disneyland prompted an expansion project called Tokyo DisneySea.[88] Tokyo DisneySea was opened in September 2001. It features typical Disney attractions and became a popular tourist location. In 2002, it reported an average of one million visitors per month.[89] Since then two new attractions, a roller coaster and a 360-degree vertical loop, debuted in 2005. Another one, Tower of Terror, was added in September 2006. DisneySea's success was aided by Disney's strong brand and the Japanese interest in anything new.[90]

DISNEYLAND PARIS, 1992

Originally known as Euro Disney, Disneyland Paris was an attempt by the Disney company to bring a well-received U.S. icon to its European patrons. Euro Disney was a joint venture with the local government. Unfortunately, the park was troubled from the beginning, financially and otherwise. Disney attributed the financial trouble to the recession and the strong French franc. Also, some said that Disney sowed the seed of failure from the very beginning, when it pitted Spain against France in a competition to be the host country, leaving a bad taste in the mouths of the French and other Europeans.[91] Experienced visitors complain that Disney Paris is merely a stripped-down version of the U.S. parks. As the attractions are few, visitors do not stay in the park and the hotels as long.

The factor that receives the heaviest scrutiny is cultural insensitivity.[92] For example, as a family oriented park, Disney naturally does not sell wine in theme parks. But that decision did not fit with the local culture. Disney now sells wine in Disneyland Paris. To placate visitors, Disney also offered more French food as they heard from visitors that American cornbread and barbecued chicken are not what they prefer. In addition, Disney has been accused by some European of cultural imperialism. The minimal adaptations carried out by the company further suggested this, and appeared to be arrogant to Europeans. In addition, Disneyland Paris later learned that Europeans use travel agents more often than Americans do. Disney had not provided adequate training to the travel agents and this resulted in lost reservations.[93]

The "intact" American experience that works in Japan is not viable in Europe. The know-how of running a theme park, the characters, the food, and the American motifs have not been successful in Europe. In sum, in the move to Paris, the transfer of core competence hit a roadblock. Disney Paris is still $2.71 billion in debt and no viable strategy has yet been announced by Disney officials.[94]

HONG KONG DISNEYLAND RESORT 2005

With its trouble in Europe, Disney has a high financial stake in the Hong Kong Disneyland Resort. The direct transfer of core competence from the United States has been only partially successful. For the Chinese market, was it going to be an "intact" American model or a modified American flavor? Disney tackled this cautiously from the very beginning. As the joint venture partner, the Hong Kong government began the adaptation by consulting a *Feng Shui* master regarding the position of the entrance and walkways in Hong Kong Disneyland. To maximize the opportunity for prosperity, it modified some of the architectural designs to preserve the energy (*chi*) for operation. Other changes, such as putting in a virtual koi pond and harmoniously arranging the five *Feng Shui* elements, were made to accelerate prosperity. To Disney officials, this is a reflection of their respect to the local culture, not to be mistaken as superstition.[95]

More adaptations can be found in the area of food. Disney officials approved the hamburger recipes prepared by local chefs even though they tasted more like meatloaf than what a hamburger would taste like in the United States. Whereas in Tokyo, signs are in English for the total American experience, in Hong Kong, Disney signs use three languages—English, Traditional Chinese, and Simplified Chinese.[96] Some of the backdrops of the rides are designed more like Asian jungles.

Hong Kong Disneyland is trying to find the optimum balance between the Tokyo and Paris models.[97] It is not clear to what extent the Chinese will accept American culture and Disney themes. On one hand, Disney wants to satisfy those who are longing for the high-speed rides and the many well-known cartoon characters. On the other hand, most Chinese do not know any characters beyond Mickey and Minnie. Disney is taking a gradual, subtle educational approach in this aspect. Take the rides as an example. Hong Kong Disney has the tamest rides among those offered in the United States. This may not suit the taste of some adventurous and experienced visitors but could be more than enough for others.

The common complaint about Hong Kong Disney is its size. Most visitors find it too small, without enough attractions. It was also the scene of chaos during the Lunar New Year holidays in February 2006. And there have been several employee issues in the theme park operation. The employees complained of not being respected by the company, having their health needs ignored, being pressed to work overtime, not being allowed to use cell phones even during breaks, female workers not being allowed to wear trousers, not being allowed to drink water until mealtime, and insufficient staff washrooms in the park.[98] Nevertheless, Hong Kong Disney is on track with their attendance expectations. In the first 100 days, it attained its goal of 1 million visitors.[99]

CONCLUSION

International expansion is a primary driver for Disney's theme park growth. Today, there are five Disney theme parks worldwide. But in the second half of 2005, unfavorable news about Disney theme parks came from various directions. The theme park in Orlando offered deeper-than-usual discounts, as much as 20 percent, signifying an aggressive move during a slow season. From Tokyo, the most successful Disney theme park also reported a drop in the number of visitors in two consecutive years, 2004 and 2005.

China is a prime location for future Disney theme park growth. It is said that the next theme park will be constructed in Shanghai in 2010, on the approval of the Chinese State Council. Given the lessons learned in Disneyland Paris, Disney should approach the Shanghai opportunity carefully. The ride to Shanghai has been a bumpy one.[100] Mishandling the situation could cost Disney a market of 1.25 billion people, and it is typically very difficult to rehabilitate a damaged relationship with the Chinese.

Even though both Hong Kong and Shanghai are physically located in China, they have had different historical experiences in recent decades. Hong Kong had ninety-nine years of direct British influence. It has been an international city and an Asian financial center for decades. In contrast, there seems to be much more education required for Shanghai to prepare for 2010. As an initial step, Walt Disney Internet Group has an agreement with Index Corporation to distribute Disney mobile content via China Mobile. The Chinese have access to Disney logos, ring-tones, animated wallpapers, games, etc.[101]

Finally, the Shanghai park will be the sixth park outside the United States and the third park in Asia. Will this cannibalize the successful parks in Tokyo?

CASE DISCUSSION QUESTIONS

1. What is Disney's core competence and distinctive competence?
2. What is Disney's business model? Is this business model transferable?
3. Is the amusement park a global industry? Why or why not?
4. What mistakes has Disney made in its domestic and international operations?
5. What strategy should Disney adopt in Shanghai?

NOTES FOR CHAPTER 3

1. James Bandler, "Ending Era, Kodak Will Stop Selling Most Film Cameras," *Wall Street Journal*, January 14, 2004, p. B1.

2. Alexandra Jardine. "Is this a Kodak?" *Marketing*, October 13, 2004, pp. 28–30.

3. Bruce Upbin, "Picture Perfect at Kodak," *Strategic Direction* 17, no. 2 (February 2001): 7–8; Jennifer Libbin, "APS Still Seeks Perfect Shot in Wake of Digital Imaging," *DSN Retailing Today* 40, no. 6 (March 19, 2001): 21.

4. Laura Heller, "Shared Technologies Give Convention New Dimension," *DSN Retailing Today* 40, no. 3 (February 5, 2001): 69–71; "Kodak Changes the Picture," *Economist.com/Global Agenda*, January 23, 2004, available to subscribers at http://economist.com/agenda/displaystory.cfm?story_id=E1_NPSPPVP.

5. Geoffrey Smith, "This Film Market Just Isn't Developing: Why the APS Film Format Has Fizzled, Despite All the Hype," *BusinessWeek* 3782 (May 13, 2002): 90.

6. Ibid.

7. Ibid.

8. Bandler, "Ending Era, Kodak Will Stop Selling Most Film Cameras," p. B1.

9. John Lippert, "Toyota Plans All Gas-Electric Vehicles by 2012," *Bloomberg News*, October 25, 2002. Available at www.auto.com/industry/iwird25_20021025.htm.

10. This section draws heavily from Spyros G. Makridakis, *Forecasting, Planning and Strategy for the 21st*

Century (New York: The Free Press, 1990), p. 21. Even so, the ideas about strategy are also synthesized from writers of strategy, specifically James B. Quinn, Henry Mintzberg, Igor Ansoff, and Penkaj Ghemawat.

11. Gary Hamel, *Leading the Revolution* (Boston: Harvard Business School Press, 2000), pp. 70–113.

12. Troy Wolverton, "Amazon, Barnes & Noble Settle Patent Suit," *News.com*, March 6, 2002. Available at http://news.com.com/2100–1017–854105.html. Example is adapted from Gary Hamel, *Leading the Revolution*, p. 76.

13. Hamel, *Leading the Revolution*. Here we simply adopt the four components of Hamel's model. In his treatise, Hamel introduces ways in which the four can be further interconnected (see Hamel, pp. 70–113).

14. While there are several treatises relating corporate to military strategy, an excellent summary of the issues is provided by Makridakis, *Forecasting, Planning and Strategy for the 21st Century*, pp. 142–62.

15. B.H. Liddell Hart, *Strategy* (London: Faber & Faber, 1957), p. 354. See Makridakis, *Forecasting, Planning, and Strategy for the 21st Century*, pp. 156–57.

16. Makridakis, *Forecasting, Planning and Strategy for the 21st Century*, p. 147.

17. See Al Ries and Jack Trout, *Marketing Warfare* (New York: McGraw-Hill, 2006), p. 3.

18. This treatment of strategy as a plan, process, position, and perspective is adapted from Henry Mintzberg, "Patterns of Strategy Formulation," *Management Science* 24 (1978): 934–48. Also see Henry Mintzberg, "The Strategy Concept I: Five Ps for Strategy," *California Management Review* 30, no. 1 (1987): 11–24.

19. George Schaeffer of Caterpillar is quoted by Jeffrey A. Rigsby and Greg Greco in *Mastering Strategy: Insights from the World's Greatest Leaders and Thinkers* (New York: McGraw-Hill, 2003), p. 6.

20. L. Schwartz, "'Great' and 'Gretzky' Belong Together," *ESPN.com*, 2004. Available at http://espn.go.com/sportscentury/features/00014218.html.

21. Al Ries and Jack Trout, *Positioning: The Battle for Your Mind* (New York: McGraw-Hill, 2001), p. 5.

22. Ries and Trout, *Marketing Warfare*, p. 38.

23. Manjeet Kripalani, "Asking the Right Questions," *Business Week* (August 22–29, 2005), p. 65.

24. Ries and Trout, *Marketing Warfare*, p. 85.

25. Mintzberg, "The Strategy Concept I," p. 14.

26. Christopher A. Bartlett and Robert W. Lightfoot, "Philips and Matsushita: A Portrait of Two Evolving Companies," Harvard Business School Case No. 9–392–156 (July 22, 1992): 10.

27. Jeffrey A. Krames, *The Jack Welch Lexicon of Leadership* (New York: McGraw-Hill, 2002), p. 51.

28. Mintzberg, "The Strategy Concept I," 11–24.

29. See Michael Roberts, *Stategty Pure & Simple II: How Winning Companies Dominate Their Competitors* (New York: McGraw-Hill, 1998), pp. 93–96.

30. Ibid., p. 237.

31. This example is taken from Roger J. Best, *Market-based Management* (Upper Saddle River, NJ: Prentice Hall, 1997), p. 12.

32. This well-established statistic provided by the American Marketing Association is cited frequently. See Douglas Pruden, Terry G. Vavra, and Ravi Sankar, "Customer Loyalty: The Competitive Edge Beyond Satisfaction," Quirks.com, article number: 19960403 (April 1996), available at www.quirks.com/articles/a1996/19960403.aspx. See also Valarie Zeithami, A. Parasuraman, and Leonard Berry, *Delivering Quality Service* (New York: Free Press, 1990), pp. 1–15.

33. Pruden, Vavra, and Sankar, "Customer Loyalty."

34. Frederick F. Reichheld and W. Earl Sasser, Jr., "Zero Defections: Quality Comes to Services," *Harvard Business Review* 68, no. 5 (1990): 105–11.

35. Manohar U. Kalwani and Narakesari Narayandas, "Long-term Manufacturer-Supplier Relationships: Do They Pay Off for Supplier Firms?" *Journal of Marketing* 59, no. 1 (1995): 1–6.

36. B. Joseph Pine and James Gilmore, *The Experience Economy* (Boston: Harvard Business School Press, 1999), p. 5.

37. Adopted from C.K. Prahalad and Venkat Ramaswamy, *The Future of Competition* (Boston: Harvard Business School Press, 2004), pp. 2–5.

38. Paul Zane Pilzer, *The Wellness Revolution: How to Make a Fortune in the Next Trillion Dollar Industry* (New York: John Wiley & Sons, 2002).

39. Kenichi Ohmae, *The End of the Nation State: The Rise of Regional Economies* (New York: Harper Business, 1995), pp. 27–28.

40. See http://pages.ebay.co.uk/aboutebay/thecompany/companyoverview.html.

41. Rick Aristotle Munarriz, "Alibaba and the IPO Thieves," *The Motley Fool*, October 10, 2007.

42. See SangMyung Lee and Gerardo R. Ungson, "Towards a Theory of Synchronous Technological As-

similation: The Case of Korea's Internet Economy," *Journal of World Business* 43, no. 3 (September 2008), forthcoming. Also see J.Y. Chae, *The Secret of Cyworld: 7 Know-Hows of Cyber King* (Seoul, Korea: JeWoo Media, 2005).

43. "California PERS (B)," Harvard Business School Case No. 9–201–091 (February 5, 2001). Also personal communication with Ted White, director of Corporate Governance, PERS, November 4, 2003.

44. Reichheld and Sasser, Jr., "Zero Defections: Quality Comes to Services," 105–11.

45. Abdullah M. Al-Obaidan and Gerald W. Scully, "The Economic Efficiency of Backward Vertical Integration in the International Petroleum Refining Industry," *Applied Economics* 25, no. 12 (1993): 1529–39.

46. Helen L. Richardson, "What Works Today . . . ," *Logistics Today* 45, no. 6 (2004): 2A–7A.

47. "Nokia Meets the Need for Speed in 3G Network Deliveries," *M2 Presswire Conventry*, March 8, 2001, p. 1. Available at http://press.nokia.com/PR/200103/811633_5.html.

48. Joan Magretta, "The Power of Virtual Integration: An Interview with Dell Computer's Michael Dell," *Harvard Business Review* 76 (2): 73–84.

49. John Hagel III and Marc Singer, *Net Worth* (Boston: Harvard Business School Press, 1999), p. 24.

50. Douglas Aldrich, *Mastering the Digital Marketplace* (New York: John Wiley & Sons, 1998), pp. 97–105.

51. The subject of "co-production" has been covered extensively in the literature on service delivery. See Peter Mills and Gerardo Ungson, "Internal Markets: Substitutes for Hierarchy," *Journal of Service Research*, no. 3 (February, 3, 2001): 252–64. Also see C.K. Prahalad and Venkat Ramaswamy. *The Future of Competition* (Boston: Harvard Business School Press, 2004).

52. Pauliina Hirvonen and Nina Helander, "Towards Joint Value Creation Processes in Professional Services," *TQM Magazine* 13, no. 4 (2001): 281–92.

53. See the following sources for detailed treatises on the three generic strategies: Michael E. Porter, *Industry Analysis and Competitive Behavior* (New York: Free Press, 1980), pp. 34–46; Robert M. Grant, *Contemporary Strategy Analysis* (Malden, MA: Blackwell Publishers, 2002), pp. 167–227; Sharon Oster, *Modern Competitive Analysis* (New York: Oxford University Press, 1999), pp. 119–40.

54. Excerpted from Grant (*Contemporary Strategy Analysis*), p. 246.

55. W. Chan Kim and Renee Mauborgne, *Blue Ocean Strategy* (Boston: Harvard Business School Press, 2005), pp. 3–21.

56. Richard D'Aveni, *Hypercompetition* (New York: Free Press, 1995), p. 14 (quotation on page 119).

57. "How H-P Continues to Grow and Grow," *Fortune*, May 2, 1994, pp. 90–100.

58. Ray Stata, "Organizational Learning—The Key to Management Innovation," *Sloan Management Review* 30, no. 3 (1989): 63–74.

59. John Redding and Ralph Catalanello, *Strategic Readiness: The Making of a Learning Organization* (San Francisco: Jossey Bass, 1994).

60. This mental exercise is well illustrated in Avinash Dixit and Barry J. Nalebuff, *Thinking Strategically: The Competitive Edge in Business, Politics, and Everyday Life* (New York: W.W. Norton & Company, 1991), pp. 85 and 272. Also see Hugh Courtney, "Games Managers Should Play," *The McKinsey Quarterly Anthologies: On Strategy*, no. 3 (2000), pp. 91–96, including his example of building capacity.

61. Courtney, "Games Managers Should Play," p. 48.

62. Ibid.

63. Ibid. Our example is a slightly modified version of Courtney's original example of Chemco versus Matco.

64. The Prisoner's Dilemma was first introduced by Merrill Flood in 1951. It was defined and formalized by Alfred W. Tucker.

65. See the *Stanford Encyclopedia of Philosophy* (Revised August 11, 2003), http://plato.stanmford.edu/entries/prisoner-dilemma. Our discussion of the dynamics of this dilemma draws from F. Heylighen, see http://pespme1.vub.ac.be.

66. B. Greenwald and Judd Kahn, *Competition Demystified: A Radically Simplified Approach to Business Strategy.* (New York: Portfolio Books, 2005), p. 169.

67. This stylized example is adapted from ibid., p. 165.

68. Ibid.

69. Robert Axelrod, *The Evolution of Cooperation* (New York: Basic Books, 1984), pp. 20, 52.

70. This section borrows from Courtney, "Games Managers Should Play," p. 49, notably his headings and core arguments.

71. Greenwald and Kahn, *Competition Demystified*, p. 230.

72. Adam Bradenburger, *Bitter Competition: The Holland Sweetener Company versus Nutrasweet (A)*, Harvard Business School Case No. 9-794-079 (November 13, 2000).

73. See Dixit and Nalebuff, *Thinking Strategically*, pp. 33–34.

74. Adam M. Brandenburger and Barry J. Nalebuff, *Co-opetition: A Revolution Mindset That Combines Competition and Cooperation: The Game Theory Strategy That's Changing the Game of Business* (New York: Doubleday Business, 1997), p. 43.

75. See Dixit and Nalebuff, *Thinking Strategically*, pp. 214–16.

76. Adam Brandenburger and Barry Nalebuff, "The Right Game: Use Game Theory to Shape Strategy," *Harvard Business Review* (July–August 1995), Reprint 95402, pp. 70–71.

77. Greenwald and Kahn, *Competition Demystified*, pp. 4–6. Also see R. Preston McAfee, *Competitive Solutions*, pp. 324–352. There are more advanced treatments of game theory that focus on business decisions, for example, see Pankaj Ghemawat, *Games Businesses Play: Cases and Models* (Boston: Massachusetts Institute of Technology Press, 2000).

78. John Trudel, personal communication.

79. "Disneyland Resort," Managing Service Quality, May 1992, p. 192. Also see Thaddeus Wawro, "Walter Elias Disney," in *Radicals & Visionaries: Entrepreneurs Who Revolutionized the 20th Century* (Irvine, CA: Entrepreneur Press, 2000), pp. 110–13.

80. See www.mickeynews.com/History/, retrieved on April 16, 2006.

81. Don Carle Gillette, "The Disneyland Story," *Barron's National Business and Financial Weekly*, January 23, 1956, pp. 9, 29.

82. Ibid.

83. "Disney's World," *The Globe and Mail* (Toronto), April 30, 2005, p. T–6.

84. Jim McLain, "Disney 'Committed His Whole Heart,'" *Knight Ridder Tribune Business News*, June 12, 2005, p. 1.

85. Yuka Hayashi, "Disney's Magic May Be Fading for Tokyo Theme-Park Operator," *Wall Street Journal*, May 18, 2005, p. 1; "Tokyo Disneyland, DisneySea Cumulative Visitors Top 300 M," Jiji Press English News Services. November 8, 2002, p. 1.

86. Tim O'Brien, "Year in Review 2000: Chart Topper: Tokyo Disneyland atop the Park World Again," *Amusement Business* 112 (51): 88.

87. Ibid.

88. Bruce Orwall and Yumiko Ono, "Disney's New Tokyo Theme Park Carries Little Risk for Company," *Wall Street Journal* (August 31, 2001), p. B6.

89. Tim O'Brien, Natasha Emmons, and Juliana Koranteng, "New Overseas Parks Push Gate Numbers Up," *Amusement Business* 114, 51(2002): 8–12.

90. James Zoltak, "Tokyo DisneySea Plans New Attractions," *Amusement Business* 115, 21(2003): 1.

91. Leslie E. Grayson, Golnar Sheikholeslami, Kunihiko Amano, Thomas Falck, and Virginia Kleinclaus, "Euro Disney or Euro Disaster?" *Darden Business Publishing Case Collection*, September 1995.

92. Laura M. Holson, "Disney Bows to Feng Shui," *The New York Times*, April 25, 2005, p. 1.

93. Beatrice S. Leung, Yim-Yu Wong, and Andre M. Everett, "Hong Kong Disneyland," in Oded Shenkar and Yadong Lou, *International Business*. Hoboken, NJ: John Wiley & Sons, Inc., 2004, pp. 42–53.

94. "Euro Disney Secures Rescue Plan," *CNN International*, September 29, 2004.

95. Holson, "Disney Bows to Feng Shui."

96. Geoffrey A. Fowler, "Disney, in Its Latest Translation: Hong Kong Theme Park Seeks to Balance Appeal to Aficionados and Novices," *Wall Street Journal* (Europe), September 16, 2005, p. A7.

97. Ibid.

98. "Worker Unrest Stirs in the Magic Kingdom," *The Standard*, September 10, 2005. Available at www. hkimail.com.hk/news_detail.asp?we_cat=4&art_id=1054&sid=4493267&con_type=1&d_str=20050910).

99. Alex Armitage, "Hong Kong Park on Target: Attendance Tops 1 Million in the First 100 Days at the Disney Theme Park," *Bloomberg News*, November 24, 2005, p. C1.

100. Geoffrey York, "The Death of Shanghai's Special Status," *The Globe and Mail* (Toronto), December 23, 2006, p. A18.

101. "Index to Distribute Disney Mobile Content via China Mobile," *Business Wire*, October 27, 2003. Available at http://findarticles.com/p/articles/mi_m0EIN/is_2003_Oct_27/ai_109257129.

PART I: THE GLOBAL CONTEXT

1. Global Strategic Management: An Overview

PART II: EXTERNAL / INTERNAL ANALYSIS

2. Analyzing the External Environment
3. Formulating Strategy and Developing a Business Model

PART III: STRATEGIC CHOICE AND POSITIONING

4. Positioning Strategic Choices in a Global Context

PART IV: LEVERAGING COMPETITIVE ADVANTAGE

5. Leveraging Advantage Through Global Marketing
6. Leveraging Advantage Through Global Sourcing
7. Leveraging Advantage Through Strategic Alliances
8. Leveraging Advantage Through Innovation

PART V: IMPLEMENTING THE STRATEGIC PLAN

9. Implementing Strategy Using Structures and Processes
10. Implementing Strategy by Cultivating a Global Mindset
11. Implementing Strategy Using Financial Performance Measures

PART VI: INTEGRATION

12. Integration and Emerging Issues in Global Strategic Management

4 Positioning Strategic Choices in a Global Context

It's not the plan that is important, it's the planning.
—Dr. Graeme Edwards

Even if you are on the right track, you'll get run over if you just sit there.
—Will Rogers

CHAPTER OUTLINE

- Asia's New Customized Dolls
- Why Strategic Positioning Is Important
- Foreign Direct Investment (FDI): A Historical Perspective
- Global and Multidomestic Industries
- A Framework for Global Strategy
- Positioning Strategic Choices in a Global Context

LEARNING OBJECTIVES

- Learn patterns of FDI and limitations as related to strategic choices.
- Understand the differences between a multidomestic and a global industry.
- Understand how to position multilocal and global strategies.
- Learn how strategic objectives, risk, and learning are part of positioning.
- Assess competitive situations characterized by industry globalization and a firm's business model.

ASIA'S NEW CUSTOMIZED DOLLS

Among many budding entrepreneurial prospects in Asia is a new type of doll that has already begun to attract attention and publicity. While many types of dolls adorn the market, these new Nenita dolls are distinguished by their intricate and detailed work, which is in itself a wonder. The creation of designer Patis Tesoro, the dolls represent facets of Filipino life; encased in protective glass cases, they are shown in several tableaux that depict quaint pastoral scenes. All are clad in lush native fabrics of the company's own creation. Interestingly, what motivated this concept of a doll was the desire to use leftover fabrics from her primary product of distinctive, high-end Filipino dress shirts (*barong tagalog*) for which the company has been the market leader in the world.

Each doll takes months to complete from design to execution, with each piece actually the result of a group effort. A minimum of ten people work on each doll: for example, there is the glassmaker, the mold maker, the carpenter who makes the base, the painter who paints the design on the base, and the painter of the face. This does not include the seamstresses, embroiderers, beaders, and other artisans involved in more complicated pieces that need extras, such as flowers and baskets.

One variation of this work—and a highly promising one—is to have dolls resemble specific people, a process that can be facilitated by computer imaging. The target clients will be business firms that will display these dolls in their front offices, replacing or complementing traditional portraits. Imagine visitors entering your office to see an impressive array of dolls in the likeness of the owners and founders adorned in real clothes, instead of the usual wall portraits. Reflecting on the potential international market, Patis Tesoro mused: "It's a very promising market, because dolls would be prominent and will arrest immediate attention. Furthermore, it will add tremendous class and distinction to the client's firm."[1]

WHY STRATEGIC POSITIONING IS IMPORTANT

With a good product and hefty domestic sales, it is tempting to bring one's product to international markets sooner rather than later. But managers and entrepreneurs with a new and innovative product need to develop a sound strategy for going abroad. Yet the competitive context varies for every company, because each one faces uncertainties on a number of fronts. Some firms might not have sufficient resources, technology, and know-how to exploit the international market opportunities needed to sustain a competitive advantage over time. Others might wonder whether the targeted market is sufficiently international, and whether market demand can justify their investment. These uncertainties provide the context for positioning strategies in international markets. Our opening vignette suggests the key questions faced by any company deciding when to sell its product internationally: What is the market potential for the product? How strong is its business model? Should it market this product abroad? If so, what strategy should it undertake?

The analysis of external environments (Chapter 2) and the appraisal of a firm's business model (Chapter 3) provide the basis and impetus for developing and positioning a firm's *strategic choices* in an international context. Historically, this discussion would fall under the rubric of **foreign direct investment** (FDI), defined generally as an investment by one firm in another, occurring across national boundaries, with the intention by the investing firm of obtaining a degree of control over the other

Figure 4.1 **Analyzing the Environment and Strategic Choice and Positioning: Positioning Strategic Choice in a Global Context**

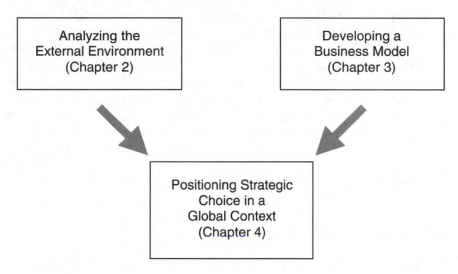

firm's operating activities. Patterns of FDI have provided an important indicator of the growth and diversity of multinational firms, in addition to different centers of production over the world. In this context, FDI also provided the motivating context for firms to go global.

Over time, scholars in strategy shifted attention away from FDI and started to identify characteristics of industries, along with attendant strategic choices, that reflected the impact of globalization. Termed "multidomestic" and "global" industries, they are differentiated by their connectedness: multidomestic consisting of a collection of separate industries, and global consisting of interconnected industries among which integration and coordination are critical. "Multilocal" strategies were hence considered to be most appropriate for multidomestic industries, while "global" strategies were considered to be appropriate for global industries. Even more recently, however, some scholars have provided a more comprehensive picture of strategic choices available to multinational firms, with consideration of strategic objectives and specific sources of competitive advantages, whether they are operating in single or multiple countries.

This chapter builds further on strategic choices as they relate to the pace of globalization and a firm's internal resources. Different combinations of strategic choices are possible when juxtaposing external market considerations, as determined by the overall pace of industry globalization (Chapter 2), against the firm's ability to exploit global markets, as determined by an analysis of its business model (Chapter 3). The integration of the two impels a competitive context that might differ for a firm that already has extensive experience in international competition. All in all, this chapter examines previous discourses on global strategy leading to strategic choices that underpin both the operations of firms that have gone global, and those of firms positioning themselves to do so (Figure 4.1).

FOREIGN DIRECT INVESTMENT: A HISTORICAL PERSPECTIVE

Historically, patterns of foreign direct investment provided the motivational context for firms that had operations overseas. According to the World Trade Organization, "Foreign direct investment (FDI) occurs when an investor based in one country (the home country) acquires an asset in another country (the host country) with the intent to manage that asset."[2] Moreover, two types of FDI are noted: **vertical FDI** occurs when a company invests in the upstream or downstream industry overseas, whereas **horizontal FDI** occurs when a firm invests in its same industry overseas.[3] The opening of a foreign market offers business opportunities for foreign direct investment, which in turn promotes globalization. Taken in this context, changing patterns of FDI are important in discerning the growth of investment, the location of this growth, the development of international production, and the underlying motivation of international strategies.

LIBERALIZED INVESTMENT ENVIRONMENT

Between 1980 and 2000, worldwide FDI exhibited periods of growth and decline (see Exhibits 4.1 through 4.4), which in itself is not unusual as firms increase or decrease their investment based on their perception of changing trends in country growth and market opportunities. Sluggish global economies in early 2000 witnessed a recession in FDI. In addition to reducing investment, some even sold foreign assets to pay off debts.[4] A more penetrating analysis shows that FDI outflows into developing countries grew by over eighteen times, much stronger than the economic growth of the developing world and the total world trade.[5] As seen in Exhibit 4.3, FDI flows in developing countries grew significantly. Industrial countries remained an attractive FDI location up until 2001.

While the United States, the United Kingdom, Germany, France, and Japan have been the main sources of FDI, China has emerged as a leading recipient. China has also begun to engage in its own foreign investment, such as the highly publicized acquisition of IBM's PC division by Lenovo in 2004. Typically, when companies in developing countries such as China expand at this level, they are supported by their governments. There are other fundamental changes and trends in FDI patterns that warrant attention:[6]

- The United States changed from a major FDI outflow nation to a major recipient nation. The United States accounted for 19.4 percent of total FDI inflow from 1991 to 1997, far more than the United Kingdom, which ranked second in the world.
- Japan grew rapidly to become an active player in FDI, going from less than US$1 billion to US$123 billion between 1974 and 1977.
- Investments in the service sector increased from 45 percent to 56 percent of world FDI between 1988 and 1997. Investments in the primary sector fell accordingly.
- In the 1980s, total FDI used to be concentrated in the hands of the United States, the United Kingdom, and Japan. In the late 1990s, the largest ten home countries for FDI outflows account for 80 percent of global FDI outflows.

Exhibit 4.1 **FDI Flows in the World** (US$ millions)

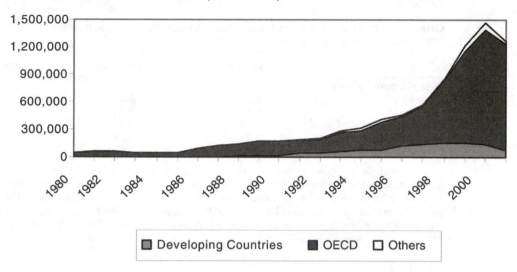

Source: Xiaolun Sun, "Foreign Direct Investment and Economic Development: What Do the States Need to Do?" p. 1. Prepared for the Capacity Development Workshops on Global Forum on Reinventing Government on Globalization, Role of the State and Enabling Environment, sponsored by the United Nations, Marrakech, Morocco, December 10–13, 2002.

Exhibit 4.2 **Trends in Global FDI Flows in the World, 1991–2003** (US$ billions)

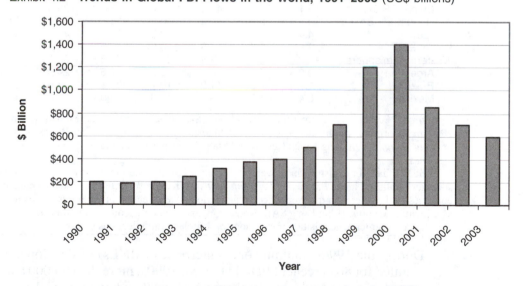

Source: United Nations Conference on Trade and Development (UNCTAD), Prospects for Foreign Direct Investment and the Strategies of Transnational Corporations, 2004–2007 (Geneva: UNCTAD, 2004).

Exhibit 4.3

Growth of Income, Trade, and Investment in Developing Countries
(1980/2000, ratio of two periods)

	1990/1980	2000/1990	2000/1980*
Gross National Income	2.2	1.62	7.48
Exports	2.0	3.03	6.20
Imports	1.8	2.81	5.14
Aggregate resource flows	1.22	2.81	3.77
Private flows	0.92	2.75	5.10
FDI flows	2.48	5.51	18.58

*For example, for Gross Domestic Income, an increase by a factor of 2.2 between 1980 and 1990; this same income increased by a factor of 1.62 between 1990 and 2000; and by a factor of 7.48 between 1980 and 2000.

Source: Xiaolun Sun, "Foreign Direct Investment and Economic Development: What Do the States Need to Do?" Prepared for the Capacity Development Workshops and Global Forum on Reinventing Government on Globalization, Role of the State and Enabling Environment, sponsored by the United Nations, Marrakech, Morocco, December 10–13, 2002, p. 1.

Exhibit 4.4

Regional Allocation of FDI inflows, 1990–2001 (US$ billions)

	1990–94 (Average)	1995	1996	1997	1998	1999	2000	2001
Total	197.7	327.9	327.9	461.4	690.4	1076.6	1489.8	729.2
Industrial countries	137.7	205.5	226.4	272.3	486.5	844.8	1241.5	513.8
Developing countries[a]	59.9	122.4	146.5	189.1	203.9	231.8	248.3	215.4
Africa	2.7	5.0	5.3	9.8	7.5	9.7	7.5	17.7
Asia	33.5	66.33	74.4	82.8	87.0	99.9	7.5	17.7
China (PRC)	16.1	35.8	40.2	44.2	43.8	38.8	38.4	44.2
Hong Kong SAR	n.a	n.a	n.a	n.a	14.8	24.6	61.9[b]	22.8
Europe	4.4	17.4	16.7	22.3	26.6	29.3	30.1	31.2
Middle East	3.6	3.2	5.8	8.0	9.3	4.9	6.5	5.7
Western Hemisphere	15.7	30.5	44.4	66.2	73.5	88.0	76.0	69.5
Argentina	3.0	5.6	6.9	9.2	7.3	24.0	11.7	3.2
Brazil	1.7	4.9	11.2	19.7	31.9	28.6	32.8	22.6
Mexico	5.4	9.5	9.2	12.8	11.9	12.5	14.2	24.7

Source: "Foreign Direct Investment Trends and Statistics," International Monetary Fund, October 28, 2003, p. 10, originally published by Census and Statistics Department, *External Direct Investment Statistics of Hong Kong, 2001* (Hong Kong: Census and Statistics Department, 2003).
Notes:
[a]The FDI data for industrial and developing countries used in this table relate to the balance-of-payments statistics published in the *Balance of Payments Statistics Yearbook* (BOPSY). The coverage of "developing countries" is broader than the World Economic Outlook classification of the group of developing countries as it includes Cyprus, Hong Kong SAR, Korea, Singapore, and the countries in transition.
[b]Reflects merger & acquisition transactions in the telecommunications sector.

- During the 1990s, multinational enterprises (MNEs) of developed nations accounted for 80 percent of FDI. In the late 1990s, more than 60,000 companies invested overseas and many of them were small and medium-sized corporations.
- In the late 1990s, there was a growth of cross-border mergers and acquisitions, which accounted for a significant part of FDI flows.

The above statistics illustrate a growing rise in FDI as well as the sources and destinations of FDI, which have become increasingly diverse. The focus of FDI as a proxy for the operations of the multinational firm is not arbitrary, since this type of larger firm is able to significantly extend national boundaries through its internationalization activities. Nevertheless, the discussion of FDI, while informative and useful, is also limited, for two reasons. First, it is unduly focused on the ownership of assets. Consequently, focusing on FDI alone does not reveal the full extent and diversity of international activities enacted by the multinational firm, some of which relate to exploiting market opportunities, while others are related with the coordination and control of these vast activities, that is, the application of a company's business model. Second, the focus on FDI congeals important information relating to *how* particular strategic choices are made, specifically the consideration of market opportunities and the pace of industry globalization. To arrive at a better understanding of FDI patterns, therefore, we turn to some theories advanced by academicians on why and how firms used FDI as a way of extending their advantages internationally.

REASONS FOR FDI

Why do firms engage in foreign direct investment? In his theory called the **Eclectic Theory of International Production**, now popularly referred to as the *Eclectic Paradigm*, Rutgers management professor John Dunning suggested that three types of advantages motivate firms to invest overseas.[7]

Dunning's Eclectic Paradigm

Ownership-specific advantages. These are the advantages arising from a company's possession; they are not available to competitors. Without the same advantages, competitors face difficulties in extending the same price for their own competing products in foreign countries. Because these advantages tend to be specific and proprietary, they are considered to endow companies with "monopoly" power.[8] Ownership-specific advantages include proprietary knowledge, patents, unique management skills, differentiation, and trade secrets. In most cases, these are knowledge-based assets. Some examples include Coca-Cola's formula, which has been closely guarded for decades; De Beers' control of diamond sources around the world; Nutrasweet's once-held patent for sweeteners; Microsoft and Intel's partnership that bundles microprocessors with operating systems ("Wintelism," see Chapter 2, pp. 68–69, and Box 2.2); and Google's extensive network of research facilities. Put simply, ownership-specific advantages are capabilities, strategic competencies, or assets that provide a company with competitive advantages that are difficult for competitors to duplicate. This is a good reason for such companies to extend their advantage on a worldwide basis.

Internalization-specific advantages. These are the advantages that a company can obtain from internally producing (internalizing) goods and services abroad instead of exporting (externalizing) or licensing (externalizing). Because exporting and licensing rely on the competency of distributors, they limit the global companies' control over the process of product distribution to end-users. Rather than selling outright, or conducting business through arm's-length relationships such as export or licensing, the firm brings in diverse competencies within its own operations. Because some companies are not adept in adopting technology and management know-how, their performance is severely compromised. To ensure the successful transfer of know-how, global companies find it imperative to internalize these critical competencies. One example is an airline's decision to bring into its fold the tasks of marketing and selling tickets through its internal online computerized service, as opposed to the traditional method of securing them from external travel agents. A good example of internationalization activities is CEMEX (Box 4.1).

Location-specific advantages. This refers to advantages a firm obtains by locating part of its production facilities overseas. They could be particular types of resources that are endowed in or unique to those locations. For example, a U.S. diamond company invests in Africa for access to minerals that are not commonly found in other parts of the world. This concept is also extended to intangible assets, such as human capital. Another type of location advantage is access to lower-cost factors such as labor. Many U.S. high-tech companies go to India, Ireland, and Spain for their less-expensive, talented workforces. In a more recent formulation of location-specific advantages, Harvard University professor Michael Porter has positioned countries in terms of "diamonds" or "clusters" with corresponding strengths in demand conditions, factor endowments, strategy, structure and rivalry, and related and supporting industries.[9]

The popularity of Dunning's Eclectic Paradigm stems from its integration of different theories of trade and foreign direct investment, and it ranks among the most extensively researched topics by international business scholars. It is also relatively straightforward.

Beyond Dunning's Eclectic Paradigm

Beyond Dunning's Eclectic Paradigm, there are several factors used by other scholars to explain the FDI activities of global companies. These relate specifically to a firm's response to competitive pressures and its objective of seeking higher levels of efficiency. Specifically, other reasons for firms to engage in FDI include:

Reduce Transportation Costs. Depending on the type of product, some products, due to their weight, incur relatively high transportation costs relative to their monetary value; examples include soft drinks and bottled water, DVDs, CDs, books, and newspapers. It would be impractical and costly to ship these products long distance. In this context, a firm might seriously consider building plants abroad, preferably close to targeted markets, in order to reduce significantly high transportation costs.

Avoid Trade Barriers. Trade barriers were the main reason for FDI during the days when world trade was characterized by protectionism. Toyota's joint venture with General Motors, NUMMI, is an example. Other Japanese automobile firms, such as

Box 4.1

CEMEX: Profile of an Emerging Multinational

We typically believe that successful multinationals emerge and are nurtured in wealthy countries. But this does not mean that companies from relatively poor countries cannot be successful in their quest for global presence and dominance. CEMEX evolved from a small company in a developing country to a big company in many rich nations. What sets CEMEX apart from its less successful counterparts is the adoption of a good and sound business model and its uncanny ability to exploit international markets.

CEMEX is a Mexican cement titan with a well-deserved worldwide reputation. Its CEO, Loranzo Zambrano, is the grandson of the founder of the same name. His strategic vision for growth involves carefully deliberated acquisitions. Since the time the young Mr. Zambrano took leadership, the company has expanded from Mexico to neighboring countries, Europe, Asia, and the United States. In 2006 it acquired the British RMC Group, which was worth $5.8 billion and instantly doubled CEMEX's size. The acquisition of RMC Group made CEMEX a leader in Europe. Before acquiring RMC, CEMEX already operated in many countries on different continents. Because the RMC Group has locations throughout Europe, Asia, the Middle East, and Malaysia, with the acquisition CEMEX instantly owned operations in more than fifty nations, grinding out 7,200 tons of cement per day.

Acquiring the RMC Group also gave CEMEX a broader product mix. Initially, the company was oriented toward plain cement. With the RMC Group's leadership in ready-mix cement, CEMEX became a leader in this category literally overnight. This new expertise brings added leverage since the company has plans for significant to large-scale construction projects to be undertaken in Mexico.

Mr. Zambrano had worked at the company since he was a teenager and had intimate knowledge of its operation and management. Before he took a top management position at CEMEX, he already had eighteen years of experience in the company and the industry. But it was his education at Monterrey Tech and Stanford's MBA program that inspired him to introduce the latest technology and to apply modern management systems to CEMEX. The company is now known for its Northern American way, instead of the Mexican way. In fact, English is its official language.

Mr. Zambrano's "CEMEX way" of management is a highly centralized yet flexible business model. It performs worldwide remote monitoring through an extensive computerized system out of the headquarters in Monterrey. This system operates with fewer work stoppages because CEMEX focuses on essential alarms, and turns off all nonessential alarms that, when activated, only delay the production process. The company believes that this system gives it increased efficiency without compromising safety. A successful turnaround for an acquisition in England, which improved its operating capacity from 70 percent to 93 percent, was attributed to the "CEMEX way."

Mr. Zambrano believes that good management will serve a company well in the long run. His goal is not to run the world's biggest cement company, but the best. But CEMEX may just be both. Unlike many other CEOs, Mr. Zambrano does not occupy a top-floor suite but rather a modest office on the ground floor. Hence, his employees credit him for keeping close contact with the day-to-day operations.

CEMEX's growth-through-acquisition strategy was largely facilitated by the Mexican government's removal of a decade-old trade and investment barrier. The primary task is to wring out continuous efficiencies within the cement empire. In 2006, CEMEX announced an investment of $500 million to increase its production capacity. After all is said and done, the next step for CEMEX would be to expand into India and China. Even so, Mr. Zambrano indicated no intention of rushing into an acquisition in either country because both places are highly complex markets.

(continued)

Box 4.1 *(continued)*

Year	Events
1906	Cementos Hidalgo is founded by Lorenzo Zambrano in northern Mexico
1931	Merges with Cementos Portland Monterrey. Renamed Cementos Mexicanos, or CEMEX
1960s	Builds plants in Ciudad Valles and Torreón
1966	Acquires Cementos Maya. Moves into Mérida
1970s	Acquires more plants in central Mexico. CEMEX becomes a national force
1976	Acquires Cementos Guadalajara and its three plants. Becomes Mexico's top cement maker
1985	Lorenzo Zambrano, the grandson of the founder, becomes CEO
1987	Acquires Cementos Anáhuac
1989	Acquires Mexico's no. 2 cement company, Cementos Tolteca
1992	Acquires Valenciana de Cementos. Acquires Sanson, Spain's largest cement market
1994	Acquires Vecemos, Venezuela's top cement business. Acquires Cemento Bayano of Panama. Adds its own plant in Texas.
1995	Acquires Cementos Nacionales of Dominican Republic
1996	Acquires Cementos Diamante and Samper, both in Colombia
1997	Invests in Rizal Cement Company in the Philippines
1998	Invests in PT Semen Gresik in Indonesia
2000	Acquires the U.S. company Southdown for $2.8 billion and becomes the largest producer in North America
Mid–2002	Acquires Puerto Rican Cement Company
2003	Acquires Mineral Resource Technologies and Dixon-Marquette Cement in the United States
2005	Acquires U.K.-based ready-mix cement giant RMC Group

Sources: Adapted from "The Master Builder: Face Value," *The Economist*, October 15, 2005, p. 88; Hoover's Company Information, Hoover's, Inc., 2006; John Lyons, "Cemex Prowls for Deals in Both China and India; Mexican Cement Maker's Appetite Hasn't Slackened After Gobbling Up RMC," *Wall Street Journal*, January 27, 2006, p. C4; Tony Illia, "U.S. and Mexico Reach Cement Import Deal," *Engineering News-Record*, January 30, 2006, p. 10.

Honda Motors, followed suit. While the intention was to avoid a trade war and the imposition of trade barriers, there were notable benefits to FDI in this context. In the cases of Toyota and Honda, not only was a prolonged trade war averted, but U.S. automobile manufacturers benefited from Japanese-style management know-how. As trade liberalization progressed over time, trade barriers become less of a factor.

Follow Customers and Competitors. A customary belief is that some companies pursue FDI as an offset to their competitors or to follow their customers. For example, Burger King's FDI initiatives were inspired by McDonald's global strategy, while Bridgestone Tire followed Toyota in coming to the United States. The flurry of firms setting operations in China is explained, in large part, to their desire to participate in China's present and future markets, and not be pre-empted by their competitors who might already be in China, or plan to do so in the near future.

Exploit Economies of Scale and Scope. When companies find it possible to realize economies of scale and scope and acquire a cost leadership position, they are also motivated to explore the foreign market. For example, as a sizable customer of coffee beans, Starbucks' buying and bargaining power, as the company expands globally, is stronger than those of coffee bean suppliers. Procter & Gamble, Nike, IKEA, and Toyota are among the many firms that have successfully exploited economies of scale and scope in global operations.

Manage the Life Cycle of the Product. According to **International Product Life Cycle Theory**, when products are standardized and become commodities, companies tend to move the manufacturing of those products to developing economies.[10] In some cases, this is done through foreign direct investment. In other cases, it is done through contracting. While this explanation of FDI might appear to be similar to Dunning's location-specific advantages that is one factor in his Eclectic Paradigm, the international product life cycle theory is broader and considers the nature of the products across different stages, specifically the mature stage.

There are generally two paths for companies to extend their advantages abroad. The first is market expansion where global companies expand overseas to new, untapped markets, or the "blue ocean" market that is not cluttered with competitors (see Chapter 3, p. 118, Box 3.3).[11] A second path is building global dominance through multiple-market penetration, such as the case of Procter & Gamble. Unlike the "blue ocean" strategy, the logic of the second path is to build presence where competitors are or are expected to be. In today's globalizing environment, the motivation to expand overseas results is prompted by competitive dynamics (Chapter 3). Such was the case with Caterpillar Inc.'s tractors, when the upstart Komatsu intruded into the United States, its traditional home market. Caterpillar responded by escalating competition in Komatsu's own market, Japan, as a consequence.[12]

In summary, the reasons for going global, as depicted in the Eclectic Paradigm, the International Product Life Cycle, and different extensions of these theories, can be rather complex and multifaceted. Recently, scholars have begun to unravel this by elaborating on the different configurations of industries—*multidomestic* and *global*—that have been affected by globalization and FDI.[13] This shifts attention from aggregate FDI trade statistics to considerations of strategic choices in an industry context. As will be discussed in detail later in this chapter, different strategies have been positioned against these industry configurations. As an extension of FDI, and as a necessary step toward examining strategic choice, the analysis of different industry configurations and attendant strategies provides a window in order to develop a better understanding of how a firm can position itself in a global context.

GLOBAL AND MULTIDOMESTIC INDUSTRIES

What distinguishes competition in domestic and international settings? While firms still compete in a variety of ways to build advantages, strategic choices tend to be enhanced in international settings because of the differences in the *scope* of the industry in which firms operate. Specifically, Harvard University professor Michael Porter argued, "The pattern of international competition differs markedly from industry to industry. Industries vary along the spectrum from multidomestic to global in their competitive scope."[14]

In a related note, INSEAD business professor Bruce Kogut states: "The fundamental change in thinking about global competition in the 1980s has been a shift in interest over the decision to invest overseas to the strategic value of operating assets in multiple countries."[15]

In a **multidomestic industry**, firms operate in several national markets that are culturally different, but competition in each country is essentially independent of competition in other countries. While globalizing processes are at work (refer to Yip's globalization drivers, chapter 2), these industries have not reached a point of convergence in which coordination is a critical requirement for success. The interactions of the firm's multiple activities across different nations are not sufficiently developed for scale and scope benefits to occur. In essence, a multidomestic industry can be considered to be a collection of national domestic industries. Therefore, a **multilocal strategy**, that is, one focused on developing advantages for each industry or business within a multidomestic context, becomes more appropriate, if not more cost-efficient.

Following World War II, Philips offered products and services in different markets across Europe, each headed by a country manager. While the company's products in the different markets were developed, any potential synergies that might have been derived from integrating their activities were significantly limited in that both markets and infrastructures in these countries had not yet developed in the wake of World War II. As a consequence, each country manager was given considerable autonomy in making decisions, and there was little by way of actual coordination, except for the pooling of corporate funds.[16]

At the other end of the spectrum is the **global industry**, defined by Porter as an industry in which a firm's competitive position in one country is significantly affected by its position in other countries and vice versa. Presumably, in contrast to multidomestic industries, the interactions between the firm's positions in each of these countries can yield scale and scope benefits, if not synergies from sharing resources, costs, or manpower across the different countries. In terms of Yip's globalization drivers, such industries exhibit a high pace of globalization, mandating close coordination and integration as a condition for superior performance. Because the industry is not simply a collection of several domestic businesses, it can be linked in terms of its market, technological, and managerial operations. Fundamentally, this is called a **global strategy**. Matsushita, a direct competitor of Philips, pursued a strategy in which its businesses (light bulbs) were tightly coordinated across the different countries of operation. As a consequence, Matsushita pursued a "global" strategy designed to pool resources, exploit common similarities between them, and attain full benefits of scale and scope economies.[17] Exhibit 4.5 depicts key differences between multidomestic and global industries.

These differences are important because strategic choices will depend on whether the industry configuration is multidomestic or global. The two configurations represent "pure" types at opposite sides of globalization. In a multidomestic industry, strategic emphasis is placed on the demands of the national or local market. This is also called a strategy of "national responsiveness" or a "country-centered strategy." Such a strategy

Exhibit 4.5

Multidomestic and Global Industries: Key Differences

Multidomestic Industries	Global Industries
Competition in each country is essentially independent of competition in other countries.	The firm's competitive position in one country is significantly affected by its position in other countries and vice versa.
The international industry is essentially a collection of national domestic industries.	The industry consists of a series of linked industries in which rivals compete worldwide.
Examples: consumer packaged goods, retailing, consumer finance, and insurance.	Examples: commercial aircraft, color television, automobiles, and digital watches.

Source: Adapted from Michael E. Porter, ed., *Competition in Global Industries* (Boston: Harvard Business School Press, 1986), pp. 46–47.

Exhibit 4.6

Positioning Multilocal and Global Strategies

Recommended Strategies: Multilocal	Recommended Strategies: Global
The firm should manage its international activities as a portfolio.	The firm must integrate its activities on a worldwide basis to capture linkages between countries.
National strategies should enjoy a high degree of autonomy.	The global competitor must view its international activities as an overall system but must still maintain some country perspective.
Country-centered strategy should be determined by competitive conditions in each country. International strategy collapses to a series of domestic strategies.	Focus is on building and exploiting economies of scale and scope on a worldwide basis by way of a standardized product. Emphasis is on leveraging a firm's competitive advantage.

Source: Adapted from Michael E. Porter, ed., *Competition in Global Industries* (Boston: Harvard Business School Press, 1986), pp. 46–47.

was appropriate in conditions characterized by strong national barriers and small market size, such as those that existed following World War II. With increased globalization (see Chapters 1 and 2), however, industries are becoming more global, or linked. This impels firms to coordinate or integrate their activities worldwide, engage in cross-subsidization activities, and develop worldwide supply chains and distribution systems. Such integration can lead to economies of scale and scope and facilitate worldwide marketing campaigns based on developing global brands. Exhibit 4.6 summarizes multilocal and global industries and the strategies that correspond to them.

A FRAMEWORK FOR GLOBAL STRATEGY

While multidomestic and global industries, in association with their corresponding multilocal and global strategies, can be intuitively clear and appealing, other scholars have considered the model to be overly simplistic. The late London Business School strategy professor Sumantra Ghoshal remarked that the concept of a global strategy

Exhibit 4.7

A Framework for Global Strategy

Strategic objectives	Sources of competitive advantage		
	National differences	Scale economies	Scope economies
Achieve efficiency in current operations	Differences in factor costs— wages and cost of capital— can lead to cost advantages	The ability to expand and exploit potential scale economies in each activity across different countries can lead to cost advantages	Sharing of investments and costs across products, markets, and businesses can reduce costs and enhance local responsiveness
Managing risks effectively	Recognition and the management of different types of risks (macroeconomic, competitive, and resource) across countries can reduce cost, improve profits, and leverage a financial position	The ability to distinguish between strategic and operational flexibility can lead to different strategies aimed at reducing future errors	Portfolio diversification and creation of options and side-bets can result in reduced risks with the proper application of financial contingency strategies
Innovate, learn, and adapt	Learning from different cultural environments can lead to a more varied firm's response set and operational flexibility	Experience derived from cost reduction and innovation in one country can be applied to other countries	Sharing and systemic learning across organizational components in different products, markets, or businesses can create synergics

Source: Adapted from Sumantra Ghoshal, "Global Strategy: An Organizing Framework," *Strategic Management Journal* (September 1987), 8 (5): 428.

was confined to how a firm structured the flow of tasks within its worldwide value-adding system.[18] Presumably, the more integrated the flow of tasks appears to be, the more global the strategy. For Ghoshal, this is not only dysfunctional in theory building but overly simplistic in practice. The use of generic strategies (multilocal versus global strategies) tends to obscure the complexities of managing large, worldwide enterprises, and inadvertently fosters false dichotomies in theory building. Moreover, the focus on tasks alone de-emphasizes the internal flows of people, technology, information, and values of the multinational firm. To this end, Ghoshal offered an organizing framework that accounts for the strategic objectives of the firm and the tools that it possesses for achieving them (see Exhibit 4.7).

STRATEGIC OBJECTIVES

The goals of the firm can be classified in terms of three categories: it must achieve *efficiency* in its current operations; it must manage the *risks* that it assumes; and it must develop *learning capabilities* in order to innovate and adapt to future changes. Competitive advantage is attained by recognizing these goals, and by taking appropriate actions to achieve them. Purposeful attention to details and good execution are essential in creating these advantages.

SOURCES OF COMPETITIVE ADVANTAGE

The firm can exploit advantage from a number of key sources: national country differences; scale economies; and scope economies. Each of these sources can be linked to the firm's strategic objectives. Specifically, to the extent that efficiency is desired, the firm can exploit differences in input and output markets, and/or expand potential scale activities within each country, and/or exploit synergies or economies of scope that might be available because of the diversity of its activities and organization. An example is Toyota, which was able to achieve cost efficiencies through global integration of its centralized production and decision making across different subsidiaries and plants around the world.

The firm also faces different types of risks when operating abroad. Some are *macro-organizational risks,* which are associated with cataclysmic events such as wars and natural disasters. Other extraneous effects, such as changes in interest rates and exchange rates, fall into this category. A second set of risks are *political risks*, or adverse consequences arising from changing governmental policies. A third type of risk is *competitive,* arising from competitors' actions and responses. These can range from simple to complex, depending on the form and intensity of competitors' responses in different parts of the world. Finally, a firm also faces *resource risks*: the firm's adopted strategy might require more resources than are available, or resources that it cannot acquire or spare. The strategic task is to consider these different risks jointly in the context of specific decisions. Currency risks, for example, can be accommodated through portfolio diversification or through various hedging mechanisms. Political risks can be reduced by setting up facilities in different countries. The use of supply chains adds operational flexibility that can balance adverse changes in scale integration.

Finally, the firm also needs to adapt and learn from the diversity of environments it faces in different parts of the world. Recall from our discussion of Dunning's Eclectic Paradigm that when a firm is able to internalize diverse activities into its operations successfully, it usually develops a competitive advantage. Typically, internalization results from the ability of the firm to learn from its international operations. For example, Procter and Gamble (P&G) reformulated ingredients in its detergent line to accommodate local tastes. In its new product, Liquid Tide, a new ingredient was introduced to help suspend dirt in the wash water. The impetus for this development came from P&G technicians in Japan and Brussels. Adapting to the local environment is a complex task, one we discuss more fully in Chapter 5 on global marketing. Needless to say, in our complex environment, many believe that learning is perhaps the only source of enduring, sustainable advantage.

Professor Ghoshal's organizing framework builds on earlier formulations about multilocal and global strategies, and how these are positioned against multidomestic and global industries. Its usefulness derives from its comprehensiveness and its depiction of the entire array of a firm's strategic objectives and how it can exploit different sources of competitive advantages. It is not a replacement of existing analytical tools but an important synthesis of them. By positing an array of possible strategic actions, the framework is also helpful in revealing consistencies and contradictions among these decisions, compelling decision makers to consider tradeoffs among them.

Exhibit 4.8   **Framework for Positioning Strategic Choices in a Global Context**

	Multilocal strategy	Incremental strategy
Embryonic	Q1: E-Loan	Q3: Komatsu
Business Model	Core formula strategy	Global strategy
Developed	Q2: Wal-Mart	Q4: Dell
	Slow	Fast
	Pace of Globalization	

In the next section of this chapter, we propose a further elaboration of these frameworks that take into explicit account the pace of globalization and the internal capabilities of the organization. Our framework integrates prior expositions about multilocal and global strategies, strategic goals, and learning. It builds further on the argument that it is no longer a question of whether a firm should globalize or not, but how fast it will do so. There is enough evidence that globalization is pervasive (Chapter 1), and that globalizing processes will continue to impact the operations of any firm. Even so, the response of the firm depends on its ability to exploit international opportunities.

POSITIONING STRATEGIC CHOICES IN A GLOBAL CONTEXT

Because the pace of globalization is different across industries, different sets of strategic options should be considered. We revisit questions posed earlier: What is the market potential for the product? How strong is its business model? Should the company market this product abroad? If so, what strategy should it undertake? To further analyze strategic choices in an international context, two factors should be considered. The first is the strength of a firm's business model, interpreted here as the firm's ability to exploit opportunities in the global market. The second is the pace of industry globalization. By juxtaposing these two factors, we arrive at a framework consisting of four distinct strategic approaches with their own sets of logic and motivation (Exhibit 4.8).

The rationale of this framework is that a firm's strategic choices will depend on its overseas ability to exploit international opportunities, and how fast its products and services targeted for international expansion are globalizing. As we have described in preceding chapters, a company needs to build sufficient competencies in order to meet its aspirations of becoming a global competitor. It must be able to leverage its strengths and competencies from its business model to the international environment in ways that create sustainable advantages. To achieve this, it must build global-scale efficiency in its existing operations and manage diverse country-specific risks and opportunities. Moreover, it has to be able to learn from its international exposure and opportunities and to exploit that learning on a worldwide basis. Writers on global strategy argue that several advantages can be gained if a firm is successfully able to exploit global scope, configuration, and coordination of its international activities.[19]

All these depend on a firm's business model, specifically *its ability to exploit the global market*. Even so, the intent to become a global player will also depend on the pace of industry globalization. A fast-globalizing industry facilitates the attainment of global scale and scope. In contrast, there are fewer opportunities to build scale and create learning opportunities if the firm's industry is multidomestic. George Yip argues that any global strategy must be tailored to match the pace of industry globalization.[20] To pursue this further, we review case studies of companies operating in each of these categories.

MULTILOCAL STRATEGY: E-LOAN

One of the entrepreneurial success stories in the recent years is the emergence of E-LOAN, an online consumer direct lender dedicated to providing borrowers across the credit spectrum with a more enjoyable and affordable way to obtain home purchase, refinance, home equity, and auto loans.[21] By making credit scores freely available to consumers and integrating them with a suite of sophisticated tools, E-LOAN pioneered debt advice—helping consumers proactively manage their debt to lower their overall borrowing costs.

The company was founded by Chris Larsen, a graduate from San Francisco State University and Stanford University. The concept was a result of an earlier experience while applying for a loan. "It was a bad experience," Larson recalls. The process was one-sided with the advantage falling exclusively on the lender. The borrower had hardly any influence at all. The lender knew all the terms that would literally preempt the entire process. The borrower did not have access to his or her credit report, which was the principal basis of the transaction.

With this as the industry standard, it is little wonder that borrowers would enter the process fearing the worst, and that most of them, like Larsen, described the process as being unpleasant and one-sided. In pioneering E-LOAN, Larsen set the following goals and strategies.

Changing the Rules of the Game

E-LOAN's business model sought to transform the traditional loan process by focusing on all three parts of the loan transaction: point of sale, transaction fulfillment, and sale of the loan to the capital markets. At the point of sale, the company reengineered the lending process to lower the cost to consumers, improve their control over the process, and expand the number of loan options compared with what consumers typically find in the offline world. By providing a clear means to compare and contrast loan products, the true cost had become as transparent as possible. The creation of E-LOAN posed as a "disruptive" technology or change within the consumer loan processing industry (more about disruptive technology in Chapter 8).

Bolstering Capital Requirements

With strong capital market relationships, the company was able to underwrite and fund loans as compared to a broker who serves as an intermediary. Control over loan fulfillment facilitated and streamlined the processes, eliminating inefficiencies and saving borrowers time and money. Finally, when selling loans, E-LOAN would sell to the highest bidder in the capital markets. This allowed the company to offer borrowers the lowest rates available from a broad range of loan purchasers in the capital markets. The ability to innovate in all three parts of the loan transaction allowed the company to take full advantage of the enormous opportunities in online consumer lending.

Low-Cost Producer Strategy

The business model started with a focus on being a low-cost producer of loans. As a low-cost provider, the company reduced the expense required to originate and sell a loan. It provided consumers great rates with fast service. As a result, highly satisfied customers helped drive overall consumer adoption and the firm's overall share of the lending market. Increased market share also drove economies of scale that further lowered costs to originate and sell loans.

Product Diversification

The company offered diversified loan products—mortgage, home equity, and auto—in order to reach more potential customers regardless of the interest rate market. It was able to shift resources such as marketing and operations expenses among its products to take advantage of seasonal and cyclical lending opportunities as the mix of business changed in response to interest rate and economic conditions. This product diversification strategy helped reduce volatility and provide more stability through a range of economic cycles. When interest rates are low, consumers are able to refinance higher-interest-rate home and auto loans to lower their overall borrowing costs. When interest rates are higher, consumers still have the need to borrow and are concerned about finding the best loan—perhaps a home equity line of credit—to meet their needs for such uses as home improvement or paying for college education.

Creating a Strong Culture

Larsen believed in building strong core values that would be the bedrock of the company's sustainable advantage. E-LOAN's core values include transparency, privacy, and efficiency. "At times, we think of ourselves as the champions of the right causes," he said, then mildly suggested, "sometimes it's like the fight between good and evil." Other companies might attempt to duplicate E-LOAN's business model, but Larsen believes that this has to be sustained by the same values. Values support the company's mission and being passionate about the values is a key part of E-LOAN's culture. Larsen also believes that if the employees feel that what they do is beneficial to society, they will work for even less compensation.

While E-LOAN holds tremendous potential for worldwide penetration, our framework suggests that two important items be considered: (1) the ability to exploit global markets through its business model, and (2) the globalization potential of the industry. Since E-LOAN is still an upstart, fledgling business in online customized banking,

Exhibit 4.9

Elements of E-LOAN's Business Model

Business model components	Present	Proposed future
Strategy	Provide highly distinctive and personalized credit for broad range of customers in multiple (corporate, individual) markets.	Create deeply loyal pockets of clientele, particularly in the consumer market; limited application to selected Asian countries.
Resources	Relatively small, but close-knit. Highly specialized skills and superior levels of service are needed.	Need to evolve with growing market, but keep proprietary competencies within targeted markets.
Customer interfaces	Personal contacts; word-of-mouth sales; Internet sales.	Deepen personalized relationships; referrals are needed.
Value partnerships	Proprietary partnerships with key agencies.	Need to establish marketing presence in targeted markets.

Exhibit 4.10

Elements of Industry Globalization Potential: Online Loan Processing

Globalization potential drivers	Current context
Market drivers	Embryonic. Markets are limited, and consumer demand in other countries is limited by existing regulatory policies.
Cost drivers	Few economies, which limits distribution on a global scale. However, because fixed costs are low, cost efficiencies can be realized with more market acceptance.
Competitive drivers	Few competitors as yet. Consumer online credit services may be fragmented worldwide.
Government drivers	Some significant regulations relating to consumer privacy and transparency of credit transactions need to be in place.

there is some question whether its business model, while viable, is strong enough to exploit markets on a worldwide basis (see Exhibit 4.9). Moreover, the pace of globalization of this business, as gauged by the position of the globalization drivers, is slower, as other countries require significant regulatory reform, much like the initiatives proposed by Larsen, in order to facilitate electronic transactions (see Exhibit 4.10). Altogether, this fits into Quadrant 1 of the framework displayed in Exhibit 4.8, which proposes use of a multilocal strategy.

In view of this situation, firms like E-LOAN are encouraged to develop a multilocal strategy oriented toward building competitive advantage in their domestic settings in anticipation of future international market expansion. Specific recommendations for pursuing a multilocal strategy include the following:

1. Develop a deep understanding of the domestic market for which a business model works well. Multilocal strategies tend to be *country-centered* with products that respond to local tastes and preferences. As firms develop competencies from repeated experiences, then the niche and focus can be appropriately extended to other countries. On occasion, strategies are built on previous mistakes. Nevertheless, as

Box 4.2

Lessons from Jollibee

From a modest beginning, Jollibee, a multinational firm hailing from the Philippines, has grown to become the number-one fast-food chain in the Philippines, with over 400 stores nationwide. It is also an international brand that has the distinction of being one of the world's most admired companies, garnering favorable ratings from the *Far Eastern Economic Review*. But for whatever accolades are bestowed on Jollibee, perhaps it is most proud to be regarded as the company that bested McDonald's at its own game in Asia.

Since its beginning in 1975, the company has expanded tremendously. The phenomenal growth is attributed to the company's unwavering quest to serve and delight the Filipino customer as well as its ability to anticipate and adapt to the ever-changing market environment. The company's name came from a vision of employees working happily and efficiently, resembling bees in a hive. The company values stressed the five "Fs": friendliness, flavorful food, a fun atmosphere, flexibility in catering to consumer needs, and a focus on families.

However, in its initial expansion into international markets, some disquieting events materialized. Under a new executive, the company expanded into eighteen new stores in eight new national markets in just two years. An international division was created to take charge of these operations. However, this division's dogmatic stance on procedures began to cause strains with Jollibee's domestic operations. The company's incursion into China also exposed a weakness in its otherwise successful business model, raising questions as to whether Jollibee's products, which had been so carefully attuned to the Filipino palate, were attractive to the Chinese local market, that is, both Filipino expatriates in China, as well as the local Chinese. Moreover, more questions arose regarding the effectiveness of adapting from the expatriate customer experience to the local customer base. Not too long later, the company found itself overextended, both financially and operationally.

In its next series of moves, Jollibee redirected its attention to targeting affluent Filipino expatriates living in California, using this as a base to broaden its appeal to the general market. Given the relative size of the Filipino expatriate community in California, this turned out to be a good strategic choice. Although it experienced both success and failures (store closings) in California, it established its competitive presence and is on its way to broadening its appeal beyond its traditional market segments. Meanwhile, Jollibee's operations in the Philippines have solidified with its purchase of another highly successful chain, Chow King, in 2005.

In 1984, Jollibee reached the P500 (pesos*) million sales mark, catapulting the company onto the list of Top 500 Philippine Corporations. In 1987, after barely ten years in business, the company joined the ranks of the Philippines' Top 100 Corporations. It then became the first Philippine fast-food chain to break the P1 billion sales mark in 1989. In 1993, Jollibee became the first food service company to be listed on the Philippine Stock Exchange, thus broadening its capitalization and laying the groundwork for sustained expansion locally and beyond the Philippines.

Sources: Adapted from Christopher Bartlett and Jamie O'Connell, "Jollibee Foods Corporation (A): International Expansion," Harvard Business School Case, 9–399–007 (July 7, 1998); personal interview with Rafael de la Rosa of the Jollibee Manila Main Office, 2003; Jollibee sources at www.jollibee.com.ph/default.htm.

*In 2005, the currency exchange rate averaged US$1.00 = 50P (pesos).

part of its learning trajectory, mistakes can reveal a lot about the company's business model, specifically where it can be strengthened as a guide for its future international forays (see Box 4.2, "Lessons from Jollibee").

2. Develop an appropriate focus for international expansion. In planning for worldwide expansion, multilocal strategies should focus on competitive advantages that

can be readily transferred abroad. It is no longer sufficient to simply be good. In the case of Jollibee, the issue is whether its new recipe for hamburgers that had worked so well in the Philippines can apply to pallets outside this country as well. Firms have to recognize that, to effectively compete abroad, they have to be able to transfer some of their competitive advantages to other places.

3. Manage the strategy as a portfolio. In finessing a multilocal strategy, it is appropriate, if not desirable, to manage the firm's international activities as a *portfolio*. In modern portfolio theory, investors focus on selecting portfolios based on their overall risk–reward characteristics and not merely on compiling portfolios from securities that individually have attractive characteristics. In short, investors should select portfolios not individual securities. Taken in this context, using a multilocal strategy implies selecting markets in which to place products and services that collectively offer the best returns or growth potential. Therefore, a firm can build synergies in managing its different local units to compensate for any lack of extensive international activities.

4. Solidify the business model in the domestic market before taking it abroad. National strategies enjoy a high degree of autonomy. It is important for a firm to focus and to learn as much about local conditions in developing a business model as possible. As many Japanese firms discovered, it was the nurturing of cost-leadership strategies first in Japan that provided an opportunity to successfully leverage advantages abroad. E-LOAN, which has plans to extend operations into China and the Philippines, should carefully examine these local contexts, particularly regulations that are related to consumer privacy, transparency of transactions, and security of electronic online transactions.

In summary, the operating logic behind a multilocal strategy lies in developing and exploiting its business model *before* going international. This means reviewing the key components of one's strategy, resources, customer interface, and value partnerships to ensure that they are mutually supportive and can lead to some degree of distinctiveness. This also means that the firm has to be competitive at the domestic level. As reflected in many of the Japanese firm strategies, it is important that a firm be competitive domestically since it can leverage its strengths abroad and also protect itself from any onslaught from foreign competitors. Only when a firm is sufficiently competitive can it build market presence in international arenas.

Core-Formula Strategy: Wal-Mart

In 2000, Wal-Mart became the biggest retailer in the world, with sales revenues of $165 billion for the year ending January 31, 2000. At the end of 2005, its revenues were a staggering $315 billion, with a return on stockholders' equity of 21.1 percent. Wal-Mart's revenues alone exceed the GDP of all but twenty-one nations.[22] Headquartered in Bentonville, Arkansas, the company operates three types of retailing outlets: discount stores that market soft goods such as clothing and linen, hard goods such as small appliances and hardware, sporting goods, and other items at low prices; Sam's Clubs, large wholesale warehouse clubs featuring purchased memberships that market merchandise displayed in bulk; and supercenters that offer the combined inventories of a Wal-Mart discount store and a full-line supermarket.

Exhibit 4.11

Elements of Wal-Mart's Business Model

Business model components	Present	Defining elements
Strategy	Provide branded products at low cost across specific target markets.	Aggressively pursue scale economies in purchasing by leveraging its 50 percent market share position.
Resources	Focus on large discount stores in small rural towns, creating lower operating costs, avoiding direct competition, and building entry barriers.	Company created a dedicated and committed staff through profit sharing, incentive bonus, and discount stock purchase plans. Wal-Mart also excelled in its management and information system, for which important information was collected.
Customer Interfaces	Distribution centers operated twenty-four hours per day to serve customers.	The company's strategy was to guarantee "everyday low prices" as a way to pull customers in.
Value Partnerships	While not entirely beneficial to all parties, Wal-Mart aggressively promotes captive loyalty by ensuring large sales to its suppliers.	In order to enhance value partnerships, Wal-Mart needs to establish marketing presence in targeted markets outside the United States.

What made Wal-Mart so successful? What elements of its business model make the company so formidable in the face of competitive opposition? Essentially, the winning strategy for Wal-Mart in the United States was based on selling branded products at low cost. Key elements of Wal-Mart's low-cost strategy are presented in Exhibit 4.11 (also see the case at the end of this chapter).

A brief analysis of Wal-Mart's industry reveals that the industry globalization potential is somewhat limited, specifically in terms of the pervasiveness of large-scale megastores for which Wal-Mart is able to implement its store operations strategy and enjoy economies of scale (Exhibit 4.12). Only a handful of countries can accommodate a store as large as Wal-Mart. Moreover, as evidenced by its expansion path in the United States, Wal-Mart faces some considerable opposition from local communities, who cite questionable wages and working conditions, along with an adverse effects on local stores, such as lost sales. How should it extend its global presence and dominance abroad? Because its core strategy and business model are formidable, Wal-Mart is better served by entering the international market through its business model, perhaps through joint ventures, in ways that accommodate some the local requirements. Wal-Mart's international chronology timeline is testimony to this direction.[23]

- 1991: Wal-Mart entered Mexico as a joint venture with Cifra. It currently has 930 retail units.
- 1992: Wal-Mart moved into Puerto Rico by purchasing a local supermarket. It currently has 54 retail units.

Exhibit 4.12

Elements of Industry Globalization Potential: Large Retailing Operations

Globalization potential drivers	Current context
Market drivers	While customers have common basic needs, and while retailing is widespread, the concept of large megastores is new and requires broader market acceptance.
Cost drivers	Economies exist in purchasing and distribution. Continuous improvements, such as the use of management information systems (MIS) and radio frequency communication, continue to lower operating costs.
Competitive drivers	There are large retailers in regions of the world, competing with the help of a wide variety of strategies.
Government drivers	High local competition favors global competitive positioning.

- 1994: Wal-Mart entered Canada by acquiring Woolco. It currently has 290 retail units.
- 1995: Wal-Mart entered Argentina. It currently has 15 units.
- 1996: Wal-Mart entered Brazil. It currently has 297 retail units.
- 1996: Wal-Mart entered China with a 35 percent interest in Trust-Mart. It currently has 185 retail units.
- 1998: Wal-Mart entered Germany by acquiring Wertkauf hypermarkets. It has exited from Germany.
- 1999: Wal-Mart entered South Korea by acquiring Makro stores. It has exited from South Korea.
- 1999: Wal-Mart officially brought in ASDA of Great Britain. It currently has 337 retail units.
- 2002: Wal-Mart purchased a minority interest in the Seiyu Ltd., in Japan. It currently has 393 retail units.
- 2005. Wal-Mart entered Costa Rica. It currently has 143 retail units.
- 2005. Wal-Mart entered El Salvador. It currently has 63 retail units.
- 2005. Wal-Mart entered Guatemala. It currently has 138 retail units.
- 2005. Wal-Mart entered Honduras. It currently has 45 retail units.
- 2005. Wal-Mart entered Nicaragua. It currently has 41 retail units.

Firms with a strong business model that are operating in an international environment that is globalizing, albeit at a slower rate, are advised to pursue a core-formula strategy (Quadrant 2). Some elements of this strategy include:

1. Leverage the core strengths of the business model. The rationale lies in the firm's ability to leverage its strong business model into various international opportunities, while avoiding massive investment in marketing in a setting that is still largely localized. Since the business model is relatively strong, the firm can partially succeed in influencing the local context in order to accommodate integral parts of its core strategy.

2. Emphasize key strengths of the business model in any global application. As firms continue to develop competencies in their home market, their distinctiveness in terms of business model will be further enhanced. In the case of Jollibee, its distinctiveness was its ability to please the Filipino palate in its products and food services. From a small brewery company, Samsung moved into fertilizer, construction, mass communication, and wireless technology to become one of the world's market leaders in communications technology today thanks to its founder Lee Byung-Chull's vision, determination, entrepreneurial zeal, and ability to overcome numerous obstacles that confronted him during Samsung's inception as a company.[24]

3. Be prepared to invest in the targeted market to facilitate the implementation of the business model. Implicit in this strategy is that the firm must be willing to invest and build the necessary infrastructure to support its strategy in the local market. This means mustering resources to influence local governments, if necessary. This entails some degree of cultural sensitivity. For example, when Microsoft's Bill Gates tried to enter China by forcing its highly successful business model, it met with resistance from the Chinese government, which admonished him to study Chinese culture. As soon as supporting infrastructures are in place, the firm can move gradually to a full-scale global strategy.[25]

In summary, the operating logic behind a **core-formula strategy** is for the firm to leverage the strengths and capabilities arising from its business model as its core strategy under conditions in which the pace of industry globalization is slow, that is, when local market conditions might not support a wholesale global strategy. In a slightly different context, this also refers to a company's ability to transplant its business model, its "DNA," to targeted overseas markets. Central to this strategy is for a firm to carefully examine its sources of competitive advantage. If Wal-Mart's advantages lie in management and corporate culture, then there is nothing to prevent it from replicating this elsewhere. If, however, its advantages arising from cost leadership are due to small-town and southern U.S. geographic differentials, then the firm might have difficulty replicating this strategy in other parts of the country, let alone in global markets.[26] As of this writing, it appears that the former is the better explanation. Even so, adapting a strong business model to worldwide markets can be a daunting task. In the case with Wal-Mart, it joined Carrefour in withdrawing from South Korea in May 2006. According to Na Hong Seok, an analyst at Good Morning Shinhan Securities in Seoul, Wal-Mart had failed to read the shopping preferences of South Korean housewives.[27] All in all, a core-formula strategy, while appropriate, still needs to be adapted to local market situations.

INCREMENTAL STRATEGY: KOMATSU LTD.

One of the more intriguing business stories is that of Komatsu Limited, currently the world's second largest earth-moving equipment (EME) company after Caterpillar Inc.[28] Of interest here is how Komatsu managed to challenge Caterpillar so successfully, when more renowned competitors, such as John Deere, International Harvester, and Clark, had failed in the past. Komatsu's story is an excellent illustration of an incremental strategy that contributes to a strong business model while avoiding head-on competition from market leaders until the firm has amassed sufficient strength (Quadrant 3).

Historically, the EME industry has been dominated by Caterpillar. Headquartered in Peoria, Illinois, Caterpillar was the recipient of good fortune and a formidable business strategy, which led to its domination of the industry. The company was fortunate to have been based in the United States, where there was a proliferation of highways, a strong automobile industry, and strong demand from construction and mining—principal users of earth-moving equipment. Moreover, World War II propelled a demand for Caterpillar's equipment from the U.S. Army. After the war, Caterpillar decided to leave behind all of its the bulky equipment (i.e., tractors, excavators, forklifts, etc.) for local use, mostly in Europe, instead of bringing it back to the United States.[29] This led to a favorable foundation for Caterpillar's business model because these products could be used immediately, as well as providing additional advertising for the company. Caterpillar's commanding market share translated into significant volume-based advantages in manufacturing costs. Manufacturing high-end equipment from a central base (Peoria) facilitated quality control and state-of-the-art automated plants. In addition, Caterpillar was able to build a vast array of loyal independent dealers who valued the company's training program and various incentives; this, in turn, led to a rapid delivery of spare parts around the world.

In contrast, Komatsu was an upstart firm in Japan, following in the wake of Caterpillar's market dominance. Established in 1921 as a specialized producer of mining equipment, its basic philosophy was driven by its need to export, and, in the postwar years, Komatsu reoriented itself toward industrial EME. Nonetheless, problems prevailed, such as poor-quality equipment, poorly motivated dealers, and poor service capability; and, despite a strong domestic demand and a tariff-sheltered market, Komatsu remained a rather puny company of $168 million in sales in 1983. A comparative assessment of Caterpillar and Komatsu at the time reinforces the argument that Komatsu lacked a strong business model (see Exhibit 4.13). An abridged summary of industry conditions is provided in Exhibit 4.14.

Unlike Deere and International Harvester, which faced Caterpillar directly and took a beating, Komatsu decided to pursue an entirely different strategy.[30] Roichi Kawai, Komatsu's chief, established two goals that he deemed necessary for survival: the acquisition of the necessary advanced technology from abroad, and the continuous improvement of product quality within the company. Komatsu entered into licensing arrangements with International Harvester and Bucyrus-Erie that led to new technologies and the establishment of the company's own research and development laboratory. Kawai also launched the first of many quality-upgrading programs reflecting the Total Quality Control concept.

Komatsu's incursion into the international setting was aggressive but selective. It first entered Argentina in 1955, followed by fledgling European operations in the mid-1960s, then the penetration, in particular, in the fast-growing industrializing countries in Asia and Latin America. Apart from avoiding head-on competition with Caterpillar, Komatsu was also able to nurture its own core competencies in working

Exhibit 4.13

Comparison Between Caterpillar and Komatsu in 1983

Business model characteristics	Caterpillar Tractor	Komatsu Limited
Strategy	Highly differentiated products supported with low operating costs that enable rapid 48-hour delivery of equipment and spare parts across the world.	Upstart producer of agricultural tractors, bulldozers, tractors, tanks, but a latecomer into EME industry; avoided direct competition with Caterpillar in secondary markets.
Resources	Enormous. Based in Peoria, Illinois, but with extensive distribution and marketing networks all over the world.	Very limited to Japanese operations.
Customer interfaces	Strong and dominant through guaranteed 48-hr. delivery.	Customer complaints about quality and poor service.
Value partnerships	Strong and loyal distributors and market dealers.	Nonexistent.

Exhibit 4.14

Elements of Industry Globalization Potential: Earth-Moving Equipment Industry

Globalization potential drivers	Current context
Market drivers	Industrial customers have common needs, such as the need for reliable equipment and fast turnaround for spare parts.
Cost drivers	Scale and scope economies exist in manufacturing, purchasing, and distribution. Additional cost-reduction benefits arise from centralized manufacturing location.
Competitive drivers	There are large manufacturers in regions of the world, competing in a wide variety of strategies.
Government drivers	Markets in industrial countries face maturity, but enormous demand arising from nonindustrialized countries. Government is a principal buyer in these markets.

with governments in less developed countries (LDCs)—a competence that Caterpillar had yet to develop. The customers in these less developed countries were offered free advice on matters such as site investigation, feasibility studies, planning of projects, selection of machines, training of operators, and so on. In Southeast Asia and Africa, where the payment for imported machines often involved some form of counter-trading, Komatsu used the services of Japanese trading companies. Organizationally, Komatsu motivated its troops by depicting itself as an underdog against the powerful Caterpillar. Only after the company developed high-quality products, deep experience in less developed countries, lower operational costs, and organizational readiness did it enter the United States for a full-fledged battle against Caterpillar. Komatsu utilized an incremental strategy designed to build strength in small pieces, with each piece representing a new pocket of strength, and with greater commitment and escalation of resources after each stage of success. This incremental strategy was organized in terms of product quality, market expansion, and organizational readiness.

Firms face a variety of circumstances when they do not have a strong business model and yet are operating in a fast-globalizing industry. In some cases, the situation results from a new business strategy (an upstart hotel chain that seeks to compete in an otherwise global industry) or simply a new entrant (Korean semiconductor manufacturers seeking to expand overseas). In summary, the operating logic behind an **incremental strategy** is for a firm to build in small steps from a low-cost/low-commitment to a higher-cost/high-commitment mode. Some key elements of this strategy include the following:

1. Avoid head-to-head confrontation with an industry leader with a superior business model. Needless to say, the firm must continue to build competencies in order to strengthen its business model. It is not unusual under such conditions that the firm is placed at a disadvantage compared to market leaders. Therefore, to avoid head-to-head confrontation, firms should locate unserved niches in the world market. In the case of Komatsu, this meant operating in countries that were not serviced by Caterpillar. One can assume that conditions are not as attractive in these places—neither physical nor legal infrastructures are likely to be as developed, and the consumer base might not be ready to accept the company's products. Therefore, patience and fortitude are needed.

2. Continue to build, improve, and refine on a business model. Firms need to build and strengthen their business models, much like E-LOAN. As in that case, strategies should focus on competitive advantages that can be transferred abroad. Firms in this category typically lag behind market leaders. Initial strategies tend to be characterized by flanking that involves building strengths in uncontested areas.[31] Firms must recognize that in order to effectively compete abroad they have to be able to transfer *some* of their competitive advantages to other places. In the case of Komatsu, these include cost efficiencies and a commitment to ever-growing quality.

3. Test the effectiveness of a business model within selected niches. Tactical surprise is an important component of this strategy. Market leaders try to protect their turf domestically and internationally. Thus they are obliged to enter any niche that might prove to be significant at a later time. For firms pursing an incremental strategy, it is important that activities related to building niches be seen as peripheral by the market leaders, discouraging immediate retaliation.

4. Learn from each incremental action. Managers need time to explore the complexities facing their organization, to experiment with options, and to assess the political consequences of various actions. They have to systematically build levels of support and commitment for the firm's core strategy, and develop a clear strategy for learning about local conditions. Finally, managers must create a widely shared consensus for action.

GLOBAL STRATEGY: DELL COMPUTERS

The pursuit of a truly global strategy is an evolving process. Very few firms have attained this level of efficiency. It was once widely acknowledged that Japan's Sony

Exhibit 4.15

Elements of Dell's Business Model

Business model components	Present	Defining elements
Strategy	Deliver superior experience through direct model that customizes product to customers' needs at superior price-performance levels.	Aggressively pursue scale economies in purchasing by forming favorable partnerships.
Resources	Enormous. Through the direct model, Dell is able to reduce total costs and compete aggressively as the industry cost leader.	Dell has lower inventory cost; it does not have to spend enormously on channel partners.
Customer interfaces	Focused on knowledgeable customers who want product stability, high-end performance, and low total lifetime costs.	Despite lower prices, Dell has been able to differentiate itself through other means and maintain customers' willingness to pay.
Value partnerships	Excellent partnerships with customers (e.g., its Premier Pages™ program) and suppliers through "seamless integration."	Close integration also facilitates just-in-time delivery of parts; co-location; reduced number of suppliers.

fit this category, as it had successfully blanketed the world with superior consumer products, along with attendant methods of coordination and control. Nevertheless, Sony's latest mistakes have considerably slowed down this pace, to the point that Samsung is beginning to seriously dislodge Sony from its esteemed market position. While Dell is selected as an example of an *evolving* global strategy, it is by no means secure in this position (Quadrant 4).

Dell computers has been phenomenally successful in its direct business-to-customer model for selling personal computers (PCs), which has proven to be popular in the United States and other countries. Its stated and demonstrated mission is to be "the most successful computer company in the world at delivering the best customer experience in markets we serve," and to "deliver a superior customer experience through a direct, comprehensive customer relationship, cooperative research and development with technology providers, computer service custom built-to-order specifications and service and support programs tailored to customized needs."[32] Despite numerous attempts by erstwhile competitors to imitate the direct model, Dell has prevailed and even built a commanding lead over them, approximated as a 10 to 14 percent price advantage by the end of 1997. A cursory glance at Dell's business model (Exhibit 4.15) reveals numerous strengths. In essence, Dell's model is internally consistent; all elements are supportive of its build-to-order operations, although Dell's competitive advantage is far from secure.[33]

In 1987, Dell ventured out of the United States and started business in the United Kingdom. By 2000, Dell had generated $7.4 billion, about 25 percent of its total revenue outside the United States.[34] With the PC market in the United States maturing, Dell considered international expansion as key to its sustained competitiveness.

Exhibit 4.16

Elements of Industry Globalization Potential: Personal Computers

Globalization potential drivers	Current context
Market drivers	Customers have common needs due to the pervasiveness of the Wintel standard; high potential exists for transferable marketing; and the top 5 companies supply 45.6 percent of global market demand.
Cost drivers	High global scale economies prevail; experience curve is steep and sourcing efficiencies are on a worldwide scale.
Competitive drivers	There are large manufacturers in regions of the world, competing using a wide variety of strategies (North America: Compaq, HP, IBM, Dell; Asia: Toshiba, Sony, Packard Bell/NEC; Europe: Zitech); exports and imports as a percentage of the world market are high.
Government drivers	Tariffs, if existent, are being reduced and eliminated; major governments are volume purchasers of PCs; government-owned competitors are relatively insignificant.

Despite serious caveats by analysts that the direct model would not work as well in other countries, Dell forged ahead. By 2000, Dell had created three regions outside the United States: Americas International (comprising Canada, Mexico, South and Central America), EMEA (Europe, Middle East, and Africa), and Asia Pacific Customer Center/Japan (APCC/Japan) (covering Asia Pacific, Australia, India, and Japan).

Dell started off in Europe, focusing first on the United Kingdom, after which it created a wholly owned subsidiary in Germany. Dell eventually had international operations in fourteen countries and had sold and supported its products in more than 100 additional markets through partnering agreements with technology distributors. Part of improving its business model involved introducing four regional call centers to broaden its scope in servicing a multilingual market. Dell also launched its direct business in Japan and Australia, with support offices in Penang, Sidney, Seoul, and Tokyo. Over the next several years, Dell introduced its direct model to Hong Kong, China, New Zealand, Taiwan, South Korea, and India. In November 1999, Dell opened its Latin America manufacturing, notably in Brazil and Chile. A review of these activities suggests that Dell had initially pursued the core-formula strategy, while nurturing actions that would facilitate the pace of industry globalization (e.g., online direct model). Exhibit 4.16 is an abridged industry analysis of how much the online direct business model has been accepted in Dell's major markets.

Dell's future success in the global scene is perhaps reflected in its move toward China. Analysts had predicted that China would soon become the second largest PC market after the United States, generating revenues of US$25 billion by 2002.[35] In September 1999 Dell ranked number seven in the China PC market; it had ambitions to achieve approximately 10 percent of its global sales and move up to a possible number-two ranking in 2000. If it did so, China would account for 50 percent of Dell's regional sales (East Asia) by 2002. China was fraught with developmental issues that threatened the successful application of the Dell direct model.[36] Staffing was a major problem. Another problem was the bureaucratic red tape involved in securing government contracts. It still appears that Dell's targeted market share might elude the company for a while. In 2004, Dell posted a 7.3 percent share of the Chinese personal computer market, behind Beijing's Lenovo Group Ltd's with 10.9 percent, and U.S. Hewlett Packard Inc.'s share of 10.8 percent. IBM Corp's share was 7.4 percent.[37]

The argument so far is that firms should position themselves in a manner that accounts for the strength of their business model and the pace of industry globalization. A fourth competitive context is when a firm has a well-developed and strong business model and intends to compete in a fast globalizing industry. Globalization increases competition, and industry conditions might propel competitors to offer commodity products that are valued on the basis of lower prices. It is for this reason that a global strategy, one that capitalizes on scale and scope economies as well as on the ability of the firm to effectively integrate its operations, is the most appropriate choice. In most cases, firms might have the scale and scope advantages, but might not have sufficient integration. Moreover, market leaders might already have advantages deriving from scale and scope economies. What is needed is to combine this with some degree of customer differentiation (or captivity) in order to secure full advantages of a global strategy.

In summary, the operating logic behind a global strategy is for a firm to integrate its activities on a worldwide basis to capture linkages between countries. Some key elements of this strategy include:

1. A strong business model and a fast pace of industry globalization. When industry globalization is high and with the ability to exploit the market, a firm can be aggressive in exploiting economies of scale and scope through "standardized" products and services.

2. The integration and coordination of all facets of global operations. The company must also be attentive to issues of coordination and integration arising out of implementing activities of global scale and scope. In addition, conditions tend to be different, giving rise to pressures for some level of localization. Moreover, the strategy must also account for cultural and linguistic similarities and differences. Because there is no such thing as a truly global strategy and because a strategy is constantly evolving; it is important that any strategy be localized to some extent. Finally, a firm should be able to utilize and enhance transferable marketing.

3. Depending on the position a firm takes within its industry, it is essential that the firm build in standardization or mechanisms for enhancing benefits from large scale and scope, as well as local adaptability or mechanisms that facilitate its ability to customize products and services to local circumstances. This has been popularized in the imperative to "think globally, but to act locally." While this might appear to be difficult to implement, some firms have been creative in positioning themselves against this dual need for integration and local adaptation.[38]

In a new book, *Redefining Global Strategy*, Harvard professor Pankaj Ghemawat criticizes positioning approaches that pit economies of scale against the need for local responsiveness and ignore the advantages derived from arbitrage.[39] For Ghemawat, the challenge of any global strategy is not the selection of a multilocal versus a global strategy (both are global strategies), but finding a balance between three strategies (called the AAA Triangle): adaptation, aggregation, and arbitrage.

• *Adaptation:* The objective is to maximize a firm's local relevance by creating units in local markets to become a part of its supply chain. For example, IBM created a number of mini-IBMs in targeted markets that responded well to local demand conditions. Moreover, these units also achieved some economies from an integrated supply delivery. A drawback noted by Ghemawat is that the focus on local adaptation can be myopic and can ignore further economies that can be achieved through integration with continued growth and expansion.

• *Aggregation:* The objective would be to derive economies from aggregating and integrating local operations on a regional and even global scale, such as Tata Consultancy Services' use of global, regional, and nearshore centers to service a broader range of customers. Similarly, Ghemawat notes Procter & Gamble's deployment of global business units (GBUs) to facilitate sales at the regional level.

• *Arbitrage:* The objective is to achieve absolute economies through specialization, either by exploiting a diverse set of countries, or by leveraging organizational vertical relationships. The basis of this strategy stems from exploiting differences in prices, resources, and knowledge across countries in ways that maximize gains while reducing or balancing risks. Ghemawat's example is that Tata previously exported software services to countries with higher labor costs as part of its overall outsourcing strategy.

While firms are occasionally tempted into adapting all three sources, Ghemawat cautions that such an approach is rarely successful. Not only are there enormous resources that are required to successfully implement all three, but that each strategy requires a different mindset, strategic orientation, and managerial skills. Instead, he recommends that every firm examine each strategy in the overall context of its resource base, its historical circumstances, and its future plans for global expansion. Thus, a correct balance between these three strategies is the key to managing differences and leveraging a firm's strategy to global markets. His case studies illustrate how firms might employ one strategy first, and then move on to combine it with another strategy (e.g., IBM's move from an adaptation to an adaptation and aggregation strategy).

Ghemawat's framework is not necessarily an abrogation of the positioning strategy that is the subject matter of this chapter, but a thoughtful critique of any positioning strategy that is excessive, deterministic, and confined to a choice between extremes. The approach to positioning adopted in this chapter is not deterministic, but builds in a contingency analysis, that is, if a firm's business model is relative weak in terms of exploiting an international market, it is prudent to scale back and to first strengthen this business model, regardless of whether the targeted international market is growing rapidly or not. Knowing a firm's position provides some guidelines for what it needs to do by way of the next steps. Moreover, positioning provides insights obtained from a strategic level that can then be applied at the granular level of tactics and operations. Managers who do strategic planning in a global context still face an array of questions that relate to marketing, sourcing, partnership, and innovation activities and decisions. Inclusive in these decisions are issues relating to the appropriate marketing mix, the choice of suppliers, the use of alliances, and the balance of new and older products and services. It is therefore to this end that our next chapters attend to these topics both as a logical extension of positioning, as well as additional venues to improve, strengthen, and leverage an existing business model.

To conclude, strategic choices result from a deliberate and purposeful process that takes into account both industry characteristics and a firm's ability to exploit market opportunities abroad. In the past, patterns of FDI provided a rough indication of a firm's motivation and strategy. More contemporary treatments have directly examined a firm's strategies, its use of resources, and the globalizing elements of its industry. In doing so, a firm's strategic position is better defined. The following chapters will examine in detail how specific capabilities and advantages can be developed to capitalize on international opportunities.

SUMMARY

1. Assessing a firm's business model and analyzing the pace of globalization are key requirements and important antecedents to building a global strategy.
2. Historically, strategic choices were subsumed under the discussion of foreign direct investment. This is defined as an investment by one firm in another, occurring across national boundaries, with the intention of obtaining control over the firm's operating activities.
3. Globalization and foreign direct investment are two forces mutually affecting each other. A liberalized investment environment allows for the rapid growth of foreign direct investment. Consequently, several changes have occurred in recent years: the United States became a major recipient nation; Japan became an active player in FDI; and investments in services grew rapidly.
4. The discussion of FDI, while informative, is limited in that it focuses unduly on the ownership of assets. It does not reveal the full extent of strategic activities and how strategic choices are made.
5. There are three types of advantages that serve as motivations for firms to invest overseas. Ownership-specific advantages refer to the advantages that a company possesses and are not available to competitors, or not available at the same price, in foreign countries. Internalization-specific advantages refer to the advantages that a company can obtain from owning (internalizing) instead of licensing or exporting (externalizing). Location-specific advantages refer to the advantages a firm can enjoy from locating part of its production facilities overseas.

6. Other reasons for FDI include transportation costs, trade barriers, corporate image, following customers and competitors, economies of scale, and the stages of the International Product Life Cycle.

7. There is a difference between multidomestic and global industries. In multidomestic industries, the firm operates in several national markets and competition in each of these markets is independent of the others. Strategic emphasis is placed on the demands of the national or local market. For global industries, a firm's competitive position in one country is significantly affected by its position in other countries. With increased globalization, industries are becoming more linked, which impels firms to coordinate or integrate their activities worldwide. In other words, operations of the same company in global industries are linked from country to country.

8. A framework for global strategy, as suggested by Sumantra Ghoshal, incorporates strategic objectives, sources of competitive advantage, and risks faced by the firm. Collectively, these determine what strategy a firm should pursue.

9. The positioning of strategic choices in a global context involves the consideration of a firm's ability to exploit international opportunities juxtaposed against the pace of industry globalization. This provides a framework for building global strategic competencies. This framework suggests four strategies: the multilocal strategy, the core-formula strategy, the incremental strategy, and the global strategy.

10. The multilocal strategy is for companies that are positioned as more multidomestic than global, and where business models are still developing. Their products and services tend to be multilocal and strategies tend to be country-centered to suit local tastes and preferences. The operating logic behind a multilocal strategy lies in developing and exploiting the firm's business model *before* going international. Only when a firm is sufficiently competitive can it build market presence in the international arenas.

11. Firms with a strong business model that are operating in an international environment that is globalizing, are advised to pursue a core-formula strategy. The operating logic behind this strategy is for the firm to leverage its strengths and capabilities in a low globalization environment.

12. The incremental strategy is recommended for firms that do not have a strong business model and yet are operating in a fast globalizing industry. The operating logic behind an incremental strategy is that the firm should build in small steps from a low-cost/low-commitment to a higher-cost/high-commitment mode.

13. When firms have a well-developed and strong business model and intend to compete in a fast globalizing industry, a global strategy is suitable. This strategy capitalizes on scale and scope economies, as well as the ability of the firm to effectively integrate its operations. The operating logic behind a global strategy is for a firm to integrate its activities on a worldwide basis to capture linkages between countries.

KEY TERMS

Foreign direct investment (FDI)
Vertical FDI
Horizontal FDI
Eclectic Theory of International Production
Ownership-specific advantages
Internalization-specific advantages
Location-specific advantage
International Product Life Cycle

Multidomestic industry
Multilocal strategy
Global industry
Global strategy
Core-formula strategy
Incremental strategy

DISCUSSION QUESTIONS

1. What are the recent trends in worldwide foreign direct investment and their implications for business?
2. According to Dunning's Eclectic Paradigm, what are the three possible advantages for firms that engage in foreign direct investment?
3. What are the reasons to support foreign direct investment that are not captured in Dunning's paradigm?
4. What is a multidomestic industry? What is a global industry? Compare and contrast these two types of industries.
5. Please briefly describe the framework for building global strategic competencies put forth by Sumantra Ghoshal.
6. What is a multilocal strategy and what is the operating logic behind it? How is it applied to the concept of the business model (Chapter 3) and industry globalization potential (Chapter 2)?
7. Discuss the recommendations given in this chapter for implementing the multilocal strategy.
8. What is a core-formula strategy and what is the operating logic behind it? How is it applied to the concept of the business model (Chapter 3) and industry globalization potential (Chapter 2)? Please use examples to illustrate your points.
9. What is an incremental strategy and what is the operating logic behind it? How is it applied to the concept of the business model (Chapter 3) and industry globalization potential (Chapter 2)? Please use examples to illustrate your points.
10. What is a global strategy and what is the operating logic behind it? How is it applied to the concept of the business model (Chapter 3) and industry globalization potential (Chapter 2)? Please use examples to illustrate your points.
11. Based on the dynamic global business environment, which strategy is most likely to be most viable in the near future?

ACTION ITEM 4.1. STRATEGIC CHOICE POSITIONING FOR THREE INDUSTRIES

Use the strategic choice positioning framework to analyze the following industries and companies.

Automobile	Renault-Nissan
	DaimlerChrysler
	Geely
	Honda
	Peugeot
Steel	Nippon
	Nucor
	China Steel
Computer	Toshiba
	Lenovo
	Acer
	Sony
	Apple

1. Analyze the pace of globalization of the industry.
2. Analyze the strength of each company's business model.
3. Identify the most appropriate strategies for each company.

CASE-IN-POINT. STORE WARS: WAL-MART TAKES ON JAPAN

MARTIN FACKLER AND ANN ZIMMERMAN[40]

A year ago, Masaaki Toyoshima made his first-ever visit to the United States—to check out his new nemesis, Wal-Mart Stores, Inc. Wal-Mart had just bought a controlling stake in struggling, debt-heavy Japanese supermarket chain Seiyu, and Toyoshima, an executive at Aeon Co., the parent company of Jusco, Japan's second-largest supermarket chain, wanted to see his new competitor first-hand.

At first he felt relieved. The sprawling Wal-Mart Supercenter that he visited in Atlanta appeared too dark and dirty to succeed in Japan. Then he grew alarmed by the low prices—so cheap he couldn't resist buying a Gillette razor for himself, at half what it costs in Japan. Even before Wal-Mart has mustered much momentum in Japan, the knives are out between Wal-Mart and its Japanese rivals. "Wal-Mart is taking its time to get ready. This is our chance to get a step ahead," says Kenichi Arai, Aeon's spokesman. Aeon and retailers like it are rushing to out–Wal-Mart, the U.S. giant, and revolutionizing Japan's notoriously backward retail system in the process. Competitors are learning from Wal-Mart's strategies, building their own megastores with large areas for parking, pouring millions into computer systems, slashing prices, and even launching a "Made in Japan" campaign to win over Japan's finicky consumers. Retailers have also taken a page from Wal-Mart's book by pressing suppliers to sell to them directly for the first time—a step toward breaking the stranglehold of middlemen over the supply chain.

All that is good news for Japanese shoppers, who would welcome lower prices and more choices after a decade-long economic slump in a country where prices are still among the highest in the world. It could also help invigorate one of Japan's most inefficient industries. But the competition will make it tougher for Wal-Mart to build a Japanese juggernaut.

Despite all the fuss, Wal-Mart has remained slow and methodical in its move into the world's second-largest retail market after the United States. It's carefully remodeling the 416-store Seiyu chain, reducing prices, and tackling cultural hurdles, like trying to figure out how far it can cut costs without alienating Japan's quality-conscious consumers. "We've been criticized for going too slowly," says John Menzer, chief executive of Wal-Mart's international division. "But we have to do it step by step. In three years we'll be fully loaded."

The company needs to avoid the costly mistakes it made when moving too quickly in other countries. In Germany, for example, it immediately overhauled the two chains it bought in 1997, lowering prices before its computerized inventory-monitoring systems were in place. Six years later, operations there were still posting losses. In Japan, Wal-Mart is working on a five-year reorganization plan that includes remodeling stores and putting in a new computerized inventory and distribution infrastructure that will take two more years to complete.

So far, results in Japan have been disappointing. Earlier this month, Seiyu reversed a previous profit forecast for the March–December period to an $83 million loss, blaming the sluggish economy and an unseasonably cool summer that led several retailers recently to slash profit forecasts. Sales at stores open for at least a year are expected to be down 4.5 percent for the first six months, far below the company's expectations.

Japan is one of the world's quirkiest and most difficult retail markets. Foreign retailers like U.S.-based computer maker Gateway, sportswear company Foot Locker, and Burger King have failed here, and even international operators such as U.S.-based Costco Wholesale Corporation, and France's Carrefour S.A. admit their progress in Japan has been slower than anticipated. Japanese customers demand the freshest food and orderly stores. And then there's Japan's complex and expensive distribution system—a labyrinth of wholesalers and transport companies with long-established ties to suppliers, which will only sell to certain wholesalers. They, in turn, sell to other wholesalers, and so on. A product might go through three or more hands before reaching a retailer.

Wal-Mart spent four years studying the market before concluding it needed a local partner. In Seiyu, Japan's fifth-largest supermarket chain, it found an established chain with plentiful, if shabby, stores and a sorry balance sheet. The forty-year-old company had overexpanded in the 1980s, leaving it saddled with debt and starved for cash. Wal-Mart bought a 6 percent stake in Seiyu for $46 million in March 2002, with the option of increasing it to 67 percent by 2007. Last December, it upped its stake to 37 percent.

Wal-Mart executives have drawn up a five-year reorganization plan, but cultural differences are stumping the company early on. Wal-Mart tried to move Seiyu toward its trademark "everyday low prices" strategy while ending weekly sales and dropping its traditional colorful newspaper ads. But it underestimated how diligently many housewives studied these ads to compare prices. It had to resume the sales and the ads when customers dried up.

Wal-Mart and Seiyu executives also admit that customers, and even employees, have had trouble understanding some of Wal-Mart's quirky English terms, like "rollbacks," which describe items with long-term price cuts. "Our biggest challenge is that Japanese people think if it's too cheap, the quality is bad," says Seiyu president Masao Kiuchi. "We have to change those perceptions. The lower price on sashimi doesn't mean it's a few days old, but that we got a better price on it."

Wal-Mart says it will announce plans for new stores in the next few months, possibly including supercenters. But its main focus now is on making existing stores more efficient. Wal-Mart is showing wholesalers and suppliers how to lower their prices by shaving costs and forecasting demand. A new computer system will soon allow manufacturers to track their product sales at Seiyu by item, hour, and gross margin, which would enable them to manufacture and deliver goods more efficiently.

Eventually, it hopes to bypass the network of suppliers and wholesalers. On this front, there's a glimmer of hope. Suppliers have, until now, refused to violate their traditional business relationships. But with the economy weak for so long, suppliers are beginning to break ranks and sell directly to retailers if it means they can earn some extra money.

Wal-Mart has held several meetings with its 400 largest suppliers to discuss buying directly, dangling the prospect that Wal-Mart might carry their products in all its stores worldwide. Since Seiyu lacks its own network of warehouses and trucks, however, Wal-Mart is working with wholesalers for the time being.

Both Wal-Mart and some Japanese competitors are trying to cut labor costs by shifting more workers to part-time, and Wal-Mart plans to eventually tackle salaries. "To improve competition, we have to crack the wage system, move it from senioritybased to merit-based," says Kiuchi.

As Wal-Mart proceeds steadily, Japanese retailers are moving fast. Aeon, with 368 stores and ¥3.1 trillion (US$25.8 billion) in sales last year, is regarded as Japan's most aggressive and innovative big retailer. It's also unabashed about its willingness to copy Wal-Mart. Aeon has sent hundreds of employees like Masaaki Toyoshima to Wal-Marts in the United States, South Korea, and China in recent years to learn from their potential competitor. Toyoshima, Aeon's vice-president of corporate strategy, concedes that Wal-Mart, with $244.5 billion in sales last year, has much deeper pockets. But he reckons his company could match Wal-Mart's low prices by copying the efficiencies of Wal-Mart's single-story supercenters.

The new Jusco stores not only look like Wal-Marts but borrow labor-saving tricks, such as displaying clothes on hangers instead of folded, and having products delivered in boxes that can be put on display without being unpacked. Aeon has opened three supercenters since 2001, and hopes to build twenty-seven more in the next three years.

At one of the Jusco supercenters opened late last year amid rice paddies outside Tenri, a small city an hour from Osaka, shoppers raved about the low prices. Sachiko Hirata, a forty-two-year-old housewife, drove 10 kilometers to the store. "Look at this," she says, holding up a brown T-shirt with the slogan "Non-Conformist." "Here, this costs ¥770. Near my home, it costs ¥2,000."

Aeon won't disclose individual store sales figures, though it says the Tenri supercenter has yet to turn a profit. But its prices are cheaper than those in most Japanese stores. A survey by Goldman Sachs found the store's nongrocery items were 9.4 percent below average prices nationwide. That's on a par with Wal-Mart's best effort so far in Japan, a newly remodeled store in the Yokohama suburb of Futamatagawa.

And Aeon has moved to squeeze out middlemen. It spent six months in 2001 convincing snack food maker Calbee Co. to buy products from it directly, rather than going through wholesalers. Since then, twenty-one more domestic companies have agreed, and Aeon plans to add another twenty by the year's end [2003].

Meanwhile, Ito-Yokado Co., Japan's largest supermarket chain, has no plans to build supercenters because land costs remain too high in Japan. And it says it's skeptical that Japanese consumers will appreciate the emphasis on price and efficiency over service and quality. For instance, Ito-Yokado isn't reducing its store staff because it feels it needs enough employees to keep shelves constantly stocked and checkout queues short. "Ito-Yokado isn't offering everyday low prices. It's offering higher quality," says Yoshinobu Naito, an Ito-Yokado board member.

But Ito-Yokado is adopting at least one strategy from the U.S. retailer. Last year, it launched a "Made in Japan" campaign reminiscent of Wal-Mart's "Buy American" drives. Local items from suits to briefcases to polo shirts have red price tags, to evoke the rising sun on Japan's flag. Ito-Yokado says it sold $171 million worth of the clothes in the first year of the campaign, about 5 percent of its total clothes sales.

Wal-Mart's best effort so far is the four-story Seiyu store in Futamatagawa, which it renovated in June. Newly widened aisles boast taller display fixtures and other Wal-Mart flourishes, like trademark yellow "smiley" faces. Tables are piled with large dog-food bags, jumbo rice sacks, and other fast-moving merchandise. Wal-Mart says sales are up 15 percent since the remodelling.

Still, only about 500 of the store's 50,000 items are being sold at Wal-Mart's rock-bottom rates. Chieko Tan, a ten-year Seiyu veteran who runs a lingerie department, has been trying to boost sales by persuading customers to use shopping carts rather than the baskets Japanese like.

Despite the efforts to change the Futamatagawa store's appearance and service, some customers say they are only mildly impressed. "I think it is easier to find things," says Yuka Nakagone, a twenty-eight-year-old housewife browsing around the food aisles. "But I don't think the items have changed very much."

CASE DISCUSSION QUESTIONS

1. What is Wal-Mart's entry strategy in Japan?
2. Evaluate Wal-Mart's strategy. What are the advantages and disadvantages of waiting?
3. What potential problems might Wal-Mart face in Japan?
4. Who are Wal-Mart's competitors in Japan and what are their strategies to counter Wal-Mart?

NOTES FOR CHAPTER 4

1. Information about Patis Tesoro and Nenita dolls was derived from the following sources: www.shangri-la.com/manila/traders/destination/en/index.aspx-38k; the *Manila Times* Internet Edition on Patis Tesoro, www.manilatimes.net/national/2003/jun/16/life/200306161if1.html-43k—Supplemental.

2. "Trade and Foreign Direct Investment," World Trade Association press release (October 9, 1996), www.wto.org/english/news_e/pres96_e/pr057_e.htm. Retrieved on March 24, 2005. A good discussion of FDI is also provided in UNCTAD. "Trade and Development Report" (United Nations, Geneva, 1996).

3. Peter Dicken, *Global Shift: Reshaping the Global Economic Map in the 21st Century* (New York: Guilford, 2003), pp. 52–54; for a deeper understanding of the context underlying horizontal and vertical FDI, see Joshua Aizenman, and Nancy Marion, "The Merits of Horizontal Versus Vertical FDI in the Presence of Uncertainty," *Journal of International Economics,* vol. 62, no. 1 (January 2004): 125–48.

4. Xiaolun Sun, "Foreign Direct Investment and Economic Development: What Do the States Need to Do?" Prepared for the Capacity Development Workshops on Global Forum on Reinventing Government on Globalization, Role of the State and Enabling Environment, sponsored by the United Nations, Marrakech, Morocco, December 10–13, 2002.

5 Ibid.

6. Saskia Sassen, "New Pattern in Foreign Direct Investment," *The Global City: New York London Tokyo,* 2nd ed. (Princeton, NJ: Princeton University Press, 2001), pp. 37–64.

7. John Dunning, *Multinational Enterprises and the Global Economy* (Boston: Addison-Wesley, 1994).

8. Stephen Hymer, *The International Operations of International Firms: A Study in Direct Investment* (Cambridge: MIT Press, 1976).

9. Michael E. Porter, ed., *Competition in Global Industries* (Boston: Harvard Business School Press, 1986), pp. 18–19.

10. See S. Hirsch, *Location of Industry and International Competitiveness* (Oxford: Clarendon Press, 1967); L.T. Wells, Jr., ed., *The Product Life Cycle and International Trade* (Boston: Harvard Business School, 1972).

11. W. Chan Kim and Rebee Mauborgne, *Blue Ocean Strategy* (Boston: Harvard Business School Press, 2005).

12. Christopher Bartlett, "Komatsu Ltd. Project G's Globalization," Harvard Business School Case (October 3, 1997), Reprint Number 398016.

13. Porter, *Competition in Global Industries*, pp. 17–19. The next section draws from this source.

14. Ibid., p. 17.

15. Bruce Kogut, "Designing Global Strategies and Competitive Value-added Chains," *Sloan Management Review* (Summer 1985): 15–38.

16. Christopher Bartlett, "Philips vs. Matsushita: A New Century, a New Round," Harvard Business School Case Study No. 302049 (September 21, 2001).

17. Ibid.

18. Sumantra Ghoshal, "Global Strategy: An Organizing Framework," *Strategic Management Journal* 8, no. 5 (September 1987): 425–40. The next two sections draw heavily from this source.

19. Michael E. Porter, *The Competitive Advantage of Nations* (New York: Free Press, 1990), p. 19.

20. George Yip, *Global Strategy* (Englewood Cliffs, NJ: Prentice Hall, 1992), pp. 28–60.

21. Based on Gerardo R. Ungson and Yim-Yu Wong, "Chris Larsen of E-LOAN in 2005: A Case Study." San Francisco: San Francisco State University College of Business.

22. See http://www.walmart.com.

23. Material for Wal-Mart, specifically its chronology of international expansion, is taken from Wal-Mart Facts—International Operational Data Sheet—August 2007, http://www.walmartfacts.com/articles/5230.aspx.

24. Gerardo R. Ungson, Richard M. Steers, and Seung-Ho Park, *Korean Enterprise: The Quest for Globalization* (Boston, MA: Harvard Business School Press, 1997), pp. 68–69.

25. Tarun Khanna, "Microsoft in the People's Republic of China—1993 and 2005 Update," Harvard Business School Case Study No. 796072 (September 14, 1995).

26. This line of inquiry was adopted from Bruce Greenwald and Judd Kahn, *Competition Demystified* (New York: Portfolio Books, 2005), pp. 85–99. Readers are encouraged to read the analysis in its entirety.

27. Choe Sang-Hun, "Wal-Mart Selling Stores and Leaving South Korea," *New York Times*, May 23, 2006.

28. Information for Komatsu was synthesized from two sources: Christopher A. Bartlett, "Komatsu: Ryochi Kawai's Leadership," Harvard Business School Case No. 390037 (September 5, 1989); and Christopher A. Bartlett and U. Srinivasa Ragan, "Komatsu Ltd.," Harvard Business School Case No. 385277 (February 6, 1985).

29. Christopher A. Bartlett and U. Srinivasa Ragan, "Caterpillar Tractor Co.," Harvard Business School Case No. 385276 (February 1, 1985), pp. 7–15.

30. Bartlett, "Komatsu: Ryochi Kawai's Leadership," pp. 1–21. This section borrows from this source.

31. Al Ries and Jack Trout, *Marketing Warfare* (New York: McGraw-Hill, 2006), pp. 75–76.

32. From the Dell mission statement in the FAQ section of their website, at www.dell.com/content/topics/global.aspx/corp/investor/en/faqs?c=us&l=en&s=corp#faq8; see also Claire Ellen Weinstein, "Writing your Mission Statement," *Becoming a Strategic Learner,* LASSI Instructional Modules, www.hhpublishing.com/_onlinecourses/study_strategies/BSL/motivation/E5.html.

33. Information about Dell's expansion is drawn from "Dell: Selling Directly, Globally," Case (07/348C), Asia Case Research Centre, The University of Hong Kong (2007), pp. 3–4; and from V. Kasturi Rangan and Marie Bell, "Dell: New Horizons," Harvard Business School Case No. 502022 (May 2002), pp. 15–16. As of this writing, however, all is not that secure for Dell. Already, Hewlett-Packard has begun to make inroads into both desktops and laptops, prompting questions as to whether Dell's Direct Model is that effective in global markets. If anything, this confirms our argument in this section that attaining a truly global strategy is more a continuing process, rather than an accomplished goal. See Bruce Nussbaum, "Dell Needs a New Business Model—Can Michael Dell Provide It?" *BusinessWeek Online* (February 1, 2007), http://www.businessweek.com/innovate/NussbaumOnDesign/archives/2007/02/dell_needs_a_ne.html.

34. "Dell: New Horizons," pp. 15–16.

35. "Dell: Selling Directly," p. 9.

36. Ibid., p. 10.

37. "Dell Aims for Bigger Market Share," *Shanghai News at People's Daily Online*, June 25, 2004, http://english.people.com.cn/200404/22/eng20040422_141254.shtml.

38. Christopher A. Bartlett and Sumantra Ghoshal, *Managing Across Borders: The Transnational Solution* (Boston: Harvard Business School Press, 1998), pp. 13–14.

39. This next section is drawn from Pankaj Ghemawat, *Redefining Global Strategy* (Boston: Harvard Business School Press, 2007).

40. Martin Fackler and Ann Zimmerman, "Store Wars: Wal-Mart Takes on Japan," *Far Eastern Economic Review,* September 25, 2003, pp. 38–41. Used with permission.

PART I: THE GLOBAL CONTEXT

1. Global Strategic Management: An Overview

PART II: EXTERNAL / INTERNAL ANALYSIS

2. Analyzing the External Environment
3. Formulating Strategy and Development a Business Model

PART III: STRATEGIC CHOICE AND POSITIONING

4. Positioning Strategic Choices in a Global Context

PART IV: LEVERAGING COMPETITIVE ADVANTAGE

5. Leveraging Advantage Through Global Marketing
6. Leveraging Advantage Through Global Sourcing
7. Leveraging Advantage Through Strategic Alliances
8. Leveraging Advantage Through Innovation

PART V: IMPLEMENTING THE STRATEGIC PLAN

9. Implementing Strategy Using Structures and Processes
10. Implementing Strategy Through Cultivating a Global Mindset
11. Implementing Strategy Using Financial Performance Measures

PART VI: INTEGRATION

12. Integration and Emerging Issues in Global Strategic Management

5 Leveraging Competitive Advantage Through Global Marketing

You miss 100% of the shots you never take.
—Wayne Gretzky, hockey great

No one has an exclusive on opportunity. When the sun rises it rises for everyone.
—Chinese proverb

CHAPTER OUTLINE

- Microsoft's Cultural Missteps
- The Need for Global Marketing
- Developing a Global Marketing Orientation
- Targeting What Markets to Enter
- How to Enter Target Markets
- When to Enter Target Markets
- Putting the Global Marketing Strategy Together: An Analytical Framework

LEARNING OBJECTIVES

- Understand the differences between a marketing and a production orientation.
- Use political risk assessment as a tool to identify market opportunities.
- Understand the pros and cons of six modes of entry.
- Learn about the correct timing of market entry.
- Synthesize global marketing strategies using an analytical framework (awareness, understanding, compatibility, and pricing).

MICROSOFT'S CULTURAL MISSTEPS

The lack of multicultural savvy can cost companies an enormous amount of money, not to mention unrealized market opportunities. Consider the case of Microsoft, the Redmond, Washington, software behemoth. Its products were banned in some of the world's largest markets because of a number of unintended mistakes:

wrongly colored pixels, a dodgy choice of music, and a bad English-to-Spanish dictionary.[1]

In developing a map of India, Microsoft colored eight of 800,000 pixels a different shade of green as a way of representing the disputed Kashmiri territory. The trouble was that the color had indicated to Indians that Kashmir was not a part of India, resulting in the product being banned in the country, and with Microsoft recalling all 200,000 copies of the offending Windows 95 operating system. In yet another blunder, the company employed the chanting of the Quran as a soundtrack in a computer game—an action denounced by the government of Saudi Arabia. Despite a new version without the chanting, the Saudi government banned the game entirely. Another fiasco was the use of a Spanish-language version of Windows targeted for Latin America markets in which users were asked to select their gender between "not specified," "male," or "bitch."[2]

Clearly none of these mistakes were intended, but they also reflect the lack of cultural sophistication on the part of Microsoft at the time. Its top geopolitical strategist, Tom Edwards, admitted as much. "Some of our employees, however bright they may be, have only a hazy idea about the rest of the world," he said.[3] Staff members are now sent to geography classes to avoid making similar mistakes in the future.

THE NEED FOR GLOBAL MARKETING

Reflecting on the passage above, some might wonder how this could have happened to Microsoft. After all, it is not only the dominant software behemoth, it is also renowned for having the best human talent among global companies. Yet Microsoft is not alone in having faced such predicaments. Well-known companies, such as Coca-Cola, Pepsi, Sony, Wal-Mart, General Motors, Ford Motor Company, and an illustrious list of others have, at one time in their histories, committed similar marketing blunders. Moreover, U.S. firms have not been the only transgressors. Yasuna, a Japanese company based in Shinagawaku that produced beef curry, had to recall its products when it discovered, amid consumer uproar, that it featured a revered Hindu god on its packaging, after learning that the Hindu religion regards cows as sacred. And six Ajinomoto officials were arrested in Indonesia for using pork enzymes in the production of a flavor enhancer sold to the world's most populous Islamic nation.[4]

In previous chapters, we discussed the process of formulating strategic choices. In the following chapters, we will examine how a firm can develop competitive advantages based on these strategic choices through global marketing strategies (this chapter), alliances and partnerships (chapter 6), and sourcing opportunities (Chapter 7). Global marketing builds on the operating logic underlying the selection of a multilocal or a global strategy that relates to cost efficiencies and local adaptation (Figure 5.1). While understanding customer nuances in different countries can be a daunting task, there are numerous benefits for firms that are able to do this effectively. The process of creating global marketing strategies requires a deep understanding of global customer needs, the selection of appropriate markets in which to enter and

Figure 5.1 **Leveraging Strategic Advantage Framework: Global Marketing**

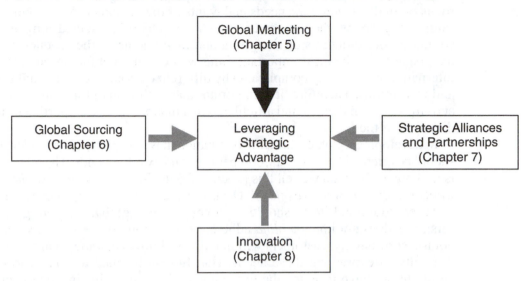

compete, and a marketing strategy that combines the unique needs of each of these markets with the core competencies of the firm.

Specifically, this chapter examines the process of appraising market opportunities and developing global marketing strategies. Marketing, as commonly understood, comprises a set of activities within the enterprise that are designed to plan, price, promote, and distribute products and services to targeted markets. The underlying assumption is that, through effective marketing, *customer value* is created in a profitable manner. Value is defined broadly as the perception by customers that what is delivered satisfies, if not exceeds, their needs and expectations. The decision to market products and services on a global scale raises additional questions: How can the firm adapt its products and services to meet the requirements of the local market, while at the same time sustain the advantages that had worked in its own market? How does the firm decide on which markets to enter, how to enter, and when to enter? What are the templates for developing a new market mix? Such questions are addressed below, and a number of analytical and organizing frameworks are proposed for ease of application.

DEVELOPING A GLOBAL MARKETING ORIENTATION

Marketing management is a relatively modern phenomenon.[5] Prior to World War II, many organizations had adopted a product orientation epitomized in the famous Ford dictum to sell customers a car in "any color they want, as long as it's black." At that time, customers were in such need of basic products that a strong producer mentality prevailed. What the company delivered was good enough for the customer. Eventually this shifted to a selling orientation, with firms focused on hiring and training salesmen to push the product. In the play *Death of a Salesman,* the principal protagonist was constantly anxious about "making the sale."

In the last two decades, this has been replaced by a market orientation, with the focus on understanding the needs and wants of the customer. As one Nike executive said: "For years, we thought of ourselves as a production-oriented company, meaning we put all our emphasis on designing and manufacturing the product. But now we understand that the most important thing we do is market the product."[6] Marketing internationally is vastly complicated by different customs, cultures, languages, laws, and institutions. Therefore, it is important that within any global strategy marketing activities be well defined and articulated in a manner that is supportive of the overall direction of the firm.

In developing a global marketing orientation, it is generally recognized that decisions should be oriented to customers, competition, and external trends. The relevant question is no longer "How do we sell this product?" but *"How are basic customer needs and wants satisfied by what we offer?"* Decisions are grounded in firm market realities.

Three additional items should be noted about a global marketing orientation.[7] First, this does not imply a *blind* adherence to customers' needs and wants. Perhaps not too surprisingly, customers will not always know what they want, or might have difficulty in expressing these needs. Had Edison listened too much to customers, he might not have invented the first commercially available incandescent light, but would have simply made improvements to the candle. With this perspective, a firm should artfully combine the best knowledge about its customers with its own product strengths and competencies. Second, satisfying the customer does not imply sacrificing reasonable profits. On occasion, what a customer articulates might be beyond the capacity of a firm to deliver within manageable costs. Firms that rarely earn sufficient profits are hardly in a position to meet their customers' needs in the long run. Third, and perhaps most important, a global market orientation is not simply a set of tools, but an underlying *philosophy*. As such, deep-seated beliefs should permeate the entire organization. When Nike places its focus on sports and athletes, this is reinforced continuously within the firm's corporate culture. The firm's central headquarters in Beaverton, Oregon, demonstrates this focus: the building walkways adorned with athletes' photos, the extensive jogging tracks, and ultra-modern training facilities are tangible hallmarks of Nike's sports orientation. Exhibit 5.1 presents key differences between a production and a marketing orientation.

DEVELOPING THE GLOBAL MARKETING STRATEGY: TARGETING WHAT MARKETS TO ENTER

Fundamentally, a marketing strategy identifies: (1) the firm's target markets, (2) the firm's products and services that are oriented to these markets, and (3) how sustainable competitive advantages are generated as a result of entering these markets. Economists Nenad Pacek and Daniel Thomiley note that students tend to reduce target markets to either China or India because of its sheer size and growing affluence. "There are 1 billion customers in India who would be potential consumers of television sets . . ." is a common response. Yet these reasons by themselves are hardly sufficient to justify any market entry. After all, most of the 1 billion will be poor and living outside the cash economy at subsistence levels. Moreover, at a lower price range, there might already be a domestic firm supplying the products at prices and costs that cannot

Exhibit 5.1

Key Differences Between a Production Orientation and a Marketing Orientation

Firm	Production orientation	Marketing orientation
American Airlines	We run an airline.	We move people and goods.
Disney	We produce movies and run theme parks.	We provide fantasies and entertainment.
Revlon	We make cosmetics.	We sell hopes and dreams.
Starbucks	We sell high-end coffee.	We provide the ultimate coffee experience.
IBM	We sell and lease computer hardware.	We provide solutions to our clients' needs.

Source: Based on a lecture by Professor Gene Johnson, Marketing Management, University of Rhode Island, MDRG Training, 1999–2000.

be matched by a foreign competitor. As such, the two other issues—the choice of products and services, and whether the firm can sustain an advantage over time—are important to consider in making this difficult decision. This section provides some ways of thinking further on these issues.

POLITICAL/ECONOMIC RISK ANALYSIS

A priority for firms is to rank potential entry markets in terms of their political and economic environment. The global market now stands at 6.6 billion, but with the largest sectors not residing in North America or Western Europe. In fact, the largest sectors in descending order are: Asia (4 billion), Africa (934 million), Europe (730 million), Latin America and the Caribbean (568 million), North America (334 million), and Oceania (34 million). The largest countries in each region are: Asia (China and India), Africa (Nigeria, Egypt), Europe (Russia, Germany), Latin America (Brazil, Mexico), and Oceania (Australia and Papua New Guinea).[8]

It is also well recognized that while many of these countries present excellent market opportunities, they are also beset with uncertainties arising from unstable economies, political regimes, and institutions. While there is more business in supposedly dangerous places, companies that understand real political risks can greatly improve their chances of operating profitably in these markets. Coca-Cola operates in many dangerous places in the world. When the firm was building its bottling plant in Angola, rebel forces were still shooting at government forces. The firm shared the risk of investment with other partners, invested heavily in security, and has since developed a presence in this country.[9]

Some core issues that a firm must recognize at the onset of any political risk assessment include the following five questions.

1. Does the Government Allow a Level Playing Field, or Are Incentives Stacked Against International Competitors?

Governments can discriminate against foreign entrants, both blatantly and subtly. For years, the U.S. government complained about the Japanese (informal) policy of favoring local semiconductor producers, despite alleged lower prices and cost savings afforded by U.S. firms.

But the uneven field does not necessarily result only from governmental policies; it can arise from societal/cultural factors as well. Take the example of Microsoft's aborted entry into South Korea's word-processing market in 1998. Microsoft announced that it would make a $20 million investment in Hangul & Computer Co. Ltd., producer of the Ah Rae Hangul program that had locked up the word-processing market in Korea. In exchange, Hangul & Computer Company would cease development of Ah Rae Hangul to focus on other software programs. Coming in the wake of Asia's financial crisis, Microsoft guessed correctly that Hangul's assets were undervalued. What Microsoft underestimated was the patriotic feelings in the aftermath of the crisis that left the country humiliated and apprehensive about foreign investment. Outraged Koreans branded Microsoft as a colonialist. In the face of public outcry, Hangul & Computer Co. terminated the deal with Microsoft and accepted a smaller counteroffer from Korean venture capitalists.[10]

2. Are Institutions Supportive of Intellectual Property Rights?

Without question, there is major concern over the theft of intellectual property, more popularly known as piracy. A subtle form of governmental protection is the sloppy application of property rights. In the past, U.S. critics have criticized China, Korea, and Vietnam for such actions, although recently these countries have stepped up their efforts at enforcing the rules. Foreign pharmaceutical companies operating in Slovenia have complained that local companies could steal and copy their formulas without regard for the consequences because of the lack of enforcement of property rights by the government.[11]

In extreme cases, governments have been accused of supporting the theft of intellectual property. The music industry association, IFPI (International Federation of the Phonographic Industry) took issue with the Ukrainian government's provision of a factory space for the production of pirated music.[12] For some time, cultural purists in China justified their use of Western products, claiming that as "innovations" these were not protected by intellectual property rights, and as a consequence, had to be "shared" for the benefit of mankind.

Such examples present any market entrant with problems, particularly if their products and services are easily imitated. Master Foods found counterfeiters even had bar codes on the packaging.[13] Intellectual property theft not only increases the victim's cost, but also entails much more effort at monitoring the market for proper enforcement.

3. What Is the Risk Involved in Dealing with Autocratic Regimes, or People with Tremendous Power?

Some firms prefer to deal with autocratic regimes because they believe that the regime's decisions can be relied upon with reasonable certainty. Yet risks abound. When Ferdinand Marcos assumed the presidency of the Philippines in 1965, he was considered to hold great promise. Throughout his oppressive regime, however, he systematically built power, neutralized his opposition, and allegedly siphoned the country's wealth to himself and his close partners.[14] But because he was a staunch anticommunist and was willing to support many of the U.S. foreign policies in the region, he was ably supported—politically and financially—by the United States. After his sudden departure from office, prompted largely by "people power," or the revolution of the masses, those foreign firms that had had extensive business with him began to unravel. The Securities and Exchange Commission filed a complaint against GTE citing payoffs of $4.5 million to well-placed Filipinos. Other companies accused of making illegal payments included McDonnell Douglas, ITT, Ford, and, in a highly publicized case, Westinghouse.

Firms that conduct business with autocrats do so at their peril. Regimes change, and so do historical circumstances. Moreover, the evil wrought by dictators can catch up with them. In current times, where new standards for "political correctness" and "transparency" have evolved, firms can also risk their reputation when it is disclosed that they offered bribes to autocrats as a cost of doing business.

4. Is the Government Stable and Efficient—Both Politically and Economically?

In contrast to the certainties coming from stable democracies or even autocratic regimes are the uncertainties of unstable governments. Such governments are also economically inefficient. This impinges on the local economy and diminishes prospects for growth. Despite great resources, Mexico has had a history of economic crises. Its 1994 financial crisis led to the so-called "Tequila effect," in which the sudden devaluation of the Mexican peso created turbulence around the world, with the hardest hit in Latin America, notably Argentina, Brazil and Columbia.

Investors know only too well the hazards of investing in unstable countries. U.S. traders in Mexico felt the pain of losing an astonishing half of their investment value in 1995. Fraport AG, a German investor and partner in Manila's heralded new high-technology international airport addition, experienced the same pain when the Philippine government of President Gloria Arroyo refused to honor financial commitments made by her predecessor because of alleged favoritism and kickbacks (see Box 5.1).

5. What Are the Risks Imposed by Government Appropriation?

Government seizure of plants and facilities has been a traditional risk for investors in foreign countries, particularly those operating in highly unstable governments. When the shah of Iran was deposed, U.S. firms that had so intimately worked with his government found themselves in dire straits. Many U.S. oil firms participated in Iran's oil-driven boom, as Iran was once considered to be among the world's hottest markets. With the onset of the new Khomeini regime, U.S. investments in Iran were promptly confiscated, resulting in more than $4 billion in losses. This accentuated the role of the political risk insurance industry, which had insured businesses against threats such as war, rebellion, and government seizure of as-

---

Box 5.1

Political Risk: The Case of Fraport AG and Piatco

Nothing could have adequately prepared the German state firm Fraport AG for the problems it faced in a project developed with its partner, the Philippine International Air Terminals Company (Piatco). Fraport AG and Piatco constructed, and would have operated, Terminal 3 of the Ninoy Aquino International. The deal with Piatco was negotiated during President Fidel Ramos's administration and the contract was completed by his successor, President Joseph Estrada.

The $650 million terminal was mothballed in late 2002 when President Gloria Arroyo revoked the "build-operate-transfer" contract with the government on the grounds that her predecessor, President Joseph Estrada, had illegally renegotiated certain terms. The Supreme Court nullified the amended and restated contracts with Piatco for being onerous and grossly disadvantageous to the government. Fraport and Piatco resorted to international arbitration for reimbursement of their investments, claiming that Terminal 3 had already cost them $650 million, although their Japanese airport contractor, Takenaka Corporation, claimed that construction costs only totaled $290 million.

These events have set off alarms on both sides of the question. Proponents of the project and Fraport regard the takeover of the terminal as a blatant breach of the law. Fraport has sought arbitration outside the country. Piatco and its Asian shareholders had earlier gone to Singapore for arbitration apart from the legal process ongoing in Philippine courts. As a German corporation, Fraport argued for fair compensation under the German-Philippine Investment Guarantee Treaty, especially in the case of expropriation. Still other supporters of Fraport maintain that this case sends signals to future investors in the Philippines that the government cannot uphold the sanctity of contracts. Specifically, the Philippine courts can invoke the issue of national interest to pave the way for a government takeover.

Opponents of the project argue that the Piatco case should serve a stern notice to everybody, especially foreign investors, that they should not trifle with Philippine laws. Businesses, they warn, must abide by legal processes, whatever they think of the courts, and not resort to bribery and corruption to clear away obstacles in their quest for profits.

In 2005, Manila Hotel signed an agreement with Fraport for the latter's entire equity. With a 60–40 interest in Piatco by Manila Hotel, and barring future complications, the much-awaited opening of the ultra-modern Terminal 3 with a capacity of 13 million passengers per year is scheduled for the near future.

The Fraport-Piatco case is a prime example of the risks confronting foreign investors in any country. The project was already 90 percent complete when the government rescinded the contract in late 2002 over allegations that the deal violated Philippine laws. Negotiations on compensating Piatco lasted for almost two years but failed to yield agreement. All in all, the case serves as another reminder to managers to seriously consider all risks attendant in operating business abroad.

Sources: Amando Dornila, "Piatco's Greed," INQ7.net (May 9, 2003), available at www.inq7.net/opi/2003/may/09/opi_amdoronila-1.htm; "Piatco Timeline," *Manila Times* (December 21, 2005), available at www.manilatimes.net/national/2005/dec/21/yehey/top_stories/20051221top3.html; Cyril Relegado, "The Piatco Fiasco," *The News Today* Online Edition, www.thenewstoday.info/20050215/columns2.htm; "Manila Hotel Corp Acquires Piatco Stake from Fraport—Report," *Forbes* (August 29, 2005), available at www.forbes.com/home/feeds/afx/2005/08/29/afx2195595.html.

---

sets. Overseas Private Investment Corporation (OPIC), which had insured U.S. firms, saw its $1 billion business in 1970 balloon to $4 billion in 1983.[15] While this threat was more salient in previous years, it is considered to be much less so in today's environment, although Russia and former states of the Soviet Union are still regarded as risks.

Exhibit 5.2

Political Risk: Rankings and Dimensions

Dimensions:
A—Government stability (12)
B—Socioeconomic conditions (12)
C—Investment profile (12)
D—Internal conflict (12)
E—External conflict (12)
F—Corruption (6)

G—Military in politics (6)
H—Religious tensions (6)
I—Law and order (6)
J—Ethnic tensions (6)
K—Democratic accountability (6)
L—Bureaucratic quality (4)

The following countries have the highest political risk based on the dimensions above:

Country	A	B	C	D	E	F	G	H	I	J	K	L	Total
Iraq	8.5	0.5	7.0	4.0	7.0	1.0	0.0	2.5	1.5	2.5	0.5	0.0	35.0
Congo, Dem	9.0	1.0	6.0	7.0	7.0	1.0	0.0	4.0	1.0	1.0	1.0	0.0	38.0
Cote d'Ivoir	6.5	2.0	5.5	7.5	9.0	2.0	1.0	2.0	2.5	2.0	2.0	0.0	42.0
Nigeria	7.5	1.5	4.5	7.5	10.0	1.0	2.0	2.0	1.5	2.0	3.0	1.0	43.5
Haiti	8.0	0.0	5.5	8.5	7.0	2.5	0.0	6.0	2.5	5.0	0.0	0.0	45.0
Zimbabwe	7.5	1.0	1.5	8.0	9.0	0.0	3.0	5.0	3.0	4.0	1.0	2.0	45.0
Myanmar	9.0	4.0	2.5	8.0	8.5	1.0	0.0	6.0	3.0	3.0	0.0	1.0	46.0
Liberia	8.5	1.0	5.0	8.5	8.0	2.5	3.0	4.0	2.0	3.0	1.0	0.0	46.5
Pakistan	9.5	6.5	4.0	6.5	8.0	1.5	0.0	1.0	3.0	5.0	1.0	2.0	48.0
Sudan	10.0	2.5	7.5	6.5	10.0	1.0	0.0	2.0	2.5	2.0	3.5	1.0	48.5

The following countries have the lowest political risk based on the dimensions above:

Country	A	B	C	D	E	F	G	H	I	J	K	L	Total
Finland	9.5	9.5	12.0	11.0	11.5	6.0	6.0	6.0	6.0	6.0	6.0	4.0	93.5
Luxembourg	10.0	9.5	12.0	12.0	11.5	5.0	6.0	6.0	6.0	5.0	6.0	4.0	93.0
Sweden	9.0	10.0	12.0	11.5	11.5	5.0	5.5	6.0	6.0	5.0	6.0	4.0	91.5
New Zealand	9.0	10.0	12.0	11.5	11.0	5.5	6.0	6.0	6.0	3.5	6.0	4.0	90.5
Netherlands	8.5	10.0	12.0	11.0	12.0	5.0	6.0	5.0	6.0	4.5	6.0	4.0	90.0
Iceland	8.5	9.5	11.0	11.5	11.0	4.5	6.0	5.5	6.0	6.0	6.0	4.0	89.5
Switzerland	9.0	10.5	11.5	12.0	11.5	4.5	6.0	5.0	5.0	4.0	6.0	4.0	89.0
Austria	8.5	9.5	12.0	11.5	11.5	5.0	6.0	6.0	6.0	4.0	5.0	4.0	89.0
Ireland	8.5	10.5	12.0	11.5	11.0	2.5	6.0	5.0	6.0	5.5	6.0	4.0	88.5
Norway	6.5	10.0	11.5	11.5	11.5	5.0	6.0	5.5	6.0	4.5	6.0	4.0	88.0

Source: Political Risk Ratings, www.prsgroup.com/icrg/sampletable.html.

Note: Numbers in parentheses represent the maximum number of points that can be allocated for that dimension. Therefore, the highest total scores (e.g., Finland) reflect low political risk; the lowest total scores (e.g., Iraq) reflect high political risk.

Fortunately there are a number of good publications that have detailed the political and economic risks for countries around the world.[16] They are very helpful in providing information that would have otherwise be rather difficult to collect and synthesize. Exhibit 5.2 provides indicators for twelve dimensions that comprise total political risk (the higher the score, the lower the political risk). For those who are curious, the United States scored 82.5, while China and India, the two hotbeds of outsourcing, scored 70.5 and 63.5 respectively. While these alone should not determine the market entry decision of a firm, they provide a rich context for making such decisions.

DEVELOPING THE GLOBAL MARKETING STRATEGY: HOW TO ENTER TARGET MARKETS

The "entry mode" decision, or *how* to enter international markets, has been a major consideration for international managers. In this section, we present more traditional approaches to market entry with an emphasis on the advantages and disadvantages of entry modes to the extent that these represent strategic choices for managers. Because of the growing complexity of this subject matter, however, we devote a separate chapter (Chapter 7) to research in the specific case of strategic alliances and joint ventures, sequential entry, and very recent offshore outsourcing.

INTERNATIONAL BUSINESS ENTRY MODES

There are six basic modes of entry to international markets. They include exporting, licensing, franchising, turnkey projects, joint ventures/cross-ownership, and wholly owned operations. Among all the modes, joint ventures/cross-ownership, and wholly owned operations involve foreign direct investment. Although exporting can also involve foreign direct investment, the level is rather low. An important consideration when analyzing possible modes of entry is the tradeoffs they present in terms of control and risk. The higher the commitment involved in a particular entry, the higher the control, but also the higher the risk. The lowest-control/lowest-risk option is exporting; generally, the highest-control/highest-risk option is the wholly owned subsidiary.

Exporting

Exporting is considered the simplest form of entering international markets and also entails the lowest level of commitment. Exporting can take on many different forms. A firm can simply let import agents manage its export sales. Thus, its responsibilities and obligations are completed once the agents take title to the products and assume the risk. Import agents take on the role of strategically moving all the products they represent abroad, and they earn commissions from the sales volume. A company can also sell products directly to distributors in foreign countries. Some firms establish offices in foreign countries for exporting and importing of their own products. This approach gives the firm more control in marketing the products and serves as a stepping-stone to further penetration of the market. Some countries use trading companies that have exclusive rights to handle all the trade activities for the countries although, under such arrangements, the manufacturer's exporting flexibility is compromised.

All in all, exporting is extensively used: it is estimated that 51 percent of U.S. companies are engaged in some form of exporting.[17] Despite the simplicity and advantages of exporting, however, it is less desirable when trade barriers, such as tariffs and quotas, are onerous. Even so, two types of exporting can circumvent trade barriers: direct selling via mail-order catalog and online selling. The risk level and resource commitments are low in both cases. Even though they now account for only a small portion of international trade, they are expected to grow significantly in the future.

Licensing

Licensing refers to a type of management contract. Under a licensing agreement, the licensor grants the licensee an exclusive right to use its copyrights, patents, trademarks, proprietary knowledge, technology, innovations, technical and management skills, or any form of intellectual property in some limited format in exchange for a royalty fee and sometimes profit sharing. Licensing can be applied to products or services. For example, Disney licenses foreign manufacturers to print Disney's cartoon characters on T-shirts, home furnishing items, jewelry, and the like for the same or other foreign markets. Florists Transworld Delivery, Inc. (FTD), licenses florists worldwide as a network for fresh flower delivery, something that would be hard for FTD to achieve through subsidiaries. Some pharmaceutical products and book publishers also use this method to expand their geographic coverage and as a way to reduce the incentive for counterfeit products produced by foreign firms. It is a low-cost approach to market expansion, but it does not always give the licensor complete control of operations. When the licensees fail to meet expectations, even though the licensors can terminate the contract, product and company images may have already been tarnished.

Franchising

Franchising is also a type of management contract. It is similar to licensing and is a fast way of expanding a company. A franchisor authorizes the right to a franchisee, another business entity, to operate the franchisor's business, either in offering products or services, in a particularly standardized way. The franchisor receives a royalty fee and/or profit sharing. The franchisees are expected to adhere to the specific procedures or the "package of operation" that the franchisor requires. Franchises usually come with a "manual" so that consistency among all franchisee operations can be maintained. McDonald's, Kentucky Fried Chicken, and Holiday Inn are among many examples of international franchising. The fast expansion nature of franchising allows a company to preempt competitors in entering the market of interest. International franchising requires a high level of coordination to maintain quality and image consistency. Franchising is not the best entry mode when the franchisee deems it necessary to enact modifications to accommodate local or regional tastes and lifestyles. In addition, another difficulty in franchising as an entry mode is that it is not easy to identify and to select qualified prospective franchisees.

Turnkey Projects

Turnkey projects are those in which a company helps its client to establish and, to some extent, operate an entity, business or nonbusiness, and provides support in many aspects for the client until the personnel of the client company is adequately trained to take over the day-to-day operation. Sometimes the project is completed as soon as the operation is up and running. Other times it can be more involved and last up to a decade. In return, the company receives compensation from their international clients. There is a high level of management and technology know-how transfer in turnkey projects. Turnkey projects can happen in many types of businesses, including accounting and computing services. For example, Quantum performed customer service, activations, billing, and collections for newly acquired markets until such a time as AT&T could conveniently merge these functions into its ongoing operations. In addition, Quantum provided switch-based prepaid wireless, including multilingual customer care for AT&T Wireless's Western Region.[18]

For international markets, turnkey projects can be found in oil refineries, power plants, and the like. Seimens AG, a German company, is a major global player in power plants and gas turbine turnkey projects. In 2005, the company has recorded success in securing US$605 million in North Africa and the Middle East.[19] In 2004, Mitsubishi Heavy Industries Ltd. of Japan entered a joint turnkey project with a German company, Balcke Durr GmbH, to build power plants for Iceland.[20] The above four modes of entry require a relatively low level of resources and managerial commitment. The following types require more commitment.

Joint Venture/Cross-Ownership

In a **joint venture**, two or more firms, in order to achieve common goals, come together to establish another business entity or to form some kind of contractual project agreement in which all parties contribute some form and level of tangible and intangible resources, such as equity, assets, technology, labor, or any other resource deemed of value. The primary purpose is often competitiveness enhancement. For example, on September 5, 2005, Hyundai Motor Company of South Korea entered a joint venture contract with Siemens AG to produce electronic parts. Hyundai will own 49.99 percent of the new venture.[21] In some cases, due to host government restrictions, a joint venture is the only way to enter a particular foreign market. A major challenge in joint ventures is finding a partner that offers complementary competencies and resources and shares the same goals. The hope to take advantage of the foreign partner's knowledge of the foreign market seems hard to realize. Nevertheless, when one of the partners in the joint venture is a native of the host country, it does provide some advantage when dealing with the host country government. The political benefits from international joint ventures include building relationships with the host country and creating the image of one's company being a team player in the host country. But the risk of losing proprietary information and the conflicts arising from profit sharing and repatriation, poor communication, distrust, and power competition often complicate joint venture operations. In most cases, companies avoid a 50–50 arrangement. Being the dominant partner is favored. The dominant partner has control over most strategic and operational decisions. Chapter 7 elaborates on strategies for using joint ventures and strategic alliances as entry modes.

A related form of joint venture, known as cross-ownership, is when two companies acquire a certain percentage of each other's joint assets or invest a certain amount of equity in each other. Typically, there is an apparent dominant party. The two parties exchange management, technology, labor, skills and know-how, suppliers, distributions, and the like. Both corporate and product identities may remain unchanged, so the two companies appear to be separate. For example, in the case of

Renault-Nissan, the two companies jointly owned each other. From 1999 to 2002, Renault increased its stake in Nissan from 22.5 percent to 44.4 percent while Nissan acquired a 13.5 percent stake in Renault in 2001, which was increased to 15 percent later in the same year.[22] The companies have their separate annual reports and their products' names are also separate. Renault and Nissan complement each other in terms of corporate image, distribution, product type, technology, and the like. Another example is when IBM sold its PC division to Chinese PC maker Lenovo for approximately US$1.25 billion, with IBM acquiring an 18.9 percent equity in Lenovo as part of the payment.[23] Lenovo opened the future enterprise-resources-planning (EPR) and high-end technology services market in China for IBM. In exchange, IBM gave its worldwide PC markets to Lenovo. In this case, even though IBM "sold" its PC division to Lenovo, IBM actually extended its influence in China through its stake in Lenovo. More will be said about strategic alliances in the next chapter.

Wholly Owned Operation

The **wholly owned operation** exists when company has complete ownership of foreign operations. This may be carried out as an acquisition or greenfield operation. In exchange for the highest level of internal control, compared to other modes, the company is taking a correspondingly higher level of risk and making a larger resource commitment. The control factor becomes critical when foreign operations play a significant role in the company's global strategic plan, for example, the interdependence between foreign subsidiaries. A wholly owned operation is essentially foreign direct investment. Compared to other modes, wholly owned operations may be up against more legal restrictions created by the home and host governments. A company with a foreign identity can also be looked upon negatively by the general public in the host country. The case of China's CNOOC's involuntary withdrawal from its acquisition pursuit of the United States' UNOCAL is an example of political and social pressures. Acquisitions represent a special case of entry. They have the advantages of rapid entry with the possibility of acquiring an established name and reputation with all the attendant benefits resulting from the experience of the acquired firm. However, the cost of acquiring such a firm might be significantly high. A recent example is Lenovo's acquisition of IBM's PC Division in May 2005 for $1.25 billion. Within a very short time, Lenovo gained access to this important market segment and became the third largest PC manufacturer worldwide.[24]

CHOOSING AN ENTRY MODE

Selecting an appropriate mode of entry depends on many factors. The internal factors refer to the condition of the company. They mostly have to do with whether the company is ready for the type of commitment involved. Basically, synergy and strategic fit play a critical role in the selection and operation process. How much by way of resources, experience, intelligence, contacts, motivation, vision, and skills does the company have in preparing for the new venture? Externally, even though the mega-trend of the open market system has provided opportunities for entering foreign markets, country conditions and requirements still pose challenges to global strategists. Entering developed versus developing economies can be quite different. The primary challenge in developing economies is the lack of adequate institutions and infrastructures, whereas the challenges in developed economies are typically in cost, competition, and deep-rooted habits that are not easily altered. Some basic advantages and disadvantages attendant to each mode of entry are presented in Exhibit 5.3.

Understanding the advantages and disadvantages of each entry mode is an important first step in analyzing entry decisions. Even so, many firms employ additional factors in making this evaluation. Below are two tables (Exhibits 5.4 and 5.5) summarizing a more detailed set of factors that affect the decisions made in selecting a mode of entry. In the first table, all factors rated 1 represent the least impact, and those rated 5 represent the most impact. In the second table, the same factors are evaluated either as disadvantageous or advantageous. If needed, a more comprehensive analysis permits a broader and more complete picture of entry decisions and avoids hasty decisions that can result in adverse long-term financial and managerial consequences.

DEVELOPING THE GLOBAL MARKETING STRATEGY: WHEN TO ENTER TARGET MARKETS

The prior sections covered two of three interrelated decisions: what markets to enter and how to enter them. Perhaps less heralded, but of crucial importance nevertheless, is the third decision: *when* to enter target markets. The timing of entry is crucial because it can bestow significant advantage over other firms. When to make a strategic move is often as crucial as what move to make. Much of what we know and understand about this timing decision is based on studies of first movers (or pioneers) and late entrants (followers). While the benefits accruing to the pioneer can be significant, such is not always guaranteed, and, in fact, the follower can gain advantage by learning from the pioneer's mistakes.

The conceptual arguments for pioneer and follower advantages are based in large part on competitive strategy, specifically the use of entry barriers as competitive weapons.[25] For the first mover, an appropriate strategy is to build barriers to entry and to forestall competitive imitation. There may also be intangible, political advantages to the first mover, such as being able to develop and nurture close relationships with the host country. For the follower, a good strategy might allow entry barriers to be overcome through a series of actions focused on a pioneer's area of weaknesses, or through an alteration of the bases of competition.

FIRST-MOVER ADVANTAGES

First-mover advantages are the advantageous positions a company gains from being the first to enter a new market. They arise under the following conditions:

- pioneering enables firms to build their image and reputation without competitive pressure;

Exhibit 5.3

Basic Advantages and Disadvantages for Each Mode of Entry

Mode of Entry	Advantages	Disadvantages
Exporting Involves selling products or services to a foreign market through an intermediary, such as a commissioned agent or trading company.	The exporting company can receive guidance and can learn know-how from the agents. It allows even a company of limited resources and manpower to achieve global presence. The agents can help the exporting company to establish business connections overseas.	The middleman fee, transportation costs, and tariffs may cause less competitive prices and less competitive positions overseas. The middleman cost lowers the company's profit margin. The company may find it difficult to manage how its products and services are delivered abroad.
Licensing/Franchising Involves assigning the firm's technology or products over to another party for exploitation in one or more foreign markets.	The capital requirements for entering foreign markets are shared by licensee and franchisee. When the business becomes unsatisfactory, the company can terminate the licensing or franchising contracts. It is a relatively low cost approach to explore a company's business opportunities overseas. The company can tap into the foreign licensee and franchisee's local knowledge in advertising and distributing the products.	The company can find that their intellectual property rights are at risk in a country of insufficient legal institutional supports. The company's technology may not be appropriately and properly utilized in the foreign markets. Technology and know-how transfer may facilitate the licensee and franchisee to grow to become competitors. The company may find it difficult to control product and service quality.
Joint Ventures/ Cross-Ownership Involves investment with a local partner to act as the firm's supplier, distributor, trading partner, or local representative.	The joint venture can promote the sharing of tasks based on specialized skills to gain greater efficiency. The company can aggressively learn and absorb its partner's skills, technology, and know-how. Having a partner significantly share the financial commitments and risks. The partners can exchange and share complementary skills, which may result in greater synergy.	The foreign partner may be too powerful that the company gradually loses its managerial power in the joint venture. Many joint ventures experience management conflicts and finally ended up with costly dissolutions. The company may be nurturing the partner to become its future competitor.

(continued)

Exhibit 5.3 *(continued)*

Mode of Entry	Advantages	Disadvantages
Wholly Owned Overseas Subsidiaries Involves setting up the firm's own office, manufacturing plant, and/or marketing facility in a foreign country.	The company can take charge of responsibilities and have complete control of its operations overseas. The company can protect its intellectual property and not worry about losing to partners. If the foreign production is designed to serve the local market, the company can avoid costs related to tariff, transportation, etc.	It often is the most expensive mode of entry to enter foreign markets. The firm may be subjected to more stringent labor laws that in its home country. The foreign market may be immature or lacking institutional supports for global business. Without a partner, the difficulties could be mounting.
Wholly Owned Overseas Subsidiaries By Way of Overseas Acquisitions	The acquiring company can achieve an instant success through a wise acquisition of a foreign firm. The acquiring company will inherit the reputation and goodwill of the acquired firm in the local market. The acquiring firm can take advantage of the acquired firm's expertise to explore new market opportunities. It significantly shortens the acquiring firm's timeline in entering the foreign market.	Typically it is costly to acquire a well-established firm that the return may not justify the cost. The company may find that the idiosyncrasies in local law, accounting, and other business practices may become barriers to success. Smooth integration and coordination may not happen due to cultural conflicts. The acquiring company may not be able to keep the talents in the acquired firm because there is a perceived glass ceiling for career advancement.

Source: Adapted from Ruth Stanat & Chris West, *Global Jumpstart: The Complete Resource Guide for Expanding Small and Medium Size Business* (Reading, MA: Perseus Books, 1999), pp. 272–276; In Joseph H. Boyett & Jimmie T. Boyett, *The Guru Guide to the Knowledge Economy: The Best Ideas for Operating Profitably in a Hyper-Competitive World* (New York: John Wiley & Sons, 2001), pp. 105–106.

Exhibit 5.4

Illustrating the Impact of Various Entry Modes (1 = low impact; 5 = high impact)

Factors	Export	Licensing	Fran-chising	Turnkey project	Joint venture	Cross-ownership	Wholly owned operation
Technology sharing and loss	1	5	5	4	4	5	1
Information sharing and loss	1	5	5	4	4	5	1
Knowledge gain	1	2	2	3	4	5	5
Experiences gain	1	2	2	3	4	5	5
Control of operation	1	2	2	4	4	4	5
Operation consistency	1	3	3	4	4	4	5
Extent of responsibilities	1	2	2	4	4	5	5
Relationship building	1	3	3	5	5	5	5
Contact building	1	3	3	5	5	5	5
Conflicts with partners	1	3	3	4	5	5	1
Political and legal risks	5	1	1	3	2	2	5
Local image	1	2	2	2	5	4	1
Local presence	1	2	2	2	5	5	5
Competitor creation	1	5	5	5	5	5	2
Speed of expansion and immediate market entry	1	5	5	4	5	5	2
International coordination requirement	1	5	5	3	3	4	2
Cost commitment	1	1	1	1	4	5	5
Management commitment	1	2	2	3	5	5	5
Other tangible resources commitment	1	1	1	1	4	5	5
Other intangible resources commitment	1	2	2	3	5	5	5

- early commitments to secure raw material suppliers, new technologies, and distribution channels can lead to advantages that might be difficult for followers to obtain;
- loyalty of first-time buyers is high and secure;
- moving first can be a preemptive strike that can discourage followers;
- securing the support of the host government by being first can be invaluable.

Box 5.2 further explores the advantages of being a pioneer.

Initial Feedback

Simply by their market presence, firms that enter first are often able to obtain quicker and richer feedback from customers. Pepsi gained an advantage in Vietnam as it was able to study patterns of consumer behavior and, in so doing, lock up important channels of distribution. Coca-Cola, by withdrawing from Vietnam in the aftermath of

Exhibit 5.5

Analyzing the Advantages of Various Entry Modes: An Illustration

Factors	Export	Licensing	Franchising	Turnkey project	Joint venture	Cross-ownership	Wholly owned operation
Technology sharing and loss	Advantage	Disadvantage	Disadvantage	Disadvantage	Disadvantage	Disadvantage	Advantage
Information sharing and loss	Advantage	Disadvantage	Disadvantage	Disadvantage	Disadvantage	Disadvantage	Advantage
Knowledge gain	Advantage	Disadvantage	Disadvantage	Advantage	Advantage	Advantage	Advantage
Experience gain	Advantage	Disadvantage	Disadvantage	Advantage	Advantage	Advantage	Advantage
Control of operation	Disadvantage	Disadvantage	Disadvantage	Advantage	Advantage	Advantage	Advantage
Operation consistency	Advantage	Disadvantage	Disadvantage	Disadvantage	Advantage	Advantage	Advantage
Extent of responsibilities	Advantage	Advantage	Advantage	Disadvantage	Disadvantage	Disadvantage	Disadvantage
Relationship building	Disadvantage	Advantage	Advantage	Disadvantage	Disadvantage	Disadvantage	Disadvantage
Contact building	Disadvantage	Advantage	Advantage	Disadvantage	Disadvantage	Disadvantage	Disadvantage
Conflicts with partners	Disadvantage	Disadvantage	Advantage	Advantage	Disadvantage	Advantage	Disadvantage
Political and legal risks	Disadvantage	Disadvantage	Disadvantage	Advantage	Advantage	Advantage	Disadvantage
Local image	Disadvantage	Advantage	Advantage	Advantage	Advantage	Advantage	Advantage
Local presence	Disadvantage	Advantage	Advantage	Disadvantage	Advantage	Advantage	Advantage
Competitor creation	Disadvantage	Disadvantage	Disadvantage	Disadvantage	Disadvantage	Advantage	Advantage
Speed of expansion and im-mediate market entry	Disadvantage	Advantage	Advantage	Advantage	Advantage	Advantage	Advantage
International coordination requirement	Advantage	Disadvantage	Disadvantage	Advantage	Disadvantage	Disadvantage	Advantage
Cost commitment	Advantage	Advantage	Advantage	Advantage	Disadvantage	Disadvantage	Disadvantage
Management commitment	Advantage	Disadvantage	Disadvantage	Advantage	Disadvantage	Disadvantage	Disadvantage
Other tangible resources commitment	Advantage	Advantage	Advantage	Advantage	Disadvantage	Disadvantage	Disadvantage
Other intangible resources commitment	Advantage	Advantage	Advantage	Advantage	Disadvantage	Disadvantage	Disadvantage

Box 5.2

Profile of a First Mover: Gillette—The Pioneer in Razor Blades

While there are many good examples of first movers, one firm that is consistently noted is Gillette. Mr. King C. Gillette was the first to devise and market a safety razor in 1903. Since that time, the company, which still bears his name, continues to be ahead of the field in a highly competitive market in which consumer requirements are increasingly diverse and demanding.

What do buyers expect out of shavers? While appearance and style have become increasingly important, for the person looking for the perfect shave, it is performance that matters most of all. Market research suggests that most people who shave find it a chore. In fact, many resent the time they devote to it. Thus, they want a shaver that not only shortens the time spent on shaving, but also performs the best job, all of which make the experience pleasurable and fulfilling. For a manufacturer, these are tough challenges.

A number of characteristics facilitate Gillette's reputation as a first mover. First, Gillette has focused on product features that improve existing technologies. Its overall emphasis is on providing premium performance, (i.e., a closeness, smoothness, and comfort, for the best value.) To illustrate, adding another blade to provide another shaving surface might be considered a marginal improvement. However, in the case of Gillette, if the additional blade also lifts the whiskers to enable the other blades to cut them cleanly, then such would be considered an advance to enhance the overall premium performance. Recent innovations include the Mach3 three-bladed razor, as well as ergonomically superior handles, notably the Sensor and Venus for Women. Gillette has also introduced the battery-powered pulsating M3 Power, and has talked about the four- and the five-razor with all the ancillary functions.

Second, Gillette has been very attentive to market segments. The market for razors is not uniform but contains different segments, the needs of which have to be met in carefully targeted, subtly different ways. Because Gillette recognized that different market segments expect different product benefits, it has developed several product categories ranging from popular disposable razors to elaborate shaving systems. In the United Kingdom, for example, an increasing number of men have switched from disposable razors to shaving systems—a trend that was noted by Gillette and that led to a new product.

A third characteristic is the company's recognition of the razor as just one component of the much broader market of "personal appearance and well-being." Not surprisingly, Gillette is heavily involved in the market for deodorants and antiperspirants. In the future, the company expects rising incomes to lead consumers to spend more on a "total package" that enhances personal appearance and personal hygiene. To this end, Gillette has developed a strategy to expand its position within this expanding market.

A fourth characteristic is Gillette's attention to human resources. Gillette has a long, distinguished history of innovation. Its scientists, technicians, and product engineers are continually trying out new features and production techniques, such as longer-lasting batteries, best-in-class electric and manual toothbrushes, and the ultimate user-friendly ear thermometer. The company's longstanding interest in being "first to get it right" remains a key element of its continuing prosperity and progress.

Source: Adapted from *Gillette: Developing New Products.* www.tt100biz.com.; William C. Symonds, "Gillette's Five-Blade Wonder," *Business Week Online* (September 15, 2005), available at www.businessweek.com/bwdaily/dnflash/sep2005/nf20050915_1654_db035.htm.

the war, had difficulties reentering the country, especially while its rival was already exploiting returns from its initial investment.

The advantages of "being first" are far from conclusive and questionable based on a survey of the empirical evidence.[26] Even so, this belief is popular and widespread, particularly among business practitioners. In the next section, we present the advantages and disadvantages of "being first," as perceived primarily from the vantage point of business practitioners.

What are the advantages of a first-mover? The first mover typically benefits from good publicity and early visibility. Mary Kay Cosmetics' early entry into China garnered the company enormous publicity. Although China was regarded to be uncharted territory, Mary Kay's business model lured Chinese women who sought not only the company's products but the opportunity to have their own businesses.[27] "If you are the first company out there, you become associated with the business that you're in, and people know your name," says Sara Zeilstra, e-commerce analyst at Warburg Dillon Read. First-mover advantage is "a head start," Zeilstra adds. "Almost anyone would be crazy not to have a head start."[28]

Secure Access to Supplies

While not always the case, first movers are also able to secure key sources of supplies. This was the case of McDonald's, for which key ingredients, such as potatoes and meat, were obtained following its early entry into key markets. Without the presence of competitors, pioneers are able to work with suppliers in setting up prices and terms of delivery. Once secured, it might be difficult for followers to obtain the same arrangements in the future.

Setting the Firm's Strategy

Being first facilitates the firm in setting the initial strategy or "rules of the game." This can lead to significant advantages in that the pioneer will likely shape the "rules of the game" in ways that favor its strengths and competencies. Following eBay's successful foray into person-to-person online trading, Chris Larsen, founder of E-LOAN (see Chapter 4), has similar dreams for his new venture, Prosper.com. The vision is to match people who need small loans with willing lenders in an online platform supported by safety measures such as credit ratings, a group of borrowers, a swath of outside collectors, and other related checks. The idea is to provide a lending venue outside of traditional sources, much like Larsen's former online broker company that disrupted the traditional reliance on mortgage lenders. Despite concerns raised by some quarters, Larsen has been able to shape a strategy, and, if the venture proves successful, perhaps even the norms and standards for this revolutionary initiative.[29]

Erecting Entry Barriers

In the long run, by being first and thus attracting the first set of customers, a firm is able to erect entry barriers that apply to other firms that follow. In business software, for example, providing a new product ahead of one's competitors is tremendously valuable, says Eric Upin, software analyst at BancBoston Robertson Stephens (BBRS): "Whoever gets in first and gets big, has a real advantage." It is not easy to erect entry barriers unless a firm has a lasting patent right on a product or service, or if entry is restricted by the government. Even so, developing highly differentiated products with a select client can result in entry barriers for followers. Gilman Louie, former

---

Box 5.3

The Myth of the First-Mover Advantage

The logic behind a first-mover advantage is that the initial occupant of a strategic position or niche develops and gains access to resources and capabilities that followers are not able to match. It is not only a compelling argument, but it can also be a seductive one. Everyone wants to be first, and firms tout their "first-mover advantage." Yet critics note that some, if not many, of these claims and advantages can be illusory. First, some claims are simply not true. Second, the success of first movers (and followers) depends largely on how well leaders are able to secure their positions, and the resiliency of followers in learning and correcting any first-mover mistakes.

Setting aside incorrect claims, the record depicting the success of first-movers versus followers is a mixed one:

- Juno was first company to offer free e-mail and it had a $20 million ad budget. Yet it was displaced by the now ubiquitous Hotmail.
- Similarly, the Osborne portable computer and the Gavilan notebook were among the first movers but are now both out of the picture.
- Netzero was not the first free ISP, and eBay was not the first firm to create auctions on the Internet.

"History imposes first-mover advantage honors," noted Roger McNamee of Integral Capital Partners. "If you asked who was the first computer game software company a lot of people might say Electronic Arts because they're still standing, but EA was about the 41st game software company to get funding."

What distinguishes between a successful first mover and an equally successful follower? McNamee argues, "Companies don't necessarily need a unique idea or service to succeed, but a *unique* business model. Barnesandnoble.com has tried—so far unsuccessfully—to compete with Amazon.com by mimicking everything the online book behemoth does. The major airlines made similar attempts to imitate the success of Southwest Airlines, only to discover that it is not so much the imitation of a successful business model but its *execution* that comprises its success."

Other cases suggest that circumstances have to favor the first mover. Dan Brown's novel, *The DaVinci Code,* has sold about 80 million copies at the time of this writing, with even more revenues expected from the box-office movie, sales and rentals of DVD, and various paraphernalia. Dan Brown was challenged in a plagiarism suit brought about by Michael Baigent and Richard Leigh. They claimed that Brown stole the theme from their earlier book, *The Holy Blood and Holy Grail,* co-written with Henry Lincoln. It did not matter much. The judge ruled in favor of Brown. All in all, the lesson is: being first is no small feat, but beating the rest of the world is an entirely different story.

Source: Adapted in part from David Needle, "The Myth of the First Mover Advantage," Silicon Valley Internet.com (April 5, 2000), http://siliconvalley.internet.com/news/article.php/3541_333311.

---

executive in In-Q-Tell, has been affectionately known as Q—a reference to James Bond's gadgetry whiz. The company is noted for its leading edge information technologies and products and it is considered the pioneer in the interactive entertainment industry. It has successfully filled what was considered to be a "IT space void" (or the application of IT in interactive space) for many of its clients, notably the CIA. Some of Louie's accomplishments include the design and development of the Falcon (expendable launch vehicle), the F-16 flight simulator (combat game flight simulator), and Tetris (puzzle video game).[30] To the extent a firm can build entry barriers, particularly when it is the first mover to secure agreements with key buyers, it can have an enduring competitive advantage.

FOLLOWER ADVANTAGES

Even so, being first is not necessarily the guarantor of success (see Box 5.3). In fact, moving early can be a disadvantage or fail to produce an advantage under the following conditions:

- costs of first-movers are significant;
- the loyalty of first-time buyers is weak;
- rapid technological changes provide learning opportunities for followers to leapfrog over the first-movers;
- strategies of first-movers are easily and quickly imitated by late movers;
- first movers are not able to create significant entry barriers.

Firms that are followers often stand to benefit from the following.

Being a First Entrant is not a Guarantee for Success

Based on the conditions discussed above, first-mover advantage is not guaranteed, nor is this advantage necessarily enduring and tangible. "I don't pay an extra dollar a share because someone has first-mover advantage," says Robert Mohn, portfolio manager of the Acorn USA fund. Because of rapid technological change, first-mover advantage might not be sustainable on the Internet.[31] One advantage of a follower is that it is able to learn from the mistakes of the first mover, thus nullifying the latter's advantage. Microsoft was a late entrant in the browser world after Netscape, yet it avoided Netscape's early problems and used its massive resources to muscle its way into this industry. Among car *afficionados*, there is the belief that one should not buy any first model, but wait for the upgraded second series where mistakes are presumably addressed and corrected.

Capitalizing on the Demand Created by the First Mover

"In large parts of the real world, there is not a first-mover advantage," Mohn adds. "Wal-Mart was not the first discount store. There was something called Korvette's."[32] Similarly, Google was hardly the first search engine. Even before Yahoo!, there were AltaVista and Archie. Another example is Sharp. Despite years of selling personal organizers, the Japanese electronics giant fell prey to the handheld PalmPilot, now a 3Com product. Other cases abound. Netscape's head start in the Web browser market, as well as Spyglass, which also began selling Web browsers at roughly the same time, could not sustain first-mover advantage when Microsoft entered the market.[33]

Providing Better Products and Services That Undermine the Leader's Initial Advantage

With better products, followers are able to successfully offset the advantages of a first mover. Successful follower strategies tend to appear in commodity markets where the ability of followers to lower costs through technology and other cost-reducing

Exhibit 5.6   **Framework for Assessing Timing Decisions**

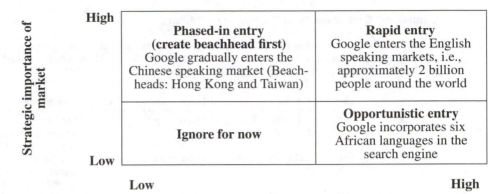

Source: Examples are from the authors. This model is adapted from Vijay Govindarajan and Anil K. Gupta, *The Quest for Global Dominance* (San Francisco: Jossey-Bass, 2001), p. 29.

measures allows them to leapfrog past erstwhile market leaders. The dramatic ascendancy of Japanese semiconductor firms (replacing U.S. firms) and Korean semiconductors (replacing Japanese firms a decade later) provides graphic testimony to how followers can gain advantage in commodity markets. Another example is how the new digital technology enabled Microsoft's CD Encarta to render Encyclopedia Britannica obsolete in 1993.

In technology-based industries, where it is difficult to gauge users' demand and consumption patterns, followers can likewise disrupt the leaders' advantage. In an incisive analysis of disruptive technologies, Harvard professor Clayton Christensen argued that it was not necessarily the "best" product demanded by the "lead" users that prevailed, but one that was "good enough" to accommodate the demands of a nascent market segment (see Chapter 8, pp. 334–335).

Thus, should a firm be the first entrant, or should it wait until it learns more about the new market? What sequence of global expansion should take place? A systematic framework is offered below that describes opportunities for firms to engage in directed opportunism rather than entering in an ad hoc, random fashion.[34] Two sets of factors need to be carefully considered. The first is the **strategic importance of the market**. This encompasses the present and future size of market demand as well as opportunities for firms to learn more about this market—specifically new technologies, demand, different strategies by rivals—that these firms can employ in their future activities. As stated earlier, market size, present and future, should be considered alongside political risks afflicting the country. Moreover, access is critical. China is a compelling market because of its sheer size, but entry is not easy, often requiring complex negotiations in the form of joint ventures to make it viable.

The second consideration is the **firm's ability to exploit the market**. In large part, this depends on the strength and transferability of a firm's business model, along with entry barriers and anticipated competition. Intuitively, the stronger the business

Exhibit 5.7

Examining Components of Global Market Share

Many new markets and most global markets are well below their full market potential. That is, there are large numbers of customers that have not entered the market. There are a number of reasons a particular market might not have reached its full potential.

Factors	Description	Market mix problem	Potential solution
Price/cost	Buyers can't afford this service at current prices	Price	Revise pricing policy through an analysis of pricing objectives and current methods
Attractiveness	Product lacks attractive benefits	Product positioning	Examine current positioning; focus market research on specific local problems
Compatibility	Product does not fit customer's use situation	Product positioning	Examine current positioning; focus market research on specific local problems
Availability	Noncustomers cannot get service	Place, logistics	Examine channels of distribution
Awareness	Noncustomers do not comprehend benefits	Promotions	Examine current promotions policy

Source: Adapted from Roger J. Best, *Market-Based Management: Strategies for Growing Customer Value and Profitability* (Upper Saddle River, NJ: Prentice Hall, 1997), pp. 280–81.

model, the stronger is the firm's ability to exploit markets. However, this is hardly an automatic consequence. Even mighty Wal-Mart experienced difficulty in penetrating the Latin American markets because of a host of regulatory constraints and community resistance to large-scale wholesale stores. Thus, the exploitation potential depends not only on the firm's business model but also on the height of entry barriers related to the market. Juxtaposing these two factors leads to a framework for assessing timing decisions (Exhibit 5.6).

PUTTING THE GLOBAL MARKETING STRATEGY TOGETHER: AN ANALYTICAL FRAMEWORK

Marketing academician and consultant Roger Best offers a way of synthesizing what we have discussed thus far into a manageable and accessible framework.[35] His work focuses on factors that impact global market demand and on understanding why a firm's market share might be restricted. Best's framework also reveals where management attention should be focused (see Exhibit 5.7).

The lead question is: *How can a firm improve its market share?* The key to unpacking this question lies in understanding the lost opportunities from a consumer's perspective. While numerous factors restrict demand, a firm cannot sell products to consumers who are not even *aware* of such products, arising from the lack of product recognition within certain international markets. **Product awareness** refers to the extent to which consumers recognize and know about a product. Logitech is best known for its computer peripherals, most notably the mouse. Few consumers, however, know that Logitech also manufactures the diNovo Edge keyboard and the NuLOOQ navigator, devices that were honored with prestigious 2007 red dot design awards. Without consumer awareness, Logitech will lose market share in the above two products.

Frequently, the lack of awareness reflects a promotional problem. The lack of a good promotional program (one of the "Ps" in the marketing mix), or worse, a wrong and incorrect promotional message, will make it difficult to market the product. Consequently, such services are not purchased.

Even if consumers are aware, products might be *unavailable*. In many cities and communities in the United States, high-speed Internet services via DSL are attractive but not available to interested customers. The lack of availability is often the result of inadequate channels of distribution (one of the other "Ps" in the marketing mix).

Another factor restricting demand is *compatibility*. Size, form, shape, color, and user requirements influence how customers use the product and incorporate them into their lifestyles. Starbucks and other coffee firms will lose share to individuals who think that drinking coffee is not good for their health. Similarly, a consumer residing in the United States might not purchase electrical appliances from Japan if these do not fit the electrical specifications in the United States.

Even with proper compatibility, however, cultural factors also temper a customer's perception of the actual *benefits* of product. In many Eastern European countries, the demand for cell phones is high not because of customer loyalty, but because the waiting time to obtain cell phones is rather lengthy. In countries such as the Philippines and Hong Kong, the use of "texting" on cell phones is much more prevalent than for customers in the United States, who prefer to talk directly to others.

Still another factor restricting global market demand is *price*. The target markets might not have sufficient discretionary income to afford the product. In such a case, these products—ranging from cars, television sets, and motorcycles, to cameras—would need to be reengineered in terms of cost to enable customers to afford them.

An excellent example of pricing and compatibility adaptation is offered by University of Michigan professor C.K. Prahalad and Cornell University professor Stuart L. Hart in their study of Third World nations, where international firms have tended to offer products at higher prices. Going against this trend, imaginative firms such as Hindustan Lever Ltd. (HLL), a subsidiary of Great Britain's Unilever PLC and widely considered to be the best-managed company in India, do otherwise.[36] In competition with a local firm, Nirma, HLL offered a new detergent, called Wheel, that was formulated to substantially reduce the ratio of oil to water in the product. Prahalad attributes plains this to the fact that the poor often wash their clothes in rivers and other public water systems. HLL changed the cost structure of its detergent business to support Wheel at a low price point. Today, Unilever has adopted the developing countries as a corporate strategic priority. (For more information about HLL, see the case-in-point at the end of this chapter). For an illustration of the opportunities and challenges faced by firms marketing in China, see Box 5.4.

In reviewing the framework, two notable areas stand out in terms of market improvement: *product positioning* and *pricing*. While not discounting the importance of the

Box 5.4

Marketing to the Masses

China's marketing potential has fascinated marketers from all over the world. Recent reports disclose that a 25-year-old professional could spend an entire month's salary on the latest Nokia mobile phone or a Scandinavian design bookshelf from IKEA. While it seems strange that such an extravagant lifestyle can emerge from a country where 80 percent of the people are living in poverty, some marketers don't seem to mind. China has over one million affluent urban households earning $13,000 annually who are regular shoppers of luxury goods. What does this mean for firms entering the Chinese market?

First, segmentation is important in the Chinese market. Coca-Cola, with China as its fourth largest market, has realized that the vast and diverse population requires product diversity. The company now offers fruit juice, water, tea and coffee, and new flavors to suit the different segments of the Chinese market. Coca-Cola's brands include Sprite Super Lemon, Sprite Ice, and Sprite on Fire in China–all introduced to accommodate different regional tastes. To maintain consumer awareness, Estee Lauder promotes a new product almost every weekend. Posters of well-groomed women have become a kind of wallpaper for Shanghai's Nanjing road.

Second, foreign and domestic retailers have aggressively added more capacity. Carrefour plans to add 40–50 more stores in Beijing by 2008, while Wal-Mart aims for 14 in six months. Gome's, a local retailer, plans to open one store every 30 hours. Advertising costs have increased by 50 percent for all consumer products in just two years, from 2002 to 2004. But advertisements that potentially clash with the Chinese culture are avoided. Nike's "Just Do It" slogan is considered too individualistic for this collectivistic, Confucius culture.

Third, the shopping experience itself has become more valued. An emerging trend in Shenzhen, the richest city in China, is "retailtainment," that incorporates a store-hosted baby crawling race (sponsored by Wal-Mart). A spacious area with a big television and chairs for shoppers is a common sight, as are air-conditioned lounging areas reserved for reading and resting while family or friends are shopping. Elegant wooden floors, wide aisles and larger shopping carts have helped a local retailer, Lianhua's Century Mart, raise its sales volume by 20 percent.

For companies targeting the rural market that is estimated to be between 700 and 900 million potential customers, the growing belief is that it's not all marketing that matters. Being partners with the local government can help. For example, in April 2007, Procter and Gamble signed an agreement with China's Commerce Ministry to train local salespersons in 10,000 villages to improve existing retail shops and add new ones. In exchange, Beijing promised to eliminate counterfeit products. With $2.5 billion in annual sales in China in 2006, P&G has noted that rural sales are fast catching up with the urban sites. To help these retailers in rural areas, P&G offers product demonstrations, posters, cardboard display stands, and samples, all of which are free.

Even so, the rural market is a challenge because of its low income, dispersed locations, logistical inconvenience, and lack of product knowledge. Moreover, rural consumers are extremely price-sensitive, and their tastes and preferences differ by group. For example, noting that many Chinese believe that salt has whitening and cleansing properties, P&G has offered Crest Salt White at a cheaper price for the smaller rural family budget. But P&G has also retained exotic flavors, such as Icy Mountain Spring and Morning Lotus Fragrance toothpaste for urbanites at a higher price.

Sources: Adapted from "China Wants the Newly Rich to Spend, Spend, Spend: Emerging Markets," *Birmingham Post*, September 19, 2007, p. 23; "Coca Cola Boss Expects China to be Largest Market," *BCC Monitoring Asia Pacific*, September 16, 2007, p. 1; "Special Report: Ready for Warfare in the Aisles—Retailing in China," *The Economist*, August 5, 2006, p. 60; Dexter Roberts, "Cautious Consumers: The Chinese Are on a Spending Spree, Right? Not Really. In Fact, They're So Tightfisted, Beijing Is Worried," *BusinessWeek*, April 30, 2007, p. 323; Dexter Roberts, "Scrambling to Bring Crest to the Masses: As Growth in Chinese Cities Slows, P&G Sets its Sights on 700 million Rural

(continued)

Consumers," *BusinessWeek*, June 25, 2007, p. 72; Frederik Balfour and David Kiley, "Ad Agencies Unchained," *BusinessWeek*, April 25, 2005, p. 50; Sheridan Prasso, "Battle for the Face of China: L'Oreal, Shiseido, Estee Lauder—the World's Leading Cosmetics Companies Are Vying for a Piece of a Booming Market," *Fortune*, December 12, 2005, p. 26.

other factors, from an international perspective these are paramount marketing issues. More frequently than not, other areas such as the lack of awareness (a promotional issue) and compatibility (a positioning issue) can be meaningfully analyzed in terms of product positioning and pricing. The next two sections amplify these two areas.

ADAPTING PRODUCTS AND SERVICES TO THE TARGETED MARKET

Product management is often considered the first "P" among the marketing Ps (the others being place, promotions, and price). Companies often assume that a product that might have fared successfully in their home market will succeed in international markets as well. Such beliefs are not often substantiated.

Even when the product appears to succeed, some companies are taken aback when they realize what the product is used for. Imagine the surprise expressed by a U.S. firm selling feminine sanitary napkins in South America when it discovered that local farmers used the napkins as dust masks. Another U.S. firm selling toothbrushes in South Vietnam during the late 1960s was surprised when it realized that the Vietcong used the product for weapon cleaning.[37] Some core questions that need be addressed include the following.

1. Are the Firm's Products Known? If They Are, Will They be Perceived in a Manner the Company Wants the Local Market to Perceive Them?

This touches on our above examples, in which products were known and, fortunately, benefited the company, despite different uses. Other firms are not as fortunate. Disney's products and services are very well known, and, in fact, desired, by French customers. Yet the company experienced numerous problems when starting its operation in Paris—a move previously considered by company insiders to be a "no-brainer."

To take another example, McDonald's products would not surprise foreign customers. Its hamburgers, developed by Ray Kroc, are considered superior and an exemplar of successful U.S. enterprise. Yet during the North Atlantic Treaty Organization (NATO) air war against the former Yugoslavia in 1999, fifteen McDonald's restaurants were closed due to angry mobs, which considered the United States to be among the "NATO criminals and aggressors," and which vented their anger by vandalizing them.

McDonald's proceeded to change its product strategy. They promoted McCountry, a domestic pork burger with paprika garnish. To heighten Serbian identity and pride, McDonald's brought out posters and lapel buttons showing the golden arches topped with the traditional Serbian cap called the *sajkaca*—a strong and unique symbol of Serbia's pride. McDonald's also handed out free cheeseburgers at anti-NATO rallies.

The results were impressive: in spite of falling wages, rising prices, and lingering anger at the United States, McDonald's restaurants were packed with Serbs. Many Serbs considered McDonald's to be "one of their own."[38]

2. How Are the Firm's Products and Services Positioned?

Positioning, according to marketing guru and Northwestern University professor Philip Kotler, is the act of designing the company's product and marketing mix to fit a place in the customer's mind, usually in regard to competitive offerings. Advertising programs attempt to build and reinforce this act of positioning. For example, Nike's famous dictum, "Just do it," is firmly associated with the sports company. Superior positioning can increase competitive leverage in that firms can place most of their resources toward further reinforcement of their position.

A firm's **global position** is inextricably related to promotions and pricing. In global markets, more marketing research might be needed to ascertain the appropriateness of a firm's positioning strategy. For example, if a firm's product is positioned in one of the lower market segments in the home market, a developed market in this example, the lack of recognition for the product in emerging markets might allow the firm to position it at a higher end and earn a higher profit margin. Volvo is positioned as a fairly unsophisticated automotive brand with a high market share in Sweden, but it is positioned as an upscale brand elsewhere in Europe. Other similar examples include Levi's jeans and Jeep Grand Cherokee. More often than not, managers will not know what customers want and need unless they question many people in different market segments. The key is continuous and relentless market research.

Developing a global brand is the key to excellent positioning and perhaps the easiest way to build global recognition. This task eluded South Korean manufacturers for decades, despite their sheer size and economic achievements, until Samsung, and to a much lesser extent, Hyundai, broke this barrier. Samsung is now recognized for its excellent products in customer electronics, while Hyundai has established its world position in lower-priced, good-quality automobiles.

Attaining a global presence, while no easy task, can lead to tremendous financial rewards. For example, Coca-Cola has been valued at over $80 billion, with another sixty brands valued at a minimum of $1 billion each. It does help to adopt a brand name that is recognizable, accessible, and noncontroversial. Volkswagen's model-series names stretch from Golf (Gulf wind), Sirocco (the hot wind from North Africa), to Passat (trade wind). It also made a successful switch from the Golf to the Rabbit in the United States.[39]

Translations must be done with utmost care, for it is in this area that cross-cultural blunders are often made. Even the most sophisticated firm, Coca-Cola, blundered when it entered China in the 1920s and wanted to introduce its product with the English pronunciation of "Coca-Cola." A translator developed a group of Chinese characters that actually translated "a wax-flattened name" or "bit the wax tadpole." The new characters now translate as "happiness in the mouth." The American Motors Corporation's "Matador" usually conjures images of vitality and strength, though in Puerto Rico, it means "killer." When Ford Motors introduced the Probe in Germany, it hardly recognized that the word translated as "test" or "rehearsal," and wondered why sales were flat.[40]

Nevertheless, with global brands, firms are able to leverage human and financial

Exhibit 5.8

The Top 100 Brands

2005 Top World Brands	2005 Top U.S. Brands	2005 Top Asian Brands	2005 Top European Brands
1. Coca-Cola	Coca-Cola	Toyota (Japan)	Nokia (Finland)
2. Microsoft	Microsoft	Honda (Japan)	Mercedes (Germany)
3. IBM	IBM	Samsung (S. Korea)	BMW (Germany)
4. GE	GE	Sony (Japan)	Louis Vuitton (France)
5. Intel	Intel	Canon (Japan)	Nescafe (Switzerland)
6. Nokia	Disney	Nintendo (Japan)	HSBC (Britain)
7. Disney	McDonald's	Panasonic (Japan)	SAP (Germany)
8. McDonald's	Marlboro	Nissan (Japan)	IKEA (Sweden)
9. Toyota	Citibank	LG (S. Korea)	Novartis (Switzerland)
10. Marlboro	Hewlett–Packard		UBS (Switzerland)
11. Mercedes-Benz	American Express		Siemens (Germany)
12. Citibank	Gillette		Gucci (Italy)
13. Hewlett-Packard	Cisco		L'Oreal (France)
14. American Express	Dell		Philips (Netherlands)
15. Gillette	Ford		Volkswagen (Germany)
16. BMW	Pepsi		Chanel (France)
17. Cisco	Merrill Lynch		Nestle (Switzerland)
18. Louis Vuitton	Budweiser		Danone (France)
19. Honda	Oracle		Adidas (Germany)
20. Samsung	Nike		Rolex (Switzerland)

Source: Adapted from "The Top 100 Brands," *BusinessWeek,* August 1, 2005, pp. 90–94.

resources in a manner that supports high-growth sales. Exhibit 5.8 depicts the world's best-known global brands.

3. In Marketing a Product Overseas, What Is the Proper Balance Between Standardization and Local Adaptation?

In the previous chapter, we introduced the difference between global and multidomestic industries and presented the strategies needed to underpin them. In this section, we elaborate on marketing strategies that are appropriate for such industries.

Achieving proper standardization and localization has been the hallmark of international market-entry decisions. Intuitively, one would think that standardization works best in global industries, while localization is more appropriate in highly domestic industries. For the most part, this is true, although, in practice, such extremes rarely exist and firms usually find an appropriate balance. In fact, global strategist George Yip argues that *"the idea of a fully standardized global product that is identical all over the world is a near myth that has caused great confusion"*[40] [italics in original].

While recognizing the need for local adaptation, it is still appropriate to think about industry characteristics in positioning the product or service. Global industries facilitate the adoption of highly standardized products. Think in terms of memory chips and semiconductors. To the extent that demand is relatively similar across international markets, then a standard product will reduce costs, improve product delivery, enhance customer preference, and facilitate competitive leverage. Yet firms can compete and differentiate themselves in the local market through creative product extensions (e.g., the use of sushi and mango pies by McDonald's in Japan and the Philippines) and high-end services (bank services that offer similar, highly competitive services).

Sodoma of France, the maker of Yoplait yogurt, used an excellent combination of standardization and localization. Roger Best explains this positioning as follows:

- In the United States, the product is positioned as a snack or dessert, emphasizes health and convenience, and is called Yoplait yogurt.
- In Japan, the product is creamier, and quality and purity are emphasized.
- In Greece, it is presented like a milk product and comes in small cartons, is drunk by adults, and is called Yovita.
- In South America, it is positioned as a between-meal snack for children and teens, and is called Kumi's.
- In Ireland, Yoplait uses humor, along with a sense of history, to portray its taste and quality, and is called Yop.[42]

Selecting the right target markets is the first step in creating global marketing strategies. After all, the premise is that what matters crucially is "location, location, location." Even so, once entrenched in the market, firms face a variety of new challenges, local and foreign competition, and the continuous need to monitor local conditions. While this effort is clearly a comprehensive one, in fact the subject matter of this entire book, there are some notable tools to help managers evaluate their progress in this continual effort.

PRICING IN AN INTERNATIONAL CONTEXT

Pricing is the application of price to products or services. Pricing is a critical part of consumer value and sustained firm profitability. More often than not, the value of a product or service is assessed through its price. The success of cost-based or differentiation strategies (Chapter 4) is validated by customer response to established prices. If prices are set high, this can be good for margins but only if perceived benefits are consistent with the price. On the other hand, when prices are set too low, even if justified by a firm's cost structure, this can result in lower-than-expected consumer sales volume if low prices are associated with inferior, lower quality.

Setting prices in international markets is even more complicated because of the difficulty of ascertaining what customers find attractive relative to competing products. Take the case of the Delacre line of luxury biscuits that was promoted under the Pepperidge Farm label and introduced into the United States with a premium prize. Unfortunately, potential customers did not regard the product to be worth the money. Only after the British firm Peek Frean sold them at a lower price did sales begin to rise. The lesson is that a "differentiated" product might not be regarded as such by customers, until the market has been clearly established.[43]

Miscues likewise occur at the low end of pricing. A manufacturer of canned luncheon meat slightly cut its prices by rounding them off to even numbers, thinking that this would provide them an advantage over competitors' products that were fractionally higher. Much to their disappointment, expected sales did not materialize. What the company failed to realize was that local retailers were promoting competition vigorously because they gained by customers not wanting small change when purchasing the fractionally higher item. In effect, this served as a "tip" that was particularly appreciated by retailers who operated with very small profit margins.[44]

Informal distribution channels can likewise compound pricing in international markets. A U.S.-based manufacturer of health supplements had decided to launch its products in an Asian country. Discussions had focused on an appropriate price. The company representative sought to price the products at a premium, one that was higher than their price in the United States, partly based on a belief that there was no other viable channel to transport products to Asia. Yet this can be a risky strategy. By setting its prices high, this manufacturer can unwittingly create a "gray" market. Hypothetically, someone can have friends in the United States purchase products that can be delivered to this Asian country—a scheme that is less costly than purchasing the products directly in the targeted country.

Collectively, price setting for products overseas—a decision that is closely intertwined with a promotions campaign—needs to be formulated in a systematic fashion. Several key steps are involved in formulating pricing policy.

Set the Pricing Objective

The company must first decide what it wants to accomplish with its particular product offering. Since there are a number of possibilities, it is critical that a company think through its objectives. Failing to do so can result in misplaced products that are inconsistent with the company's overall strategy. Some pricing objectives include:[45]

- *Survival.* Companies pursue survival if they are plagued with overcapacity, price wars, intense competition, or a significant reversal in consumer needs that renders their positions untenable in their home markets.
- *Maximum current profit.* Some companies try to set the price that will maximize current profits or some established targeted rate of return. When Dell Computers entered China, it sought to have a 20 percent market share in a specified number of years. Pricing of its products was consistent with this objective.
- *Maximize sales growth and market share.* Some firms want to maximize sales growth based on a belief that higher sales volume leads to lower cost and higher long-run profits. A popular strategy used by Japanese multinationals in the 1970s and 1980s was to reduce their entry prices in an effort to grab market share. This worked successfully in maturing products and services.
- *Maximum market skimming.* Some companies favor setting high prices to "skim" the market. This strategy has been attributed to Intel, which priced its new line of microprocessors at a premium price, only to reduce them later.
- *Establish product quality leadership.* A company might aim to be the product quality leader in the field. Cray Computers often priced its line of supercomputers at a premium level based on the belief that it offered the fastest and most reliable supercomputer at the time of entry and that consumers could well afford them.

Estimate Costs

Knowing the company's costs is fundamental to any pricing decision. Absent this, prices might fail to cover associated costs, leading to disastrous results. By under-

---

Exhibit 5.9

Pricing Considerations

Pricing decisions are generally under the control of manufacturers. Even so, the wrong price can result in significant changes in company profits. To illustrate a pricing decision, a simplified example is presented.

Assume the cost structure for a manufacturer of steel-lined drums for sale in Asia:

Variable cost per unit	$20
Fixed cost	$600,000
Expected unit sales	100,000
Manufacturer's unit cost	= Variable cost + fixed costs/unit sales
	= $20 + ($600,000/100,000) = $26

Assume that a 20 percent markup is desired. Thus, price is given by:

Markup price = unit cost (1-desired rate of return) = $26 / (1 − .20) = $32.50

The manufacturer will charge dealers $32.50 in order to make a profit of $6.50 per unit. The dealers, in turn, can mark up the unit, depending on their own cost and profit considerations.

Even so, other issues need to be considered. McKinsey consultants propose the following:

1. At the industry level, does the manufacturer anticipate changes in costs, supply, and demand patterns? If so, the manufacturer's unit cost might need to be revised accordingly.
2. At the product/market level, the manufacturer might consider how its steel cans compare against competitors. This decision entails a very understanding of competitors' response patterns and customers' consumption or buying patterns.
3. At the transaction level, the manufacturer has to consider the exact price that includes discounts, allowances, rebates, incentives, terms, warranties, and bonuses for favored customers.

Source: Adapted from Philip Kotler, *Marketing Management* (Upper Saddle River, New Jersey: Prentice Hall, 1997), p. 503 (figures are slightly revised); Michael V. Marn, Eric V. Roegner, and Craig C. Zawada, *The Price Advantage* (New Jersey: John Wiley & Sons, 2004), pp. 23, 43–44, and 77.

---

standing its cost structure, a company is also able to decide whether to enact markup pricing, or to pursue target return pricing. Both are illustrated in Exhibit 5.9.

Understanding Competitors' Response Patterns

In addition to a company's own costs, it is essential to understand those of the competition. Granted that competitors' costs are not readily available, it behooves the company to anticipate the far-reaching implications of any price policy. Will competitors react fiercely and match them in order to maintain market share? Or will they sit back and allow the company to pursue its intended course of action?

One method of anticipating competitors' response is to examine previous patterns of behavior. Some competitors do not react quickly or strongly to a rival's aggressive action. Anheuser-Busch pretty much ignored Miller's aggressive stance, until after the latter achieved a 60 percent market share. Other firms are selective, that is, they elect to respond only to certain behaviors. Oil companies generally respond only to competitors' prices but not promotions. Still others are particularly ferocious, such as Procter & Gamble, which zealously guards its turf. When attacked by Lever Brothers in the "ultra" detergent market, P&G vastly outspent Lever in support of its brand, to the point that Lever could not even get shelf space among retailers.[46] Thinking through competitors' actions supplements managerial decisions about pricing policy.

In conclusion, developing appropriate global marketing strategies is essential in properly leveraging a firm's advantage in the international arena. The process involves identifying target markets, selecting an optimal mode of entry, and deciding on the timing of entry. It also involves consideration of product adaptation, in tandem with promotional, positioning, and pricing decisions. International marketing is one of the first forays into international markets, and comprises perhaps the most central of decisions made by managers.

SUMMARY

1. Marketing internationally is vastly complicated by different customs, culture, languages, laws, and institution. The goal of marketing is to satisfy customer needs with what a company offers.
2. Global marketing orientation is an underlying philosophy that does not imply a blind adherence to customers' needs and wants nor sacrificing of reasonable profits.
3. Ranking political and economic environment in terms of potential for entry should be a priority when developing a global marking strategy. Core issues in political risk assessment include: (1) a level playing field between foreign and domestic business; (2) support of intellectual property rights; (3) autocratic versus democratic regimes; (4) stable and efficient political and economic environments; and (5) government appropriation.
4. There are six basic modes of entry and they all come with advantages and disadvantages. Exporting involves the fewest resource commitments and offers the least control. Licensing, a type of management contract, is a low-cost approach for fast market expansion, but it does not always give the licensor complete control of operations. Franchising requires a high level of coordination among all international markets to maintain quality and image consistency. A company can gain international experience with almost no investment through turnkey projects. Joint venture is often used for enhancing competitiveness. A major challenge is finding compatible partner(s). Wholly owned operations require the highest level of resource commitments and offer the highest level of control. Selecting a mode requires the examination of both internal and external factors.
5. Timing of entry can favor one firm over another. First movers, or pioneers, enjoy the advantages of (1) having initial feedback; (2) securing access to supplies; (3) setting rules of the game; and (4) erecting entry barriers. Followers offer the advantages of (1) learning from the first entrant's mistakes; (2) capitalizing on the demand created by the first mover; and (3) providing better products and

services that undermine the leader's initial advantage. Two sets of factors need to be taken into account when considering timing: the strategic importance of the market, and the firm's ability to exploit the market.

6. There are five factors affecting international market mix. They are price/cost, attractiveness, compatibility, availability, and awareness. A high level of brand recognition benefits market expansion. The global positions of products can vary from market to market. A product positioned at the low-end segment in one market can be positioned at the high-end segment in another.

7. Striking a balance and optimal combination of product standardization and localization in the global market requires a thorough investigation of industry characteristics. The growing of global industries facilitates the adoption of highly standardized products.

8. There are several steps involved international pricing: setting pricing objectives; estimating costs; and understanding competitors' response patterns. When setting pricing objectives, companies consider the following five options: survival, maximum current profit, maximize sales growth and market share, maximum market skimming, and establishing product-quality leadership.

KEY TERMS

Exporting	Strategic importance of the market
Licensing	Firm's ability to exploit the market
Franchising	Product awareness
Turnkey project	Positioning
Joint venture	Global position
Wholly owned operation	Pricing
First-mover advantages	

DISCUSSION QUESTIONS

1. This chapter suggests several core questions to be addressed for political risk assessment. How can a company protect itself from these risks? In today's international global environment, what are some of the most commonly found political risk levels in foreign markets?

2. Compare and contrast the six modes of entry. In what way is one strategically better than the others? How does a host country's economic growth affect the investor's choice of entry?

3. It is said that the choice of entry mode is affected by the external and internal factors. Select a multinational company and analyze how these factors have affected its entry mode and evaluate whether its choices are justifiable.

4. Discuss the advantages of being a first mover and under what circumstances this would be a viable strategic move.

5. Discuss the advantages of being a follower and under what circumstances this would be a viable strategic move.
6. Select a company of your choice to illustrate how the following two factors affect the choice of entry timing: (1) the strategic importance of the market, and (2) the firm's ability to exploit the market.
7. What are the five components of global market? How do they affect the problems in the market mix? What are the solutions to these problems? Please use examples to illustrate.
8. What are the core questions in adapting products and services to the targeted international market? Select a company to illustrate how successful this company is in addressing these questions.
9. How does a brand's level of recognition, that is, known versus unknown, affect its international market potential? Will the trend of globalization enhance or reduce the power of brand?
10. What is global positioning? How do companies develop global brands through positioning? Please use cases to help illustrate your points.
11. There are five international pricing objectives stated in the text. Discuss the pros and cons of each and how the current global environments affect a manager's choice of pricing strategy.

ACTION ITEM 5.1. ENTRY STRATEGY SELECTION

A small U.S. company recently obtained a patent from the U.S. government (worldwide patent is pending) for a handheld machine tool that combines the functions of screwdriver and chainsaw. It is designed for both industrial and household use. Only low-level technical skills are required to operate and use the tool. There is no apparent high-tech requirement for producing this tool. If producing in the United States, for every 100,000 units manufactured, the average production cost is $23 and the products can be sold at retail stores for $81 each. The company is open to both domestic or overseas manufacturing. Among the strategic options studied in this chapter, please evaluate each combination of options below. Please specify the factors that should be taken into consideration and offer your recommendations.

	Export	Licensing	Joint venture	Greenfield wholly owned subsidiary	Merger or acquisition wholly owned subsidiary	Primary reasons
Canada						
Germany						
Japan						
China						
India						
Argentina						
Mexico						

Case-in-Point. Unilever Raises Its India Game

By Chris Prystay, October 2003[47]

Priti Loyalka dips litmus paper into a facial cleanser to show housewife Rachna Garg how mild it is compared to a popular baby soap. Garg asks what alpha hydroxy creams do, then tries on a lipstick. For years, Garg has shopped in the cluttered family-run stores scattered throughout her upmarket beach-side Mumbai suburb for things like shampoo and cosmetics. These days, she's happy to pay more—and buy more—from Loyalka, who peddles a high-priced portfolio of Hindustan Lever products made exclusively for door-to-door sales. "We need expert advice, and there's nowhere to get it," says Garg. "Shopkeepers can't explain all these new products well."

Hindustan Lever—Unilever's Indian subsidiary—has deftly tapped India's hinterland by making products affordable to even the poorest consumer. Now, the company hopes to tap India's growing middle class by offering value-added services and sales—a departure from the classic "we make it, retailers sell it" manufacturing-based business model used by consumer-goods companies worldwide. In the last three years, the company has experimented with a number of services businesses, from a home-laundry service to an online grocery store. But the most promising is its fast-growing direct-sales business and a chain of beauty salons run by Lakme Lever, the company's retail-cosmetics unit.

Hindustan Lever's quest for new growth areas comes at a time when myriad foreign and low-priced local players are starting to erode the company's dominant grip. The company, however, sees fresh opportunities in the changing habits of Indian consumers. As more Indian women join the workforce, they've got less time to shop and groom, but more money to spend. Other women, like Garg, want expert advice on new products—something India's fragmented mom-and-pop retail industry can't provide.

"People are willing to pay for those value-added services, at home and in a salon," says Dalip Sehgal, director of new ventures at Hindustan Lever. The Indian service ventures aren't Unilever's first, but they might be the first to succeed. Unilever's London office opened a three-branch pilot men's salon, designed to leverage their Lynx male personal-care line, and Myhome Services, a home-laundry and cleaning service, in 2000. It shut the first and sold the second a year later. Critics cite Unilever's lack of experience in retailing, slow scale-up, and the high cost of the pilot salons, located on London's pricey Bond Street, as reasons for the project's failure.

Undeterred, Unilever set up Unilever Ventures, a venture-capital fund designed to invest in and manage service-oriented start-ups that leverage the company's food, home, and personal-care product portfolio in Europe. Last year, that unit opened a new Persil-brand laundry and dry-cleaning chain, run this time as a concession in Sainsbury's, a British supermarket chain.

The unit has opened fifteen outlets so far. Unilever Ventures has also taken control of another trial salon venture, run under the Pond's Institute brand, set up in 2000 in Spain. The ventures unit has opened two more Pond's Institute salons, which offer facials, manicures, pedicures, massage, and waxing, in Madrid this year. Unilever Venture executives, who hope to roll out salons countrywide, say Lakme Lever's own chain offers up plenty of ideas.

"Lakme is a long way down the line compared to us; we're just at the start. They've been sharing knowledge with us, particularly on things like roll-out costs," says Brendan Stewart, principal of Unilever Ventures. In India, Lakme executives opted to franchise the salon instead, an option Unilever Ventures is "seriously considering" for Pond's. Unilever, meanwhile, has already set up direct-sales units in Thailand and South Africa, modeled on the three-year-old Indian Hindustan Lever Network venture.

The challenges facing Hindustan Lever mirror challenges faced by the industry in developed markets, analysts say. "In developed markets, growth is stagnant and one of the issues is no-name or in-store brands, made and sold by big retailers," says Patrick Medley, a consumer-sector specialist at IBM Global Services' business-consulting unit in Singapore.

That makes innovation in developing markets, the last bastion of strong growth, all the more important. But here, too, companies are facing competition from a plethora of new, and cheaper, local brands that mirrors the threat posed by low-cost, in-store brands in the West. Innovation, however, is easier here.

Developing markets like India, which has a fragmented retail sector, offer consumer-goods companies more room to experiment with new business models. The retail sectors in Britain and the United States may have the power to block their suppliers from becoming their competitors, but not so in a place like India. In Britain, for example, four big retail chains account for 70 percent of Unilever's sales. In India, most of the company's goods are sold through millions of small, independent shops that can't complain if Lever starts selling competing goods, for example, door to door.

"A lot of organizations have struggled to do this in developed markets where you have strong relationships with the retailer. In India, there's no conflict with the retail channels," says Medley. At Hindustan Lever, executives maintain that manufacturing mass-market consumer goods will remain the company's core focus. But longer-term, these new ventures will be important additions to the company's revenue stream. Seghal estimates the salons and the direct-sales unit, plus a sampling of other small services projects, will together account for 15 percent of Hindustan Lever's revenue within five years. Hindustan Lever posted a 17.6-billion-rupee ($382 million) net profit in 2002, up 7 percent over the year before.

Some projects have fared better than others. The home-laundry business floundered, because it couldn't compete on price with myriad dhobis, or local launderers, who offer home delivery of washing done by hand. It has had more success with services that India's cheap labor pool can't necessarily provide—like the advice Loyalka gives on which beauty products each customer should use to suit her particular complexion and skin.

The direct-sales business in India is worth just $350 million a year and employs about 1 million, according to the Indian Direct Selling Association. Hindustan Lever is making a long-term bet that as the middle class grows, so will the demand for value-added services. "The man behind the counter at your neighborhood shop can't provide advice on what color suits you," says Sehgal.

HIGH-END COSMETICS

The company began direct sales in 2000 with Aviance, a new line of high-end shampoos, skin creams, and cosmetics that cost about 40 percent more than Lever brands sold in stores. Earlier this year, the company renamed the direct-sales unit Hindustan Lever Network, and added home, dish, and laundry detergents, plus male grooming products and oral care to the door-to-door line. The company hopes to add health supplements and specialty foods to its direct-sales portfolio early next year. Hindustan Lever Network now has 75,000 direct-sales staff, and plans to recruit 1 million more in the next five years.

Over at Lakme, a fifty-one-year-old cosmetics company in which Hindustan Lever acquired a 50 percent stake in 1995 (and fully bought in 1998), executives are banking on services to help boost sales and shore up the brand's current 50 percent market share. In the past ten years, excise taxes on cosmetics have dropped to 16 percent from 120 percent, making the products more accessible to consumers—and more appetizing to foreign investors.

L'Oreal, which also owns the Maybelline brand, came to India in 1991, as did Revlon in 1995, and they have since grabbed a combined 16 percent share of the market from Lakme. Executives began looking for ways to revamp Lakme's image, known by many young women as their mothers' brand.

"You can't compete on price alone. If you don't evolve your brand into something the modern woman aspires to, you'll be overtaken by international companies like L'Oreal," says Anil Chopra, business head of Lakme Lever. Three years ago, Chopra noticed that India's salon business had begun to flourish as more women joined the work force. Chopra estimates that India's salon business is growing by 15 percent per year and is worth as much as the country's $200 million skin-care business—and far more than the $50 million cosmetics industry.

That presented Lakme with an opportunity to cash in on the growing beauty-services niche and at the same time leverage both its image and sales. Lakme has franchised 50 salons in the last three years and plans to open 200 more in India's wealthier cities in the next three. The salons use and sell Lakme cosmetics and nail polish. The real winners for the company, however, have been services like hair cuts, waxing, and facials. Product sales account for just 5 percent of sales in most of the salons.

"We're not selling as much product as we'd planned, but in terms of turnover we're doing much better. The average bill value per customer is higher than planned," says Chopra. "It's really been about the services." "Product sales should get a boost as the salons build repeat customers," he says. "That's slowly starting to happen."

In a bustling Lakme salon in downtown Mumbai, Priya Jaikishan, a sales manager at a nearby hotel, gets her monthly head massage while a manicurist paints her nails with Lakme polish. Stacks of Lakme products sit by the till. On the way out, Jaikishan, who usually favors Estee Lauder, grabs a lipstick and an eyeliner. "I wouldn't go out and look for Lakme, but it's here," she says, pointing to the counter display. "So every time I pay, I end up buying something."

The salons also offer fresh marketing opportunities to bolster the brand, from professional staff who promote the product to a growing customer database built up through a loyalty-card program. "If you want to defend your 50 percent share, you either find innovation in product or find another business opportunity that will help strengthen brand credentials," Chopra says. He expected the salon business to contribute 40 percent of Lakme Lever's sales by 2005.

One of the biggest challenges in the move to the services sector is the company's own legacy as a manufacturing company. "We have the skills in consumer understanding, technology, product knowledge. What we did not have and something we need to build is a service culture," says Sehgal.

At Lakme, Chopra opted to franchise the salons, selecting entrepreneurs with a strong service history. At the Hindustan Lever Network, unit head K.K. Rajesh hired a fresh team of twelve managers from the services sector, mostly hotels and banks. "I've learned a lot of things. At Hindustan Lever we tend to be a little arrogant when we deal with retailers. We know his stake with you is as high as your stake with him. But this business is about relationship building," says Rajesh.

Those lessons are trickling back. Hindustan Lever is looking at ways to teach its sales managers to treat their customers—the distributors and retailers—more like consumers. The board of Hindustan Lever is also looking at ways to copy the motivational programs—such as bonuses and tiered-reward plans—they use to motivate their direct-sales consultants to spur the 10,000 salesmen, employed by distributors, who sell Hindustan Lever's goods to shopkeepers.

"Our culture is one of interacting with customers rather than consumers. We could say to a stockist, 'I don't have these three products today. You can get it tomorrow.' You can't do that with a consumer," says Sehgal. "With consumers, there's a moment of truth in every interaction."

CASE DISCUSSION QUESTIONS

1. How did HLL approach the Indian market?
2. Specifically discuss HLL's approach in regard to the following: (a) product policy, (b) promotions, (c) positioning, and (d) pricing.
3. To what extent was HLL's marketing strategy successful in India?
4. Can HLL continue its successful marketing activities in the future? What needs to be changed?

NOTES FOR CHAPTER 5

1. Adapted from Nic Fleming, "Geopolitical 'Illiteracy' Blamed in Microsoft Fiasco." *The Vancouver Sun*, August 19, 2004, p. A9.

2. Nic Fleming, Microsoft Feels the Pain of Tricky World," *The Ottawa Citizen*, August 19, 2004, p. C1.

3. Nic Fleming, "It's a Tricky World in Computers, Says Microsoft Chief," *The Daily Telegraph*, August 19, 2004, p. 05.

4. Both examples are taken from "How Not to Sell Food in Asia," *Asia Times*, February 12, 2001.

5. Richard Lutz and Barton Wietz, "Strategic Marketing—Delivering Customer Value," in *What the Best MBAs Know*, ed. Peter Navarro (New York: McGraw-Hill, 2005), p. 89.

6. Ibid.

7. Ibid.

8. World Factbook 2006–07, Central Intelligence Agency. https://www.cia.gov/library/publications/the-world-factbook/index.html.

9. This section is based on Nenad Pacek and Daniel Thorniley, *Emerging Markets: Lessons for Business Success and the Outlook for Different Markets* (London: The Economist Newsletter, 2004), p. 33.

10. Marvin Zonis, Dan Lefkovitz, and Sam Wilkin, *The Kimchi Matters: Global Business and Local Politics in a Crisis-Driven World* (Chicago: Agate Publishers, 2003): xv–xviii.

11. Nenad Pacek and Daniel Thornliey, *Emerging Markets: Lessons for Business Success and the Outlook for Different Markets*, p. 34.

12. Ibid., p. 39.

13. Ibid.

14. Zonis, Lefkovitz, and Wilkin, *The Kimchi Matters: Global Business and Local Politics in a Crisis-Driven World*, pp. 4–9.

15. Ibid., p. 95.

16. A particularly good source is Economist.com.

17. This figure is for 1999. Updated monthly information is provided by the U.S. Census Bureau.

18. See www.quantumcomm.com.

19. "Siemens AG: Power-Plant Orders Are Won from Mideast and North Africa," *Wall Street Journal*, June 15, 2005, p. 1.

20. "Siemens AG: Power-Plant Orders Are Won from Mideast and North Africa," p. 1.

21. "Mitsubishi Heavy Industries Ltd.," *Wall Street Journal*, September 15, 2004, p. 1.

22. *Nissan Annual Report 2001*, 2002, p. 10.

23. "Lenovo Group Ltd.: Share Repurchase Price Is Set; IBM Will Receive $152 Million," *Wall Street Journal*, May 5, 2005, p. 1.

24. Ibid.

25. The literature on pioneer and follower strategic advantages is extensive. See Kerin, Roger, P. Rajan Varadajaran, and Robert A. Peterson, "First-Mover Advantage: A Synthesis, Conceptual Framework, and Research Propositions," *Journal of Marketing* 56 (1992): 33–52; M.B. Lieberman and D.B. Montgomery. "First Mover Advantages," *Strategic Management Journal* 9 (1998): 41–58. Luo Yadong and Mike Peng, "First Mover Advantages in Investing in Transitional Economies," *Thunderbird International Business Review* 40, no. 2 (1998): 141–163; Julio Castro and James J. Chrisman, "Order of Market Entry, Competitive Strategy, and Financial Performance," *Journal of Business Research* 33 (1995): 165–177.

26. Marvin B. Lieberman and David B. Montgomery, "First-Mover (Dis) Advantages: Retrospective and Link with the Resource-Based View," *Strategic Management Journal*, 1998, 19 (2): 1111–1125.

27. Cecilia Yang (Mary Kay General Manager). Lecture for the Age of the Pacific Series, University of Oregon and Portland State University, May 8, 1998.

28. Quoted in George Mannes, "First Mover Advantage: What It's Really Worth," *TheStreet.com*, January 26, 1999. Available at http://thestreet.netscape.com/tech/internet/682198.html.

29. Robert Hof, "Prosper: The eBay of Loans?" *Business Week* (February 13, 2006).

30. See Wikipedia, "Gilman Louie," at http://en.wikipedia.org/wiki/Gilman_Louie.

31. Quoted in Mannes, "First Mover Advantage."

32. Ibid.

33. Ibid.

34. This is adapted from Vijay Govindarajan and Anil K. Gupta, *The Quest for Global Dominance* (San Francisco: Jossey Bass, 2001), pp. 28–30.

35. Roger J. Best, *Market-based Management: Strategies for Growing Consumer Value and Profitability* (Upper Sadde River, NJ: Prentice Hall, 1999), p. 280.

36. C.K. Prahalad and Stuart L. Hart, "The Fortune at the Bottom of the Pyramid," *strategy+business,* 26 (First Quarter 2002): 54–67; also see update at C.K. Prahalad, *Fortune at the Bottom of the Pyramid: Eradicating Poverty Through Profits* (Philadelphia, PA: Wharton School Publishing, 2006), p. 213.

37. David A. Ricks, *Blunders in International Business*, 3rd ed. (Oxford, UK : Blackwell, 1999), p. 3.

38. Robert Block, "How Big Mac Kept from Becoming a Serb Archenemy," *Wall Street Journal*, September 3, 1999, p. B3.

39. Examples are taken from David A. Ricks, *Blunders in International Business*, 3rd ed., pp. 39–40.

40. Ibid., pp. 78–90.

41. George S. Yip, *Total Global Strategy II* (Upper Saddle River, NJ: Prentice Hall, 2003), p. 90.

42. Best, *Market-Based Management*, p. 322.

43. Ricks, *Blunders in International Business,* 3rd ed., p. 71.

44. Ibid.

45. Philip Kotler, *Marketing Management* (Upper Saddle River, NJ: Prentice Hall, 1997), p. 239.

46. Ibid.

47. This section is adapted from Cris Prystay, "Unilever Raises Its India Game," *Far Eastern Economic Review*, October 30, 2003, pp. 50–54. Reprinted with permission.

6 Leveraging Competitive Advantage Through Global Sourcing

The buyer needs a hundred eyes . . . the seller but one.
—Italian proverb

*You don't need face-to-face communication. So why pay
someone sitting in Ohio $60,000 a year when it could
be done in Cebu, Philippines, for $12,000 a year?*
—Eugene Kublanov, neoIT's vice president of corporate development

CHAPTER OUTLINE

- IKEA: From Retailer to Cult Brand
- Why Global Sourcing?
- From Domestic Purchasing to Global Sourcing
- Types of Global Sourcing
- Global Sourcing: Five Levels of Development
- Locating Global Sourcing Partners
- Key Success Factors for Global Sourcing
- Guidelines for Implementing Global Sourcing
- The Benefits of Global Sourcing
- From Sourcing to Outsourcing: Emerging Patterns
- Outsourcing from "Make-or-Buy" to Strategic Transformation
- A Framework for Examining Outsourcing Decisions

LEARNING OBJECTIVES

- Understand the needs and benefits of global sourcing.
- Know the different types of sourcing and the process of a firm's development toward full participation in global sourcing.
- Understand the progression from global sourcing to outsourcing.
- Know the difference between global sourcing and outsourcing.

- Learn about the benefits and costs of outsourcing.
- Know how a firm can progress in outsourcing.
- Understand what makes a job activity at risk for outsourcing.
- Learn how to use the Outsourcing Index for managerial decisions.

IKEA: FROM RETAILER TO A CULT BRAND

Which mass-market retailer has had more success globally? Chances are you might guess Wal-Mart, or Carrefour. The right answer is IKEA, a Swedish retailer founded by Ingvar Kamprad that has become a global cult brand. For all that has been said about Wal-Mart's power and growth, it stumbled in Brazil, Germany, and Japan. France's Carrefour, in turn, has yet to make it in the United States. In contrast, IKEA had 250 stores in thirty-four countries in 2007. Its operating margins of approximately 10 percent compare quite favorably against erstwhile competitors, such as Target and Pier One. And about 1.1 million people visit an IKEA store *every day*.[1]

But success did not occur overnight, nor did it come easily. Prior to IKEA's entry, the furniture industry was cartelized—for both manufacturers and retailers. IKEA's ability to break into this otherwise intransigent industry is testimony to Ingvar Kamprad's vision, creativity, and persistence. He realized that a new market segment of newly established middle-class families had emerged. He targeted this segment with products along simple contemporary lines, yet affordable because products came in ready-to-assemble knocked-down parts. Kamprad located his stores in the suburbs with features that were simple, unpretentious, and friendly, making them nonthreatening to the young, middle-class buyer. Kamprad sought to lure customers to the store, where he relied on good layout, product display, and catalogue information to guide customers. His pricing was not constrained by industry practice.[2]

Perhaps less pronounced in IKEA's history and business model is its sourcing strategy. This is important when considering the economics of growth. If IKEA keeps growing at its historical pace, it will need to source twice as much material by 2010. Lennart Dahlgren, IKEA's country manager for Russia, explains further: "We can't increase more than 20 stores a year because supply is the bottleneck."[3] Supply is further challenged by different requirements for local customization. In China, 250,000 plastic placemats were launched to commemorate the Year of the Rooster. Americans like to fold their clothes, requiring features like deeper drawers. Large Hispanic families like dining tables and sofas that fit more than two people, in contrast to the Swedish norm, and they prefer bold colors.[4]

Equally demanding is the need for materials sourced at competitive prices. Eager to cash in on relatively inexpensive raw materials and cheap but skilled labor, IKEA has made Vietnam its largest Asian supply center after China and India. In 2003, IKEA purchased close to $110 million in products from Vietnam, outstripping purchases from Indonesia, Malaysia, and Thailand. IKEA keeps its retail prices low by driving hard bargains with its Vietnamese suppliers. Even so, in return for its continued service, IKEA offers its suppliers the prospect of a stable, long-term partnership with high-volume business. Suppliers also receive advice from IKEA, ranging from sourcing raw materials to improving productivity, and information about new equipment. For the future, IKEA is interested in bamboo products that are not only environmentally sustainable, but also less expensive than wood and in abundant supply. If this need materializes, Vietnam and other neighboring countries are ready.[5]

WHY GLOBAL SOURCING?

Perhaps more so than before, heightened global competition has placed increasingly high performance demands on business. Customer expectations for product and service improvements have escalated over time. Ignoring these expectations places any company at risk of being replaced by a competitor. Yet it has been difficult for companies to exert pricing power while keeping costs under control. As a consequence, firms now have to scramble and explore new ways to make their prices competitive with increased quality to boot. For a company like IKEA, these constitute pressure points for which a new and effective sourcing strategy is needed. What many firms have discovered in this process is that reducing costs through more efficient sourcing activities can boost the bottom line, keep abreast of customers' expectations, and leverage the competitive advantage.

To shore up sourcing activities, firms have now repositioned sourcing as a key strategic activity, instead of one of many functional activities.[6] For IKEA, the use of global sourcing has reaped significant benefits in terms of sustaining its cost leadership strategy. In fact, international sourcing has become a fundamental element of its overall corporate strategy. Global sourcing differs fundamentally from such traditional conceptions as purchasing. **Global sourcing** is defined as "the integration and coordination of procurement requirements across worldwide business units, looking at common items, processes, technologies, and suppliers."[7] Moreover, the "ultimate objective of global sourcing strategy is for the company to exploit both its own competitive advantages and the locational advantages of various countries in global competition."[8] Global sourcing involves the development and transformation of the firm's logistics and supply chain, with longer inventory pipelines and reliable suppliers becoming key components of a firm's international strategy.

This chapter builds on global sourcing as the second path for a firm to exploit opportunities in a global context, and to leverage its business model accordingly (see Figure 6.1). In Chapter 5, international marketing was introduced as the first path toward sustaining advantage through new international markets, and products and services aligned with the needs and requirements of those markets. International marketing comprises the demand side of the performance equation. Global sourcing involves the coordination of supply lines to reduce costs and to ensure quality and timely delivery. With its focus on costs, global sourcing comprises the supply side of the performance equation. International marketing and global sourcing are twin, complementary paths by which a firm can transform its business model into an effective one in international markets.

The organization of this chapter is as follows. First, we review different patterns

Figure 6.1 **Framework for Leveraging Strategic Advantage: Global Sourcing**

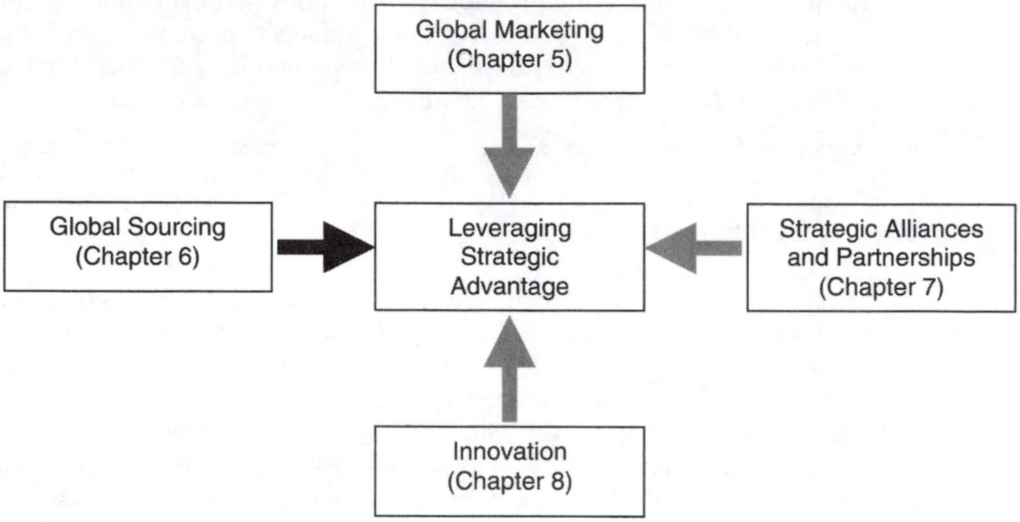

of sourcing and the methods of developing competencies in this area. Second, we discuss how sourcing has evolved from a domestic to an international/global platform. Third, we provide guidelines to develop sourcing programs recommended by various researchers and industry experts. Finally, we discuss the most recent wave of global sourcing—outsourcing—focusing specifically on how this has shifted from a "make-or-buy" decision to a strategic transformation of a firm's competencies. We introduce new templates for thinking about activities that are likely to be outsourced, and a framework to make these decisions appropriately. The central theme of the chapter is that sourcing (and outsourcing) constitutes an integral element of a firm's global strategy. While global sourcing is a laudable objective for many firms, it still has not been done effectively. The objective of this chapter is to help managers understand how to integrate global sourcing as part of global strategic management.

FROM DOMESTIC PURCHASING TO GLOBAL SOURCING

Historically, the progression of sourcing practice has evolved from domestic to international to a global platform. Because of its front-end position in a firm's value chain, sourcing on the basis of costs and quality provides crucial indicators of the efficiency of the actual production process. A concern for costs, along with the availability and the quality of materials, are among many factors in the production process that have a significant impact on the final price or value of the end product or service.[9] Therefore, the choice of suppliers is critical for controlling costs and ensuring quality. In relatively stable and tranquil times, this choice of suppliers, while important, was considered an operational, not a strategic, issue for many firms. As competition has intensified, however, firms have sought new ways to reduce costs and improve quality, prompting a shift from purely domestic to international suppliers.

Within an international context, cross-cultural communication is important because firms have to work with suppliers from different cultures. Despite these potential difficulties, firms have realized that sourcing from other countries, particularly those with lower cost structures and with comparable quality, provides a "window of opportunity" for a head start in keeping ahead of competition. In other words, they have been willing to accept this tradeoff between handling cross-cultural problems and the potential savings from using international suppliers. Thus far, the pattern of global sourcing is compelling: in 2001 alone, the United States imported more than $1.3 trillion worth of goods and services.[10] In a survey of CEOs, nearly 80 percent cited cost reduction and quality improvement as their top priorities in international purchasing decisions.[11] It was also mentioned that for every sales dollar generated, about fifty-five cents was spent on purchasing goods and services for production.[12] Reflecting these statistics, successful companies reported realized savings ranging from 10 to 60 percent.[13]

Global sourcing has become an integral part of a firm's corporate strategy. In order to think strategically in the context of numerous potential suppliers all over the world, firms require an entirely different mindset. In contrast to domestic sourcing alone, global sourcing expands a firm's strategic options: it can introduce competition to the domestic supply base, establish a presence in a foreign market, satisfy offset requirements, and increase the number of available sources.[14] For example, aircraft manufacturer Boeing's decision to source significant components from China led to the opening of the Chinese market to its airplanes.[15] In addition to lower costs and improved quality, the firm also found itself in a position to learn about better product design, better delivery performance, better customer service, and improved technology from coordinated and integrated activities, all through interaction and mutual learning with different suppliers.[16]

Despite recognizing the importance of global sourcing to business success, these companies still conduct global sourcing in selected opportunistic moments, oftentimes in an ad hoc manner, instead of folding it into their business model.[17] Yet many companies are *not* capable of making this transition. In the sections that follow, some methods of facilitating the shift from domestic to a global sourcing, and from an operational to a strategic perspective, are introduced. The first step is to understand the current types and methods of domestic and international sourcing.

TYPES OF GLOBAL SOURCING

What are specific methods of domestic and international sourcing? In this section, common practices in sourcing are presented and analyzed—from traditional multiple suppliers to selected suppliers or hybrid-supplier structures.

MULTIPLE SUPPLIERS SOURCING

The traditional method of sourcing involves the use of **multiple suppliers**. The logic is to avoid overdependence on one supplier that might place the buyer at risk in the event the supplier fails to deliver the product, raises prices, or lowers quality. Another reason for using multiple suppliers stems from the inability of any one supplier to provide the necessary volume to buyers. By using multiple suppliers, a firm enjoys better leverage and opportunities for added flexibility, reduced dependence, reduced risk, and the ability to compare price/quality with other suppliers.[18] Competing suppliers also have to provide evidence of their competencies, cost, quality, technology, and expertise during the bidding process in order to be attractive to the buyer-firm.[19] Because firms can play one supplier against another, it is generally assumed that buyers have stronger bargaining power over their suppliers.

Even so, the use of multiple suppliers has a number of drawbacks. First, it can be taxing for a buyer-firm, as it requires a lot of time and effort obtaining information, securing documentation, engaging in negotiation, and finalizing contracts with a large group of suppliers. Other costs include the allocation of time and management needed to maintain and build supplier relationships. Second, because these relationships are not secure and tend to be ad hoc, that is, activated only when formal negotiations are conducted, both the firm and its supplier tend to be opportunistic. Since the relationship is not built on mutual trust, it can be quite adversarial, with each party closely protecting its personal interests at the expense of the other. Thus, while the use of multiple suppliers has the potential of reducing costs and ensuring some level of reliability, it is not without risks and limitations.

Even so, a firm can excel using multiple sources in two ways. First, the firm has to be able to leverage these suppliers into learning platforms. For example, Li & Fung, a Chinese–based global trading group, works with 7,500 business partners in 37 countries and employs a network of specialists to manufacture everything from high-end wool sweaters to synthetic slacks. Quite conceivably, a parka supplied by Li & Fung might have been assembled in China with fabric from Korea, elastic and studs from Hong Kong, and a zipper from Japan. Instead of limiting suppliers, Li & Fung has chosen to expand its suppliers in order to gain access to their specialized skills. What is noteworthy about Li & Fung is the amount of attention it devotes to building and sustaining a good relationship with a number of these suppliers to help all parties build their capabilities more quickly. It is through such a commitment that Li & Fung has been able to sustain its successful strategy.[20]

A second way to leverage the use of multiple sources for learning is by using the latest technology as a means to foster systemic and worldwide learning. Dartmouth professor David Pyke reports that with the Internet, some firms have been able to position their use of multiple sourcing on an entirely new level.[21] For example, General Electric (GE) purchases a significant number of components over the Internet by way of its Trading Process Network (TPN), in which needed parts are posted electronically for bids by prequalified vendors. Pyke reports GE does $1 billion worth of business with 1,400 suppliers on the TPN, with the length of bidding decreasing from 21 to 10 days, and with a growing percentage of the business going to international suppliers.[22]

SINGLE SOURCING

With the successful application of just-in-time (JIT) management, firms began to reevaluate the effectiveness and viability of multiple-supplier sourcing in favor of

single sourcing. Central to the concept of JIT management is eliminating waste and increasing value-added activities by placing inventory orders for the right amount, at the right time, at the right place, and with the right quality. When JIT is done properly, inventories are minimized significantly, along with holding costs, warehouse management, insurance, obsolescence, and the costs from possible theft and pilferage. To ensure the proper implementation of JIT, however, a strong and reliable relationship must be forged between the firm and its suppliers. Such a relationship is not possible if the firm is suspicious of its suppliers, and if the suppliers in turn have little sense of security. To the extent that opportunism and an adversarial relationship prevail, JIT management will not work. While the importance of single sourcing might have been motivated in the context of JIT, it is important to note that single sourcing has had viability outside the JIT context, assuming that issues of reliability and performance are effectively considered.

Recognizing this need to build strong, trust-based relationships, firms have to carefully select and nurture their suppliers, treating them as partners as opposed to adversaries. A motivated supplier can lead to the following benefits: avoid customer loss by providing greater customer satisfaction, improve operating stability with better coordination and communication, increase volume due to greater efficiency, and obtain cost advantages through close connection with suppliers.[23] Other benefits that cut across both buying and supplying parties include cost reduction, flexibility, stability, and improved communication. With a strong, committed supplier–buyer relationship, barriers to entry are also erected, and competitive advantages are established for both sides—a classic case of a "win-win" scenario. When the availability of technical support and the reliability and the price of the product are assured, single sourcing becomes the preferred method.[24] For example, Michael Dell, CEO of Dell Computers, describes his relationship with suppliers as "seamless integration." Part of Dell's relationship with its suppliers involves sending suppliers product and order information frequently, including product and process updates, effectively folding them as partners into Dell's business model.

The besieged U.S. automakers embarked on a painstaking process of pruning down multiple suppliers to a select few when they were confronted by market-share losses to the Japanese. Chrysler, for example, established a "value-managed relationship" in which it consolidated component manufacturers into a few suppliers. Moreover, it has lengthened its average contract time to secure a better long-term relationship with its suppliers. In another example, Xerox has reduced its supplier base from about 5,000 to about 400, with lamps in copiers now sourced from a single multinational firm.[25]

The critical task is the selection of the single source. This decision is of utmost importance in that a single supplier or a few suppliers create the risk of nonperformance. That is, should one single supplier fail to deliver, even for a trivial reason, it could spell disaster for the buyer. Accordingly, the selection of a single supplier is a painstaking process that is best carried out not by one person, but rather by a team of experts in quality assurance, design engineering, manufacturing engineering, purchasing, industrial engineering, and accounting.[26] A team works best under these circumstances because of the need to accomplish multiple tasks, often in a short time

Exhibit 6.1

Evaluating Potential Global Sources: A Checklist

Specification review	Is each element included in material specification really necessary?
Equipment capability	Is the supplier's equipment capable of producing the product?
Quality assurance	Is the supplier able to ensure a good output?
Financial capability	Is it risky to do business with the firm?
Cost structure	What does the item cost?
Supplier value analysis effort	Is the supplier capable of performing value analysis with the buyer's technical personnel?
Production scheduling	What are the supplier's production scheduling and procedures?
Contract performance	How is performance measured?

Source: Adapted from Richard G. Newman, "Single Source Qualification," *International Journal of Purchasing and Materials Management* 24(2) (1988): 10–17.

period. These tasks include obtaining information on performance attributes collected from plant visits, financial reports, vendor surveys, trade journals, and other sources. In addition, the team must evaluate the aspects that are typically considered "weaknesses" on the foreign supplier side. These include trustworthiness, scheduling, on-time delivery, and the lack of domestic presence.[27] A comprehensive guide for this process, based on consulting practice, is presented in Exhibit 6.1.[28]

HYBRID NETWORK SOURCING

Hybrid network sourcing combines the best features of single- and multiple-suppliers sources.[29] It uses both single and multiple suppliers depending on the task at hand. The system arranges suppliers into a hierarchy, in which the most skilled, technologically advanced, and knowledgeable are placed at the top tier and are charged with selecting and managing all other subcontractors. Therefore, the lower-tiered subcontractors become the suppliers of their upper-tiered counterparts. Ideally, there is continuous communication between firms in each tier during the entire process. After careful coordination with the subcontractors, the top-tiered suppliers can then bring complete turnkey systems to buyer-firms, instead of simply individual components. Buyer-firms can then further add to the value of their final products with customized features. By reducing their involvement with multiple suppliers, but still obtaining a final product that is a result of multiple parties, the buyer-firm is able to minimize its overall purchasing activities without compromising the quality of purchased goods.

Hybrid sourcing is most appropriate for assembly-type manufacturing organizations, particularly those that carry a high purchased content of parts made specifically for the firm, as seen in Mazda and other automobile manufacturers. Dartmouth professor David Pyke reports that such arrangements can lead to greater depth and interaction. For example, Air Products and Chemicals, a Pennsylvania-based manufacturer of chemicals and industrial gas, has developed a multitiered system of rating vendors—a form of hybrid network system. Once certified through this process, the selected supplier is offered a long-term contract including opportunities to increase its share of Air Products and Chemicals' total purchases and to work directly with Air Products and Chemicals' marketing staff.[30]

Because of the close relationship between the firms and suppliers under this system, there is also substantial technology transfer among firms and suppliers, as evidenced in the following examples. The Anglo-Dutch multinational Unilever has developed alliances with a few suppliers with the end-in-view of achieving the lowest system cost in the industry by reducing cycle time and inventory.[31] Despite having scale advantages, American Express (Amex) handed off its transaction-processing business in 1992 and entered into a service contract with First Data. As a spinoff, First Data could aggregate American Express' volume with that of other companies, avoiding the concern held by issuing banks that First Data was outsourcing processing to Amex—a move that would have aided a perceived competitor.[32] The practice employed by Amex is an example of a reverse auction. While traditional auctions involve a single seller and many buyers, a **reverse auction** generally involves many sellers and one buyer and is organized as a fixed-duration bidding event. It is reported that reverse auctions can lower the cost of procuring products and services by as much as 20 percent. As such, reverse auctions are the favored choice for companies faced with declining sales and margins. GE Chief Information Officer Gary Reiner claims the company saved approximately $600 million by using reverse auctions in 2001, which was a net savings of 8 percent.[33]

GLOBAL SOURCING: FIVE LEVELS OF DEVELOPMENT

Knowing the types of sourcing arrangements is the first step toward developing a strategic mindset; understanding how sourcing evolves over time constitutes the next step. Although terms like *global sourcing* and *supply chain management* might appear to be new, the problems they address are not. Historically, sourcing was part of an organization's manufacturing function, referred to as procurement or purchasing, and based at the operational level of the organization hierarchy. Considered ancillary to the functions of production and manufacturing, sourcing was focused on buying from suppliers at low prices and at the desired quality levels.

As firms competed in international markets and faced new global competitors, the consideration of purchasing decisions shifted from domestic to international sources, with firms actively seeking cheap materials overseas. Even so, although recognized as important, sourcing was still considered an operational rather than strategic function within the firm. In late 1980s, with crucial resources becoming a critical factor, the need to link sourcing to cost leadership strategies became even more compelling, prompting a shift to a strategic perspective. What differentiates operational thinking from strategic thinking is the consideration of scope and complexity, and the centrality of sourcing within a firm's core strategy. For many, this means "proactively integrating and coordinating common items and materials, processes, designs, technologies, and suppliers across worldwide purchasing, engineering, and operating locations."[34]

Supply chain experts Robert Trent and Robert Monzcka have suggested five levels of development, depicting a progression in sourcing activities.[35] Exhibit 6.2 presents the five levels of activities ranging from purely purchasing domestically to integrated, coordinated sourcing. It depicts how a firm can evolve in its sourcing activities, from domestic to global, and from operational to strategic positions. Level I represents a case of purely domestic sourcing. Level II and Level III represent international purchasing,

Exhibit 6.2

Five Levels of Sourcing (in percentages)

The table below summarizes the results of a survey on 162 firms. These firms reported their current and future sourcing plans.

	Level I	Level II	Level III	Level IV	Level V
2003	13.4	21.3	31.0	18.1	16.1
2007–2010	7.8	7.8	14.3	15.6	54.5

Level I: Engage in domestic purchasing only
Level II: Engage in international purchasing as needed (International purchasing)
Level III: International purchasing as part of sourcing strategy
Level IV: Integration and coordination of global sourcing strategies cross worldwide buying locations
Level V: Integration and coordination of global sourcing strategies with other functional groups

Both Levels II and III are in the international purchasing mode.
Both Levels IV and V are in the global sourcing mode.

Source: Adapted from Robert J. Trent and Robert M. Monczka, "International Purchasing and Global Sourcing—What Are the Differences?" *Journal Supply Chain Management* 39, no. 4 (2003): 12–37.

and Level IV and Level V represent cases of global sourcing. Pundits anticipate that global sourcing will be the dominant practice in sourcing in the foreseeable future. What follows then is a five-stage developmental process that describes how firms can evolve through different phases of sourcing activities.

LEVEL I: ENGAGE IN DOMESTIC PURCHASING ONLY

At this level, firms are mostly engaged in **domestic purchasing**. Typically, these are small businesses, such as mom-and-pop stores, or retail stores alongside gasoline stations that do not yet recognize international sourcing as viable or economical, given their limited scope of operations. In our view, it is simply a matter of time before such firms realize the value of international sourcing. For these firms, moving to Level II tends to occur on an ad hoc or reactive basis, triggered by an unexpected shortage of domestic suppliers, or when they are disappointed in the quality or cost level provided by their domestic suppliers. Other conditions include a disruption in the firm's supply chain, dwindling domestic sources, inflation in the domestic market, and more intense competition from abroad. It is also likely to occur when competitors have gained advantages from international purchasing, at which time the laggard firms react in a similar fashion.

LEVEL II: ENGAGE IN INTERNATIONAL PURCHASING

Firms operating at Level II are typically those that have only recently extended their purchasing from domestic to international suppliers. Since this new activity is embryonic, it is often seen as a transitional stage preceding the time when international sourcing can became a more significant activity within a firm's core strategy. Purchasing remains at the operational and tactical levels.

LEVEL III: INTERNATIONAL PURCHASING AS PART OF SOURCING STRATEGY

The transition to this stage signals an initial step in **integrating purchasing** into a larger sourcing activity within the firm. While there is recognition of the importance of cost and quality, there is still no concerted effort to integrate purchasing across locations and functions. For many firms, this is their first level of participation in international markets. Therefore, learning from experience becomes the crucial key in terms of escalating the activity further, or scaling it back to former levels. What is central to learning lies in establishing long-term business relationships with suppliers. Purchasing carries some strategic significance at this stage, but the effort in elevating it to a higher organizational level is still inadequate. Most U.S. firms fall into this category.

LEVEL IV: INTEGRATION AND COORDINATION OF GLOBAL SOURCING STRATEGIES AROUND WORLDWIDE BUYING LOCATION

This level represents a more sophisticated sourcing activity. To quote the experts: "Operating at this level requires worldwide information systems, personnel with sophisticated knowledge and skills, extensive coordination and communication mechanisms, an organizational structure that promotes central coordination of global activities, and executive leadership that endorses a global approach to sourcing."[36] Note that, at this stage, although sourcing is worldwide, it is focused on managing across locations, not across functions at the same time. IKEA and Nike are firms at this stage of development.

LEVEL V: INTEGRATION AND COORDINATION OF GLOBAL SOURCING STRATEGIES WITH OTHER INTERNATIONAL GROUPS

This represents the most sophisticated level of sourcing, from which maximum returns are attained if the system is properly implemented. At this stage, firms have already transcended Level IV, in which integration across different locations has been established. Firms then proceed to Level V, which involves the integration of activities and processes, designs, technologies, information systems, knowledge, technical know-how, suppliers and transporters, engineering, and other functional areas. Implementation can vary across different functions and locations, but the imperative to integrate and coordinate is diffused throughout production, marketing, and after sales, as part of the firm's corporate strategy and philosophy. Typically, at this stage, firms will assign critical functional responsibilities to the most capable units within the company's worldwide network, such as sourcing. Only firms that possess worldwide design, development, production, logistics, and procurement capabilities can handle an integrated and coordinated approach at this level. Few firms have reached this stage. Toyota and Honda are among such firms, that have exploited local sources on a global scale to their advantage.[37]

LOCATING GLOBAL SOURCING PARTNERS

Despite the advantages of global sourcing, research also indicates that supplier contracts fail to deliver their full worth—or anything close to it. According to a survey conducted in August 2004 by Vantage Partners and the International Association for Contract and Commercial Management, only 13 percent of companies said that their contracts realized their anticipated value.[38] The root of the problem lies partly in poor selection of vendors and a control process that fails to implement key provisions of the supplier contract. In identifying qualified sources of supply, firms have encountered challenges arising from differences in social culture, language, laws, personnel skills and competencies, and business practices between their domestic and foreign suppliers.

To understand this further, a pattern of supplier engagement has been defined based on the experiences of managers in global sourcing.[39] Because different countries and regions have their particular strengths, they become the dominant suppliers for certain industries. For example, Japanese suppliers are strong in high-tech areas such as computers and electronics. Taiwanese suppliers excel in the provision of computer motherboards. What makes them successful is their ability to offer quality products at low cost and maintain state-of-the-art of technology. Governmental policies play a role as well. In the 1960s and 1970s, the Japanese government, specifically the Ministry of International Trade and Industry (MITI), supported Japanese suppliers through its "preferred supplier" policy. Such support was maintained through the 1980s when investment in R&D and new product development were given priority, enabling Japanese suppliers to become the preferred choice by the electronic and high-tech industries.

Other Asian suppliers, such as Taiwan, Singapore, South Korea, and Hong Kong, also excelled in small electronics and automotive and industrial equipment (see Box 6.1). Their advantages stemmed from producing good-quality, reliable, and fairly standardized products at very competitive prices. As these countries upgraded their technological capabilities and moved to higher-end production, other Asian countries, notably China, Malaysia, Vietnam, and Indonesia, applied similar cost leadership strategies to assume leadership in low-end production. Sourcing from European suppliers focused on pharmaceutical, chemical, and industrial equipment industries, reflecting their technical expertise, such as the German and Italian competence in industrial machine tools. European suppliers were very adept and precise, capable of producing highly customized equipment, and flexible in terms of accepting small orders. Moreover, they were most appreciated for "trustworthiness"—keeping their word and honoring their promises over the long run.

Among these worldwide suppliers, China and India have emerged as prominent global sources and have seen a corresponding increase in their share of foreign direct investment. Exhibit 6.3 details the largest offshore service exporters.

KEY SUCCESS FACTORS FOR GLOBAL SOURCING

A firm should not pursue global sourcing without a carefully crafted supporting structure, a deliberately designed process, teams possessing international competencies, intelligence, and foreign-language skills, and top management commitment. Effective global sourcing requires interaction with a diverse set of people, organizations, and cultures on both a personal and a professional level. There are a number of key factors associated with effective global sourcing.[40]

Box 6.1

Taiwan as a Global Source: From the Old to the New

In their quest for global dominance, firms have scoured the world for suppliers that can deliver excellent prices at better or comparable quality. Yet the world is constantly in flux. Even within the world of global suppliers, the economics of production have changed, creating new learning trajectories and opportunities for new erstwhile suppliers. Such changes can be gleaned in the case of Taiwan.

Not many years ago, Taiwan was the world's preferred source for Barbie dolls. The Taiwan factory was opened by Mattel, Barbie's American maker, in 1967, and was clearly the trailblazer for the "outsourcing" phenomenon in Asia. At one point, half the world's Barbie dolls ware made in Taiwan.

Within twenty years, Taiwan's labor force had became more prosperous, forcing Mattel, in 1987, to the Chinese mainland, where wages are lower. While the world's favorite plastic model is no longer made in Taiwan, Barbie is still so revered that the town of Taishan has dedicated a museum to her.

To get a glimpse of how globalization has altered the underlying economics of labor, the science park in the city of Hsinchu is Taiwan's exemplar of its economic prominence. It is responsible for making vast quantities of the world's ubiquitous laptops, personal organizers, and MP3 players. Asustek makes iPods and Mac minis for Apple, along with the motherboards for one in three of the world's desktop computers. Quanta is the world's largest manufacturer of laptop computers. Along with other Taiwan firms, it makes 75 percent of the world's laptops, including the Dell or Sony brands. TSMC is the world's largest manufacturer of outsourced computer chips, a task shared with neighbor UMC, just opposite in the Hsinchu science park.

A look at the very latest sourcing trends suggests that Taiwan is carrying its global source status to an even higher plane. Total purchases made by international procurement offices (IPOs) in Taiwan of foreign (IT) firms from the island are expected to grow 11.3 percent from 2004 to reach US$54 billion, and the figure is expected to exceed the level of US$60 billion for 2005, according to the statistics released by the Ministry of Economic Affairs (MOEA).

An IT report notes the following: "Among the buyers in 2004, the top six, namely Hewlett-Packard (HP), Dell, Sony, Apple, IBM, and NEC, were recently awarded by MOEA for their great support for Taiwan's IT industry during that year. They together accounted for US$40 billion, or about 75 percent of the total purchasing value, with HP taking a lion's share of US$18 billion, followed by Dell's US$8–9 billion, Sony's US$5–6 billion, and Apple's US$3–4 billion. NEC and IBM each recorded total procurement values of US$2.5 billion."

Taiwan's current concern? To catch up with the world trend of environmental protection. Recently, Hsiao Kuo-kun, general manager of HP's IPO in Taiwan, encouraged Taiwan's IT product manufacturers to develop more green products and join the world's green supply chain.

Sources: Adapted from Richard Spencer, "Barbie Sends a Shiver Through Taiwan with a Lesson in Globalisation," June 26, 2005, http://news.telegraph.co.uk/news/main.jhtml?xml=/news/2005/06/25/wtaiwan25.xml; "IT Firms Expected to Make Record Purchases from Taiwan," *Taiwan Headlines,* November 17, 2004, http://news.cens.com/php/getnews.php?file=/news/2004/11/17/20041117018.htm&daily=1.

1. Develop Logistical Infrastructures and Supporting Processes

A supplier contract is a necessary first step, but is hardly enough. A firm has to develop its own logistical infrastructure and process, or ensure a low-lead-time logistics system that allows a seamless delivery of goods at the most efficient cost and at predetermined times through an arrangement with transportation companies. An intimate understanding of the availability of global transportation resources and logistics becomes essential in this process. If this operation is not available through international transportation companies, the logistical process can become nightmar-

Exhibit 6.3

Locations of Sourcing Opportunities: The Largest Offshore Sourcing

I. *High labor costs, high quality skills*

Canada
Israel
Singapore
Spain

II. *High labor costs, low quality skills*

Brazil
Mexico

III. *Low labor costs, high quality skills*

India
Philippines

IV. *Low labor costs, low quality skills*

China
Czech Republic
Hungary
Malaysia
Russia
Vietnam

Source: Original data obtained from A. Vashistha and A. Vashistha, *The Offshore Nation: Strategies for Success in Global Outsourcing and Offshoring* (New York: McGraw-Hill, 2006), p. 15. Two countries were added by the authors of this book.

ish, with the daunting task of managing a complex array of small and medium-sized transportation companies operating worldwide. The success of FedEx, DHL, and UPS in developing such structures and processes is testimony to the importance of properly designed supporting infrastructures.

2. FORMALIZE PURCHASING AND SUPPLY CHAIN PROCESSES AND PRACTICES

Global purchasing and supply chain management require knowledge about the location of core merchandise, experience in purchasing and negotiation, competencies in knowing and working with foreign suppliers, and experience in establishing long-term relationships and partnerships. Firms should also design schemes and methods for approaching and handling foreign suppliers and transporters with the necessary incentives. Within global supply chain management, it is critical to set up an evaluation system for selecting qualified suppliers. The best practice is to find a qualified global supplier who can offer cheaper cost in bulk and can ship to multiple locations within its own global network. In some cases, using multiple suppliers is desirable for quality of products and quality of services comparisons. Our earlier discussion of Air Products and GE are good examples of how formalized processes can enhance the sourcing relationship. In other cases, constant interaction is necessary. For example, during the new product development phase, engineers from Boeing maintain offices at their suppliers' facilities, and suppliers have similar arrangements at Boeing's headquarters. Having offices in both locations ensures that manufacturing several million components that have to be done at the right time can be tightly coordinated and lead to on-time delivery.[41]

Another requirement is the need for a close examination of the technical requirements of the global sourcing activity. For example, in contrast to retailing and services, or simple "ramp-up" manufacturing sourcing, new manufactured products entail an additional level of complexity associated with the design or prototype. This requires different capabilities, technologies, and processes for which only highly qualified suppliers can do the job. These capabilities are vastly different from those used by qualifying suppliers to build volume, or to deliver in a just-in-time environment.

3. DEVELOP THE SUPPLY CHAIN INFORMATION SYSTEM

A critical element of success in the global marketplace is to set up a supply chain information system that can bring together suppliers and transporters with global companies as part of their corporate strategies. This requires interorganizational information sharing on a global basis. It entails the establishment of a network between the suppliers, the transporters, and the companies in order to connect with each other, resulting in the ability to share information across global organizational boundaries. The end result is a highly integrated global information system shared by all parties involved. Boeing has three alliances with aero-engine manufacturers: GE, Rolls-Royce, and Pratt & Whitney. With extremely complex interfaces between the engines and the airframes, the use of information systems to coordinate simultaneous design is not only desirable, but necessary.[42]

Even so, in practice, this is an extremely difficult goal to attain for three reasons. First, this task can be highly complex because of differences and incompatibility in technical competencies among all the suppliers and transporters. The entire supply chain involves a diverse group of suppliers and transporters. Second, the system is complicated by the geographical and business unit boundaries, characterized by a combination of national and professional cultural uniqueness and differences. Third, some companies may be reluctant or very conservative about becoming part of the integrated system due to the possibility of losing strategically critical and confidential information to other users. Despite these obstacles, if successful, global companies can shorten cycle times, improve inventory positions, reduce cost, expedite delivery, and enhance the quality of customer services and other key performance areas.

4. STRENGTHEN GLOBAL BUSINESS CAPABILITIES

A strong global sourcing structure and process involves, a priori, the establishment of global business capabilities. The awareness of cross-cultural business practices is absolutely critical to the task of implementing an effective global sourcing strategy.

A global company has to develop sourcing managers with skills that apply to the company's global settings, and this involves knowledge of geographic issues, cultural boundary uniqueness and differences, as well as the skills pertinent to their professions. There are several reasons for this. First, managers have to possess high-level strategic and analytical skills that include the ability to recognize opportunities and threats in the global environment, and persistence in exploiting opportunities that contribute to the attainment of organizational goals and objectives. Second, managers must be capable of managing instability, risks, and uncertainties arising in foreign countries, and they must be agile in avoiding or overcoming such challenges. Third, global sourcing managers should possess crucial knowledge of the business practices in foreign countries, such as foreign business customs, international rules and regulations, and foreign countries' relations with their trade partners. Fourth, managers must also be knowledgeable in identifying the best sources of information and locating the latest technology on a global basis. Fifth, managers must develop business insights in their international dealings. All of this comes from an accumulated pool of knowledge over time, long and extensive experience, and open-mindedness. Some companies use a team-based approach, in which they choose groups of employees and managers who are considered to be outstanding in their area of expertise, select the skills required for each class of employee, and offered training to them. Coupled with appropriate reward systems and other skill-building processes, managers and employees are given opportunities to develop the required skill sets. Germany's automaker Volkswagen (VW), in its truck assembly plant at Resende, Brazil, employs seven major parts suppliers who manufacture the parts with their own equipment and install them on trucks with their own workers. In doing so, VW has reduced its investment, cut its inventory, and obviated union pressure.[43]

5. BUILD COMMUNICATION AND NEGOTIATION SKILLS IN THE GLOBAL CONTEXT

Effective communication skills refer to the ability to send, receive, and interpret correspondence and contracts from one's foreign business partner. Studies have found that foreign-language capabilities have a very large effect on the development of global sourcing business capabilities. Many U.S. firms still believe that English is the universal business language, and they expect their foreign partners to make the effort to learn English, instead of the opposite.

Unfortunately, without knowledge of a foreign language, U.S. managers are at a disadvantage in terms of obtaining critical information and promoting closer relations through constant contacts with their partners. In addition, the inability to speak or to read partners' languages could slow down the negotiation process and delay much-needed decisions. Therefore, effective negotiation skills begin with the ability to choose the most appropriate words when presenting one's conditions and terms. During negotiation, a substantial degree of respect is paid to the other parties, necessitating a thorough understanding of foreign cultures. This is critical because, for example, a common gesture in one culture can be offensive in another. Therefore, firms need to develop their employees' international language and negotiation skills through improved hiring, training, and rewarding processes. Jorge Machicado, chief marketing office at Tecmedica in the United Kingdom, discussed how his company takes advantage of learning from international operations: "Our view of innovation is that it is fully concentrated in some countries, and we want to distribute innovation in other countries. As we look at what is going on in Chile, we see what is going on in the United States or in Europe and try to replicate best practices and great innovations."[44]

6. ENGAGE TOP MANAGEMENT COMMITMENT IN GLOBAL SOURCING ACTIVITIES AND DECISIONS

Studies have found that top management commitment is critical to global sourcing effectiveness. At the same time, any global sourcing effort undertaken without the necessary commitment and support of top management is unlikely to succeed. Top management commitment is composed of: "(1) executive management's recognition of the benefit of coordinating purchasing and supply chain strategies, practices, and approaches between business units or buying centers across national boundaries; and (2) the degree to which executive management [is] committed to coordinating and integrating purchasing/supply chain strategy and approaches across national boundaries."[45] For example, Bill Gates would seclude himself each year in the San Juan Islands, northwest of Seattle. His objective? To ponder Microsoft's next leap forward. Any Microsoft employee can submit a written proposal for a new product or service to Gates for consideration. If Gates likes the idea, he will return to launch the new initiative. It is rare, but refreshing, to see support from the very top when it comes to assessing proposals from the rank-and-file.

7. BUILD STRATEGIC ALLIANCES

Some companies adopt the viewpoint that external collaboration is an essential component in the development of their internal capabilities. Suppliers constitute the logical partners for a strategic alliance because they are at the front end of the value chain. In evaluating suppliers as potential strategic allies, three aspects should be given special attention for compatibility and long-term stability: interorganizational relationships, organizational capabilities, and country-specific factors.[46] The success of Sun Microsystems in the 1980s can be attributed to working with outside organizations as strategic partners to provide value-creating activities. Alliances come in many forms. When General Electric coupled service contracts with its manufactured electric turbines, new synergies were created when customers bought the package of hardware and service as bundled products. It also set the industry standard requiring competitors to master both hardware and service to remain competitive.[47]

GUIDELINES FOR IMPLEMENTING GLOBAL SOURCING

The next step toward developing a strategic perspective is effective implementation. Global sourcing represents both a strategic direction and an organizational process. When it comes to setting up a system from scratch or converting an existing system to a truly global system, a company should proceed with caution. The following guidelines are recommended:[48]

- An open, public message from the top executives to the entire organization is pivotal to the process. This legitimizes the strategic position of global sourcing in the company. It is preferred that top executives participate on a steering committee. Other functional areas quickly recognize this and are encouraged to make resources available, including human and informational resources, to support global sourcing projects. At the same time, subsidiaries can "buy into" this new strategic direction as well.
- The company must immediately follow up with financial and human resources for the development of the global sourcing project and process.
- The company must obtain the commitment of all operational levels to support the global processes.
- The concept of a global team project must be planted in managers' and employees' minds. Cross-functional teams, with members from the headquarters and subsidiaries, must be pooled together to identify areas of commonality, standardization, and synergy in procurement and design. Issues that need to be addressed on both a short-term and a long-term basis include product specifications and future replacement and maintenance requirements. Ideally, individuals who directly and indirectly participate in this are sourcing and engineering representatives, executives, executive steering committee members, and so forth.
- Moving from international to global sourcing exposes companies to more rapid changes to product and process technology. Companies must be flexible enough managerially and infrastructurally to adapt to the changes.
- Operational units such as design and procurements departments are now closer to the strategic level and should align their unit-level strategies and operating philosophy with the company's business strategy.
- Beyond functional levels of the headquarters and subsidiaries, a formal process is needed to develop consistency and understanding within the organization. Ideally, the goal should be innovation by management in building best practices within the company.

Exhibit 6.4 provides more features supporting the complexity that is inherent to the global sourcing process.

THE BENEFITS OF GLOBAL SOURCING

When global sourcing is properly implemented, the benefits accruing from it can be significant. In a survey of practicing managers, seven benefits were identified: (1) quality improvement, (2) product and process technology development, (3) price/cost reduction, (4) shorter new product development cycle times, (5) responsiveness to customer improvement requirements, (6) on-time delivery improvement, and (7) overall customer service improvement.[49] The overall result is better management of supply chain inventory for companies, increased global market penetration, reduced environmental risk,

Exhibit 6.4

Features and Characteristics of Global Sourcing Organizations

- Regular sourcing strategy review meetings with worldwide purchasing managers
- Use of international purchasing offices
- Formally established process for developing global sourcing strategies
- Worldwide purchasing database or data warehouses
- Development of global suppliers
- Worldwide integration of technical design specialists, operations personnel, and sourcing personnel
- Formal information sharing through electronic information systems across worldwide buying units
- Coordinated sourcing strategy development efforts across regions
- Cross-functional/cross-locational commodity management teams
- Sourcing analysis tools available electronically
- Centralized sourcing strategy development
- Common worldwide part of commodity coding schemes
- Worldwide supplier performance measures and measurement systems
- Worldwide buyer–supplier executive councils
- Post-selection site visits to suppliers
- Pre-selection site visits to suppliers
- Procurement engineers used for supplier visits

Source: Adapted from Robert J. Trent and Robert M. Monczka, "International Purchasing and Global Sourcing—What Are the Differences?" *Journal of Supply Chain Management* 39(4) (2003): 26–37.

the creation of a learning organization, and the reduction of noncore company-owned assets and resources. The following are a selected group of price and nonprice benefits of global sourcing, combining inputs from published research.[50]

1. PRICE/COST BENEFITS

Cost savings is the goal and one of the outcomes of global sourcing. The extent of cost benefits varies and depends on the length of commitment to global sourcing and other management efforts. It has been reported that some companies were able to realize 2 to 25 percent savings for their supplies even though price differences of the same products within the region had gone down to 10 percent.

2. IMPROVED QUALITY

Improved quality is one of the results from global sourcing. Yet unlike cost reduction, the improvement usually requires a certain amount of time to materialize. Some companies indicated obvious improvements, such as a 10 to 50 percent reduction in material defect rates, although most of them reported a 10 to 20 percent reduction.

3. PRODUCT AND PROCESS TECHNOLOGY DEVELOPMENT

The continuous pressures from competition and customer demand drive companies to improve existing products and to introduce innovations in both product and production processes from competent suppliers. This in turn drives the companies to a higher level of sourcing capabilities and to secure greater access to technology. To accommodate this change, the overall technological infrastructure of the companies is correspondingly enhanced.

4. IMPROVED SUPPLIER RESPONSIVENESS

Working closely with suppliers, increasing the strategic importance of global sourcing, and the competition between domestic and foreign suppliers all result in greater supplier responsiveness to global companies. The benefits from this include better overall supplier relationships, improved on-time delivery, improved information sharing with suppliers and development of critical information systems, greater cooperation and coordination to meet customer needs, shorter and more stable lead times, greater access to new materials and critical materials, and more consistent procurement practices. In just-in-time delivery, some companies enjoy an improvement in on-time delivery ranging from 5 to 30 percent, while others report shortening lead times 20 to 60 percent.

5. IMPROVED COMMUNICATION

One of the biggest improvements is in communication. With the help of advanced technology, coordination between global companies and their global sourcing network participants is facilitated through communication tools such as groupware, video and phone conferencing, and Web-based instruments. Regular strategy review meetings between locations and joint training sessions involving worldwide team members are more easily conducted. Improved communication can happen along the supply chain, between different sites within the company, and between functional units. Well-established systems and methods in communication will help overcome the complexities inherent in a process that involves subsidiaries across continents.[51] Exhibit 6.5 provides a summary of some benefits in global sourcing.

In summary, global sourcing is not without risks and difficulties. Some are due to faulty planning, others arise from inadequate implementation. Mostly commonly cited problems include the need for additional inventory, longer lead time when ordering materials, cost of rejects, unfamiliar supply, high total costs versus low unit cost, brokerage costs, damage in transit, currency differences, rising customs duties, inventory holding costs, technical support, language and cultural barriers, business practice differences, differences in institutional environment, transportation costs, manager travel costs, reduced flexibility, involuntary sharing of new technologies advantage, the cost of using foreign representatives or trading companies, and more.[52] Moreover, we emphasize that if global sourcing decisions are to be made at the strategic level, they cannot be made without full consideration of other impacts, which include the speed of industry evolution (Chapter 4), country and currency risk assessment (Chapter 5), the risks of ownership and strategic partner unreliability (Chapter 7), and risks associated with multinational investment. All told, global sourcing is a complex and multifaceted process that can add significant value if properly implemented, but can also create significant problems if implementation goes awry.[53]

Exhibit 6.5

Global Sourcing Benefits: A Checklist

To achieve the full advantages of global sourcing, the firm needs to evaluate how global sourcing can lead to the following benefits. The more benefits, the better.

___	Better management of total supply chain inventory
___	Greater supplier responsiveness to buying-unit needs
___	Greater standardization or consistency to the sourcing process
___	Greater access to product technology
___	Improved supplier relationships
___	Greater access to process technology
___	Improved sharing of information with suppliers
___	Greater early supplier involvement during new product/service development
___	Lower purchase price/cost
___	Shorter ordering cycle time
___	Higher material/component/service quality
___	Improved delivery reliability
___	Improved environmental compliance
___	Greater appreciation of purchasing by internal users
___	Lower purchasing process transactions costs
___	Higher user satisfaction with the purchasing process

Source: Adapted from Robert J. Trent and Robert M. Monczka, "International Purchasing and Global Sourcing—What Are the Differences?" *Journal of Supply Chain Management* 39(4) (2003): 26–37.

FROM SOURCING TO OUTSOURCING: EMERGING PATTERNS

Given the importance of global sourcing, it is not surprising that all facets of cost reduction and quality enhancement need to be explored by firms so that they can maintain their competitive edge. One prominent development is the escalation of global sourcing into an outsourcing activity. While global sourcing entails the purchase of input necessary for producing a product or service internally, outsourcing involves the displacement of an internal activity that is assigned or contracted to an outside supplier or vendor, generally for purposes of cost reduction and/or quality enhancement. Moreover, **outsourcing** goes beyond consulting contracts in that activities are *ongoing.* Not only are activities transferred, so are factors of production and decisional rights.[54] Some additional distinctions and definitions are provided in Exhibit 6.6.

A belief that has gained widespread recognition is that companies should outsource activities that are not their strong points, that is, **peripheral** or **noncore activities**, particularly if the activity can be provided at lower cost than that done in-house.[55] By outsourcing peripheral or noncore activities, the firm is able to focus on its core competencies, reduce its costs, and enhance its flexibility to keep up with agile competitors. For example, Cisco, Nortel Networks, and 3Com have outsourced their manufacturing to companies like Solectron, Sanmina, and Flextronics in order to capitalize on economies of scale.[56] Outsourcing trends have shifted from traditional vertical integration, back office work, product support, and customer service to advanced software, advanced engineering, business development, and full product design—the latter of which can

Exhibit 6.6

Different Perspectives on Outsourcing

Make-or-buy	Company retains outside domestic and/or foreign suppliers to provide products and services. Typically this is contracted to domestic suppliers to reduce its costs.
Business process outsourcing	Company unbundles its business services, including its vertically integrated processes, and then sources them back from domestic or foreign providers.
International in-house sourcing	Company uses services supplied by its own foreign-based affiliates or subsidiaries.
Domestic outsourcing	Company uses services supplied by another domestically based company on a recurrent basis.
Offshore outsourcing	Company uses services supplied by another foreign based company on a recurrent basis.
In-sourcing	Company produces products and services internally that had been previously sourced to domestic or international suppliers.

be considered as high-end services that have strategic importance to a firm's corporate strategy.[57] The reasons why firms outsource generally parallel the reasons for global sourcing, but perhaps have more intensity with regard to cost and quality needs. For example, it is generally held that firms engage in offshore outsourcing if they are able to realize 20 to 30 percent cost savings. This is particularly compelling in that they must anticipate more difficulty in communicating and coordinating with their international suppliers (see Box 6.2). Moreover, recent studies have begun to indicate far-reaching benefits of outsourcing. Specifically, a 2003 study by the McKinsey Global Institute (MGI) showed that offshoring (outsourcing to international suppliers) creates wealth for the United States as well as for India, the country receiving the jobs.[58] For every dollar of corporate spending outsourced to India, the U.S. economy captures more than three-quarters of the benefit and gains as much as $1.14 in return. Far from being a zero-sum game, offshoring creates mutual economic benefit. Findings from another study that detailed reasons for outsourcing are presented in Exhibit 6.7.

OUTSOURCING FROM "MAKE-OR-BUY" TO STRATEGIC TRANSFORMATION

The theoretical antecedents of outsourcing stem from the need for organizations to specialize—a process that is typically accomplished through organizational differentiation.[59] In an early classic, Adam Smith noted that when output is small, one worker is forced to perform all tasks involved in manufacturing, but as the scale of operations increases, efficiency is enhanced by focus and specialization.[60] While specialization can alleviate the problems of an overburdened hierarchy, it does not completely eradicate the need for added coordination. Beyond production costs, the expense of management layers, the slowness and inflexibility of making decisions, and corporate politics can create coordination problems.[61]

Probably the greatest costs are agency costs, which arise when individuals act in their own self-interest rather than acting to maximize corporate performance. The employment relationship between a firm and a subcontracting vendor reflects the basic

Box 6.2

Hidden Costs of Outsourcing

Despite the vaunted benefits of outsourcing, it is still a risky proposition. Take the case of IT sourcing. In one published study of fifty companies by Audencia Nantes' professor Jérôme Barthélemy, about 14 percent of sourcing operations were deemed a failure. While this figure might not be so imposing (when compared to the failure rate of joint ventures as discussed in the next chapter), it is bound to get worse if all major costs are not taken into account. An informative paper by Jeffrey Pfeffer talks about these "hidden costs" that are not likely to be immediately recognized by firms venturing into initial outsourcing forays.

Hidden Cost 1: Vendor Search and Contracting

This involves a firm's underestimating the expense of identifying and evaluating suitable IT vendors, selecting the finalist, and negotiating and drafting the contract. Companies incur such costs even before spending the first dollar on the actual work. Remember that outsourcing is a process, from the beginning of the project to its conclusion. Thus, hidden costs can pop up anytime in the process unless properly managed.

Recommendations. Define your search and contracting goals at the outset. It's tempting to go with a convenient vendor, but it might prove to be a mistake in the end. Take time to select a trustworthy vendor, using firsthand information. Define your goals and know what you want. Finally, be very attentive to the details of the contract. Include evolution and reversibility clauses. Even well-intentioned parties end up with serious miscommunication if contractual details are incomplete and confusing.

Hidden Cost 2: Transitioning to the Vendor

Switching in-house IT activities to a vendor presents the most elusive hidden cost because most companies don't realize how much they will have to spend until the transition is complete. It can take a long time for the new vendor to completely understand the internal operations that are being outsourced. Meanwhile, costs can mount in a hurry.

Recommendations. Try to determine transition costs before they occur. Then, based on this understanding, reduce them. Transition costs are lower when a company knows what it wants from the outsourced activity.

Hidden Cost 3: Managing the Effort

This is the largest category of hidden costs because it covers three areas: monitoring to ensure that vendors fulfill their obligations; bargaining with them, with appropriate sanctions, if necessary; and negotiating needed contract changes. Estimates approximate these costs at 8 percent of the yearly contract amount.

Recommendations. Determine the cost of managing vendors; work with experienced vendors; build and cultivate trust; define and clarify goals.

Hidden Cost 4: Transitioning After Outsourcing

This cost arises from switching vendors or reintegrating IT activities internally—very difficult to quantify since most managers are reluctant to think about the end of a contract.

Recommendations. Determine the cost of transitioning after outsourcing (e.g., finding a new vendor, defining a new contract, transitioning resources); then reduce costs accordingly (be aware of post-outsourcing activities; you may need to call back employees transferred to the vendor; and maintain a sufficient level of IT internally).

Source: Adapted from Jérôme Barthelémy, "The Hidden Cost of IT Outsourcing," *MIT Sloan Management Review* 42 (3) (Spring 2001): 60–69; Jeffrey Pfeffer, "The Hidden Costs of Outsourcing," CNN Money (March 1, 2006), available at http://money.cnn.com/2006/03/01/magazines/business 2/costofoutsourceing/index/htm.

Exhibit 6.7

Reasons for Outsourcing

Reasons		Percentage of Respondents
Labor cost savings (% cost savings, offshore versus U.S. operations)	No cost savings	6
	1–20%	17
	21–40%	44
	41–60%	28
	Over 60%	6
		100
Quality ratings (offshore versus U.S. operations)	Higher	28
	Same	50
	Lower	22
		100
Productivity ratings (offshore versus U.S. operations)	Higher	33
	Same	50
	Lower	17
		100

Source: Manuel Serapio, *International Outsourcing in Information Technology (IT): Trends, Developments, and Implications for Colorado* (Denver, CO: Colorado Institute of Technology, November 2004), p. 20.

agency structure of a principal and an agent who have different goals and attitudes toward risk. Specifically, agency theory postulates that when there is little or incomplete information, two problems arise: *adverse selection* and *moral hazard*. **Adverse selection** refers to the difficulty in ascertaining whether the agent (e.g., the source) has the right abilities for the job. **Moral hazard** refers to the lack of effort on the part of the agent (e.g., the source) to fulfill the agreed-upon goal.[62] To the extent that agency costs are involved, then misrepresentation of abilities and shirking become problems, compounding administrative and coordination costs. When costs become too high, outsourcing is seen as one solution to this problem.

Taken altogether, outsourcing represents a form of organizational specialization in which relatively costly activities are contracted outside the firm, that is, externalized, in order to allow managers to focus on the organization's most critical activities. The motivation to outsource occurs when some activities become more expensive than others, leading to the search for opportunities to carry them out more cheaply elsewhere. In contrast to purchased inputs that are sourced externally, outsourced activities reside in the firm's value chain. However, there are similarities between global sourcing and outsourcing. Much like global sourcing, outsourcing has progressed through different stages, reflecting historical circumstances and changing patterns of competition (see Exhibit 6.8).

SUBCONTRACTING: THE "MAKE-OR-BUY" DECISION

Traditionally, specifically in the pre-1980 period, subcontracting was an outgrowth of the "**make-or-buy**" decision and related issues of vertical/horizontal integration.

Exhibit 6.8

Stages of Strategic Outsourcing

	Manufacturing-based (pre-1980)	Service-based (1980–2000)	Technology-based (2000 and beyond)
Context	Make-or-buy	Core vs. noncore	Technological and strategic transformation
Criteria	Cost	Cost, durability, uniqueness, centrality	Technology/service metrics
Key events	Production efficiency	Unbundling of value chain	Advent of new technology (fiber optics, Internet)
Patterns of jobs outsourced	Buyer–seller Manufacturer–subcontractor	Manufacturing Chip manufacturing	Software writers Customer service
		Call centers Medical transcriptions Telemarketing	Accounting Payroll services Insurance claims Paralegals Computer programmers IT services Tax preparation Brokerage services Human resource assistants Technical writers, animation (3D) Assisted digital services Desktop publishing R&D
			At risk of being outsourced (2000 and beyond) Legal analysts and attorneys Market analysts Consultants Projects managers Reports Retail sales Actuary Mechanical Draftsman Statistician Editors Life science Architeture Business operation Art and design

Sources: Adapted from Steve Hamm, "How to Keep Your Job Onshore," *Business Week*, August 20 and 27, 2007, pp. 68–71; Pete Engardio, Aaron Bernstein, Manjeet Kripalani, Frederik Balfour, Brian Grow, and Jay Greene, "The New Global Job Shift," *BusinessWeek*, February 3, 2003, p. 50.

Because many researchers and practitioners believed that outsourcing was a natural outcome of a maturing industry, it made sense for companies to purchase products and services that could be produced at a cheaper rate elsewhere. Typically such products and services were not closely linked to the firm's strategy or its "technical core."[63] Thus, the need to reduce cost in order to increase production efficiency was the major consideration in early "make-or-buy" decisions.

CORE VERSUS NONCORE COMPETENCIES

During the 1980–2000 period, outsourcing moved beyond "make-or-buy" manufacturing decisions and began to cover some service-related components of a firm's value chain.[64] In this context, outsourcing decisions were centered on whether activities were core or noncore.[65] Earlier conceptions of **core competencies** (Chapter 4) relied heavily on manufacturing operations for which it was easy to identify standardized subcomponents that cost more to produce in-house. As technologies improved and reduced the costs of activities within the firm's value chain, further economies were realized and effectively unbundled the value chain, creating viable candidates for outsourcing.[66] Correspondingly, research attention shifted to distinguishing between core and noncore activities in order to retain core competencies in-house, while outsourcing noncore activities.

Another significant shift was toward offshoring or offshore outsourcing (outsourcing to international suppliers). Unlike previous practices that concerned mainly manufacturing or the service activities of what are regarded as blue-collar jobs, the current environment includes high-end services that are most notably associated with white-collar jobs. Software and IT are notable examples. Moreover, while previous outsourcing occurred between firms within the same country (United States), current jobs have been reconstituted in other countries: India (software), China (manufacturing), Eastern Europe (manufacturing), and Southeast Asia (call centers). The shift toward offshore outsourcing was enabled by three forces: the explosion of undersea fiber-optic cable and bandwidth; the diffusion of PCs around the world; and the convergence of software programs, from e-mail, to Google, to Microsoft Office, to specially designed outsourcing programs.[67] Today it is possible to transmit and store huge amounts of data for virtually nothing. The rise of India and China as sourcing and outsourcing destinations has not escaped the attention of firms around the world. A comparative profile of the two countries is presented in Box 6.3.

While control, coordination, and communications—problem areas identified in domestic outsourcing—remain central, these are exacerbated in international transactions. While these applied to global sourcing as well, the internationalization of outsourced service activities adds to the *complexity* and to the *scope* of the contractual arrangements. The risks and dangers of expropriation and intellectual property theft are enlarged, particularly with service transactions. New issues related to vendor trust occur with greater cultural distance. The selection of foreign vendors entails more requirements, with some emphasis on the previous experience of the vendor with U.S. firms.

STRATEGIC TRANSFORMATION

The third phase of outsourcing occurs when it is used as a restructuring and transformational tool for creating strategic change. Because the objective of outsourcing is far-reaching and involves a fundamental change in value creation within a firm, it is referred to as **strategic transformation**, or "transformational outsourcing."[68] At General Electric, Jack Welch started a process of orchestrating a corporation-wide dialogue of ideas, including an assessment of suppliers, in order to shake up and change the existing corporate culture.[69] Another facet of strategic transformation is when outsourcing is used to significantly restructure a firm's business model. Old-line multinationals used

Box 6.3

China vs. India as Global Sourcing Opportunities

China	India
China relies on scale-driven, commodity-intensive manufacturing jobs, which are not stable for employment. In furniture, foreign retailers can source a new design from China's megaplants for delivery in two months.	India's growth is in design, service, automobiles, medicine, technology, and finance, which will provide more steady growth.
China is weaker than India in innovation. Taiwan is the conduit of electronic migration to China. It is forecasted that all electronic hardware manufacturing will be produced in China in the future. Much hardware is also designed in China.	Companies went to India for low costs, stayed for quality, and now invest for innovation.
Being a one-party government, China is efficient in building infrastructure. Power plants, bridges, airports, and the like are developed into the inland areas. China is building a 20,000-mile highway network, the world's second largest next to the United States.	In the short-term, pluralistic systems and the worry about losing at reelection slow down radical changes. The lack of well-planned transportation systems result in traffic horrors.
The one-party system has caused political uprisings.	The democratic system "sunk costs" will reap handsome dividends and could benefit foreign investors in the future.
Aggressive government support in acquiring foreign firms, reducing trade barriers, increasing foreign investment ownership.	More aggressive government support in reducing tariffs (from 300 percent down to 15 percent) and foreign ownership just recently.
Weak legal system and less legal protection.	Stronger legal protection for foreign investors.
Economic growth is heavily U.S.-investment reliant.	Economic growth is based on the growing consumer class.
Only 10 percent of China's engineers have the skills for multinational enterprises.	About 25 percent of India's engineers can be readily used by multinational enterprises.
Chinese companies' average profitability was at around 13 percent in 2004.	Indian companies' average profitability was at about 16.5 percent in 2004.
In 2003, nonperforming loans in China were up to approximately 22 percent.	In 2003, nonperforming loans in India were close to 9 percent.
Bigger aging population in China than in India.	By the 2050s, India could have more people than China and the average age will be younger than that of China.
There is a wide economic gap between the coastal and inland regions. The government has been trying diligently to close that gap.	There is no strong sign of a closing economic gap in India.

Both India and China are considered the emerging superpowers. It is forecasted that their economies combined will account for almost 50 percent of the world's GDP in the next forty-five years. Both offer more innovation, better goods, more competitive prices, and newer manufacturing plants than the United States. Many attribute their current success to the abundant supply of young and inexpensive labor. The two countries complement each other's strengths. An accelerating trend is that technical and managerial skills in both China and India are becoming more important than cheap assembly labor.

Sources: Adapted from Patrick Barta, "India Isn't Devouring Commodities," *Wall Street Journal,* January 9, 2006, p. A11; P. Chidambaram, "A Passage to Prosperity," *Wall Street Journal,* March 4, 2005, p. A14; Pete Engardio, "A New World Economy," *Business Week,* August 22–29, 2005, pp. 52–58; Pete Engardio, Dexter Roberts, and Brian Bremner, "The China Price," *Business Week,* December 6, 2005, pp. 102–112; Diana Farrell, "India Outsmarts China," *Foreign Policy*, vol. 152 (January–February 2006), pp. 30–31; Dexter Roberts, "Go West, Westerners," *Business Week,* November 14, 2005, pp. 60–61; Marcus Walker, "India Touts Its Democracy in Bid to Lure Investors Away from China," *Wall Street Journal,* January 30, 2006, p. A2.

outsourcing as a catalyst to overhaul outdated office operations, and to prepare for new competitive battles.[70] For example, Genpact, Accenture, or IBM Services would send a team to dissect processes of a given firm, after which they would build a new IT platform with all redesigned processes for which they administer the program as a virtual subsidiary. It is reported that Procter & Gamble, DuPont, Cisco Systems, ABN Amro, Unilever, Rockwell Collins, and Marriot were among those who have signed similar megadeals.[71] In a 1997 survey of CEOs by *Chief Executive* magazine and Anderson Consulting, 382 CEOs reported that 50 percent of their outsourcing was considered strategic, compared to 47 percent that was tactical, and 3 percent that was a combination of both.[72] These results were corroborated in a later 1997 survey of senior-level executives in large companies across the United States conducted by KMPG Peat Marwick. Specifically, based on 189 responses, close to 89 percent indicated that outsourcing was a strategic tool, with the rest in disagreement.[73]

While strategic outsourcing appears to be in vogue, there is a question of whether any transformation can occur without changing or transforming a firm's core competencies. In the case of Jack Welch's General Electric, for example, the transformation led to a new emphasis on service activities and the elimination of key product areas to arrive at a sharper corporate identity and focus. Yet, what is not fully resolved in theory and practice is *how* core competences *develop,* or—even more fundamentally—how they might *change* over time.[74] For early research, the choice of core competencies was not problematic, that is, companies appeared to recognize their internal strengths and weaknesses. While subsequent conceptualization attempted to define core competencies in more specific terms, empirical research illustrated the difficulty in applying generic definitions to more specific applied settings.[75] And while we now have a sprawling list of outsourced activities, we also have less compelling arguments for their classification as core or noncore, and some question whether some of these activities have, in fact, been transformed into core competencies.

Changing core competencies is incorporated in the notion of **dynamic competencies**, defined as "the firm's ability to integrate, build, and reconfigure internal and external competencies to address rapidly changing environments."[76] Such reconfigurations entail new resource combinations as markets emerge, collide, split, evolve, or simply die out.[77] Proponents of dynamic competencies call for proactive attempts to transform the firm on an ongoing basis, even if it might mean actually killing off highly successful products for which competencies were built, in order for new emerging ones to flourish.[78] Even so, there remains the question of what constitutes a core competency, and how this might be strengthened further to endure over time. In the next section, we synthesize theoretical and empirical arguments into a framework for better understanding of the outsourcing decision.

A FRAMEWORK FOR EXAMINING OUTSOURCING DECISIONS

Two questions are posed in developing a framework for assessing outsourcing decisions. First, what inherent factors in a particular job activity put it at risk, or vulnerable to becoming outsourced? Second, how can outsourcing decisions be made on the basis of the vulnerability and the costs of job activities?

FACTORS THAT MAKE AN ACTIVITY A CANDIDATE FOR OUTSOURCING

By way of an exercise, let's ask a basic question: *Under what circumstances might an activity be outsourced, or not outsourced at all?* A closer examination of the outsourcing context suggests that some elements of core competency bear greater weight than others.[79]

1. An Activity Is Likely to Be Outsourced If It Is Interchangeable or Fungible

Fungibility has received considerable attention in economics, finance, and international relations. **Fungibility** refers to "the degree to which all instances of a given commodity are considered interchangeable" (*Dictionary of Economics*). In economics, gold is fungible because one gram of gold is equivalent to any other gram of gold. In international relations, fungibility relates to the power of states to reinforce each other. Applied to a job context, fungibility refers to specific portions of the job that are interchangeable and unbundled, often prompted by the extent to which they lack differentiation, or have become commodities. For example, IT and various programmable tasks have become interchangeable. Because they are considered as commodities, that is, not differentiable, it does not matter whether a worker from the United States or India pursues a particular task; the task can be disaggregated (it is fungible) and it is interchangeable (a commodity).

Fungibility, or interchangeability, is related to the degree of inherent uniqueness or the extent to which a task is **idiosyncratic**. For example, there is an emerging job activity in graphic arts and animation called the "morph artist."[80] This involves a special knowledge of how animated characters can morph, or transform their appearance in a seamless fashion. Because this is a relatively new job in an embryonic industry (cartoon animation), it is considered to be relatively unique skill—one that is found in only a very few persons. To the extent that this job is considered unique and highly idiosyncratic, it is not likely be outsourced in the near future.

2. If an Activity Is Tacitly Specialized, It Is Less Likely to Be Outsourced

Pushed along by the philosopher Michael Polanyi's concept of tacit knowing, **tacit specialization** refers to an individual's automatic (often unconscious) skills that are highly contextual (interpreted in a specific context), bound to the individual's experience (specific to an individual or job), and difficult to codify or transfer.[81] This is contrasted against explicit knowledge, which is formal (conscious), invariant (applies across different contexts), and codifiable (manifested in formal expression). Tacit specialization is very difficult to measure, while explicit knowledge is amenable to measurement.

As an example, let us contrast two jobs: the IT programmer and the CEO. In the case of the IT programmer, much, if not the entire job, can be explicitly described and formalized as it involves using mathematical programs to represent events or transactions. Uncertainty is reduced by formal guidelines, and there is rarely an exception to the rule. In contrast, the CEO's job is multifaceted, involving managerial, technical, and human relations skills. It is nearly impossible to describe every aspect of the job as it involves managerial judgment and intuition. At this time, one can argue that the CEO's job, when compared to that of the IT programmer, has greater tacit specialization, and that it is impervious to formal measurement.

There are a number of factors that lead to a higher level of tacit specialization. First, face-to-face contact and information exchanges tend to be highly contextual and specific. Think, for example, of an emergency room doctor, a nurse, or a stockbroker with an intimate knowledge of the market. Second, the more relational the activity, that is, the more oriented at building reciprocity ties, the higher its tacit specialization. This is because relational activities are specific and difficult to transfer or replicate elsewhere. Imagine a college business dean engaged in various types of fundraising activities involving alumni, parents, students, faculty, staff, and business firms. In addition to the need for point-to-point flexibility (as in the case of negotiating contracts) and multiple communication channels, more social interaction also requires different levels of teamwork across the entire university. Will this job be outsourced? In our view, it is unlikely.

3. If an Activity Is Not Measurable, It Is Less Likely to Be Outsourced

It has been opined that "you cannot outsource what you cannot measure." This is because potential outsourced activities are typically evaluated in terms of their cost and quality relative to their production outside the company. **Measurability** is closely aligned with tacit specialization, that is, if the knowledge of skills and competencies associated with a job activity cannot be codified, or made explicit, it is not likely to be outsourced. Let's consider one specific example.

Guanxi is a central concept in Chinese culture and describes, in part, a "personal connection between two people in which one is able to prevail upon another to perform a favor or service" (Wikipedia). It describes the basic dynamic in personalized networks of influence and is considered by sociologists as a form of social capital. Because they are highly relational, relationships developed from *guanxi* are hardly transferable. While perhaps not as extensive, nor as consequential, deeply forged connections in the Western world are likewise highly relational. To the extent that any job is highly relational, it reinforces its tacit specialization and is not likely to be outsourced.

4. Even If an Activity Is Interchangeable or Fungible, It Is Not Likely to Be Outsourced If It Is Anchored or Interconnected to Other Jobs in the Organization

Let's assume that a job is fungible, specialized, and measurable. Will the job be outsourced? Not necessarily. It is *not* likely to be outsourced if it is connected, anchored, and embedded to other critical activities within the organization.[82] In contrast to the first three factors (fungibility, tacit specialization, and measurability), **interconnectedness** relates to how a particular activity is linked to the strategy of a firm, and thus is company specific. Connectedness can take the form of various types of dependencies. The late organizational sociologist James Thompson classified dependencies as pooled, sequential, and mutual interdependence based on the reciprocity of two actors.[83] **Pooled interdependence** refers to the common sharing of the same resource (functional units sharing a common budget); **sequential interdependence** refers to a unidirectional transfer of knowledge and resources (the case of automobile assembly); and **mutual interdependence** refers to inputs and outputs that are exchanged by parties (as in the case of medical diagnosis or management consulting). In the outsourcing context, mutual interdependence provides that tightest form of interconnectedness, that is, if activities are mutually interdependent and interconnected to other activities, they are less likely to be outsourced. Outsourcing these interconnected activities can have adverse effects since unbundling them can create disruption and dislocation with other units of the organization. For example, at Southwest Airlines, the job activities of the flight attendants are tightly bundled with routine cleaning and maintenance of the aircraft, as well as ticketing. Unbundling one of these activities for purposes of outsourcing is not likely to improve the company's cost position and could lead to disruption in that uncertain delivery schedules are now added to the firm's value chain.

Consideration of the above factors can be structured in terms of a decision methodology for students and managers (see Box 6.4). Four questions are sequenced that closely parallel the propositions above: Is the job activity interchangeable or fungible? If so, can it be measured? How much, if at all, does the activity involve tacit specialization? If it is fungible and measurable, is it anchored or tightly interconnected to other activities? Using a modified decision tree, one can compute a range of values that comprise the **Outsourcing Index**. Depending on the range of values, a particular job activity can be classified in terms of risk, that is, whether it is vulnerable to outsourcing, or conversely, not likely to be outsourced in the near future. In practice, the characteristics of fungibility, specialization, measurement, and connectedness rarely lead to a binary choice, that is, whether or not the job activity is fungible or not. More than likely, it involves a question of the extent to which a job is fungible, eliciting a response that can be rated along a scale of 0 to 100. In such a case, the values along the Outsourcing Index can be improved even further (see Box 6.4).

Taken as a whole, evaluating jobs and activities in terms of the Outsourcing Index, is important not only for the job holder, but also for firms that are planning to outsource as part of their corporate strategy. Two possible errors are noted. An error of commission occurs when a firm decides to outsource a job activity that should otherwise been retained in-house. This can entail significant costs of internal adjustment and dislocation within the organization, as well as the hidden costs of having the vendor fully understand the complexities of the job activity. On the other hand, by not outsourcing jobs that can save enormous costs for the company, a firm will lose valuable opportunities to focus on its core competencies, if not lose its competitive advantages to rivals who take advantage of this opportunity. A framework that positions jobs and activities more explicitly in terms of outsourcing decisions is presented next.

EXAMINING THE OUTSOURCING DECISION

Given the seismic shift toward strategic outsourcing, it's important to review the basic arguments in the outsourcing literature. Current conceptions that call for simply

Box 6.4

Illustrating the Use of the Outsourcing Index

Under what circumstances might an activity be outsourced, or not outsourced at all?

Outsourcing Index (OI)*

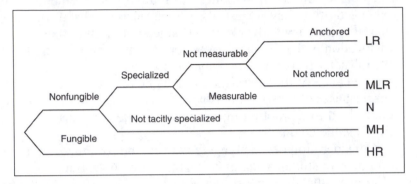

Index: LR = Low risk; MLR = Moderately low risk; N = Neutral; MHR = Moderately high risk; HR = High risk.

*Computed as the joint multiplicative product of four components: *fungibility, tacit specialization, measurement,* and *anchoring.* The higher the index, the less susceptible to outsourcing; the lower the index, the more vulnerable to outsourcing. While estimates are preliminary, a cutoff of .0400 is consistent with interviews conducted with IT firms (see Manuel Serapio, "International Outsourcing in Information Technology," Presentation, the Colorado Institute of Technology, November 2004).

Job activity: IT Consultant**

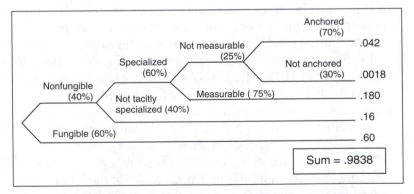

Outlook: Despite some degree of tacit specialization, this job is at moderately high risk for being outsourced in the future. Its outsourcing index, that is the composite risk of *not* being outsourced, is a low .042 (slightly above IT application). To prevent outsourcing, the activities that lead to a higher level of tacit specialization should be enhanced.

**Note that the sum should add up to 1.00, or very close to it, since fractional probabilities encompassing a certain event should add up to certainty (1.00).

classifying competencies as "core" and "noncore" tend to be overly simplistic, if not outright tautological. Moreover, by simply outsourcing noncore activities, one might inadvertently create internal dislocation within a company.[84] For example, Honda's core competency is its ability to make internal combustion engines, since this is a common core underlying its uniform strength in many diverse products: cars, motorcycles, lawnmowers, power generators, outboard motors, snowblowers, and garden tillers. Less emphasized are Honda's brand management, marketing, design of new vehicles, ability to make components, and management of suppliers. Should these be considered noncore and subsequently outsourced, this could create serious problems since they are anchored or closely connected to Honda's core competency of making internal combustion engines.[85] Relating back to the factors to consider, the first three—fungibility, tacit specialization, and measurement—are generic features of any job or activity. The factors of anchoring or connectedness relate to how the job is linked to the firm's strategy or competitive advantage.

By extending the Outsourcing Index, we arrive at a framework for examining the outsourcing decision. It is organized along two variables: outsourcing vulnerability (based on the Outsourcing Index), and the costs associated with outsourcing. Note that this attention to costs underscores our earlier discussion about the relationship between hidden costs and outsourcing (Box 6.2, p. 247). In retrospect, hidden costs arise when circumstances attendant to outsourcing are not properly anticipated and documented, even with tight monitoring of the outsourcing structure, because it is difficult, if not impossible, to verify *every* activity within an outsourcing venture.[86] Therefore, in addition to the costs of outsourcing a product/service delivery, hidden costs that include coordination, control, and enforcement should be incorporated fully into the decision. This juxtaposition of outsourcing vulnerability with the costs of outsourcing leads to an assessment framework for outsourcing decisions (Exhibit 6.9).[87]

Within each cell, there are managerial implications for logical action. More conventional recommendations are reflected in Cells 2 and 3, that is, core competencies should be retained in-house, while cheaper noncore activities should be outsourced. Cells 1 and 4 represent "gray" areas for which outsourcing will depend on whether costs can be reduced (Cell 1), or whether core competencies remain significant in the face of lowered costs (Cell 4). Implicit in these recommendations are the performance implications within each cell. If effectiveness, determined by vulnerability and costs, is high, then it makes sense to keep the activity in-house, assuming that the company can maintain this effectiveness in the future. To the extent that a firm's strategy is attractive, managerial attention should be directed at increasing the value of the core/distinctive competencies through less fungibility, more tacit specialization, and interconnectedness.

Migrations within each cell take into account changing competencies that might be in response to a changing and dynamic environment. One possible trajectory is the movement from noncore/high cost (Cell 1) to noncore/low cost (Cell 3). Intuitively, firms will attempt to manage noncore activities in ways that reduce their costs for maintaining them. Let's assume, for discussion, that the human resources hiring that once served a firm well has now become less valuable in that outside firms have developed more state-of-the-art practices at presumably lower prices. All things being

Exhibit 6.9   **Outsourcing Assessment Framework**

	Noncore *Fungible* *Not highly specialized* *Nonconnected* *Measurable*	Core *Nonfungible* *Highly specialized* *Connected* *Not readily measured*
High-cost *Product/Service* *Delivery* *Coordination* *Control* *Enforcement*	1 Gray area for outsourcing: *Do cost benefits significantly exceed total costs?* *Can coordination/control costs be reduced through training?*	2 Strong and preferred in-house candidates: *How to enhance distinctiveness/uniqueness?*
Low-cost *Product/Service* *Delivery* *Coordination* *Control* *Enforcement*	3 Strong and preferred outsourcing candidates: *Do we anticipate further standardization?*	4 Preferred in-house, but also a gray area for outsourcing: *Are cost benefits significant? Can staff be retrained? Are resources scarce?*

equal, the firm will want to reposition this as a possible candidate for outsourcing (see Exhibit 6.10).

In examining the characteristics of core competencies, stability and durability are important to the extent that these support and reinforce the requirements of a given strategy. Yet core competencies are not preordained to succeed forever. As such, the movement from Cell 2 (core) to Cell 1, 3, or 4 (noncore) might occur. To illustrate, in the 1950s, business schools built their competencies around superior teaching. This was the first gateway toward tenure and promotion. With the recognition of research as a necessary way of legitimizing the business profession—a charge articulated by later commissions (Carnegie, Ford Foundation)—the good schools slowly began to wean away from good teaching alone toward intellectual contributions and scholarship.

But movements can also occur in a different direction, that is, from noncore to core. One example is a food-retailing firm in Philadelphia, whose legal department in the early 1970s was regarded as having a peripheral support function. With the passage of new laws and the resolution of legal challenges to the company, however, the legal department became more central. Lawyers became an integral part of the firm's competitive strategy. Other departments within the firm had to coordinate with the legal department as the latter was in a better position to define the firm's critical

Exhibit 6.10   **Outsourcing Assessment Framework Migration Patterns**

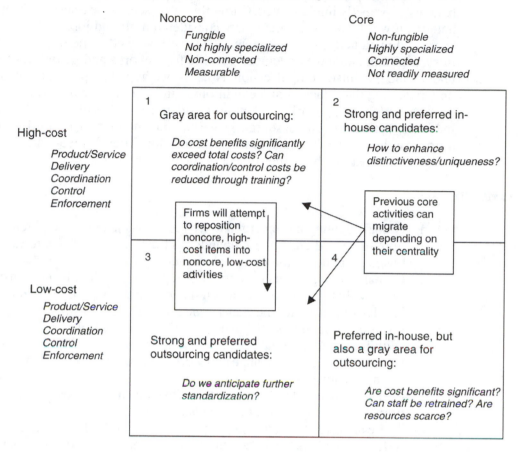

contingencies. In this scenario, the legal department increased its stature and influence and became a core competency.

In summary, global sourcing and outsourcing provide a firm with the opportunity to further leverage its business strategy and business model in an international context. In the case of global sourcing, this is principally attained by reducing costs significantly through improved relations with suppliers. Traditionally, relations with suppliers were viewed as arms-length transactions, with underlying assumptions of suppliers as being passive and, even worse, adversaries. More enlightened views characterizing strategic perspectives position suppliers as thoughtful partners that are actively engaged in the decision-making process with their buyer-firms. While many U.S. firms are still new at organizing their supply chains in a manner that reveals their competencies, there are numerous processes and procedures offered by industry experts that can make this happen, some of which are detailed in this chapter. Moreover, we are witness to a new type of transformation—offshore outsourcing—that has the potential of restructuring supply chains further, if not reconstituting a firm's mission and business strategy itself. While outsourcing, particularly offshore outsourcing, has been a contentious issue, even a national political debate, there is an emerging belief that it can yield significant benefits, if properly implemented. Currently we are seeing the transition in outsourcing patterns toward what were previously considered high-end jobs and activities, even "core" competencies. In this chapter, we have reviewed some important aspects of this transition, and have developed specific frameworks and guidelines to help you understand the outsourcing decision. Notably, we hope that practicing managers, by understanding these factors and conditions, can use outsourcing more effectively to operate in globalizing markets. Having considered elements of demand (international marketing) and costs (global sourcing), we turn our attention to the third path by which a firm can leverage advantage in its quest for global dominance—through strategic alliances and partnerships, the subject of the next chapter.

SUMMARY

1. Global sourcing has emerged as a strategic issue due to heightened competition, increased customer demands, and the desire of firms to leverage their business model in international markets.

2. Global sourcing differs from traditional purchasing. The latter is an operational activity that assures a firm a continued source of supplies. Global sourcing involves the development and transformation of a firm's supply chain and logistics through worldwide coordination and control.

3. Within an international context, global sourcing is complicated because of the need for firms to manage and work with suppliers from different cultures. Even so, statistics bear the pattern of significant increases in global sourcing over several decades. Yet, despite the benefits, many firms are still not capable of making the transition to global sourcing.

4. There are three types of sourcing. The first is multiple sourcing, or the use of different suppliers to reduce a firm's dependence on any one supplier. However, this can be time-consuming and unwieldy. Successful firms invest in good relationships with their suppliers and learn from them. The second is single sourcing, which emphasizes just-in-time management methods. Because it creates dependence on the supplier, firms have to select this partner carefully. The third is a single/dual hybrid network, or a combination of the above two. It is appropriate for assembly-type manufacturing and oftentimes employs teams to work with multi-rating systems.

5. The progression of a firm from domestic to global sourcing typically takes on five distinct stages: domestic purchasing (Level I), some international purchasing (Level II), international purchasing as part of sourcing strategy (Level III), integration and coordination of global sourcing (Level IV), and integration and coordination with worldwide groups (Level V). Published research suggests that most U.S. firms are in Level III.

6. As globalization has accelerated, the pattern of global sources has shifted. Currently, the popular sources include many Asian countries, notably India, China, Malaysia, Indonesia, and Vietnam.

7. Effective global sourcing requires the interaction with a diverse set of people,

organizations, and cultures on a personal and professional level. This includes developing a logistics infrastructure and supporting processes, formalizing purchasing and supply chain practices, developing a supply chain information system, strengthening global business capabilities, building communication and negotiation skills globally, engaging top management commitment throughout the process, and building strategic alliances.

8. When properly implemented, the benefits of global sourcing include: price/cost savings benefits, improved quality, product and process technological developments, improved supplier responsiveness, and improved communication.

9. Among the recent trends in global sourcing is outsourcing. While global sourcing entails the purchase of materials, albeit on a strategic level, outsourcing involves the displacement of an internal firm activity, which is assigned or contracted to an outside vendor on a recurring basis. Otherwise known as offshoring, or contracting with vendors outside a firm's home country, the practice has gained prominence in recent years.

10. The antecedents of outsourcing date back to organizational specialization and how it has led to organizational efficiency. Nevertheless, specialization can be risky since agency costs can arise. This is when individuals act in their self-interest, rather than in maximizing corporate performance. Two types of agency costs are distinguished: adverse selection (when owners cannot discern whether a manager has accurately represented his/her work) and moral hazard (when owners are not sure whether a manager has put forth maximal effort).

11. Because of agency costs and others relating to coordination, some activities have become more expensive. If they are not considered core or central to a firm's strategy, they are outsourced in order for the firm to concentrate on others with a more strategic function.

12. Similar to global sourcing, outsourcing has assumed different levels of development: considerations include subcontracting (make-or-buy), core versus noncore, and strategic transformation. The first decision relates to considerations of relative cost and quality. The second involves retaining core activities in-house while outsourcing noncore activities. The third occurs when outsourcing is used as a tool for achieving change, for a fundamental change in a firm's value creation, and when it is used to reconstitute a firm's business model.

13. There are four factors that make any job activity vulnerable or less vulnerable to outsourcing: fungibility, or the extent to which the job is interchangeable; tacit specialization, or the extent to which knowledge is implicit; measurability, or the extent to which knowledge for the job can be codified; and anchoring, or the extent to which the job is tightly interconnected with others in the organization.

14. The consideration of all these four factors results in an Outsourcing Index. This is the composite value determined by a joint multiplicative product of all four factors, ranging from 0 to 1.00. The higher the Index, the higher the risk and vulnerability to outsourcing. Generally the median value of .40 demarcates between job activities that are vulnerable to outsourcing against those that are not.

15. The organizing framework consists of two factors: outsourcing vulnerability and costs. By examining how jobs are arrayed in this framework, managers can view job activities that are at risk, not at risk, and possible migrations across cells (core to noncore, and vice versa) as a guide for examining their outsourcing decisions.

KEY TERMS

Global sourcing	Core competencies
Multiple suppliers	Strategic transformation
Single sourcing	Dynamic competencies
Hybrid network sourcing	Fungibility
Reverse auction	Idiosyncratic
Domestic purchasing	Tacit specialization
Integrating purchasing	Measurability
Outsourcing	Interconnectedness
Peripheral activities	Pooled interdependence
Noncore activities	Sequential interdependence
Adverse selection	Mutual interdependence
Moral hazard	Outsourcing Index
Make-or-buy	Migrations

DISCUSSION QUESTIONS

1. Why is global sourcing an option for managers to leverage their firm's strategy and business models internationally? How does global sourcing complement international marketing?

2. What are the three different types of global sourcing? What are the advantages and disadvantages of each type? Using company websites, classify what type the following companies have used in their sourcing activities: Nike, Solectron, Cisco Systems, Amazon.com, and Asea Brown and Boveri.

3. Discuss the five levels of global sourcing. Using the cases from the preceding question, classify each company in terms of its stage of development.

4. Discuss the specific steps involved in establishing a global sourcing program. What are the most difficult steps to implement? Why?

5. Discuss the advantages and disadvantages of offshore outsourcing. Why do companies engage in offshore outsourcing despite the short-term disadvantages of employee disruption and dislocation?

6. Discuss the four factors that determine a job's vulnerability to being outsourced. Take the case of your class instructor. Using the Outsourcing Index (Box 6.4), what is the risk of this job being outsourced? Why or why not?

ACTION ITEM 6.1. ROLE PLAYING

As part of an in-class exercise, you will be assigned to one of two groups: a buyer-firm or a potential vendor. Your instructor will decide whether the potential vendor will represent a pure supplier, or an offshore outsourcing vendor (see scenarios below).

SCENARIO ONE

First Brands, Inc., the maker of Glad sandwich bags, has partnered well with Kmart in the past. The company has an existing arrangement in which vendors are responsible for ensuring appropriate inventory levels to Kmart at all times. Kmart provides a three-year sales history that is used by First Brands in its own planning. The contract is up, and Kmart would like to expand the service across more of its distribution centers. First Brands would like to see such an expansion, but also a significant increase in its fees.

SCENARIO TWO

Nike, the world's leader in athletic shoes and apparel, seeks to broaden its market presence in Asia. It is exploring the possibility of a marketing distributorship, possibly even a Nike Center, in either the Philippines or Indonesia. Initial inquiries reveal that reliable parties in these two countries are interested.

In negotiating the terms of a contract or agreement, write down what both groups decide on with regard to the following steps in the process:

- Strategy phase: the objectives and scope of the relationship
- Scope phase: the baselines and service levels required from the vendor
- Negotiation phase: the total effort in terms of time, resources, and a preliminary budget
- Implementation phase: terms of the contract
- Management phase: the management relationship with the vendor
- Termination phase: terms that define the termination of the contract—continuation, a new contract, or a new vendor

---

CASE-IN-POINT. HUAWEI'S GENERATION—THE NEXT GLOBAL SUPPLIER?

SHERMAN SO[88]

China Motion Telecom, the Singapore and Hong Kong Internet IDD [international direct dialing] Company, needed a VOIP (voice-over Internet protocol) solution that would work for telephone numbers in more than one country, but there was nothing remotely similar on the market. Executive Vice President Chow and his colleagues listened patiently to ideas from Canada's Nortel and Lucent of the United States, among others, but nothing quite seemed to fit.

The outlook brightened, though, when they sought a proposal from Huawei Technologies, far and away China's largest telecoms vendor but, like most mainland companies, saddled with a reputation as a cheap, off-the-rack producer. Huawei engineers descended on the company en masse—there were so many that Chow eventually lost count. It took them three months to design a prototype exclusively for China Motion and six months to present the company with a finished product. The price was US$5 million (HK$39 million), a "real bargain," says Chow, for a product that supports 2 million customers.

Huawei has two ambitions, according to Fu Jun, its director of corporate communications—one is to be a world leader, the other is to survive. These two preoccupations seem contradictory unless you remember that glittering names like Nokia, Ericsson, and Cisco are just as intent on invading Huawei's mainland patch, where its market share is estimated at 30 percent, as it is on invading theirs.

Huawei, based in Shenzhen, is one of the first Chinese companies to try to gain recognition abroad as more than just a cheap producer. To do this, it is making greater use of its undoubted cost advantages to win contracts that showcase its ability to innovate and tailor products to client needs. In 2004, overseas business accounted for about 41 percent of Huawei's US$3.82 billion in sales; this year, it will probably account for over 50 percent, says Fu. The company has fifty-five offices around the world. Almost 6,000 of its 24,000 staff are located abroad, and about 3,400 are non-Chinese.

Outside China, Huawei has research facilities in India, Russia, and the United States. Asked if Huawei considers itself a world leader, Fu opts for modesty. "The customers decide who the leading players are, not us," he says. Applying this test, Huawei has some way to go before it breaks into the ranks of the elite. Most of its overseas clients are in emerging markets or smaller players in developed markets. For Brazil's Telemar, for example, it has supplied Internet equipment for use in the home.

Etissalat, the telecoms carrier in the United Arab Emirates, picked Huawei to build its third-generation mobile network. It also built the 3G [third generation] networks of Sunday, Hong Kong's smallest mobile operator, and the small Dutch operator Telfort. In 3G, one analyst says, the threat posed by Huawei is an "excuse" for the weak and "no problem" at all for the strong. The combined global 3G equipment market share of Huawei and its main domestic competitor, ZTE, was 2.5 percent, worth just under US$1 billion, in 2004, according to a report by New York–based Bernstein Investment Research and Management. By comparison, Ericsson alone had more than 40 percent of the market. As yet, neither mainland manufacturer has the installed base, the track record, or the global support organization necessary to win major deals in the West, Bernstein concluded in its report, due out in February 2005. But the breadth of Huawei's product line is impressive, as any visitor to its exhibition center in Shenzhen can testify. Wireless, fixed line, voice, data, 2G, 3G, base stations, mobile phones, optical fiber networks, switches, and routers—you name it and Huawei probably makes it.

Huawei even designs its own integrated circuit chips to keep costs down. Still, says China Motion's Chow, many of its offerings remain prototypes that will require a lot of work before they reach the market. For smaller players like China Motion, Huawei is a good partner by all accounts. "One thing that is impressive about the company is their willingness to customize their products to suit your requirements," says Chow, who has worked closely with the Huawei engineering team since October 2003.

In his opinion, Huawei is using its contract with China Motion to learn more about NGNs (next-generation networks), which combine fixed-line voice and data services, a technology that could be crucial to its future. Its 3G project with Hong Kong's Sunday can be seen in the same light: "Huawei's 3G solution needs a lot of help, and a key reference deployment that it can show to its future clients," says Chow.

To obtain a 3G showcase, Huawei did not shy away from aggressive financing terms. It loaned Sunday HK$859 million over seven years to help finance its 3G rollout and HK$500 million over two years to repay financing previously provided by Nortel, Sunday's original equipment supplier. In January, to win 3G a contract in Thailand, Huawei bid US$187 million, 46 percent below the customer's original estimate.

"Huawei is learning what is needed in the market from the operators," says Chow. And with senior engineers who earn a quarter of what most of their foreign counterparts earn, and junior engineers earning just half as much as their seniors, sending out teams to work hand-in-hand with the customer makes a lot of sense.

If the strategy works, Huawei will establish itself as a leading supplier of both NGN and 3G equipment just as major operators the world over are introducing the new technologies. There are some signs that Huawei has started to win the endorsement of first-tier operators. BT, Britain's largest phone company, became the first blue-chip operator to use Huawei for a major project, naming it and seven others, including Lucent, Ericsson, Fujitsu, and Cisco, as preferred suppliers for its US$19 billion, five-year network upgrade project, which straddles fixed-line, mobile, and Internet services. Vodafone, the world's largest cellphone operator, is also evaluating Huawei's gear. But for the real boost that transforms its status, Huawei may have to wait a few more years—and, ironically, it may have to come home to get it. Huawei is expected to get a handsome share of coming 3G equipment orders in China. Research firm Bernstein expects that of the total US$8–$10 billion, Huawei and ZTE will get 30 or 40 percent.

If so, it will be the chance both mainland firms have been waiting for to establish a track record that allows them to achieve the same ranking as their foreign competitors. It could happen as soon as 2007, the target for completing the first phase of China's 3G project. It is not uncommon for equipment vendors to be involved in projects with low or even negative margins at the same time that they reap good profits on others.

The danger for Huawei, however, may be in having too many of the first kind and too few of the second. The company's 2004 balance sheet (though unlisted, Huawei publishes annual financial results) showed some signs of strain. The item "trade and other payables," which is usually the amount due to suppliers, was exceptionally high, at US$1.461 billion, when compared with the company's cost of sales at US$1.918 billion. This means that on average it took nine months for suppliers to get paid.

But it is hard to imagine this well-connected company being allowed to fail. Local government officials point to Huawei as one of the most brilliant successes of the Shenzhen special economic zone, which, though it owns no stake in the company, is certainly in a position to offer it subsidies, tax breaks, and cheap land. Huawei is also rumored to have strong ties to China's military, whose appetite for new technology is growing by the day. Few journalists are allowed inside Huawei's Silicon Valley–like headquarters.

The honor tends to be reserved for recent and current presidents and premiers—Jiang Zemin, Zhu Rongji, Li Peng, Hu Jintao, and Wen Jiabao have all taken the grand tour—and a smattering of less-recognizable but undoubtedly key figures from the Central Military Commission and the State Council. Huawei has its own highway access from which VIPs can be whisked in and out in safety and comfort. State banks stand ready to help the company realize its international ambitions. China Development Bank, for one, agreed in December to put a massive US$10 billion, five-year credit facility at the disposal of both Huawei and its foreign source.

CASE DISCUSSION QUESTIONS

1. Evaluate the steps Huawei has taken to establish itself as a major global source for NGN and 3G.
2. Do you consider Huawei's current relationship with the Chinese government to be an advantage or a disadvantage in their aspiration to be a global source? Please substantiate your answer.

NOTES FOR CHAPTER 6

1. Kerry Capell, "IKEA: How the Swedish Retailer Became a Global Cult Brand, " *Business Week* (November 14, 2005), pp. 96–106.

2. Christopher A. Bartlett and Anish Nanda, "Ingvar Kamprad and IKEA," Harvard Business School Case Study, No. 9–390–132 (originally published May 7, 1990; revised July 22, 1996). Teaching Note (5-395-155), p. 4.

3. "IKEA Bets on Vietnam," *Far Eastern Economic Review* (September 25, 2003), pp. 56–59.

4. Youngme Moon, "IKEA Invades America," Harvard Business School Case Study, No. 504–094 (April 27, 2004).

5. "IKEA Bets on Vietnam," p. 57.

6. Robert J. Trent and Robert M. Monczka, "International Purchasing and Global Sourcing—What Are the Differences?" *Journal of Supply Chain Management* 39, no. 4 (2003): 26–36.

7. See Larry C. Giunipero and Robert M. Monczka, "Organizational Approaches to Managing International Sourcing," *International Journal of Physical Distribution & Logistics Management* 20, no. 4 (1990): 3–12; Robert M. Monczka and Robert J. Trent, "Global Sourcing: A Development Approach," *International Journal of Purchasing and Materials Management* 11, no. 2 (1991): 2–8; Robert E. Spekman, "U.S. Buyers' Relationships with Pacific Rim Sellers," *International Journal of Purchasing and Materials Management* 27, no. 1 (1991): 2–10.

8. Masaaki Kotabe, "Efficiency vs. Effectiveness Orientation of Global Sourcing Strategy: A Comparison of U.S. and Japanese Multinational Companies," *Academy of Management Executive* 12, no. 4 (1998): 107–19.

9. Philip B. Crosby, *Quality Without Tears* (New York: McGraw-Hill, 1984).

10. Tim Minahan, "Global Sourcing: What You Need to Know to Make It Work" (Boston, MA: Aberdeen Group, August 11, 2003), SearchCIO.techtarget.com/generic/0,295582,sid182_gci1049457,00.html.

11. Trent and Monczka, "International Purchasing and Global Sourcing—What Are the Differences?" pp. 26–36.

12. Shawn Tully, "Purchasing's New Muscle," *Fortune* (February 20, 1995): 75–83.

13. Carl R. Frear, Lynn E. Metcalf, and Mary S. Alguire, "Offshore Sourcing: Its Nature and Scope," *International Journal of Purchasing and Materials Management* 28, no. 3 (1992): 2–11.

14. Joseph R. Carter and Ram Narasimhan, "A Comparison of North American and European Future Purchasing Trends," *International Journal of Purchasing and Materials Management* 32, no. 2 (1996): 12–23; Monczka and Trent, "Global Sourcing: A Development Approach," pp. 2–8.

15. David Pyke, "Strategies for Global Sourcing," in *Mastering Global Business: The Complete MBA Companion in Global Business* (London: FT/Prentice Hall, 1999): p. 107.

16. Mary S. Alguire, Carl R. Frear, and Lynn E. Metcalf, "An Examination of the Determinants of Global Sourcing Strategy," *Journal of Business & Industrial Marketing* 9, no. 2 (1994): 62–74; Laura M. Birou and Stanley E. Fawcett, "International Purchasing: Benefits, Requirements, and Challenges," *International Journal of Purchasing and Materials Management* 29, no. 2 (1993): 27–37; Robert M. Monczka and Larry C. Giunipero, "International Purchasing: Characteristics and Implementation," *International Journal of Purchasing and Materials Management* 20, no. 3 (1984): 2–9.

17. Pyke, "Strategies for Global Sourcing," p. 107; A. Coskun Samli, John M. Browning, and Carolyn Busbia, "The Status of Global Sourcing as a Critical Tool of Strategic Planning: Opportunistic Versus Strategic Dichotomy," *Journal of Business Research* 43, no. 3 (1998): 177–87.

18. A. Ansari and B. Modarress, *Just-in-Time Purchasing* (New York: The Free Press, 1990).

19. Jay Heizer and Barry Render, *Principles of Operations Management* (Englewood Cliffs, NJ: Prentice-Hall, 2004), pp. 401–02.

20. Michael Yoshino and A.S. George, "Li & Fung (A): Beyond 'Filling in the Mosiac': 1995–1998," Harvard Business School Case No. 398092.

21. Pyke, "Strategies for Global Sourcing," p. 109.

22. Ibid.

23. Mark Treleven, "Single Sourcing: A Management Tool for the Quality Supplier," *Journal of Purchasing and Materials Management* 23, no. 1 (1987): 19–25.

24. Cathy Owens Swift, "Preferences for Single Sourcing and Supplier Selection Criteria," *Journal of Business Research* 32, no. 2 (1995): 105–12.

25. Pyke, "Strategies for Global Sourcing," p. 109.

26. Richard G. Newman, "Single Source Qualification," *International Journal of Purchasing and Materials Management* 24, no. 2 (1988): 10–17.

27. Robert B. Handfield, "U.S. Global Sourcing: Patterns of Development," *International Journal of Operations & Production* 14, no. 6 (1994): 40–51.

28. Newman, "Single Source Qualification."

29. Peter Hines, "Network Sourcing: A Hybrid Approach," *International Journal of Purchasing and Materials Management* 31, no. 2 (1995): 18–24.

30. Pyke, "Strategies for Global Sourcing," p. 110; Trent and Monczka, "International Purchasing and Global Sourcing—What Are the Differences?" pp. 26–27.

31. Ibid., p. 110.

32. Mark Gottfredson, Rudy Puryear, and Stephen Phillips, "Strategic Sourcing: From Periphery to the Core," *Harvard Business Review* 83, no. 2 (February 11, 2005): 132.

33. Mohanbir Sawhney, "Forward Thinking about Reverse Auctions," *CIO Magazine* (June 1, 2003). Alibaba.com is another example of a firm that successfully utilized reverse auctions for online procurement.

34. Trent and Monczka, "International Purchasing and Global Sourcing—What Are the Differences?" p. 26.

35. Ibid., pp. 26–37; Giunipero and Monczka, "Organizational Approaches to Managing International Sourcing," pp. 3–12; Monczka and Trent, "Global Sourcing: A Development Approach," pp. 2–8; Spekman, "U.S. Buyers' Relationships with Pacific Rim Sellers," pp. 1–10.

36. Trent and Monczka "International Purchasing and Global Sourcing—What Are the Differences?" pp. 26–37.

37. It has been pointed out to us, specifically by Jay Jayaram, that considerations of sourcing sources, inclusive of the progression of escalated sourcing over time, should be made in tandem with product life cycles as well as multinational investment decisions. This is because there are risks along the product life cycle that inextricably impact sourcing decisions, in addition to considerations relating to the speed of industry evolution. The notion of the total cost of ownership and isolating vendor risk, country risk, and economic risk are crucial in global sourcing decisions. While we cover these topics in other chapters, we did not integrate these into this chapter. Nevertheless, some useful references on this treatment include: Charles H. Fine, *Clockspeed: Winning Industry Control in the Age of Temporary Advantage* (New York: Perseus Books, 1998); G. Tomas M. Hult, "Managing the International Strategic Sourcing Function as a Market-driven Organizational Learning System," *Decision Sciences* 29, no. 1 (1998): 193–216.

38. Jonathan Hughes, "Why Your Supplier Relationships Fail to Deliver Their True Value," *HBR Supply Chain Strategy*, June 1, 2005.

39. This section summarizes findings from Handfield, "U.S. Global Sourcing: Patterns of Development," pp. 40–51.

40. Monczka and Giunipero, "International Purchasing: Characteristics and Implementation," pp. 2–9; Kenneth J., Petersen, David J. Frayer and Thomas V. Scannell, "An Empirical Investigation of Global Sourcing Strategy Effectiveness," *Journal of Supply Chain Management* 36, no. 2 (2000): 29–39.

41. Pyke, "Strategies for Global Sourcing," p. 111.

42. Ibid., p. 110.

43. Ibid., pp. 111–12.

44. "Ben Franklin Forum on Innovation: How Companies Use Innovation to Build Value," *Knowledge@Wharton* (February 27, 2006).

45. Shanthakumar Palaniswami and B.P. Lingaraj, "Procurement and Vendor Management in the Global Environment," *International Journal of Production Economics* 35, no. 3 (1994): 171–76.

46. Janet Y. Murray, "Strategic Alliances–based Global Sourcing Strategy for Competitive Advantage: A Conceptual Framework and Research Propositions," *Journal of International Marketing* 9, no. 4 (2001): 30–58.

47. Tony Davila, Marc Epstein, and Robert Shelton, *Making Innovation Work: How to Manage It, Measure It, and Profit from It* (Philadelphia: Wharton School Publishing, 2005).

48. Monczka and Giunipero, "International Purchasing: Characteristics and Implementation," pp. 2–9; Petersen, Frayer, and Scannell, "An Empirical Investigation of Global Sourcing Strategy Effectiveness," pp. 29–39; Trent and Monczka, "International Purchasing and Global Sourcing—What Are the Differences?" pp. 26–37; Amy Zhaohui Zeng, "A Synthetic Study of Sourcing Strategies," *Industrial Management & Data Systems* 100, no. 5 (2000): 219.

49. Petersen, Frayer, and Scannell, "An Empirical Investigation of Global Sourcing Strategy Effectiveness," pp. 29–39.

50. The section is drawn from the following sources: The first three benefits (price/cost; improved quality; and product technology) are from a study by Petersen, Frayer, and Scannell, "An Empirical Investigation of Global Sourcing Strategy Effectiveness," pp. 29–39; the fourth benefit (improved supplier responsiveness) is synthesized from Trent and Monczka, "International Purchasing and Global Sourcing—What Are the Differences?" pp. 26–37; Birou and Fawcett, "International Purchasing: Benefits, Requirements, and Challenges," *International Journal of Purchasing and Materials Management* 29, no. 2 (1993): 27–37; Frear, Metcalf, and Alguire, "Offshore Sourcing: Its Nature and Scope," *International Journal of Purchasing and Materials Management* 28, no. 3 (1992): 2–11; Paul D. Arson and Jack D. Kulchisky, "Single Sourcing and Supplier Certification: Performance and Relationship Implications," *Industrial Marketing Management* 27, no. 1 (1998): 73–81; Palaniswami and Lingaraj, "Procurement and Vendor Management in the Global Environment," *International Journal of Production Economics* 35, no. 1–3 (1994): 171–76; Swift, "Preferences for Single Sourcing and

Supplier Selection Criteria," *Journal of Business Research* 32, no. 2 (1995): 105–12; Ann K. Willis, "Creating Win-Win Customer–Supplier Partnerships," *Hospital Materials Management Quarterly* 9, no. 3 (1998): 15–22.

51. Trent and Monczka, "International Purchasing and Global Sourcing—What Are the Differences?" pp. 26–37.

52. Handfield, "U.S. Global Sourcing: Patterns of Development," pp. 40–51; Trent and Monczka, "International Purchasing and Global Sourcing—What Are the Differences?" 26–37.

53. See note 33 in particular for other considerations. Also see Joseph R. Carter and Shawnee K. Vickery, "Currency Exchange Rates: Their Impact on Global Sourcing," *Journal of Purchasing and Materials Management* 25, no. 3 (1989): 19–25.

54. Maurice Greaver, *Strategic Outsourcing* (San Francisco: AMACOM, 1999).

55. James B. Quinn, "Strategic Outsourcing: Leveraging Knowledge Capabilities," *Sloan Management Review* 40 (Summer 1999): 9–21.

56. Ling Ge, Prabhudev Konana, and Huseyin Tanriverdi, "Global Sourcing and Value Chain Unbundling," University of Texas at Austin, Department of Management Science and Information Systems, McCombs School of Business, 2004.

57. "The New Jobs Migration," *Economist*, February 21–27, 2004, p. 11; Stephen Baker and Manjeet Kripalani, "Software: Will Outsourcing Hurt America's Supremacy?" *BusinessWeek*, March 1, 2004, pp. 84–94.

58. "Offshoring: Is It a Win-Win Game?" Report, McKinsey Global Institute, San Francisco, CA, August 2003.

59. Paul Lawrence and Jay Lorsch, *Organization and Environment: Managing Differentiation and Integration* (Cambridge: Harvard University Graduate School of Business Administration, 1967).

60. Adam Smith, *An Inquiry into the Nature and Causes of the Wealth of Nations* (Oxford: Clarendon, 1776; repr., 1869).

61. Harvey Leibenstein, *Inside the Firm: The Inefficiencies of Hierarchy* (Boston, MA: Harvard Business School Press, 1987).

62. Definitions are from Kathleen Eisenhardt, "Agency Theory: An Assessment and Review," *Academy of Management Review* 14, no. 1 (1989): 61; also see Mary Logan, "Using Agency Theory to Design Successful Outsourcing Relationships," *International Journal of Logistics and Management* 11, no. 2 (2000): 21–32.

63. James Thompson, *Organizations in Action: Social Science Bases for Administrative Theory* (New York: McGraw-Hill, 1967).

64. Quinn, "Strategic Outsourcing: Leveraging Knowledge Capabilities," pp. 9–21.

65. James B. Quinn, T.L. Doorley, and P.C. Pacquette, "Technology in Services: Rethinking Strategic Focus," *Sloan Management Review* (Winter 1990): 79–87.

66. Ibid.

67. Thomas L. Friedman, "Small and Smaller," *New York Times* (March 4, 2004), E1; also see George Gilder, "The Bandwidth Tidal Wave," *Forbes ASAP* (December 5, 1994). Available under "Gilder Article Index," at www.seas.upenn.edu/~gaj1/bandgg.html.

68. "The Future of Outsourcing: How It's Transforming Whole Industries and Changing the Way We Work," *BusinessWeek,* January 30, 2006, www.businessweek.com/magazine/content/06_05/b3969401.htm.

69. Noel Tichy and Stratford Sherman, *Control Your Own Destiny or Someone Else Will* (New York: Doubleday, 1993).

70. "The Future of Outsourcing," p. 20.

71. Ibid.

72. Michael Winkleman, "View from the Top—Raise High the Roof Beam," *Chief Executive*, April 1997, p. 67.

73. "KPMG Survey: Companies Increasingly Look to Outsourcing for Competitive Advantage," KPMG Peat Marwick LLP, 1997, p. 6.

74. See Pete Engardio and Bruce Einhorn, "Outsourcing Innovation." *BusinessWeek*, March 21, 2005, pp. 84–90.

75. Mansour Javidan, "Core Competence: What Does It Mean in Practice?" *Long Range Planning,* 31, no. 1: 60–71.

76. David Teece, Gary Pisano, and Amy Shuen, "Dynamic Capabilities and Strategic Management," *Strategic Management Journal* 18, no. 7 (August 1997): 509–33.

77. K.M. Eisenhardt and J.A. Martin, "Dynamic Capabilities: What Are They?" *Strategic Management Journal* 21 (2000): 1105–21.

78. Clayton M. Christensen, *The Innovator's Dilemma: When New Technologies Cause Great Firms to Fail* (Boston: Harvard Business School Press, 1997).

79. The ensuing discussion is drawn from an earlier argument made by Thomas L. Friedman, *The World Is Flat: A Brief History of the Twenty-First Century* (New York: Farrar, Straus, and Giroux, 2005), pp. 238–239.

80. Ibid., p. 242.

81. Michael Polanyi, *The Tacit Dimension* (London: Routledge & Kegan Paul, 1966).

82. Thomas Friedman, *The World Is Flat*, p. 239. The definition of *guanxi* in the earlier section is taken from Wikipedia (April 5, 2008).

83. James Thompson, *Organizations in Action* (New York: Wiley, 1967).

84. "The New Jobs Migration," *Economist*, February 21–27, 2004, p. 11; Baker and Kripalani, "Will Outsourcing Hurt America's Supremacy?" pp. 84–94.

85. This example is taken from Carlos Cordon, Thomas Vollman, and Jussi Heikkila, "Thinking Clearly about Outsourcing," in *Mastering Global Business* (London: FT Management, 1999), pp. 113–18.

86. David Wessel, "The Future of Jobs: New Ones Arise, Wage Gap Widens," *Wall Street Journal*, April 2, 2004, p. A1.

87. Modified from an earlier version, Application Management and Outsourcing Services, 2004 META Group (Stamford, CT: META, 2004). However, we used two completely different factors.

88. Adapted from Sherman So, "Huawei's Generation," *The Standard,* July 18, 2005, with permission.

7 Leveraging Competitive Advantage Through Strategic Alliances

If you do not seek out allies and helpers, then you will be isolated and weak.
—Sun Tzu, "The Art of War"

The forces of a powerful ally can be useful and good to those who have recourse to them . . . but are perilous to those who become dependent on them.
—Niccolo Machiavelli, "The Prince"

CHAPTER OUTLINE

- Which of the Two Scenarios Will Prevail?
- Strategic Alliances: Lessons About Partnerships
- Why Strategic Partnerships?
- Defining Strategic Alliances
- Benefits of Strategic Alliances
- Alliances in the New Competitive Landscape
- The Risks of Strategic Alliances
- The Causes of Alliance Failure
- Managing Strategic Alliances
- Emerging Global Alliances and Partnerships

LEARNING OBJECTIVES

- Understand the need for strategic partnerships.
- Know the different types of strategic alliances.
- Understand the reasons why alliances fail.
- Know how strategic, cultural, and operational fit improves alliance management.
- Understand the concept of transparency and how this relates to the collaborative membrane.
- Learn more about new forms of alliances and the need to build new competencies.

WHICH OF THE TWO SCENARIOS WILL PREVAIL?

The story of the Fuji Xerox joint venture is often hailed as the poster child of stable alliances. In 1962, Fuji Xerox, a 50–50 joint venture between Fuji Photo

Film and Rank Xerox, was established to sell photocopiers and related products and services to the Japanese market, as well as to some Asian countries. While initially rebuffed by the Japanese government, Fuji Xerox eventually emerged from a local organization into a global partner for Xerox, despite some resistance from Japanese firms such as Canon and Ricoh. Its strategy included a number of initiatives, such as Total Quality Management (TQM) and new product development for small photocopiers that solidified the market position of this joint venture against the likes of Canon. As of 2001, the joint venture has been a global partner of Xerox and has been involved in R&D and the manufacturing of products and services throughout Asia. On one occasion, the alliance aided Xerox when Japanese competitors chipped away at Xerox's copier empire in Japan. With the assistance of Fuji Xerox's design, manufacturing capacity, and management ideas, Xerox was able to overcome the onslaught of low-end copiers from Canon, Ricoh, and Minolta, and a high-end attack from Kodak and IBM. What made Fuji Xerox so successful? Management professor and analyst Ben Gomes-Casseres attributes such stability to good management, proper levels of specialization, a long-term focus, learning, and partner flexibility.[1]

DaimlerChrysler, a joint venture incorporated in 1998, brought together Daimler and Chrysler with the vision of combining the quality reputation of Daimler Benz with the mass manufacturing capability of Chrysler. Specifically, Chrysler would tap into Mercedes–Benz technology, and Chrysler would give Mercedes–Benz some buffer in the event that the luxury car market declined or plateaued.[2] Despite the fanfare, nothing materialized as planned. Chrysler's financial setbacks led to a massive rescue job that absorbed the attention of Mercedes-Benz management for years, while Mercedes-Benz, in turn, lost share, reputation, and profits.[3] According to University of Chicago professor and automobile expert James Schrager, the alliance was doomed from the start: "They were a mistake because the strategies—for Mercedes and Chrysler and all of its associated brands—were so different. For years, Mercedes' car brand sat at the top of the world as far as prestige, durability, and reliability . . . it was the finest-engineered car you could buy. Contrast this with Chrysler. . . . Were it not for the minivan, introduced in 1982, Chrysler would have been gone sometime in the 1980s . . . we have a huge mismatch here."[4]

STRATEGIC ALLIANCES: LESSONS ABOUT PARTNERSHIPS

The debate on the effectiveness of strategic alliances often conjures two contrasting scenarios:[5]

- Alliances are formed for reasons that are not completely disclosed by partners at the outset. Despite good intentions, there still remains strong rivalry within the alliance. In time, competitive pressures lead to opportunism that erodes good intentions. Moreover, coordination activities are exacerbated by misunderstandings that lead to further mistrust and the eventual demise of the alliance.

- Alliances are formed by rivals who might not completely trust each other, but believe that gains from the alliance far exceed costs. Accordingly, structures, incentives, and communication channels are designed that effectively incorporate differences in their organizational structures and cultural backgrounds. Despite these differences, the partners learn to work with each other, and the alliance maintains high stability.

WHY STRATEGIC PARTNERSHIPS?

As the globalization of the competitive landscape intensifies, there is growing pressure for companies to develop an international market presence. To meet this challenge, a firm must be able to acquire, outsource, or internalize specialized assets, technological knowledge, organizational competence, finance, production, supplier and customer networks, and market intelligence on a global scale. And a firm in today's environment has to build these competencies much *quicker* and at *less cost* than its competitors.[6] Thus far, in the previous two chapters, we have discussed how a firm can leverage its ability to exploit international opportunities through international marketing (Chapter 5) and global sourcing (Chapter 6). Given pervasive globalization pressures, however, it is widely believed that no firm, including the dominant market leader, can generate all these capabilities internally. This necessitates a shift from direct, individual competition to increasingly cooperative forms of competition, such as a partnership with another firm in the form of a strategic alliance. The ability to learn quickly from experiences and to develop dynamic capabilities is a key requirement in any successful endgame. Forging strategic alliances is the third path by which a firm can leverage its advantage in international competition (see Figure 7.1).

Yet, as the opening vignette indicates, having a global partner does not ensure that a firm will sustain its competitive advantage. For whatever benefits might accrue to an alliance, the failure rate—meaning the inability of the alliance to meet objectives, oftentimes resulting in the termination of the partnership—is a dismal one. For every successful alliance, such as Fuji Xerox, one can come up with a failed one, such as DaimlerChrysler. Why one alliance succeeds while another fails is the subject matter of this chapter. We begin with definitions of strategic alliances. Then we review the rationale and benefits of alliances, particularly as these apply to global competition. We will discuss why alliances fail—a perspective borne out of much published research. We will then present a framework of alliance formation and management, and examine new managerial competencies needed for the management of strategic alliances and large-scale global networks.

DEFINING STRATEGIC ALLIANCES

Basically, a **strategic alliance** is "a form of cooperative linkage entered for strategic reasons . . . [to provide] . . . a means by which firms can attain the levels of efficiency and effectiveness necessary to remain competitive."[7] There are a number of benefits that result from a successful alliance, including economies of scale, new skills and technologies, risk reduction, and effective resource sharing. These may explain the

Figure 7.1   **Framework for Leveraging Strategic Advantage: Strategic Alliances and Partnerships**

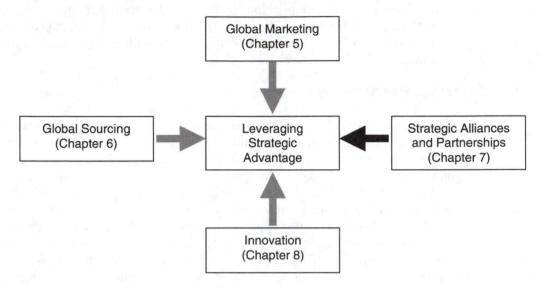

variety of joint ventures, R&D partnerships, technological alliances, licensing, franchising, and cross-manufacturing arrangements. Among these, the most popular form of a negotiated alliance is the joint venture, where two firms provide equity shares toward a company with some specific goal.

Even so, defining a strategic alliance is elusive as it can take on many forms. Strategic alliances can be joint ventures, mergers, acquisitions, and even traditional contractual agreements, such as licensing and franchising. To add clarity and focus, Harvard professor Michael Yoshino and Babson professor Srinivasa U. Rangan have suggested a restrictive definition that specifies three necessary conditions for qualifying as a strategic alliance that are excerpted below:

- The two or more firms that unite to pursue a set of agreed-upon goals remain independent subsequent to the formation of the alliance.
- The partner firms share the benefits of the alliance and control over the performance of assigned tasks—perhaps the most distinctive characteristic of alliances and the ones that make them so difficult to manage.
- The partner firms contribute on a continuing basis in one or more key strategic areas, for example, technology, products, and so forth.[8]

Under these definitions, mergers and acquisitions (including takeovers) do not constitute strategic alliances. Similarly, overseas subsidiaries of multinational firms are not considered to be strategic alliances. Nor are licensing and franchising agreements considered as strategic alliances. While these cases call for continuous transfer of technology, products, or skills between partners, they are considered one-way exchanges, not the mutual exchanges on a continuous basis that characterize strategic alliances.

Taken collectively, we can further distinguish strategic alliances in terms of their underlying *function* and *capital structure.* By function, we refer to the purpose of the alliance; and by capital structure, we refer to whether the alliance is structured as having a formal equity-sharing arrangement. Let's define each of these and provide some examples.[9]

FUNCTIONAL ALLIANCES

Some partnerships can be defined in terms of their basic functions, hence **functional alliances**, but entail no form of equity participation.[10]

- *Product and service alliances.* Two or more companies jointly market their complementary products or a new product. In March 2007, Cisco and IBM expanded their Global Service Alliance to provide product maintenance services for mutual enterprise customers in 46 countries. Cisco provides its expertise in networking technology solutions, while IBM contributes its extensive service-delivery capabilities.
- *Promotional alliances.* One company agrees to carry a promotion for another company's product or service. PepsiCo forged alliances with Adidas, Microsoft, Yahoo!, and Indian partners for World Cup Cricket 2007. Among the promotional products included cricket accessories, T-shirts, wristbands, a viral campaign, and an exclusive game, Yuvraj Singh International Cricket 2007.
- *Logistical alliances.* One company offers logistical support services for another company's product. More computer manufacturers are forming logistical alliances with providers of logistics services to improve their efficiency. For example, the Ford Motor Company and United Parcel Service Inc. (UPS) alliance will facilitate the delivery of vehicles from Ford plants to dealers and customers in North America.
- *Pricing collaborations.* Two or more companies join in special pricing collaboration, such as in the case of rental car companies, provided that these do not violate antitrust laws.
- *Research and development alliances.* One or more companies agree on co-developing and sharing basic research in the development of a new product or service. Pharmaceutical giant Pfizer has formed numerous alliances with smaller firms with the goal of developing new medicines that address unmet medical needs.

EQUITY SHARING ARRANGEMENTS

Equity sharing arrangements refer to the establishment of a new company or organizational unit based on equity contributions by two or more companies. These are more popularly known as equity joint ventures. An **equity joint venture** is usually structured as a limited liability company with both partners contributing a designated share of their registered capital.[11] The underlying logic is that the profit and risk sharing of equity joint ventures is proportionate to the equity of each partner. Thus, the success of a joint venture relies very much on the partners complementing and supporting one another. Equity joint ventures can be structured in terms of 50–50 equity participation, or can be uneven when partners have disproportional contributions. Two examples are provided.

- Tata International has formalized a joint venture with the Italian company Graziella to export footwear. Structured as a 50–50 equity joint venture, the objective is to co-manufacture, package, and sell footwear in the international market. The venture brings complementary skills: Graziella, a high-end footwear manufacturer, is promoted by the Dante Group of Italy and operates in India through its base in Chennai. Tata International will use this joint venture as an opportunity to expand business in footwear, garments, accessories, and finished leather in Europe, the United States, and China.[12]
- For some time, the Pixar-Disney alliance, structured as a 50–50 joint venture, was considered to be an exemplar of a partnership in which both partners complemented each other. Pixar, under the leadership of Steve Jobs, developed and produced the films, while Disney, under the embattled (now departed) Michael Eisner, marketed them. In late 2005, the partnership was dissolved. Pixar offered to pay production costs and give Disney 6 percent of studio film revenues, while Disney could keep Pixar's old films and agreed to a long-term contract to market Pixar's merchandise.[13]

BENEFITS OF STRATEGIC ALLIANCES

The first benefit of an alliance is *flexibility* achieved through collaboration. Even with scarce capital, a company can expand into new markets, fund research and development, and market new or existing products by entering into a joint venture. Partnering provides the firms with access to additional resources such as technology, management, brands, distribution systems, and customers. The second benefit is *risk–sharing,* achieved through shared equity participation. By sharing risks and costs, a company is able to pursue multiple opportunities that might be unaffordable for any one firm that does it alone. The third benefit of an alliance is *co-specialization* achieved through synergy. The IBM-Cisco alliance, for example, combines IBM's global leadership in the services marketplace, coupled with its complete portfolio of technology, hardware platforms, middleware, and management software, with Cisco's leadership in networking products for the Internet. Research and practice have disclosed additional benefits of alliances:[14]

- Broadening the scope of a firm's international operations without incurring the full expenses of market entry.
- Allowing the firm to reconfigure its value activities to achieve the necessary cost and differentiation advantages.
- Increasing response times to meet market needs. Alliances allow firms to bring technology to the marketplace faster.
- Facilitating learning by exposing firms to differing managerial systems and take the initiative to learn from other firms.

As indicated in Chapter 3, value partnerships have become a critical part of any firm's business model. Strategic alliances and partnerships have fueled the growth of the world's most successful companies. One published report declares that firms with alliances outperform their unallied counterparts by a considerable margin.[15]

This is because alliances permit firms to enter new markets and launch new products and services that they otherwise could not. While the motivations behind strategic alliances have been traditionally explained in terms of cost–benefit considerations, recent research based on competitive dynamics indicates that other important reasons factor in as well. Specifically, research by Seung Ho Park, an executive at the Samsung Economic Research Institute in Beijing and strategy professor at the China Europe International Business School, indicates that the underlying motives of strong and weak firms differ. That is, weaker firms join alliances to protect themselves against losses that could be incurred should their competitors do so. Moreover, stronger firms might avoid alliances altogether since it is easier for them to do so when circumstances dictate otherwise.[16] In some special cases, two strong firms will combine (Yahoo! and eBay) to position themselves more adequately against even a potentially powerful rival (Google). All in all, alliances have become an integral part of the business landscape and of contemporary strategic thinking.

ALLIANCES IN THE NEW COMPETITIVE LANDSCAPE

Alliances are hardly new. In fact, they have pervaded international business for many decades. Even so, there are distinguishing features of new alliances that are emerging and defining the new competitive landscape (see Exhibit 7.1).

PARTNERSHIPS ARE EXTENSIVE ON A GLOBAL SCALE

Whereas traditional alliances tended to be partnerships between firms from the same country, new alliances tend to transcend national borders. These reflect the pace of globalization and the developing competencies of firms operating in the global market. Even giant corporations such as AT&T, IBM, Dell, Philips, and Siemens cannot sustain market leadership without some form of alliance. In cases aimed at enhancing international market presence, companies have determined that traditional contractual arrangements—export agreements, licensing, and franchising (see Chapter 5)—can be limited and can only take them so far.

In global industries in which new products and innovations are launched almost simultaneously and by different firms, competition has become even more intense, requiring firms to develop new managerial skills. Moreover, since different countries excel in particular products and services, it is becoming critical that firms also develop a presence in these countries. These so-called **lead countries** are important sources of customers as well as emerging innovation (also see Chapter 2, pp. 73–74). China, with its vast population and improved infrastructure for innovation, is one example of a lead country. For all these reasons, developing strategic alliances has become a critical cornerstone of a firm's business model and international strategy.

PARTNERSHIPS ARE INCREASINGLY BETWEEN ERSTWHILE RIVALS

What differentiates the growth and development of joint ventures during the 1980s and the 1990s is the dramatic increase in alliances formed between competitors or

Exhibit 7.1   **Alliances at a Glance**

Exhibit 7.1A

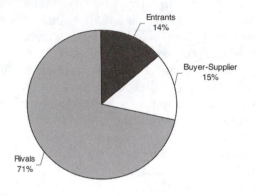

PATTERN: Contemporary alliances are increasingly between rivals.

    IMPLICATION: *Failure rates can even be higher in untested territory.*

Exhibit 7.1B

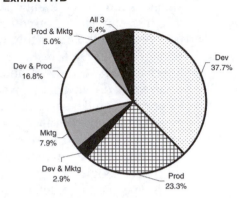

PATTERN: Strategic alliances have shifted from production to development/production.

    IMPLICATION: *There will be more pressure on alliances for pre-competitive activities with cooperation expected down the line.*

Exhibit 7.1C

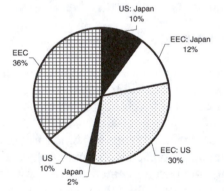

PATTERN: Up until 1994, a majority of strategic alliances have been between European and U.S. firms.

    IMPLICATION: *Despite the attractiveness of Asia and other regions/countries, U.S./European firms are still more comfortable with each other as partners.*

    EEC = European Economic Community is the former name of the European Union.

    US : Japan = Alliances between U.S. and Japan
    EEC : Japan = Alliances between EEC and Japan
    EEC : US = Alliances between EEC and U.S.

United States: 54% (cross border); 46% (domestic)
Latin America: 92% (cross border)
Europe: 90% (cross border)
Japan: 84% (cross border)
Asia Pacific: 90% (cross border)

PATTERN: Of the 20,000 alliances formed worldwide from 1994 to 1996, approximately 75% have been across borders.

    IMPLICATION: *The rise of cross-border alliances will be more challenging, requiring cross-cultural management skills.*

Source: Adapted from the Harvard Multinational Project. This was also based on a similar version from Seung Ho Park, "Failure of Strategic Alliances," Ph.D. Dissertation, University of Oregon, 1989. Data on cross-border alliances are drawn from Booz-Allen interviews and analysis published in C. Freidheim, *The Trillion-Dollar Enterprise* (New York: HarperCollins, 1998), p. 44.

potential competitors, as opposed to the vertically linked firms that characterized earlier periods (see Exhibit 7.1). For example, the alliances between Toyota and General Motors, NUMMI (see case-in-point at the end of this chapter), and between Ford and Nissan would have been unthinkable years ago. Similar associations between rival firms exist in consumer electronics, semiconductors, computers, office equipment, telecommunications, and biotechnology. Moreover, not only rival firms and firms in different countries, but firms in industries thought to be entirely unrelated, are now joined by the new alliances.

In September 2005, Palm, Inc., a pioneer in handheld devices, announced the release of its latest Treo smart phone using an operating system, Windows Mobile 5.0 OS, developed by its rival Microsoft.[17] Previously, the two firms had clashed over the type of software to run the expanding arena of sophisticated cell phones. Among the many projected features of the new products are the ability of users to dial phone numbers by photo, and the ability to call someone who just e-mailed them with a simple click. Microsoft sees the collaboration as tapping into the expanding lucrative mobile enterprise market. For Palm, Inc., it provides an opportunity to get into Microsoft's accounts.

PARTNERSHIPS ARE INCREASINGLY CROSS-BORDER

Cross-border alliances, or partnerships between firms from two different nationalities, can become an important arsenal within a firm's global strategy. Because foreign firms have different core competencies, such as the Japanese and Koreans in manufacturing, or Southeast Asian firms in terms of lower labor costs, an alliance with a U.S. firm that is skilled in research and product design offers complementary benefits. For example, British Airways' marketing joint venture with United Airlines is cited as a successful way of expanding the geographical scope of both firms. By sharing ground facilities with United, British Airways can route passengers from United's domestic flights to its international flights. In turn, United can explore transatlantic routes.[18]

While cross-border alliances are soothing in tone and reassuring in content, they also pose unresolved questions: Do cross-border alliances perform as well as national alliances, and vice versa? United Airlines' decision to seek transatlantic flights through an alliance with British Airways could transform it from a present "friend" to a future "foe" of British Airways. While this is generally true for any alliance, it is particularly so for cross-border alliances because of cross-cultural differences. Even with the best intentions, cross-cultural alliances still face complex problems relating to control and coordination.

PARTNERSHIPS ARE MORE COMPLEX WHEN INVOLVING MORE THAN TWO FIRMS IN SOME FORM OF CONSORTIUM OR NETWORK ARRANGEMENT

While traditional alliances and joint ventures were relatively simple, that is, an arrangement between two firms, today's alliances can be complex. Because no one firm can "do it alone," firms have bounded together as consortia or global networks. A

consortium is an array or constellation of firms that can include buyers, sellers, suppliers, specialized firms, and even competitors—all working together in a concerted fashion to meet pre-established goals. These networks have begun to exert themselves as powerful blocks in global competition. Because of their sheer complexity, the participants in such consortia should approach them with long-term planning, a desire to cooperate with others, and a strong resolve to address future problems in order to succeed. The level of complexity transcends the traditional two-firm joint ventures and requires new competencies, which will be discussed further in the final section of this chapter.

An example of a consortium is SEMATECH (SEmiconductor MAnufacturing TECHnology).[19] Formed in 1986 as a response to the Japanese challenge in semiconductors, fourteen U.S.-based semiconductor manufacturers and the U.S. government came together to solve common manufacturing problems by leveraging resources and sharing risks. Its initial focus was on improving the industry infrastructure, particularly by working with domestic equipment suppliers to improve their capabilities. Currently, the consortium has augmented its membership to include firms from other countries. In recognition of its new global membership base, the consortium was renamed International SEMATECH, and it completed its first year of operations as a unified global consortium in 2000, with members from Asia, Europe, and the United States dedicated to cooperative work on semiconductor manufacturing technology.

THE RISKS OF STRATEGIC ALLIANCES[20]

Despite the popularity of strategic alliances and the purported benefits for participating firms, they fail as often as they succeed (see Exhibit 7.2). The following studies illustrate this point:

- Coopers and Lybrand's study found that 7 out of 10 alliances fail.[21]
- Harrigan's study disclosed a failure rate of over 50 percent.[22]
- In a study of thirty-three randomly chosen, largely diversified U.S. companies during the 1950–1986 period, Porter reported the dissolution rate of joint ventures to be 50.3 percent. This dissolution rate was as high as that for mergers and acquisitions in new industries (53.4 percent), and higher than internal venturing (44.0 percent) and corporate buyouts (21.4 percent).[23]
- Other studies have noted that the outcomes of joint venture dissolution, such as loss of face, damaged reputations, operational difficulties, disagreements, and anxiety over the loss of proprietary information, are often devastating.[24]

This pattern is consistent across different operationalizations of alliance failure, whether these relate to alliance stability, survival, or goal attainment.[25] Does this mean that firms should avoid alliances altogether? As we have suggested earlier in the chapter, alliances provide critical value partnerships, especially in the new context of international competition. It behooves managers to understand why alliances fail, if only to develop better templates for making them successful.

Exhibit 7.2

Empirical Findings on Joint Venture Instability

Author	Sample size	Period	Type of Alliance	Instability rate (%)
Franko (1971)	1,100	1967	International	29[b]
Killing (1983)	37	1974–80	International	30[c]
Stuckey (1983)	64	1955–79	International	58[c]
Beamish (1984)	66	n/a	International	45[c]
Kogut (1988b)	78	1975–83	International	40[a]
Kogut (1988b)	70	1975–83	Domestic	53[a]
Harrigan (1988)	384		International	58[d]
Harrigan (1988)	511	1974–85	Domestic	
Park and Russo (1996)	204	1979–88	International	27.5[e]

Source: Adapted from Seung Ho Park and Gerardo R. Ungson, "Why Cross Border Alliances Endure: An Institutional Analysis," *Business and Contemporary Society,* 10, no. 2 (1998): 249–77. L. G. Franko, *Joint Venture Survival in Multinational Corporations* (New York: Praeger Publishers, 1971); J. P. Killing, *Strategies for Joint Venture Success* (New York: Praeger Publishers, 1983); J. A. Stuckey, *Vertical Integration and Joint Ventures in the Aluminum Industry* (Cambridge: Harvard University Press, 1983); P. W. Beamish, "Joint Ventures in LDCs: Partner Selection and Performance," *Management International Review*, vol. 27, (1987): 23–37; B. Kogut, "Joint Ventures: Theoretical and Empirical Perspectives," *Strategic Management Journal*, vol. 9 (1988): 319–22; K. Harrigan, "Strategic Alliances and Partner Asymmetries." In *Cooperative Strategies in International Business*, ed. F. Contractor and P. Lorange (Lexington, MA: Lexington Books, 1988); M. Porter, "From Competitive Advantage to Corporate Strategy," *Harvard Business Review*, vol. 65 (1987), 43–59; Seung Ho Park and Michael Russo, "When Competition Eclipses Cooperation: An Event History Analysis of Joint Venture Failure," *Management Science*, vol. 42, no. 6 (1996): 875–90.

Note: Despite the popularity of strategic alliances, various researchers have reported high failure (instability) rates, even with the use of different measures. A sampling of such studies is presented above.

[a] Includes dissolutions and acquisitions.

[b] Includes dissolutions, acquisitions, and major reorganizations.

[c] Includes major reorganizations and liquidation.

[d] Includes ventures that did not survive longer than four years in the overall sample of 895 ventures.

[e] Includes dissolutions and acquisitions, although analyzed separately. Instability is a specified hazard rate using event history analysis.

THE CAUSES OF ALLIANCE FAILURE

Why do alliances fail? On the surface, there is no dearth of explanations as to why failure occurs: poor management, poor communications, lack of trust, competitive rivalry, lack of top management commitment, cultural differences, and so forth. Research on strategic alliances is compounded by the problems of defining "failure." While there is clear merit in specifying objective measures, such as survival, or loss in market share, it can be argued that subjective measures, such as satisfaction with the other partner, may be as meaningful, if not more appropriate.[26]

Because joint ventures are formed primarily for participating firms to gain core skills that would otherwise be very difficult for them to obtain on their own, the stability of any joint venture is dependent on the **complementarity** between joint venture partners. In other words, a joint venture will remain stable as long as partners continue to build core skills from the partnership that lead to economic benefits. A number of research studies have addressed the question of failure within alliances (see Exhibit 7.3).[27] Some key arguments and findings based on published research are discussed next.[28]

Exhibit 7.3 **Framework for Understanding Joint Venture Instability**

National culture
"Simple" case: Alliances between firms from two or more different cultures can be difficult to manage (+)

"Complex" case: Different cultures moderate the performance of alliances depending on values and institutions (+/–)

Economic characteristics

High levels of product/market (+)
Codifiable technology transfers (+)

Organizational compatibility
Age of organization(+/–)

Size of organization(+/–)

Source: Adapted from Seung Ho Park and Gerardo R. Ungson, "Why Cross Border Alliances Endure: An Institutional Analysis," *Business and Contemporary Society* 10, no. 2 (1998): 249–77.

Notes: (+) means that the factor is likely to increase the probability of joint venture instability; (–) means the opposite, that is, the factor is likely to decrease the probability of joint venture instability.

The vulnerability of a joint venture to instability is influenced by the following "control" variables: (1) repeated or prior experiences reduce the probability of instability; (2) equity-sharing joint ventures are more likely to succeed when there is a clear, dominant partner, and (3) scope of operations are more likely to succeed when firms have greater scope in their respective operations.

CROSS-CULTURAL DIFFERENCES ARE SIMPLY TOO OVERWHELMING FOR ALLIANCES TO HANDLE

The case against cross-border joint ventures is generally based on the proposition that the dissimilarity of cultural values may reduce misunderstanding between the partners, and that culturally distant joint ventures experience greater difficulty in their interactions. While cultural differences abound, it was Geert Hofstede, an expert in cultural theory, who provided a significant theoretical direction in systematically defining differences across cultures in terms of specific dimensions: power distance, uncertainty avoidance, individualism, and masculinity.[29] No culture is identical to another; however, similarities exist. In Hofstede's research, for example, the United States—characterized as having "high individualism" and "moderate power distance"—is closely related to other Anglo cultures, including Australia, Great Britain, and Canada. Other cultures, such as Asiatic or Middle Eastern, are significantly different from the United States in terms of individualism and power distance.[30]

It has been argued that "cultural compatibility between partners is the most important factor in the endurance of a global alliance."[31] In an empirical study, some researchers reported that joint ventures are more susceptible to cultural difficulties because they have to contend with both national and corporate cultures, that is, "double layered acculturation."[32] The failure of a Dutch company, Fokker, and the German company VFW was attributed to cultural differences, with one executive lamenting, "If you have a Dutch company, a German company and a headquarters, you don't have a partnership. You have a Dutch company, a German company, and a headquarters."[33]

While the effects of national culture on behavior and management systems can be rather subtle, they can still lead to destabilizing effects within joint ventures. Generally, it is reasoned that cross-border alliances experience more differences in their organizational and administrative practices, employee expectations, and their interpretation and response to strategic issues, compounding coordination problems that already exist in any generic partnership. Because of poor communication and mutual distrust, the transfer of management practices and technologies—a condition for successful alliances—can be very costly. Thus, the joint venture is vulnerable to managerial conflicts and early dissolution, as is highlighted in a study by the late management professor William Dymsza:

> A U.S. TNC involved in a 50% joint venture in industrial machinery with a family-run firm in South Korea strived to impose a major part of its strategic and operational planning system, budgeting, reporting and information system, and financial and other controls on the affiliate. The Korean partner resisted the imposition of these management processes on the grounds that they were unsuitable and irrelevant for the management of the affiliate and would interfere with its actual management. As a result of this conflict, along with other disagreements in the management of the joint venture, the operation was terminated within five years.[34]

COMPETITIVE RIVALRY CANNOT BE COMPLETELY ERADICATED IN AN ALLIANCE

While firms form joint ventures with expectations of reducing rivalry among them, such competitive forces cannot be completely redressed and can be destabilizing over time.[35] Since firms establish joint ventures to improve their competitive positions, the partnership is sustained to the extent that partners gain access to each other's core skills such as know-how and assets, as well as fulfilling human resource needs, market access needs, government and political needs, and knowledge needs. Accessibility assures the necessary balance that keeps the alliance intact.

At the other extreme, these same reasons contribute to instability, that is, joint ventures will be less stable when contributions by partners become less balanced, asymmetrical, and inequitable over time. These conditions create one-sided dependency between partners and encourage opportunistic behavior. Three specific cases underscore this argument.

1. Direct vs. Indirect Competition

Joint ventures formed between direct competitors are more vulnerable than those between indirect competitors.[36] This is particularly pronounced in joint ventures between firms competing in the same market, where present "friends" can easily become future "foes." In contrast, joint ventures between indirect competitors are less likely to fail because the partners are not directly in competition in the same market/product segment. This might explain why firms that anticipate future competition are hesitant to engage in "pre-competitive" alliances. In a joint venture between direct competitors, goals of the two parent companies are also likely to be in conflict, and as the joint venture evolves, ensuing activities may run counter to these goals. Given similar strategic objectives and, in many cases, a similar resource base, partners have the abilities to identify, appreciate, and then assimilate the other partner's know-how, that is, if either of the partners decides to behave in an opportunistic fashion. What might be then conceived as a cooperative exchange of information might ultimately lead to future opportunistic behavior when the alliance is terminated and partners become direct competitors. For example, the practice of "second sourcing"—when a competitor is licensed to produce the host firm's products—has led Intel and AMD to carry their disputes into the courtroom.

2. Complementary vs. Noncomplementary Overlap

The success of an alliance also depends on the extent to which the alliance activities are complementary in terms of the current strategic and operational activities of both firms. For example, where the joint venture is an expansion of the partners' current operation, such as movement into new international markets or new product areas, there will be synergy between the activities of the joint venture and the firm. Another example is when there is an expected positive spillover of new products and technology from the alliance onto the parent firm's activities. In these cases, learning from the cross-border alliances results from activities that occur outside the scope of the parent firm but that are complementary in terms of any anticipated benefits and spillovers.

However, in situations where the joint venture operates in the same product/market scope of either partner, learning and spillovers are not as extensive, and the economic benefits tend to be minimal and less visible. Such joint ventures, perceived as peripheral to the parent firm's strategy, will yield few opportunities for the transfer of new knowledge, leading to insufficient and inconsistent interaction with the parent management and resource commitments to the management of the collaboration. Accordingly, these types of alliances are less stable.

3. Technological vs. Nontechnological Ventures

A **technological joint venture** is characterized by an exchange of know-how and technology. In such a case, it is difficult to codify or to translate tangible knowledge or procedures, thus the relationship requires direct communication between the partners. Such joint ventures are vulnerable, particularly in cases where one partner is more technologically proficient. In such a case, the less proficient partner might engage in opportunistic behavior aimed at copying or replicating the specific assets of the more technologically proficient partner.[37] Thus, a joint venture characterized by an exchange of technologically specific know-how can be more vulnerable than one that involves more discrete contributions, such as financing or physical resources, that are more defined. In contrast, a **nontechnological joint venture**, which is not based on the exchange of technology, can be more stable in that the scope of operation and boundary of appropriation can be specified more clearly in contractual terms, making it relatively easier to estimate the partners' contributions and monitor their behavior.

ALLIANCES FAIL TO MANAGE COMPLEX STRUCTURES AND PROCESSES SUCCESSFULLY

In addition to interfirm rivalry, the dissolution of joint ventures is also affected by how compatible the partners are in regard to organizational structures and processes. Since a joint venture is typically a hybrid of two independent firms, dissimilarities in organizational structures and processes can create problems in coordination that can, in turn, lead to dissolution of the joint venture. On the other hand, similarity in partners' organizational structures and processes can facilitate mutual understanding and collaboration. This view is consistent with management consultants Joel Bleeke and David Ernst, who found that cross-border joint ventures per se are not as problematic as joint ventures between companies with strong and weak cultures, or those between companies with asymmetric financial ownership.[38] Other researchers have argued that the compatibility of organizational processes may be more significant than national cultures in explaining the dissolution or duration of a joint venture.[39]

As dissimilar partners will likely expend time and energy to establish standard managerial routines to facilitate communication, they may incur higher costs and mistrust relative to a joint venture with similar partners, for which easier coordination is expected. While there may be a number of organizational structures and processes that come to bear on this relationship, three cases have direct implications for the dissolution of a joint venture: (1) breadth and scope of strategic activities, (2) size difference, and (3) organizational age.[40]

1. Breadth and Scope

Firms differ in terms of their **breadth and scope**, defined broadly as their underlying structure, system, process, management focus, control system, and internal value systems. These differences are generally measured in terms of their diversity and strategic scope. Highly diversified firms experience a higher level of diversity and uncertainty than single-business firms, requiring more complex information-sharing and decision-making processes. Accordingly, diversified firms require greater decentralization, self-containment of divisions, less important roles for corporate staff, higher monitoring costs, and more rules. Differences between diversified and single-business firms are directly shaped by their organizational cultures, which typify how resources are used, how patterns of interaction evolve, and how strategically important information is conveyed. On this basis, joint ventures between partners of similar breadth and scope are less likely to dissolve than those involving partners that are more different.

2. Organizational Size

Organizational size, or the number of employees, is an important factor that shapes behaviors and decisions in joint venture management. Size becomes a compatible factor in that larger firms tend to behave differently from smaller ones on account of advantages derived from sheer size alone. INSEAD Professor Yves Doz indicated that joint ventures between large and small firms experience difficulties because of idiosyncratic incentives for partners, cultural variation, and asymmetric policies in information distribution.[41] In cross-border joint ventures, where large foreign parent firms tend to be systematic and have a long-term approach, their local partners often are entrepreneurs with no established operational system and policy that are looking for more immediate financial returns.

3. Organizational Age

The **age of an organization**, meaning its length of operations, is relevant to the extent that partners of similar ages are able to share common experiences and empathize with one another. Harvard management professor Michael Tushman and Marsh & McLennan Companies (MMC) Vice Chairman David Nadler have argued that "an organization's history has a very strong influence on the values and beliefs that develop over time."[42] Specifically, historical forces that influence organizational culture also reflect the circumstances of the birth of the organization, the crises that it has faced, how those crises have been resolved, and the organizational referents admired or used as an ideal in its history. Management problems and principles are rooted in time, and the age of an organization reflects institutionalized managerial attitudes and beliefs. Studies on organizational mortality suggest that younger organizations are vulnerable to failure because their structures and processes are not as stable, their organizational politics are unstable, and links with the environment are irregular. Newness liabilities also can be attributable to size because new organizations are typically small organizations.[43]

In summary, competitive rivalry, organizational factors, and cross-cultural differences all contribute to the difficulty in managing alliances. They also provide a good picture as to why the rate of failures and dissolutions within alliances are so alarmingly high. Even so, it is important to note that these differences are not absolute (see Box 7.1). That is, with proper management, alliances can be managed effectively.

MANAGING STRATEGIC ALLIANCES

Now that we have a better idea and understanding of why and how alliances fail, we can develop methods and skills to manage them effectively. As with any generic partnership, management can be classified in three stages: (1) ensuring proper partner selection; (2) developing appropriate structures and process over the course of the alliance, and (3) managing performance goals.

ENSURING PROPER PARTNER SELECTION

As with any partnership, selecting the right partner is crucial. The right partner can reduce the risk of opportunism or the inflexibility of behavior over the course of the alliance. As a first step, it is recommended that a firm examine the reasons why it wants to enter into an alliance. According to a number of scholars, there are numerous reasons to enter into an alliance:[44]

Box 7.1

A Contrarian View of Cross-Border versus National Joint Ventures

While it is intuitive to assume that cross-border alliances will fail more often than local alliances, this is not necessarily true and has not been borne out in at least two research studies.

In a study of forty-nine strategic alliances featuring both cross-border and national partnerships, management consultants Joel Bleeke and David Ernst reported that cross-border alliances are not different from national firms in terms of their vulnerability. What matters in terms of stability and survival are partnerships that involve strong and weak companies, or those with significantly unequal financial ownership. Later studies of joint ventures between U.S. firms and foreign multi-nationals by H. Lane and Paul Beamish suggest that instability tends to develop more often when partners start out with uneven shares of equity and when contracts have been negotiated before. Asymmetry in ownership and the lack of flexibility are factors contributing to this instability. Overall, these studies suggest that other key variables impacting the stability of alliances go far beyond partners' national cultures. Consideration of these differences using a synthesis of economic and organizational factors provides a more fruitful way of addressing the viability of these alliances.

In a study of over 186 international alliances involving U.S., European, and Asian firms, and 187 cross-border and domestic alliances, management professors Seung Ho Park and Gerardo Ungson examined the causes of joint venture instability and dissolution and the duration of the alliance over time. Their results validated a long-held belief that dissolution and the length of the alliance are primarily determined by rivalry conditions. Even so, in a somewhat surprising finding, they reported that cross-border alliances generally survived longer than domestic alliances and that there were significant differences in survival rates. Findings suggest that cross-border alliances have a lower rate of dissolution and that U.S.–Japan joint ventures last significantly longer than domestic (U.S.–U.S.) joint ventures.

In these studies, the authors implore managers to go beyond "simple" explanations, such as that alliances fail because of cultural differences or because partners are opportunistic. Rather, managers need to explore ways of facilitating the exchange of knowledge and information, and ways to build trust over time. Far beyond cultural differences, the authors also encourage a closer examination of the underlying institutions that provide the necessary infrastructures that facilitate interaction. For example, in an economy that is oriented toward having buyers and sellers come together, it is important to have mechanisms for enforcing contracts, a clear and meaningful regulatory system, and a well-defined system of property rights. Because one misdeed by one company can irrevocably damage the reputation of the larger entity, the concern for upholding one's reputation provides a haven where contracts are respected.

Source: An earlier version of this narrative was published by S.H. Park and G. Ungson, "The Effect of National Culture, Organizational Complementarity, and Economic Motivation on Joint Venture Dissolution," *Academy of Management Journal,* 40, no. 2 (1997): 279–307. This box incorporates two studies: Joel Bleeke and David Ernst, eds., *Collaborating to Compete* (New York: Wiley, 1993), chapter 1; and H. Lane and P. Beamish, "Cross-Cultural Cooperative Behavior in Joint Ventures in LDCs," *Management International Review* 30 (special issue) (1990): 411–32. Other studies supportive of the proper design of cross-border alliances are J. Slocum and D. Lei, "Cultural and Economic Factors in Global Alliances," in *Organizational Change and Redesign*, ed. G. Huber and W. Glick (New York: Oxford University Press,

- Enhance competencies through a learning partnership
- Extend market presence in new markets
- Fill gaps in your current technological bases
- Turn excess manufacturing capacity into profits
- Reduce your risk and entry costs in new markets
- Accelerate product introduction
- Produce economies of scale

- Overcome legal and trade barriers
- Extend the scope of existing operations
- Cut exit costs when divesting operations
- Establish presence in a "lead" country

A related step is to carefully examine the business model of one's prospective partner. As much as the firm would like to select the "right" partner, it can be assumed that any such partner is likewise seeking areas in which to leverage its competencies. Therefore, for effective partner selection, it is important that the bases of complementarity be firmly established. Not too surprisingly, the assessment for partner fit corresponds closely to our earlier discussion of alliance failure. Partner selection consists of determining the fit or similarity of potential partners along the following dimensions: strategic fit, organizational fit, and cultural fit.[45] Let's examine each in detail.

Strategic Fit

Strategic fit refers to whether the partner can provide the complementary skills and resources that the focal firm cannot acquire or possess in ways that constitute a strategic advantage. These can cover market, technology, capital, distribution, and even organizational assets. Underlying this selection is an examination of the strategic intent and objectives of each partner in entering into an alliance. This involves answering the following questions:

- What are the reasons for entering this particular alliance?
- Do partners have a shared vision on the outcome of the alliance?
- How critical is this alliance for each partner?
- Do they need an alliance to achieve their objectives?
- What is the relative competitive position of each partner?
- Do the partners have complementary assets and competencies?

Ideally, the partners' reasons for entering the alliance complement each other. When AT&T entered into an alliance with Olivetti, it wanted access to the European market, while Olivetti sought out AT&T's technological skills. While the alliance subsequently failed for other reasons, its pre-alliance objectives appeared to be complementary with strategic fit. Moreover, each partner should share the extent of importance or criticality of the partnership. Should one partner view its participation in the alliance as proportionally less than its partner, future problems are bound to arise. This is particularly apparent if the partners have a different time frame for achieving their objectives within the alliance. Rather than joining forces to save a few dollars, it is best that partners share a common time frame for gains that can be harvested for years to come.

Since alliances can change the competitive market positions of each partner, it is likewise important that they enter the alliance with a clear understanding of each other's competitive position. This is particularly true for partners that are direct rivals, knowing that they might have to compete again in the future, or when the alliance is terminated.

Assessing complementary skills and competencies is perhaps the most critical aspect of partner selection. Without complementary resources and competencies, there is really no reason to enter the alliance. This assessment comes along with knowing the strategies of each other's firm, that is, knowing each other's business models. It also entails an in-depth understanding of where there are overlaps in a market and technological sense inasmuch as overlaps tend to enhance rivalry even if both firms are entrenched in an alliance mode.

Organizational Fit

Organizational fit refers to how well the partners share common features in terms of their organizational structures, processes, and history. It also refers to the degree of flexibility, for alliances can only last if they are flexible and adaptive to change. Key questions include:

- Do the partners have goals, experiences, and behaviors that facilitate cooperation?
- Do the partners have a history of successful collaboration?
- Is there "chemistry" among the key players?
- Are the corporate cultures similar or potentially compatible?

Current research has focused on the similarity of age and size of each partner's organization, although results have not been conclusive. Historically, firm size has been related to market power in both domestic and international contexts. As stated earlier, size becomes a compatibility factor in that larger firms tend to behave differently from smaller ones on account of advantages derived from sheer size alone. Larger firms are able to compete in a broader spectrum of products and markets using scale and scope economies. They are able to make preemptive moves that limit or prevent later entrants from gaining access to suppliers, markets, customers, and other scarce assets.[46] Larger firms have more resources to invest in innovations, to pursue aggressive expansions, to be able to incur the costs and bear the risk, and to achieve a better performance. Other advantages include access to privileged learning channels, risk reduction through wider portfolios, and stronger bargaining power to gain concessions and incentives from host country governments.[47] Note that the arguments are premised on the effects of firm size, not necessarily on size alone.

What is emerging as a key consideration is the *compatibility* of the corporate culture of each firm. Corporate culture comes from the history of the firm, its ownership structure, and its management style (see Chapter 10). Former Hewlett-Packard CEO Carly Fiorina's failure was attributed to implementation problems, specifically her difficulty in merging the diametrically opposed cultures of Hewlett-Packard and Compaq Computers.

Finally, another variable—prior relationship—should be examined as part of partner selection. Research indicates that familiarity and trust evolve relatively easily as partners develop mutual understanding from prior collaborative experiences.[48] Opportunistic risks are obviated by partners' expectations in anticipation of repeated transactions in the future, or by their respect for transactions that occurred in the past. Since partners know each other's strengths and weaknesses, they may be able to minimize organizational complexity. Thus, destabilizing influences (such as cross-cultural differences) could, in fact, be negated by prior experiences between the partners that leave them disposed toward potential cooperation in anticipation of building better relationships.

Cultural Fit

Cultural fit refers to the extent to which partners share common norms and values. In cases of cross-border alliances, in particular, the success of the alliance will depend on how the values and institutions that are imbedded within the nationalities of each partner lead to potential cooperation (or competition) in the presence of potential competition between them. Cultural differences in this context, are significant but not absolute, in determining the success or failure of an alliance. Firms from trust-based cultures that hold reputation at a high premium are more likely to endure as partners in an alliance, as compared to firms from cultures where trust and reputation are not regarded as highly. Key questions include:

- How similar or different are the national cultures of each partner?
- How efficient are their formal and informal institutions?

By defining acceptable and unacceptable rules of conduct, institutions reduce uncertainty and provide a structure to economic and noneconomic exchanges.[49] Without trust, transaction costs tend to be high because higher costs of monitoring and safeguards against opportunistic behavior are needed. But, a strong culture based on trust can overcome problems that formal procedures—based on monitoring compliance—cannot. For example, University of Washington management professor Charles Hill explained how a trust-based society, such as Japan, led to lower transactional costs and provided Japanese enterprises a competitive advantage over their (Western) competitors.[50] It was likewise illustrated that multinational corporations choose market-like entry strategies over direct investment in such high-trust cultures because of the lower threat of opportunistic hazards.[51]

While strategic, organizational, and cultural "fit" remain important considerations, there are more specific considerations that apply for strategic alliances and their choice of suitable partners for operating in the international environment. These include level of internationalization, scope economies, and competitive intensity.

Level of Internationalization

Level of internationalization refers to a company's engagement overseas. Firms that have a significant overseas engagement can benefit from the learning and experience associated with their operations in foreign markets, as well as their extensive market networks.[52] Because they can leverage their accumulated knowledge and experience more readily, firms with a higher degree of international experience are more likely to enter a newly opened international market earlier. They can cross-support and cross-subsidize their entry in the new market with their existing operations in other foreign locations. While there is no guarantee that a firm can successfully leverage its experience from one market to another, experienced firms are in a better position to overcome the risks and uncertainties in the initial phase of the market entry and thus enter markets earlier.

Scope Economies

Scope economies refer to the breadth of a company's products and services. A broader scope of products and services means a wide portfolio of offerings to choose from, and thus a better chance of providing the right product and service to the newly opened market. In this case, firms with a broader strategic scope are better prepared to handle the uncertainty about the types of product that are needed in the new market. In addition, a broader scope of products enables the firm to develop a synergy across different product sectors. This synergy gives rise to both efficiency and quality in product development, product line extension, production, distribution, and market support. Firms with a broader product scope have a higher likelihood of entering the market early. Thus, firms with the capacity for scope economies are likely to leverage their skills into early entry into foreign markets.

Competitive Intensity

Competitive intensity refers to the level of competition. In markets of high uncertainty and risk, firms tend to be influenced by what other firms in their industry do.[54] Thus, competitive behavior, as reflected in the entry decisions of competitors is a significant signal for market entry decisions for two reasons. First, in the absence of their own calculations, firms use the behavior of other firms as a justification of their own behavior. When many firms are observed to be investing in an overseas market, hitherto nonentrants infer from their competitors' behavior that such entry is profitable and that the earlier they enter the faster they too will be able to earn such profits. Second, firms often have a sense of paranoia and fear that either an opportunity will be completely gone, or those that have entered will put up entry barriers high enough to deter subsequent entries.

A contrasting position is that some firms might avoid entering markets for which they anticipate intense competition.[55] Firms might also choose to delay their entry and await new information, but they do not always have the opportunity to do so. Specifically, strategic conditions might make it imperative for the firm to invest quickly and preempt existing or potential competitors.[56] In such a scenario we would expect firms to take competitive behavior in the form of the number of prior entries into the host market (in its product sector) as a signal of profitable opportunities in that market.

Developing Appropriate Processes over the Course of the Alliance

After the formation of an alliance, each partner embarks on a learning trajectory about the other. Dynamic considerations become important. For a perspective on what is needed to achieve long-term value and short-term goals, see Box 7.2. In most, if not

---

Box 7.2

Achieving Long-term Value and Short-term Goals

A U.S. software developer, a pharmaceutical company in France, a British hospital information systems company, a Germany auto components supplier, and a U.S. telecommunications company had a common experience: all had failed in managing strategic alliances. Professor Will Mitchell, Jack D. Sparks/Whirlpool Corporation Research Professor at the University of Michigan, has offered three imperatives for an alliance to achieve long-term value and short-term goals.

Pre-Alliance Planning. The emphasis is on knowledge acquisition.

- Know what the company wants to achieve in the short run.
- Identify who can help the company to achieve the goal.
- Design a process to attain short-term and long-term goals.
- Inform the appropriate people about the alliance.
- Determine what the company wants to learn from the partner.
- Determine what to allow the alliance partner to learn, and what to prohibit the partner from learning.

Post-Alliance Education. The emphasis is on education creation.

- Identify the individuals as the "learners" in the alliance.
- Identify the individuals as the "teachers" who transfer the knowledge back to the company.
- Design a reward system for alliance education.
- Watch the changes occurring in the alliance.
- Detect what the partner has learned from us.

Corporate Alliance Management Capabilities

- Manage alliance portfolios—a company must be able to evaluate the needs and opportunities in a portfolio of alliances and separate the needs and values of each alliance.
- Treat the alliance with a dedicated alliance management unit. A company must see the alliance as more than a minor part of corporate development. It needs to recognize the strengths of the alliance and the risks involved when failing to manage it.

Source: Adapted from Will Mitchell, "Alliances: Achieving Long-term Value and Short-term Goals," *Financial Times* "Mastering Strategy" series, October 1999.

---

all, cases, changes in the alliances start to occur. External environments can change, shifting the initial premises and agreements of the alliance. Host country policies might change, such as China's specific shift from favoring entry into Special Economic Zones to areas within China where import expertise was needed. The firms themselves will change as they begin to learn more about each other and about how to compete in the local environment. The reduction of uncertainty and the firm's assessment of risk are key factors that temper the alliance's performance over time. Key processes that are now critical in managing the alliance will next be discussed.

Learning Trajectories

Learning is generally discussed in the context of reducing uncertainty, fostering transparency, and building trust. Specifically, it is a process in which growing insights and successful restructuring of organizational problems reflect themselves in structural elements and outcomes.[57] Prior knowledge permits the effective utilization of new knowledge. In related formulations, organizational learning is viewed as a critical determinant of a firm's strategic intent. Taken from the perspective of joint ventures, the objectives of the alliance partners to learn from each other can be usefully characterized as a form of internalization, that is, acquiring or internalizing the competence of the other. As the alliance unfolds, each partner will accumulate knowledge of the other partner, as well as relationships with the local government, suppliers, and customers. This extended experience fosters an understanding of the local environment, which enables each partner to decide on whether to invest further in the alliance.

Former secretary of labor and U.C. Berkeley professor Robert Reich and management professor Michael Mankin have unleashed outright arguments that cross-border alliances, particularly with Japanese firms, do greater harm than good, specifically regarding the contention that U.S.–Japan partnerships in high-technology industries are "part of a continuing, implicit Japanese strategy to keep higher-paying, higher value jobs in Japan and to gain the project engineering and production process skills that underlie competitive success." [58] Another study also suggests that Japanese firms "plan ahead to increase the benefits they extract from the alliance across the '**collaborative membrane**,' or areas of shared collaboration between partners, leaving the European or American partner in a worse strategic position."[59] In both cases, the argument is that, because Japanese partners learn much faster than their Western counterparts, they create an imbalance in terms of expectations and dependencies that eventually destabilizes the alliance.

If anything, these opinions provide an imperative that each partner needs to formulate learning objectives within the course of the alliance. If both partners are learning at their own predetermined pace, the alliance can be stable. If, however, one partner earns at the expense of the other, then a **dependency spiral** occurs in which one partner become overly dependent on the other.[60] In such cases, alliances become unstable and even subsequently fail. Thus, setting learning objectives becomes a critical process in the management of alliances (see Exhibit 7.4).

Fostering Transparency

The stability of an alliance is influenced by the extent to which firms or partners can learn from each other, particularly as trust and commitment result from the successful exchange of both explicit and tacit knowledge. Failed joint ventures, particularly in the case of Japanese and American firms, can be traced to asymmetries in learning, that is, in the ability of the Japanese to more quickly learn the core skills of its partner (American). Learning is determined by: (1) the propensity or desire for one partner (firm) to learn the core skills of another, and (2) the degree to which partners are "transparent," that is, easy to learn about.[61] **Transparency** refers to the degree to which a partner can see through or interpret the actions and intent of the other partner.[62] Naturally, transparency is achieved when partners adopt clear and explicit learning goals as they become the object of purposeful search, rather than having to

Exhibit 7.4   **The Collaborative Membrane**

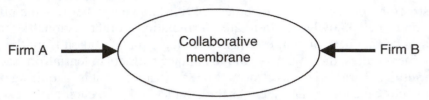

Design Issue: Two firms, A and B, which are partners in a strategic alliance, seek to cooperate and co-ordinate their activities in what is referred to as a "collaborative membrane." The more that is shared, the larger the collaborative membrane. To assess cooperative patterns, key questions need to be addressed:

- How do the firms complement each other in terms of assets and skills?
- Where are the likely sources of synergies, economies of scale, and scope?
- Do the firms have compatible corporate cultures?
- Do the firms have previous track records of successful cooperation?
- Do the firms understand each other's expectations, objectives, and intent?

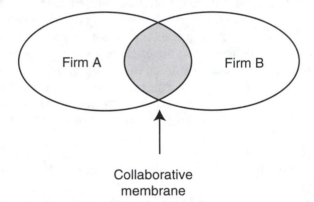

In the case depicted below, firm A has contributed disproportionately more than firm B. Until this is corrected, it can create an unstable situation in which B becomes overly dependent on A.

Source: Adapted from Gary Hamel, "Competition for Competence and Interpartner Learning within International Strategic Alliances," *Strategic Management Journal* 12 (1991): 83–103.

occur surreptitiously in a partner's actions and behavior. In addition, transparency is enhanced to the extent to which partners are less arrogant and strive to learn each other's customs and traditions. It is now widely believed that Americans tend to be more "transparent" about their work and attitudes compared to their Japanese or Korean counterparts.

Favorable dispositions toward cooperative relations enhance the viability of strategic alliances. Moreover, learning that is perceived to occur simultaneously, or at least within acceptable threshold levels, also enhances the stability of exchange relationships. Conversely, unfavorable dispositions toward cooperation and asymmetric learning are hypothesized to destabilize exchange relationships, eventually leading to the dissolution of the alliance (see Exhibit 7.5).

Exhibit 7.5 **Overcoming Barriers to Transparency**

Transparency is the degree to which a partner can see through or interpret the actions/intent of the other partner. To the extent that transparency is increased, greater trust can be built between firms A and B, improving their desire to cooperate and to enlarge the collaborative membrane.

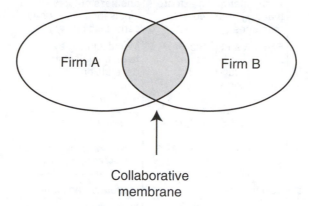

Transparency can be improved through the following actions.

Behavioral actions:

- Set learning goals.
- Eliminate arrogance.
- Learn the language.
- Involve key people.

Design considerations:

- Create serial versus parallel structures, which affect learning and trust.
- Understand information/diffusion flows.
- Build "win-win" payoff scenarios.

Monitor/coordinate activities:

- Foster information exchange.
- Have frequent reviews that are broad in scope.
- Learn to resolve conflicts.

Source: Adapted from Gary Hamel, "Competition for Competence and Inter-partner Learning within International Strategic Alliances," *Strategic Management Journal* 12 (1991): 83–103.

The degree of transparency is also tempered by the structure or design of the alliance.[63] Two basic generic forms can be distinguished: serial or sequential dependence, and pooled and simultaneous exchange. Trust and learning also depend on how well participating firms are able to understand how they are interdependent. Any exchange of information and core skills will be influenced by whether contributions by participants are made in serial, in parallel, or in pooled relationships.[64] In **serial dependence relationships**, the contributions of each participant occur at distinct stages of the work flow.[65] Thus, the contribution of firm A will precede or follow the work of firm B. In contrast, participants working in **parallel dependence**

Exhibit 7.6   **Pooled, Sequential, and Reciprocal Dependence: Implications for Strategic Alliances**

Type of dependence	Pooled	Sequential	Reciprocal
Definition	Firms are dependent on each other to the extent that they share common resources.	A firm depends on another's outputs as inputs for its own use in a serial fashion.	A firm's inputs are another's outputs, and vice versa.
Prototype/example	Firms A and B share a common budget in a simple functional organization.	Manufacturing systems (e.g., manufacturing depends on R&D.)	Consulting, hospitals, high-end services. Both firms contribute to the final product, and are interdependent.
Graphic structure	Budget ↑ Firm A ↑ Firm B	Firm A → Firm B / B depends on A; it cannot proceed without it.	A ⇄ B / Firm A's inputs are Firm B's outputs, and vice versa
Transparency level	Low transparency	Moderate transparency	High transparency
Implications for learning within alliances	Learning is constrained; firms do not interact except for sharing resources in a pool.	Moderate learning occurs. Firm learns from the output of another, similar to buyer–supplier, or R&D and manufacturing relationships.	Extensive learning occurs. Because both firms share in the creation of value, cooperation and trust are needed.

Sources: Adapted from James Thompson, *Organizations in Action: Social Science Bases of Administrative Theory* (New York: John Wiley & Sons, 1967) and from Gary Hamel, "Competition for Competence and Inter-partner Learning within International Strategic Alliances," *Strategic Management Journal* 12 (1991): 83–103.

relationships engage in value-creating activities at the same time. That is, firms A and B work on concurrent projects. Finally, participants working in pooled relationships do not necessarily interact directly but are related in terms of their mutual dependence of common sources of funds or governance. In this case, firms A and B may be in different workstations but are linked together in terms of a common budget (see Exhibit 7.6).

In serial or sequential dependence, the task is structured as a sequence, whereas one partner takes on a task and completes it before transferring the product. This has been characteristic of many alliances featuring product design and development, mostly between U.S. firms in partnership with each other. While this schema is helpful in securing the benefits of specialization, it is not ideal from the standpoint of access and transparency because learning is not facilitated. In contrast, pooled and simultaneous learning occurs when each partner participates in each stage of the project's development. This was a characteristic of the Japanese approach to R&D, and also of Hewlett-Packard's former style of project management. While there are circumstances that favor either schema—for example, specialization is particularly effective when deadlines abound—there are also consequences for learning and facilitating transparency. Therefore, it behooves managers of alliances to understand their objectives and timetables, and to design task schemas accordingly.

Building Trust

The stability of interfirm relationships within any alliance is influenced by the degree of trust between partners. In general, trust is sustained by previous performance, a relatively open relationship, and a concern for one's reputation. Management professor J.C. Jarillo argued that trust in any network linkage can be generated by: (1) knowing the values and motivations of the partners involved; (2) understanding that the intrinsic relationship is bound to fail should opportunistic behavior displace trust; and (3) emphasizing the long-term relationship as mutually beneficial for all participants.[66] A relatively open relationship, such as an information-sharing network, also enhances the stability of the relationship by allowing mutual and instantaneous verification of contributions.

DESIGNING CONTROLS AND COORDINATION MECHANISMS

The decision to cooperate or compete depends on the effectiveness of administrative incentives and controls. Incentives to cooperate can be intrinsic and/or extrinsic in nature; controls refer to organizational arrangements designed to direct attention and effort to alliance goals. Because it is critical to exchange information and resources on a continual basis, measuring performance outcomes on an interim basis becomes a critical feature of alliance management. In the successful Fuji Xerox alliance, both partners maintained multiple points of contact—from their CEOs down to bench engineers—and entwined all operations, from R&D to marketing.

Approaching the Exchange of Technical Information

The more subtle point in information exchange in an alliance relates to the uncertainty involved in the transmission of technical information between partners.[67] It is generally recognized that a joint venture contract does not specify in detail what technical expertise each partner will contribute. This is, in fact, what differentiates a joint venture from a licensing agreement. The more uncertain the partner about its technological competence, the greater the risk the partner assumes in specifying what to expect from a joint venture; also, the partner assumes some risk of accepting an obligation to provide specific technical services.

In an environment of constantly shifting technologies, products, and processes, it is now argued that the only sustainable competitive advantage is the ability of a firm to learn, accumulate, and diffuse knowledge.[68] Knowledge, in turn, is differentiated as being explicit, which is formal, codified, and easily transmitted, and tacit, which is implicit, hard to formalize, and highly personal. These distinct classes of knowledge have to be sustained by appropriate communication systems within a strategic alliance. It can be assumed that explicit knowledge is what is communicated and exchanged in formal negotiating phases of a pre-alliance structure. It can also be argued that explicit knowledge is the type of information that is communicated during the management of the alliance. The presence of **tacit knowledge** suggests that the partners may not have a conscious or focused perception of their mutual expectations, and the exchange of this type of information can become a problem in alliance management. Also, because the accumulation of tacit knowledge results from shared experiences and core values, it is much more difficult to transfer across organizational boundaries, and even more so in a cross-border alliance. This is perhaps why the prior experiences of alliance partners are significant enough to offset cultural differences and rivalry within an alliance.

Establishing Controls through Structural Arrangements

Controls may also encompass punitive measures for those firms that fail to provide expected levels of information exchange, whether these are material or psychological. **Controls** are administrative/structural arrangements to ensure consistency of work effort. Again in the Fuji Xerox alliance, the design and management of the alliance evolved continually in response to competitive challenges and the changing capabilities of the partners.

Contingency frameworks linking controls to different types of structures are developed to explain ensuing performance. For proper coordination, controls via tight product deadlines and impact analyses are needed for serial relationships. Group-reward structures are often related to parallel relationships. Finally, institutional-type rewards (consortia-wide bonus schemas) are regarded as appropriate for pooled relationships. Theorization follows a contingency framework: success accrues from the "fit" between appropriate structures and controls, and inappropriate linkages often lead to inefficiency and eventual failure. To conclude, the stability of cross-border joint ventures may ultimately depend on the ability of the parties to understand, access, and adopt innovative practices within joint ventures that can mitigate the compounding effects of cultural differences.

Four facets are relevant here.[69] First, partners need to know the metrics that define the performance of the alliance. While each partner might have different goals and metrics, it is important that the alliance itself be evaluated in terms of achievement over time. Second, partners need to understand the structure of information exchange. How is information exchanged? Formally or informally? Written or oral? By e-mail or through personal telephone conversations? Moreover, it is important to designate key personnel who might represent the essential components and contributions of each partner in the alliance. Third, it is important that the scope and the frequency of information exchange be firmly established, whether this is daily, weekly, monthly, or yearly. Formal points of communication provide the basis not only for the actual exchange, but also for ensuring that adequate preparation is made before exchanges take place. Fourth, it is critical that partners learn, formally and informally, ways to resolve conflicts between them.

Conflict resolution is paramount, as changes will occur in any alliance. Research on alliances reveals that changes are likely to happen in the following areas: personnel, a partner's interest in the alliance, diminishing commitment on the part of one or more partners, and new conflicting values. In such cases, open communications and creative problem solving become avenues for conflict resolution. Rangan suggests that new contractual arrangements will be raised, for example, can the alliance be restructured in terms of a merger acquisition or licensing agreement? Absent this, discussion should center on whether the alliance can be dissolved amicably. Management professor U. Srinivasa Rangan offers the following action steps in response to important changes in the alliance:[70]

- Recognize the evolution of your firm's own strategy and capabilities.
- Understand the evolution of your partner's strategy and capabilities.
- Assess the implications of changes in the competitive environment.
- Shape, adjust, and recalibrate the alliance over time.

EMERGING GLOBAL ALLIANCES AND PARTNERSHIPS

In *The Trillion-Dollar Enterprise: How the Alliance Revolution Will Transform Global Business,* author Cyrus Freidheim presents a compelling picture of how alliances will transform from episodic, such as joint ventures, into megacorporations or networks with assets exceeding 1 trillion dollars (see Exhibit 7.7).[71]

In Freidheim's depiction, the 1970s was the era of product performance, whereby the imperative was to gain access to the latest technologies and international markets. Also, the demarcation between industries was clear cut, with a focus on product development. In the 1980s the emphasis shifted to positional focus, that is, companies used alliances to build industry structure, consolidate position, and utilize economies of scale and scope. The emphasis also shifted to capabilities. With industry lines blurring (also see Chapter 8) and markets globalizing, the emphasis in the future will evolve into relationship-based, long-term enterprises.

Specifically, the **relationship-based enterprise** will exhibit four distinguishing characteristics:[72]

- *Size and global reach.* Relationship-based enterprises will be large and global, with assets in the trillion-dollar range.
- *Network of independent companies.* They will comprise independent companies, large and small, based in several countries.
- *Common mission.* They will be bonded together by a common mission with broad strategies, a single agenda, and a recognition that they will succeed as a group.
- *Act as a single company.* The member companies will develop and execute a common strategy as a single company.

In a study of future organizational forms, Raymond Miles (UC, Berkeley) and Charles Snow (Pennsylvania State University) make an outright case for a global network: "Correspondingly, the new form of enterprise will be the global network, which will eschew the traditional ingredients of corporate success, such as, 'do everything yourself.' It will not call for complete vertical integration or tall management hierarchies. It will rely on new ingredients, such as value-chain location based on core competencies, strategic alliances, outsourcing, and, whenever possible, the substitution of market forces for hierarchical controls."[73]

In building competencies for international expansion and dominance, firms are

Exhibit 7.7 **Changing Patterns of Skills for Strategic Alliance**

1970s Product-focused	1980s Position-focused	1990s Capabilities-focused	2000s Network-focused
• Learn and use latest technology • Select markets beyond national borders that match product specifications • Sell product stressing performance	• Strengthen business model • Consolidate position • Exploit economies of scale and scope • Enhance industry stature	• Introduce constant stream of new prospects with advancing technologies • Anticipate and maximize delivered value • Recognize core and distinctive competencies • Optimize total cost by product/customer segment • Gain advantage in response to changing conditions and opportunities	• Create a network of alliances to lead industry transformation globally

Source: Adapted from Cyrus Freidheim, *The Trillion-Dollar Enterprise: How the Alliance Revolution Will Transform Global Business* (Reading, MA: Perseus Books, 1998), p. 47.

constantly exploring ways to build bridges with one another. While strategic alliances may not always work, they make a lot of sense. When properly implemented, alliances can provide significant advantages by way of flexibility, access to markets, avenues for learning, sharing risks and expenses, and working with partners who possess specialized skills that are not part of the firm's repertoire of skills. In international competition, alliances are an indispensable path to extending a firm's business strategy and leveraging its competitive advantage. Keep in mind that the underlying logic of strategic alliances is to gain the benefits of expanding operations, while minimizing the risks of having to do it alone, or to outright buy this expertise. However, strategic alliances should be pursued and considered with the same due diligence as in international marketing and global sourcing. While the benefits are widely recognized, many firms (as evidenced from high failure rates) are still unable to work within partnerships in ways that optimize overall performance. Thus far, we have discussed ways in which a firm can build on its strengths, both internally and externally. We next discuss the fourth pathway for international success, that is, the ability of the firm to innovate and to continuously transform itself in the context of a highly competitive environment, specifically in a digitally based economy (Chapter 8).

SUMMARY

1. Forging strategic alliances and partnerships provides the third path toward leveraging a firm's competitive advantage in international competition. This is based on a well-acknowledged belief that partnering is the quickest and most effective way to build and extend a firm's core competencies.

2. While a strategic alliance can be defined as any form of partnership with a strategic rationale, a more restrictive definition specifies three conditions: (a)

two or more firms that unite to pursue a set of goals remain independent subsequent to alliance formation; (b) the partners share the benefits and control over the performance of specific tasks; and (c) the partners contribute on a continuing basis in one or more key strategic areas.

3. Strategic alliances can be further distinguished by function and capital structure. Functional alliances are defined by their basic intent, but entail no form of equity participation. An equity joint venture is usually structured as a limited liability company with both partners contributing a designated share of their registered capital. Equity joint ventures can be structured in terms of 50–50 equity participation, or can be uneven when partners have disproportional contributions.

4. Three basic benefits of strategic alliances are: (a) flexibility achieved through collaboration; (b) risk sharing achieved through shared equity participation; and (c) co-specialization shared through synergy. Other benefits include access to new markets, providing opportunities for a firm to reengineer its activities, facilitating speed to entry, and organizational learning.

5. The distinguishing characteristics of contemporary alliances are: (a) they are extensive on a global scale; (b) they increasingly involve erstwhile rivals; (c) they are increasingly cross-border in structure; and (d) they are more complex, involving more than two firms in the form of consortia or network.

6. Despite the popularity of strategic alliances, the failure rate, using multiple measures, is high, ranging from 20 to 70 percent.

7. Failure of strategic alliances can be attributed to instability arising from disproportionate contributions and the lack of complementarity between the partners. Specific reasons based on published research include: (a) competitive rivalry cannot be completely eradicated, and an untenable situation emerges in which there is direct competition, a lack of operational overlap, and know-how is not codifiable; (b) alliances fail to effectively manage complex structures and processes such as scope, size, and age; and (c) cross-cultural differences are simply too overwhelming for partners to handle.

8. The proper management of alliances occurs in three stages: (a) ensuring proper partner selection; (b) developing appropriate structures and processes; and (c) managing performance goals.

9. Considerations relating to partner selection involve issues of strategic, organizational, and cultural "fit."

10. Considerations relating to designing structures and processes include the extent to which management addresses the level of internalization of the partners, scope economies, and competitive intensity. This also entails as assessment of learning trajectories, fostering transparency, and building trust.

11. Considerations relating to managing performance goals relate to designing controls and coordination mechanisms, managing the exchange of technical information, and establishing controls through structural arrangements.

12. Contemporary alliances are shifting to megacorporations and network structures. The emphasis in the future will evolve into relationship-based, long-term enterprises that address four characteristics: (a) size and global reach, (b) network of independent companies, (c) common mission, and (d) acting as a single company.

KEY TERMS

Strategic alliance	Organizational fit
Functional alliance	Cultural fit
Equity joint venture	Level of internationalization
Lead countries	Scope economies
Cross-border alliances	Competitive intensity
Consortium	Collaborative membrane
Complementarity	Dependency spiral
Technological joint venture	Transparency
Nontechnological joint venture	Serial dependence relationship
Breadth and Scope	Parallel dependence relationship
Organizational size	Tacit knowledge
Organizational age	Controls
Strategic fit	Relationship-based enterprise

DISCUSSION QUESTIONS

1. Discuss the differences between a generic definition of a strategic alliance and that proposed by Professors Yoshino and Rangan. Using the latter, how would you classify the alliance between Hewlett-Packard and Compaq?
2. What are the benefits of a strategic alliance? Why are partnerships considered a strategic competence for firms in the contemporary business world?
3. What are the costs and risks of an alliance? Discuss ways in which an alliance (or a joint venture) can fail. What are the early warning signs that an alliance is unstable or leading to failure?
4. Let's assume that you have just formed a group of four classmates to work on your final group presentation. How would you structure this group project to enhance learning on the part of the four partners involved? How might you enhance transparency among the partners? How might you reduce overdependency on the part of some, if not all, of the partners?
5. What are the key competencies needed to manage large-scale alliances and networks?

ACTION ITEM 7.1. RECOMMENDATIONS FOR A JOINT VENTURE

Provide your recommendations on a proposed joint venture (JV) between companies A and B below. Specifically, should you recommend a joint venture? What are your recommendations to make the venture effective (if management decides to pursue this venture)? Present any assumptions, if appropriate.

	Company A	Company B
Nationality	United States	Netherlands
Primary product	Semiconductors (65%)	Semiconductors (80%)
Other products	Advanced semiconductors; televisions	High-definition television (HDTV)
R&D/Sales	12%	18%
Age	32 years old	5 years old
Size	30,000 employees	10,000 employees
Market growth rate	8% per year	12% per year
Sales	$40 billion	$8 billion
Return on investment	12.2%	19.0%
Discretionary cash	$3.2 B	$800 M
JV partners	30 worldwide	35 worldwide
Proposed capitalization	51%	49%
Proposed joint product	HDTV using advanced semiconductor/television technologies. Company A will do marketing in the U.S., while company B will do R&D in Europe. Both will manufacture the joint product in Europe and the U.S.	
No. of seats on board	11	9
Proposed structure	Chairman and president	Chief operating officer

Note: Semiconductors are electrical devices used to store memory or operating programs. These are main inputs to computers and a host of electrical products. High-definition television refers to state-of-the-art receivers with detailed compression limits that are superior to conventional televisions.

CASE-IN-POINT. ALLIANCE DYNAMICS WITHIN NUMMI
by Edwin Duerr, Mitsuko Duerr, Gerardo Ungson, and Yim-Yu Wong[74]

In 2004 General Motors and Toyota celebrated the twentieth anniversary of the formation of their 50–50 joint venture, New United Motor Manufacturing, Inc. (NUMMI). The processes underlying NUMMI, particularly the learning opportunities afforded to General Motors and Toyota, have been touted as the exemplar of best management practices, offering a benchmark for erstwhile alliances in the future. The success of NUMMI stands in stark contrast to the gloomy statistics depicting the failure rates of joint ventures and other forms of strategic alliances. Established in 1984 in Freemont, California, NUMMI was designed as a partnership between two competitors to bring complementary resources together for the purpose of achieving a higher level of synergy.

BACKGROUND OF THE JOINT VENTURE

During the 1970s and 1980s, the growing demand for small cars in the United States was largely met by imported cars because U.S. automakers were not able to produce them efficiently at the same quality level. Japanese automakers' success aroused protectionist sentiments within the United States, prompted by a 33.6 percent loss in employment, or about 347,000 jobs, within the U.S. auto industry. Accordingly, in 1981, the Voluntary Export Restraint (VER) agreement was reached between the Reagan administration and Japan. Under this agreement, only 1.68 million Japanese cars, approximately 17.5 percent, would be allowed to enter the U.S. automobile market. The pressure on Japanese auto exports continued unabated as the limits were increased in 1984 and 1986. Yet, such trade barriers did not hurt the Japanese automakers since they began to export higher-end models, placing more required choices on their cars, and ultimately raising their prices. It was estimated that the Japanese increased their profits by $1 billion to $1.6 billion in 1983, and by $1.6 billion to $2.6 billion in 1984. These experiences by both U.S. and Japanese automakers kindled sentiments toward more cooperation in the form of strategic alliances and partnerships.

TOYOTA AND GENERAL MOTORS: MOTIVATIONS FOR A JOINT VENTURE

After its first attempt in the U.S. market in 1958, which ended in failure, Toyota redesigned its styles and improved the quality of its products when it returned to the United States. Toyota's primary objective behind manufacturing in the United States was to increase its market share significantly. Its long-term goal was to take over General Motors' worldwide leadership position in the industry. Thus, any joint venture with a U.S. firm was meant to (1) provide Toyota experience with U.S. suppliers and the American-style unionized labor force, and (2) help ease the trade friction between the two countries.

General Motors, on the other hand, already bruised by skirmishes with local and Japanese rivals, had aimed at: (1) gaining access to Toyota's extremely efficient and cost-effective production system, and (2) attaining high-quality production of the Chevrolet line of automobiles. The experiences and know-how obtained from its joint venture with Toyota, ultimately called NUMMI, were expected to be transferred and diffused within the entire GM operation.

What aroused interest in NUMMI was its success, despite early skepticism and conditions that hardly seemed ideal. The manufacturing plant used was a General Motors facility that had been closed in 1982 due primarily to poor productivity, poor quality, and labor problems. Understandably, the first steps taken by NUMMI were designed to signal a new form of labor–management relations. Prior to the actual incorporation of NUMMI, representatives of the United Auto Workers (UAW), General Motors, and Toyota had already signed a Letter of Intent formalizing a new, cooperative approach to union–management relations. Following the incorporation of NUMMI, applications were sent to some 5,000 former GM-Fremont employees; this gesture was taken as a sign of good faith.

CHARACTERISTICS OF THE JOINT VENTURE

In the original division of responsibilities for the joint venture, Toyota was to be responsible for manufacturing while General Motors was to market all of the output. Some of the modifications to policies used in Japan that Toyota made at NUMMI were relatively minor, though quite effective. The joint venture provided only one cafeteria to serve both workers and managers, something that is not done in their Japanese plants (nor in typical American plants). The parking lot at NUMMI is on a first-come, first-served basis without reserved spaces for managers (though reserved spaces are provided for visitors).

Developing Cooperative Management–Labor Relations

Management–labor relations in major industries in Japan, at the time NUMMI was formed and for many years afterward, were generally cooperative rather than confrontational. This was supported and reinforced by a system sometimes called "lifetime employment." Regular employees could expect to be kept on the job even when improvements in productivity or reduced demand made positions redundant. They also shared in increases in profits. In turn, employers could expect their workers to give total loyalty as well as support for productivity and quality improvements.

While NUMMI could not offer lifetime employment, the UAW was invited to participate in the development of a collective bargaining agreement along with Toyota and GM representatives (including former U.S. secretary of labor W.J. Usery). The final result was a labor agreement offering the highest level of security in the U.S. automobile industry. It provided for advance consultation with the union on major business decisions and nonconfrontational problem-resolution procedures based on discussion and consensus, gave team members (workers) the right to stop the line, and contained a limited no-strike provision.

A unique feature of the contract was that the company would not lay off employees unless compelled to do so by severe economic conditions threatening the company's long-term financial viability. This commitment was tested in 1987 when reduced demand for the automobiles caused line slowdowns and an excess number of workers. Even so, NUMMI did not lay off any workers. They reduced the number on the assembly line, but reassigned the excess workers to "continual improvement teams" and training to upgrade their skills. NUMMI lost $80 million in 1988 and additional money in 1989. Similarly, in 2004 when the company shut down the truck line to set up for a new model, it did not furlough any workers. Instead, the time was spent retraining team members to work more productively on the remodeled line.

Careful Selection and Training of Workers

Applicants for positions at NUMMI were carefully selected. They were told that all employees needed to be willing to contribute to an atmosphere of trust and cooperation. Potential production employees went through a three-day assessment that included production simulations, individual and group discussions, and written tests and interviews. Those hired go through a four-day orientation covering the team concept, production system, quality principles, attendance policies, safety policies, labor–management philosophies, and the competitive position of the auto industry. The former union officers, now NUMMI hourly workers, were invited to help in interviewing and evaluating additional applicants for jobs. They participated in orientation sessions, played an important role in training, and participated in discussions about the selection of supervisors.

Stressing Teamwork and Responsibility of the Individual

From the beginning of discussions with the union, there had been an emphasis on a team approach. Each team was responsible for doing the work assigned to it, and each team member is responsible for supporting his/her team. Individual members were responsible for improving their own productivity and efficiency, and teams were responsible for improving operations in their areas of responsibility. Teams were kept informed of company objectives in quality, cost, production, and safety, as well as the teams' roles in meeting these objectives. Team members received training in problem-solving methods. In the production groups, each member was cross-trained to do every job. When a person was absent from the team, the other members were expected to do that person's job in addition to their own. This provided peer pressure to be on time and do one's full share of the work. NUMMI stressed consensus decision making and channels for staff feedback, obtaining input from all areas concerned and holding discussions until agreement was made. While this resulted in slow decision making, managers did not experience surprise changes.

Worker Responsibility and Control in Safety and Quality

From the beginning, NUMMI recognized that for safety and quality to be given primary emphasis, the workers had to have some control over the process and operations. First, any assembly line worker could stop the line in the event of safety or quality problems simply by pulling an overhead cord. No prior consultation with a supervisor was required. Second, there were electric signboards located throughout the plant that were controlled by the workers. Each board has three lights: green, yellow, and red. The workers were empowered to stop the production line using this set of colors.

Each worker and each team were responsible for ensuring that the materials, parts, and components coming to them did not have identifiable defects and fit properly into the product they were assembling. In August 1990, parts that had been received from a new supplier were defective. Rather than continue production with parts that might have later required replacement, the plant was shut down for three days until new parts could be obtained. Cars that had already been produced were not shipped to dealers but were held for part replacements. Since it was not the workers' fault that the parts were defective, and NUMMI wanted to encourage them to report defects, the company offered the workers full pay for the period the plant was shut down.

IMPLEMENTING THE TOYOTA PRODUCTION SYSTEM

The successful implementation of the Toyota Production System at NUMMI required and was based upon the development of cooperative labor–management relations, careful selection and training of workers, development of teamwork, and giving workers the authority to assure safety and quality as outlined above. The elements of the lean production system include: a just-in-time inventory system; a quality assurance system under which workers do not allow defective parts to pass from one workstation to the next; continuous improvement to eliminate waste in machinery, materials, labor, and production methods; and standardizing of improved procedures.

Continuous improvement and standardization of improved processes have resulted from suggestions made by teams and individual team members. Adopted by the company and made into standard practices, these have resulted in making work safer, easier, and/or more productive. A continuing pressure for improvement comes from the electric signboards indicating the status of each process step at all times.

Evaluating NUMMI

NUMMI's success is evidenced by statistics. For example, employee attendance was at 98 percent in the first two years, and employee grievances were almost completely resolved. Productivity, attendance, and labor relations remained admirable throughout the two decades. The success with NUMMI gave Toyota the experience and confidence for more ambitious projects in the United States and other countries. Today, Toyota has become the largest and the most profitable automobile company in the world. In 2004, 43 percent of Toyota's long-term assets, including production sites, were held overseas. From 1993 to 2002, Toyota's share in the U.S. passenger car market rose from 7.4 to 12.8 percent and its share in the sport/utility segment rose from 4.1 to 9.2 percent. In 2003, Toyota passed Ford to become the second-largest automaker worldwide. Sixty percent of Toyota's U.S. sales are manufactured in the United States and 70 percent of Toyota's profits come from the United States.

GM was less successful in achieving its goals through the joint venture. Even though it had learned to enhance productivity and quality, as well as about lean production systems, the results were not significant. In addition, there was insufficient knowledge and know-how transfer from NUMMI to other GM plants, partly due to the strong resistance of these plants to the NUMMI managers. GM later corrected its approach by sending managers to NUMMI for training in groups and returning them to their GM plants as a group, instead of isolated individuals. In sum, GM is still behind Toyota even after the experiences gained at NUMMI.

Case Discussion Questions

1. What made NUMMI different from other joint ventures?
2. How did NUMMI overcome the problems that potentially arise from a partnership between firms from two cultures?
3. Evaluate NUMMI from the standpoint of the following topics discussed in the chapter: (a) selection of partners, (b) designing appropriate structures and processes, (c) enhancing learning and transparency, and (d) designing control and coordination mechanisms.
4. Check the websites of Toyota and General Motors regarding their current financial profiles. Which company appears to have learned more from this joint venture? Why? What recommendations would you make for Toyota? For General Motors?

NOTES FOR CHAPTER 7

1. Information for this section is drawn from Ben Gomes-Casseres, "Xerox and Fuji Xerox: From the Corporate Intensive Care Ward, Lessons About Partnerships," (March 5, 2001), www.alliancestrategy. com/PDFs/BGC%20FujiXerox%200pEd01.pdf; and K. McQuade and B. Gomes-Casseres, Xerox and Fuji Xerox, Harvard Business School Case, 9–391–156 (December 8, 1992).

2. "Dark Days at Daimler," *BusinessWeek*, August 15, 2005, available at www.businessweek. com/magazine/content/05_33/b3947016_mz001.htm.

3. Ibid.

4. Ibid. See also "DaimlerChrysler: Divorce, German Style?" *Business Week*, August 15, 2005, available at www.businessweek.com/magazine/content/05_33/b3947001_mz001.htm.

5. Seung Ho Park and Gerardo Ungson, "To Compete or to Collaborate: A Conceptual Model of Alliance Failure," *Organizational Science* 12 no. 1: 37–53.

6. Michael Borrus and John Zysman, "Wintelism and the Changing Terms of Global Competition: Prototype of the Future?" Working Paper 96B, Berkeley Roundtable for the International Economy. Berkeley, California, February 1997.

7. Alan I. Murray, *Joint Ventures and Other Alliances: Creating a Successful Cooperative Linkage* (Morristown, NJ: Financial Executive Research Foundation, 1989).

8. Michael Yoshino and U. Srinivasa Rangan, *Strategic Alliances: An Entrepreneurial Approach to Globalization* (Boston: Harvard Business School Press, 1995), p. 5.

9. See Philip Kotler, *Marketing Management* (Upper Saddle River, NJ: Prentice Hall, 1997), pp. 85–86. Other examples are drawn from two additional sources: Press Release, "Cisco and IBM Expand Global Service Alliance to Collaborate on Maintenance Services in 46 New Countries" (March 12, 2007), http://newsroom.cisco.com/dlls/2007/prod_031207.html; and Prabir K. Bagci and Helge Virum, "Logistical Alliances: Trends and Prospects in Integrated Europe," *Journal of Business Logistics,* 1998, http://www.pfizer.com/home/.

10. The PepsiCo. example discussed in this section is from http:www.southasiabiz.com/2007/02/world_cup_cricket_2007; the UPS-Ford alliance is from http://query.nytimes.com/gst/fullpage.html.

11. Technically a limited liability company (LLC) is not a corporation. However, owners of an LLC have the liability protection of a corporation. An LLC exists as a separate entity much like a corporation. Members cannot be held personally liable for debts unless they have signed a personal guarantee.

12. "Tata International, Graziella in 50:50 JV for Export of Footwear," *Financial Express,* March 16, 2001, http://www.tata.com/tata_international/media/20010316.htm.

13. Garry Barker, "Pixar Terminates Disney Alliance," Fairfax Digital, February 2, 2004, http://www.smh.com.au/articles/2004/02/01/1075570290214.html?from=storyrhs.

14. Yoshino and Rangan, *Strategic Alliances: An Entrepreneurial Approach to Globalization*, p. 68.

15. See Cyrus Freidheim, *The Trillion-Dollar Enterprise* (Reading, MA: Perseus Books, 1998).

16. Seung Ho Park, R. Chen, and S. Gallagher, "Firm Resources as Moderators of the Relationship between Market Growth and Strategic Alliances in Semiconductor Start-ups," *Academy of Management Journal* 45, no. 3 (2002): 527–50; Seung Ho Park and Densheng Zhou, "Firm Heterogeneity and Competitive Dynamics in Alliance Formation," *Academy of Management Review* 30, no. 3 (2005): 531.

17. Palm and Microsoft Announce Smartphone Market Strategic Alliance, September 27, 2005, PalmInfoCenter, http://www.palminfocenter.com/view_story.asp?ID=8109.

18. George S. Yip, *Total Global Strategy: Managing for Worldwide Competitive Advantage* (Englewood Cliffs, NJ: Prentice Hall, 1992), p. 74.

19. See SEMATECH History, http://www.sematech.org/corporate/history.htm.

20. Pages 280–286, and 290–297 are slightly revised from previous publications: Seung Ho Park and Gerardo R. Ungson, "The Effect of National Culture, Organizational Complementarity, and Economic Motivation on Joint Venture Dissolution," *Academy of Management Journal* 40, no. 2 (1997): 279–307, and from Seung Ho Park and Gerardo R. Ungson, "Why Cross Border Alliances Endure: An Institutional Analysis," *Business and Contemporary Society* 10, no. 2 (1998): 249–77.

21. Coopers & Lybrand, *Collaborative Ventures: An Emerging Phenomenon in Information Technology* (New York: Coopers & Lybrand, 1986). The following section draws heavily from an earlier published paper by Seung Ho Park and Gerardo R. Ungson, "Why Cross Border Alliances Endure: An Institutional Analysis," *Business and Contemporary Society* 10, no. 2 (1998): 249–77.

22. K. Harrigan, "Strategic Alliances and Partner Asymmetries," in *Cooperative Strategies in International Business*, ed. F. Contractor and P. Lorange (Lexington, MA: Lexington Books, 1988), pp. 205–26.

23. M. Porter, "From Competitive Advantage to Cooperative Strategy," *Harvard Business Review* 65, no. 3 (1987): 43–59.

24. P. Buckley and M. Casson, "A Theory of Cooperation in International Business," in *Cooperative Strategies in International Business*, ed. Contractor and Lorange, pp. 31–53.

25. See review by Seung Ho Park and Michael Russo, "When Competition Eclipses Cooperation: An Event History Analysis of Alliance Failure," *Management Science* 42 (1996): 875–90.

26. Developing their hypotheses in separate studies, Park, Russo, and Ungson have used the "longevity" of an alliance as a measure of stability. The dependent variable—duration of joint ventures—was measured in terms of years and months from their formation to their dissolution. Consistent with previous studies, these researchers used liquidation of joint ventures (and a few sell-offs to third parties) as the operational definition for dissolution. In addition, to ensure that dissolution (i.e., liquidation) of the joint ventures would be treated as an unexpected event, they excluded joint ventures that specified the period of operation or included an option for governance change, such as acquisition by one of the partners, in their initial contracts—a fact further confirmed by contacting the managers in the U.S. parent firms of the dissolved ventures.

27. See Park and Russo, "When Competition Eclipses Cooperation," pp. 875–890; W.A. Dymstra, "Successes and Failures of Joint Ventures in Developing Countries: Lessons from Experience," in *Cooperative Strategies in International Business*, ed. F. Contractor and P. Lorange (Lexington, MA: Lexington Books, 1988), p. 407.

28. Park, Russo, and Ungson have acknowledged that this is also an imperfect measure. Failure is a complex phenomenon that entails perceptual self-reporting and archival measurement. Moreover, institutional attributions (i.e., stock market indices) can also signal instability in an alliance. The study by Park and Russo cited in note 27 justified the adoption of unexpected termination in terms of its usage by others, specifically Porter, Harrigan, and Kogut, among others (cited in their journal articles), to permit comparisons across findings.

29. Geert Hofstede, *Culture's Consequences: International Differences in Work-related Values* (Beverly Hills, CA: Sage, 1980).

30. We will discuss Hofstede's research in detail in Chapter 10 of this volume, "Implementing Strategy by Cultivating a Global Mindset."

31. H. Lane and P. Beamish, "Cross-Cultural Cooperative Behavior in Joint Ventures in LDCs," *Management International Review* 30 (1990 Special Issue): 411–32.

32. H. Barkema, J. Bell, and J. Pennings, "Foreign Entry, Cultural Barriers, and Learning," *Strategic Management Journal* 17 (1996): 151–66.

33. Reported by Wendy J. Hall as part of her interview with F. Van der Jagt, vice president of Marketing and Sales, Fokker Aircraft Company, 1989. In W. Hall, *Managing Cultures: Making Strategic Relationships Work* (Chichester, U.K.: John Wiley & Sons, 1989), p. 250.

34. Dymstra, "Successes and Failures of Joint Ventures in Developing Countries," p. 407.

35. See Park and Ungson, note 20. Bruce Kogut has addressed this problem specifically in the context of alliances. See B. Kogut, "Joint Ventures and the Option to Expand and Acquire"; *Management Science* 37 (1991): 19–32.

36. Competition between firms within an alliance is a much treaded research path. See Kogut, "Joint Ventures and the Option to Expand and Acquire," J. Hennart, "The Transaction Costs Theory of Joint Ventures," *Management Science* 3 (1991): 483–97; K.J. Hladik, *International Joint Ventures* (Lexington, MA: Lexington Books, 1985). This section draws much from their work.

37. M. Porter and M. Fuller, "Coalitions and Global Strategy," in *Competition in Global Industries*, ed. M.E. Porter (Boston: Harvard Business School Press, 1985).

38. Joel Bleeke and David Ernst, eds., *Collaborating to Compete: Using Strategic Alliances and Acquisitions in the Global Marketplace* (New York: John Wiley & Sons, 1994).

39. L. Brown, A. Rugman, and A. Verbeke, "Japanese Joint Ventures with Western Multinationals: Synthesizing the Economic and Cultural Explanations of Failure," *Asia Pacific Journal of Management* 6 (1989): 225–42.

40. The literature on age, history, and breadth is a robust one that filters across studies of life cycles, population ecology, sociology of organizations, and organizational theory. Our section draws from

L. Griener, "Evolution and Revolution As Organizations Grow," *Harvard Business Review* 50, no. 4 (1972): 37–46; J.P. *Killing, Strategies for Joint Venture Success* (New York: Praeger, 1983); M. Hannan and J. Freeman, "Structural Inertia and Organizational Change," *American Sociological Review* 49 (1984): 149–64.

41. Y. Doz, "Technology Partnerships between Larger and Smaller Firms: Some Critical Issues," in *Cooperative Strategies in International Business*, ed. F. Contractor and P. Lorange (Lexington, MA: Lexington Books, 1988).

42. David Nadler and Michael Tushman, *Strategic Organization Design* (New York: HarperCollins, 1988).

43. Hannan and Freeman, "Structural Inertia and Organizational Change."

44. Julie Mason, "Strategic Alliances: Partnering for Success," *Management Review* (May 1993): 10–15.

45. While strategic, organizational, and cultural fit are part of the alliance management nomenclature, one of the early papers on the subject was by Marc Douma, Jan Bilderbeek, Peter Idenburg, and Jan Kees Looise, "Strategic Alliances: Managing the Dynamics of Fit," *Long Range Planning* 33, no. 4 (2000): 579–598. For a more recent treatment, see Andrew Inkpen and Kannan Ramaswamy, *Global Strategy* (New York: Oxford University Press, 2006), pp. 94–96. This section is drawn from these two sources.

46. S. Kobrin, *Managing Political Risk Assessment: Strategic Response to Environmental Change* (Berkeley: University of California Press, 1982); Martin Lieberman and David Montgomery, "First Mover (Dis)advantages: Retrospective and Link with the Resource-based View," *Strategic Management Journal* 19 (1998): 1111–125.

47. Benjamin Tan and Ilan Vertinsky, "Foreign Direct Investment by Japanese Electronics Firms in the United States and Canada: Modeling the Timing of Entry," *Journal of International Business Studies* 27, no. 4 (1996): 655–81; Sea-Jin Chang, "International Expansion Strategy of Japanese Firms: Capability Building through Sequential Entry," *Academy of Management Journal* 38, no. 2 (1995): 383–407; Yigang Pan and Xiaolian Li, "Joint Venture Formation of Very Large Multinational Firms, *Journal of International Business Studies* 31, no. 1 (2000): 179–81.

48. Park and Ungson, "The Effect of National Culture . . ."

49. Douglass North, *Institutions, Institutional Change and Economic Performance* (Cambridge: Cambridge University Press, 1990).

50. Charles L. Hill, "National Institutional Structures, Transaction Cost Economizing, and Competitive Advantage: The Case of Japan," *Organizational Science* 6, no. 1 (1995): 119–31.

51. S. Shane, "The Effect of National Culture on the Choice between Licensing and Direct Foreign Investment," *Strategic Management Journal* 15 (1994): 627–42.

52. Sea-Jin Chang, "International Expansion Strategy of Japanese Firms"; J. Myles Shaver, Will Mitchell, and Bernard Yeung, "The Effect of Own-Firm and Other-Firm Experience on FDI Survival in the United States, 1987–92," *Strategic Management Journal* 18, no. 10 (1997): 811–24.

53. Roger Kerin, P. Rajan Varadarajan, and Robert Peterson, "First-Mover Advantage: A Synthesis, Conceptual Framework, and Research Propositions," *Journal of Marketing* 56 (1992): 33–52; Shaver, Mitchell, and Yeung, "The Effect of Owner Firm and Other Firm Experiences on FDI"; Mary Lambkin, "Order of Entry and Performance in New Markets," *Strategic Management Journal* 9 (1988): 127–40; Donna Green, Donald Barclay, and Adrian Rynas, "Entry Strategy and Long-Term Performance: Conceptualization and Empirical Examination," *Journal of Marketing* 59 (1995): 1–16; Srivinas Reddy, Susan Holak, and Subhod Bhat, "To Extend or Not to Extend: Success Determinants of Line Extensions," *Journal of Marketing Research* 31 (1994): 243–62.

54. Mark Casson, *The Economics of Business Culture* (New York: Oxford University Press, 1987); Michael Porter, "Towards a Dynamic Theory of Strategy," *Strategic Management Journal* 12 (1991): 95–117.

55. F. Knickerbocker, *Market Structure and Market Power Consequences of Foreign Direct Investment by Multinational Corporations* (Washington, DC: Center for Multinational Studies, 1976).

56. Pietra Rivoli and Eugene Salorio, "Foreign Direct Investment and Investment under Uncertainty," *Journal of International Business Studies* 27, no. 2 (1996): 335–57; Martin Lieberman and David Montgomery, "First Mover (Dis)advantages."

57. Alfred Chandler, *Strategy and Structure* (Cambridge, MA: MIT Press, 1962); B.S. Chakravarthy, "Adaptation: A Promising Metaphor for Strategic Management," *Academy of Management Review* 7

(1982): 735–744; C.M. Fiol and Marjorie Lyles, "Organizational Learning," *Academy of Management Review* 10, no. 4 (1985): 803–13; Gary Hamel, "Competition for Competence and Interpartner Learning within International Strategic Alliances," *Strategic Management Journal* 12 (1991): 83–103.

58. R.B. Reich and E.D. Mankin, "Joint Ventures with Japan Give Away Our Future," *Harvard Business Review* 64, no. 2 (1986): 78–139.

59. Cited in F. Contractor and P. Lorange, eds., *Cooperative Strategies in International Business* (Lexington, MA: Lexington Books, 1988).

60. Our treatment in this chapter is adapted from Gary Hamel's research that was initially presented in a working paper based on his dissertation ("Competitive collaboration: Learning, power and dependence in international strategic alliances." Unpublished doctoral dissertation, Graduate School of Business Administration, University of Michigan, 1990). This research was later expanded and refined in Gary Hamel, "Competition for Competence and Interpartner Learning within International Strategic Alliances," *Strategic Management Journal* 12 (1991): 83–103.

61. Ibid., p. 87.

62. Ibid.

63. Ibid.

64. This was initially formulated by J. Thompson, *Organizations in Action: Social Science Bases of Administrative Theory* (New York: John Wiley & Sons, 1967).

65. This section builds on arguments initially proposed by Gary Hamel, "Competition for Competence and Interpartner Learning within International Strategic Alliances."

66. J.C. Jarillo, "On Strategic Networks," *Strategic Management Journal* 9 (1988): 31–41.

67. This argument has been advanced by P. Buckley and M. Casson, "An Economic Model of International Joint Venture Strategy," in *Cooperative Strategies*, ed. Paul Beamish and J. Peter Killing (San Francisco: New Lexington Press, 1997).

68. While there have been numerous discourses on organization knowledge, our section draws heavily from the work of Chong Ju Choi and Soo Hee Lee, "A Knowledge-based View of Cooperative Interorganizational Relationships," in *Cooperative Strategies*, ed. Paul Beamish and J. Peter Killing (San Francisco: New Lexington Press, 1997); M. Polanyi, *The Tacit Dimension* (New York: Anchor Books, 1966); D. Teece, "Profiting from Technological Innovation: Implications for Integration, Collaboration, Licensing, and Public Policy," *Research Policy* 15 (1986): 285–305.

69. Gary Hamel, "Competition for Competence and Interpartner Learning within International Strategic Alliances."

70. U. Srinivasa Rangan, "Strategic Alliances: The Management Challenge." Lecture at the Amos Tuck School of Dartmouth, October 1997, excerpted from Slide 19. Also see Yoshino and Rangan, *Strategic Alliances: An Entrepreneurial Approach to Globalization*, pp. 123–46.

71. Cyrus Freidheim, *The Trillion-Dollar Enterprise* (Reading, MA: Perseus Books, 1998), pp. 63–64.

72. Ibid., p. 63.

73. Excerpted from Raymond Miles and Charles Snow, *Fit, Failure, and the Hall of Fame* (New York: The Free Press, 1994), p. 56. The authors propose three types of networks: *dynamic*, where a lead firm retains core activities within its value chain and links other independent units in loose alliances to cover non-core activities; *stable*, where a few large firms provide upstream and downstream services; and *internal*, where units within the organization exchange products and services for which decisions and resource allocations are guided by market forces.

74. The material on the NUMMI–GM joint venture was adapted from Edwin C. Duerr, Mitsuko S. Duerr, Gerardo R. Ungson, and Yim-Yu Wong, "Evaluating a Joint Venture: NUMMI at Age 20," *Journal of International Business and Economy* 6, no. 1 (Fall 2005): 111–35. Used with permission.

Leveraging Competitive Advantage
Through Innovation

*When I started eBay, it was a hobby, an experiment to see if people
could use the Internet to be empowered through access to an efficient market.
I actually wasn't thinking about it in terms of a social impact. It was really about
helping people connect around a sphere of interest so they could do business.*
—Pierre Omidyar, founder, eBay

Innovation distinguishes between a leader and a follower.
—Steve Jobs, CEO, Apple

*As we go forward, I hope we're going to continue to use technology to make
really big differences in how people live and work.*
—Sergey Brin, founder, Google

CHAPTER OUTLINE

- Apple Computers: Championing Strategic Innovation
- Why Innovation?
- The Emergence of a Knowledge-based Digital Economy
- Key Drivers of a Knowledge-based Digital Economy
- The New Structure of Individual Consumption
- New Logics and Institutions of Realignment
- How the Digital Economy Will Affect Business
- Types of Innovation
- Emerging Context of Innovation and Creativity
- Toward Strategic Innovation

LEARNING OBJECTIVES

- Understand the knowledge-based, digital economy.
- Understand how the innovative context has changed in the knowledge-based, digital economy.
- Become familiar with the different types of innovation.
- Know three models of innovation in the knowledge-based, digital economy.

- Learn more about strategic innovation, and ways to attain it.
- Understand the obstacles to the successful transition to strategic innovation.
- Learn new perspectives on how firms can build innovation in their corporate cultures and at all stages of the corporate life cycle.

APPLE COMPUTERS: CHAMPIONING STRATEGIC INNOVATION

"What does Apple mean to you?" *MacWorld*, a popular magazine on consumer electronics, found in an online poll that 36 percent of *MacWorld* online readers believed that innovation is Apple Computer's defining characteristic. This result is further supported by a poll conducted by another magazine, *Advertising Age*, which wrote that Apple Computer's CEO Steve Jobs is "once again at the forefront of innovation."[1]

It is apparent that the prevailing characteristic of Apple's image is its innovativeness. Many consumers like Apple's products for several reasons: ease of use, "cool" look, sleekness, inspiring software, and better and improved hardware. Apple's innovations embody user-focused design efforts and creativity. Apple's flurry of new products reflects an underlying understanding of the way its consumers think. In addition to developing new products, Apple has also taken the lead in selecting parts, components, and accessories that are the best of their kind to go along with their products.

One of Apple's latest innovations is the iPod series. It combines Apple's usual creativity with the growing interest in digital entertainment, particularly downloading music and videos. Interestingly, iPod came to the market during a period of slow economic growth, when many companies slashed investment in research and development (R&D). So how does Apple do it?

In an interview with *BusinessWeek* computer editor Peter Burrows, Steve P. Jobs disclosed the following reasons for Apple's success as an innovator.[2] First, Apple has a product-oriented culture, which is considered to be necessary in a technological environment. Even with the consumer in mind, Apple needs to fully exploit the production capabilities of its talented workforce. This product orientation provides a gravitational force that pulls the efforts of different organizational units together and gives designers and engineers a sharp focus. Otherwise, resources would be spent on bits and pieces that might not be adequately integrated into a whole product offering.

Second, Apple has nurtured a need for consistency. Jobs remembered the days when Apple lost its graphical user interface monopoly to competitors. In his opinion, this occurred because there was no consistent effort in pushing this technology forward. Apple was busy marketing its whole line of products and overlooked the production end.

Third, Apple hires people who are driven and passionate about making the best products in the world. They are dedicated and committed to devising solutions to every possible problem and issue that end-users will face before they happen, perhaps months down the road after the purchase of Apple's products.

Fourth, Apple has an excellent creative process in place that facilitates and encourages innovation. Innovative ideas come from frequent meetings and the constant exchange of ideas among Apple's employees.

Fifth, Steve Jobs is personally involved in the creative processes, even though he has two full-time CEO positions, at Apple and at Pixar. He spends half of his time on new products and forward-looking matters.

To conclude, Apple does not jump into a market without diligent deliberation. When Apple chose to produce iPod, Steve Jobs knew that they could make a significant contribution that went beyond CD or DVD players. Jobs has the desire to own and control the primary technology in everything Apple does, which is an ambitious principle. Meanwhile, the flurry of innovations continues. Apple introduced iTunes on the software side. With this product, along with well-designed hardware, Apple believes that it can dominate the music business. With iPod, Apple is back on the list of most innovative companies in the world.

WHY INNOVATION?

Not too long ago, the United States was the undisputed leader in business and in technology. Pundits point to the videocassette, the computer, the first silicon chip, and the microprocessor as among the many products that were invented by U.S. firms. Inventing new products and bringing them quickly to market comprised the cherished hallmark of competition at the time. With relentless innovation, firms unleashed new products, transformed their business models, and created new industries. While many U.S. firms still dominate the landscape today, new competitors—domestic and international—have introduced new strategies in maturing industries based on low cost, and have challenged incumbents that had previously built their leadership based on innovation and differentiation. Young upstarts from these developing economies have been able to achieve a level of quality and cost at a quicker pace and with even more efficiency.[3] Our opening vignette highlights one of the rare exceptions, Apple Computers, which had been dismissed as an "also-ran" firm by pundits not too long ago, but has since regained its competitive footing under Steve Jobs's leadership with a flurry of new products and services.

With the advent of a knowledge-based, digital economy—one based on know-how, timing, and rapid commoditization—the need for innovation is even more compelling. While the so-called latecomers (Japanese, Koreans) were once characterized as low-cost leaders, their new competitive weapon is their ability to innovate at a rate that has challenged traditional market leaders. That Samsung has been able to dislodge Sony as the premier firm in consumer electronics is testimony to this transition. In fact, Samsung is regarded as being among the most innovative firms today, holding its own against the likes of Sony, Nokia, Ericsson, General Electric, and others. Innovation has become a new addition to their strategic arsenal; in some ways, the "innovation playing field" has reached parity.

Developing innovative capabilities constitutes the fourth way in which a firm can leverage its competencies in the global market (see Figure 8.1). Core competences based

Figure 8.1   **Framework for Leveraging Strategic Advantage: Innovation**

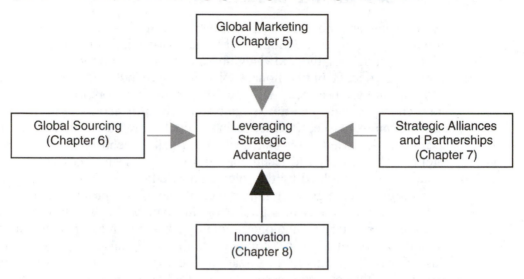

on innovation go beyond exploiting market opportunities, sources of reliable materials, and strategic partnerships that are focused on demand, supply, and reach. Innovation is a transformation process, the ability to think outside of the box using creativity and imagination.[4] A proverbial adage that necessity is the mother of innovation applies to the current competitive context. Firms have to harness their innovative capabilities in response to cost differentials that they might not be able to overcome.

While the need to innovate is widely acknowledged, current research suggests that firms do not quite understand how to make this happen.[5] Consequently, firms have not been able to respond adequately to new competition for at least two reasons. As we will develop further in this chapter, the first reason is the lack of a meaningful process for strategic innovation. The second reason is that innovation does not occur in a vacuum, but now in a context that is defined only by knowledge but also by new technologies. This inability to distinguish how invention and innovation occur in the knowledge-based, digital economy, as opposed to the previous capital-intensive based industrial economy, adds to this difficulty. Much as U.S. firms had to understand the industrial economy in order to thrive in it, current firms have to understand the key characteristics of this knowledge-based, digital economy in order to place innovation in its proper context.

This chapter is organized as follows: we begin our discussion by defining characteristics of a knowledge-based, digital economy and its differences from the industrial age. We describe how the creation of value differs in the knowledge-based, digital economy and the implications for global business. We discuss different models of innovation, distinguishing those that were appropriate for industrial production, and those appropriate for today's knowledge-based, digital environment. The concept of strategic innovation is introduced, and we present ways of achieving this state using key recommendations from industry experts. The rest of the chapter discusses the imperatives for new managerial thinking based on strategic innovation and transformation.

THE EMERGENCE OF A KNOWLEDGE-BASED, DIGITAL ECONOMY

Business has entered a new age with far-reaching implications for firms operating in international markets.[6] Some call it the post-capitalist or post-industrial era, the information age, or the knowledge-based, digital economy. It is also described in terms of the decline of traditional capital-intensive industries and the rapid growth of information-based services. Despite differences in jargon, most agree that this new era is characterized by a **knowledge-based, digitally economy** in which knowledge plays a prominent role. Knowledge, in this context, refers to intellectual capital, more specifically knowledge associated with information technology, intellectual property, intellectual research, and technology transfer. Thus, the knowledge-based, digital economy is highlighted by the role of knowledge, the prominence of science and technology, and the growing importance of knowledge professionals.

This knowledge-based, digital economy can be further described in terms of new complementary technologies, notably advances in semiconductors and related miniaturization of electrical components into a digital format (see Semiconductor Case, Chapter 2). This miniaturization of components facilitates the digitalization of anything that can be measured into information that can be connected, shared, and communicated. As we will discuss in this chapter, digitalization has accelerated product maturity for older products (e.g., transistors, vacuum tubes), while opening up lucrative market niches through new innovative products and services (the iPod, digital telephones, HDTV).

While these technological changes have been occurring for the past four decades, firms have not always noted their effects or appreciated their implications. While it was widely conceded that U.S.-based textiles, steel, machinery, automobiles, and consumer electronics had lost their competitiveness to Japanese and European competitors, conventional wisdom still held that semiconductors, software, and computers were impervious to foreign competitors. After all, the transistor, the integrated circuit, the computer—products that had spurred the high-tech revolution—were all invented in the United States. Moreover, America's scientists were the technological leaders, U.S. high-technology industries were the vanguards of future innovation, and U.S. education was the envy of the rest of the world. In 1985, the editors of *BusinessWeek* sounded a belated alarm: America's high-tech industries were in crisis.[7]

The *BusinessWeek* editors detailed how Japanese semiconductor firms had derailed America's stranglehold on the global memory chip market. For many observers, the unthinkable had occurred: the Japanese succeeded in semiconductors, employing entry strategies similar to those previously used to penetrate the textiles, machinery, consumer electronics, steel, and automobile industries.[8] Despite warnings by the editors and actions taken by the U.S. semiconductor industry, a similar event would occur several years later with the next generation of memory circuitry, the 256k DRAM, and again with the 1 M DRAM and further, with successively larger sizes of each. Korean and other firms have used similar tactics to capture portions of the high-technology market. After some deliberation, it was recognized that myopia, while significant, was not the overriding cause.[9] Central to this deliberation was the recognition of the emergence of a new knowledge-based economy, based on the power of digitalization, for which different rules of management and the need for a different logic of enterprise had become imperative.

KEY DRIVERS OF A KNOWLEDGE-BASED, DIGITAL ECONOMY

What are the new guiding principles of the new knowledge-based, digital economy? Shoshana Zuboff (Charles E. Wilson professor at Harvard Business School), and James Maxmin (chairman and CEO of Volvo-UK, Thorn Home Electronics, and Laura Ashley), have suggested that revolutions, such as the older industrial revolution and the knowledge-based, digital economy, arise from the interplay of three "drivers": *technologies; new structures of consumption;* and *new logic or institutions that align people, markets, and technologies in a new way.*[10] Let us examine how all three determine a knowledge-based, digital economy.

NEW TECHNOLOGIES

At the center of the knowledge-based, digital economy are **new technologies** that emanate from the simultaneity of rapid advances in computing power, information storage, and exploding communications capacity.[11] To illustrate, the highly touted "information superhighway" is an enfolding group consisting of the hardware configurations of digital industries (semiconductors, consumers, and electronics), the transmission industries (telephone and cable), and the software industries (publishing, video games, and television marketers). Such would not have been possible without core technological trends that are so pervasive that they are dubbed as "laws."

Moore's Law

First postulated in 1964 by Gordon Moore, co-founder of Intel, **Moore's law** refers to the ability of new technology to double the density of transistors on a chip about every eighteen months. While it is not a law in a physical sense, it has proved to be remarkably accurate: between 1971 and 2001, transistor density has doubled every 1.96 years.[12] As a consequence, the cost of information processing has been reduced to the point that it is now economical for hundreds of millions of people to have access to computing power previously reserved only for highly trained scientists and researchers (see Exhibit 8.1).

Increasing computational speeds in personal computing devices have also accelerated the maturity of certain industries, while obscuring the boundaries of others. A laptop has the computing power that only a few mini-computers had a few years ago. In effect, the boundaries between the laptop computer, mainframe computer, and mini-computer have been blurred, resulting in higher levels of productivity. For example, consumers today have access to notebook computers that exceed the computational capacities that

Exhibit 8.1   **Moore's Law**

Year	Intel Microprocessor	Transistors	Incremental Capacity Increase	Time Required to Increase Capacity
November 1971	4004	2300	—	—
April 1972	8008	3300	1.43	5 months
April 1974	8080	6000	1.82	24 months
June 1978	8086	29000	4.83	51 months
February 1982	80286	134000	4.62	45 months
October 1985	386 DX	275000	2.05	45 months
April 1989	486 DX	1200000	4.63	55 months
March 1993	Pentium	3100000	2.58	48 months
November 1995	Pentium Pro	5500000	1.77	33 months
May 1997	Pentium II	7500000	1.36	19 months
February 1998	Pentium III	9500000	1.27	19 months
November 2000	Pentium IV	42000000	4.42	34 months
May 2001	Itanium	25000000	.59	6 months
September 2001	Xeon	42000000	1.68	4 months
July 2002	Itanium 2	220000000	5.23	10 months
July 2006	Dual-Core Itanium 2	1700000000	7.72	48 months

In 1965, Intel co-founder Gordon Moore's prediction, popularly known as Moore's Law, states that the number of transistors on a chip doubles about every two years. This prediction about silicon integration is validated per the table above. It has fueled the worldwide technology revolution.

Source: Adapted from Steve Gilheany, Evolution of Intel Microprocessors: 1971–2007 (http://www.cs.rpi.edu/~chrisc/COURSES/CSCI-4250/SPRING-2004/slides/cpu.pdf) "Innovation from the start," http://download.intel.com/museum/Moores_Law/Printed_Materials/Microprocessor_Poster_Ltr.pdf; "Intel Delivers Dual-Core Itaniums," *High Productivity Computing Wire*, http://www.hpcwire.com/hpc/732289.html.

guided the 1969 moon landing. A new laptop computer today with significantly more computing power than one of three years ago can be purchased for the *same* price.[13]

The significance of Moore's law is seen most markedly in the downward spiral of costs and prices. It only took three years for the price of semiconductors to drop by 85 percent, and in the next ten years, production increased twenty times.[14] As a point of comparison, it took seventy years (1780–1850) for the price of cotton to drop by 8 percent during the Industrial Revolution. During the 1960s, better chip design and more efficient manufacturing methods cut the average price of an integrated circuit from $50 in 1962 to $1 in 1971.[15] The giant leap forward came in 1971 with the invention of the microprocessor by Ted Huff. In one estimate, computer power now costs only one-hundredth of 1 percent of what it did in the early 1970s.[16] Never before in the history of industrial applications have we seen such a dramatic fall in prices, and this trend is continuing, as illustrated in the declining cost of accessing and using informational tools later in this section.

METCALFE'S LAW

With computing power doubling every eighteen months and storage densities doubling at an even faster rate of every twelve to fifteen months, bandwidth is moving ahead at an astonishing rate: the amount of information that can be transferred between nodes on a network is doubling every four to six months. Bob Metcalfe, co-inventor of Ethernet and founder of 3Com, observed that the value of the network increases by the square of the number of users. This is now known as **Metcalfe's law** (Exhibit 8.2). Moore's law and Metcalfe's law are interrelated. Moore's law refers to the ability of new technology to double the density of transistors on a chip about every eighteen months. Consistent with this increase in computational power, Metcalfe's law stipulates that the increasing number of computers on the network acts in the same way by amplifying the effect of each node on the whole network. In 2000, some 90 million host computers were connected to the Web, creating more computational/communications bandwidth rather than constraining it.[17]

The "laws" of the knowledge-based, digital economy reflect the relentless technological progress and the falling cost of accessing and using the new information tools. In 1970, the cost of processing 1 million computer instructions per second (MIP) was $1 million; the cost of storing 1 million bits of information (megabits) was $5,000, and sending 1 trillion bits of information cost $150,000. Today, one MIP costs less than 17 cents, one megabit of storage is 17 cents, and sending one trillion bits over the Internet is 12 cents.[18] Combined with the rising affluence of customer groups, lower prices have accelerated the speed of adoption and diffusion over time. Classical economics used the term "diminishing returns" to describe how value decreases with each additional increment of a given product. For example, the yield from the second or third harvest of a piece of land will not be as valuable or as fertile as the very first. Traditional industries, such as agriculture and coffee, fit this pattern well. In the case of knowledge-based, digital economy, however, economists have used the phrase **increasing returns** that describe how benefits amplify with increased product usage.[19] That is, the more you buy a particular product (software), the value of this product product increases because others are likely to buy it as well. Industries such as computers, software, telephones, fax machines, software, telecommunications, and fiber optics exhibit this pattern of behavior. Because of increasing returns, markets are hypothesized to be "winner-take-all," particularly when products from different vendors are commodities, or considered identical.[20] The firm whose product become the industry standard is positioned to garner a significantly large share of the market (e.g., Microsoft's Operating System).

Increasing returns are closely associated with network effects (see Metcalfe's law). **Network effects** refer to the benefits accrued by participating in a network that becomes proportionately faster as the number of network users grows.[21] Network effects apply to products and services for which benefits expand geometrically with each addition of users in the network. For example, the user of a fax machine benefits from other users of fax machines. Each new addition or use of a fax machine geometrically increases the value to all current participants. Therefore, each new customer on the Internet increases its value to sellers, and vice versa.

Exhibit 8.2   **Metcalfe's Law**

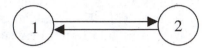

Metcalfe's law states that the value of a network equals approximately the square of the number of users of the system.

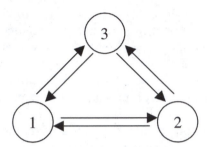

The law is often illustrated with the example of a telephone. A single telephone is useless, but the value of every telephone increases with the total number of telephones in the network, because the total number of people with whom you communicate increases.

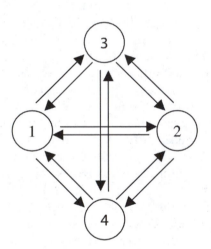

Network effects are further distinguished in terms of complementary bandwagon effects. **Complementary bandwagon effects** occur when products benefit from the use of more competitively supplied complementary products. For example, as more customers purchase a hardware product, software vendors have greater incentives to produce more software for the product. Microsoft prospered as software vendors wrote complementary programs for its operating system, not for the Mac or other rivals. As innovations diffuse in large quantities, there is a self-reinforcing cycle where the positive impact of this diffusion leads to increased demand for the product and the growth of complementary products. In short, new digitally based products do not always mature and die in the conventional sense. Instead, they set off new patterns of renewal and growth based on the amplification of customer demand. Increasing returns or the widespread adoption of an industry standard is a key characteristic of this new environment.

The combined effects of Moore's law and Metcalfe's law have changed the information and computational boundaries that had previously constrained human analytic capacities. Together, they have placed individuals in control of information with limits on problem solving that are limited only by human intelligence and imagination.

THE NEW STRUCTURE OF INDIVIDUAL CONSUMPTION

New technologies by themselves do not create economic revolutions. Because individuals sustain and nurture themselves and their families through their consumption patterns, it is this centrality of **individual consumption** that defines the different levels of economy.[22] In the the industrial age, or of mass consumption specifically, most people were limited by their income and assumed that they had to make do with whatever they could earn and viewed mass-produced goods and services as basic necessities. When goods were produced cheaply, for example Ford's Model T, they were appreciated and consumed accordingly, since cost reductions resulting from scale and scope economies had made cars affordable to mass consumers. In contrast, with even newer and cheaper products spawned by Moore's and Metcalfe's laws, today's consumers express a different view of consumption compared to the generations that preceded them. Let us examine some of these basic differences.

One-on-One: Individuation of Consumption

A description of the "new consumer" goes as follows: "People no longer want to bend to antiquated rules of business. They do not want to be the objects of commerce, treated like anonymous pawns in the exploitative games of market segmentation, penetration, and manipulative pseudo-intimacy. Instead they want to 'opt in' and make their own choices, controlling their destinies and their cash. They want their voices to be heard, and they want them to matter."[23]

In contrast to their precedessors who lived in decades of mass production, the new consumers of today are not passive but seek fulfillment in their lives that goes beyond material security and comfort. They satisfy their quest for influencing the final form of the products they purchase through self-expression, choice, and control. Unlike their predecessors, the new consumers are much more adept in accessing and using information technologies, as reflected in their participation in creating blogs, chat rooms, wikis, social networking, and peer-to-peer downloading.

These traits have become important hallmarks of the new consumer mindset. Emboldened by the power of the computer and the Internet that permit quick access to information, individuals can research and read about almost any topic. Notably, through use of the Internet, many modern consumers might have already determined their purchase choices even before visiting a retail store. As noted by automobile retailers, this has reduced the impact of on-site retailing, once the preferred marketing channel, and this tendency to surf the web before making an actual purchase has resulted in an emphasis by retailers on promotion design and off-site advertising on the Internet. Some visionary companies have moved from traditional mass-produced items to one-on-one, personalized marketing as a way to capitalize on this growing mindset. For example, consumers can log onto the Nike website and design their own athletic shoes and apparel, specify their personal preferences, and order manufacturing to their specifications. The same can be done by those seeking individualized bicycles, or even custom-made suits. Individuality, autonomy, and self-determination have trumped conformity, authority, and hierarchy.

Personalized Experience/Co-creation

An emerging component in a knowledge-based, service economy is **personalized experience** or the proactive role of consumers in defining their consumption experience. The success of Starbucks is attributed in no small part to the firm's ability to tout "affordable luxury" as part of the customer's consumption experience. When consumers buy a specially made $4.95 cappuccino, for example, they consider themselves to have a similar consumption experience as movie actors and actresses, sport celebrities, politicians, and CEOs, who are held to indulge in high priced, specialized, and customized coffee products. When taken in tandem with Starbucks' store ambience and its knowledgeable *baristas*, it is an experience that is difficult to top elsewhere. It is little wonder that Starbuck's coffee recipes number into the thousands to accommodate many diverse consumers (Chapter 1).

Service management research has focused on the interaction between a firm and its clients and the role of the clients in this interaction. Yet the firm's management of these interactions at various levels of client involvement also affects the firm's performance. Among the various models, some require more active customer involvement. They involve the actions of a consumer actually defining the value of the end product, a process referred to as "**co-production**" and "**co-creation**."[24] This is typical in high-end services, such as financial services that can purchase stock using specially designed outlets (Charles Schwab) and online services where customers can prepare their own investments (prospect.com). Our earlier example of a consumer designing his own Nike shoe to his unique specifications using the company's website is an example of the "co-creation" process. This is much different from traditional service encounters, which require very limited involvement because all customers can do is choose from the products that are displayed by the on-site brick-and-mortar retailer.

New Enterprise Logic

The knowledge-based, digital economy is grounded in new technologies and new patterns of individual consumption. However, meeting the needs of the new consumers using new technologies is hardly sufficient to ignite a revolution without a supportive ideology or enterprise logic. The third pillar of the knowledge-based, digital economy depends on a new logic of enterprise that links new technologies with new markets that results from patterns of individual consumption.[25] The industrial revolution of the early twentieth century, for example, came about not only from new technological advances of the day (i.e., transportation, and communication) nor from the growing affluence of consumers that made them predisposed to buy mass produced, standardized products. It was also facilitated by a new enterprise logic called managerial capitalism Under managerial capitalism, the primary form of control and coordination was a managerial hierarchy that was controlled by management and designed to ensure the proper flow of increasingly complex processes of production and distribution. A tightly-knit hierarchy ensured consistency in mass-produced products and services. As we will discuss in the next section, managerial capitalism (i.e., standard enterprise logic) worked effectively during the industrial era. However, it is limited in terms of accommodating a knowledge-based, digital economy.

Limitations of Standard Enterprise Logic

An enterprise system carries with it a whole philosophy and theory. Once this system is adopted by an organization, its logic becomes part of the organization as well. Specifically, during the industrial age, the standard enterprise logic proved to be quite effective for production methods designed to achieve high levels of standardized throughput and low unit costs. The essential elements of **standard enterprise logic** included the following: (1) an internal focus that requires the consolidation of once-scattered resources into a single enterprise and chain of command; (2) a professional breed of salaried managerial hierarchy to oversee internalized management of the resulting functional units; and (3) the separation of ownership and management.[26] The financial assumptions associated with this logic were constituted in "**transactional economics**," that is, the transactions between buyers and sellers. Each transaction was regarded as a wholly contained unit of analysis, and value was maximized to produce shareholder wealth.[27]

While useful in the past, standard enterprise logic is limited in the knowledge-based, digital economy. For one, transactions are virtual and not always visible as tangible exchanges. Physical distance on the Internet has become irrelevant, because everything is virtually connected and just "a click away." Value realization does not revolve around the acquisition of goods and services in an arms-length transaction, but involves ongoing relationships. Whereas value was added inside organizations, specifically the end of a firm's value chain in traditional organizations, value is distributed or dispersed throughout the organization. In fact, ownership and control are similarly dispersed, now shared with customers and broader stakeholders. Taken collectively, the demands of the knowledge-based, digital economy call for different institutions and logic to support emergent needs of customers and new technologies.

Deep Support and Distributed Economies

According to the old logic, standardization was required to serve the masses. This created a divergence of interests that insulated producers from their customers. In their quest to achieve their profit goals, firms "created" value by emphasizing cost reductions and productivity enhancements that did not necessarily work to the benefit of their consumers. These methods led to disgruntled consumers and this was exacerbated by higher but unfulfilled expectations of product quality and service. Moreover, the focus on transactional economics within the organization precluded an appreciation of the new digital medium for which consumers could participate in the "co-creation" process. For these reasons, managerial capitalism proved to be significantly limited as the underlying enterprise logic for the knowledge-based digital economy.

To support the new digital medium and emerging patterns of individual consumption, Zuboff and Maxmin have touted a new enterprise logic based on **deep support** and **distributed economies**. The new logic supports the convergence of interests between advocates and individuals, as well as among participants. Zuboff and Maxim argue that the individuation of consumption will place immense pressure for a logic that can support collaboration and coordination across highly dense and embedded networks. Though still preliminary, Zuboff and Maxmin offer some fundamental elements of this new logic that includes the following affirmations:

1. Value resides in individuals, that is, customers are recognized as the source of value and cash flow.
2. Value is distributed, or lodged in every individual, thus necessitating distributed production, ownership, and control.
3. Relationship-based economics become the framework for wealth creation and sustainable advantage. Enterprises and federations have to invest in commitment and trust with individuals in order to realize value.
4. Unlike traditional markets that are targeted, attacked, penetrated, and saturated by organizations, markets for deep support are self-selected and self-defining, that is, individuals and advocates opt into these markets.
5. New structures and processes based on convergence, configurability, and adaptability become essential implementation elements. This means a perpetually adaptive and proactive attention to the evolving needs of an individual.[28]

Taken all together, these elements have important implications for firms operating in the new knowledge-based, digital economy. A summary of arguments is presented in Exhibit 8.3.

Digital technologies will render any new imperatives for transparency and openness. Accordingly, these will create numerous opportunities for individuals to collaborate, communicate, and connect across space and time. In the next section, we will shift from the individual to the organizational level and discuss some specific ways in which the knowledge-based, digital economy will affect business.

How the Knowledge-based, Digital Economy Will Affect Business

The knowledge-based, digital economy upholds the power of information over physical factors in ways that depart from traditional conceptions. In the knowledge-based, digital economy, wealth is created by codified knowledge. In manipulating and trans-

Exhibit 8.3

Key Drivers of the Knowledge-based, Digital Economy

New Technologies: These have dramatically reduced costs and increased the consumer installed base.	*New Patterns of Individual Consumption:* Knowledgeable and empowered consumers have demanded a new role in value creation.	*New Logics and Institutions of Realignment*: A new logic based on deep support is needed to link new technologies and new patterns of individual consumption.
Specific Characteristics:	**Specific Characteristics:**	**Specific Characteristics:**
1. Moore's law: Doubling of computing capacity every 18 months.	1. One-to-one individuation of consumption: Focus on individual needs.	1. Need for realignment: Standard enterprise logic is limited because transactions are impersonal and based primarily on creating value for producers.
2. Metcalfe's law: Increases in the value of the network by the square of the number of users.	2. Personalized experience/co-creation: Empowered consumer is actively involved in creating value with producers.	2. Need for alternative logic: This new logic is based on deep support and distribution economies.
Summary: New technologies have led to rapid commoditization, fast-changing life cycles, and affordable products and services.	*Summary:* Consumer is an active not passive, agent. There is heightened pressure to engage consumers through mass customization and "co-creation."	*Summary:* A new logic based on deep support is needed to bridge new technologies and new patterns of individual consumption.

Source: Based on Shoshana Zuboff and James Maxmin, *The Support Economy* (New York: Penguin Books, 2002).

mitting information at electronic speeds, value is added. When competitors are able to copy and replicate innovations expeditiously, firms will have to rely more on their intellectual capital (their arsenal of knowledge, experience, expertise, and soft assets) rather than their hard physical and financial capital, to sustain advantage.[29] Viewed in this context, information creates value and enhances functionality.

With the knowledge-based, digital economy, attention shifts from mere processing of information to its transmission and transformation into new knowledge. There are four reasons for this.[30] First, because the cost of information transmission is so much lower, in many cases, information is readily accessible. The computer is available for sale on almost every street corner. Unlimited Internet access is a reality, and long-distance telephone charges are now routinely a few cents a minute. Second, enhanced communications create greater linkages and interconnectivity, partly through network effects. A stock trader in Montana with a satellite feed can have the same timely data as his colleagues on Wall Street. Third, greater linkages and interconnectivity facilitate transactions. Information per se becomes transactions. Information was long regarded as involving a tradeoff between richness (content) and reach (connections), such that one can only rise at the expense of the other. In today's new economy, this tradeoff is no longer true as advances in communications technology can accommodate both (e.g., the richness of information provided on the Internet).[31] Fourth, virtual transactions reduce the importance of physical distance, eroding locational monopolies. That is, using the Internet can reduce the reliance by firms on physical closeness to their suppliers and customers. As virtual corporations, teams, agencies, and units abound, the interactions of individuals, teams, and institutions can become transformed through self-empowerment. The speed of transmission is crucial to a company's ability to respond quickly to consumer demands. Barring disruptive technologies, Internet-based businesses can grow, prosper, and continuously transform themselves.

Beyond significant cost reductions induced by Moore's law and the rapid diffusion of products and services enabled by Metcalfe's law, the other characteristic of a knowledge-based, digital economy is how "winner-take-all" markets can be established through "lock-in" processes. In winner-take-all markets, it is essential to build a large customer base (also called an "installed base") in order to gain the largest market share, then "locking in" the market. Creating a **locked-in market** is tantamount to making the company's product and services the "industry standard," thus ensuring that this large customer base is secured and that competitors are held at bay.[32] This can happen even when the accepted standard is clearly inferior to other designs.

In industries where standards are important, the ability of a firm to successfully establish its technology as the standard becomes the basis of its long-term success and viability.[33] The diffusion of such technological standards or "drivers" increases the innovative uses of the product, as well as the development of complementary products. Once technologies are "locked in," they are difficult to change unless there is another revolutionary breakthrough.

The classic example of the market locking in to an inferior technology is the QWERTY layout for typewriters (referring to the order in which letters are placed), now extended to computer keyboards.[34] Originally developed by trial and error in the 1860s to compensate for a design deficiency in typewriters, it became a locked-in standard even when better engineering alleviated the initial problem. Despite superior keyboard formats that could have increased typing speeds considerably, the QWERTY layout prevailed. This was sustained when the first touch-typists, who had trained in the QWERTY format, developed this preference. Eventually, training on the QWERTY format was so widely adopted that it became institutionalized.

The proponents of lock-in argue that it is important to be first to market because switching costs restrain customers from adopting a newer and superior product. While quality is important, it is not the overriding issue. With costs dropping precipitously in high-tech products, product life cycles are much shorter, with the premium accruing to firms that manage continuous iteration of new products effectively. If products are similar, customers will select the one available soonest, that is most proven, most accepted, and cheapest. If market growth is high, but product life is short, then the greatest determinant of profits is getting to market early.

What are the implications for inventing and innovating in the knowledge-based, digital economy? The new rules for operating in this environment transcend agility, speed, and discipline. They call for redefining value in an economy where the cost of raw technology is plummeting to near zero, and where value is in establishing a goodwill relationship with present customers. The seemingly endless cycle of cost reduction and increased market demand creates an environment in which the only thing that matters is that the exponential growth of the market is faster than the exponential decline of prices. This inverted logic results from rapid technological advances that lead to lower prices, which, in turn, spur market demand. Having introduced the key characteristics of this new digital environment, we now turn our attention to the process of innovation, what worked previously, and what is likely to work in this environment.

TYPES OF INNOVATION: PRODUCT, PROCESS, AND SERVICE

Innovation is inextricably tied to wealth or value creation, specifically how value is derived from a firm's internal activities and created in the provision of its products and services. The process of **innovation** leads to new products and services and results in improved profits, added rents, or a larger market share.[35] Within this perspective, innovation is placed in the context of adding value to consumer satisfaction. We start with a discussion of innovation in a generic business environment in the next section, and then relate the process to the knowledge-based, digital context in the later sections. Philip Kotler, marketing professor at Northwestern University and a renowned marketing guru, suggests that value is created in three ways:[36]

- *Providing a material that is in short supply.* Conceivably, this is the easiest path to adding value. In this case, demand is already there (i.e., oil, food, groceries, office supplies, etc.), and fulfilling consumer orders simply closes the gap between expectations and realization.
- *Adding useful features to an existing product.* This involves creative product extensions, since consumers are already familiar with the product. Thus, extensions such as call waiting, caller ID, and call forwarding improve the service for landline telephones, much in the same manner as different ring tones, different screen sizes, and colorful designs augment the value of cell phones.
- *Offering a new product or service altogether.* This is probably the most challenging of Kotler's options since it involves an invention or radical transformation of existing products to meet previously undefined consumer needs. The invention of the integrated circuit paved the way for future products and services (computers, telecommunication devices) and transformed existing industries (consumer electronics, defense, health care).

While all three involve some level of creativity, it can be said with certainty that the second and third options are direct examples of innovation enabled by an innovative process. **Market-based innovation** is a phased process through which a new idea is *discovered* (invented), *developed*, and *executed,* or brought to practice. The three phases are underscored because some firms that invented a product (e.g., Philips and the CD-ROM, or the commercial videocassette) failed to fully capitalize on this due to an inability to bring the product successfully to market. To succeed, a firm has to effectively manage all three phases. Accordingly, for many innovations, the process is complex, involving interacting managerial, technological, and social transitions.[37] Moreover, the process can be convoluted and time consuming, following patterns

Exhibit 8.4

The Development of the Creative Organization

Organization development has moved to a new era. Creativity and innovation drive a new corporate model to take shape. This new model offers a new pathway for corporations.

Stage 1	The company recognizes that the globalization and commoditization of technology and information has changed the source of competitive advantage. Making products and offering services based on better features, speed, and low cost is no longer enough to sustain profit margins.
Stage 2	Corporations find that commoditization allows core advantage to be performed overseas through offshoring to China, India, and Eastern Europe. Jobs that are offshored extend from manufacturing through knowledge-based jobs.
Stage 3	Six Sigma (a measure of quality that strives for near perfection), the principle that previously held supreme, gives way to design strategy. Design is now the dominant factor differentiating products and appealing to consumer emotions.
Stage 4	Organizational growth is mostly driven by creative innovation. Any unmet demand, unarticulated expectation, or unfulfilled desire will be met by new thinking in creative product design.
Stage 5	The creativity approach has been rewarding. A new DNA for innovation was found in successful corporations. They establish fast-moving, highly appealing, innovative designs to beat out their rivals.

Source: Adapted from Robert Berner and Diane Brady, "Get Creative," *BusinessWeek,* August 1, 2005, pp. 60–68.

of peaks and valleys, often with frustrating setbacks and unexpected delays. The discovery and invention process is largely nonrational, relying on intuitive insights along with purposeful research. One framework for examining the evolution of a creative company is presented in Exhibit 8.4. Within this perspective of innovation, three types have been distinguished.

PRODUCT INNOVATION

Some of the most innovative products are solutions to specific problems, such as Post-it Notes, Teflon, penicillin, and incandescent light. **Product innovation** is a multifaceted process that is driven by the need to provide solutions to existing needs. These include adding advanced functions, new features, and better designs. The explosion of mobile phone (cell phone) technology is an example. The mobile phone started as a bulky, heavy device that looked like a brick. Today, it is candy-bar sized, with many features packed inside, and can fit in the hand of a five-year-old child.

Related product innovations are illuminating. Today's mobile phone can work as a personal digital assistant (PDA) and high-end camera with advanced optics.[38] The technology to support this product had gone from 1G to 4G (first generation to fourth generation) by 2006. It is said that 5G will come in less time than it took to reach 4G. New features do not necessarily mean high-tech. Nokia added a flashlight to some of its mobile phones in India and China. In India, the feature was requested by consumers because of frequent blackouts in some areas.[39] In China, it was mostly for fun. Lenovo has a mobile phone available in China that has a small chamber to be

Box 8.1

The Freitag Bags

Markus Freitag, a twenty-two-year-old Swiss art student, needed a durable, waterproof bag for his art supplies as he often biked on the roads of Zurich, where it rains an average of 127 days a year. One day, while overlooking the Autobahn A3, the freeway used by trucks between Germany and Italy, Freitag was inspired by the materials used by truckers in Europe and invented a messenger bag made out of recycled waterproof vinyl tarpaulins that have been heavily used by trucks running on autobahns daily. In the United States, cargos are placed in enclosed trailers, but in Europe they are covered by tarpaulins decorated with colorful logos of different companies. Aside from its novelty, recycling the used tarpaulins fits in with Markus's concern for the environment. After cleaning off the oil and dirt, using an industrial sewing machine, and adding a few other notions, Freitag's company churns out thousands of very durable messenger bags—no-two-bags-alike merchandise loved by the likes of bike messengers in San Francisco. Freitag's bags are sold in 250 stores and on the Internet worldwide. In 2004, Markus and his brother sold more than 100,000 bags. Prices range from $70 to $250.

Source: Adapted from Siri Schubert, "From the Autobahn to Fifth Avenue," *Business 2.0.* August 1, 2005, p. 42.

filled with the user's favorite fragrance.[40] Nokia produced a mobile phone that has a speaking alarm clock and iconic address book targeted for illiterate users in developing economies.[41] For innovation in product appearance, the focus is not to add more features but to make the current features and layout more appealing. For example, Samsung, although not known for offering the most advanced technology, made "some of the coolest gadgets on earth"[42] that were smaller, slimmer, and sleeker.[43]

While most people equate product innovation with advanced technological features, this is not necessarily the case. The Freitag story is about the use of recycling materials to solve a common problem (see Box 8.1). Whichever way a product innovation is positioned, it should go beyond the surface (e.g., adding new colors or changing appearance) to creating new consumer experiences. For example, Birkenstock updated its earth-toned sandals to add new styles, such as the colorful slip-on beach Birkis to accommodate consumers' preferences for a more informal lifestyle. And radio users now have the choice of satellite radio to broaden their musical spectrum, news outlets, and features.[44] These innovations add unique emotional experiences to the consumer's daily life.

INNOVATION IN SERVICES

Services have taken a big share of the knowledge-based, digital economy, particularly in developed economies where many businesses are carried out in cyberspace. With the growing use of the credit card and the ATM, more **innovative services**, such as online ordering and bill payment, are now available. Many of these services are driven by the pursuit of convenience. Beyond credit and debit cards is the cash card, which eliminates the need to carry cash for small expenses. For a completely cash-free world, the next stage is electronic cash that can be stored on cell phones.[45]

Online search engines such as Yahoo! and MSN, which originally provided access to free information, have now become magazine-style websites and interactive personal communication platforms offering features such as instant messaging (IM). This combination of a search engine and communication platform eventually became an online entertainment portal for many people. Breaking away from the old style of broadcasting television shows, both NBC Universal and CBS Broadcasting are experimenting with the option of making top TV shows available via on-demand video. Along with pay-per-view movies and iPod's podcast, the United States has moved to an on-demand era.[46] Service lead time is shortened and customers control delivery time. John Hagel III, an independent management consultant, and John Seely Brown, the former head of Xerox's Palo Alto Research Center, have suggested that on-demand services are made possible by innovation in three areas: service-oriented architectures, virtualization architectures, and interaction tools.[47]

As mentioned above, innovation that creates new consumer experiences takes place in fields other than technology. An innovation in entertainment was created by Cirque du Soleil. As discussed in an earlier chapter, the circus has dramatically reexamined what it can provide through modern costumes, beautiful dancing, gymnastics, fluid flow of actions, and imaginative fairy tales that transcend the stunts and animal tricks found in the traditional circus.[48]

PROCESS INNOVATION

Typically, **process innovation**, or new inventions and directions in information flows, is driven by operational efficiency. For example, in insurance, it is in consumer underwriting and pricing; in e-commerce, it is promotional-offer personalization; in retailing, it is inventory replenishment; in transportation, it is asset deployment; in brokerage, it is trading and fraud detection; in energy, it is service-delivery management; in telecommunications, it is provisioning optimization; and in government, it is fraud detection and security.[49]

In addition to pushing for technological advancement, innovation in process can stem from simply a good idea. Brown and Hagel point out that Aravind Eye Care System in Madurai, India, has adopted the concept of chain hospitals and manufacturing centers for medical needs to create high-quality eye care.[50] By specializing in eye care, the doctors are able to hone their skills and may operate on as many as twenty-five patients in half a day. And the hospitals can work out the flow of patients smoothly and efficiently. This is an example of an innovative approach arising from the challenge of serving low-income customers with high-quality outcome. After researching why patients could not receive treatment, Aravind was able to provide medical accessories and eyeglasses conveniently and at low cost.[51] This approach inspired other entrepreneurs in the Indian health care industry, notably in the field of cardiology. The company's success has already attracted patients from foreign countries. It is estimated that medical tourism in India could reach revenues of $2 billion per year by 2012.[52]

Another example of process innovation is Toyota Motor Corporation's reduction from using 50 braces to a single brace to hold auto frames together during the production process. Given the complexity of Toyota's production process, this change may not seem significant, but the outcome is a Global Body Line system that allows Toyota to reduce refitting costs by 75 percent. Now Toyota can make different models using a single line of production. The resultant total saving on manufacturing costs for 2003 was $2.6 billion.[53]

Process innovations typically lead to opportunties for customers to create value. Amazon.com provides one such example. The company saw that those who want to sell their products on the Internet find that eBay provides easy access. In response, Amazon opened up its platform to other sellers. This way, Amazon has not only reached more buyers and sellers with more varied merchandise, but it also can provide more convenience to individuals who only want to sell their goods and not get involved in auctions.[54] While there are other types of innovations that will be introduced later in this chapter, the above constitute the main sources of innovation.

THE EMERGING CONTEXT OF INNOVATION AND CREATIVITY IN A KNOWLEDGE-BASED, DIGITAL ECONOMY

Despite the touted benefits of innovation, there is a downside: the innovation success rate is a mere 4.5 percent.[55] In fact, John McAfee, the founder of the antivirus company McAfee Associates, suggests a "rule of thumb": the first firm to take an invention to market almost always fails.[56] Part of this failure is the inability of the firm to recognize the changing context of innovation and creativity in the knowledge-based, digital economy. Traditional models of innovation, based on the industrial age, conceptualize creativity in two basic ways: first, as a sequential process, much like a linear production system of inputs and outputs; and second, as a deterministic S-shaped product life cycle (see Exhibit 8.5). In contrast, innovation in a knowledge-based, digital economy embraces the logic of open innovation. In this section, we discuss the differences between closed and open innovation.

The **sequential process**, also a "closed" system of innovation, yielded useful product and process improvements in the past. Consistent with the traditional view of organizations as sequential and incremental value chains, most innovation was organized within research and development (R&D). This concentration of the innovation function in one department did produce a number of significant inventions in the past, such as telephone and telecommunication devices by Bell Laboratories. Similarly, the use of the **S-shaped innovation curve** was particularly successful in planning for the transition of many products as they entered different stages in their life cycles.[57] Nevertheless, the relevance and application of these models in a knowledge-based, digital environment is limited for several reasons.

The new rules for competing in a knowledge-based, digital economy entail imperatives for speed and agility and for know-how and collaboration. Given the complexity of the current environment, taken in tandem with the steep costs of research and development, it is unlikely that any one firm, no matter its size, can do it alone. Successful innovation systems have to connect inventors to needs and users almost simultaneously in time, while nurturing the informal and unstructured environments where new ideas can flourish and develop into feasible commercial applications. Therefore, the reliance

Exhibit 8.5 **Traditional Models of Innovation**

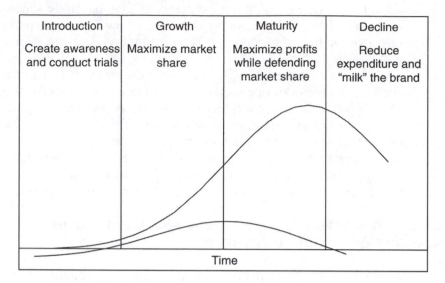

Introduction	Growth	Maturity	Decline
Create awareness and conduct trials	Maximize market share	Maximize profits while defending market share	Reduce expenditure and "milk" the brand

Time

Critique: While helpful in planning transitions, the underlying logic is deterministic. Moreover, innovations can occur at any stage of the life cycle. The upper curve is the sales curve. The lower curve is the profit curve.

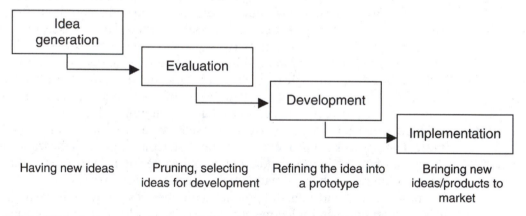

Idea generation	Evaluation	Development	Implementation
Having new ideas	Pruning, selecting ideas for development	Refining the idea into a prototype	Bringing new ideas/products to market

Critique: While the sequence is reasonable and helpful, the more important insights probably flow within each stage and from activities linking each stage, from inception to implementation.

on R&D alone might prove insufficient in an environment where the cost of new innovations is steep, where industry boundaries are blurred, and where innovations are likely to occur outside of a firm's boundaries. Moreover, the deterministic character of the S-shaped innovation curve, which suggests deterministic phases of innovative activities, might also be limiting. Many innovative products arise from serendipity or are outcomes of accidents. Many managers claim that their approach is "not to manage" but to "let the market manage it." Others believe that "innovations are made, not born."[58] Innovative breakthroughs do not happen overnight but come about through people who have been working on some similar ideas or lines of research for years.

Thomas A. Edison's invention of the incandescent light is an example.[59] So is the discovery of the double helix, the basic structure of DNA. Successful innovation in the current environment, therefore, needs a new process with attendant ideologies and principles. Next, we discuss three leading-edge perspectives that have direct relevance to innovation in a knowledge-based, digital economy.

OPEN INNOVATION VS. CLOSED INNOVATION

Henry Chesbrough, professor at the Haas Business School at the University of California, Berkeley, has championed "open innovation" as the appropriate model of innovation for the current time. In contrast to the "closed innovation" model, successful **open innovation** often requires the transformation within the business model (R&D activities) itself to allow reliance on external agents as the potential source of value along with the firm.[60] In case studies contrasting Xerox, IBM, and AT&T, where all had previously used "closed innovation against firms that employed open innovation," Chesbrough reported performance differentials between the two innovative approaches. Firms operating under "closed" innovation typically confined their innovative activities within R&D; new ideas were simply integrated into the existing old business model, a classic formula that has proven ineffective in the current environment.

Within the emerging knowledge-based economy, new ideas spring not from a single unit within the firm but from numerous outside sources: suppliers, customers, complementors, and partners, oftentimes in an unstructured manner. This is one reason why new firms mostly from outside of the industry are typically the first ones to embrace radical ideas that change the existing patterns of competition. They are able to access new ideas that are either outside the industry or are not as appreciated by incumbents. In earlier decades, IBM had championed the cause of "closed" innovation by restricting innovation for its acclaimed IBM 360 series to within the organization. It was forced to open up sourcing and software opportunities to all interested parties for its personal computer, in contrast to the old Apple model that restricted its research activities to within the company. Interestingly, IBM was forced to play this hand because of its lateness in recognizing the potential of the personal computer.[61]

Despite the intuitive appeal of the open innovation model, not as many companies have adopted this practice as one might expect. One reason is that Chesbrough's initial study covered high technology and research and development organizations, prompting some question about the applicability of the open innovation model to more traditional manufacturing firms. Another reason, one acknowledged by Chesbrough, was that adopting an open innovation model required significant changes in organizational processes, and that firms were not willing to enact these changes without sufficient justification.[62] Adopting a new innovation, even a highly promising one by itself can be a risky decision: "If a rising corporate star brings forth a risky innovation that ends up failing, his career is apt to be damaged considerably more than that of the executive who squelches an innovation that could have been a winner."[63]

Even so, for firms that have adopted open innovation practices, the results have been quite favorable. Consider the case of Eli Lilly's wholly owned subsidiary, InnoCentive, that functions as a Web-based community to link its clients (called "seekers") to top scientists around the world.[64] Companies first register with Inno-Centive as "seekers" and post their research and development challenges, including a description, requirements, a deadline, and a reward, to the InnoCentive website. Scientists around the world, called "solvers," then submit their proposals for consideration. If their proposal is accepted, these "solvers" receive award amounts ranging from $10,000 to $100,000. InnoCentive's success rate is reported at 50 percent, which is not bad, considering that the internal R&D units of the "seekers" were not able to solve these research problems.[65] Since 2001, InnoCentive's website has reported over 75,000 "solvers" from 175 countries around the world who have served more than 30 "seekers."[66]

With open innovation, large companies have to open their research departments and include partners outside the firm as sources of new technology. Successful innovation entails the right balance between internal R&D with the acquisition of the results of external R&D, and the commercialization of internal R&D internally and externally to the company. Open innovation is consistent and co-aligned with a knowledge-based, digital environment in which consumers are better educated and inextricably woven into a co-creation process with companies. Within this perspective, consumers, suppliers, partners, and so on, become potential sources of new ideas for innovation.

DISRUPTIVE VS. CONTINUOUS INNOVATION

An informative study by Clayton Christensen, a professor at the Harvard Business School, reveals another perspective of innovation in the context of a knowledge-based, digital economy. Christensen observed that industry stalwarts such as Sears, IBM, DEC, Data General, and others were often blindsided by competitors, even after they had built what appeared to be insurmountable advantages based on their ability to lock in their technologies.[67] Remarkably, firms failed not because they did anything wrong; in fact, they appeared to have done everything right, including listening to their customers and investing in new technologies that were oriented to serving their customer base. Does this contradict our preceding discussion about open innovation?

What is insightful about this research is its distinction between two types of technologies that have the potential for influencing market performance. To explain and resolve this dilemma, Christensen contrasted "sustaining" technologies from "disruptive" technologies. **Sustaining technologies** continue the rate of improvement of established products, much like process innovations. For example, in the disk drive industry, established companies sought to improve the drives they were making in order to offer higher capacity at a lower cost per megabyte. **Disruptive technologies**, on the other hand, typically result in less product improvement but offer features that are valued by new customers. These innovations are typically smaller, simpler, and more convenient to use. In Christensen's research, for example, the 14" diameter hard disks were superior to the 8" diameter, but the latter replaced the former. Similarly, the 8" diameter was replaced by the 5.25" diameter, which was, in turn, replaced by the 3.5" diameter disk. What is notable here, however, is that these technologies were considered inferior to or to have a lower level of performance than existing products at the time—which is why existing customers favored the existing ones, even when new customers favored the newer, inferior products. In effect, the manufacturers of the 14" diameter disk, for example, were held captive by their existing customers and failed to change even when the 8" diameter disk became more accepted in the marketplace.

Because disruptive technologies were associated with small startups, the reigning market leaders considered them to be unimportant. Since they were outside of the incumbents' primary markets, they were not considered threatening.[68] Therefore, they are ignored or de-emphasized by both market leaders and their leading consumers. Christensen's early research noted that the makers of 14-inch disk drives failed because they listened, perhaps too intently, to their established mainframe customers, who said that they did not want a smaller drive. Yet technologies can progress faster than the demands of the market. In efforts to satisfy their customers, firms can "overshoot" the market, giving customers more than they can handle, when in fact disruptive technologies that offer less may be sufficient. Because of the rapid pace of technological developments, disruptive technologies soon catch up with customers' needs. Meanwhile, firms that introduce these disruptive technologies may have already established their competitive advantage over more entrenched rivals. Previously established firms have no recourse other than to belatedly jump on the bandwagon to defend their customer base, starting yet another cycle of competitive maneuverings. The implication is that firms must nurture internally and develop markets for them, rather than forcing the application of these products to mainstream markets.

Christensen has subsequently expanded his research with recent examples of disruptive innovations: the Prius of Toyota, the BlackBerry, the USB flash drive, PlayStation, TiVo, the Segway and Skype.[69] Inventors of disruptive technological products work diligently to move upward in the market and eventually are able to challenge the incumbent firms, particularly when their products fulfill the needs of an emerging market segment.[70] This disruption perspective of innovation fits well within the mantle of a knowledge-based, digital economy. Shorter product life cycles accelerate the maturity of older products that pave the way for newer products and applications. Digitalization facilitates this process of disruption, leading to new innovations. Firms operating in this environment have to be mindful of technological changes, and, to the extent possible, have to be prepared to defend all market niches. To do this, they have to be vigilant about anticipating key changes. Since it is almost impossible to expect a firm to do all of this, firms can still benefit from the use of open innovation discussed in the preceding section.

THE TECHNOLOGY ADOPTION LIFE CYCLE

In a pioneering book, *Crossing the Chasm*, Geoffrey A. Moore, a marketing expert on new product development and Managing Director of TCG Advisors, introduced a reformulation of the S-shaped normal innovation curve that addresses managerial needs of a knowledge-based, digital economy.[71] In this book, the landscape of the

Exhibit 8.6 **The Technology Adoption Life Cycle**

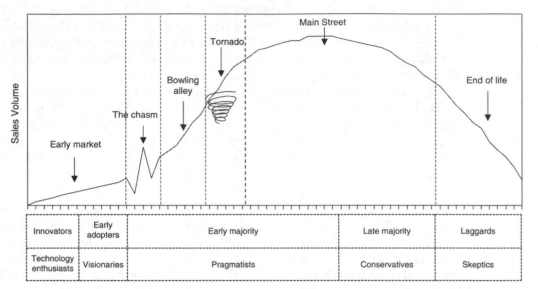

In this formulation, the Technology Adoption Life Cycle is divided up into six zones (early market, the chasm, the bowling alley, the tornado, main street, and the end of life). Corresponding to these zones are consumer types (technology enthusiasts, visionaries, pragmatists, conservatives, and skeptics). The key is to understand these divisions and the processes involved in making transitions. The most difficult passage is crossing the chasm because customers are radically different. The next step is then to carefully select a niche and to "place all the eggs in one basket."

Source: Adapted from Geoffrey A. Moore, *Crossing the Chasm* (New York: HarperCollins, 2002), p. 10.

Technology Adoption Life Cycle is divided into six distinct zones that correspond to the S-shaped normal innovation curve (see Exhibit 8.6). One difference, however, is Moore's introduction of the "chasm," which is the gap separating embryonic innovation activities from the mass adoption phases within the technological life cycle. The idea of a chasm is a simple one: despite the attraction and promise of any new technology, it faces a challenge in terms of becoming widely diffused as a mainstream product to broader market segments (including late adopters, laggards, and skeptics).[72]

Some managers may note that the formulation is not significantly different from previous discourses about the S-shaped innovation curve. In the older S-shaped normal innovation curve, even if late adopters did not match the excitement (and the expenditures) made by the innovators and early adopters, it was a matter of time before this transition occurred and typically in a deterministic manner. In Moore's research, however, the real world shows anything but the pattern described above. He provides deep insights into the traits and thinking of the consumer segments that comprise these segments, specifically the difference between the visionaries (innovators, early adopters) of the early market and the pragmatists (late adopters) in the mainstream: the "former are willing to bet 'on the outcome,' whereas the latter want to see solutions 'in production' before they commit and buy."[73]

How do firms spin out of this chasm and make the necessary crossing? In *Inside the Tornado*, a sequel to *Crossing the Chasm*, Moore has argued: "As markets move from stage to stage in the Life Cycle, the winning strategy does not just change—it actually reverses your prior strategy. The very skills that you've just perfected become the biggest liabilities; and if you can't put them aside to acquire the new ones, then you're in it for the hard times."[74] Beyond this difficult change in attitudes, Moore suggests that firms then need to carefully and purposefully identify a beachhead of pragmatic customers in the mainstream market, that is, a niche, and to focus on these market niches, pursuing in effect the counterintuitive course of "placing all your eggs in one basket."[75]

Even so, the wholesale subscription to a niche might not be as important as understanding the process of crossing the chasm. The process is inextricably tied to "tipping" tendencies. Introduced earlier as escalating patterns of neighborhood migration, today the term **tipping** is generally understood as a point in time when sales become self-sustaining. In a rather provocative book, *The Tipping Point, New Yorker* writer Malcolm Gladwell provides a more behavioral/sociological account of how self-sustaining, lock-in behaviors occur, much in the same manner firms are able to cross the chasm. Ideas, behaviors, messages, and products often spread like outbreaks of infectious diseases.[76] Eschewing more traditional economic explanations, Gladwell relates tipping to particular personality types (connectors) and to a "stickiness" factor. **Connectors** are people who are at the center of influence and are instrumental in sharing and spreading information by virtue of their central and influential position. By knowing whom to share information with one can greatly increase the likelihood that that information will spread. **Stickiness** is a particular way of packaging information that, under certain circumstances, locks consumers into iterative and sequential engagements. As one example, Malcolm cites the popularity of *Sesame Street*, although the logic of "stickiness" can be extended to the astounding success of J.K. Rowling's *Harry Potter* book series, or that of television's *American Idol*. In the latter, through their votes, viewers are induced to keep returning to the series, only to see if their selections are still in the running. Such are the origins of fads or self-reinforcing behaviors, which can also lend deeper insights into how successful firms are able to cross the chasm and become leaders in the mainstream market.

Taken collectively, three perspectives of innovation (open/closed innovation, disruptive technologies, and the Technology Adoption Life Cycle) offer new ways of examining the innovative process in a knowledge-based, digital economy. While they share some features with the traditional models of innovation, notably the importance of carrying though an innovative idea from its generation to its implementation, they also differ in fundamental respects that can be explained in reference to the emerging environment. Open innovation provides the stern reminder that the origins of innovations are now more than likely outside the industry, a fact to which firms should pay attention. Disruptive technology presents a picture in which customers overshoot technological requirements, and occasionally a product-idea considered "inferior" could be the eventual winner. In regard to the Technology Adoption Life Cycle, it reinforces the argument that customers are fundamentally different at different stages of a product's life cycle and that transitions are far from being predestined in a deterministic manner.

Toward Strategic Innovation: The New Innovative Context

In a recent book, *Ten Rules for Strategic Innovators*, Vijay Govindarajan and Chris Trimble, both professors at the Tuck School at Dartmouth, conducted a survey of hundreds of Fortune 500 companies in an effort to identify factors that differentiated between successful and unsuccessful innovators.[77] Their research examined numerous cases, from Xerox to Sears to Polaroid. The authors differentiated between product, process, service, and strategic innovations. By **strategic innovations**, they refer to innovations in a company's business model. Strategic innovations result when executives reinvent their strategies by redefining *who* the customer is, *what* value the company delivers, and *how* the company delivers it.[78]

Their findings and conclusions reinforce earlier statistics regarding the success rate of innovation.[79] They conclude that most attempts at strategic innovation fail. Failure is related to a poor process. Typically, a CEO calls for breakthrough initiatives. This leads to creative new ideas that fly around, seeking funding. The CEO commits by funding some ideas. A talented leader is assigned to lead the initiative, and a senior executive is appointed as a sponsor. However, when the CEO returns to business as usual, the initiative falls apart. The resulting process, though well-intended, is unlikely to overcome the myriad of difficulties of working within an organization that was oriented for an entirely new business. Other mistakes take the form of myths about the innovation process and can contribute to failure as well (Exhibit 8.7). For the researchers, strategic innovation is primarily an organizational challenge. They provide an astute reminder that innovation is not just the invention or the inception of a new idea, but development and execution as well. For perspective, the world's top twenty innovators in 2005 are presented in Exhibit 8.8. We will turn to a discussion of how organizations can build new processes for enhancing strategic innovation.

Formalize the Process of Forgetting, Borrowing, and Learning

Professors Govindarajan and Trimble suggest that the coexistence of a new business and a mature business within the same company is unnatural and unlikely to succeed. Thus, before an organization can pursue new ideas, it has to forget old ways of doing things. The specifics include the following:[80]

- *Forgetting.* The venture must be able to forget three things: its established business definition, that is, who the customers are and what are the value propositions; its old competencies, that is, it has to develop new ones; and its established emphasis on exploiting the system, that is, it needs to explore new possibilities. As an example, General Motors had to do all three when it decided to develop OnStar, a new information, safety, and communication system.
- *Borrowing.* The organization needs to leverage existing customer relationships, brands, manufacturing capacity, expertise, and so forth, by borrowing good ideas from established companies. When the *New York Times* launched New York

Times Digital, the old company could only offer the new company its journalistic content.
- *Learning*. This entails learning how to succeed in a new and uncertain environment, including the company's ability to improve predictions of its own business performance.

All three of the above require recreating the organization's DNA, or its staff, structure, systems, and culture. The rationale for Govindarajan and Trimble's recommendations stems from the difficulty in changing any organization. Specifically, strategies and routines that worked well in the past also become the basis of failure when they inhibit or obstruct the evolution of new ones that are needed to accommodate the requirements of any new environment. With constant application, successful routines become institutionalized and reified as part of the organization's deep-seated beliefs and values.[81] This paradoxical nature of change creates dilemmas for managers, and the lack of adaptability by firms has led to failures. How then does constructive change happen? Research indicates that such change occurs when the older routines start to fail, precipitating a crisis, but oftentimes too late for the afflicted organization.[82] Such crisis can assume global visibility, such as the 1997 Asian financial crisis that led to changes in the financial and governance structures of many Asian firms, or can be more prosaic events, such as coaches being fired after a losing season.

In a recently published book, *The Future of Management*, Gary Hamel argues that old business models based on nineteenth-century concepts of control and operational efficiency are no longer adequate in the present time; in effect, he sees management thinkers to be "prisoners" and "partisans" of older paradigms.[83] While such thinking might not yet be at a crisis level, Hamel urges managers to go beyond operational, product/service, even strategic innovation, to what he calls management innovation, or radical innovations within management thinking itself. Rather than presenting a definitive description of management innovation, Hamel provides the process for firms to engage in transforming their mental models, transforming their business models, and realizing their vision. To achieve these end-states, Hamel recommends a two-pronged change-agenda.[84] First, managers should recognize the blind spots when it comes to management innovation. These include the belief that managers are not supposed to innovate but to focus on control and efficiency, and that bold management innovation is not possible. Second, managers need to respond to the three challenges: first, to accelerate the pace of strategic renewal; second, to make innovation a part of everyone's job; and third, to create a highly engaging work culture that can motivate anyone to innovate.

REVITALIZE THE COMPANY THROUGH RENEWAL AND TRANSFORMATION

In the late 1990s and early 2000s, Procter & Gamble's CEO Alan G. Lafley not only replaced half of the top executives but quadrupled the design staff.[85] P&G sent designers to work directly with researchers in R&D. It also made the entire innovation

Exhibit 8.7

Innovation Myths

Myths	Facts
Performance measures ensure higher success rates.	Metrics are only part of the entire innovation strategy. Too much emphasis on them will slow down growth opportunities.
High failure rate suggests the need for hundreds of ideas.	Large companies can afford to pursue many ideas at one time. Most companies focus on a smaller number with good potential.
Innovation is costly and time-consuming.	Commoditization of high-tech products hastens the process of obsoleteness. But the cost lagging behind is more expensive.
Innovation is best characterized by crazy creativity.	Although creativity is essential to innovation, other organizational and management issues, such as performance measures, leadership, discipline, and focus are critical too.
Innovation stems from new products.	Not all companies have the creative cultural DNA. An innovation audit may uncover areas of potential in any company.

Source: Adapted from Robert Berner and Diane Brady, "Get Creative," *BusinessWeek,* August 1, 2005, pp. 60–68.

Exhibit 8.8

Top Twenty World-Class Innovative Companies in 2005

Rank	Company	Innovative areas
1	Apple	Consumer experiences and product design
2	3M	Cultivated creative culture through formal incentives
3	Microsoft	Continuous improvements
4	GE	Innovative management practices in competition
5	Sony	Converging technology in media
6	Dell	Cost-cutting and supply-chain management
7	IBM	Advanced IT
8	Google	Online search to solve complex problems
9	P&G	Products designed for consumer lifestyle
10	Nokia	Updated designs and additional features
11	Virgin	Created lifestyle through air travel
12	Samsung	Designs that capture consumer's pulse
13	Wal-Mart	Efficient logistics and supply-chain management
14	Toyota	Quality and technology advancement such as hybrid automobile
15	eBay	Customer empowerment
16	Intel	Use of disruptive approaches to combat competition
17	Amazon	Nontraditional retailing and customer experience
18	Ideo	Process innovation consultancy
19	Starbucks	Created a lifestyle brand from coffee
20	BMW	Design, technology, and Internet marketing

Source: In 2005, Boston Consulting Group polled 940 senior executives in 68 countries. The results were reported in Robert Berner and Diane Brady, "Get Creative," *BusinessWeek,* August 1, 2005, pp. 60–68, from which this was adapted.

process consumer-centric, instead of completely technology driven.[86] In addition, it launched the new idea of "connect and develop" to link apparently unrelated product lines. One of its most popular innovative products is Mr. Clean AutoDry, a handheld sprayer. It is a product combining existing technologies: deionized water from P&G's PUR unit water filter, and water-spot-minimization dish-washing detergent from Cascade. Instead of creating a new brand, P&G capitalized on the widely recognized Mr. Clean brand and image. It was an instant success and boosted the sales of other products under the Mr. Clean brand.[87] CEO Lafley also set up an innovation "gym" in which managers are trained for design thinking. He established a Design Board consisting of non-P&Gers in order to obtain an independent perspective.[88] To further the renewal process, Lafley also mandated that up to half of the company's new product ideas must be sourced externally. The result has been a series of acquisitions and successful products, including Olay Regenerist, a skin-care item. This was obtained from the acquisition of a French company. Overall, this strategy helped P&G's fourth quarter profits jump 44 percent in 2001.

A new standard, such as Six Sigma, a type of management program, can also be renewed and transformed. There were concerns that these programs were not strong enough in quality improvement and process management to suit creative areas in research and new-product development. Critics and academicians even argued that the programs would have negative effects on the exploratory process.[89] It was then proposed that Six Sigma be replaced as a key element in organizing activities.[90] This might explain why GE created CENCOR (calibrate, explore, create, organize, and realize) as a post–Six Sigma initiative.[91] CEO Jeff Immelt even created the new position of chief marketing officer in charge of generating innovation and creativity. Coupled with inputs from outside consultants, the results include soaring sales to China, one of the toughest consumer markets.

INSTITUTIONALIZE ACTIVITIES THAT GENERATE INNOVATION

When asked what methodology they used for their design strategy, CEOs such as Lafley, Immelt, and others shared similar opinions.[92] The three steps are observation, storytelling, and building an organizational process to put these together.[93] Similar thoughts were also shared by Tom Kelley, general manager of IDEO and co-author of *The Ten Faces of Innovation,* published in 2005. Kelley finds that innovation does not generate itself and does not pass on to anyone by itself. It takes the human element to make it work. Tom Kelley developed ten people-centric roles for innovations.[94] Each has a different persona but they fall into three general categories:

The *Learning Persona* collects information to continually expand the knowledge pool. Roles include:

- *The Anthropologist* observes human behavior by staying with subjects or "living" their lives.
- *The Experimenter* tests and tries new ideas and keeps learning from mistakes.

- *The Cross-Pollinator* brings cultural, disciplinary, and market differences from place to place for inspiration.

The *Organizing Persona* moves ideas forward. Roles include:

- *The Hurdler* detects barriers and is able to break them.
- *The Collaborator* brings people of diverse backgrounds together and seeks solutions by interweaving multiple disciplines.
- *The Director* pools innovative talents together and inspires such people to maximize their potential.

The *Building Persona* applies the thoughts of the learning persona and empowers the organizing persona to bring innovative ideas to fruition. Roles include:

- *The Experience Architect* designs experiences to connect deeply with customers, such as giving them a chance to participate in the production process.
- *The Set Designer* provides physical space and an environment that facilitate the innovation process, such as the use of off-site innovation labs.
- *The Caregiver* looks for care that can be provided customers beyond the concept of services. It is the extra touch and concern that reach the hearts of customers.
- *The Storyteller* uses compelling stories and legends to inspire, reinforce, and further strengthen corporate values.

Other experts have offered ways of enhancing creativity within the organization. Robert Iger, CEO and president of the Walt Disney Company, offers five tips for enhancing creativity (Exhibit 8.9). They reinforce those presented in earlier subsections.

BUILD A SYSTEMIC CORPORATE CULTURE

Innovation is related to **learning dynamics**. That is, innovation can be vastly enhanced when individuals are positively predisposed to it. A new academic discipline has been developed at Stanford University with a "D-school" that was established for managers to learn innovation dynamics. The new D-school is headed by David Kelley, co-founder of IDEO, a winner of seven *BusinessWeek* 2005 Design Awards. Kelley believes that innovation culture and routine can be built through design thinking.[95] Other managers with similar views include Jack Welch, former CEO of General Electric, who said that innovation is the business application of creativity and imagination.[96] Thus, managing both creativity and imagination are prerequisites for successful innovation. In the case of Amazon.com, its CEO, Jeffery P. Bezos, said that innovation should be "culture of divine discontent." He believes many people could be innovators if their creative talents were unleashed.[97]

Another example of learning dynamics within a systemic corporate culture can be gleaned from Sony in competition with Apple Computers. Sony Corporation has a long history in the personal music-player business. The Walkman and Discman, two major innovations by Sony, were favorites of a billion music lovers of all

Exhibit 8.9

Pointers for Managing Creativity

Point 1	Eliminate the hierarchical approach.
Point 2	Reduce undue rigor in the approval process.
Point 3	Do not dumb down ideas, and keep the passion high.
Point 4	Delegate decision making to those who are in charge.
Point 5	Focus on the company, not the staffers.

Source: Adapted from Merissa Marr, "Redirecting Disney: CEO Iger's Push for Change Goes Far Beyond iPod Deal; Fewer Films, Evolving Parks," *Wall Street Journal,* December 5, 2005, p. B1.

---

ages. Even MP3 players at the time could not dent Sony's reputation. Nevertheless, Apple Computer, backed by its competency in computer technology, was able to challenge Sony with a digital music player that offered multiple functions beyond simply playing music. The impetus behind this development was a newly revitalized culture at Apple, led by Steve Jobs. Since then, Apple has assumed market leadership of this sector, leaving Sony in a rebuilding mode. This case of Apple Computer reinforces the power of a facilitating corporate culture that successfully leveraged its competencies in PC manufacturing to the upcoming mega-trend of digital entertainment.

A systemic corporate culture of innovation incorporates an ingrained belief in relentless and continuous improvement, notably "out-of-the-box" thinking (see Box 8.2). In managing innovation, a fundamental belief is that nothing stays constant.[98] Toyota's *kaizen* system calls for making an effort to seek even the smallest innovation for improvement. It may be a small change out of many changes but, at Toyota, people are thinking about improvements every day and every minute.[99] Making changes is part of the lifestyle and corporate culture at Toyota. As far as "out-of-the-box" thinking is concerned, some innovative ideas are inspired not on whiteboards but in nature, such as the new field of biomimicry or the biologically inspired design.[100] Both Mercedes-Benz's bionic car and DaimlerChrysler's Pontiac Aztec were designed using the streamlined shape of the boxfish. Teijin Limited in Japan adapted the structural color concept found in morpho butterflies to develop fibers that show color not from pigment but from their inner structure, to produce colored fabric without the use of dyes. This achievement was made possible by employing nanotechnology in its development. Observing how geckos walk up walls with billions of points of contact produced by millions of tiny split hairs, the Defense Advanced Research Projects Agency is developing a robot that can climb vertical surfaces.[101]

Another feature of a systemic culture is a proactive effort to eradicate barriers to communication across organizational units. Henry Chesbrough, whom we introduced earlier, has proposed a two-pronged approach to achieving this. First, the company has to eliminate the internal barriers between research and manufacturing or marketing. The lack of communication stifles the emergence and fruition of good and novel ideas. Second, the company has to be proactive in searching for new ideas externally.[102] Toyota's new hatchback Prius, the second-generation hybrid vehicle,

Box 8.2

Creativity in Corporations

It has been documented that the new product failure rate is up to 96 percent. Companies around the world realize the importance of innovation, but very few of them are able to bring ideas to fruition. Consulting firms such as IDEO, Doblin Group, and BCG have provided guidelines and tips to help. Innovation requires the courage to change the rules of the game in the following areas: business model, networking, enabling process, core process, performance, product system, service, channel, brand, and customer experience.

But exactly how does innovation happen? Washington University psychologist R. Keith Sawyer, author of *Explaining Creativity: The Science of Human Innovation*, shared some of the secrets with us. First, when a person is creative, the person's brain is utilizing the same mental building blocks as they typically use in daily life, not unlike what one does when facing a traffic jam. Second, there are multiple subareas in our brains. We use different parts of our brain when we relax or work. Creative ideas can come from any part of the brain. Therefore, the "a-ha" moment might happen during dinner or in the shower, depending on the proximity of the problem needing to be solved to the part of the brain being used. Third, ideas do not come from one single incident. They are the products of what came before. The key is collaborating with people of different disciplines. Fourth, nobody is creative at everything. But one must know a particular subject very well and everything about that area before they can try to be creative with cross-pollination within different categories of the subject.

Technology is a prime area for product innovation. But a simple idea such as Netflix's convenient process and the sliding cutter on the Saran Plastic Wrap box are examples of non-high-tech innovations. This type of innovation comes from attention paid to details of what the product can do "for the customers," not what the company can sell to the customers. Some of the innovative inspirations are from fashioning products, visualizing the future, and understanding customer emotion.

To be creative, a company must start with the belief that creativity can come from both external and internal sources. External sources include co-creation with customers and other noncompany-related labs. Top management must take revolutionary action for the journey to successful innovations. Designated individuals such as change managers will further reinforce the importance and urgency. Like any good management, success should be closely tied to rewards. Below is a summary of what some of today's innovative leaders say about innovation in their corporations.

Innovative Leaders	Thoughts on Innovation
Craig Wynett, P&G	Make innovation the norm.
Thomas Fogarty, Three Arch Partners	Accept that what you create may not be the best.
Lieutenant General Ronald T. Kadish, U.S. Department of Defense	Reorganize frequently and allow the new structures to stimulate people.
Michael Dell, Dell Computers	Innovation is about taking risks and learning from failure. Make sure that people are not afraid of failure.
Hal Tovin, Citizens Financial Group	Hire people who have experience outside of the company.
Larry Keeley, Doblin	Look in places your competitor overlooked.
Nolan Bushnell, uWink	There is no such thing as a bad idea. Let others participate in the development of your ideas.
Luciano Maiani, European Organization for Nuclear Research	Do not underestimate science. Pure science is often a major driver of innovation.
Mike Lazaridis, Research in Motion	The key is building conviction. The company must go on despite differing opinions.

(continued)

Box 8.2 *(continued)*

Mark Dean, IBM Fellow	People should be encouraged to ask "what if?" and pursue what appears to be worthwhile.
John Talley, Microbia	Have passion. The mandatory partner of passion is diversity.
Marcian E. "Ted" Hoff, FTI/Teklicon	Bend the rule of "doing what the customer wants." Do something better.
Betty Cohen, Turner Broadcasting System	Use an experimental approach to encourage innovation. The biggest danger is complacency.
Daniel Vasella, Novartis	Make innovation meaningful by aligning business objectives with the company's ideals.
David Falvey, British Geological Survey	Stop internal competition. Use a matrix structure to spur innovation.
Esther Dyson, EDventure Holdings	Don't try to innovate for its own sake, but to find creative solutions to real problems.

Sources: "A Creative Corporation Toolbox," *BusinessWeek,* August 1, 2005, p. 72; "Inspiring Innovation," *Harvard Business Review,* August 2002, p. 39; David Kirkpatrick, "Throw It at the Wall and See If It Sticks," *Fortune,* December 12, 2005, pp. 142–150; Jason Pontin, "The Rules of Innovation," *Technology Review,* May 2005, p. 12; Serge Bloch, "The Hidden Secrets of the Creative Mind," *Time,* January 16, 2006, p. 89.

---

was built in 2004 by a team of electrical, computer, and mechanical engineers lead by Shigeyuki Hori, an engineer at Toyota. Hori says that it was the first time the three groups of engineers had worked together. The result is greater fuel-efficiency, fewer smog-forming emissions, and a better-handling vehicle with improved acceleration. In 2005, Toyota sold more than 54,000 Priuses and kept a waiting list six months long.[103]

Another example of good teamwork is the development of the Razr, Motorola's very thin and ultra-light cell phone model. The project was undertaken at an off-site location, the innovation lab in Chicago. To expedite production, engineers, designers, and marketers came together away from the usual laboratory and the company campus to avoid distractions.[104] The innovation lab was not designed like the traditional R&D unit. In the innovation lab, scientists and engineers worked together, not independently as they did in the traditional R&D center. Ideas and products were passed back and forth among team members. In this innovative lab, things happened almost simultaneously. Glitches could be worked out on the spot. The process cut down on lead time and red tape and brought energy and inspiration. These barrier-minimizing labs have been used at Mattel, Boeing, Wrigley, and other well-known U.S. firms.[105]

Another barrier breaker was to encourage mingling and social time among units. After having some social contact, even mechanics were comfortable enough to bypass the bureaucracy and contact the engineers directly for changes.[106] Exhibit 8.10 presents ideas about how to build a successful innovation lab by Tom Kelley, general manager of IDEO.

Exhibit 8.10

Tom Kelley's Four Best-Practice Ideas for a Successful Innovation Lab

Establish a "home" for idea development.	Set aside a location to welcome staffers; encourage them to visit frequently and bounce ideas back and forth with each other.
Use pictorials.	Provide ample space, flip charts, whiteboards, writing pads, and other types of writing and sketching surfaces.
No idea is too foolish.	Encourage as many ideas as possible during brainstorming and avoid judgment. Avoid any structural issues that could get in the way at this stage.
Create the "lab" atmosphere.	Like any lab, the innovation lab should be stocked with items such as prototyping materials, markers, sticky notes, glue, coloring pens, and the like.

Sources: Adapted from Joseph Weber, with Stanley Holmes and Christopher Palmeri, " 'Mosh Pits' of Creativity," *BusinessWeek,* November 7, 2005, pp. 98–100.

INNOVATING AT ALL STAGES OF THE LIFE CYCLE

A widespread belief is that firms need to innovate at the early stages of a product life cycle, but as the product grows and matures, attention should be placed more on managing price points and volume sales. The underlying assumption is that a product becomes more of a commodity when it matures, in which case differentiating it further through innovation is not cost efficient, nor is it effective, as the focus should be on new product development in order to start the next phase of the innovation cycle. Even so, in a recent book, *Dealing with Darwin*, Moore suggests that firms have to deal with innovation in every phase of a product's life cycle, regardless of whether a product is at the introductory or the maturation, or even the declining phase.[107]

This is accomplished by an understanding of two distinct and opposing modalities in business, each with its own logic: complex systems and volume operations. **Complex systems** specialize in tackling complex problems to arrive at customized solutions, a case where the logic of differentiation dominates. **Volume operations**, on the other hand, specialize in serving volume markets through standardized products and transactions, a case in which the logic of standardization dominates. Sustainable competitive advantage is built on either of these two logics, but not by a combination of the two.[108]

Based on this underlying logic, different innovation types can be mapped against different stages of a product's life cycle (see Exhibit 8.11). Moore organizes various innovation types into four clusters or innovation zones: (1) **The Product Leadership Zone**, where innovations occur within the growth phase of a product category; (2) **The Consumer Intimacy Zone**, where innovations occur within the growth phase of a product category; (3) **The Operational Excellence Zone**, where innovations occur on the supply side with the end-in-view of lowering the firm's cost structure; and (4) **The Category Renewal Zone**, where innovations occur within the declining stage.[109]

While it is good to know the different types of innovation, it is even more im-

Exhibit 8.11   **Innovation Across the Technology Adoption Life Cycle**

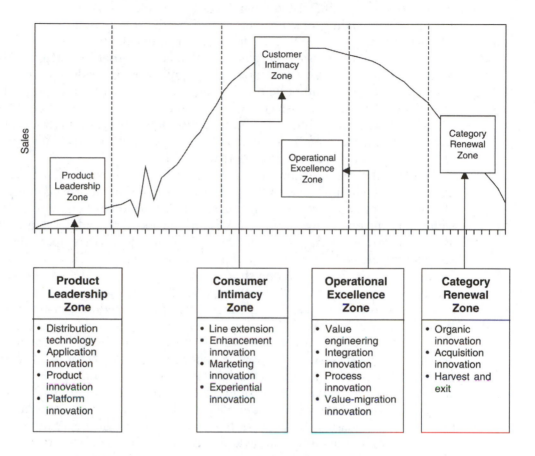

Product Leadership Zone	**Consumer Intimacy Zone**	**Operational Excellence Zone**	**Category Renewal Zone**
• Distribution technology • Application innovation • Product innovation • Platform innovation	• Line extension • Enhancement innovation • Marketing innovation • Experiential innovation	• Value engineering • Integration innovation • Process innovation • Value-migration innovation	• Organic innovation • Acquisition innovation • Harvest and exit

Source: Adapted from Geoffrey A. Moore, *Dealing with Darwin: How Great Companies Innovate at Every Phase of Their Evolution* (New York: HarperCollins, 2005), p. 62.

portant to place them into the context of the firm's overall strategy. In this regard, Moore recommends a number of tasks.[110] Management has to recognize and choose the appropriate innovation strategy (i.e., conduct a "core-context" analysis) that is oriented to differentiation (complex systems) or standardization (volume operations) in each innovation zone. Depending on this selection, management can then build a portfolio of programs and core competencies to support them in ways that lead to a deep advantage over the firm's strongest competitor. Finally, Moore argues for widespread implementation activities, including team management, aggressive planning, the involvement of top performers, and continuous attention to these processes.

Any extension to a global context entails the development of even more distinctive competencies. Specifically, the emphasis on the consumer intimacy zone requires a deep understanding of customers' needs in the local culture (see Chapter 5 on international marketing). Within the operational excellence zone, the firm needs to know how volume transactions can be scaled across broad segments of the market. Komatsu's success in the earth-moving-equipment (EME) industry can be attributed to its ability to hone and build quality and cost efficiencies in its products in Japan (product leadership zone), selecting geographical markets where it could harness its advantages while avoiding direct competition with its main adversary, Caterpillar (consumer intimacy zone), and then enter the U.S. market only after it was capable of challenging Caterpillar (category renewal zone).

All in all, there is little question that innovation has become one of the key imperatives for organizations today. One reason arises from the improved competitiveness of new competitors. Firms from China and India, as well as neighboring Vietnam, in addition to the emerging markets in Eastern Europe, have entered the world market using entry strategies that are typically based on low-cost leadership. Firms that are not able to compete in this light have to refashion their capabilities and actions elsewhere. Exciting new products based on strategic innovation provide an alternative route to success. Moreover, as this chapter has pointed out, even in markets that have yet to be challenged by low-cost leaders, incumbent firms need to transform themselves. With the knowledge-based, digital economy, consumers are more educated and more empowered. They are most likely waiting for new and better improvements, as reflected in their expectations for new cell phone features, new forms of entertainment, and new fashion designs. Within this Internet-centric environment, consumer changes and technologies designed to accommodate them are constantly in flux. Companies that sit too long on their laurels are bound to find themselves left behind in the race to capture new market segments or to defend old ones. Strategic innovation entails radical rethinking about the innovation process itself (i.e., open rather then closed innovation), as well as revolutionary ways to reignite corporate cultures in order to ensure continuous renewal and transformation.

SUMMARY

1. Developing innovative capabilities is the fourth way in which a firm can leverage its strategy and competitive advantage in international markets. It complements international marketing, global sourcing, and strategic partnerships. It involves the basic transformation of a firm's business model.
2. Despite the need for innovation, many firms have not been able to harness this capability for at least two reasons: first, they are unable to distinguish the innovative context in a knowledge-based, digital economy, as opposed to the traditional industrial age; second, they lack a meaningful process for innovation.
3. The three drivers of the knowledge-based, digital economy are: (a) new technologies, (b) new structures for consumption, and (c) new logic or institutions that align people, markets, and technologies.
4. Two technological truths dominate the knowledge-based, digital economy, and

are dubbed as "laws" because of their pervasiveness: (a) Moore's law refers to the doubling of computing (density) power every eighteen months, and (b) Metcalfe's law says that the value of a network increases by the square of the number of users. Taken together, they have changed the informational and computational boundaries that previously constrained human analytic abilities.

5. The new structure of consumption relates to: (a) one-to-one consumption, or the mass customization of consumers' needs, and (b) personalized experience/co-creation, or the proactive involvement of the consumer in value creation, particularly in high-end services.

6. A new logic and institution of realignment is needed because the standard enterprise logic that is based on transaction economics may no longer be adequate. Instead, deep and distributed economies based on relational support should be the appropriate paradigm.

7. The knowledge-based, digital economy affects business in the following manner: (a) it upholds the power of information over physical resources, (b) it shifts attention from mere processing of information to its transmission and distribution, (c) it creates greater linkages and connectivity, and (d) it can establish a "winner-take-all" market based on lock-in mechanisms.

8. Innovation is inextricably related to wealth and value creation. Value is created by providing a material that is in short supply, by adding useful features to an existing product, or by offering a new product and service altogether.

9. Three types of innovation are distinguished: product innovation (a new product, e.g., the iPod), process innovation (a new and refined process, e.g., just-in-time), and service innovation (a high-end experience, e.g., Cirque du Soliel).

10. The innovation success rate is a paltry 4.5 percent. Part of the problem is the inability of firms to recognize the changing context of innovation and creativity. Three concepts highlight this distinction and offer direct relevance to the knowledge-based, digital economy: (a) open innovation, or the sourcing of creative ideas outside of the firm, even outside of the industry; (b) disruptive innovation, or the offering of technologies with fewer product improvements but with significant customer value, which effectively trump conventional technologies; and (c) the Technology Adoption Life Cycle, which involved assessment of stages of a life cycle in terms of prospective consumers, and how the cycle can accommodate discontinuous or disruptive innovations.

11. Some recently published research touts the adoption of strategic innovation. This occurs when a firm redefines the consumer, its value proposition, and its delivery mechanism. Failure is often related to a poor process. To improve the process, the firm must do the following: (a) forget old ways of doing things in a systemic manner, (b) borrow systemically from others, and (c) learn relentlessly from multiple sources. Other suggestions include the following: The firm should (a) revitalize the company through renewal and transformation, (b) institutionalize activities that generate innovation, and (c) innovate at every stage of the firm's life cycle.

KEY TERMS

Knowledge-based, digitally economy
New technologies
Moore's law
Metcalfe's law
Increasing returns
Network effects
Complementary bandwagon effects
Individual consumption
Personalized experience
Co-production
Co-creation
Standard enterprise logic
Transactional economics
Deep support
Distributed economies
Locked-in market
Innovation
Market-based innovation
Product innovation
Innovative services
Process innovation
Sequential process

S-shaped innovation curve
Open innovation
Sustainable technologies
Disruptive technologies
Technology Adoption Life Cycle
Tipping
Connectors
Stickiness
Strategic innovations
Learning dynamics
kaizen
Complex systems
Volume operations
Product leadership zone
Consumer intimacy zone
Operational excellence zone
Category renewal zone

DISCUSSION QUESTIONS

1. Select one of the following high-technology sectors: semiconductors, computers, nanotechnology, or biotechnology. Discuss how one such industry has been affected by (a) new technologies, (b) new structures of consumption, and (c) a new logic or institution that aligns people, markets, and technologies.
2. What are the distinguishing characteristics of a knowledge-based, digital economy?
3. How does the innovation context differ between a knowledge-based, digital economy and the traditional economy based on the industrial age?
4. From your experience, define some new products, processes, and service innovations that you or your friends have or are using.
5. In what industries has open innovation been used? Why have firms been slow to recognize disruptive innovation and technologies? What are ways of "crossing the chasm"?

6. Look through *Fortune's* most recent issue on the World's Most Admired Companies. Select one or two of these firms. In your opinion, how have these firms been able to develop a systemic corporate culture that is also receptive to innovation?

ACTION ITEM 8.1. MINI-CASES

You will be divided in groups to discuss selected cases below.[111]

CASE 1

The Pacific Northwest has been stricken with a major earthquake, and there are indications that this tragic event might encompass California in the near future. Medical equipment, power, and resources are in extremely short supply. What kinds of logistical, strategic, and political solutions may need to be created to work effectively and quickly?

CASE 2

Doctors Without Borders has discovered that there is an epidemic of depression running rife through several large Brazilian tribes in a remote area of the Amazon. Disappearance of the rain forests is suspected as one causal agent; however, a second problem exists. In this particular tribal culture, there is a strongly held belief that admitting to depression is anathema to a person's strength and social worth. How can the doctors creatively come up with a solution to get people the treatment they need?

CASE-IN-POINT. THE SEOUL OF DESIGN

BILL BREEN[112]

Samsung used to be known for cheap knockoff electronics. Now it's a red-hot global brand, thanks to sleek, bold, and beautiful products. It transformed itself by opening to the outside world—and looking deep within its Korean heart.

On the third floor of the Time Warner Center in New York, just below Thomas Keller's $210-a-plate and perpetually booked restaurant Per Se, is Samsung's equally sleek offering, where you don't need a reservation. Walk through the glass doors that look out onto Columbus Circle, pass by a forest of plasma screens, and you'll see the future as the Korean electronics giant would have it.

Elegant and austere, the Samsung Experience showroom invites visitors to live, work, and play in a luxurious, fully operational world of network-controlled refrigerators, "hygienic power" vacuum cleaners, nanotechnology-enabled air purifiers, steam-cleaning microwave ovens, ultra-light notebook computers, sumo-sized liquid-crystal display TVs, near-silent laser printers, all-in-one digital cameras, and dozens of do-everything cell phones. The place amounts to a temple for the hip and technocentric; on a typical Saturday, it draws more than 1,500 acolytes.

Twelve years ago, Samsung's enigmatic chairman, Kun Hee Lee, endured a different kind of experience when he visited a decidedly inelegant electronics retailer in Los Angeles. Lee found his company's products gathering dust on the store's back shelves, ignored by even the salespeople. American consumers, he realized, regarded the Korean company's wares as cheap, toylike knockoffs, best suited for the discount bin. Right there, he decided that Samsung's very survival in the U.S. market was in peril.

Not long after that visit, Lee issued a manifesto to Samsung's top executives, which he later repeated in a book, *Change Begins With Me.* "Management is still clinging to the concept of quantity at the expense of quality," he declared. "We will become a third-rate company. We must change no matter what." He implored workers to "change everything except your wife and family"—a decree that is still talked about within Samsung. To shatter old work habits, he ordered that henceforth, every Samsung employee must report for work two hours early.

Lee's ultimate aim was simple and audacious: To seize the future, Samsung would have to catapult to the uppermost ranks of the world's first-class brands; it would have to become a company whose vast array of digital products not only met people's needs but also captured their imaginations. Today, Samsung has come a long way from its humble, homely past. The consulting outfit Interbrand calculates that it's the world's fastest-growing brand over the past five years: Samsung is now the world leader in CDMA cell phones; it's battling Motorola for the number-two spot, behind Nokia, in total handsets sold; it also tops the global markets for color televisions, flash memory, and LCD panels—key battlegrounds in its quest to one day dominate the digital era. Last year, Samsung racked up $10.3 billion in earnings on $55.3 billion in sales, which made it the world's most profitable tech company.

This year, to be sure, Samsung has hit some headwind in the form of plunging profits and a political scandal in Korea. And in October, the company agreed to pay a $300 million criminal fine for conspiring to fix computer-chip prices in the United States. Despite those woes, Samsung's shares are trading at a near record high; it has just launched a global marketing campaign, and it's on pace to ship 28 million units in the United States alone. Back in its homeland, Samsung might be unloved, but it is greatly respected for its growth, its technological prowess, its 20.7 percent share of Korea's total exports, and for transforming the tagline "made in Korea" from a pejorative to a source of pride. Samsung has, indeed, changed everything.

The change began with Lee's bet that in a world where products are rapidly becoming commodities, Samsung would never thrive through scale and pricing power alone. It had to create stylish, premium digital products that sparked customers' emotions with elegant, human-centered design. Lee foresaw that Samsung could wield design as a competitive weapon and use it to transform itself from an also-ran imitator to a world-class innovator. Steve Jobs may be the rock star of product design, but the reclusive Lee, a sixty-three-year-old billionaire who is little known outside his native country, has arguably done more, on a larger scale, to seize on design's ability to create great business opportunities. And by some measures, Samsung has even surpassed

Apple in the quest for design excellence. Over the past five years, Samsung has won more awards from the Industrial Design Society of America (IDSA) than any other company on the planet. "Samsung is one of the world's most respected companies for its designs," says Michelle Berryman, executive vice president of IDSA and a principal at Echo Visualization, an Atlanta-based design consultancy. "Its flat-panel TVs, for example, are so elegant that people are willing to pay a premium for them, just like the iPod."

Samsung's success is all the more remarkable given that it was more than a decade in the making. Twelve years ago, Lee dispatched his design adviser, Tamio Fukuda, to assess the state of Samsung design. Fukuda's conclusion: Samsung lacked a design identity; its product development process was primitive; and its top managers discounted design's value. In other words, Samsung was not unlike most corporations of the day. To change that, the company put years into building a sustainable design culture—one that is simultaneously innovative and global, yet reflective of Korea's ancient culture.

WIRED NATION

Today's Korea just might be the most technologically advanced country on earth. More than 75 percent of its households are wired with high-speed Internet connections, which operate at many times the speed of U.S. broadband. An equal percentage of Koreans own cell phones; Seoul commuters often pass the time watching live, satellite-TV broadcasts on their handsets. For Samsung, the country amounts to one vast lab for testing consumer reactions to bleeding-edge digital technologies.

For all of its striking modernity, though, Korea remains in many ways a traditional society. Over the past twenty-three centuries, the Korean peninsula was repeatedly conquered and occupied by China, Mongolia, and Japan, each of which left behind its own indelible cultural imprint. Chief among these is a neo-Confucian mode of thinking that values authority and order above all else. As chairman, Lee commands absolute respect within Samsung; as one designer put it, his pronouncements "are like a page out of the Bible." In one such pronouncement, Lee issued a clarion call for making design a core asset in the company's bid to transform itself: "An enterprise's most vital assets lie in its design and other creative capabilities. I believe that the ultimate winners of the 21st century will be determined by these skills." The quotation, framed, occupies a place of honor in a corner office belonging to Kook Hyun Chung, chief of Samsung's Corporate Design Center. "To hear, from the chairman's own mouth, how much he valued design was absolutely shocking," Chung says.

Lee could issue edicts. He could send a delegation of Samsung executives to the Art Center College of Design, in Pasadena, California, to lay plans to launch an in-house design school at Samsung. He could quickly build a $10 million, state-of-the-art facility in downtown Seoul to house the result, the Innovative Design Lab of Samsung, or IDS. And he could add millions more to fund the school's programs and pay the student designers' salaries. But even the Emperor of Samsung couldn't change the corporate mindset, which was imitative, hypercompetitive, and ultra resistant to change.

Samsung—the name means "three stars" in Korean—was founded by Lee's father in 1938 as an exporter of rice, sugar, and fish. And Samsung, at its core, remained a commodity company well into the 1990s. Many of its managers couldn't—or wouldn't—value design. "Samsung was a technology company whose management thinking came out of exporting rice," says Gordon Bruce, a veteran design consultant who, along with fellow Art Center faculty member James Miho, helped Samsung set up IDS. "There was no design involved. It was all about keeping the price down and outselling the other guy."

When Bruce and Miho, a pioneering graphic designer, audited the state of Samsung design, other problems quickly surfaced: the company's neo-Confucian culture led its designers to imitate the masters of their industry, which at that time were Sony and IBM. The result: Samsung had failed to develop a distinctive design identity of its own. The company's middle managers were so competitive that they kept ideas to themselves—"the place was just shark infested," says Brace—which stymied efforts to create a collaborative, risk-taking environment. And because Samsung's engineers controlled the product-development process, engineering constraints choked off any notion of design becoming an end in itself.

Bruce and Miho soon realized that a Western-style curriculum modeled on the Art Center's program would never meet the needs of Samsung's designers. They had to find a way to make managers allies of design. But the biggest challenge of all was to unlearn old, ingrained ways of thinking—to create a new Samsung mind.

SUMMONING THE GAIATSU

Bruce and Miho threw out the Art Center's curriculum and invented something new. Some of the resulting initiatives were highly tactical—quick hits aimed at forging a collaborative work environment. Designers were required to take a yearlong course in mechanical engineering to better prepare them to defend their ideas. "Before they could design a product, they had to know how to make it work," Bruce says. Up-and-coming engineers and managers from other disciplines were also brought into IDS so they could learn to work with designers—and designers could learn to work with them. Such partnerships are the principle behind Samsung's Creating New Business Group, an elite team of designers, technologists, and experts in marketing and manufacturing, who study consumers and create what-if scenarios, all in an effort to glean the world's future buying habits.

IDS also took on the larger challenge of breaking the Korean practice of education through memorization. Now the students would learn by doing. To gain a better understanding of their own cultural heritage, for example, they produced a DVD on Sokkuram, a mountain shrine that houses a peerless eighth-century statue of Buddha.

Often, progress came slowly. In one class assignment, Bruce asked his students to present what they considered to be a perfectly designed object. His own choice: a banana. "Nature is the best designer," he told them. "The banana fits in your pocket. It comes in its own sanitary package. It's biodegradable. And the color indicates when the fruit is ripe." For a moment, a befuddled silence cloaked the class. Then came a question: "You mean," asked one student, "you want us to design a cell phone in the shape of a banana?"

Miho decided that Samsung's designers most needed a *gaiatsu*, the Japanese term for an outside force that delivers great change. He wanted IDS's students to experience profoundly original ideas at the source. And so Samsung's *gaiatsu* became the world at large. Miho and Bruce launched the Global Design Workshop, a traveling tutorial in which a couple dozen students visited the world's great design centers: Athens, Delhi, Florence, London, New York, and beyond. "In Paris, we discussed the designs of the Imperial Class of Louis XIV," Miho recalls. "In Berlin, we saw how Germany was once divided, just like Korea is now—and yet the Germans still produced incredibly original designs, like the Mercedes-Benz. We visited the Smithsonian Institution in Washington and saw the earliest model of the Apple computer. They were surprised by how primitive it looked, but they finally understood that it's the idea that matters."

Samsung has continued, through its Design Power Program, to send its most promising designers to study at the world's top universities and institutions. And the company has beefed up its global presence by launching design studios in London, Los Angeles, Milan, San Francisco, Shanghai, and Tokyo.

DEFINING AN IDENTITY

Samsung's in-house school gave its designers the tools and confidence to risk thinking differently. But there remained an equally vexing challenge: the company lacked a universal design ethos—a measurable, clearly defined set of principles that its designers could replicate and its customers could intuitively understand. Samsung's instinct was to develop a design language that grew out of Korean culture. But that proved equally hard to define. China's Han, Ming, and Tang dynasties, as well as the Mongols, Russians, Japanese, and even American missionaries had all left elements of their cultures on the peninsula. Unearthing a true Korean character proved difficult, but Samsung discovered it in the Tae Kuk—the yin-yang symbol found on the South Korean flag that represents the simultaneous unity and duality of all things. From the Tae Kuk, Samsung developed its touchstone: "Balance of Reason and Feeling."

"Reason and feeling are opposites, but they are essential to each other," says Sangyeon Lee, who heads Samsung's San Francisco design studio. "In design terms, 'reason' is rational, sharp-edged, and very geometric. 'Feeling' is soft and organic—it makes an emotional connection with the user. Taken together, reason and feeling give us a way to frame our design identity, which is always evolving."

A task force spent a year developing and perfecting a scale, with reason at one end and feeling on the other, which is now used to ensure that every single product design hews to Samsung's brand positioning. That generally falls near the scale's center, thereby striking a balance. Samsung did the same with two other key words: "simplicity" and "complexity." Here, Samsung generally hews closer to simplicity—it wants its designs to be intuitive and humanistic. Samsung even maps its competitors on the two scales: In one recent analysis, Apple occupied the "simplicity/feeling" zone, with Sony in the "complexity/reason" field. Samsung seeks out the areas where there are no competitors—that's where opportunity lies.

Samsung undertook a particularly difficult balancing act with its design for the YP-T8 portable media player, which hit the North American market this fall. The company's product planners landed heavily on the "reason/complexity" end of the spectrum by stuffing the palm-sized gadget with features: FM radio, voice recorder, photo viewer, text viewer, game functions, and video and audio playback. The device was packed with so many functions that its initial, rough design was "machinelike and rectangular—not so user friendly," recalls Miri Lee, the T8's Seoul-based designer.

To strike the right balance on the T8's design continuum, Miri Lee had to pull the device back to the center, toward "feeling/simplicity." Lee began by drawing a series of squares, each containing a different product spec. She layered the squares on top of one another, hoping to find a form that could elegantly contain the device's functions. "Each square was like a black hole that took in all my thoughts," she says. "The more squares I drew, the more design problems I had to resolve."

Lee strove to give the device a soft, feminine feel, with a curved shape so users could grip and operate it easily with one hand. Her design team struggled to pare away as many control keys as possible. Eventually, they came up with three clickable buttons that are centered beneath an outsized, horizontal LCD screen. They spent additional weeks tweaking every detail, from the fit and finish of the T8's silicone case to the color and size of the fonts on the display screen, all in an effort to give the device a minimalist look and feel. Lee refined the T8's cell-phone-like shape by dipping into Samsung's Idea Bank—a global database of design concepts that initially failed to find their way to market but are valuable enough to be recycled into new products at a later date. There, she found the basic design language for the T8's rounded shape and large screen, then translated it to better fit the tiny media player.

How did Lee know she had struck the right balance between form and function? She says she simply felt it in her gut. And that's a sure sign, as Sangyeon Lee suggests, that designers have found a Tae Kuk unity and duality of their own: they are simultaneously thinking for themselves and thinking the Samsung way.

CASE DISCUSSION QUESTIONS

1. What are Samsung's achievements in the design area?
2. How did Samsung accomplish this level of success?
3. How did Samsung combine the traditional and global culture together?
4. What is *gaiatsu*? How does it help Samsung?
5. Is the innovative design model carried out by Samsung transferable? Why and why not?

NOTES FOR CHAPTER 8

1. "Poll: Innovation Defines Apple," *MacWorld Daily News*, Wednesday, November 19, 2003, available at www.macworld.co.uk/mac/news/index.cfm?newsid=7314.

2. This section summarizes the article, "The Seed of Apple's Innovation," *BusinessWeek Online*, October 12, 2004, available at www.businessweek.com/bwdaily/dnflash/oct2004/nf20041012_4018_db083.htm.

3. See Donald Sull with Yong Wang, *Made in China: What Western Managers Can Learn from Trailblazing Chinese Entrepreneurs* (Boston: Harvard Business School Press, 2005).

4. Robert Berner and Diane Brady, "Get Creative," *BusinessWeek*, August 1, 2005, pp. 60–68.

5. Vijay Govindarajan and Chris Trimble, *10 Rules for Strategic Innovators* (Boston: Harvard Business School Press, 2006), pp. 1–2.

6. This section is based largely from Gerardo R. Ungson and John Trudel, *Engines of Prosperity* (London: Imperial Press, 1999), pp. 37–38.

7. John W. Wilson, "America's High-Tech Crisis: Why Silicon Valley Is Losing Its Edge," *BusinessWeek*, March 11, 1985.

8. For a good discussion from one involved in trade negotiations when the leadership changed, see Clyde Prestowitz, *Trading Places: How We Allowed Japan to Take the Lead* (New York: Basic Books, 1988).

9. See Ungson and Trudel, *Engines of Prosperity*, pp. 202–204.

10. Shoshana Zuboff and James Maxmin, *The Support Economy* (New York: Penguin Books, 2002), pp. 31–33.

11. James L. Koch and Regis McKenna, "Where Technology and Tradition Meet," *STS Nexus* 1, no. 1 (Winter 2001), pp. 5–11.

12. "Less is Moore," *Economist*, May 10, 2003.

13. Koch and McKenna, "Where Technology and Tradition Meet."

14. Joel Mokyr, *The Lever of Riches: Technological Creativity and Economic Progress* (New York: Oxford University Press, 1990).

15. Ibid.

16. "The Hitchhiker's Guide to Cybernomics," *Economist*, September 28, 1996, p. 8.

17. Koch and McKenna, "Where Technology and Tradition Meet."

18. Ibid.

19. W. Brian Arthur, "Increasing Returns and the New World of Business," *Harvard Business Review* (July/August 1996): 92–144.

20. See W. Brian Arthur, "Positive Feedback in the Economy," *Scientific American* (February 1990): 92–144; also see Arthur, "Increasing Returns," p. 102.

21. A good discussion of network effects is found in Arthur, "Positive Feedbacks in the Economy," p. 99. For complementary bandwagon effects, see H. Leibenstein, "Bandwagon, Snob, and Veblen Effects in the Theory of Consumers' Demand," *Quarterly Journal of Economics*, 64, no. 2 (May 1950): 183–207 and Jeffrey H. Rohlfs, *Bandwagon Effects in High Technology Industries* (Boston: MIT Press, 2003).

22. This section is based on Zuboff and Maxmin, *The Support Economy*, pp. 93–102.

23. Zuboff and Maxmin, *The Support Economy*, p. 11. This next section draws heavily from this source.

24. C.K. Prahalad and V. Ramaswamy, *The Future of Competition* (Boston: Harvard Business School Press, 2005), pp. 8–10; also see Peter Mills, *Managing Service Industries: Organizational Practices in a Postindustrial Economy* (New York: Ballinger, Harper & Row, 1986).

25. See Zuboff and Maxmin, *The Support Economy*, pp. 318–382.

26. Ibid., p. 179.

27. Ibid.

28. Ibid., pp. 321–22. Another perspective of how firms can build wealth through a collaborative community is presented by Raymond E. Miles, Grant Miles, and Charles C. Snow, *Collaborative Entrepreneurship* (Stanford, CA: Stanford University Press, 2005).

29. See Stephan Haeckel, *Adaptive Enterprise: Creating and Leading Sense-and-Respond Organizations* (Boston: Harvard Business School Press, 1999).

30. The section draws heavily on Gerardo R. Ungson and John Trudel, *Engines of Prosperity:*

Templates for the Information Age (London, United Kingdom: Imperial College Press, 1998), pp. 38–47.

31. Philip Evans and Thomas Wurster, *Blown to Bits: How the New Economics of Information Transforms Strategy* (Boston: Harvard Business School Press, 2000); and Jim Taylor and Watts Wacker, *The 500-Year Delta* (New York: Harper Business, 1997), p. 115.

32. Arthur, "Increasing Returns," p. 102.

33. Charles W. Hill, "Establishing a Standard: Competitive Strategy and Technological Standards in Winner-Take-All Industries," *Academy of Management Executive* 11, no. 2 (May 1997): 7–26.

34. P.A. David, "Clio and the Economics of QWERTY," *American Economic Review* 75, no. 2 (1985): 332–37.

35. Rafael Ramirez, "Value Co-production: Intellectual Origins and Implications for Practice and Research," *Strategic Management Journal* 20, no. 1 (January 1999): 49–65.

36. Philip Kotler and Gary Armstrong, *Principles of Marketing,* 7th ed. (Englewood Cliffs, NJ: Prentice Hall, 1996), p. 308.

37. James Brian Quinn, "Software Sparks an Innovation Explosion," in *Mastering Global Business* (London: Financial Times Management, 1999), pp. 96–102.

38. Andy Reinhardt and Elizabeth Johnson, "Cell Phones for the People," *BusinessWeek*, November 14, 2005, p. 65.

39. Om Malik, "The New Land of Opportunity," *Business 2.0*, July 2004, pp. 72–79.

40. Telis Demos, "Lenovo's Sweet Cell of Success," *Fortune*, November 28, 2005, p. 38.

41. Reinhardt and Johnson, "Cell Phones for the People," p. 65.

42. David Rocks and Moon Ihlwan, "Samsung Design," *BusinessWeek*, December 6, 2004, pp. 88–96.

43. "The Best Product Designs of 2005," *BusinessWeek*, July 4, 2005, pp. 60–72.

44. Robert Berner and Diane Brady, "Get Creative," *BusinessWeek*, August 1, 2005, pp. 60–68.

45. Roger O. Crockett, "Will That Be Cash, Credit, or Cell?" *BusinessWeek*, June 27, 2005, p. 42.

46. David Kiley, Tom Lowry, and Ronald Grover, "The End of TV (As You Know It)," *BusinessWeek*, November 21, 2005, p. 40.

47. John Hagel III and John Seely Brown, "The Shifting Industrial Landscape," *Optimize*, April 2005, p. 30.

48. Berner and Brady, "Get Creative," p. 64.

49. Colin Snow, "Managing Process Innovation," *Optimize*, September 2005, pp. 81–84.

50. Hagel III and Brown, "The Shifting Industrial Landscape," p. 30.

51. Mannijeet Kripalani, "Getting the Best to the Masses," *BusinessWeek*, October 11, 2005, pp. 174–78.

52. Hagel III and Brown, "The Shifting Industrial Landscape," p. 30.

53. Robert D. Hof with Peter Burrows, Steve Hamm, Diane Brady, and Ian Rowley, "Building an Idea Factory," *BusinessWeek*, October 11, 2004, pp. 192–200.

54. Ibid., p. 198.

55. "A Creative Corporation Toolbox," *BusinessWeek*, September 5, 2005, p. 72.

56. Jason Pontin, "The Rules of Innovation," *Technology Review*, May 2005, p. 12.

57. A S-shaped innovation curve is characterized by the rapid diffusion of new innovations creating a steep S-curve, followed by a slower rate of adoption of other technologies, which explains the gradual sloping of the curve. See Everett Rogers, *The Diffusion of Innovations* (New York: The Free Press, 2003).

58. Hof, "Building an Idea Factory, " p. 194.

59. Ibid.

60. Henry W. Chesbrough, *Open Innovation: The New Imperative for Creating and Profiting from Technology* (Boston: Harvard Business School Press, 2003), pp. 2, 8.

61. Ibid., pp. 93–95.

62. "From Open Innovation to Open Business Models: An Interview with Henry Chesbrough, by Michael Docherty," *PDMA Visions Magazine*, June 2007.

63. Ibid.

64. For more information, see InnoCentive website at www.innocentive.com/.

65. John Seely Brown and John Hagel III, "From Push to Pull: The Next Frontier of Innovation," *McKinsey Quarterly* 3 (June 2005). Available at www.mckinseyquarterly.com/article_page.aspx?ar=1642&L2=21&L3=37.

66. Darren J. Carroll, "Distributed R&D Case Study: InnoCentive," Lecture notes, Managing Innovation: Emerging Trends (March 5, 2005), Boston, MA: MIT OpenCourseWare.

67. Clayton M. Christensen, *The Innovator's Dilemma: When New Technologies Cause Great Firms to Fail* (Boston: Harvard Business School Press, 1997), particularly pages 4–23.

68. Ibid., p. 18.

69. Clayton M. Christensen, "Riding the Waves of Disruptive Change," *Electronic Engineering Times*, December 5, 2005, pp. 9–10.

70. Rick Merritt, "The Zen of Disruption," *Electronic Engineering Times*, December 5, 2005, p. 3.

71. Geoffrey A. Moore, *Crossing the Chasm* (New York: HarperCollins, 2002).

72. Geoffrey A. Moore, *Inside the Tornado: Strategies for Developing, Leveraging, and Surviving Hypergrowth Markets* (New York: HarperCollins, 2004), p. 19.

73. Ibid., p. 20.

74. Ibid., Preface, Book Jacket.

75. Ibid., p. 22.

76. Malcolm Gladwell, *The Tipping Point: How Little Things Can Make a Big Difference* (New York: Little Brown, 2000), pp. 9–11; also see pp. 42–43 (Connectors) and pp. 92–93 (Stickiness factor).

77. Vijay Govindarajan and Chris Trimble, *10 Rules for Strategic Innovators* (Boston: Harvard Business School Press, 2005).

78. Ibid., xvii–xviii.

79. Ibid., pp. 3–4.

80. Ibid. The three points were abridged from pp. 7–9.

81. The topic of organizational change has been well researched over the past decades by numerous academic fields. Among the early pioneers was Kurt Lewin who introduced the triadic concepts of unfreezing, changing, and refreezing that correspond to Govindarajan and Trimble's most recent formulation of forgetting, borrowing, and learning. See Kurt Lewin, "Frontiers in Group Dynamics: Concept, Method, and Reality in Social Science," *Human Relations* (1947) 1: 5–40.

82. This topic has been extensively researched and represented in the following sources: "How Organizations Learn and Unlearn," in Paul C. Nystrom and William H. Starbuck (eds.), *The Handbook of Organizational Design* (New York: Oxford University Press, 1981), pp. 3–27; and William H. Starbuck, Arent Greve, and Bo L. Hedberg, "Responding to Crisis," *Journal of Business Administration* (1978), no. 9: 111–37. An excellent article on adaptation is Alan D. Meyer, "Adapting to Environmental Jolts," *Administrative Science Quarterly* 27, no. 4 (1982): 515–37.

83. Gary Hamel (with Bill Breen), *The Future of Management* (Boston, MA: Harvard Business School Press, 2007).

84. Ibid., pp. 35–41.

85. Berner and Brady, "Get Creative," p. 66.

86. Ibid., p. 63.

87. Hof, "Building an Idea Factory," p. 178.

88. Berner and Brady, "Get Creative," p. 67.

89. Erin White, "Theory & Practice: Rethinking the Quality-Improvement Program," *Wall Street Journal*, September 19, 2005, p. B3.

90. Berner and Brady, "Get Creative" p. 63.

91. Ibid.

92. Ibid.

93. Ibid.

94. Tom Kelley with Jonathan Littman, "The 10 Faces of Innovation," *Fast Company*, October 2005, pp. 74–77.

95. Berner and Brady, "Get Creative," p. 67.

96. Ibid.

97. Hof, "Building an Idea Factory," p. 195.

98. Ibid., p. 200.

99. Ibid., p. 198.

100. Anne Underwood, "Nature's Design Workshop," *Newsweek*, September 26, 2005, p. 55.

101. Ibid.

102. Hof, "Building an Idea Factory," p. 198.

103. "The 2005 Wired Rave Awards," *Wired*, March 2005, pp. 83–96.

104. Joseph Weber with Stanley Holmes and Christopher Palmeri, " 'Mosh Pits' of Creativity," *BusinessWeek*, November 7, 2005, pp. 98–100.

105. Ibid., p. 99.

106. Ibid., p. 100.

107. Geoffrey A. Moore, *Dealing with Darwin: How Great Companies Innovate at Every Phase of Their Evolution* (New York: Penguin Books, 2005).

108. Ibid., pp. 29–30.

109. Ibid., pp. 62–72.

110. Ibid., pp. 256–60.

111. Some of the examples are drawn from Joel Nicholson's teaching notes (IBUS 330-International Business and Multicultural Relations, San Francisco, California).

112. Bill Breen, "The Seoul of Design," *Fast Company* 101, December 2005, pp. 90–95. Reprinted with permission.

PART I: THE GLOBAL CONTEXT

1. Global Strategic Management: An Overview

PART II: EXTERNAL / INTERNAL ANALYSIS

2. Analyzing the External Environment
3. Formulating Strategy and Developing a Business Model

PART III: STRATEGIC CHOICE AND POSITIONING

4. Positioning Strategic Choices in a Global Context

PART IV: LEVERAGING COMPETITIVE ADVANTAGE

5. Leveraging Advantage Through Global Marketing
6. Leveraging Advantage Through Global Sourcing
7. Leveraging Competitive Advantage Through Strategic Alliances
8. Leveraging Advantage Through Innovation

PART V: IMPLEMENTING THE STRATEGIC PLAN

9. Implementing Strategy Using Structures and Processes
10. Implementing Strategy by Cultivating a Global Mindset
11. Implementing Strategy Using Financial Performance Measures

PART VI: INTEGRATION

12. Integration and Emerging Issues in Global Strategic Management

9 Implementing Strategy Using Structures and Processes

*I like to tell people that all of our products and business will go through three phases.
There's vision, patience, and execution.*
—Steve Ballmer, CEO, Microsoft

*The best thought-out plans in the world aren't worth the paper they're
written on if you can't pull them off.*
—Ralph S. Larsen, chairman and CEO, Johnson & Johnson

CHAPTER OUTLINE

- Nokia's Revitalization Initiatives
- Why Strategic Implementation?
- Why Is Implementation Crucial?
- Fundamental Principles of Implementation
- The Basic Design Variables
- The First Design Principle: Congruence
- The Second Design Principle: Stage-of-Growth
- Organizing Framework
- Designing the Global Organization
- Human Resource Management: Its Role in Strategic Implementation

LEARNING OBJECTIVES

- Understand how crucial implementation is to strategy
- Learn the fundamental principles of implementation
- Learn to apply the basic design variables for implementation
- Learn to apply the basic design principles for implementation
- Understand the role of human resources (HR)
- Understand the "centric" approaches in human resource management

NOKIA'S REVITALIZATION INITIATIVES

"When the Finns are under pressure, that's when the *sisu* comes out," said Jorma Ollila, former CEO of Nokia. *Sisu* is a Finnish word meaning "courage" and "perseverance."[1] At one time, Nokia was a Finnish manufacturing conglomerate, with products ranging from wooden flooring, rubber boots, telephone and telegraph cables, and toilet paper to telecom equipment. It was little known to people outside of the Scandinavian market. After Ollila became the chief financial officer in 1985, Nokia changed its business direction and was restructured. Resources were allocated to technology-oriented businesses such as consumer electronics, and eventually to mobile phones, networks, and wireless systems. Businesses that belonged to the old economy, such as papers, rubber, and cable, were divested.

Nokia's restructuring came just in time for the telecommunication boom of the 1990s.[2] Between 1998 and 2004, Ollila brought Nokia from a domestic company to the top cell-phone giant in the world, controlling one-third of the $100 billion phone market and making it the world's largest vendor of telecom equipment. But even with its success, it wasn't long before aggressive Asian competitors, such as LG Electronics, Sony-Ericsson, and Samsung, begun to introduce phones equipped with jazzier images, better cameras, and a wider selection of styles and features to appeal to customers. Nokia's market share dropped from about 38 percent worldwide in 2003 to 30 percent during the first nine months of 2004. Its share went down even more dramatically in the European market, from 51 percent to 32.6 percent that same year. As profits declined, Wall Street expressed concern and stock prices dropped by 14 percent over the next one-and-a-half years.[3] While focusing on technology and functions, Nokia had ignored elements such as phone size, ease of use, colors, screen size, sleek styling, and the like, features that appealed to customers. Also, Nokia appeared to have overlooked a very important player in the industry—the mobile operators, such as Vodafone. In effect, they were the lead customers because they chose which handsets to carry. Finally, Nokia had not as yet experienced the full brunt of competition from Asian companies, which were much more aggressive.[4]

Another reason for Nokia's downfall—and perhaps part of the reason why it missed key market signals—was its internal organizational structure. Mr. Ollila had created three separate units: business, multimedia, and mass-market phones. Even with a new initiative called "restructuring for growth" undertaken in late 2003, the structure was not designed to identify and capitalize on emerging customer trends. In fact, the initiative proved to be distracting.[5]

On August 1, 2005, Ollila announced that he would step down in June 2006 and Olli-Pekka Kallasvuo would take over. Kallasvuo's challenges included a mediocre stock, new growth opportunities, falling profit margins, and very tough rivals like Motorola, Samsung, and LG Electronics.[6] Fortunately for Nokia, the bad years of the telecom industry depression were over and mobile phone operators had begun to invest in new services and networks.

Early results of Kallasvuo's strategy suggest a new surge of creative products. At least fifty new models were introduced in 2005, offering state-of-the-art features such as Carl Zeiss optics, 3G capability, easy-to-download music, and so forth. Kallasvuo, a self-proclaimed pragmatist, believes in a very customer-centric approach, and thus the company had to offer what customers wanted as quickly as possible. Short in flip phone supplies, Kallasvuo turned to Taiwanese manufacturers, a move that Nokia would not have undertaken in the past. He also opened new channels of distribution to accommodate a wider range of lower cost products. Kallasvuo also brought in a new generation of managers to help him fight the battle, hoping their diversity and youthfulness would energize Nokia.[7]

Under Kallavuo's leadership, Nokia has regained part of its lost market share, from 29 percent in 2004 to 33 percent in 2005. Nokia now churns out new products at a faster rate than before. Kallasvuo has also aggressively pursued both the high-end and low-end market segments. Participating in emerging markets has further expanded Nokia's range of products to suit different tastes.[8]

WHY STRATEGIC IMPLEMENTATION?

The selection of a good strategy by itself does not guarantee success. The importance of strategic implementation is reflected in a belief that a strategy that is not implemented effectively is more frequently the cause of poor performance than a strategy that is developed inadequately.[9] Implementing strategy basically involves choices about how to allocate tasks and responsibilities most efficiently in line with organizational goals, strategies, and individual needs and aspirations. It is a multifaceted task that entails the creation of "fit" or "congruency" between these elements of the organization in order to support the firm's strategy.

It is necessary because organizational and individual goals do not necessarily match, creating mismatches between different goals, strategies, and individual needs. Finally, implementation can be interpreted as a control process, not only for linking individual and organizational goals, but also in ensuring that sufficient resources are allocated in line with the firm's financial and operating performance goals that reflect its strategy. A successful implementation effort means that strategy is executed in an efficient, timely, and proficient fashion.

This chapter focuses on the first view, that is, the creation of fit between organizational elements, but with particular attention to structures and processes. We also emphasize the role of the human resource management (HRM) function in strategic implementation. Our view is that another important perspective—developing and cultivating a global mindset—is imperative in the proper understanding and functioning of strategic implementation in a global context. This is addressed in the next chapter (Chapter 10). Finally, we discuss the control function in strategic implementation using financial performance measures in Chapter 11. All three chapters provide different perspectives about implementing strategy and are essential in understanding its proper application (see Figure 9.1).

As the opening vignette about Nokia ably illustrates, organizations fail or succeed

Figure 9.1 **Implementing the Strategic Plan: Using Structures and Processes**

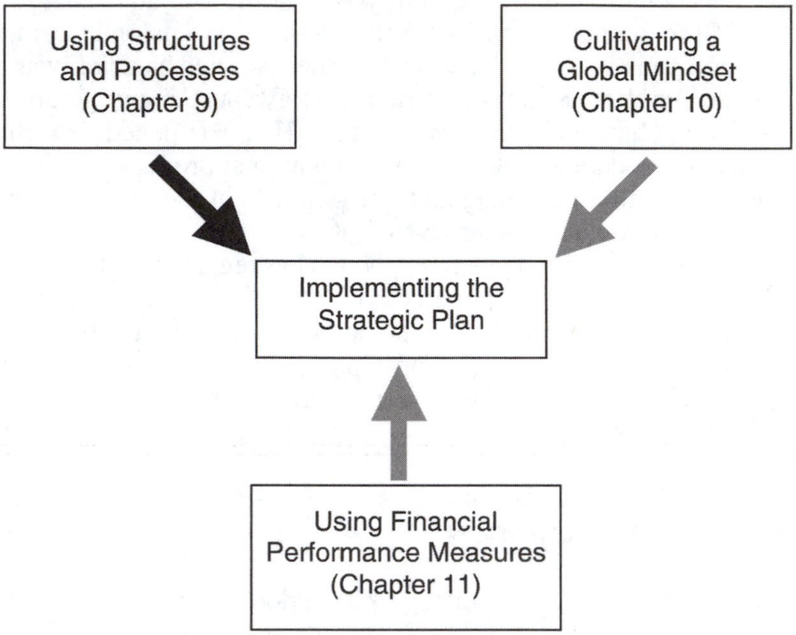

to the extent that appropriate strategies are formulated *in tandem* with organizational structures and processes that are designed to accommodate and support them. Implementing strategy is a complex task that involves individuals, structures, processes, cultures, and rewards in a systemic and holistic interaction. Taken altogether, implementing global strategies is a daunting challenge. A widely acknowledged belief among seasoned executives is that firms that excel in implementation possess a competence that is very difficult for others to imitate. Southwest Airlines, Emerson Electric, Dell Computers, Nordstrom, and Toyota are among firms that have been recognized for their excellence in developing structures and processes that are strongly supportive of their corporate strategies.

The organization of the chapter is as follows. First, we discuss reasons why implementation fails based on several published research studies. Second, we introduce fundamental approaches to implementation that require the coordinated interaction of five design variables—strategy/tasks, formal structures, processes, individuals, and corporate culture. Each of these variables is discussed and developed in an international context. Then we expand on two design principles: *congruency/fit* and *stage-of-growth*. This discussion covers how the design variables evolve and change in response to a fast-changing environment in which competitive rules are not likely to be defined with great confidence beforehand. Specifically, we discuss how various levels of implementation are related to different stages of growth and development. We then discuss how the HRM function has evolved in response to growing global complexity, and how it can be designed as a powerful tool in facilitating the implementation of a firm's global strategy.

Exhibit 9.1

Why Implementation Fails

Various researchers have examined why implementation fails. A recent study by Wharton professor Lawrence G. Hrebiniak provides a comprehensive summary of obstacles to effective implementation based on the Wharton–Gartner Survey and the Wharton Executive Education Survey. Some of the notable reasons that cut across these findings are ranked below.

1. Inability to manage change effectively or to overcome the internal resistance to change.
2. Trying to execute a strategy that conflicts with the existing power structure.
3. Poor or inadequate information sharing between individuals or business units responsible for strategy execution.
4. Unclear communication of responsibility and/or accountability for execution decisions or actions.
5. Poor or vague strategy.
6. Lack of feelings of "ownership" of a strategy or execution plan among key employees.
7. Not having guidelines or a model to guide strategy execution efforts.
8. Lack of understanding of the role of organizational structure and design in the execution process.
9. Inability to generate "buy-in" or agreement on critical execution steps or actions.
10. Lack of incentives or inappropriate incentives to support execution objectives.
11. Insufficient financial resources to execute the strategy.
12. Lack of upper-management support of strategy execution.

Source: Adapted from Lawrence G. Hrebiniak, *Making Strategy Work* (Upper Saddle River, NJ: Wharton School Publishing, 2005), p. 17.

WHY IS IMPLEMENTATION CRUCIAL?

A seasoned executive from California's Silicon Valley opined in a class talk: "Formulating strategy is a necessary step in strategic planning. However, if a firm cannot implement or executive this strategy, it will fail . . . and there is nothing worse than implementing a *bad* strategy with ruthless abandon." Without a good design for implementation, strategies are bound to fail. What this underscores is that, while managers view implementation as a critical task, it is not as well understood. Moreover, some, if not many, managers think—incorrectly—that implementation is a matter of "common sense," reduced to "directing people to do the necessary work." While common sense is clearly involved in implementation efforts, there has also been a growing body of knowledge, including templates that have been validated by research and practice, that provide key reasons why implementation fails and important guidelines to aid in any implementation effort (see Exhibit 9.1). A study by Wharton management professor Lawrence G. Hrebiniak disclosed that managers need a logical model as a guide to execute decisions. He adds: "Without guidelines, execution becomes a helter-skelter affair. Without guidelines, individuals do the things they think are important, often resulting in uncoordinated, divergent, even conflicting decisions and actions."[10]

Whatever problems a firm faces in implementing its strategy within its domestic market are magnified in an international context. The paramount challenge to a multinational company lies in coordinating and integrating activities that take place in different countries. Jay Galbraith, formerly a management professor at the International Institute for Management Development (IMD) in Lausanne, Switzerland, and currently the head of Galbraith Management Consultants, Ltd., has proposed four specific issues that exacerbate the problems of global implementation and integration.[11] The first is *global complexity*. There are simply a large number of countries, currencies, tax policies, languages, cultures, legal statutes, and host government policies that need to be considered. The second is the need to *recreate the sources of a firm's competitive advantage* as discerned by its business model. While Japanese firms have the strong support of their suppliers, workforce, and government at home, they have to contend with recreating these resources and assets in a different country. The third is *geopolitical uncertainty*. Multinationals are constantly beset with the politics of integration (the European Economic Community being a prime example), religion (the continuing flux of resettlements prompted by Arab-Israeli negotiations), and emerging nongovernmental forces (such as the power of NGOs in developing countries). The fourth is the *globalization of consumers*. Cross-border and cross-business complexities increase as suppliers try to coordinate purchasing and delivery activities to meet the demands of global customers.

FUNDAMENTAL PRINCIPLES OF IMPLEMENTATION

As a guide to developing a logical framework for effective implementation, we start off with basic operating principles that have been developed by various researchers and validated in practice.

IT STARTS WITH STRATEGY

Any type of implementation effort needs to come to grips with how organizations support their basic strategies. Thus, for perspective, it is important to frame the implementation process with the question: *What is the firm implementing*? What is implemented is the firm's *strategy*. As discussed in Chapters 1–3, strategy sets the vision and the firm's position within its environment. It also provides the context and consistency to a firm's current and future decisions. Thus, it is critical that a strategy be defined at the outset. This basic yet fundamental premise pervades all issues and considerations of implementation and organizational design.

IMPLEMENTATION REDUCES UNCERTAINTY AND RISK THROUGH COORDINATION ACTION

Any strategy entails the specification of tasks needed to implement and support it. Since strategy involves risks, there is uncertainty attendant to the specification and differentiation of such tasks. Let's consider Google's efforts to implant its U.S.-based strategy in China. Will potential customers perceive the benefits in a similar manner as in the United States? What additional tasks, structures, and processes are needed to make Google's strategy more applicable to the Chinese market? To reduce some of the uncertainty surrounding these questions, it is essential that Google coordinate its structure, processes, people, and resources in a manner that is supportive and accommodating of its corporate strategy.

REDUCING UNCERTAINTY ENTAILS AN INCREMENTAL AND SEQUENTIAL PROCESS

Implementation is not a one-step process but involves a continuous assessment of a firm's strategy as it grows and develops over time. What might be important to a new startup is different from the interests of a maturing firm, and certainly different from those of a firm engaged in international operations. Nike's first incursion into the Asian region was to locate low-cost but efficient manufacturers of shoes and apparel. Now that Nike is poised to move beyond contract manufacturing into marketing in Asia, it will need different uses of resources. Implicit in this principle is that effective implementation designs are also cost efficient. In what some authors refer to as "the principle of minimum intervention," it is maintained that the choice of resources to coordinate should be tempered by its costs of implementation and relative effectiveness.[12]

THE BASIC DESIGN VARIABLES

The starting point of strategic implementation is some form of diagnosis. Due to the complexity of this task, there are many ways to approach it. In early years, approaches tended to be universalistic in scope, that is, theorists of different persuasions would recommend bureaucracies (mechanistic) or participative management (organic) as the "best" way to manage organizations.[13] Adopting systems thinking, much later theorists argued that there was no one best way, but that organizations should adopt either form depending on the environments they faced, or the technologies they used. Over the past decades, there has been a consensus among theorists and business practitioners that effective implementation entails the consideration of organizations not as static classical military models, but as social systems.[14]

Within a social systems perspective, organizations consist of fundamental design variables. Because these variables are inputs in an implementation effort, a good understanding of each variable and how it works will facilitate success. Various authors and consultants have proposed design variables that underlie strategic implementation (see Exhibit 9.2).[15] Notwithstanding some slight differences in formulation, there is agreement on the fundamental design variables: (1) the *strategy* to be implemented, including requisite *tasks*; (2) the *individuals* involved in the implementation effort, (3) *formal organizational structure*, (4) organizational *processes*, and (5) the informal organization or *corporate culture*. These are generic in that they apply in any implementation initiative. Effective organizations design these variables in ways that are internally consistent and supportive of global strategies. We elaborate on these variables in the following sections.

STRATEGY/TASKS

Strategy, as we have discussed and developed in the book, is the subject matter of what is being implemented. In a basic sense, this can refer to how a firm chooses to be different, or how it competes differently—its source of competitive advantage. In previous chapters we have established that this can be accomplished through

Exhibit 9.2 **Different Design Perspectives**

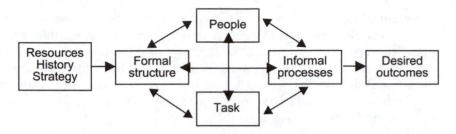

David Nadler and Michael Tushman introduced the congruence model, which conceptualized the organization as a basic system of inputs, throughputs, and outputs. The basic input was the firm's strategy. The throughput picture indicates elements of organizational design. Within this, four elements are defined: task, structure, formal, and informal organization. All four elements had to "fit" together to support the requirements of a firm's strategy. Goodness-of-fit was hypothesized to lead to organizational performance.

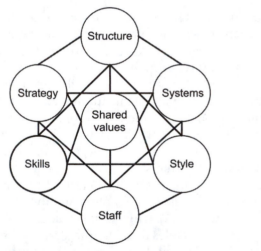

The McKinsey Consultants have popularized what they call the 7s Model based on the premise that an organization is not simply structure, but also consists of "hard" and "soft" elements: strategy, systems (formal and informal), style, staff, skills, and shared values/superordinate goals. McKinsey Consultants implore managers to be attentive to both the hard and the soft elements when diagnosing and planning organizational change.

Jay Galbraith has developed the "star" model (shown above). Design elements include strategy, structure, task, people, and rewards. Fit among and between these elements is hypothesized to lead to higher organizational performance.

Sources: Adapted from David Nadler and Michael Tushman, "A Congruence Model for Diagnosing Organizational Behavior," in *Resource Book in Macro-Organizational Behavior*, ed. Ray Miles (Santa Clara, CA: Goodyear, 1980), pp. 30–49; Robert Waterman, Jr., T. Peters, and J.R. Phillips, "Structure Is Not Organization," *Business Horizons* 23 (June 3, 1980): 14–26; Jay Galbraith and Daniel Nathanson, *Strategy Implementation: The Role of Structure and Process* (St. Paul, MN: West Publishing, 1978).

cost leadership, differentation, or the selection of a market niche using either of the above two strategies (Chapter 3). Taken in a global context, strategy can also refer to a firm choosing to have a multilocal, incremental, core formula, or a global strategy (Chapter 4). Whichever the context, strategy constitutes the primary context for which structures, processes, and informal cultures can be properly designed in ways to support or facilitate it.

Inclusive in any discussion of strategy are **tasks**, or the basic or inherent work to be done to meet the requirements of a specific strategy.[16] The emphasis is on the specific work activities or functions that need to be done, and their inherent characteristics. Analysis of the task would include responses to the following questions: What are the basic work flows and functions, such as the knowledge and skill requirements? What kinds of rewards does the work inherently provide to those who do it? What is the degree of uncertainty associated with the work? What are the specific constraints inherent in the work (such as critical time demands, cost constraints, etc.)? Understanding how tasks logically derive from a firm's strategy is the key to assessing how these are mutually interdependent, and how tasks should be matched against the other design variables.

INDIVIDUALS

Individuals, or people, implement strategies. Thus, people's policies influence and define the quality of employees' mindset, and skills. As a design variable, this consideration of individuals recognizes that the workforce has to be managed in order for a strategy to be implemented effectively. Central to any assessment of individuals are assumptions related to motivating them. Motivation generally refers to that which energizes, directs, and sustains human behavior. The study of motivation is best undertaken in a dynamic systems perspective. In specific terms, the consideration of individuals involves the assessment of the nature and characteristics of individuals, individual knowledge and skills, differential needs and preferences, the perceptions or expectations that they develop regarding their motivation and opportunity to perform, and other demographic information. Since the understanding of what motivates individuals requires a multifaceted approach, one basic schema (i.e., the performance equation) for integrating the above involves the consideration of how individual attributes and the capacity to perform are related to individual motivation (Exhibit 9.3).[17]

The individual's motivation to perform is influenced by his/her belief that whatever effort is expended will lead to a particular outcome.[18] If individuals believe deeply that good grades will result in a lucrative and meaningful job, then they will be motivated to work very hard to get good grades. Even so, one's motivation to perform is tempered by other important factors. First, in order to perform well, employees must have the *capabilities* to perform, meaning the abilities, experience, and traits necessary to carry out the tasks assigned to them. Second, it is important that they clearly understand what is expected of them (*role clarity*). Third, they should have the *opportunity* to perform. If they are assigned to the wrong place, for example, assigning highly energetic and motivated salespeople to an area with little sales poten-

Exhibit 9.3 **Factors Affecting Individual Performance**

```
                          ┌─────────────┐
                          │  Employee   │
                          │  traits and │
                          │  abilities  │
                          └──────┬──────┘
                                 │
                                 ▼
┌──────────────┐  ┌────────────┐  ┌─────────────┐  ┌─────────────┐
│  Belief that │  │  Employee  │  │             │  │ Role clarity│
│  individual  │  │ motivation │  │     Job     │  │     and     │
│ effort will  │─▶│ to perform │─▶│ performance │◀─│ acceptance  │
│  lead to     │  │            │  │             │  │             │
│  particular  │  └────────────┘  └──────┬──────┘  └─────────────┘
│  outcomes    │                         ▲
└──────────────┘                  ┌──────┴──────┐
                                  │ Opportunity │
                                  │ to perform  │
                                  └─────────────┘
```

Source: Adapted from Richard M. Steers, *Introduction to Organizational Behavior*, 2d ed. (Glenview, IL: Scott, Foresman, 1984), p. 179.

tial, then it is unlikely that they will be motivated to reach their potential in the long run. Moreover, the lack of sufficient funding, lack of time, inadequate personnel, or lackadaisical management support are conditions that constrain the opportunity to perform. It is important to understand and identify which factor might be causing a drop in individual performance.

FORMAL STRUCTURE

This includes the proper selection of organizational structures that are explicitly and formally developed to get individuals to perform tasks consistent with organizational strategy. **Formal structure** generally refers to stable and relatively fixed relationships that exist among jobs in the organization, and represents the skeleton of the organizational system. John Child, a prominent management professor from the University of Birmingham, defines structure as the "formal allocation of work roles and the administrative mechanisms to control and integrate work activity, including those that cross formal organizational boundaries."[19] Tasks are allocated within the organization over time that reflect their underlying differentiation or segmentation into work roles. Structure also encompasses the ways in which different jobs are coordinated and controlled. Thus, we may also say that structure consists of stable, enduring relationships reflecting task differentiation and control and integration.[20]

Differentiation refers to the cognitive and emotional demarcation of the firm's environment, or the number of constituencies that a firm needs to deal with. For example, in a university setting, school administrators have to deal with students, faculty, staff, parents, recruiters, other universities and colleges, and governmental entities. In general, the greater the differentiation, the greater the need for integration and control.[21]

Firms employ different methods of grouping that reflect both organizational differentiation and structural control. Grouping can be determined by function, product, division, geography, and some combination of these groupings, such as a matrix organization (see Exhibit 9.4). These structures range from being relatively simple (functional) to very complex (matrix). As we will discuss in this chapter, the choice of each of these groupings depends on the historical circumstances, strategy, and the stage of growth of the firm. Another point to remember about formal structures is that they are very difficult to change. Despite high expectations, Germany's Siemens AG CEO, Klaus Kleinfeld, found it difficult to change the old-style German management structure. His management board—a formal committee mandated by German law—is packed with former rivals for the top job. Moreover, his predecessor did retire but became chairman of the firm's supervisory board, which functions in Germany more like a board of directors. Many think that Germany's consensus-based two-tier system of corporate governance will hinder any aggressive actions by Kleinfeld to restructure the company.[22]

PROCESSES

Because not every facet of differentiation and control can be fixed and enduring over time, processes are necessary. In contrast to formal organizational structure, a **process** is defined as the "direction and frequency of work and information flows linking the differentiated roles within and between departments of the complex organization."[23] More recent treatises define processes as the "collection of activities that takes one or more inputs and creates an output that is of value to customers"; a structured, measured set of activities designed to produce a specified output for a particular customer or market; or a "specific ordering of work activities across time and space, with a beginning, an end, and clearly identified inputs and outputs."[24] While structure resembles the skeleton of a human body, processes are akin to basic bodily functions, such as those performed by the circulatory, cardiovascular, neurological, pulmonary, and other systems that comprise the human anatomy and physiology. Therefore, structure and processes are inextricably related, and, when well designed, the two can be complementary and mutually reinforcing.

In the context of organizations, processes are likewise described in terms of systems of work and information flows. Examples are procurement, information and budgeting systems, management development, training, supply chain management, management succession, acquisitions, strategic planning, incentives, and so on—many of which have been discussed in our previous chapters. All these systems facilitate the exchange of resources and information necessary for the organization to function properly; as such, they have consequences for the company's bottom line. IT consultant Peter Keen

Exhibit 9.4 **Basic Organizational Structures**

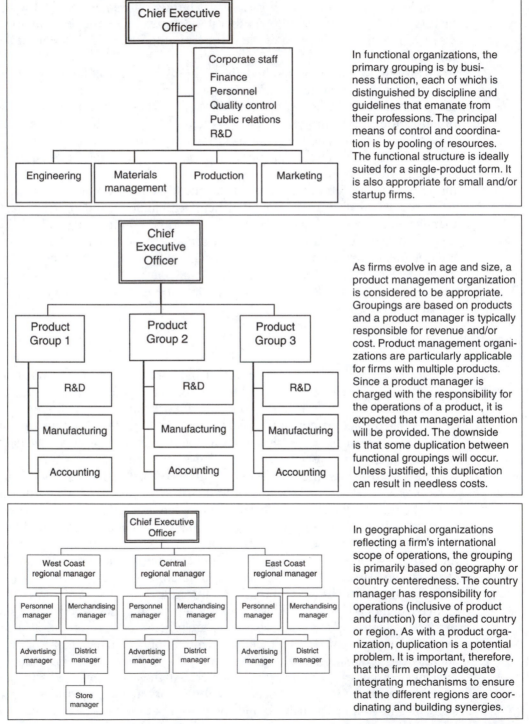

In functional organizations, the primary grouping is by business function, each of which is distinguished by discipline and guidelines that emanate from their professions. The principal means of control and coordination is by pooling of resources. The functional structure is ideally suited for a single-product form. It is also appropriate for small and/or startup firms.

As firms evolve in age and size, a product management organization is considered to be appropriate. Groupings are based on products and a product manager is typically responsible for revenue and/or cost. Product management organizations are particularly applicable for firms with multiple products. Since a product manager is charged with the responsibility for the operations of a product, it is expected that managerial attention will be provided. The downside is that some duplication between functional groupings will occur. Unless justified, this duplication can result in needless costs.

In geographical organizations reflecting a firm's international scope of operations, the grouping is primarily based on geography or country centeredness. The country manager has responsibility for operations (inclusive of product and function) for a defined country or region. As with a product organization, duplication is a potential problem. It is important, therefore, that the firm employ adequate integrating mechanisms to ensure that the different regions are coordinating and building synergies.

(continued)

Exhibit 9.4 *(continued)*

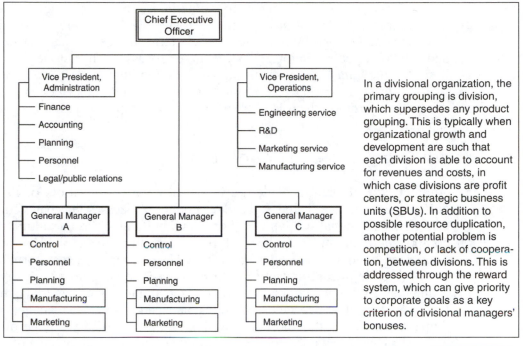

In a divisional organization, the primary grouping is division, which supersedes any product grouping. This is typically when organizational growth and development are such that each division is able to account for revenues and costs, in which case divisions are profit centers, or strategic business units (SBUs). In addition to possible resource duplication, another potential problem is competition, or lack of cooperation, between divisions. This is addressed through the reward system, which can give priority to corporate goals as a key criterion of divisional managers' bonuses.

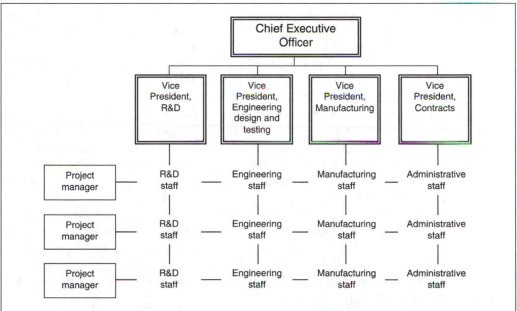

Perhaps the most complex of organizational forms is the matrix. Grouping is made on the basis of two, or more, dimensions. A typical matrix is a combination of product and function (shown accordingly). Matrix organizations are particularly applicable in complex situations when there are two or more thrusts on the organization for which simultaneous attention and resource-sharing are needed, Nevertheless, it is difficult to operate within a matrix since this entails vigilance in monitoring the balance between the two groupings. In the case of Asea Brown and Boveri, the total of six groupings are used. The use of matrix organizations should be justified in terms of cost, efficiency, and organizational development.

provides a specific definition that captures this appraisal of organizational processes: "A process is any work that meets four criteria: it is recurrent; it affects some aspect of organizational capabilities; it can be accomplished in different ways that make a difference to the contribution it generates in terms of cost, value, service or quality; and it involves coordination."[25] While these processes affect strategic implementation, it is the human resource management system that lends coherence to a firm's strategy through its prime responsibility to manage the firm's workforce. Because of this critical position, the role of HRM in strategic implementation is developed in a separate section within this chapter.

THE INFORMAL ORGANIZATION, OR CORPORATE CULTURE

Another critical element of design is the informal organization, or its **corporate culture,** defined as "shared values and implicit processes that have consequential effects on individual behavior."[26] For many, building a strong culture is a critical component of an implementation effort. In research on this topic, Harvard Business School professors John Kotter and James Heskett reported that corporate culture can have a significant impact on a firm's long-term economic performance. They found that firms with cultures that emphasized all the key managerial constituencies (customers, stockholders, and employees) and leadership from managers at all levels outperformed firms that did not have those cultural traits by a huge margin. Over an eleven-year period, the former increased revenues by an average of 682 percent versus 166 percent for the latter, expanded their work forces by 282 percent versus 36 percent, grew their stock prices by 901 percent versus 74 percent, and improved their net incomes by 756 percent versus 1 percent.[27]

Culture is important because it involves deeply ingrained beliefs and values held by individuals in an organization. To the extent that these beliefs are widely shared with significant consequences, they can be a powerful element in strategic implementation. Corporate culture has two important components: consensus *(sharing)* and intensity *(consequentiality)* (see Exhibit 9.5). Both lead to a strong and cohesive culture. Unless beliefs and values are widely shared, then the culture becomes a vacuous one. Moreover, unless they have consequential effects, then these do not operate as effectively as norms or guides to proper behavior. Norms are also closely tied to situational cues, or external artifacts that have strong consequences. For this reason, individuals' behaviors can be strongly influenced by what they feel as expectations of others around them. For example, studies suggest that people wash their hands after using the bathroom more frequently when they are in the presence of others. For an interesting context on this relationship between norms, values, and situational cues, see the example of the Good Samaritan (Box 9.1, page 378).

THE FIRST DESIGN PRINCIPLE: CONGRUENCY

Having described the basic design variables, we now turn to how they are employed as models or frameworks for strategic implementation. The first design principle is

Exhibit 9.5

Corporate Culture as a Design Variable

Categories of Corporate Culture	Design Considerations		
	Description	Typical Examples	Implications for Design
Low consensus, low intensity	No established culture. Few, if any, norms are shared and those that shared have no consequences for individual or organizational performance.	New start-up firms. Firms with extremely high personnel turn-over. Firms in crisis. Firms that are not able to transition from different environments.	Firms will face significant difficulty in implementing their strategies. Remedial measures include the building a corporate culture to effectively manage social culture.
Low consensus, high intensity	Vacuous cultures (i.e., unclear mission, strategies, and goals). Norms are not widely shared; in practice, individuals are rewarded or punished for actions reflecting norms that are not widely shared.	Firms with an unclear vision, and/or when the mission and strategy are not adequately diffused nor understood. Firms that are in a transition from one strategy to another. Newly formed mergers and acquisitions.	Firms will need to formulate/clarify their mission, strategy, and build their business model. High conflict is to be anticipated. Communicating the mission and strategy becomes a critical action item.
High consensus, low intensity	Ineffectual cultures (i.e., poor linkage between performance and rewards.) There is high consensus on norms, but they have no consequences for individual or organizational performance.	Firms with severely limited human and financial resources. Firms with poor incentives and compensation structures.	Firms will most likely experience resistance to implementing their mission and strategies. A recurring problem will be units and departments declining key responsibilities without sufficient authority. Firms should link rewards to performance.
High consensus, low intensity	Strong and cohesive cultures. There is consensus on norms and beliefs that also have significantly high consequences for individual and organizational performance.	Firms with a long history of clear strategies and good implementation practices. Religious sects. Clans.	Successful firms are able to link corporate cultures to overall strategy. However, strong cultures lead to significant resistance-to-change if a major strategic shift should occur.

Source: The categories of corporate culture are drawn from Charles O'Reilly, "Corporations, Culture, and Commitment: Motivation and Social Control in Organization," *California Management Review*, 31, 1989: 9–25; information for the next columns was synthesized from other sources including: Terrence E. Deal and Allan A. Kennedy, *Corporate Cultures* (Reading, MA: Addison-Wesley Publishing Company, 1982); Michael L. Tushman and Charles O'Reilly, *Winning Through Innovation* (Boston: Harvard Business Review Press, 1997); and Michel Robert, *Strategy Pure & Simple II* (New York: McGraw-Hill, 1998).

that of **congruency**. Between each pair of variables, there exists in any organization a relative degree of congruency, consistency, or "fit." Generally speaking, congruency is a measure of the fit between pairs of components.[28] Consider, for example, two components: strategy/task and individual. At the simplest level, the task can be thought of as the most basic requirements of work demands. By matching work de-

Box 9.1

The Parable of the Good Samaritan, Revisited

Some years ago, two Princeton University psychologists, John Darley and Daniel Batson, decided to conduct a study inspired by the biblical story of the Good Samaritan. As you may know, that story, from the New Testament Gospel of Luke, tells of a traveler who has been beaten and robbed and left for dead by the side of the road from Jerusalem to Jericho. Both a priest and a Levite—worthy, pious men—came upon the man but did not stop. The only man to help was a Samaritan—a member of the despised minority—who bound up the wounded man and took him to an inn.

Darley and Batson decided to adopt this parable in a study at the Princeton Theological Seminary. Seminarians were instructed to report to another building to give a talk about religious vocations, or about the parable of the Good Samaritan. In some cases, they were then told "You're late. They were expecting you five minutes ago." Some others were told, "(they) are ready for you. Please go right over." In other cases, they were told, "it will be a few minutes before they are ready for you, but you might as well head there now."

Along an alley to a nearby building to present the talk, each student passed a "victim" slumped in a doorway, eyes closed, head down, coughing, groaning, and not moving. The dependent variable was whether the seminarians would stop and how they would assist the "victim."

"It's hard to think of a context in which norms concerning helping those in distress are more salient than for a person thinking about the Good Samaritan," said Darley. Yet, this did not significantly increase helping behavior.

What really mattered? The answer is whether or not they were in a rush. Of the group that was rushed, only 10 percent stopped. Of the group that knew that they had a few minutes to spare, 63 percent stopped.

It is no small wonder that the words "you are late" would literally make people forget—even temporarily—years of seminary training.

Source: Adapted from John Darley and Daniel Batson, "'From Jerusalem to Jericho': A Study of Situational and Dispositional Variables in Helping Behavior," *Journal of Personality and Social Psychology* 27 (1973): 100–19.

mands against individual qualifications and characteristics, the task-individual fit can be properly assessed. For example, if a person is either overqualified or underqualified for the job, then a misfit between the person and the task occurs. Operationally, there are other ways of determining congruency:

- *Internal Consistency:* Management processes need to convey priorities and information that are consistent with strategic requirements. If a firm's strategy, for example, is to develop new products and innovations, its information systems (e.g., accounting systems and budgets) should reflect this priority. Likewise, reward and compensation systems should support this strategic direction.
- *Contingency:* Different environments impose pressures on firms to organize in different ways. To be successful, firms facing complex and fast-changing environments need to adopt flexible structures. Conversely, firms facing stable and predictable environments would fare better if they adopted bureaucratic structures oriented toward providing consistent products and services. Incongruent relationships (and possible organizational failure) occur when firms adopt structures that are not appropriate for environmental requirements.[29]

Exhibit 9.6

Four Design Variables, Definitions, and Problem Symptoms

Design variable	Definition	Problem symptoms
Strategy/Task	The basic or inherent work to be done by the organization.	• Unclear direction • Confusion • Misplaced attention and focus
Individuals	The nature and characteristics of individuals that the organization currently has as members.	• Low morale • High training costs • Absenteeism • Turnovers • Strong resistance to change
Formal Structure	This includes the range of structures that are explicitly and formally developed to get individuals to perform tasks consistent with organizational strategy.	• Slow decision making • Unclear direction • Lack of innovation • Paralysis • Strong resistance to change
Informal Structure and Processes	Shared values and implicit processes that have consequential effects on individual behavior.	• Unclear incentives • Lack of norms • Lack of shared values • Strong resistance to change

- *Efficiency:* A firm in a highly volatile environment needs more complex management information systems, which are costly to maintain. During this period, top management may need to determine whether levels of information processing are justified in terms of financial returns.
- *Balance:* As organizational structures become more complex and differentiated, coordination becomes even more necessary. Conflict inevitably results when highly differentiated units have to be integrated. Therefore, a proper balance between organizational flexibility and control is needed for a firm to be continuously successful.

As a diagnostic framework, the congruency or co-alignment between tasks, individuals, formal and informal organizations, and processes helps managers see where discrepancies occur, and where they might focus their attention (see Exhibit 9.6). Yet the four design variables are hardly static. As these have to be supportive of strategy, these also change in response to change and organizational transformation. The example of the pharmaceuticals (see Box 9.2) exemplifies how changes in basic strategy can affect the four design variables. Understanding the fundamental decisional variables and how these interact in the context of implementation are indispensable elements of a diagnosis. Specifically, this diagnostic method provides critical cues to what is going wrong or might go wrong in implementation. Thus, before more complex approaches of implementation take place, it is essential that a manager understand the operation of the basic decisional variables.

Box 9.2

How New Strategies Can Change Implementation in the Pharmaceutical Industry

While the global pharmaceutical industry includes biotech firms, makers of generic drugs, contract research manufacturers, wholesalers, and retailers, it is the top pharmaceutical firms that have been the main focus of attention due to their size and prominence. Global drug sales have almost doubled since 1997 and are projected to grow to $700 billion by 2008. By the standards of other industries, the industry has consistently attained operating margins of 25 percent, compared to 15 percent for consumer goods. In 2004, health care spending in the United States alone reached an estimated $1.8 trillion, more than 15 percent of GDP, and $200 billion went to prescription drugs. All in all, the industry is widely recognized to be among the most profitable in the world and has been so over several decades.

Much of this can be attributed to the industry's success in implementing its strategy. For many pharmaceutical companies, the objective is to develop and introduce a continuous array of pharmaceutical products and services from which some will emerge as "blockbuster" drugs that can enhance a firm's profitability and ensure the development of future products. Notable examples of blockbusters include Lipitor, Viagra, Valium, and Vioxx, which have more than $1 billion in worldwide sales.

Successful implementation results from the co-alignment of the four variables—task, individuals, formal and informal structures, and processes. These are strongly aligned and mutually reinforcing. The main *task* is focused on research and development, followed by intense lobbying with the FDA and aggressive marketing to doctors. Research and development is the lifeblood of the industry. This is complemented by its *people* (individuals), or human resources, who are many leading research scientists. Since it takes an average of twelve years to develop a drug from start to finish, *formal* and *informal* structures and processes support this investment in R&D. Drug companies have been increasing R&D by about 6 percent per year. In a forecast for 2005, $55 billion in R&D expenditures was projected for the industry, three-fifths of it by the big drug makers. Incentives and informal norms are stacked to enhance the research and development process. Upon development, an army of "detail persons," many of whom include ex-medical students, visits or invades doctors' offices to promote products. All these activities are staged to develop and promote the blockbuster drugs.

Even so, there are some trends that tend to undermine the strategy and the alignment of the

(continued)

The Second Design Principle: Stage-of-Growth

In this section, we introduce the second design principle that explicitly recognizes the additional imperatives that exist for a firm in response to its growth in size and scope, changes in its strategy, and what new structures and processes might be necessary to accommodate the requirements of growth and a new strategy. Fittingly, such designs are called **stage-of-growth** models of implementation.

Historical Research on Stage-of-Growth Models

Present theory and research evidence suggest that strategies have to be consistent or congruent with organizational structure and processes for the organization to succeed. The empirical foundations of strategic consistency can be traced to the research by Harvard historian Alfred Chandler in 1972.[30] On the basis of an historical study of seventy of America's largest firms, he proposed that organizational structure is

---

Box 9.2 *(continued)*

four variables. The blockbuster drugs have had their patents and market share seriously challenged by cheaper generic competition. This problem is compounded by a broader social debate about the purposes and practices of the industry. But perhaps the most serious threat comes from a fundamental *shift* in how drugs are developed. The traditional business model was targeted at developing blockbuster drugs that could be used by the general population. In the case of cancer treatments, however, the results have been disappointing: response rates are stuck at a low 20 percent. Moreover, it has been recognized that adverse side effects and highly toxic nature of some chemotherapy can kill the patient. Therefore, the new trend advanced by biotechnology firms lies in *targeting*—a concept of delivering the cancer-killing agent only to the cancer cells and leaving the rest of the body alone. Some have hailed this as the coming of age of personalized medicine. Within the next fifteen years, it is projected that targeted and multitargeted therapies that perform much like multiple-warhead missiles will be perfected for cancer treatment.

Because the traditional business model of pharmaceuticals is not geared to personalized treatment, and because biotechnology firms are at the forefront of this development, there is some question whether the pharmaceutical industry will respond adequately. Sidney Taurel, Eli Lilly's boss, observes: "The industry was living a little fat and happy." Now firms see change as the imperative. Some are cutting costs; some are diversifying into specialized health treatments; some are in the midst of mergers; some are consolidating.

Should personalized treatments ensue, then misalignments between tasks, people, formal and informal structures, and processes will occur. The use of current R&D that is aimed at universal application (task) will clash against that of personalized targeting (strategy). Moreover, it is not clear that current R&D personnel and the "detail persons" are necessarily able and equipped to pursue the development and selling of personalized drug treatments. In systemic fashion, the formal organization and informal cultures also need to change. Barring such changes, the new strategy of personalized treatment will led to misalignment, creating problems in implementation. A new set of tasks, people, formal and informal structures, and processes will be needed to support a strategy aimed at capitalizing on the new trends.

Sources: Adapted from the following sources: "Prescription for Change: Survey of Pharmaceuticals," *Economist,* June 18, 2005, pp. 3–42; Catherine Arnst with Arlene Weintraub, John Carey, Kerry Capell, and Michael Arndt, "Biotech, Finally: Yes, the Business Remains Risky, But Medical Progress Is Stunning," *BusinessWeek,* June 13, 2005.

---

determined by the growth strategy of the firm. That is, as firms move from volume expansion, through vertical integration, to diversification, their structural forms evolve from simple functional units to multidivisional firms. Chandler's research suggested that for each type of growth strategy there was an appropriate organizational form. In fact, companies that had a good "fit," or consistency between strategy and structure, tended to financially outperform firms that did not.

In another landmark study in 1972, Paul Lawrence and Jay Lorsch, both professors of business at the Harvard Business School, found that successful firms in rapidly changing environments tended to have more flexible and organic structures, while those in stable, predictable environments developed more mechanistic or bureaucratic structures.[31] Like Chandler, they found out that firms that had a good "fit" also outperformed those that did not. The Lawrence and Lorsch study triggered a flurry of empirical studies for about a decade that attempted to replicate or corroborate the "congruency" hypotheses.[32] While this stream of research is inconclusive and has resulted in conceptual and methodological dead ends, the concept of "congruency" or "consistency" has been extended and further refined to describe how structures and processes might support and accommodate the requirements of different strategies.

Metamorphosis models are typified by the approach suggested by Larry Greiner, a management professor at the University of Southern California, in 1978.[33] Age and the size of organizations provide the driving force that underlies metamorphic change. Therefore, as organizations develop in terms of size and age, they face different types of "crises" that are overcome with more complex structures and control processes. In spite of its intuitive appeal, the model has been criticized as oversimplistic and lacking in specificity.

Jay Galbraith and his colleague, Daniel Nathanson, provided the necessary embellishment in their "stage-of growth" model.[34] Based on an extensive review of the experiences of both American and European companies, Galbraith and Nathanson expanded the works of Chandler, Lawrence and Lorsch, and Greiner that take into account global strategies. The key premise is the same as Chandler's—that is, starting from a simple form, any source of diversity can be added to promote evolution into a new form. In their formulation, Galbraith and Nathanson see organizational structures evolving to meet the requirements of a changing growth strategy. Internal processes such as performance rewards, measures, careers, leadership styles, and organizational choices are used to support the requirements of strategy and structure.

ORGANIZING FRAMEWORK

Our organizing framework incorporates the two design principles: congruency and stage-of-growth. As established in our historical review of published research, the congruence between strategies, structures, people, and formal and informal processes is the critical element that underlies this stage-of-growth model. Firms offering multiple products in distinctly different markets will need a multidivisional structure with the corresponding processes. The failure to adopt such a structure can lead to inefficiencies. Similarly, it might be quite costly for firms that offer a few related products in similar markets to have a multidivisional structure. A functional structure with some controls might be more efficient and effective. Overall, these studies have provided the criteria with which to assess linkages between strategy, structure, and processes. We illustrate this further, first, with a relatively simple example (no international operations), followed with a more involved one that incorporates international operations in the next section.

A relatively straightforward way of thinking about strategic implementation is to start with a simple startup company for which we adapt Jay Galbraith's stage-of-growth model to illustrate the principles of organizational design (see Exhibit 9.7).[35] In a typical case of a startup, the company is small (1–3 people), entrepreneurial, with probably a single product. It should not surprise managers that a formal organizational chart might not even exist. Processes consist of largely extensive, personalized exchange of information. As the firm begins to grow, however, such informality is not likely to be sustained (much to the dismay of some true-blooded entrepreneurs). Typically, small and new companies foster specialization through functional group-

Exhibit 9.7

A Framework for Analyzing Implementation at Different Stages of Growth and Development

STEP ONE: Analyze the company's current position using the factors below.

Factors Affecting Levels of International Development:
- Scope of products and services (low to high)
- Number of countries served (few to many)
- Level of customer sophistication (low to high)
- Capital investment intensity (low to high)

As all these factors increase in intensity, stage-of-growth evolves from Level I to V as depicted below. For example, Level I is characterized by a low scope of products and services, a few countries served, low customer sophistication, and low capital investment intensity. Level V would be the obverse of these factors.

STEP TWO: Determine the appropriate stage-of-growth for the company and use contingency table below to apply implementation parameters.

Implementation parameters \ Levels	I (low)	II	III	IV	V (high)
Stage of industry globalization	Local	Multidomestic	Multidomestic internationalization	Internationalization	Transnational/ Global
Primary strategic focus	Domestic	Multilocal	Incremental/core formula	Internationalization	Transnational/ Global
Strategy driver	Product adaptability	Product adaptability/ brand enhancement	Risk sharing/ learning	Local learning/ commitment	Systemic sharing and resource transfers
Formal structure	Business function	Business function plus international office	Business function/ country-based equity-based venture	Internationalization	Matrix/ country-based investment
Key integrative processes	Export function; marketing	Legal contractual	Coordination mechanisms; team building	Transferring firm DNA/business model; cross-cultural teams	Institutionalized learning and knowledge transfers
Informal structures	Entrepreneurial	Marketing	Cross-cultural incentives	Knowledge transfer	Institutionalized learning

Source: Adapted in part from Jay R. Galbraith, *Designing the Global Corporation* (San Francisco: Jossey Bass, 2000), pp. 23; 46–47.

ings, such as marketing, accounting, finance, and human resources. These different functions are then coordinated by clear programs that delineate areas of responsibility and integration. Functional organizations work most effectively when a firm has a single product.

With more growth, particularly when a firm begins to produce and market more products to multiple markets, functional structures can get overtaxed and overwhelmed as personnel are not able to pay adequate attention to more than a single product. It is at this point that the firm will shift to a product-line structure, or even a divisional structure, depending on the complexity of its operations and the scale of its business. With these newer structures, attention can be placed on numerous products with explicit task responsibilities. Specifically, a product manager is given the responsibility for the performance of a particular product and is held accountable for results. In a much larger organization, it is the divisional manager who takes on this role. Since differentiation is increased significantly, there is the corresponding need for integration and control. In typical cases, such integration is seen in the increased employment of integrating mechanisms, such as rules, hierarchy, goal-setting operations, direct contact between personnel, task forces, and integrators.[36] It is unusual for organizational systems and processes (i.e., procurement, staffing, IT, supply chain, and so on) to take an enlarged role. The use of more integrating mechanisms usually reflects a firm's commitment to a more complicated and expensive mechanism for control.

From this vantage point, it is not difficult to see how some implementation plans go awry. When rules and other forms of integrating mechanisms become overwhelming, then bureaucratic tendencies creep in, stifling creativity and innovative activities within the organization. However, the opposite might likewise occur, that is, the firm fails to adopt sufficient integrating mechanisms, such that there are frequent lapses in communication between different parts of the organization. Depending on how the firm diagnoses the problem, new structures and processes can be employed, ushering in yet another set of requirements and imperatives. Such variations of structures and processes are covered in detail in other books.[37] Our intention in drawing on this relatively simple example is to illustrate how differentiation and the need for control arise from a firm's growth strategy, and how congruency and stage of growth are employed as design principles to fashion new structures and processes (see Exhibit 9.8). As we will discuss in our next section, the inclusion of an international context adds even more complexity to organizational design. In early research, it was determined that this relatively "simple" stage-of-growth model did not apply as well to European firms.[38] This suggests that implementation in a cross-cultural context is more complex and tied to different cultural institutions. Therefore, our third design principle reflects the added embellishment of international growth and development.

DESIGNING THE GLOBAL ORGANIZATION

Cast in the context of international growth, a firm faces a series of organizing conditions that transcend purely domestic considerations: (1) levels of international development, (2) the need for cross-border coordination, and (3) its investment in capital and fixed costs, also called its capital intensity.[39]

LEVELS OF INTERNATIONAL DEVELOPMENT

The stage of international development reflects the firm's response to the differentiation imposed by its external environment. Specifically, the scope of products and

Exhibit 9.8 **Changing Design Imperatives**

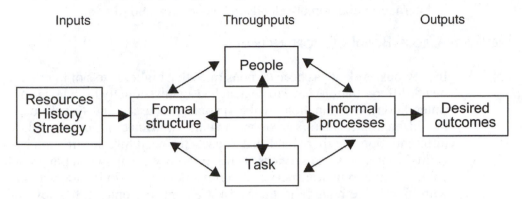

Inputs   Throughputs   Outputs

Previous treatises regarding congruence or "fit" centered on the co-alignment between design variables (strategy/task, formal structures, informal processes, and people).

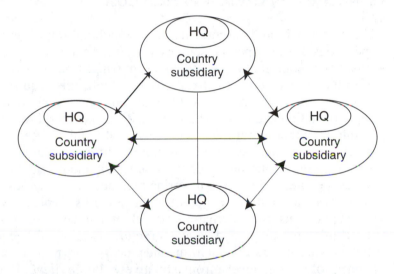

In a recent formulation that incorporates extensive internationalization, congruence and "fit" are now extended to co-alignment between networks. As companies increasingly link their subsidiaries and partners through internal trade networks, a network becomes the preferred way of establishing balance between strategic forces and organizational dimensions.

Source: Adapted from Jay Galbraith, *Designing the Global Corporation* (San Francisco: Jossey Bass, 2000), p. 12.

services reflects the firm's market strategy. In the case of Procter & Gamble, which offers a multitude of products across the world, such a scope is extensive. A related factor is the number of countries served outside the firm's home country. Again, in the case of P&G, the company serves customers in 170 countries all over the world. Still a third factor is the relative sophistication of the firm's worldwide customers.

When customers are aggressive, knowledgeable, and demanding of services, the level of internationalization also tends to be complex and diverse.

NEED FOR CROSS-BORDER COORDINATION

In previous work, it has been demonstrated that higher levels of international development (differentiation) have to be matched against equally high levels of coordination (integration). Coordination involves people, processes, and systems designed to align the differentiated factors in order to attain coordination and control. In addition to differentiation, another factor that impacts the need for coordination is the transportability of products and services. Transportability occurs when the product has a high value relative to its transport cost. Semiconductors provide an example of products with high value relative to their cost. Cement, in contrast, has low value but high transport cost.

THE FIRM'S INVESTMENT IN CAPITAL AND FIXED COSTS

This factor is more consequential in international implementation than in domestic operations. Firms expend resources, both fixed and variable, in extending operations outside its domestic border. When a firm's investment, particularly in factories and subsidiaries that represent fixed costs, is high, this requires an organizational arrangement that is more complex than one in which such investment is low. Stage of implementation in global markets depends on the interplay of the above three factors, an interplay that, in turn, leads to levels that require different sets of organizational structures and processes. Whereas more traditional organizing principles focused on the principle of congruency between organizational elements, that is, structure, processes, people, and culture, the principle underlying the design of global structures focuses on the co-alignment of different networks. Typically when each of the above three conditions (i.e., international development, need for cross border coordination, and firm's investment and capital structure) escalate or become more intense, new strategies and organizational forms and processes are needed that are further delineated in terms of varying levels, from a relatively simple (Level I) to very complex (Level V). We illustrate the stage-of-growth principle using an adaptation of a recent work by Jay Galbraith (see Exhibit 9.7).

LEVEL I: THE LOCAL/EXPORT MODE

The simplest level of internationalization characterizes a primarily domestic organization. This firm might have a single product and a simple business model. In most typical cases, it is also relatively new and small in size. Therefore, its main preoccupation is building market presence in the domestic market. Let's take an example of a firm that offers specialized training, such as GMAT or GRE review sessions, for prospective students seeking to join an MBA or other graduate program. As its target market will include those at work, the firm might offer evening classes that provide flexibility for this sample. In such a case, internationalization is not, as yet, an imperative. However, to the extent that the product or service is appealing in international markets, then a firm might fold international sales within the marketing function, or create a separate export unit.

When international sales become more significant, an alternative arrangement is for the firm to create an export department (see Chapter 5), such as typified in Exhibit 9.7. The **export department** becomes responsible for promoting sales, coordinating activities with the marketing department, and acting as an important conduit for local information that is channeled to headquarters. The export unit involves transferring products and services abroad through sheer exports, or exports with a simple sales subsidiary office. It provides the primary link with distributors or direct customers. It can also be used for consulting, advertising, or banking services. A good number of firms seeking to sell abroad for the first time often take this organizing mode before moving into more complex arrangements that involve foreign direct investment (FDI) and the transfer of resource advantages (see Chapter 4).

Processes support the functions of international sales and the export unit. In early stages of internationalization, the marketing department might handle international sales with all operations coordinated through this department, and with international sales being supplements to the income earned from home country operations. This works best when international sales are not as extensive and when value added from international sales is not a significant portion of the firm's total sales.

Coordination is achieved through functional integration for which the export unit plays a role. Marketing is involved with product adaptability, using information from the export unit to realign product and service offerings. Generally, because the firm tends to be new and small, informal norms support an entrepreneurial orientation.

LEVEL II: PARTNERING MODE

When a firm invests in another country, it can go beyond sheer exports and select a partner—usually a local company—to join in the investment. This **partnering** is usually a joint venture, although a number of strategic alliances in the form of marketing and R&D will work as well (Chapter 8). While a primary objective behind a joint venture or strategic alliance is to gain access into the targeted country, it behooves any firm to build in learning objectives as well. Specifically, we argue that firms formulate entry strategies with learning as one component of the decision-making process. Since learning is most fundamentally facilitated by frequent interaction, those firms entering in collaborative modes (nonequity ventures and equity joint ventures) proactively seek local market knowledge through partnerships. On the other hand, firms entering through sales contracts or wholly owned subsidiaries prioritize shorter-term sales or manufacturing efficiencies over market knowledge acquisition.

As such, we argue that firms entering through collaborative modes enhance their abilities to absorb greater knowledge of the market, and attain the requisite skills for working within a joint operation. In contrast, firms entering through noncollaborative modes will absorb less knowledge of the market and maintain either low-control (sales) or high-control (wholly owned subsidiary) modes of foreign activity.

Level III: International Groups and Divisions

As the level of internationalization increases, a reasonable response is to enhance the adaptive capabilities of the firm by way of more intensive functions and activities by the firm's subsidiary. In most cases, the subsidiary's role shifts from that of a mere export liaison to that of a multifunction business that can encompass its own supply chain, advertising, and further investment in the host country. Structurally, a common form of organizational differentiation, one popularized by Procter & Gamble, is through products and divisions. In contrast to functional organizations, product-management groups place primary emphasis on products, supported by the business functions. Such characterized the cases of Procter & Gamble, Kellogg Corporation, and Colgate Palmolive at their early inception.

Product groupings typically occur when the firm graduates from a single product into multiple ones that need varying degrees of attention. To the extent that these product groups become entrenched in market positions, they are treated as profit centers, where product managers assume responsibility for sales and costs. With more even growth that led to more autonomy and accountability, product organizations can be better organized in terms of divisions that perform all the functions required to carry out their operations. General Motors is the prototypical example of the divisional organization. Even so, some inefficiencies may develop because each division maintains its own inventories, which can result in redundancy and resource overlaps.

The international prototype in a divisional organization is a separate **international division** that centralizes all international operations. This enhances the role of international operations, while reducing the burden of overseas responsibilities by the local divisions. Because the international division is located in the host country, there is a risk of its become too detached from central headquarters, leading to problems in control and coordination. One such example was Jollibee, the fast food manufacturer based in the Philippines (see Chapter 3), which created international divisions in Taiwan and Hong Kong that repeatedly clashed with central headquarters and eventually had to be dismantled.

Level IV: Internalization

With greater level of complexity, more responsibility is given to the subsidiary, most notably that of local implementation. Within this level, the challenge lies in incorporating or recreating the firm's business model into the scope of local operations. Some authors refer to this as "transferring the company's DNA," while others simply call it **internalization** (see Chapter 4, pp. 149–150). The scope can include product development, brand management, R&D, or some modification of the firm's distinct advantage. Thus, the challenge for Wal-Mart might be transferring its advantages emanating from sheer warehouse size and strong supplier relationships to Latin America and Europe, where it faces more resistance.[40]

Firms step up international efforts in the form of global structures that are either product-based or area/country-based. A global product structure provides domestic divisions with worldwide responsibilities. In this arrangement, each product division sells its output throughout the world. In each case, the manager of the product division has internal functional support (akin to a functional organization) providing support to worldwide operations. This arrangement provides the necessary focus for a product group seeking to promote and sell its products throughout the world, as the product group is unencumbered by concerns of other products.

A related structure is the area/country organization. This structure, based on geographical location, is particularly suited for firms that serve markets in different areas. The rationale is to be as close as possible to the action. In the United States it has been popular to split the market into eastern, southern, western, and northern regions. Because each region has a different growth rate, the geographic structure allows each regional unit to monitor change in its own area. As with divisional organizations, some inefficiencies may exist and control might emerge as a serious problem.

LEVEL V: TRANSNATIONAL/GLOBAL FORM

The highest level of international development is the **transnational global form,** which occurs when "subsidiaries assume a leadership or contributory role in developing strategies and advantages for business. The transnational global form has all the international challenges of the preceding levels plus the task of coordinating the intensive complexity of multiple strategy centers."[41]

Mixed/matrix structures combine the elements of at least two types of organizational forms (e.g., functional and product management organizations) in ways that maintain flexibility in the face of complex environmental conditions. These mixed/matrix structures are particularly appropriate in complex environments that mandate simultaneous attention to both product and business functions and mandate sharing of resources. Even so, the arrangement creates a dual command system emphasizing functions and outputs. (see Exhibit 9.4, p. 374). Nevertheless, some firms can employ an even more complex set of mixed/matrix structures when more than two types of organizational forms are used. In the case of Asea Brown and Boveri, a merger between Asea AB of Sweden and BBC Brown Boveri Ltd. of Baden, Switzerland, in 1988, for example, the focus spans beyond functions and products to include considerations of countries, strategic focus, and timing that collectively result in a very complex matrix that does not have a geographic center.[42] While complex, ABB's mixed/matrix structure allows three internal contradictions to operate: it can be global and yet local, big and yet small; and decentralized and yet with centralized reporting and control.[43] Managers from different subsidiaries and factories are allowed to learn from each other, as well as compete for accomplishments.[44] Even so, at this level of complexity, ABB managers have to constantly adjust structures and processes to ensure that its mixed/matrix structure is able to retain its flexibility. Another company that has adopted a mixed/matrix, Philips Ltd., employs a special process "strategic conversations" to facilitate communications in its complex structure (see end-of-chapter case).

In terms of process, systemic and institutionalized learning become key prerogatives. While some learning is assumed in the previous levels, it is of prime importance for firms operating in global structures. Learning involves intricate transfers of knowledge and resources across the different subsidiaries, a process that a less internationalized firm is less inclined to undertake.

Decisions relating to the choice of organizational structure are time-consuming because they involve permanent or enduring investments in specific task allocations and groupings. These choices are often made over a long time period, and, because structural changes are also expensive and entail far-reaching consequences (such as a change in power), they are infrequent. Nevertheless, in periods characterized by crisis and significant transitions, structural changes reflect changes in basic strategy and resource competencies. It is then important to recognize how structural changes might, in fact, occur together with other processes in the "star" model.

As has been true of economic transformations, management and organizational innovations evolve in response to new pressures and opportunities presented by new technologies. Greater access to information enabled by new technology and the emergence of more educated knowledge workers form a symbiotic relationship as they are mutually reinforcing. Rather than producing large quantities of standardized products, companies have to reach their global customers directly. Moreover, since customers are better educated, more knowledgeable about the product, and more demanding of services, companies have to be able to respond in a fashion customized to consumers' needs. To meet this challenge, companies use their information-processing capabilities to change their internal operations, coordinate activities with suppliers and retailers, empower their employees to make decisions, and provide sufficient incentives for employees to retain their services. New and emerging organizational structures and processes are beginning to evolve in response to the growing requirements of the new global order (see Box 9.3).

HUMAN RESOURCE MANAGEMENT (HRM) ITS ROLE IN STRATEGIC IMPLEMENTATION

Designing organizational structures and processes is a complex and lengthy task that involves a combination of analytical as well as intuitive decision making. As companies progress from domestic to global, managers face a greater degree of complexity that requires the competency to grapple with cross-cultural issues and emergent locally based problems. In this context, human resource management becomes critical to strategic implementation in that it ensures a consistent talent flow throughout the company over stages of its life cycle.

Traditional **HRM** serves the function of integrating a number of key processes: recruiting, selection, training and development, and the performance appraisal system. Taken in this aggregate, HRM relates to the management of the entire work force, both domestic and international. Because cultures and institutions differ across countries, a firm that competes internationally needs to enlarge the scope of its HRM function in a manner that reflects these differences. Factors that

Box 9.3

The New Organizational Structures

In its survey of the new organization, the *Economist* (January 21, 2006), presented a sobering indictment that "the way people work has changed dramatically, but the way their companies are organized lags far behind." A major part of this problem is what the *Economist* writers call the "addiction to hierarchy." By this they meant specifically that the attachment to functional and product silos has not matched the growing complexity of environmental, competitive, and technological advances. Yet some firms have pioneered the development of new structures and processes. Some key examples, with their accompanying logics, are presented here.

Horizontal Structures: The Logic of Speed

While suited to the demands of consistency and reliability, top-heavy hierarchies have proved cumbersome in fast-globalizing organizations. The response time to consumer demands and competitive pressures was inadequate. Worst, however, was the inability of hierarchies to renew themselves and encourage a stream of innovations. Because knowledge is quickly transformed and information rapidly transmitted, it is imperative for firms to respond and adapt quickly to their environments. In this context, new organizational forms, specifically "lean-and-mean horizontal" structures, have been proposed. Horizontal structures aim at flattening the hierarchy by focusing on lateral activities, not up and down a top-heavy hierarchy. In contrast to a structure around functions or departments, the horizontal company is built around three to five "core processes" with specific performance goals with an "owner" assigned to each process. By reducing supervision, combining fragmented tasks, and eliminating nonessential work, response time is vastly improved. A horizontal structure uses autonomous teams as the building block of the organization, and its motivational force is meeting consumer demands more quickly and effectively than competitors. Among the firms that have adopted the horizontal structure to improve response time are the newly organized AT&T, which is now structured around processes; Eastman Kodak, which consists of over 1,000 teams to facilitate lateral exchanges; and General Electric, which boasts a horizontal design consisting of more than 100 processes and programs designed to improve their responsiveness to customers.

Hybrid Organizations: The Logic of Connectivity

The adaptability of firms depends on the manner in which information is processed. This, in turn, is tied to how decisions are made in organizations. A hybrid organization allows the achievement of the benefits of centralization and decentralization simultaneously. Rather than segregating operating processes, managers seek to connect them in creative ways. This is essential in coordinating the flow of activities and in providing decision makers with a thorough understanding of process dynamics. In addition, processes are managed by cross-functional teams to ensure that authority is not vested in a single individual but in teams that represent a range of expertise and accountability to make decisions. An example is Lexmark International, which utilizes cross-functional teams to respond to different customer groups.

Hybrid structures are closely aligned to learning structures that enhance the timely provision of information. Analysts John Redding and Ralph Catalanello suggest that broad-based learning can be achieved through a learning cycle characterized by continuous planning, improvised implementation, and deep reflection. As learning systems, hybrid organizations exhibit openness, systemic thinking, creativity, self-efficacy, and empathy. This imperative to learn is reflected in the belief that "the ability to learn faster than your competitors may be the only sustainable competitive advantage."

At the Shell Planning Group, systemic learning was achieved through scenario planning with the aid of computers. Other examples of hybrid organizations include Kao, which likens organizing to a "bio-function," Buckman Laboratories, which uses a global electronic communications network called K'Netix, and Ameritech-SBC, which uses a virtual company called Worldview Systems to enhance learning and connectivity.

(continued)

Box 9.3 *(continued)*

Quasi-Internal Networks: The Logic of Self-Organization and Empowerment

In service-oriented industries, information and knowledge are acknowledged to be the crucial drivers of corporate performance. If information is more accessible and pervasive across levels of hierarchy, employees can be empowered to exchange information and resources akin to democratic work practices and self-organization. A new organizational form, the "quasi-internal market structure," consists of numerous small, self-guided units that can adapt to their local environment more quickly, creating a form of organization that operates from the bottom up. Management professor William Halal has argued that modern economies require organic organizational systems composed of numerous small, self-guided units that can adapt to their local environments more easily. The logic of empowerment and self-organization is grounded in the need for managerial accountability and creative entrepreneurship. Therefore, the ideal situation is to treat each unit as though it were a small, separate company with relative freedom to carry out transactions inside and outside the firm.

There are numerous emerging quasi-internal markets, but the most prominent include the following: Cypress Semiconductors allows each business to have its own board of directors. Johnson & Johnson is organized into 166 separate chartered organizations. Au Bon Pain reports that each store owner is now part owner. Nucor Corporation has small teams running the company, while Merck and Company allows free choice of selection into teams by scientists. The Linux operating system is an evolving collaboration of thousands of software writers around the world that create and provide Linux-oriented services. EBay is the premier Internet auction site, where buyers and sellers create all the content by bundling work with key customers. At MutualMinds.com, the investors themselves pick the stocks that are publicly posted in the Internet, updated regularly, and evaluated for accuracy and consistency.

Sources: "The New Organization: A Survey of the Company," *The Economist* (January 21, 2006), pp. 1–15 (see www.economist.com/surveys); "The Horizontal Corporation," *BusinessWeek*, December 20, 1993, pp. 76–81; Dan Dimancescu, Peter Hines, and Nick Rich, *The Lean Enterprise* (New York: The American Management Association, 1997); Lynda Applegate, "Managing in an Information Age: Organizational Challenges and Opportunities," Harvard Business School (HBS) (9–196–002); "Designing and Managing the Information Age Organization," HBS (9–196–003); "Managing in an Information Age: IT Challenges and Opportunities," HBS (9–196–004); Peter Keen, *The Process Edge* (Boston: Harvard Business School Press, 1997); David Klein, ed. *The Strategic Management of Intellectual Capital* (Woburn, MA: Butterworth-Heinemann, 1998); W. Halal, "From Hierarchy to Enterprise: Internal Markets Are the New Foundation of Management," *Academy of Management Executive* 8, vol. 4 (1994): 69–83; W. Halal, A. Geranmayeh, and J. Pourdehnad, *Internal Markets: Bringing the Power of Free Enterprise Inside Your Organization* (New York: John Wiley & Sons, 1993); J. Redding and R. Catalanello, *Strategic Readiness* (San Francisco: Jossey Bass, 1994).

differentiate domestic and international human resource management include the following: different labor markets, mobility of managers, management styles and practices, national or global orientation of companies, and strategy and control systems of the companies.

Nevertheless, the gap between what is needed to accommodate these differences against what firms actually do is much wider in practice for a number of reasons. First, an international assignment is typically treated as an extension of the functional areas and departments of the company's domestic operation, or its human resource department. Therefore, the activities that comprise this international assignment are influenced by domestic policy rather than the needs that arise from the international context. The global strategy and environment drive the configuration of the HRM function. HRM, in this context, has a rather modest role in strategy formulation (i.e., the behavioral-based view).[45] Second, the focus on firm resources (the resource-based view), while valuable to the point of identifying a company's driving forces and motivation for a particular strategy (Chapter 3), is limited as it tends to ignore the potential value of the external market, specifically international opportunities.[46] Both tangible and intangible assets are considered organization-specific because they are part of the history of the company and they define the company through its competencies. Within the traditional perspective, the HRM program is not tightly coupled with strategic planning, and is more often referred to as the "personnel" department. It is no wonder that failures in international assignments, or in the primarily domestic HRM function, broadly defined, occur frequently, costing up to an estimated $2 billion a year for U.S. corporations alone.[47] Moreover, intangible costs such as damaged relationships with the host country can be more significant than the financial cost.

With these alarming figures, some firms have begun to reorient their HRM programs in ways that reflect their underlying international strategies and priorities. Current approaches to HRM reflect the belief that different stances or HRM approaches are contingent on a firm's propensity and priorities for global engagement. When complex global environments require dynamic strategic changes, human resource management becomes critical in selecting and training employees suited to new strategies.

Two particular challenges are paramount. First, when the capabilities are imitable or surpassed by other companies, a firm's competitive position can be seriously compromised. Second, organizations need a consistent inflow of talents to achieve a desirable pool of intangible assets in order to cope with emergent environmental changes. This requires well-defined human resource management goals and processes. Further, when HRM is dispersed among different subsidiaries in various locations, these must be connected and integrated to facilitate resource sharing and information transfer as ways to enhance new organizational competencies.

THE "CENTRIC" APPROACHES

In order to address these problems, HRM has to be correctly positioned in terms of a firm's strategy and international priorities. In the preceding section, we discussed strategic implementation using a stage-of-growth approach. We now adapt this approach to discuss the potential positioning of the HRM function. Historically, there are three developmental phases of international staffing (see Exhibit 9.9).[48]

The Ethnocentric Approach

An **ethnocentric approach** would entail the assignment of parent-country nationals, or expatriates, in all key management positions of a firm's subsidiaries. This is particularly applicable during the early stage of internationalization when many companies still maintain a predominantly domestic focus and believe that the most qualified individuals can only be found in home country of the headquarters. Management change and succession are all organized and handled from the headquarters. This approach allows the parent company to keep both formal and informal control

Exhibit 9.9

Comparison of Three "Centric" Approaches in Staffing

Approaches	Pros	Cons
Ethnocentric	• Ensures that what is practiced at home will be transferred abroad. • Maintains corporate culture across foreign subsidiaries. • Simplifies coordination and control among subsidiaries.	• Overlooks country-specific environmental factors. • Fails to recognize the ability of local talent. • The cost of using expatriates is high. • Local talent has limited upward mobility.
Polycentric	• Locally hired managers are familiar with local conditions, customs, languages, cultures, and general business practices. • Less expensive than using expatriates. • Subsidiaries can work independently.	• Limits career mobility for local talent. • Complex coordination and control system is required. • May risk internal consistency. • Managers in headquarters have less access to international experiences.
Geocentric	• Allows the transfer of competence and expertise from country to country. • Maximizes the use of talents.	• Using expatriates is costly. • Very challenging in coordination and maintaining internal consistency.

over foreign subsidiaries. In addition, it helps maintain a unified corporate culture and makes transfer of corporate competency relatively smooth. A total ethnocentric approach can be very expensive and impractical as international business grows. In addition, the control over expatriates can become complex as their responsibilities expand. Most companies, including Procter & Gamble, adopted this approach in their early stage of internationalization.

The Polycentric Approach

Using the **polycentric approach**, parent companies fill some management positions in subsidiaries with nationals of the host countries while keeping key positions in the headquarters filled by nationals of the parent companies. This approach greatly deemphasizes the use of expatriates. It allows the parent company to fully utilize the local talents and their social capital, by encouraging some level of autonomy on the part of subsidiaries. This is achieved by keeping subsidiaries at arm's length. This is particularly applicable in the developmental phase of internationalization when the subsidiaries mature and their managers become more aligned with the parent companies' corporate cultures, and when the parent companies allow the subsidiaries to operate with autonomy in some aspects of HRM. In a less-developed economy, this approach may not be as practical to implement, and parent company managers are still needed. This approach is commonly adopted when a company has gradually developed local talents into responsible positions. Again, using Procter & Gamble as an example, after over twenty years of company experience in China, many key positions in P&G China are held by Chinese. Some of these are home grown—local people educated locally. Many acquired their tertiary education outside China.

The Geocentric Approach

The **geocentric approach** focuses on the use of global managers on a worldwide basis, regardless of their nationality. As overseas subsidiaries grow in size and maturity and come more in line with the parent companies, a selection system that goes beyond geographic boundaries can be put in place. This will increase the size of the talent pool and will nurture a group of managers who have multiple country experiences. International managers will become well acquainted with individuals and the organizational network. This approach is particularly applicable for firms with extensive international operations and relatively developed global strategies. Under this approach, headquarters still control the appointment of key positions in subsidiaries. For newly established subsidiaries, there is still a tendency to use managers from the parent company to secure and harmonize the corporate system. The downside of this approach is the high cost of having expatriates moving between locations. Companies such as GM develop their managers for positions beyond their national base. For example, GM used Mexican nationals in Mexico and later transferred them to start up new ventures in Austria, Hungary, and China as they become more experienced.[49]

The "centric" management approaches served as useful guides for planning and staffing decisions when the stage-of-growth cycles were predictable and clearly demarcated. Even so, with growing complexity arising from the diversity of geographic coverage, cultural backgrounds, and institutional differences, the application of the "centric" approaches became much less compelling. Accordingly, more recent formulations of an international HMR function are more extensive, more systematic, and more balanced. Two are discussed next: the system-based and the competency-based HRM functions.

THE SYSTEM-BASED APPROACH

The **system-based approach** entails a three-level system to achieve the goal of creating co-alignment between a firm's strategy, organization structure, and its HRM function.[50] Specifically, it is recognized that HRM is an integral part of corporate policy. At the corporate level, any gap between headquarters and the firm's foreign subsidiaries is not considered a tactical issue, but a strategic one. The wider the gap, the more effort is required in preparing, planning, training, and making adjustments to ensure the success of the firm's international activities. At the business strategy level, the HRM department plans and identifies the preferred profiles of candidates and their placement within the organization. At the tactical level, the HRM department provides a multitude of methods, including psychological examinations, interviews, and cultural adaptability training to maximize the likelihood of a successful talent search.

The approach is distinctive because it builds the HRM function with the firm's strategy-making operation and structure. As indicated earlier, traditional HRM tended to be regarded as a "personnel" issue that was important at the tactical level, but not at the strategic level. Within this approach, HRM is deeply ingrained in decisions relating to current and future staffing, and, by extension, to the development of the firm's future core competencies.

The application of a system-based approach lends further insight into how a firm can manage locals or expatriates as part of its overall global activities. For perspective, locals are those hired to work in their country of origin. Expatriates are those hired by the companies of their home countries to work overseas. The decision of whether to use locals or expatriates mostly depends on how much local knowledge is required for the assignments, the availability of technical and specialized talents in foreign countries, the need to control subsidiary operations, and the need to acquire foreign experiences.

In general, the cost of expatriates is significantly higher than that of hiring locals. The decision to use locals instead of expatriates is mostly made because of its motivational value and cost benefit. If gaining foreign experience as part of management development is critical to the headquarters, expatriates will be preferred even though the cost is higher. Among many issues involved, the need to look beyond using locals and expatriates necessitates the use of inpatriates.[51] Inpatriates are individuals hired from foreign subsidiaries, due largely to their competencies, and brought into the headquarters for key positions. Their value goes beyond fulfilling job expectations. They are expected to infuse the corporate culture with new perspectives and build a global network of experts who can be transferred to different subsidiaries of a multinational organization.

THE COMPETENCY-BASED APPROACH

This **competency-based approach** recognizes the dynamic nature of the global environment and acknowledges the need for a dynamic set of global competencies to sustain global competitive advantage. In other words, "competencies are broader sets of human attributes than the narrowly defined knowledge, skills, and abilities of the past."[52] A set of dynamic global competencies is created through the continuous renewal and improvement of current competencies. This means that a company's strategic intent includes a relentless process of discovery and the transformation of current competencies into new ones.

To ensure this, capable global managers are needed throughout the process to provide an enduring source for a firm's competencies. Competencies are organized as follows: (1) input competencies—capital, labor, physical assets, and other factor inputs to the organizations; (2) managerial competencies—top management team capabilities, social knowledge, informal internal/external networks, and personal social capital of individual managers that can be used to accomplish the mission of the organization; and (3) transformation-based competencies—the ability of management to accomplish the tasks necessary to gain a competitive position in the marketplace, which assumes adaptability and learning capabilities embedded in the organization.[53] The greater the stock of competencies is, the larger the amount of strategic options that can be executed by management.

The function of HRM is to directly link all three categories. In input competencies, HRM identifies and selects qualified individuals for the companies. Employees can be from different ethnic and social backgrounds. In the case of managerial competencies, HRM provides the necessary training and development. As part of the training,

Exhibit 9.10

Factors That Determine the Use of Inpatriates

1. The stage of globalization. There are different needs at different stages of globalization. A company tends to be more involved in the global market when it advances from one level up to another.
2. The existing heterogeneity of global operations. The breadth and depth of global operations determines the heterogeneity of the internal environments. The more heterogeneous it is, the more complex it is and the greater the need to introduce a new level of knowledge, coordination, and control through the use of inpatriates.
3. Future strategic direction. An organization's perspective on the future affects its needs in terms of global talents and resources.

Source: Adapted from Michael G. Harvey, Milorad M. Novicevic, and Cheri Speier, "An Innovative Global Management Staffing System: A Competency-based Perspective," *Human Resource Management* 39, no. 4 (2000): 381–94.

managers of diverse backgrounds are given opportunities to exchange knowledge and share experiences. Some managers may possess country-specific knowledge and connections that can potentially make up the institutional void for the company's global and subsidiary operations. The more heterogeneous the group of managers is, the more diverse the competencies, which in turn generates better opportunities for enhanced organizational performances. These can be manifested through a change of manager's views of business environments in other countries, a reshaping of their thinking, and a renewal of their visions for the companies as well as oneself.

In the case of the need for new strategies, HRM training and development focuses on creating a collective experience base and/or organization learning capability that can lead to an organizational culture or a learning environment.[54] To build diversity, managers from outside the firm's headquarters or even outside of the organization are employed. These individuals may possess specific social capital that can provide the firm more leverage with its suppliers and customers, if not the social capital to facilitate strategic connections. Managers of such backgrounds and talents are often limited in supply and may be difficult to retain.

A competency-based approach focuses on diverse bases of knowledge that can complement and reinforce each other. Managers who are trained within these multicultural, multidisciplinary environments tend to develop a mindset that tends to provoke proactive thinking and visionary breakthroughs for their organizations (see Chapter 10). An important aspect in this perspective is the emphasis on the value of quasi-cultural control through inpatriates' coordination/integration of functional responsibilities between headquarters and subsidiaries. Exhibit 9.10 summarizes the factors affecting the use of inpartriates by multinational enterprises.[55]

A specific application of competency-based approach is the **competency cube** (see Exhibit 9.11), which integrates three competency dimensions: cultural, functional, and product competencies.[56] All three dimensions are measured by breadth and depth. Cultural literacy can be enhanced by cross-cultural training. Functional breadth is based on common expertise, experiences, and use of common infrastructural resources, such as accounting, marketing, production, and so forth, while functional depth re-

Exhibit 9.11   **The Competency Cube**

Cultural competency	Functional competency	Product competency
• Cultural literary	• Expertise • Experience • Use of infrastructural resources • Level of specialized expertise	• Ranges of differentiation from commodities to specialty products

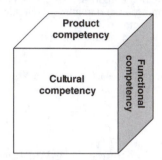

Source: Adapted from Allen D. Engle Sr., Mark E. Mendenhall, Richard L. Powers, and Yvonne Stedham, "Conceptualizing the Global Competency Cube: A Transnational Model of Human Resource," *Journal of European Industrial Training* 25, no. 7 (2001): 346–53.

fers to the level of specialized expertise available in the field. Product breadth ranges from industrial goods and commodities of very little differentiation to consumer and specialty products of high differentiation. Organization strategies directly affect the competencies required of their global managers.

These three dimensions construct a model that allows an organization to identify its "location" within these underlying competencies. This location of the company will vary, depending on the strategy of the company, and the complexity of the environment. A balance between competencies and organization strategies is critical to the multinational enterprise. An organization can gain competitive advantage through the enhancement of one or more of these dimensions. In human resources, all functions are going to be based on these three dimensions. Managers are selected based on their competencies in the breadth and depth of cultural, functional, and product dimensions. Companies will maximize their selection efficiency when using these as hiring criteria. Managers' imbalance in these competencies will result in more training and fewer rewards.

CONCLUSIONS

As organizations move from domestic to global operations, fierce competition drives firms to attend to issues of strategic implementation, with the realization that properly implemented strategies, achieved in large part through the design of appropriate structures and processes, will create competitive advantages that are more difficult for others to copy, thereby more sustainable. These drastic changes in strategic levels, structures, unit of analysis, organization environments, unit of control, and performance expectations require a fundamental rethinking of all design issues, as well as the major responsibilities in international human resource management.[57] For organizational theorists, what matters is the congruency or fit between different elements of the organization. The extension to an international context adds on the imperative that "fit" extends to networks, or to different international subsidiaries as well. For HRM pundits, what matters is maintaining a stream of human capital to flow into and remain in the organization so as to constantly generate competitive advantage renewal and rejuvenation, both in the headquarters and subsidiaries. Able employees must be capable of coordinating the company's global strategic efforts while attending to host country strategies.

In this chapter we consistently pointed out demarcations between traditional and contemporary approaches to organizational design and to the HRM function. While the design principles of congruency and stage of growth are viable and applicable across different settings, we are beginning to see the emergence of different types of structures and processes that transcend traditional functional, product, divisional, and geographical structures. Within a global context, stage of growth now underlies the linkages between international subsidiaries, and, within HRM, it is widely recognized that a top management team must possess complementary international and multicultural intelligence and be capable of converging different global competencies.[58] All these require a systematic, purposeful, and focused approach to linking subsidiaries and functional units in different parts of the world. Our discussion of competency-based HRM, for instance, offers a perspective that balances the diffusion of competencies across organization units along with the need to share this depth of competencies. The global game raises the stakes for those involved in organizational design and HRM. For example, an organization may redesign human resource service and delivery, streamline information accessibility and availability, automate administrative tasks, outsource payroll and benefits function, and outsource information systems.[59] For this to happen, however, it is imperative that managers have the training to be involved in corporate-level policy and strategy decisions. Consequently, there is a corresponding level of expectations for the human resource specialist's knowledge in strategy development and process planning, understanding of behavior and motivation, and organizational learning practices, processes, and resources.[60]

Taken as a whole, strategic implementation involves purposeful and intricate design, a thorough understanding of organizational structure and processes, and a deep understanding of human behavior in a cross-cultural context. Although going global is not an entirely new idea to business, there are still a very limited number of global managers around who have the requisite skills. A fundamental trait in global managers is an exceptionally open mind, an unusual respect for how things are different from country to country, and an appreciation of why these things are different. Moreover, global managers need to be adaptive and should have "the capacity to comprehend world trends as they affect business, governments, and standards of competition."[61] For these managers, success may not reside only in their technical or specialized skills, but in their capacity to communicate, exude broad-based sociability, exhibit cultural flexibility and a cosmopolitan orientation, and cultivate a collaborative negotiation style.[62] In our view, this comes by way of

a developed and cultivated global mindset, the second anchor of strategic implementation, and the subject matter of our next chapter.

SUMMARY

1. This chapter discusses implementing global strategies through structures
   and processes. Organizations require appropriate strategies that are formulated in tandem with organizational structures and processes. Professor Jay Galbraith has proposed four specific issues that exacerbate the
   problem of global integration. They are global complexity, the need to
   recreate the sources of a firm's competitive advantage as discerned by its
   business model, the firm's geopolitical uncertainty, and the globalization
   of consumers. These problems suggest the importance of well-designed
   structures. A sustainable, hard-to-imitate advantage is often dependent
   upon excellent implementation.

2. Without a good business model, strategies are bound to fail. Implementation
   guidelines and logical models are used to help managers execute decisions
   throughout the model. Three fundamental principles of implementation
   are recommended in this chapter. First, firms must understand that what is
   implemented is the firm's strategy. Hence, strategy must be defined clearly.
   Second, efficient coordination and allocation of tasks and responsibilities
   reduces uncertainty and risk. Three, continuous assessment entails an incremental and sequential process that underpins a firm's stage of growth
   and development.

3. There is no one best way for strategic implementation. However, it helps
   to understand the three basic characteristics that can be found in organizations. They are: internal interdependence, capacity for feedback, and system
   equilibrium. The latter means that an organization will seek ways to achieve
   balance when needed. This chapter suggests four basic variables for designing an organization. First, task specification reduces uncertainties. Second,
   individual differences in knowledge, skills, needs, and preferences constitute
   part of organizational characteristics. Third, the formal side of the organization, such as structures, processes, methods, procedures, policies, and the like,
   provides it with consistency and stability. Fourth, the informal organization
   encompasses shared values and implicit processes resulting in corporate
   cultures that affect individual behavior.

4. Organizational congruence is determined by the fit of any pair of the four
   variables. There are four ways of determining congruence: internal consistency, contingency, efficiency, and balance. In other words, strategic priority
   and reward systems should be consistent in order to motivate employees.
   Different environments require different structures, and a highly volatile
   environment requires a very flexible structure for fast adaptation. A proper
   balance between flexibility and control is essential to complex and differentiated organizations.

5. Different environments and situations call for different structures. The stages

of growth of an organization also affect implementation. It has been suggested that for each type of growth strategy there is an appropriate organizational form to go with it. Firms in rapidly changing environments tend to have more flexible and organic structures, while those in stable, predictable environments foster more mechanistic or bureaucratic structures. Changes in size and age are also said to have an impact on the types of "crises" that require more complex structures and control processes. Last but not least, any source of diversity promotes the evolution of new organizational forms.

6. International growth affects congruency and consistency among strategies, structures, people, and formal and informal processes. The higher the level of international development and the more complex and diverse the environment is, the stronger the need for better coordination and control. The higher the cost of investment, the more complex the arrangement is.

7. There are five levels of international growth. Level I is the local/export mode. Its main task is building market presence in the domestic market. Typically, an export unit can be used to fulfill that need until the firm moves into foreign direct investment. The organization remains as functional management structure, and coordination is achieved through functional integration. Level II is the partnering mode. It includes joint ventures and strategic alliances of various sorts. Learning is often the primary objective, and business is carried out in a collaborative fashion. Level III is the international product and division mode, for example, area/country organizations, in which geographical location is the focus or in which the product management mode is emphasized. This mode allows each unit to monitor changes in its own environment for higher adaptability and intensive functional operations. Level IV is the internalization mode and is designed for the handling of a greater level of complexity. Subsidiaries are authorized with more responsibilities and are expected to incorporate or recreate the firm's business model in their own operations. This comes into play with either product-based or area/country-based modes, each possessing its own functional supports. Level V is the transnational/global form in which subsidiaries assume a leadership or contributory role in developing strategies and competitive advantages for the firm. Its mixed/matrix forms combine the elements of functional and product management in ways that maintain flexibility in the face of complex environmental conditions. It has a dual command structure. A systemic and institutionalized learning process is a key prerogative. The success of learning involves intricate transfers of knowledge and resources across subsidiaries.

8. HRM ensures a consistent flow of talent throughout the company. There are three general approaches in HRM. The "centric" approach consists of the ethnocentric, polycentric, and geocentric approaches. The system-based approach entails a three-level system: corporate, business, and tactical. The competency-based approach focuses on diverse bases of knowledge that can complement and reinforce each other: cultural, functional, and product competencies. A balance between competencies and organization strategies is critical to the multinational enterprise.

KEY TERMS

Strategy
Tasks
Individuals
Formal structure
Differentiation
Process
Corporate culture
Congruency
Stage-of-growth model
Export department
Partnering

International division
Internalization
Transnational/global form
Mixed/matrix structures
HRM
Ethnocentric approach
Polycentric approach
Geocentric approach
System-based approach
Competency-based approach
Competency cube

DISCUSSION QUESTIONS

1. Why is implementation crucial to strategic success?
2. What are the fundamental principles of implementation?
3. What are the basic characteristics of organizations?
4. What are the four fundamental decision variables?
5. What is the concept of "congruency" in organization structure and how is congruency determined?
6. What are the three factors that affect organization decisions? Please provide examples when illustrating your points.
7. Discuss the local/export mode, its appropriate type of organization structure, and how a firm can attain strategic success through its strategy-structure fit.
8. Discuss the partnering mode, its appropriate type of organization structure, and how a firm can attain strategic success through its strategy-structure fit.
9. Discuss the foreign mode, its appropriate type of organization structure, and how a firm can attain strategic success through its strategy-structure fit.
10. Discuss the internalization mode, its appropriate type of organization structure, and how a firm can attain strategic success through its strategy-structure fit.
11. Discuss the transnational mode, its appropriate type of organization structure, and how a firm can attain strategic success through its strategy-structure fit.
12. What is the ethnocentric approach in HRM? In what situation does this approach fit a global company?
13. What is the polycentric approach in HRM? In what situation does this approach fit a global company?
14. What is the system-based approach in HRM? Select a global company as a case study and explain why this approach fits this company.

15. What is the competency-based approach in HRM? Select a global company as a case study and explain why this approach fits this company.
16. Compare and contrast the "centric" approach, the system-based approach, and the competency-based approach.

ACTION ITEM 9.1. APPLYING CONGRUENCY ANALYSIS TO YOUR ORGANIZATION

This exercise is best done in groups. Based on the team experiences, select one organizational unit or a specific group to illustrate the congruence model. Please use Exhibit 9.6 as a guide in answering the following questions:

1. Describe the basic nature of each of the four components with an emphasis on their critical features:

A. Key Strategy/Task to Be Done

_____

_____

_____

B. Nature, Background, and Skills of Individuals/Managers

_____

_____

_____

C. Type of Formal Organization

_____

_____

_____

D. Nature of Informal Organization (Corporate Culture)

_____

_____

_____

2. Analyze to determine the relative "fit" among components. Specifically, where are the "mismatches"? (Use the text discussion on pages 378–379.)
3. Identify areas where there are significant and meaningful differences between desired and actual outputs in the organization (unit). Discuss how the (possible) lack of congruency among components might be contributing to this problem.
4. Indicate what possible actions might deal with the causes of problems.

CASE-IN-POINT. TRANSFORMING IWDS's BUSINESS IN ASIA: THE ROLE OF GLOBAL HRM

BY: ANNMARIE NEAL AND MANUEL SERAPIO[63]

In preparation for her meeting with the executive committee, Elizabeth Ryan took inventory of her global HR team's key initiatives over the past five years. Elizabeth had joined International Warehouse and Distribution Solutions (IWDS) in early 2001 as senior vice-president of global human resources. During the past five years, she has worked with IWDS's top leaders in overseeing the transformation of the company's business in Asia. Elizabeth has focused on major strategic HR issues, including rebuilding of the leadership team in Asia, aligning IWDS's HR strategy in Asia with the company's growth objectives, and integrating the company's acquisitions in Hong Kong and Singapore.

IWDS is one of the world's leading providers of distribution facilities and services. Based in St. Louis, Missouri, the company had 2005 revenues in excess of $5 billion, 4,500 employees, and over 2,300 distribution facilities owned and managed worldwide. IWDS's customers include the world's largest multinational companies, such as Wal-Mart, General Motors, Procter & Gamble, and Nestle. The company has traditionally concentrated its business in North America and Europe, where it has developed over two-thirds of its total distribution facilities. In recent years, however, IWDS has embarked on an aggressive Asian expansion—in response to the rapid growth of transpacific trade and its customers' business in the region. Since 2004, the company has developed or acquired over 400 distribution facilities, most notably in China, Hong Kong, Japan, and Singapore.

As she looked back at Global HR's accomplishments over the past five years, Elizabeth organized them into three scenarios, each representing an important milestone in the transformation of IWDS's business in Asia. For each scenario, she identified the opportunities and challenges facing IWDS and then outlined corresponding actions that Global HR took to address them. Finally, Elizabeth addressed the future challenges facing HR and IWDS in Asia.

SCENARIO 2001

Assessing the Opportunities and Challenges in Asia

IWDS expanded into Asia in the mid-1990s. One of its major customers—a large U.S. retailing firm—asked IWDS to set up distribution facilities to serve its stores in Japan and Hong Kong. IWDS's business in North America and Europe was growing rapidly at that time and the company did not want to venture into Asia. However, the U.S. customer gave IWDS very little choice. Fearing the loss of an important account to competitors, IWDS reluctantly followed the U.S. customer to Asia.

When Elizabeth joined IWDS in 2001, the company's operations in Asia represented less than 10 percent of total revenues and were barely breaking even. Its Asian operations were headquartered in Hong Kong, where a management team and staff of 40 people managed about 70 distribution facilities and 350 employees in 6 markets: Hong Kong, China, Japan, Taiwan, South Korea, and Australia.

Following the Asian crisis in 1997, international trade to and from Asia showed signs of recovery. Leading this recovery was China. A growing number of U.S. and European companies set up production operations in the Pearl River Delta region (Southern China and Hong Kong) and Shanghai. Many of these companies were customers of IWDS in North America and Europe.

Despite these signs of recovery and the strong growth projections of over 50 percent per year in Asia, IWDS's top management showed little interest in the region. Elizabeth attributed this, and the lackluster performance of IWDS's Asian operations, to three factors.

- First, corporate headquarters was still very much United States and Europe-centric. Asia was viewed as less important and was not on the radar screen of corporate headquarters. In fact, two executives at headquarters, namely, the executive vice-president of real estate and the chief technology officer, had a general "fear of doing business in Asia," particularly China.
- Second, because of the percentage of revenue it represented at that time and its lack of visibility at corporate headquarters, Asia was not considered an important market. Mr. Takashi Tanaka, the managing director of Asia, was ineffective in selling the region to top management at corporate headquarters. He operated the business in Asia largely as an "autonomous" unit and had very limited interaction with corporate headquarters.
- Third, management and employee morale in Asia were at the lowest levels in the company. A 2000 corporate employee pulse survey revealed that Asia had the lowest scores companywide. The survey specifically identified three areas of particular concern to employees: (1) issues with strategy and direction; (2) issues with management; and (3) too few resources with which to grow the business.

Global HR's Response

Elizabeth was initially brought into the company by the executive vice-president of Human Resources to help address morale issues in the region. She spent her first six months at the company listening to the employees and understanding the dynamics of IWDS's business in Asia. Specifically, she probed into the results of the 2000 employee survey by conducting focus groups of employees at the Hong Kong headquarters and in the company's six Asian markets. She also spent time exploring the cultural dynamics of the region versus corporate expectations.

From these conversations Elizabeth confirmed that the majority of IWDS's Asian employees were highly dissatisfied with the current state of affairs. They felt that the company failed to articulate a strong sense of direction and strategy. Most employees sensed that Asia took a back seat to North America and Europe and that the company did not appreciate the growth potential of the Asian markets. Further, the managers at the Asian headquarters in Hong Kong and the six country managers—all of whom were recruited from Asia and Australia—had very limited, and thus unproductive, interactions with corporate headquarters. Mr. Tanaka closely controlled and monitored communication with headquarters in St. Louis. Finally, although the Asian operations were run in a relatively autonomous manner, they were prohibited from doing their own marketing as this fell under the purview of the Global Marketing group at headquarters. IWDS's Asian business was conducted mainly as an operating arm of the company and its responsibility was to help the business establish or acquire warehouse facilities and offer distribution services in their respective markets.

SCENARIO 2003

Stabilizing the Region

Elizabeth knew that the first priority for the company was to stabilize its operations in the region. Based on her recommendations, IWDS released Mr. Tanaka from his contract and replaced him with Blair Underwood.

IWDS recruited Blair from United Parcel Services (UPS), where he was president of European and Asian Operations. A British national, Blair had lived in Hong Kong for twenty years. He is an Asian expert and was responsible for successfully launching UPS's business in China. In addition to UPS, Mr. Underwood had worked for McKinsey Consulting, Federal Express, and Li & Fung.

Blair set very high expectations for his team and for the company's business performance in Asia. He set out to put Asia on the CEO's radar screen. He forged strong partnerships with top business leaders in St. Louis, as well as his counterparts in major IWDS markets in North America and Europe. Blair set ambitious growth projections for the region. He lobbied for and received approval from corporate headquarters to transfer marketing responsibility for Asia to his team. Additionally, he procured the budget he needed to incrementally add critical resources.

Signaling a stronger commitment to Asia, corporate headquarters expatriated two vice-presidents (VP of Operations and VP of Finance/Controller) from the United States to Hong Kong and Shanghai. Not only did these two expatriates help open communication lines from Asia to the United States, but they also played an important role in assisting Blair in fast-tracking the growth of IWDS's business in Asia.

Global HR's Response

Elizabeth worked closely with Blair on several strategic HR initiatives that were instrumental in transforming IWDS's business in Asia. These included:

- *Anchoring strategy.* Business strategy for Asia was aligned directly with corporate objectives for growth. To accomplish this effectively, strategy was translated directly into measurable operating objectives, management processes, and performance management systems.
- *Applying talent management strategies.* Assessments were made that compared organizational capabilities against business strategy. Critical positions were identified based on these assessments. Evaluations were made about the current talent skills and capabilities and gaps were identified.
- *Consulting on performance management and culture change.* To create strong

links between performance and objectives, direct alignments were made between the two, creating a culture of performance that was enforced with pay-for-performance initiatives. Aggressive performance management standards were also put in place to provide the basis for terminating nonperforming managers.

- *Hiring much-needed talent.* Aggressive recruiting strategies were put in place to fill requisites while evaluating the top talent in the region (this process is also referred to as "top grading").
- *Improving global compensation.* An innovative rewards and recognition strategy was implemented that directly supported strategy execution. The program was closely aligned with the corporate office's compensation system.
- *Coaching senior leaders in Asia.* Intensive coaching was given to high-level executives in Asia to improve their understanding of corporate ("mother ship") dynamics and politics, and how to get things done effectively at corporate.
- *Promoting ongoing feedback and communications.* Feedback mechanisms were formalized to ensure ongoing information was received from employees about organizational dynamics and employee–corporate communications.

SCENARIO 2006

Explosive Growth in the Region

In 2006, industry growth in the region exploded, along with IWDS' business. Several drivers converged to bring about this development. The first driver was the explosive growth of the Chinese market—both in the external sector and the domestic economy. Direct beneficiaries of this growth were other Asian economies, most notably Japan, where IWDS had a meaningful presence. Moreover, several of IWDS's largest customers in North America and Europe launched very aggressive expansion campaigns into China and Asia, prompting IWDS to expand its operations in Asia as fast as these customers expanded into the region. Blair's successful marketing programs and the resources that the company dedicated to boosting its business in Asia only added fuel to the fire as growth in the region far exceeded corporate expectations. At the end of 2005, IWDS has signed contracts to build and deliver over 500 distribution facilities to its customers by 2009. Revenue growth of the region was north of 65 percent.

In 2005 IWDS acquired Tiger Warehouse Ltd., one of the largest warehouse and distribution facilities operators in Asia. This company—with headquarters in Singapore and subsidiaries in Hong Kong, Japan, and China—helped IWDS address the explosive demand for distribution facilities in Asia.

However, throughout this period of rapid growth, operational excellence trailed top-line growth. The operating team had a very difficult time keeping up with growth in selected markets, such as Southern China. These markets were adding employees at an accelerated pace—in most cases doubling headcount in each market per year. One particular problem facing IWDS was a lack of employer brand awareness among potential recruits. IWDS found itself competing against large and successful multinationals and regional employers with well-recognized corporate brand names who were also aggressively recruiting talent for their Asia operations.

To address operational excellence issues, IWDS brought managers from its North American and European subsidiaries to help fill the talent gap in the Asia region. Also, corporate headquarters put in place processes and policies to encourage greater formalization and harmonize service quality in all of its Asian markets. Blair greeted the latter with mixed feelings—he knew that this will help increase quality consistency but was concerned that such formalization would constrain the entrepreneurial spirit and innovation among his management team.

Blair also found himself spending more time in Saint Louis. By this time, the CEO had been giving more attention to the region and was talking about bringing Blair to the United States for succession assignment. The investor community had also noted IWDS's strong performance in Asia and required more communication time with Blair in New York and at corporate headquarters.

Global HR's Response

To address the pressing issues facing IWDS's Asian business in 2006, Elizabeth's team put in place a number of fast-track measures focused on talent management in the region. These included employer branding, talent acquisition, expatriation, leadership development, and succession management.

IWDS hired a consulting company to boost its employer brand in Asia. The company also leveraged the reputation of the newly acquired subsidiary, Tiger Warehouse Ltd., in Asia. IWDS launched an aggressive recruiting campaign and showcased the company as one of the largest distribution facilities companies in the world as well as an employer of choice. This campaign partially worked, as more entry and mid-level people applied for jobs. However, recruitment problems persisted at senior levels and for specialist and senior management positions (e.g., global supply chain managers, real estate specialists).

As noted previously, IWDS launched an expatriation program to move talent into the region. Each year, about half a dozen mid-level and high-potential employees from headquarters accepted one-to-two-year developmental rotations to Asia. In addition, the company recruited several expatriates from its European operations.

Elizabeth also launched an ambitious emerging leadership development program for high-potential leaders within the region. The program consisted of three key elements:

1. Developing unique skills needed to support the growth in the region (innovation, marketing, project and operations management, and global supply chain management);
2. Installing a manager development program to build skills needed to keep pace with growth (e.g., managing managers, managing functional and business units, etc.),
3. Sending high-potential leaders from Asia to St. Louis's executive development program for exposure.

Finally, Elizabeth developed a solid succession planning process for senior leadership roles including assessment, deployment, and development.

GLOBAL HR'S FUTURE CHALLENGES

In two weeks, Elizabeth Ryan was scheduled to give a presentation to the CEO, executive vice-president of Human Resources, and the executive committee. In this presentation, she planned to review the progress that her team had made vis-à-vis the Global HR initiatives launched in Asia. She would also outline the current and future challenges facing the business in Asia and recommend strategic and tactical measures to address the company's challenges. These challenges included:

1. Elizabeth knew that a serious risk facing the business was the possible loss of Blair Underwood. Elizabeth was concerned that the CEO would soon decide to bring Blair to corporate headquarters for a substantial succession assignment. Blair had signaled that he was interested in taking on the position of president of one of IWDS's business units in St. Louis, and Elizabeth knew that Blair was under serious consideration for the job. Elizabeth was also aware that other major multinational companies and headhunters had approached Blair to lead their regional headquarters in Asia. Elizabeth expected the executive committee to ask for her recommendation about Blair's next career move at IWDS and how best to retain him should the CEO decide not to offer him a job at headquarters.
2. The CEO commissioned a major study on the feasibility of outsourcing and offshoring more of the company's operations to Asia, including customer support facilities, data centers, shared services, and internal call centers. The recently completed study called for the company to increase its offshoring to Asia and recommended that this effort be championed by IWDS's Asian operations. Elizabeth was not sure whether IWDS should take on this responsibility particularly in light of the fact that IWDS's business in Asia was growing at full speed.
3. Finally, although Elizabeth was very pleased with the progress that her team has made in Asia, she knew that there was a lot more work to be done to lead and support IWDS business' transformation in Asia. She wanted to make sure that she asks for and get the CEO and executive committee's commitment and support for the next phase of her work in Asia.

CASE DISCUSSION QUESTIONS

1. What role should HR play in a strategic, operational, financial, and cultural transformation—and especially when entering an emerging market?
2. Critique Elizabeth and HR's responses to the opportunities and challenges in each of the scenarios (Scenario 2001, Scenario 2003, and Scenario 2006). Identify two to three "best in class" practices that Elizabeth adopted in order to provide strategic HR services to her company's Asian operations. What would you have done differently?

3. Elizabeth has a challenging task as she carefully navigates cultural dynamics of both the Asian market and the corporate infrastructure. Identify some of these challenges. How should Elizabeth deal with these challenges?

4. How should Elizabeth deal with IWDS future challenges? What are her next "to do's" to take the region to the next level? Going forward, what should Elizabeth "not do"?

5. What type of centric approach has IWDS adopted at the three stages of its Asian operation: 2001, 2003, and 2006?

6. What are the implications for HR should the company decide to offshore more of its operations (e.g., data centers, customer support facilities, etc.) to Asia? How should Elizabeth and her team deal with this move?

CASE-IN-POINT. CAN PHILIPS LEARN TO WALK THE TALK?

BY IAN WYLIE[64]

Royal Philips Electronics is a global technology powerhouse, and it always has been. Since Anton and Gerard Philips began making light bulbs in 1891, inventors in the Netherlands-based company's Eindhoven labs have been churning through patent applications at a rate of 3,000 a year. Relentless investments in R&D have generated such breakthrough inventions as the rotary head shaver in 1939, the compact cassette in 1963, and CD and DVD formats in the 1980s and 1990s.

But ask a shopper at Wal-Mart to name her favorite Philips product, and she may not be able to come up with one. Where is Philips' Walkman? Its iPod? Its killer app?

With annual sales of $28.8 billion, Philips is Europe's largest electronics outfit. The company produces 2.4 billion incandescent lamps a year and fits picture tubes to one in seven TV sets worldwide. But in the critical consumer-electronics sector, neither Philips' size nor its innovation has produced satisfactory business results. Here's the troubling technology punch line: While the consumer-electronics sector accounts for one-third of Philips' sales, it contributes none of its profits.

That is the reason why Gerard Kleisterlee, who became Philips' president in April 2001, has announced his bold, unyielding challenge to everyone at Philips: The consumer-electronics division must make money in the United States, the world's biggest market for consumer electronics, within the next few years, or he'll simply shut it down.

There's nothing in Philips' recent performance to suggest that Kleisterlee's ultimatum will be easy to meet. Just ten years ago, Philips was close to bankruptcy after a series of strategic blunders and operational mishaps. A decade of financial restructuring has restored order to the balance sheet, but the legacy of limp branding and lazy diversification remains. Record losses in 2001 combined with a fifteen-year losing streak in the United States set the stage for Kleisterlee's arrival.

But Kleisterlee clearly believes that he knows what it will take to make Philips profitable. He has already made a number of textbook moves: He's selling nearly thirty noncore businesses with combined annual sales of about $1 billion. He's outsourcing the unprofitable production of cell-phone handsets. And, in a split from the policies of Cor Boonstra, his predecessor, Kleisterlee is now moving aggressively to centralize a number of service functions, such as human resources, payroll, and finance.

But what is at the heart of Kleisterlee's plan to create "One Philips" isn't technology or tactics: It's talk. In order to build internal confidence, stimulate cross-boundary cooperation, and spark new-product speed to market, Kleisterlee is sponsoring what he calls "strategic conversations": dialogues that center around a focused set of themes that Kleisterlee believes will define Philips' future.

CAN WE TALK?

When Kleisterlee took the reins, he found a company that was rigidly segmented into six business divisions, with little or no communication among them. "We had become an armada of independent companies that all acted independently," he says.

His first step was to define four key themes that would describe a technology future that Philips could win: display, storage, connectivity, and digital video processing. By definition, those themes crossed technology boundaries. Winning, Kleisterlee saw, would require new and fresh dialogues across the business divisions. "Those four themes are critically important in a converging, interconnected world," he says. "Whether your vision is of a PC, consumer-electronic, or telecom-centric world, it's all about capturing information, sorting it, transmitting it, and displaying it."

Kleisterlee's strategic conversations for each theme begin by gathering together everyone who has a contribution to make—regardless of rank—for a one-day summit. Attendees exchange views, debate scenarios, and, ultimately, agree on strategies and road maps for key projects. "These meetings result in very clear goals and much better cooperation between the different divisions," says Kleisterlee.

As a result of their strategic conversations, for example, the board of management determined that winning in optical storage meant winning in the DVD-recorder market. The project team that was tasked with developing and bringing to market the first DVD recorder based on the new DVD+RW (rewritable) standard pulled in managers from Philips' semiconductors, components, and consumer-electronics divisions. The benefits, Kleisterlee proudly points out, are already visible: cross-boundary collaboration allowed Philips to cut its typical development time by a stunning nine months. Philips' range of DVD recorders (including a sub-$1,000 model) now claims 60 percent of the U.S. market.

Strategic conversations in the display category have identified a similar technology path. There, the cross-boundary team determined, winning means leading in the flat-screen-TV market. "Through strategic conversation, it became clear that we had too many resources invested in conventional TV development," says Kleisterlee. So at this month's consumer-electronics show in Las Vegas, Philips will unveil a full range of LCD TVs and a projection TV based on liquid crystal on silicon technology.

BACKING THE TALK

Philips staffers are no strangers to false starts and broken promises. But Kleisterlee appears to have their support. "Before he arrived, we were bitterly divided," says one senior manager who has worked for Philips in the United States and in the Netherlands. "But I know of many people who are sticking with Philips just because they have faith in Kleisterlee."

Kleisterlee—an electronics engineer who, like his father, has worked for Philips for his entire career—knows that a lot is riding on what happens in the move from technology to market, including the fate of the entire U.S. operation. Kleisterlee has written off 2002 as a "lost year." That means that the next twelve months will reveal whether his strategic conversations are truly inspired collaboration—or just a whole lot of talk.

* * *

Philips president Gerard Kleisterlee's strategic conversations have become a part of redesigning the company's R&D labs, changing the practice of innovation. Philips' 8,000 R&D workers from all six business divisions are dispersed around Eindhoven in the Netherlands. By 2006, Kleisterlee aims to move them all to a single 1,873,900-square-foot high-tech campus in that city. The new buildings will be flexible, making it possible for "theme teams" to assemble and disband as the need arises.

Philips will also be turning to a new source of inspiration: its consumers. Eindhoven is also home to HomeLab, an ambitious experiment in developing "ambient intelligence": homes and offices where spoken requests or even facial expressions will trigger music and movies to play, control environments, and respond to owners' particular needs. The lab rats in this modern homemaking experiment are flesh-and-blood humans who volunteer to live in the home 24 hours a day while Philips' researchers observe how they interact with the company's electronic prototypes. It's another part of Philips' attempt to break down boundaries between R&D and the rapid commercialization of innovation.

CASE DISCUSSION QUESTIONS

1. Despite being a global technology powerhouse, Philips still had some problems to be resolved. What are they? What do you think are the primary factors attributing to these problems?
2. Gerard Kleisterlee had made some "textbook" moves for Philips. Please analyze these moves in terms of the fundamental decisional variables (Exhibit 9.2).
3. What has Gerard Kleisterlee achieved in creating "One Philips"? Please analyze to what extent his tactics are structural changes or human resource management changes.

NOTES FOR CHAPTER 9

1. This introductory section draws on two sources: Nelson D. Schwartz, "Has Nokia Lost It?" *Fortune* (January 24, 2005): 41; and Nelson D. Schwartz, "The Man Behind Nokia's Comeback," *Fortune* (October 31, 2005): 39.

2. This paragraph is drawn from Andy Reinhardt, "Nokia: Answering the Call Won't Be Easy," *BusinessWeek* (August 15, 2005): 46.

3. "Special Report: The Giant in the Palm of Your Hand—Nokia's Turn," *The Economist* 37 (February 12, 2005): 72.

4. Ibid.

5. Ibid.

6. Information on Nokia's turnaround is adapted from Mark Veverka, "Nokia Strikes Back," *Barron's* (November 14, 2005): 26.

7. Andy Reinhardt, "Will Rewiring Nokia Spark Growth?" *BusinessWeek* (February 14, 2005): 46.

8. Ibid.

9. Based on personal communication and lecture notes, Professors Raymond Miles and Charles Snow.

10. Lawrence G. Hrebiniak, *Making Strategy Work* (Upper Saddle River, NJ: Wharton School Publishing, 2005), p. 33.

11. Jay R. Galbraith, *Designing the Global Corporation* (San Francisco: Jossey Bass, 2000), pp. 4–7.

12. Lawrence Hrebiniak and William Joyce, *Implementing Strategy* (New York: Macmillan, 1984), pp. 8–9.

13. A number of books have addressed the differences between universalistic and contingency approaches to organizational design. Historically, universalistic designs were supported by proponents of bureaucracy, administrative management, and human relations as the "one" best design. With the advent of contingency theory, however, pundits argued that the choice of organizational structure and processes depended on the environment, technology, strategy, and size. See accounts by Charles Perrow, *Complex Organizations: A Critical Essay* (Glenview, IL: Scott Foresman, 1979), pp. 178–218; D.S. Pugh, D.J. Hickson, C.R. Hinings, and C. Turner, "The Context of Organizational Structures," *Administrative Science Quarterly* 14 (1969): 91–114; Paul Lawrence and Jay Lorsch, *Organization and Environment: Managing Differentiation and Integration* (Cambridge: Harvard University Press, 1967).

14. David Nadler and Michael Tushman, "A Congruence Model for Diagnosing Organizational Behavior," in David Nadler, Michael Tushman, and Nina G. Hatvany (eds.), *Managing Organizations: Readings and Cases* (Boston, MA: Little, Brown and Company, 1982), p. 36. Also see David Nadler and Michael Tushman, "The Organization of the Future: Strategic Imperatives and Core Competencies for the 21st Century," *Organizational Dynamics* 28, no. 1 (Summer 1999): 45–46. Lawrence and Lorsch, *Organization and Environment*, pp. 6–7. Contingency theories have been among the organizing frameworks popularized by D. Hellriegel and J.W. Slocum, *Organizational Behavior*, 10 ed. (St. Paul, MN: Thomson/South-Western, 2006).

15. These four variables were introduced as part of an overall congruence model by Nadler and Tushman, "A Congruence Model for Diagnosing Organizational Behavior," pp. 35–48. See the updated version in Nadler and Tushman, "The Organization of the Future." These variables correspond to the variables of the "star" model developed by Jay Galbraith, *Designing Organizations: An Executive Briefing on Strategy, Structure, and Process* (San Francisco: Jossey-Bass Inc., 1995), pp. 11–17.

16. Nadler and Tushman, "A Congruence Model for Diagnosing Organizational Behavior," p. 41. The following section paraphrases the questions contained in the "task" section of their Figure 2.

17. Adapted from Jack Wood, *Organizational Behavior: An Asia-Pacific Perspective* (Queensland: Jacaranda Wiley Ltd., 1998); Original model is from Richard M. Steers and Lyman Porter, compilers, *Motivation and Work Behavior*, 4th. ed. (New York: McGraw-Hill, 1991); adaptation is used with permission.

18. Based on the work by L. Porter, E. Lawler and J. Hackman, *Behavior in Organizations* (New York: McGraw-Hill, 1975). Also see Richard Mowday, Lyman Porter, and Richard Steers, *Employee-*

Organization Linkages (New York: Academic Press, 1982). Early expectancy motivational models were developed by Victor Vroom, *Work and Motivation* (New York: John Wiley & Sons, 1964).

19. John Child, "Organizational Structures, Environment, and Performance," *Sociology* 6 (1972), pp. 1–22.

20. Lawrence and Lorsch, *Organization and Environment: Managing Differentiation and Integration*, pp. 9–11.

21. Ibid., pp. 156–158.

22. Matthew Karnitschnig, "Too Many Chiefs at Siemens?" *Wall Street Journal,* January 20, 2005, page A12.

23. Jay Galbraith and Daniel Nathanson, *Strategy Implementation: The Role of Structure and Process* (St. Paul, MN: West Publishing, 1978), p. 5.

24. Peter G.W. Keen, *The Process Edge: Creating Value Where It Counts* (Boston: Harvard Business School Press, 1997), p. 17.

25. Ibid., pp. 19–20.

26. Personal communication and lectures by Professor Charles O'Reilly.

27. John Kotter and James Heskett, *Corporate Culture and Performance* (New York: The Free Press, 1992).

28. Nadler and Tushman, "A Congruence Model for Diagnosing Organizational Behavior," p. 42. They acknowledge the earlier works on the congruence concept by George Homans, Harold Leavitt, James Seiler, Paul Lawrence, Jay Lorsch, and Alan Sheldon (page 38). The congruence hypothesis was later enlarged to the general concept of a "contingency theory" in a landmark book by Lawrence and Lorsch, *Organization and Environment: Managing Differentiation and Integration*, pp. 156–158.

29. Lawrence and Lorsch, *Organization and Environment: Managing Differentiation and Integration*, p. 156.

30. Alfred Chandler, *Strategy and Structure* (Cambridge, MA: MIT Press, 1962).

31. Lawrence and Lorsch, *Organization and Environment: Managing Differentiation and Integration*, pp. 156–158.

32. Professor Claudia Bird Schoonhoven implored researchers to be very specific about what they mean by congruence, "Problems with Contingency Theory: Testing Assumptions Hidden Within the Language of Contingency 'Theory'," *Administrative Science Quarterly* 26, no. 3. (Sept. 1981), pp. 349–377. Another excellent critique is by William H. Starbuck, "A Trip to View the Elephants and Rattlesnakes in the Garden of Aston," in Andrew Van de Ven and William F. Joyce (eds.), *Perspectives of Organization Design and Behavior* (New York: John Wiley & Sons, 1981), pp. 167–198. Even so, the debate about structural contingency theory is far from over. In a spirited rebuttal, Australian School of Graduate Business professor Lex Donaldson staunchly defends the theory. See Lex Donaldson, *The Contingency Theory of Organization* (Thousand Oaks, CA: Sage Publishing Company, 2001).

33. Larry Greiner, "Evolution and Revolution as Organizations Grow," *Harvard Business Review* 50, no. 4 (July/August 1972): 37–46.

34. Galbraith and Nathanson, *Strategy Implementation: The Role of Structure and Process*; also see Jay Galbraith and R. Kazanjian, *Strategy Implementation: Structure Systems, and Process*, 2nd ed. (St. Paul, MN: West Publishing, 1986).

35. This organizing framework draws from Galbraith, *Designing the Global Corporation*, pp. 35–42.

36. Galbraith and Nathanson, *Strategy Implementation,* pp. 64–65.

37. Ibid., pp. 63–71; Hrebiniak and Joyce, *Implementing Strategy*, pp. 65–92; also see Raymond Miles and Charles Snow, *Organizational Strategy, Structure, and Process* (Stanford, CA: Stanford University Press, 2003), pp. 116–130.

38. See Bruce R. Scott, "The Industrial State: Old Myths and New Realities," *Harvard Business Review* (March–April 1973).

39. Galbraith, *Designing the Global Corporation*, pp. 13–23.

40. Geri Smith, "Mexico's War of the Megastores," *BusinessWeek Online* (Sept. 16, 2002), http://www.businessweek.com/magazine/content/02_37/b3799143.htm.

41. Quoted from Jay Galbraith, *Designing the Global Corporation*, pp. 42–43. For a broader treatise about the transnational organization, see Christopher Bartlett, Sumantra B. Ghoshal, and Julian Birkinshaw, *Transnational Management: Text, Cases and Readings in Cross-Border Management*, 4th ed. (New York: McGraw-Hill/Irwin, 2004).

42. William Taylor, "The Logic of Global Business: An Interview with ABB's Percy Barnevik," *Harvard Business Review* 69, no. 2 (March/April 1991): 89–104. Also see Jay Galbraith, *Designing the Global Corporation*, pages 98–105 on how ABB has refined its matrix organization. For an excellent primer on the nature, logic, and operations of a matrix organization, see Galbraith and Kazanjian, *Strategy Implementation: Structure, Systems, and Process*, 2nd ed. For an empirical application of matrix organizations, see William F. Joyce, "Matrix Organization: A Social Experiment," *Academy of Management Journal* 29, no. 3 (1986): 536–562.

43. Quote from Percy Barnevik, William Taylor, "The Logic of Global Business: An Interview with ABB's Percy Barnevik," p. 95.

44. Taylor, "The Logic of Global Business," pp. 90–91. Also see Ted Agres, "Asea Brown Boveri—A Model for Global Management," *Research & Development* 33, no. 13 (December 1991): 30–33.

45. Michael G. Harvey, Milorad M. Novicevic, and Cheri Speier, "An Innovative Global Management Staffing System: A Competency-based Perspective," *Human Resource Management* 39, no. 4 (2000): 381–94.

46. Ibid., pp. 381–383.

47. Michael G. Harvey, "The Selection of Managers for Foreign Assignments: A Planning Perspective," *Columbia Journal of World Business* 31 (1996): 102–18.

48. Charles Hill, *International Business: Competing in the Global Marketplace*, 6th ed. (New York: McGraw-Hill/Irwin, 2007) pp. 620–623. For a perspective that relates training and selection procedures to performance among U.S., Japanese, and European multinationals, see Rosalie L. Tung, *The New Expatriates: Managing Human Resources Abroad* (Cambridge, MA: Ballinger Publishing Co., 1988).

49. M. Gowan, S. Ibarreche, and C. Lackey, "Doing the Right Things in Mexico," *Academy of Management Executive* 10, no. 1 (1996): 74–81.

50. Harvey, "The Selection of Managers for Foreign Assignments."

51. Harvey, Novicevic, and Speier, "An Innovative Global Management Staffing System."

52. Juan I. Sanchez and Edward. L. Levine, "Is Job Analysis Dead, Misunderstood, or Both?" in Allen I. Kraut and Abraham K. Korman (eds.), *Evolving Practices in Human Resource Management* (San Francisco: Jossey Bass, 1999), p. 57.

53. Harvey, Novicevic, and Speier, "An Innovative Global Management Staffing System."

54. Ibid.

55. Ibid.

56. Allen D. Engle Sr., Mark E. Mendenhall, Richard L. Powers, and Yvonne Stedham, "Conceptualizing the Global Competency Cube: A Transnational Model of Human Resource," *Journal of European Industrial Training* 25, no. 7 (2001): 346–53.

57. Robert W. Rowden, "The Strategic Role of Human Resource Management in Developing a Global Corporate Culture," *International Journal of Management* 19, no. 2 (2002, part 1): 155–61.

58. Rakesh B. Sambharya, "Foreign Experience of Top Management Teams and International Diversification Strategies of U.S. Multinational Corporations," *Strategic Management Journal*, 17, no. 9 (1996): 739–46.

59. Diane McGinty-Weston, "Raising the HR Game to Support Company Goals," *Human Resource Management International Digest* 8, no. 3 (2000): 8–11.

60. Ibid.

61. Mary Beth Stanek, "The Need for Global Managers: A Business Necessity," *Management Decision* 38, no. 4 (2000): 232.

62. John D. Daniels and Lee H. Radebaugh, *International Business: Environments and Operations*, 9th ed. (Upper Saddle River, NJ: Prentice Hall, 2001), pp. 872–874.

63. This case was prepared by Annmarie Neal, vice president, Worldwide Talent Management and Development, Cisco Systems, and Manuel G. Serapio, University of Colorado at Denver and Health Sciences Center. IWDS is not a real company; the actors and data presented in the case are fictitious. The case was prepared as a basis for class discussion and is intended to deepen students' comprehension of strategic and global human resource management. This case is not intended to serve as an illustration of effective or ineffective management.

64. Ian Wylie, "Can Philips Learn to Walk the Talk?" *Fast Company*, January 2003, pp. 44–45. Reprinted with permission.

10 Implementing Strategy by Cultivating a Global Mindset

*A cultivated mind is one to which the fountains of knowledge have been opened,
and which has been taught, in any tolerable degree, to exercise its faculties.*
—John Stuart Mill

No culture can live, if it attempts to be exclusive.
—Mahatma Gandhi

CHAPTER OUTLINE

- Geography of Thought
- A Global Mindset and Strategic Implementation
- Culture and Managerial Behavior
- Synthesizing the Frameworks
- The Global Mindset
- Ethnocentrism: Limiting Influences on a Global Mindset
- A Learning Program for Addressing Ethnocentrism and Developing Cross-Cultural Skills
- An Assessment Methodology

LEARNING OBJECTIVES

- Understand the relation between a global mindset and strategic implementation.
- Understand different cultural perspectives and how culture affects managerial behavior.
- Learn the general theories of culture.
- Understand different perspectives on the global mindset.
- Understand how ethnocentrism affects management.
- Understand how cultural relativism affects the development of a global mindset.
- Learn to build a global mindset.

GEOGRAPHY OF THOUGHT

While popular cultural stereotypes abound, it is generally assumed that everyone uses the same tools for perception, for memory, and for reasoning. Such an assumption was once held by University of Michigan psychologist Richard Nisbett, Theodore M. Newcomb Distinguished University Professor and co-director of the Culture and Cognition Program. Nisbett observed that many cognitive scientists, much like himself, believed that "all human groups perceive and reason in the same way."[1] Whatever the skin color, nationality, or religion, a logically true statement should hold true. The same should apply when looking at graphic information, that is, everyone *should,* at least, see the same picture.

In his provocative book *The Geography of Thought,* Nisbett challenged this assumption of universality or invariance across cultures. Using an arsenal of experimental studies conducted mostly by himself and his colleagues, Nisbett builds a case that East Asians and Westerners think differently, and he also establishes the grounds for why this is so.

Prompted by a Chinese student who opined that the world is a circle, not a straight line, Nisbett embarked on an intensive reading of the comparative literature on the nature of thought by philosophers, historians, and anthropologists—both Eastern and Western. His finding, the core argument of the book, is that Westerners (primarily Americans, Europeans, and citizens of the British Commonwealth) tend to be categorical. They focus on particular objects in isolation from their context and believe that if they can know the rules governing objects, they can control the objects' behavior. In contrast, East Asians (principally the people of China, Korea, and Japan) tend to be broader and contextual. They believe that events are highly complex and cannot be properly interpreted without considering their underlying context. Moreover, because events are determined by many factors, they are much more difficult, if not impossible, to control.

Nisbett compares two views of the future—Francis Fukuyama's vision of convergence toward Western values, against Samuel Huntington's disruptive vision featuring a "clash of civilizations." Nisbett argues for a third view—a convergence based on the blending of Western and Eastern social systems and values. While Western traditions dominate, he adds, "The entry of East Asians into social science is going to transform how we think about human thought and behavior across the board." On an optimistic note, he concludes, "I believe the twain shall meet by virtue of each moving in the direction of the other."

A GLOBAL MINDSET AND STRATEGIC IMPLEMENTATION

A casual stroll down any sidewalk will reveal the incredible variety of human beings. Physical differences are noted and occasionally translated into salient differences in the culture or ancestry of others. This propensity to sort people into cultural cat-

Figure 10.1   **Implementing the Strategic Plan: Cultivating a Global Mindset**

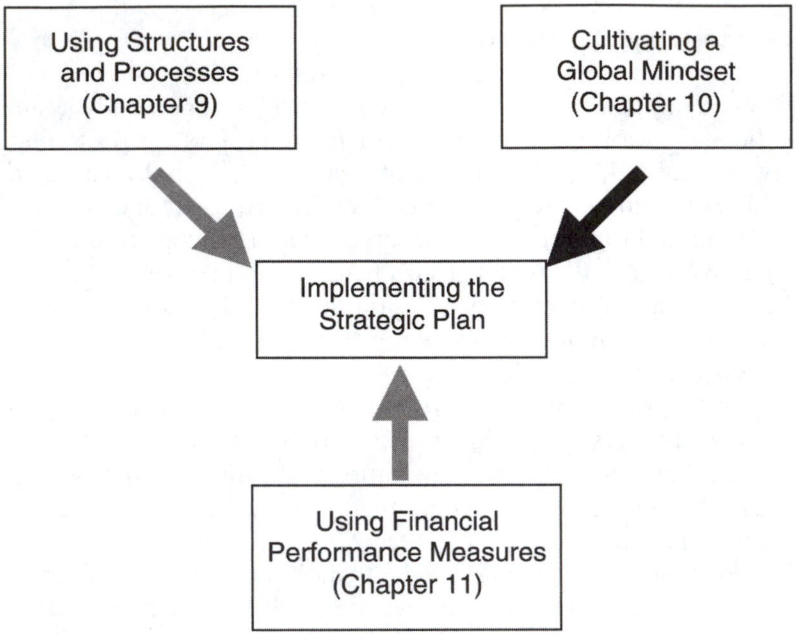

```
┌──────────────────────┐              ┌──────────────────────┐
│  Using Structures    │              │   Cultivating a      │
│   and Processes      │              │   Global Mindset     │
│    (Chapter 9)       │              │    (Chapter 10)      │
└──────────────────────┘              └──────────────────────┘
              ↘                          ↙
                 ┌──────────────────────┐
                 │  Implementing the    │
                 │   Strategic Plan     │
                 └──────────────────────┘
                           ↑
                 ┌──────────────────────┐
                 │  Using Financial     │
                 │ Performance Measures │
                 │    (Chapter 11)      │
                 └──────────────────────┘
```

egories has led to stereotypes, some of which are intuitively plausible, but many of which are unjustified and unwarranted. For example, Asians are generally regarded as reserved, shy, and reticent, though Indians and Koreans can be forthright and outspoken. Americans and Europeans are cast as being aggressive, extroverted, and opinionated, although significant exceptions continue to be noted. The stereotypes go on and, over the course of history, have resulted in cross-cultural mishaps, frustrated objectives, and human suffering.[2]

Individuals differ in terms of how they make sense of the world around them. Such differences tend to be more pronounced, however, when different cultures are involved. While the design of structures and processes (Chapter 9) holds a central position in strategy implementation, the cultivation of a global mindset might prove to be as consequential in practice (Figure 10.1). In this chapter, we introduce and build on the concept of a global mindset. By **mindset**, we mean "a set of deeply held internal mental images and assumptions, which individuals develop through a continuous process of learning from experience. They exist in the subconscious, determining how an individual perceives a specific situation, and his or her reaction to it."[3] A mindset has also been defined a paradigm, a cognitive schema, or a mental map.[4] When individuals come together in a company, their collective thinking comprises the mindset of the organization. It is "the origination point of all workplace behavior."[5] In extending the mindset to a global context, we heed management and anthropology scholars who maintain that thinking reflects what we learn and experience from our particular cultures.

This harkens back to the old adage, "Your behavior is based on *what* and *how* you think." Our opening vignette brings into focus the question: "Do Asians think differently from Westerners?" In our work, we have come across countless individuals who intellectually subscribe to cultural differences but still act in a manner that suggests otherwise. Consistent with Nisbett and his associates, the important question for us is not so much whether individuals across different cultures think differently. They do. In relating cultural differences to strategic implementation, what matters is *why* individuals from different cultures think differently, and what the consequences are for implementation. Learning to understand why cultural differences exist and to act in a manner that reflects this understanding is what we refer to as "cultivating a global mindset."

Culture dictates the learning and experience of managers, which shape the way they think (mind) and the way they act (managerial behavior). We start off this chapter with a discussion of culture and its consequences. We discuss three theories of culture that have influenced management practice significantly. Following this, we address the problem of ethnocentrism, or the tendency to interpret events and behavior in terms of one's primary culture. We argue that cultivating a global mindset entails a good understanding of ethnocentrism, its problems, its relevance in particular settings, and ways to overcome it. As a method of building cross-cultural competencies, we introduce a learning platform, reinforcing our belief that global mindsets are founded on a deep appreciation of different cultures, as well as a solid moral grounding. Finally, we introduce a practical methodology for assessing and diagnosing cross-cultural skills and how this can be further used to facilitate global strategic implementation.

CULTURE AND MANAGERIAL BEHAVIOR

While we all have some level of proficiency in dealing with individuals from different cultures, it is an elusive task to define and understand what culture really means. Professor Geert Hofstede, Extramural Fellow, Center for Economic Research, University of Tilburg, and a widely respected expert on culture, proposed that **culture** is something that is learned and deeply embedded in a society or country.[6] It informs a mental state that is first cultivated during childhood and consistently reinforced from experiences over a lifetime. For us, culture refers to values, norms, and beliefs that are widely shared in a given society and transmitted from generation to generation.

What makes culture difficult to grasp is that, much like an onion, it is revealed through continuous unfolding. The center of the cultural onion comprises the core values of the members of the society, while the outside layers represent the extended habits and rituals associated with those values.[7] Another way to view this is to classify culture into three levels: national, corporate, and professional. **National culture** refers to shared values and norms in a particular country. This is what we commonly refer to as a country's culture. In Chapter 9, we introduced *corporate culture* as expressed and transmitted through the behavior of the employees of a company. Finally, *professional culture* is the aggregate behavior of the members of the same profession, including their ethical orientation.[8] For example, accountants, lawyers, and engineers tend to operate along their own predefined set of rules and conventions. Typically, national culture is the one that affects us first and most deeply among the three cultures. Individuals become members of corporate and professional cultures as their

Exhibit 10.1   **A Model of Culture**

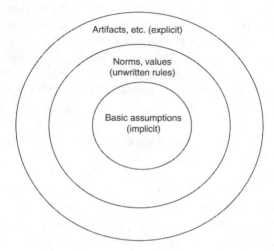

Source: Adapted from Fons Trompenaars, *Riding the Waves of Culture: Understanding Diversity in Global Business* (Burr Ridge, IL: Irwin, 1994), p. 24.

careers develop. National culture can be understood in the model shown in Exhibit 10.1. Nevertheless, all three types of culture come into play as we interact with other individuals. As a consequence, proper understanding of these levels of culture is a key requirement behind the cultivation of any mindset, particularly a global one.

The outer layer of culture is the explicit culture, something that can be observed directly. It includes language, design, art, food, and general expression of views and feelings. Phrased differently, this is much like the "first impression" when an individual visits a new country or meets a foreigner for the first time. Insiders in the culture can adapt to this explicit culture in varying degrees, and outsiders can acquire it without much difficulty. The second layer is the manifestation of shared beliefs in terms of norms, values, and other commonly accepted unwritten rules. These rules govern human behaviors. One example is how the Japanese (and other Asian cultures) make attributions about a person's economic standing and hierarchical social status based on the person's age and/or position in a firm. This is why the exchange of business cards is considered to be very important in business meetings. In social settings, age carries more weight. In western societies, the tradition may be "ladies first," but in the oriental societies, it is often "senior first." These beliefs and norms must be internalized by outsiders who desire to be part of the culture. The innermost layer is the core of a culture, that is, its most basic assumptions about human existence. The rigidity and persistence of these basic assumptions are reflected in numerous, continuous battles for survival in human history. We fight for certain beliefs and values that are of utmost importance to us. For example, if members of a society believe that freedom is valuable to humankind, this will become a bedrock belief within their cultural values and a building block of their country. We can extend this to organizations and smaller social groups when we enact democratic principles. Because core cultural values are deeply embedded, it is very difficult for outsiders to give up their own values for a dramatically different kind. In this regard, socialization becomes an integral part of learning another culture. It is only by having an open mind, however, that socialization and assimilation can take place.

While there have been numerous attempts to classify cultural dimensions, we have selected three in particular that have influenced management thinking and practice: Edward Hall's depiction of culture as a silent language at the unconscious level;[9] Fons Trompenaars's integrative framework, which is oriented to building cross-cultural competencies;[10] and Geert Hofstede's cultural dimensions, which are cited frequently and have provided a major theoretical base for research in international business.[11]

EDWARD HALL'S SILENT LANGUAGE

Edward Hall, a world-renowned cultural anthropologist, is best noted for his seminal work on nonverbal behavior that applies theories of cultural anthropology to the context of business and commerce. His fundamental argument is that we are not always aware of the influence of culture in our thinking and behavior because it influences us at a tacit or subconscious level through "silent language."[12] Specifically, the basic premise underlying "silent language" is that, because cultural experiences are poorly captured in verbal language, culture can be described in several "silent" languages that incorporate different sensory worlds. Hall specified five such silent languages: time, space, things, friendship, and agreements. In subsequent work, he amplified his ideas about time and space by distinguishing time as being either *monochronic* (i.e., linear, in which things occur sequentially) or *polychronic* (i.e., parallel or simultaneous, as in the case of multitasking).[13]

Among other key contributions is Hall's description of underlying contexts in terms of their salience in communication.[14] Hall characterized societies as being either low-context, which is typical of northern Europe and the United States, or high-context, most notably represented by Japan. In a low-context system, the message itself conveys its meaning. Thus, explicit communication rules become the guide for interpreting behavior. In most cases, these rules are also formal, or written out. In contrast, in a high-context system, much of the communication is nonverbal or interpreted in terms of its shared context. Thus, implicit cues, such as friendship, relationships, family background, education, and so forth, are important in interpreting patterns of behavior. In Japan, for example, responsibility is diffused throughout the organization and difficult to pin onto one person. Teamwork, previous friendships and affiliations, and having been peers at the same university are critical components underlying collective responsibility and accountability, and they provide richness in interpreting actions and decisions in this culture.

While other frameworks have evolved that have either integrated the above dimensions, or have enlarged them, Hall's early writings are important in that they illuminate the difficulty we all experience about culture, that is, we can talk about culture in cognitive terms, and yet we are not always aware of its subtleness in influencing our behaviors and actions. Hall's works highlight how our conceptions of space and time, and, by extension, our expectations of privacy are influenced by national culture. Unless these expectations are recognized, significant communication problems will occur between persons from different cultures. But because cultural influences are tacit and operate at a subconscious level, oftentimes internalized within a person, these are not readily accessible. We will revisit this premise later when we discuss ethnocentrism.

FONS TROMPENAARS'S EXTENSION TO MANAGEMENT PRACTICES

Fons Trompenaars, founder of the Centre for International Business Studies in 1989, now Trompenaars Hampden-Turner, an Amsterdam-based consultancy firm, developed a seven-point orientation framework to provide more detailed connections between national culture and management practices.[15] Based on research conducted over fourteen years, Trompenaars suggested that the first five orientations are about relationships with people; the last two are about people's attitudes toward time and the environment. We discuss these orientations in this section using his published results relating to the classification of countries as specific cultural types, and develop these orientations further into cultural dilemmas at the end of this chapter.

Universalism vs. Particularism

Universalism is the belief that what is right and what is good are clear and can be defined. Countries with universalistic cultures include Canada, the United States, Switzerland, Australia, and Norway. Particularism is the belief that rules can be adjusted to accommodate situations and conditions. Rules are allowed to give way to relationships and obligations. Countries with particularistic cultures include South Korea, Venezuela, Russia, Indonesia, and China.

Individualism vs. Collectivism

In an individualistic culture, members believe that an individual's success has priority over the group's success, whereas members of collectivist cultures consider that group benefits should come first, that is, an individual's welfare has to give way to that of the group. Countries such as Canada, United States, Norway, Spain, and Australia are individualist societies, whereas Kuwait, Egypt, France, South Korea, Thailand, and Singapore are collective societies.

Neutral vs. Emotional

In a "neutral" culture, emotions are not displayed as a way of getting business done. Members refrain from showing their feelings in a demonstrative way. Countries of this type include Japan, Indonesia, the United Kingdom, and Norway. On the other hand, members of an "emotional" culture feel it is legitimate to use feelings and emotions if these will help one's point to come across. On some occasions, members can resort to demonstrative actions that can be considered dramatic ways of getting their points across, such as banging fists on the table or even abruptly leaving a meeting during negotiations. Countries of this type include Italy, France, the United States, and Singapore.

Specific vs. Diffuse

People in a culture of a "specific" nature have social roles that are clear and well defined. They do not see the need to play any role beyond the one they are supposed to. The emphasis is on analysis, results, facts, and feedback. This cultural dimension includes countries like Australia, the Netherlands, the United Kingdom, Switzerland, Sweden, and the United States. In a "diffuse" culture, people see their roles as going beyond their specified titles and responsibilities. The emphasis is on the whole person, not just the specific relationship prescribed in the contract. Facts, results, and feedback are also important, but these have to be considered in the broader context in which they are made. This cultural dimension applies to countries like China, Japan, Nepal, Indonesia, Singapore, Thailand, Egypt, and Malaysia. These differences between a specific and a diffuse culture are typically manifested in attributions about a problem, for example, a case when a product is found to be defective. A specific style would tend to look for a primary cause or reason (e.g., a defective drill), while a diffuse style would look into the entire process by which this product is designed and manufactured, from a specific defective part to the broader context of training, incentives, and design (as exemplified in Toyota's production system).

Achievement vs. Ascription

In an achievement-oriented culture, members are evaluated and judged based on what they accomplish on their own. Countries such as Denmark, Australia, the United States, Canada, the United Kingdom, France, and Norway are examples of this type. In a culture of an ascription orientation, members are locked in by birth, family background, gender, age, kinship, school reputation, and so on. Countries such as Indonesia, Austria, Thailand, Russia, the Philippines, and Pakistan are examples of this type.

Attitude Toward Time

In some cultures, an individual's past accomplishments are as important as what they plan to do in the future. For example, in France and Mexico, there is an emphasis on people's past histories and achievements. The opposite is true in other cultures, such as the United States, which is considered to be more future-oriented in terms of evaluating plans and performance. Also, in some cultures, such as China, members believe that what happens in the past, the present, and the future comprises one big circle. The past, present, and the future overlap synchronously, such that the past informs the present, and both inform the future.

Attitude Toward the Environment

In some cultures, members believe that the origin of virtue is from within. Thus, an individual is more powerful than the environment and is able to conquer the environment. The United States, Switzerland, Pakistan, Canada, Argentina, Australia, and

Spain fall into this category. In other cultures, members feel the opposite, and they tend to submit to and/or work within the environment, or to achieve harmony with nature. China, Egypt, Japan, Turkey, and Singapore belong to this category.

Trompenaars and his consultancy firm have since extended these cultural dimensions to represent knowledge-structures. Their current initiative lies in conceptualizing knowledge-structures in the form of cultural dilemmas that illuminate significant cross-cultural differences (see Box 10.1).

GEERT HOFSTEDE'S CULTURAL DIMENSIONS

Another scholar, Professor Geert Hofstede, whom we introduced earlier, identified a set of cultural dimensions to capture the impact of national cultural characteristics on the workplace. Between 1968 and 1970, Hofstede collected questionnaire data from close to 100,000 IBM employees working in more than fifty countries. Based on these data, he developed a typology of four cultural dimensions, with a fifth developed and subsequently refined in his research with Michael Bond.[16] These five dimensions are power distance, uncertainty avoidance, individualism versus collectivism, masculinity versus femininity, and long-term versus short-term orientation. Exhibit 10.2 presents a summary of Hofstede's research on the original four dimensions.[17]

Power Distance

Power distance refers to how much a society accepts or rejects the inequalities among its people. Managers in countries of low power distance do not rely on power to manage subordinates. Nor do their subordinates feel themselves to be inferior to their supervisors. Switzerland, Sweden, and the United States are examples. Managers in countries of high power distance see their superior status as a way to ensure obedience. The Arab world, China, Malaysia, Indonesia, and India are examples.

Uncertainty Avoidance

Uncertainty avoidance refers to the extent to which members of a society tolerate uncertain and ambiguous situations. Managers from cultures with a low level of uncertainty avoidance are risk takers, such as those in Singapore, the United Kingdom, the United States, and Jamaica. Managers from cultures with a high level of uncertainty avoidance are risk-averse, such as those in Guatemala, Japan, Hungary, Spain, Portugal, and Greece. They look for information, instructions, rules of thumb, regulations, guidelines, and the like to minimize guesswork.

Individualism versus Collectivism

Individualism versus collectivism refers to the relationship between members of a society. In some cultures, members are closely tied to each other, but this is not necessarily so in other cultures. In an individualistic society, members find opportunities

Box 10.1

Building Cross-Cultural Skills Using Cultural Dilemmas

In an effort to redress the problems associated with ethnocentrism, some scholars have suggested the development of cross-cultural competencies—an important step in developing a global mindset. The concept of **cultural relativism**, as advanced by cultural anthropologists, is that all cultures are equally worthy of tolerance and respect, and that in studying another culture, we need to suspend judgment, empathize, and try and understand that particular culture. Fons Trompenaars and Charles Hampden-Turner have introduced the use of cultural dilemmas to build cross-cultural skills.

In an interview with Simon Lelic, Trompenaars explained this approach: "It is the process of structuring that adds meaning. And since different cultures have different ways of structuring meaning, you can see that, by definition, knowledge management is a cultural construct." Since many managers and academicians still fail to grasp this significance, Trompenaars and Hampden-Turner have developed a holistic, systemic approach to understand cross-cultural decisions using dilemmas. Through extensive research and ongoing work with clients, five central dilemmas were defined:

Dilemma 1: You are asked to lie for your friend who has hit a pedestrian while driving over the speed limit in an underdeveloped country. By testifying that your friend was driving less then the speed limit, you could save him from severe punishment.

Dilemma 2: An error was made in an assembly plant that required significant repairs. You know the person who committed the error, and by reporting this, you could save the entire group from bearing the responsibility for the mistake.

Dilemma 3: In a joint project, the Americans spent considerable amount of time codifying their knowledge and writing it up in handbooks and procedures, while the Japanese refrained from formalizing information, claiming that knowledge was tacit and stored in their networks. This infuriated the Americans and you are asked to intervene.

Dilemma 4: In a choice of a person to promote, one was from an Ivy League university, while the other was not. At the time of the decision, the latter was the more deserving person by virtue of performance, but the former had better contacts.

Dilemma 5: You are consistently getting late deliveries from a prime supplier from a foreign country where "being late" is acceptable. You have tried to explain the importance of prompt deliveries in the past, but such has not worked.

In all these dilemmas, "the context of organizational culture dictates the starting point of reconciliation," says Trompenaars, "but effective knowledge management is dictated by the integrated scorecard of rules and exceptions, group and individual, explicit and implicit, top and bottom, and inner and outer worlds." Trompenaars has argued that "the only real competence an effective leader needs is the ability to integrate opposites."

Sources: Dilemmas were adapted from Charles Hampden-Turner and Fons Trompenaars, *Building Cross-Cultural Competence* (New Haven, CT: Yale University Press, 2000). All quotations are taken from "The Knowledge: Fons Trompenaars," interview by Simon Lelic, *Inside Knowledge* 6, no. 8, www.kmmagazine.com/xq/asp/sid.0/articleid.1A6014BC-399A-47C4-A330-D9DE2BB7BEE7/qx/display.htm.

Exhibit 10.2

Hofstede's Original Four Cultural Dimension Indices (L = low, M = medium, and H = high)

	Power distance	Uncertainty avoidance	Individualism	Masculinity
Argentina	M	H	M	M
Australia	L	M	H	M
Austria	L	L	M	H
Belgium	H	H	H	M
Brazil	H	M	M	M
Canada	L	L	H	M
Chile	M	H	L	L
Colombia	H	H	L	H
Denmark	L	L	M	L
Finland	L	M	M	L
France	H	H	H	L
Germany (F.R.)	L	M	M	H
Great Britain	L	L	H	H
Greece	M	H	L	M
Hong Kong	H	L	L	M
India	H	L	M	M
Iran	M	M	M	L
Ireland	L	L	H	H
Israel	L	H	M	M
Italy	M	M	H	H
Japan	M	H	M	H
Mexico	H	H	L	H
Netherlands	L	M	H	L
New Zealand	L	L	H	M
Norway	L	L	H	L
Pakistan	M	M	L	M
Peru	H	H	L	L
Philippines	H	L	L	H
Portugal	M	H	L	L
Singapore	H	L	L	M
South Africa	M	L	M	H
Spain	M	H	M	L
Sweden	L	L	H	L
Switzerland	L	M	M	H
Taiwan	M	M	L	M
Thailand	H	M	L	L
Turkey	H	H	M	M
U.S.A.	M	L	H	H
Venezuela	H	M	L	H

Source: Adapted from Geert Hofstede, *Culture's Consequences: International Differences in Work-Related Values* (Thousand Oaks, CA: Sage Publications, 1984).

to stand out in a group for career growth. The United States, Australia, the United Kingdom, the Netherlands, and Canada are examples of an individualistic culture. In a country with a collective culture, employees feel that it is important to blend in with groups, rather than isolating themselves from peers. Guatemala, Ecuador, Panama, and Indonesia are examples of this type.

Masculinity versus Femininity

Masculinity versus femininity refers to the extent to which assertiveness, success, and competition are valued by a society (masculine traits) as opposed to an emphasis on need and feeling (femininity). As such, reward systems have to match preferences. Countries such as Costa Rica, Denmark, Norway, and Sweden are examples of masculine cultures. In a masculine society, members are motivated by extrinsic rewards, whereas the opposite is true in a feminine culture. Countries such as Japan, Hungary, Austria, Switzerland, and Venezuela are examples of feminine cultures.

Long-term versus Short-term Orientation

In a culture of long-term orientation, individuals believe that the hard work they put in today will eventually be rewarded in the long run. Traditions are well respected and observed. Outsiders have to take the time to develop business networks to be accepted as insiders for easier, smoother business dealings. China, South Korea, and Japan are countries of this type. Societies with short-term orientation are not bound by tradition as much. Changes happen frequently and tradition will give way occasionally to expediency. The Philippines, Norway, New Zealand, Canada, and Australia are countries of this type.

SYNTHESIZING THE FRAMEWORKS

With heightened globalization, three general theories have emerged that hypothesize the impact of globalization on culture and the converging or diverging direction of multiple cultures. The first—**convergence theory**—suggests that technological developments and industrialization have changed business practices to the extent that cultures are beginning to become more homogenized, rather than different. Pundits of convergence theory make their case by heralding globalization as the homogenizing force, and local cultures are continuously transformed by globalization (see Chapter 1). As a consequence, business environments and managerial behaviors have become more similar and more uniform. Moreover, consumers' interest in global products, their sense of belonging to the elite culture, and their use of the Internet all facilitate and reinforce this process of convergence. Thus, convergence, or the homogenization of cultures, is a product of several factors.[18] These include the widespread use of one language (English), the consumption of a highly popular beverage (Coca-Cola), the passion for one type of food (McDonald's and other fast food), the preference for a few cars (notably Toyota), and the emergence of a world view that is influenced by media outlets (*Wall Street Journal, Newsweek,* CNN, etc.).[19]

The second theory—the **divergence theory**—proposes that each culture retains unique characteristics that cannot be transformed by the forces of globalization. Even with globalization, each culture is held to be unique. Such unique cultural characteristics, centered in the inner core of the proverbial cultural "onion," become even more solidified with frequent and repeated interactions between members of a particular culture. In fact, homogenizing forces discussed earlier tend to uncover

Exhibit 10.3

Characteristics of an Emergent Global Culture

Educated	Members have a better-than-average education as compared to their peers. They are well-informed and knowledgeable about the current global environments.
Connected	Members stay connected with the world by traveling and communicating via technological devices.
Self-confident	Because of their experience and success in their global endeavors, members are very self-assured. They pursue high-risk ventures and activities that many others would not. As a result, they have tremendous confidence.
Pragmatic	Members are concerned about getting things done. To achieve this, they are committed to exploiting creativity and innovative thinking.
Unintimidated by national boundaries or cultures	Because of their high level of self-confidence, members are unintimidated by cultural differences or the separation created by national boundaries.
Democratic and participatory	Members tend to be democratic and participatory. They take initiative to share their views with others, and expect others to reciprocate.
Individualistic but inclusive	Members are comfortable taking the lead in trying new ideas, fashions, equipment, or anything distinctive. This makes them unique, but they do not exclude others from joining the trend.
Flexible and open	Members are adaptive to uncertainties and surprises. Because of their adventurous and novelty-seeking nature, they also demonstrate a high degree of openness to unusual subjects and thoughts.
Begin in a position of trust	Members approach relationships with trust, but not blindly. They are willing to listen but may or may not approve.

Source: Adapted from Allan Bird and Michael J. Stevens, "Toward an Emergent Global Culture and the Effects of Globalization on Obsolescing National Cultures," *Journal of International Management* 9, no. 4 (2003): 395–407.

these unique characteristics rather than change and transform them. The emergence of various regional blocks and the rise of nationalism in developing countries reflect this divergence theory.[20]

The third theory—the **cross-vergence theory**—maintains that the interdependency and integration of economies beget the creation of a new type of culture that combines the old and the new, the domestic and the foreign.[21] This theory can also be interpreted as the hybridization of culture.[22] The subcultures that emerge from cross-vergent cultures tend to be very local, or so-called "dialectical" cultures. These represent a deeper, micro level of cross-vergence. The second or third generation of a particular culture (e.g., the Filipino as influenced by the United States) that exhibits bi-cultural traits and understanding (i.e., fluency in both languages and a cohabitation of Filipino-U.S. cultural values) is one example of cross-vergence. Another example is a Chinese-Cuban restaurant, or the various forms of "fusion" cuisine that are fast developing throughout the world.

A related perspective comes from scholars who argue for the development of a global culture.[23] The members of the global culture are educated, connected, self-confident, pragmatic, democratic and participatory, and not intimidated by national boundaries or cultures. They are individualistic but inclusive, flexible and open, and begin from a position of trust (Exhibit 10.3).[24] These characteristics can lay the foundation for people who eventually become global managers.

Exhibit 10.4

Executive Traits Now and in the Future

Now	The Future
Know it all	Learn as the manager leads
Adopt local perspective	Adopt global perspective
Use historical data to project the future	Use intuition to predict the future
Focus on individuals	Focus on both individuals and institutions
Emphasize the top manager's vision	Help others to find their visions
Exercise power to achieve	Facilitate to achieve
Determine goals and methods for others	Offer specific process
Single-handedly manage at the top	Consider oneself as part of the management team
Favor things to be done in order	View chaos positively and allow disruption of order
One-culture mind	Multicultural mind
Earn trust from shareholders and boards	Earn trust from owners, customers, and employees

Source: Adapted from Patricia A. Galagan, "Executive Development in a Changing World," *Training and Development Journal* (June 1990): 23–41.

THE GLOBAL MINDSET

The concept of a global mindset was introduced to the management field in the early 1990s when globalization had become the dominant force of change in society and industry (see Chapter 1). In a survey about expectations for the future, managers' responses emphasized the development of global skills. Key elements such as "global vision," "intuits the future" and "multicultural" were among the most valued attributes (see Exhibit 10.4). This pattern signifies the budding interest in the global mindset and the growing realization that it is a managerial imperative (Box 10.2).[25]

A global mindset extends the concept of a mindset to the global perspective. Its motivation stems from a belief that managers need to develop an appreciation and an empathy for cross-cultural differences and global issues. A global mindset also incorporates sound strategic skills since it emphasizes a manager's knowledge structure as providing the basis for decisions and actions. Having a global mindset also affects how the manager processes disparate pieces of information. Since the mindset predisposes the individual to react to various cues, this person may accept or reject particular information, resulting in a potential change in his or her knowledge structure.[26] New information can reinforce or contradict existing beliefs and values, but whatever is processed becomes the seed of something new. As part of an iterative process, new information is continuously assimilated into the person's mindset. It is precisely for this reason that the development and cultivation of a global mindset is needed. If a person is parochial in his thinking, this is reflected in his attitudes and actions regarding people from different cultures. With continuous exposure to foreign cultures, taken in tandem with a genuine desire to understand any differences, subsequent patterns of decisions and actions will define an individual's global perspective and his propensity to accept and accommodate attitudes and behavior that might be different from his own.

Box 10.2

The Imperative for a Global Mindset: A Survey and Results

Occasionally, students and managers wonder whether a global mindset is *truly* necessary, or whether this is simply another subject taught in international business courses. Korn/Ferry International, the premier provider of executive search and leadership development solutions, conducted a survey of managers and executives to ascertain the structural, economic, social, and political challenges facing U.S. industry and their impact on management. Their findings:

The most critical attributes of the next generation of leaders for America's industrial sector are passion, vision, and a global mindset.

  Key leadership attributes are the following:
- *Cultural and intellectual openness.* For more than four decades, the United States has been the dominant economic force in the world. This leadership position has fostered executives who are innovative, aggressive, and focused on winning. But it has also bred complacency and an ethnocentric view of the world.
- *Long-term view.* Many of the troubles facing U.S. multinationals were fomented by a Wall Street–driven focus on quarterly results. To succeed in a global game, leaders must be able to withstand the short-term pressure and stay focused on the end game—as their foreign-based competitors are.
- *Diversity.* Diversity will be a hallmark of global executives of the future. Diversity of thought, diversity of the workforce, diversity of the customer base, diversity in design philosophy—these are the hallmarks of a truly global company and must be embraced and advanced by the leadership team.

  Source: "Passion, Strategic Vision and Global Mindset Identified as Key Attributes for Future Leaders of America's Industrial Sector: Korn/Ferry Study Examines the Leadership Challenges Facing the U.S. Industrial Sector." Press release, December 13, 2004. Available at http://kornferry. com/Library/Process.asp?P=PR_Detail&CID=866&LID=1 (accessed November 17, 2006). Used

A global mindset can also be interpreted beyond the individual level, that is, the collective or aggregate thinking of individuals can reflect the mindset of the organization. Even with different backgrounds, an organization is a social collectivity for which decisions are interpreted to represent the views of individuals. Gradually, the corporate mindset will be dominated and shaped by more influential employees through their more active participation. To the extent that firms participate more in global activities, it behooves them to develop a global perspective.[27] Even if companies do not go global, they still need to develop this perspective, particularly if and when their global competitors encroach on their domestic markets. The application of a global mindset has since taken on the imperative to "think globally, but act locally," emphasizing the benefits of thinking globally while not abandoning one's local roots.[28]

THE RHINESMITH PERSPECTIVE

In the early 1990s, Stephen H. Rhinesmith, currently a partner of Mercer Delta Executive Learning Center in Portland, Oregon, developed a framework to explain the relationship between personal characteristics and competencies.[29] He proposed six approaches to global management, requiring six personal characteristics to facilitate them (Exhibit 10.5). By combining these two sets, managers can develop the neces-

Exhibit 10.5

Six Personal Characteristics of Managers with a Global Mindset

Characteristics	Approaches
Knowledge	• They strive for the bigger, broader picture. • They are never satisfied with one task.
Conceptualization	• They accept life as a balance of contradictory forces that must be appreciated, pondered, and managed. • They develop conflict management as a key skill to handle contradictory ideas, feelings, and interests.
Flexibility	• They use process rather than structure to deal with the unexpected. • They recognize that process is more powerful than structure and that organizational processes are the key to organizational adaptability.
Sensitivity	• They value diversity and multicultural teamwork. • They believe that teamwork and interdependence are basic tenets of global management.
Judgment	• They flow with change as opportunity and are comfortable with surprises and ambiguity.
Reflection	• They continuously seek to be open to themselves and others by rethinking boundaries, finding new meanings, and changing their directions and behavior.

Source: Adapted from Stephen H. Rhinesmith, "Global Mindsets for Global Managers," *Training & Development* 46, no. 10 (October 1992): 63.

sary skills to manage a global enterprise. These constitute the global competencies required for global success (Exhibit 10.6). This perspective was later extended to include to a relationship between the global mindset and requisite behavioral skills (Exhibit 10.7).[30]

These approaches recognize that the global mindset is manifested into two ways: the intellectual and the emotional intelligence of managers. **Intellectual intelligence** refers to information and knowledge about businesses and responsibilities. **Emotional intelligence** includes a manager's self-management of her emotions and the extent to which she possesses cultural acumen. Global cultural acumen includes traits such as "cultural self-awareness, understanding other cultures, managing cross-cultural effectiveness, and successfully adapting business practices to a global context."[31] The combined effect of intellectual and emotional intelligences is a set of global behavioral skills. In other words, global mindsets manifest global skills.

THE HERBERT PAUL PERSPECTIVE

The development of a global mindset is a corporate issue for which a system needs to be developed to facilitate its management. This requires "increased cross-national coordination and a more centralized, uniform strategy."[32] Herbert Paul, professor of international management at the University of Applied Sciences in Mainz, Germany, suggests four external forces and five ways to shape a corporate global mindset.

Top Management's View of the World

Leaders of organizations can exert influence on corporate operations. When leaders of companies adopt a geocentric view, the company will be driven to expand globally;

Exhibit 10.6

Six Necessary Competencies for a Global Mindset

Global competencies	Description
Managing competitiveness	Constantly scanning the environment for changes in market, competitive, and supplier conditions, as well as socioeconomic and political trends that might affect the organization and its strategic intent.
Managing complexity	The skills necessary for managing tradeoffs among many competing interests, as well as managing the inherent contradictions and conflicts that exist in all global organizations.
Managing adaptability	Developing a global corporate culture with the values, beliefs, systems, and norms of behavior that allow it to be responsive to constant change, and with the ability to deal with ambiguity.
Managing teams within a multicultural environment	The cultural sensitivity and managerial skills to lead, understand, manage, and supervise people from a wide range of cultures in a broad range of work situations.
Managing uncertainty	A fundamental skill for dealing with the increasing chaos of the environment in a way that provides for continuous improvement, while providing structure or taking advantage of opportunities that arise from a lack of structure.
Managing learning	This requires that managers not only learn about themselves on a continuing basis, but also train and develop others and facilitate constant organizational learning so that the organization can be responsive and adaptive to global change and challenges.

Source: Adapted from Stephen H. Rhinesmith, "Global Mindsets for Global Managers," *Training & Development* 46, no. 10 (October 1992): 63.

Exhibit 10.7   **Global Mindset for Managing Global Paradox**

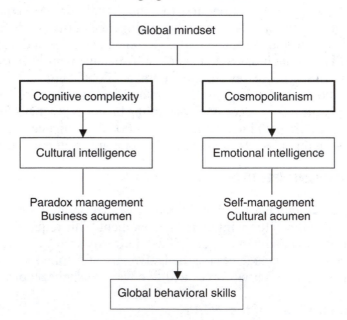

Source: Adapted from Stephen H. Rhinesmith, "How Can You Manage Global Paradox?" *The Journal of Corporate Accounting & Finance* 12, vol. 6 (September/October 2001): 3–9.

adopting an ethnocentric view, defined later in this chapter, will put the focus on domestic expansion.

Administrative Heritage

A company's history and legacies influence its position in terms of developing a global mindset. Companies that traditionally delegate decision-making authority to foreign subsidiaries tend to become multidomestic, and such delegation might make find it harder for these companies to develop a global vision. This was the experience of many U.S. multinationals during the early stages of their international expansion.

Structural Solutions

A company with a strong product orientation tends to think globally because it is driven to seek market opportunities for its products. Procter & Gamble and Nike are good examples of companies with strong product orientation. In contrast, a company with a geographic orientation, such as a local bookstore, tends to view the market by regions and this limits a global view.

Industry Forces

Industry forces relate to economies of scale, global sourcing, and lower transportation costs, which provide the motivation for companies to capitalize on the benefits by expanding globally. Other factors, such as homogeneous demand, uniform technical standards, and the like also provide the rationale for global expansion (see George Yip's framework, Chapter 2). However, the external environment can only provide the motivating context. It is up to the company to fully develop a corporate-level global mindset through the training and proper socialization of its employees. This places heavy emphasis on the human factor. With the support of an efficient corporate program, however, individual managers can be groomed to develop and cultivate a global mindset.

Composition of Top Management

Typically a global company starts with a board of directors and top executives who are already multicultural in nature. In such a case, top management composition can bring in a broad global perspective and knowledge to the entire firm.

Focusing on Vision, Processes, and People

Global companies should be visionary and create management processes that encourage employees from all levels to participate in ways that are adequately recognized, rewarded, and incorporated into the organization agenda. Lateral (cross-departmental) processes also reduce the dependence on "silo" thinking in favor of more structures that facilitate employee interactions and promote interdisciplinary thinking. The company's main goal is to build global attitudes and skills through processes, structures, rewards, and supportive relationships among employees (Chapter 9).

Developing and Coordinating Networks

Global companies must have extensive external networks that give them access to key resources worldwide. The players in such networks include suppliers, customers, contractors, and so forth. One exemplar of this is Asea Brown and Boveri, a Swiss company that has excelled in coordinating various internal and external networks.

Employee Selection, Career Path Planning, and International Assignments

A global company's human resource program is more oriented at a geocentric approach to individual development. As such, it draws and attracts talent from diverse sources around the world. As a consequence, broad and diverse perspectives and experiences enrich the management team. When Matsushita entered the United States, it appointed U.S. managers and others from around the world as key officers, instead of the traditional method of using its nationals for key executive positions. Moreover, in order to broaden its horizon, a global company should also rotate managers for local and overseas assignments. Not only does this practice provide the necessary first-hand experience, it also builds self-confidence, credibility, personal networks, and cultural experiences for managers.

GOVINDARAJAN AND GUPTA'S PERSPECTIVE

For Professors Vijay Govindarajan and Anil Gupta, a global mindset consists of three elements: openness to diversity across cultures and markets; knowledge about diversity across cultures and markets; and the ability to integrate diversity across cultures and markets (Exhibit 10.8). To determine whether a company can adequately develop a global mindset with this perspective, some diagnostic tests have been proposed (see Exhibit 10.9).[33]

They argue that, the primary purpose of instilling a global mindset in a company is to prepare managers for a dynamic and volatile global environment. With a global perspective, a company can benefit on several fronts. It can perform more open-minded environmental analysis, as well as an assessment of the mega-environments affecting its consumers and competitors. This also enables the company to respond by introducing new products in a timely manner, thus meeting consumers' expectations. Moreover, the company is able to make sound decisions on its mix of local and global products, coordinate among functional entities and subsidiaries, and efficiently benchmark the best practices that can be diffused throughout the company. With a global perspective, the company is likely to reduce expatriate failures.

Cultivating a global mindset is similar to the work of education and training. It is a project with no end, but one that involves several milestones. Professors Govindarajan and Gupta have proposed several stages of learning in developing a global mindset. First, individuals should have a deep curiosity about how the world works and evolves. Curiosity is typically shaped at a very young age and partially affected by national culture. Curiosity motivates people to seek answers to questions that interest them and is a positive way to gain new knowledge, thus encouraging innovation and creativity.

Second, individuals need to examine the underlying premises and assumptions of

Exhibit 10.8 **Three Elements of a Global Mindset**

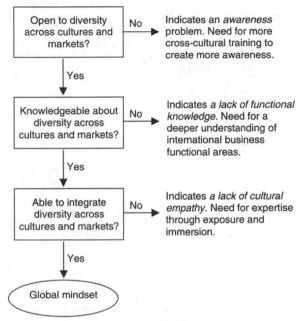

Source: Adapted from Vijay Govrindarajan and Anil Gupta, *The Quest for Global Dominance* (San Francisco: Jossey-Bass, 2001), p. 112.

their current thinking. This step forces them to take a critical look at their assumptions about other cultures. By objectively comparing their views with those of others, they might be able to see the differences, and to appreciate why these differences exist. Such differences serve as a reminder that individuals should maintain an open mind and accept diversity in the world. We will say more about this is our next section.

Third, individuals should cultivate knowledge regarding diverse cultures and markets in a continuous manner. Knowledge about other cultures is typically obtained through learning and exposure. Through formal education, the learning process includes acquiring new language skills, knowledge about the global markets, participation in cross-border teams and projects, experience in working overseas, immersion in foreign cultures, and, if appropriate, the establishment of headquarters in foreign locations. These provide an all-around, hands-on, multicultural, and multifaceted experience so as to broaden any individual's view of the world.

Fourth, individuals have to integrate new knowledge in their daily activities and operations. The success of cultivating a global mindset depends on how new knowledge can be applied in a meaningful way. Thus, the acquisition of global knowledge and the cultivation of a global perspective must be a part of the company's core values and culture. Since core values are deeply shared (Chapter 9), a sense of ownership is inculcated in the mindset of the individual. As stated earlier, processes, such as job rotation across regions, reinforce the goal of developing a global mindset by enriching the individual. To perpetuate the cultivation of a global mindset, reward systems should be used to explicitly relate individuals' actions and accomplishments to the

---

Exhibit 10.9

Characteristics of an Individual and an Organizational Global Mindset

Professors Govindarajan and Gupta have formulated a number of diagnostic questions to determine whether you and your organization have a global mindset. Key characteristics based on these diagnostic questions are presented below.

Characteristics of an Individual Global Mindset

- In interacting with others, national origin has no impact on whether or not they are assigned equal status.
- As open to ideas from other countries and cultures as to those from one's own country and culture of origin.
- Exposure to a new cultural setting does not result in undue excitement, fear, and anxiety.
- Sensitive to differences arising from another culture, without necessarily becoming totally captive to these differences.
- When interacting with people from other cultures, recognizes that the most important consideration is to understand them as individuals, not simply as representatives of their national cultures.
- Values that are a hybrid of those acquired from multiple cultures, not just from a single culture.

Characteristics of an Organizational Global Mindset

- The company is regarded as a leader (rather than a laggard) in the industry in discovering and pursuing emerging market opportunities in all corners of the world.
- The company regards each and every customer, wherever they live in the world, as just as important as a customer in their own domestic market.
- Employees are drawn and recruited from the worldwide talent pool.
- Employees from every nationality have the same opportunity to move up the career ladder.
- In scanning the horizon for potential competitors, the company examines all economic regions of the world.
- In selecting a location for any activity, the company seeks to optimize the choice on a truly global basis.
- The company views the global arena not just as a market to exploit but also as a source of new ideas and technology.
- The company is perceived as having a universal identity with many locations, as opposed to a singular national identity.

Source: Adapted from Vijay Govindarajan and Anil K. Gupta, *The Quest for Global Dominance* (San Francisco: Jossey-Bass, 2005), pp. 114–115.

---

company's core values that promote global thinking. In other words, rewards should be based on merit. Despite all these imperatives for developing a global mindset, however, some companies fall short in achieving this objective. One obstacle is a deep-seated and tacit bias for one's own particular culture, and this is developed in detail in the next section.

ETHNOCENTRISM

Understanding the influence of culture is the first step toward developing and cultivating a global mindset. Nevertheless, knowing a particular culture, perhaps too well, might have its pitfalls as well. **Ethnocentrism** (from the Greek *ethnos*, or "nation" + centrism) is the tendency to look at the world primarily from the perspective of one's own ethnic culture. While the origins of ethnocentrism can be traced to the nineteenth century, it was formalized into a social science concept in 1906 by William Graham Sumner (1840–1910), a social evolutionist and professor of political and social science at Yale University, in his classic volume *Folkways*.[34] He defined it as the viewpoint that "one's own group is the center of everything," against which all other groups are judged.[35] Ethnocentrism, as commonly used and understood in popular usage is even more restrictive: "thinking one's own group's ways are superior to others" or "judging other groups as inferior to one's own."[36] It is little wonder that Hofstede said: "Culture is more often a source of conflict than of synergy. Cultural differences are a nuisance at best and often a disaster."[37]

Ken Barger, a cultural anthropologist at Indiana University/Purdue University at Indianapolis (IUPUI) argues that ethnocentrism is built into every society and is something that all cultures have in common.[38] Because our experiences form the basis of our "reality," it is generally assumed that others interpret events as we do. As a result, we make false assumptions based on our own limited experience.[39] This argument builds further on Edward Hall's position that cultural influences are internalized within ourselves, and that we might not be even conscious about how these influences affect our behavior. Our cultural blinders serve a useful role as a buffer in processing information and in reducing complexity. Specifically, our own perceptions of ourselves, our time frames, our values, our social roles, and our religious beliefs are helpful in managing the uncertainty in our daily activities. Even so, because we are dealing with deep-seated beliefs and assumptions, we may not be even aware that we are ethnocentric. Even with good intentions, we tend to interpret events in terms of our primary culture. Because ethnocentrism is deeply lodged within our belief system, and because we are not always conscious about how this affects our interactions with others, ethnocentrism is insidious and cannot be avoided or willed away by a simple positive attitude[40] (see Box 10.3).

When we use our own cultural norms to make assumptions or generalizations about other cultures and customs, this is the product of ignorance, or very little exposure to other cultures. To the extent that we assume one culture to be superior to others, we fall into ethnocentric thinking. Such generalizations—often made without a conscious awareness that we have used our culture as a universal yardstick—can be inaccurate and misleading as they distort what is meaningful and functional to other peoples.[41] We interpret their ways in terms of *our* life experience, not in terms of *their* context.[42] Our cultural blinders, while useful in reducing uncertainty, are a double-edged sword in that they limit our appreciation of the ways of others that have their own meanings and functions, just as our ways have for us. The dysfunction associated with ethnocentrism is manifest in both our attitudes and our behavior. Consider the following examples:

- On a trip to Japan, one of the authors took a bus to his hotel. While in the bus, an American asked the question: "Why do the Japanese drive on the wrong side of the road?" It had not occurred to him (and others in the bus) to have simply said "opposite side" or even "left-hand side." In observing the Chinese or the Hebrew read text, someone might observe that they are reading "backward." Again, it might be more appropriate to simply say "from right to left" or "in the opposite direction from English."
- Ethnocentrism is likewise manifested in those who view the problem of world

---

Box 10.3

Ethnocentrism and Managerial Sentiments

The origins of ethnocentrism stem from a basic survival need: when faced with a hostile environment, people have to find ways in which to survive. Depending on this interaction, ethnocentrism can be determined by cultural, political, economic, historical, social, psychological, and nationalistic institutions.

Ethnocentrism is manifest in an individual's lack of openness to foreign cultures. It is captured in the following sentiments:

- I prefer working in a domestic company instead of a foreign company, but I do not have that option.
- I experience difficulty in adapting to the foreign management style.
- I can work in an international corporation but I would not like this assignment.
- I find it difficult to work in an international corporation with only colleagues of foreign backgrounds.
- More often than not, my values trump those of the local culture.

To reduce the impact of ethnocentrism, company training should be focused on knowledge of the other culture, guided management activities, mentorship, rotation of key management positions, language acquisition, cooperation, organizational, social and political support, media coverage, and diversity training.

Sources: Adapted from Michael Harris Bond, "We Are All Ethnocentric—Origins, Features, Results and Treatments for a Necessary Human Condition." Paper presented at the Pacific Region Forum, Simon Fraser University (Vancouver, BC, February 2, 1995); Rudolf Sinkovics and Hartmut Holzmüller, "Ethnocentrism—A Key Determinant in International Corporate Strategy Formulation?" Paper presented at the European International Business Academy (EIBA) conference (Warsaw, August 2–6, 1994).

---

poverty as arising from the inability of people in poorer countries to adopt modern structures and policies to lift themselves from their affliction. The question, "What is wrong with the poor?" underlies the belief that deviations from First World economic standards are the result of faulty adaptation, while ignoring the social conditions and institutions that maintain poverty, if not the previous actions and policies of First World nations (i.e., multinationals) that some critics argue have created the plight of Third World nations in the first place.[43]

- The concept of time in the English culture is oftentimes depicted linearly (i.e., the past, the present, and the future). In contrast, there are no future tenses in the Chinese language. Time cycles are typically represented as overlapping circles of life events, rather than in a straight, linear manner. In light of these differences, English speakers may inadvertently impose a linear time frame or schedule when a different conception of time exists.[44]

Cultivating a global mindset forces us to come to grips with the problems associated with ethnocentrism. Americans are particularly vulnerable on account of their dominant position (due to the military and commercial power of the United States) and the near-universal use of the English language in business. Nevertheless, ethnocentrism is not confined to the United States, but applies to every part of the world.

As stated earlier, overcoming ethnocentrism is not a matter of trying *not* to be ethnocentric. Unless we are able to experience every situation in the world—an impossible task—our best route is to be aware of our own ethnocentrism, as well as that of others, and to deal with situations accordingly. An analogy with cognitive psychology might be appropriate in this context. In studies of human information processing, in which cognitive biases and heuristics were identified, it was shown that recognizing and controlling biases was an effective way of reducing, not eliminating, them.[45] This type of academic thinking is helpful in gaining a clearer view of what we *do* understand in the context of what we do *not* understand. While it is now widely acknowledged that ethnocentrism limits our understanding of other cultures, an encouraging development is that we can develop new learning skills that allow us to become functional in new social settings. Some are presented here; other methods—developing cross-cultural competencies—are discussed in the next section.

A LEARNING PROGRAM FOR ADDRESSING ETHNOCENTRISM AND DEVELOPING CROSS-CULTURAL SKILLS

As the pace of globalization accelerates, the ability of managers to interact, engage, and adapt to different cultures will become more essential for developing and sustaining an organizational advantage. Reflecting more intensified business activities, there has been a flurry of books and periodicals on cross-cultural communications, along with touted programs such as cultural literacy, global mindsets, and cultural intelligence. In this section, the theories and frameworks presented earlier in this chapter are synthesized into a program for developing cross-cultural skills.

Our own experiences suggest that such a program is an ongoing process that is enhanced by a healthy dose of curiosity, a motivation for self-improvement, and a continuing effort to engage other cultures. Building these skills will not occur overnight and that miscues will be part of the learning experience. Therefore, the logic is a sequential, incremental, and evolutionary based on experiential learning over time. While we present this program in stages, the sequence is not intended to be deterministic. Some of you will be more proficient than others in cross-cultural communication and might be better positioned at the later steps.

1. *Address ethnocentrism directly and then conduct an assessment of your skills and competencies in international business.* Change is frequently an outcome of a perceived deficiency, an unpleasant experience, or a desire for improvement. Let's start by addressing how to reduce ethnocentrism, or at least be able to place this in proper perspective. Remember that this tendency is innate and internalized within people, the result of socialization and experiences. One way to reduce ethnocentrism is to recognize the limitations of false assumptions (i.e., that we might be assuming something that is not the case).[46] We can observe our own reactions, check underlying assumptions, and reflect on why these assumptions might not apply in a particular situation. When we take into account another person's reactions, we then have more ample opportunities to learn more about ourselves. In most cases, unexpected reactions and behaviors that disconfirm our expectations are those that prompt our attention.

Rather than reacting in a negative manner, we can reexamine the entire situation to understand what led to these unexpected outcomes.

While the practice described above is helpful on a personal level, it might be helpful to expand this assessment from ethnocentrism to a general assessment of international business skills. Extending the scope of analysis can be helpful in two ways. First, a broader appraisal can provide more clues into understanding our ethnocentric tendencies, or why we think the way we do. Second, the assessment and diagnosis can provide important insights into one's strengths and weaknesses that, in turn, can be the basis of a future platform for self-goals and strategies. While there are a number of ways to do this, we present a specific methodology in the next section of this chapter as a starting point for such an assessment. Because we will cover this method in more depth later, we simply mention it here as a point of reference.

2. *Develop an increased awareness of cultural similarities and differences through personal experiences.* Change is unlikely to occur without an awareness of a problem or the need to change. The lack of cultural curiosity and sensitivity is acute if one is not motivated to understand cultural differences, a problem that can quickly escalate if one is also highly ethnocentric. While awareness can be enhanced in formal classes or from reading a book, it's honed by personal experiences and actual engagements with people from a different culture.

Most books about culture are replete with stories about a person's experience in another country. Many of you are more likely to remember stories than statistics or facets of a particular theory, particularly if the stories do not confirm your beliefs and assumptions. Thus, building awareness is inextricably related to one's everyday experiences. We present two examples to underscore this point.

Edward Hall (introduced in this chapter) recounts an incident when he encountered a stranger in his hotel room in Japan. Sensing a mistake, he contacted the front desk to find out that he had been transferred to another room. Apparently his former room had been reserved in advance by somebody else. What shocked Hall, however, was that his personal items (clothes, toiletries, and other material) had been meticulously laid out in exactly the same manner in his new room as if he had never been moved. Several months later, this same arrangement reoccurred but in a completely *different* Japanese hotel![47] This experience provided the impetus for his arguments that culture influences one's conceptions of time and space, as well one's expectations about privacy.

Hall is not alone in reconstructing everyday observations into theories about culture. Karl Polanyi, considered to be among the world's most famous economic anthropologists and philosophers, observed that the Triobriand Islanders did not conduct transactions based on economic criteria depicted by the classical economists but on gift-giving, reciprocity, and redistribution.[48] Later studies disclosed that gift-giving among the Triobriand Islanders has a special significance rooted in deep-seated communitarian values. Specifically, objects are considered to retain a spiritual essence with the gift giver. Even when exchanged, these objects still retain this meaningful link. Without an understanding of the significance of this link, outsiders might unwittingly treat gifts as alienable objects or commodities and unknowingly offend other cultures.[49]

While direct exposure to a different culture is one way of increasing awareness, international travel and cultural immersion are not the only opportunities to build a rich cultural experience. Increased diversity in education and the workplace facilitates interaction with persons from different cultures and provides an alternative way for those who do not have an opportunity to travel abroad.

3. *Deepen your understanding of cultural differences by observing how people derive meanings from activities they perform.* One way to deepen one's understanding of different cultures is to carefully observe how people attach meanings and interpretations to activities they perform. In studies of consumer behavior, marketers have termed this as patterns of consumption. By examining how people use (or consume) products, valuable insights can be applied to future ones. For example, China's Haier, a world leader in manufacturing white goods, discovered that its rural customers frequently used washing machines not only to launder clothes but also to clean vegetables. Accordingly, Haier was able to develop and market a versatile machine and it has since become the market leader.[50]

When applied in a cross-cultural context, this can lead to surprises and unpredictable outcomes. Consider the case of a U.S. agency that attempted to improve the plight of women in one African village.[51] The women would trek miles each day to collect clean water that they carried in large pots on top of their heads. From the point of view of outsiders (certainly the foreign agency), this was a daunting, if not a physically laborious task. To alleviate their plight, the agency installed a water well right in the center of their village. To the dismay of the agency, however, the well was constantly plugged and hardly used by the women.

It turned out that the women had plugged the well, rendering it inoperative. Contrary to the agency's assumptions, the women actually enjoyed the long walk for it afforded them the opportunity to socialize and to spend some time outside of their normal household chores. When the new well was installed inside their village, it eliminated the need to make the two-hour hike, and the women were considered to have more time to perform additional work and tasks.

What the story underscores is that patterns of use can provide information that might be otherwise difficult to obtain from casual observation. Understanding how patterns of use are related to meaningful interpretations can be helpful in uncovering local knowledge. Used in tandem with more sophisticated programs, such as cultural dilemmas, cultural intelligence, and global literacy, interpretations based on patterns of use can go a long way in building your skills in accessing local knowledge.[52]

4. *Develop a "cultural recovery" system of transforming negative to positive experiences.* Even with a well-organized program of preparedness and development, cross-cultural mistakes and gaffes are likely to occur. Why? It's because cultures around the world are not only complex and even obtuse but frequently changing. Rather than waiting for these mistakes to occur, or to leave these to chance, it's better to be prepared and to know in advance what to do when miscues happen.

In service management, there is a term called *service recovery*. Basically this means turning a potentially negative experience into a positive one. Let's consider one example from service management before applying it in a cross-cultural context. When a devastating storm struck New York's John F. Kennedy International Airport on February 2007, the embattled JetBlue Airways decided to cancel more than 1,000 flights over six days, stranding disgruntled passengers and, even worse, trapping them on planes for hours.[53] By all accounts, this potential fiasco threatened to undo all of JetBlue's prior efforts to differentiate itself as a consumer-friendly airline. JetBlue's CEO David Neeleman quickly apologized publicly, offered immediate refunds and travel vouchers for customers who were stuck more than three hours, and mandated a new Customer Bill of Rights that exceeded the terms of other airlines at the time. For many, he had transformed a potentially adverse situation into a positive one—a classic case of good service recovery.

In applying this in a cross-cultural context, we emphasize that service recovery has to take into account the form, timing, and flexibility of actions that affect all parties. It does not matter who made the mistake, but how the situation is reframed into a positive outcome. Consider the experience of Fons Trompenaars when he found out that his book (with Hampden-Turner) was (illegally) translated by a local firm in an Asian country.[54] Immediately, their publisher considered a lawsuit against the offending party. This transgression was particularly difficult for Trompenaars and Turner-Hampden because the translation reflected a deep respect for their work. Moreover, it had already been widely circulated throughout the company, and the reaction had been "most enlightening." Trompenaars and Turner-Hampden had every right to sue, but circumstances compelled them to do otherwise. After all, the translation was of the highest quality. They would have had to spend more if they did this on their own (without the guarantee of high quality). Rather than suing the company, they paid respect to the host firm, thanked them warmly for the translation, expressed delight that they found the book worthwhile, and then asked advice on how to locate a suitable local commercial publisher. Within a month, a legal contract was sealed that protected their copyright. Moreover, they maintained good relations with the local firm—a "win-win" outcome for all parties. The story underscores the need to develop a "cross-cultural recovery plan"on your own. If this is done proactively, even with potential gaffes, a favorable resolution will be the likely outcome.

5. *Develop cross-cultural skills as a portfolio of experiments.* As you are developing your skill-set, you might want to consider its overall variety. Among systems-theorists and pundits of cybernetics, there is Ashby's famous *Law of Requisite Variety*.[55] We rephrase this as follows: *adaptation to a complex external environment should be matched and accommodated by an equally complex response set.* Why is a varied skill-set favorable?

To place this in perspective, let's return to what has become the central issue in strategy, that is, how a firm can adapt to its environment and create an advantage over competitors for a prolonged time period. McKinsey consultant Eric Beinhocker cites two recent studies to provide light on this issue.[56] The first study, conducted by former McKinsey consultants Dick Foster and Sarah Kaplan, examined the survival pattern of the largest 100 U.S. companies listed annually by the business periodical *Forbes* since its inception in 1917.[57] Of the original 100 companies, 61 had ceased to exist or had gone bankrupt, and of the survivors, 21 companies had dropped out of the list. In fact, a more rigorous assessment disclosed that only one firm—General Electric—had survived and outperformed the Standard and Poor's (S&P) market over the past eight decades.

The second study, by Robert Wiggins of the University of Memphis and Tim Ruefli of the University of Texas, undertook an even more rigorous study that employed a series of rolling five-year time frames with an improved methodology.[58] They reported that only 5 percent of their sample of 6,722 companies from different industries from 1974 to 1997 had a period of superior performance lasting ten years or more. Only three companies (American Home Products, Eli Lilly, and 3M) sustained high performance past the fifty-year mark.

In a sobering assessment, Beinhocker suggests that firms should refrain from adopting one "right" strategy, but instead to think of strategy as a "portfolio of experiments" and "bring evolution inside" or within their four walls.[59] Following the precepts of evolutionary theorists, firms should develop a steady stream of products and services that should be introduced in the market where the efficient ones are continued, with the less efficient ones weeded out.[60] The antecedents of evolutionary thinking goes back historically to an experiment by the Russian biologist Gause who compared the survivability of two similar organisms placed in one jar with limited amount of food versus two entirely different organisms in another jar under exactly the same conditions (the diverse organisms survived).[61] For evolutionary theorists, firms will not survive by offering highly similar products. The best way for firms to survive and endure in highly unpredictable and implacable environments is to increase variety in their adaptive repertoire.[62] Some firms already maintain such a posture. As part of their new product strategy, Sony Corporation, Capital One, Nike, and Apple typically unleash a multitude of new product designs and features that are constantly modified, refined, and discarded until the next iteration of new product development cycle.

Applied in the context of cross-cultural learning skills, the import of these arguments is that the most efficient way to survive the rugged contours of cross-cultural differences is to continuously strive for a varied portfolio. This portfolio of skills can include interpersonal competencies, cultural and global literacy, adeptness in reconciling polar opposites in cultural dilemmas, and enhancement strategies for improving cultural intelligence. There is also the slew of populist books that recommend ways of doing business in other countries. Ideally, a wider variety of skills should include *different*, if not *competing* cultural interpretations of anticipated cultural encounters.[63]

With growing complexity in the global environment, mistakes are bound to happen (we have contributed our own share in this regard), even with a thorough preparation and the best intentions in mind. Even so, with a tolerance for cross-cultural differences, an interest in engaging other cultures, a well-developed deployable platform for continuous improvement, a plan for "cross-cultural recovery," and a varied adaptive response repertoire, one can turn a cultural miscue into a positive experience, if not a competitive advantage. Our next section deals specifically to a methodology for assessing your capabilities for conducting international business as part of the process of implementing strategy.

An Assessment Methodology

Firms and individuals with a global mindset are in the best position to create responsive strategies through effective and efficient implementation. In the previous sections, we discussed various frameworks centered on enhancing cross-cultural competencies and reducing ethnocentrism. Regardless of what might be said in corporate speeches and annual reports, a firm's response is only as good as the global mindset that is shared among individuals.

One way of assessing the propensity or the readiness of any organization to go global is through a methodology that measures the capabilities of the firm in several key areas of international business. As an illustration, three key areas of international business competencies were identified based on a careful review of cultural theorists such as Edward Hall, Fons Trompenaars, and Geert Hofstede. Exhibit 10.10 lists sample questions and attitudinal statements that measure these capabilities.

- *International business functional skills.* These relate to cognitive understanding of the functional skills underlying the conduct of international business. They include international accounting, finance, marketing, systems theory, culture, legal systems, and negotiations.
- *Contextual information about international business.* These relate to basic knowledge about key international institutions (World Trade Organization, World Bank, United Nations), regional agreements (EU, Mercosur, SEATO, etc.), and geographical contexts (emerging markets, North-South differentials, etc.).
- *Cultural understanding and empathy.* Contrasted with the above two, this relates to attitudes and some sense of relatedness to different cultures. This includes the understanding of cultural dimensions, an awareness of ethnocentrism, and a level of comfort in dealing with the types of cultural dilemmas delineated by Trompenaars.

In Exhibit 10.11, these competencies are represented in terms of a "spider web" chart that has been used in business and economics journals.[64] Numbering the dimensions starting at the center, we can position the level of proficiency in each competence by its relative distance from the center. A company that exhibits very low competencies or a limited propensity for engaging in international business would have a fairly small footprint. Contrariwise, one with extensive competencies would have a much larger footprint.

This demarcation of international business competencies facilitates strategic thinking and the cultivation of a global mindset in many respects. First, by delineating the range of competencies, firms are able to appreciate a relatively complete repertoire of skills that they need in order to develop and cultivate a global mindset. Second, this method illuminates the gaps that need to be bridged in order to facilitate a global mindset. For example, one firm might excel in international market research but might be deficient in international negotiations. Third, this method also can provide insights on competencies that either facilitate or impede the firm's strategy. For example, if an aggressive differentiation is desired, but analysis reveals the lack of competencies in identifying

Exhibit 10.10

Sample Questions Relating to International Business Competencies

Summarized below are commonly expressed attitudes of individuals. Using the scale below, rate each statement with respect to the degree to which you either agree or disagree with it.

Strongly agree	Moderately agree	Slightly agree	Neither	Slightly disagree	Moderately disagree	Strongly disagree
1	2	3	4	5	6	7

_____ When I am in a different culture, I am more excited than anxious or fearful.
_____ When I find people from other cultures having difficulty understanding me, my first reaction is to state my thoughts more clearly, if not more forcefully.
_____ When in a different culture, I occasionally have "culture shock."
_____ When other cultures challenge my core beliefs and values, I tend to explain to others why I hold these beliefs.
_____ While there are different forms of market structures, I think that capitalism trumps all others.

Summarized below are commonly expressed attitudes of organizations. Using the scale below, rate each statement with respect to the degree to which you either agree or disagree with it.

_____ My company is a leader, not a follower, in introducing international initiatives.
_____ My company leaders visit foreign countries at least three times per year.
_____ My company has a clear and cogent international strategy that is known to most every employee.
_____ In selecting between applicants with exactly the same qualifications but with different nationalities, my company will select the person from a different culture.
_____ Incentives are tied closely to international training and assignments.

Summarized below are different areas of individual international business expertise. Using the scale, rate each statement with respect to the degree to which can you perform each activity.

Expert	Moderately Proficient	Marginally Proficient	Neutral	Moderately able	Marginally able	Not able
1	2	3	4	5	6	7

_____ International negotiations   _____ Competitive analysis
_____ Market research   _____ SWOT analysis

distinctive product and service features, then this is an area that would warrant closer managerial attention. Thus, the method can be valuable not only for purposes of enhancing a global mindset, but for facilitating strategic implementation as well.

In conclusion, this chapter attends to an area that has not, until recently, drawn the attention of top managers. In consideration of strategic implementation, it is important to attend to designing appropriate structures and processes (Chapter 9). Yet, one key process is having the right attitude or state of mind that is appropriate for a particular strategy. This is because what we believe (global orientation) is tempered by what we know (knowledge-based structures), that is, it is turned and shaped by our collective experiences (shared cultural experiences). Even so, interpretations of other cultures are at risk when one is ethnocentric, and bad decisions will occur as a result. Accordingly, managers need to minimize this result by enhancing their cross-cultural competencies, honed in part by the acquisition of technical skills and in part by a deeper apprecia-

Exhibit 10.11   **A Spiderweb Representation of International Business Competencies**

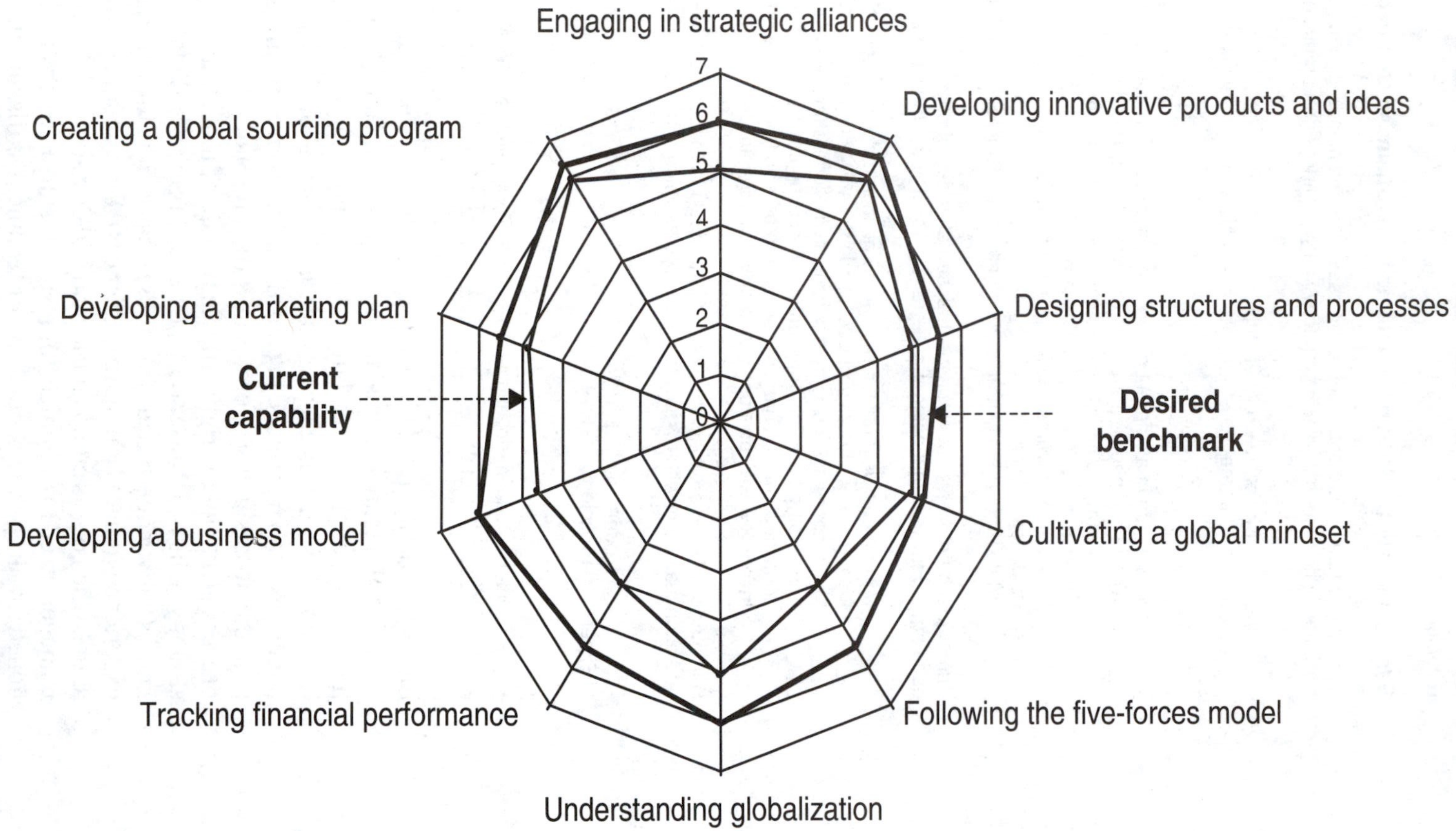

tion and empathy for other cultures. Because what we believe ultimately determines how we act, developing and cultivating a global mindset will go a long way toward realizing any firm's quest to be a participant, if not a leader, in global business. The next skill set in strategic implementation is understanding the company's performance through financial reports—the subject matter of Chapter 11.

Summary

1. This chapter introduces the concept of the global mindset and proposes a practical methodology for mapping a global mindset for global strategic implementation.

2. Every individual is affected by national, corporate, and professional cultures. Edward Hall, Fons Trompenaars, and Geert Hofstede have their ways of interpreting cultures and their impacts on management thinking and practice.

3. Edward Hall's contributions include the introduction of "silent language" and the low-context vs. high-context cultures. Silent language includes time, space, things, friendship, and agreements. Low-context culture uses explicit communication rules. High-context culture uses implicit cues, such as friendship and relationships.

4. Fons Trompenaars developed a seven-orientation framework. Five of them deal with relationships between people: universalism versus particularism; individualism versus collectivism; neutral versus emotional; specific versus diffuse; and achievement versus ascription. Two relate to people's attitudes toward time and the environment.

5. Geert Hofstede's cultural dimensions include power distance, uncertainty avoidance, individualism versus collectivism, masculinity versus femininity, and long-term versus short-term orientation.

6. The impact of globalization has been proposed and organized in terms of three theories. The convergence theory suggests that cultures become more homogenized. The divergence theory proposes that the uniqueness of culture is not transferable. The cross-vergence theory maintains that the interdependency and integration of economies beget the creation of a new type of culture.

7. A global mindset represents a global perspective, global knowledge, and sound strategic skills. In developing a global mindset and global competency, Stephen H. Rhinesmith proposed the use of six approaches to combine with six personal characteristics. The combined effect of intellectual intelligence and emotional intelligence is manifested in a set of global behavioral skills.

8. Herbert Paul suggested four external forces and five ways to shape a corporate global mindset. The four forces are "top management's view of the world," "administrative heritage," "structural solutions," and "industry forces." External forces provide opportunities and should be supported by an efficient management process.

9. To develop a global mindset, Vijay Govindarajan and Anil Gupta have suggested four steps: an openness to diversity across cultures and markets, or curiosity about the world; the articulation of a current mindset that acknowledges the diversity in our world; an active learning process to cultivate knowledge

regarding diverse cultures; and the integration of new knowledge achieved through sharing, job rotation, and a reward system based on merit.

10. Ethnocentrism entails the belief that one's own race or ethnic group is the most important or that it is superior to others. Ethnocentric individuals will then judge other groups in relation to their own. Ethnocentrism can become a cultural blinder and affects management attitudes and behaviors.

11. A learning program to address ethnocentrism and to develop cross-cultural skills includes the following sequence of recommended steps: First, address ethnocentrism directly and conduct an assessment of your skills and competencies in international business. Second, develop an increased awareness of cultural similarities and differences through personal experiences. Third, deepen an understanding of cross-cultural differences. Fourth, develop a "cultural recovery" system for transforming negative to positive experiences. Fifth, develop cross-cultural skills as a "portfolio of experiments."

12. A methodology to build a global mindset is presented for managers. Three distinct factors are identified: international business functional skills, contextual information about international business, and cultural understanding and empathy.

KEY TERMS

Mindset

Culture

National culture

Power distance

Uncertainty avoidance

Individualism vs. collectivism

Masculinity vs. femininity

Convergence theory

Divergence theory

Cross-vergence theory

Intellectual intelligence

Emotional intelligence

Ethnocentrism

DISCUSSION QUESTIONS

1. What is a "mindset?" What is culture? What is the linkage between the two and how do they affect international managers?

2. How does Edward Hall characterize culture and how do his interpretations help international managers?

3. Fons Trompenaars developed a seven-orientation framework. What are the seven orientations and how are they applied to international management?

4. What are the cultural dimensions developed by Geert Hofstede? How are they applied to international management?

5. Compare the interpretations and practical values offered by Hall, Trompenaars, and Hofstede in terms of culture.

6. Explain convergence theory, divergence theory, and cross-vergence theory. Discuss the validity of each theory in light of the future trend of globalization.

7. What is Rhinesmith's perspective on the global mindset? How practical is his framework in practicing global strategic management?

8. What is Herbert's perspective on the global mindset? Please use examples to illustrate how the four external forces and the five ways can be applied to shape a corporate global mindset.

9. What is Govindarajan and Gupta's perspective on the global mindset? Please use examples to illustrate how the three elements and the four steps are applied to shape a corporate global mindset.

10. What is ethnocentrism and how does it affect global managers? Please use examples to illustrate how to understand ethnocentrism.

11. Discuss how each of the five dilemmas presented in Box 10.1 can be creatively reconciled.

ACTION ITEM 10.1. TESTING FOR ETHNOCENTRISM

At this juncture, you might wonder whether you are ethnocentric, or, more accurately, about the degree to which you hold (unconscious) ethnocentric tendencies. If your score suggests that you are, you are advised not to worry too much since you are simply part of the rest of the universe. The key, as we suggest in this chapter, is to recognize our ethnocentric beliefs and to broaden our cultural skills in trying to overcome or reduce their effects.[65]

1. I apply the norms of my culture to judge people of different cultural backgrounds.

Not true		Sometimes		Always true
1	2	3	4	5

2. I see people with similar opinions to mine as "correct."

Not true		Sometimes		Always true
1	2	3	4	5

3. I see people with viewpoints different from mine as being wrong.

Not true		Sometimes		Always true
1	2	3	4	5

4. I prefer to hang around with people who think and act differently from me.

Not true		Sometimes		Always true
1	2	3	4	5

5. I have little faith in people who are different from me.

Not true		Sometimes		Always true
1	2	3	4	5

SCORING YOUR ANSWER

Your score	Interpret with care
5	Very low: You are a culturally literate person. You need to write a book on how you do it.
6–10	Low: You are quite adept at evaluating other cultures. You're cool.
11–15	Medium: You often lapse into some form of cultural stereotyping, like most of us.
16–20	High: You have a tendency to be highly ethnocentric—join the rest of us.
21–25	Very high: You see your culture as central, if not superior, to others.

CASE-IN-POINT. MINDTREE AND CULTURAL DIVERSITY

ASHOK SOOTA[66]

> "Happy people lead to happy customers," says Ashok Soota, head of MindTree Consulting, an international IT and R&D services company, which in FY05 achieved a gross revenue of $55 million, representing growth of 90 percent over the previous year. And how do you create an environment where people can be happy? Read on . . .

When we launched MindTree Consulting in August 1999, we were about the 1,500th IT services company out of India. We set to differentiate ourselves by providing customers the best of both worlds: the high consulting capability of companies in the West with the low cost and scalability of India. We were able to do this as the founders and early team members came from a variety of global companies such as Cambridge Technology Partners, KPMG, Lucent, PricewaterhouseCoopers, Wipro, and others. Equally important, within a brief period after our launch, we had team members of seven different nationalities.

The initial positioning and the rich cultural diversity led to a flying start. Yet, we found that there were significantly different approaches in thought processes, style, and approach to building an organization among the senior team members who were brought up in different milieus. We saw these as a source of potential conflict and were concerned.

CULTURAL OPPORTUNITY

It was at this juncture that we had the opportunity to interact with Professor Jukka Laitamakki, who taught at the Fordham MBA program in New York. We asked his advice on how we could manage cultural diversity.

To our surprise, Jukka told us that instead of managing diverse culture, we must celebrate it as a source of different ideas. "Nobody likes his or her culture to be managed. Instead, you must focus on building values that are shared and adopted by everyone in the organization," he said. He added that a common set of values would surpass cultural differences and bind the organization together. That was an eye opener for us.

When we launched the company, we started by defining a set of values, and when Jukka made this observation, I invited our team members to articulate the company values. The entire middle management and senior leadership were present and it soon became apparent that virtually no one remembered more than one or two of the six values we had defined. I immediately realized that if people could not remember the values, we were miles away from internalizing them.

During the next few months my colleagues and I interacted with almost of all of the team, which was then about 500 MindTree Minds. The question we asked was: "What do you think MindTree stands for? What would you like MindTree to stand for?" Many ideas emerged and when we pieced all these together, what we call our CLASS values virtually jumped out. The values that MindTree Minds collectively chose were *Caring, Learning, Achieving, Sharing,* and *Social Responsibility.* The values were simple, comprehensive, and the acronym of a "CLASS" company conveyed the message that the whole is greater than the sum of its parts. We built the values into our performance management system. When we did that, we soon realized that the words meant different things to different people. To give a common perspective, we defined attributes and indicative descriptions for each of the values.

TESTING TIMES

At the end of our first year, MindTree's exclusive focus was on e-business solutions and engineering services in the telecom domain. As we began our second year, we witnessed the dotcom bust, followed by the telecom bust. It was like pulling the rug out from under the feet of a toddler learning to walk. This was followed by September 11, when we were just two years old. It was evident that we had more delivery people than we could effectively utilize with the business in had. Yet, we were determined not to lay off a single person. We called in the entire team, shared the situation with them, and came to an agreement that everyone would take salary cuts ranging from 10 percent to 25 percent with senior people taking heavier cuts. We had added some staff positions, which seemed a luxury in the changed circumstances. We debated whether we should give these persons notice to seek alternative jobs. The middle management learned of this, got together, and volunteered to take a higher salary cut, but insisted that no one from the team should be asked to leave for reasons other than nonperformance.

At that time I realized how well our team had imbibed our values. That year, in spite of the salary cuts, we took a heavy loss, but we emerged from the same stronger and more resilient—poised to take advantage of the revival in the global economy. It was our values that kept us together in those difficult times.

WALKING THE TALK

Sometimes our customers inquire how the values will be of value to them, to which I respond that the caring value will be of value to them, that the caring value will be manifested by the "extra mile" our teams will walk for them; the sharing and learning values will create more skilled teams—critical in this knowledge-intensive business; the social responsibility objective helps to build more committed people; and our achievement objective would ensure excellence, on-time delivery, and customer satisfaction.

At our startup stage we had appealed more to the emotions of our prospects to assess us on what we could be, rather than what we were. A few early customers, like Hindustan Lever and Volvo, took the trouble of examining our capabilities and took the leap of faith. To them we remain ever grateful. In the post-9/11 situation, a different approach was needed. The global recession had introduced uncertainty, leading to conservatism in decision making. Customers were hesitating to sign up with us, saying how do we know you are going to be around for the future.

We did a quick assessment of our customers' needs and looked for areas where budgets were being less heavily cut. This led to the development of new practices and competencies: we advanced what we would otherwise have done a few years later. We accelerated our efforts to enter into new geographies. We looked at new vertical markets and invested in new IPs.

Although these investments led to heavy losses, we saw them as investments for our future. We had faith in our team and in our ability to achieve our five-year vision. We were convinced that the tough times had to be used to prepare for better times ahead. By the end of our third year, we were confident that, if markets revived, we were well positioned to grow much faster than the competition. Which, indeed, is what happened.

KNOWING WHAT WE DON'T WANT TO DO

There's always a temptation to enter a booming sunrise business. At MindTree, we defined our business as "IT services," which requires the skills of consulting, architecting, design services, building solutions, developing expertise in multiple technologies, and understanding technology directions with a view to taking investment decisions on the same. We see the BPO (business process outsourcing) field as a completely different business, requiring a different profile of persons. Also, the rhythm is different—more like running a factory than a design center. Likewise, the products business requires single-minded focus on the one product and we don't want to compete with our customers. Accordingly, we have been able to stay away from the "temptation" of entering these areas, to which many of our competitors have succumbed for a variety of different reasons.

The approach to customer selection is based on the premise that we seek strategic relationships in preference to having hundreds of customer accounts. Every account must meet the criterion of being a partnership and must provide the potential for profitability as the account grows. I can't say that we have been 100 percent spot-on in terms of decisions in meeting this criterion, though we have been fortunate that we were able to start several of our practices to fulfill existing customer needs. For example, Volvo took us into the SAP area; Hindustan Lever drew us into business intelligence.

We see and project ourselves as the best mid-sized company out of India, but we have formidable competitors and we respect them. Due to their strong brands and the enormous press coverage they receive, they get many walk-in customers and are in the consideration set for increasingly larger deals. Yet, there are several advantages to being mid-sized. Large organizations are increasingly finding it more comfortable to work with mid-sized IT companies, and this trend is prevalent across the globe. Many customers don't want to be the 1000th customer of a company. They seek MindTree for agility, access, and attention.

Likewise, many young persons don't want to be the 30,000th or 50,000th employee of a huge entity. It's all about Mindshare. Accordingly, just as we are able to attract talent from the bigger players, we find there are customers who are more comfortable in a partnership with a mid-sized company. And when we do get a chance to compete, we win more often than not. Our challenge is to expand our reach and enhance our brand to reduce the cost of getting new customers.

Though we have a smaller number of practices compared to the larger players, we try to succeed through depth rather than breadth. For customer satisfaction, our philosophy is a simple one: 100 percent of our customers must be referenceable. At any point of time, there will be one or two who are not. Since we closely monitor the relationships and we will always go the extra mile, we are confident of bringing a temporarily unhappy customer to a stage of referenceability. We place a large importance on Joy and creating a joyous environment for MindTree Minds. Our people, in turn, define "Joy" as the satisfaction of a job well done.

Happy People Lead to Happy Customers

We strongly believe that culture drives behavior and behavior drives results. Indeed, our performance and results demonstrate the impact of our culture and values. MindTree is the first Indian IT services company to have achieved $50 million in revenues within five years of its inception and we are well on the way to becoming the fastest to reach $100 million. Over a three-year cycle, we are growing at about two to three times the industry average. More importantly, the recognition that MindTree is one of the best places to work is also a testimony to our people practices and values. All through this, we never forgot our social responsibility value, which was recognized by our becoming the youngest company to receive the Helen Keller Award, instituted by Shell and the government, for our work with differently abled persons.

Our ability to attract people from across almost all companies in the industry is truly a unique characteristic of MindTree. About 65 percent of our people are lateral hires, and of these almost 40 percent are references from MindTree Minds. This shows that MindTree's Minds are not only happy to be with MindTree but happy to bring their friends here. Due to the high percentage of lateral hiring, the average experience profile of our team is almost double that of the larger players in the industry. We see that as our investment for ensuring higher satisfaction for our customers. We also do our share of hiring at campuses and try to build close relationships with a few rather than spread ourselves thin. On these campuses, MindTree often gets dream company status and this facilitates quality in hiring.

I am sometimes asked, "What do employees want more: money, titles, a learning environment, or the fast track?" We recently did some research on the needs and concerns of the young IT professional. We found that, in the services sector, many of them are not enthused since they do not get the satisfaction of seeing the end product. Since our proportion of new project work is very high, our people are able to see the impact of the work they are doing for our customers, which enhances job satisfaction. Compensation is indeed important, but if several companies are within the same ballpark range, the choice of one company in preference to others is influenced by multiple factors such as challenging work, career path, and feeling of inclusiveness.

The research referred to above also revealed that in this industry, there is high pressure due to the ongoing and continuous need to meet customer deadlines. Through a variety of programs, we try to ensure that this pressure does not translate to stress for our people.

THE 95:95:95 RULE

We believe in the concept of 95:95:95—i.e., we believe that 95 percent of our people must have 95 percent of all information, 95 percent of the time. Let me illustrate this with an example. Every quarter, we present to our board a qualitative document of "What Went Well and What Could Be Better." The leadership team of about seventy persons provides inputs for the same and it analyses threadbare improvement areas. This same document is shared with all MindTree Minds after the board meeting. We want our team to know that success is not a projection of the past, but meeting the challenges identified in this strategic document. We want them to relate to the challenges and contribute toward addressing them for MindTree's ongoing success and the team's satisfaction.

Regarding processes, we planned from the beginning to be a large company and made the investments in systems in advance—like installing an integrated ERP package in our first year. All our people processes run off the net, through the interface of our PeopleNet portal. Notwithstanding this, processes need continuous review for assessing scalability and ensuring that cross-functional baton passing is smooth and seamless. We do this through cross-functional task forces and a fledgling Six Sigma program. While our profitability has enhanced significantly year after year, we still have a way to go before we can compare our profit to sales with industry leaders. In terms of Returns on Capital Employed (ROCE) we are better placed for being in the top rung.

I believe that visitors will see and perceive this difference as they walk through our premises. They will sense the energy and enthusiasm of our teams. They will, of course, see the cheerful work environment we have created. They will also notice and admire the vibrant colors, which make all our buildings art galleries of work done by children with cerebral palsy.

TABLE 1. MINDTREE'S VALUES

- Caring for each other, for our clients, and for our stakeholders
- Learning personal development and innovation
- Achieving aspiration, accountability, and action orientation
- Sharing teamwork and knowledge creation
- Social responsibility, corporate citizenship, and integrity

TABLE 2. MINDTREE'S VISION FOR 2007–08

- To achieve $231 million in revenue
- To be among the top 10% in our business in terms of profit after tax (PAT) and return on investment (ROI)
- To be one of the top twenty globally admired companies in our industry
- To give a significant portion of our PAT to support primary education

CASE DISCUSSION QUESTIONS

1. Identify the five core values of MindTree. How were they put in practice in this company?
2. The company employees and executives took pay cuts during a financially difficult time to preserve jobs. The company feels that this helped to build commitment. Will this be an effective approach in other cultures?
3. Describe the company's culture and how the culture was built and fostered.

NOTES FOR CHAPTER 10

1. This section is adapted from G. Ungson and D. Braunstein, "The Geography of Thought. Book Review," *Journal of Marketing* 68, no. 13 (July 2004): 14–18; used with permission. Quotes by Nisbett (cited in above article) from Richard Nisbett, *The Geography of Thought* (New York: The Free Press, 2003), pp. 226 and 229.

2. Ibid.

3. Herbert Paul, "Creating a Global Mindset," *Thunderbird International Business Review* 42, no. 2 (2000): 187.

4. Vijay Govindarajan and Anil K. Gupta, *The Quest for Global Dominance* (San Francisco: Jossey-Bass, 2001). Also see N. Boyacigiller, S. Beechler, S. Taylor, O. Levy, "The Crucial but Illusive Global Mindset," in H. Lane, M. Maznevski, M. Mendenhall & J. McNett (eds.), *The Handbook of Global Management* (Oxford: Blackwell, 2004) for additional dimensions of a global mindset.

5. Paul, "Creating a Global Mindset."

6. Geert Hofstede, "The Cultural Relativity of the Quality of Life Concept," *Academy of Management Review* 9, no. 3 (1984): 389–398.

7. D.K. Tse, K. Lee, I. Vertinsky, and D.A. Wehrung, "Does Culture Matter? A Cross-Cultural Study of Executives' Choice, Decisiveness, and Risk Adjustment in International Marketing," *Journal of Marketing* 52, no. 4 (1988): 81–95.

8. Fons Trompenaars, *Riding the Waves of Culture: Understanding Diversity in Global Business* (Homewood, IL: Irwin, 1994), p. 24.

9. Edward T. Hall, *The Silent Language* (New York: Anchor Books, 1959).

10. Fons Trompenaars and C. Hampden-Turner, *21 Leaders for the 21st Century* (New York: McGraw-Hill, 2001).

11. Geert Hofstede and Michael H. Bond, "The Confucius Connection: From Cultural Roots to Economic Growth," *Organizational Dynamics* 16, no. 4 (1988): 4–21; Geert Hofstede, *Culture's Consequences: Comparing Values, Behaviors, Institutions, and Organizations Across Nations*, 2d ed. (Thousand Oaks, CA: Sage Publications, 2001).

12. Hall, *The Silent Language*, p. 2.

13. Edward T. Hall, *The Hidden Dimension* (New York: Anchor Books, 1966).

14. Edward T. Hall, *Beyond Culture* (New York: Anchor Books, 1976).

15. Fons Trompenaars, *Riding the Waves of Culture: Understanding Diversity in Global Business*; also see Charles Hampden-Turner and Fons Trompenaars, *Building Cross-Cultural Competence* (New Haven: Yale University Press, 2000).

16. Hofstede and Bond, "The Confucius Connection: From Cultural Roots to Economic Growth."

17. Geert Hofstede, online materials, www.geert-hofstede.com/hofstede_dimensions.php, retrieved on October 24, 2005. Also see Geert Hofstede, *Cultures and Organizations: Software of the Mind* (London: McGraw-Hill, 1991; New York: McGraw-Hill, 1997). Entirely rewritten Third Millennium Edition, by Geert Hofstede and Gert Jan Hofstede, New York: McGraw-Hill, 2005.

18. Nader Asgary and Alf H. Walle, "The Cultural Impact of Globalization: Economic Activity and Social Change," *Cross Cultural Management* 9, no. 3 (2002): 59–75.

19. Allan Bird and Michael J. Stevens, "Toward an Emergent Global Culture and the Effects of Globalization on Obsolescing National Cultures," *Journal of International Management* 9, no. 4 (2003): 395–407.

20. Ibid.

21. D.A. Ralston, D.H. Holt, R.H. Terpstra, and K-C Yu, "The Impact of National Culture and Economic Ideology on Managerial Work Values: A Study of the United States, Russia, Japan, and China," *Journal of International Business Studies* 28, no. 1 (1997): 177–207.

22. Asgary and Walle, "The Cultural Impact of Globalization: Economic Activity and Social Change."

23. Bird and Stevens, "Toward an Emergent Global Culture and the Effects of Globalization on Obsolescing National Cultures."

24. Ibid.

25. Stephen H. Rhinesmith, "Global Mindsets for Global Managers," *Training & Development* 46, no. 10 (October 1992): 63.

26. Govindarajan and Gupta, *The Quest for Global Dominance*, p. 107.

27. Ibid.

28. Mark E. Mendenhall and Gunter K. Stahl, "Expatriate Training and Development: Where Do We Go from Here?" *Human Resource Management* 39, no. 2, 3 (Summer/Fall 2000): 251–265. Also see Rosalie Tung and Ed Miller, "Managing the Twenty-first Century: The Need for Global Orientation." *Management International Review* 30, no. 1 (1990): 5–18 for related proposals that enhance a global mindset.

29. Rhinesmith, "Global Mindsets for Global Managers."

30. Stephen H. Rhinesmith, "How Can You Manage Global Paradox?" *The Journal of Corporate Accounting and Finance* 12, no. 6 (September/October 2001): 3–9.

31. Ibid., p. 5.

32. Paul, "Creating a Global Mindset."

33. Govindarajan and Gupta, *The Quest for Global Dominance*, pp. 126–34.

34. Thomas Pettigrew, "Ethnocentrism," http://208.164.121.55/reference/SOME/Outlines/ethnocentrism.htm. William Graham Sumner, *Folkways: A Study of the Sociological Importance of Usages, Manners, Customs, Mores, and Morals* (Boston, MA: Ginn, 1934, first published, 1906).

35. See William Graham Sumner, http://en.wikipedia.org/wiki/William_Graham_Sumner.

36. Ibid.

37. Quoted from a speech made by Professor Hofstede.

38. Ken Barger, quoted in "Putting Empathy to Work," www.sisr.net/ncgcd/pdf/GM2003VO14issue1.pdf.

39. Ibid. Even so, Thomas E. Maher, professor emeritus of California State University–Fullerton,

and one of our reviewers, astutely pointed out that we need to distinguish between correct and false generalizations, however critical. Critical comments, such as attributions of corruption in some cultures, are accurate and can be validated empirically. These are not construed as ethnocentric.

40. "Putting Empathy to Work."

41. Ken Barger, "Ethnocentrism," Working Paper. Department of Anthropology, Indiana University-Purdue University Indianapolis, December 20, 2004.

42. Ibid.

43. This is the debate between modernization and dependency theorists. The modernists, notably Walt Rostow, maintain that poor countries have failed to enact the proper policies that could have transformed poor agricultural states into successful industrialized ones. Dependency theorists, such as Paul Prebisch and Immanuel Wallerstein, counter that underdevelopment is not a condition, as stipulated by modernization theorists, but a process of impoverishment that has been created in large part by developed countries themselves. See John Isbister, *Promises Not Kept: Poverty and the Betrayal of Third World Development*, 7th ed. (Bloomfield, CT: Kumarian Press, 2006); also Ethnocentrism: Definitions and Examples.

44. Hall, *The Silent Language*, pp. 168–85.

45. For a review, see G. Ungson, D. Braunstein, and P. Hall, "Managerial Information Processing: A Research Review," *Administrative Science Quarterly* 26, no. 1 (1981): 116–134.

46. Barger, "Ethnocentrism."

47. Hall, *Beyond Culture,* pp. 58–60.

48. Karl Polanyi, "The Economy as Instituted Process," in K. Polanyi, Conrad M. Arensberg, and Harry W. Pearson (eds.), *Trade and Market in the Early Empires: Economics in History and Theory* (Glencoe, IL: The Free Press, 1957).

49. Annette B. Weiner, *Inalienable Possessions: The Paradox of Keeping-While-Giving* (Berkeley: University of California Press, 1992).

50. Donald Sull, Alejandro Ruelas-Gossi and Martin Escobari, "Innovating Around Obstacles." *Strategy & Innovation* (November–December 2003), pp. 3–6.

51. Personal communication. George Orbelian, Global Trade Council, San Francisco, November 15, 2007. Original story is from Peter Cook.

52. See Charles Hampden-Turner and Fons Trompenaars, *Building Cross-Cultural Competence* (New Haven: Yale University Press, 2000); P. Christopher Earley and Soon Ang, *Cultural Intelligence: Individual Interactions Across Cultures* (Stanford, CA: Stanford University Press, 2003); and Robert Rosen, Patricia Digh, Marshall Singer, and Carl Phillips, *Global Literacies* (New York: Simon & Schuster, 2000).

53. "An Extraordinary Stumble at JetBlue," *BusinessWeek Online* (March 5, 2007), http://www.businessweek.com/magazine/content/07_10/b4024004.htm.

54. Hampden-Turner and Trompenaars, *Building Cross-Cultural Competence*, pp. 46–47.

55. This is attributed to W.R. Ashby, who defined the term in 1956.

56. Eric Beinhocker, *The Origin of Wealth* (Boston, MA: Harvard Business School Press, 2007), pp. 334–36.

57. Richard Foster and Sarah Kaplan, *Creative Destruction* (New York: Doubleday, 2001).

58. Robert Wiggins and Timothy Ruefli, "Sustained Competitive Advantage: Temporal Dynamics and the Incidence and Persistence of Superior Economic Performance," *Organizational Science* 13, no. 1 (2002): 81–105.

59. Beinhocker, *The Origin of Wealth*, pp. 334–36.

60. Richard Whittington, *What Is Strategy, and Does It Matter?* (New York: Routledge, 1993), pp. 18–19.

61. Ibid., p. 19.

62. Ibid., pp. 18–19.

63. An emerging initiative by Professor Horacio Borromeo, Asian Institute of Management, is a

collaborative program with University of Malaysia focused on Islamic management that significantly complements the traditional coverage of management theories in international business. For those interested, see Khaliq Ahmad, *Management from Islamic Perspective* (Kuala Lumpur, Malaysia: International Islamic University Malaysia, 2007).

64. See Jean-Pierre Jeannet, *Managing with a Global Mindset* (Great Britain: Financial Times/ Prentice Hall, 2000).

65. These questions were adapted and modified from Keith Fenwick, *Buildings, Bridges and Walls* (Paint a Watercolour Landscape in Minutes) (London: Arcturus Publishing, 2002).

66. Reprinted with permission from Ashok Soota, "90% Growth through Cultural Diversity," *The Smart Manager* (December 2005/January 2006): 27–32.

11 Implementing Strategy Using Financial Performance Measures

You can't manage what you can't measure.
—William Hewlett

Financial statements are like fine perfume; to be sniffed but not swallowed.
—Abraham Brilloff

CHAPTER OUTLINE

- Cooking the Books at Woolworth
- The Role of Financial Analyses in Strategic Implementation
- The Financial Statements: Accounting Conventions
- Strategic Objectives and Performance Measures
- Assessing Financial Health Through Financial Ratios
- Analysis by Disaggregation: The DuPont Formula
- Using Marketing Ratios
- Revisiting the Value Problem: ROE versus EVA
- Economic Value Added (EVA) and Market Value Added (MVA)
- Testing the Sustainability of Business Strategy
- Relating Valuation to Strategy
- Toward a Balanced Scorecard
- Financial Reporting in the Context of International Operations

LEARNING OBJECTIVES

- Understand the use of financial statements.
- Learn about the different measures of financial and operating performance.
- Understand the debate underlying the value problem.
- Learn different methods of assessing the sustainability of a firm's current and future operations.

COOKING THE BOOKS AT WOOLWORTH

On March 30, 1994, Woolworth Corporation, the eighth largest retailer in the United States, announced that it had launched an internal investigation of "allegations of accounting irregularities." A whistle-blower, John H. Cannon, the company's treasurer, reported to John W. Adams, an outside director, about possible wrongdoing in at least three of the company's late quarterly reports. It was said that Brian Flood, then controller of Woolworth's operation in Canada, was told to report monthly financial performances that did not closely resemble the accounting records. Selig Adler, then chief financial officer (CFO) of Kinney, one of Woolworth's shoe stores, said that he was told by CFO Charles T. Young to report rosier figures than the realities when submitting the second and the third quarters of the 1993 fiscal year report.[1]

Mr. Adams found "some substance" to justify an internal investigation and a special committee was formed. In 1994, the special committee of the board hired a law firm, Paul, Weiss, Rifkind, Wharton & Garrison, which had retained accounting from KPMG Peat Marwick to assist the investigation. It appeared that the problems could be more than typical year-end reviews of merchandise-discount policies. This announcement raised questions about Woolworth's operations. From 1992 to 1994, the retailer closed and sold some stores in order to boost the low operating results.[2]

While several top Woolworth executives were under investigation, only the chairman and chief executive, William K. Lavin, and the chief financial officer, Charles T. Young, had stepped aside temporarily during the investigation to allow the company to operate as usual. Both insisted there was no wrongdoing. The focus was on whether they knowingly reported inaccurate gross profit margins in three quarterly reports during fiscal year 1993.[3]

At the end of March 1994, Woolworth stock fell 5.6 percent, reaching a fifty-two-week low. Two major ratings agencies took a closer look and launched intensive reviews of Woolworth's financial liabilities. Moody's Investors Service, Inc., announced that they might downgrade the company based on the "details of possible weaknesses," "internal controls," among other concerns. By placing Woolworth's debt on the CreditWatch list, Standard & Poor's (S&P) sent negative implications to the financial communities about Woolworth. S&P maintained that the investigation could reveal a deeper problem that had to do with more than the integrity of financial management.[4]

Specifically, this problem referred to the fact that Woolworth had posted revenues of $9.63 billion along with a gross margin of US $16 million for the fiscal year that ended in January 1994. The gross margin was misstated, leading the board to report a moderate interim after-tax profit, rather than after-tax losses, for at least two quarters, which would have been discovered with correct accounting reporting. While the discrepancies were modest, the impact was damaging to Woolworth's integrity and credibility. Since the news about the investigation was reported in newspapers, suppliers were advised to hold shipments to Woolworth until more information about the investigation was released. A series of lawsuits were filed by shareholders in federal count. Some claimed that Lavin "knew, or was grossly reckless in not knowing, of the fraud alleged" and that he concealed "adverse material information" in order to "increase and maintain an artificially high market price for the common stock of Woolworth."[5]

The investigation prompted the company to announce that it would restate the correct gross profit margin in its interim financial results for 1993 or even the fiscal year before that. Some said that the company had already corrected the gross profit margins in the last quarterly report. Woolworth executives maintained that these adjustments would not have an impact on the full-year results of both 1992 and 1993.

After listening to a number of allegations made by some executives in the company, the Special Committee found "no facts" to support them. On April 14, 1994, it was reported that Woolworth restated quarterly results for 1993 but did not change the year-end numbers. Thin profits in the first and second quarters were restated to losses for the first and second quarters and a larger loss in the fourth quarter was also restated. The dividend was maintained. The company still had enough working capital and liquidity to pay the bills and meet its mature obligations.[6]

The investigation placed Lavin and Young under a "hard look." CFO Young subsequently resigned. The board considered Lavin's presence to have hampered the company's turnaround efforts by bringing about embarrassing investigations and allegations (Lavin ultimately resigned as well). There was much to do to salvage the unstable confidence in Woolworth among the stakeholders, credit analysts, suppliers, and factoring companies. There were other pending lawsuits that sought class-action suits alleging "misleading disclosures" on the part of directors and officers.[7] Reflecting a more accurate financial picture, for the first and second fiscal quarters 1994, the company reported a losses of $38 million and $42 million, respectively.

THE ROLE OF FINANCIAL ANALYSES IN STRATEGIC IMPLEMENTATION

While the role of financial management has assumed center stage in the world of business, it has not arrived without controversy. The events described in our opening vignette about the pressures faced by Woolworth's accountants in disclosing financial information could be seen as an ominous portent of the events of the current day. Two top executives from once-acclaimed Enron Company (Jeffrey Skilling and Kenneth Lay) were tried and convicted of conspiracy and fraud, but Lay passed away before sentencing. The fall of Enron marked a series of similar embarrassing setbacks for WorldCom, Arthur Andersen, Quest, World Crossing, and others that used questionable financial transactions that violated ethical standards and transgressed legal statutes. The misuse of financial statements is certainly not the sole province of U.S. firms; in fact, such events occur in all parts of the world (Box 11.1).

While these events are disquieting, they also provide graphic testimony of the importance of financial analysis in business. Financial analysis is an essential skill that applies across a number of professional occupations, from financial accountants to corporate finance and investment analysts, and from commercial lenders to merger and acquisition analysts. For those engaged in this task, there have been two traditional roles and fundamental approaches.[8] The first approach, more oriented to a

Box 11.1

The Pervasiveness of Financial Irregularities

While U.S. firms are the unglamorous centerpiece in matters of financial irregularities, foreign firms are not exempt from this fray. South Korea's *chaebol*s are the symbol of that country's rapid rise from poverty to global emerging economy. But their mounting debt was also the primary reason for South Korea's financial crisis that forced the International Monetary Fund to bail it out with $58 billion in rescue loans in the late 1990s. In May 2006, executives in charge of Dutch retailer Royal Ahold were convicted of fraud that arose from a financial scandal.

South Korea's Fair Trade Commission launched an investigation into SK Group. SK Global is a trading subsidiary of SK Group, the third largest industrial conglomerate *chaebol* by assets. On the February 23, 2003, Chey Tae-won, chairman of SK Corp, was arrested for his part in the $1.2 billion (1.6 trillion won) fraud dating from 2001, aimed at concealing huge losses at affiliate SK Global. The restated financial results for SK Corp showed a 50 percent decline in profits and a negative net worth of $3.7 billion by the end of 2002. On March 14, 2003, SK Corp's share price fell to an eighteen-year low. In June, Chey Tae-won was convicted and jailed for his part in accounting fraud, shaking the SK Group conglomerate, of which SK Corp is a key trading unit. SK Group chairman Son Kil-Seung was also found guilty of illegally drawing more than $680 million from the Group for private investment overseas and given a three-year suspended sentence. Eight other SK Group executives were indicted and given suspended sentences.

In December 2004, South Korea's financial regulators announced that they uncovered $1.13 billion of accounting irregularities at Hyundai Merchant Marine. The company inflated its net profit in 2000 by overstating sales and understating costs. The Financial Supervisory Service also said that they found $170 million in additional accounting violations. Even though the past wrongdoing was corrected in Hyundai's 2002–2003 books, accounting problems found in SK Networks, Nynix Semiconductor (spun off from Hyundai Group), and Kookmin Bank, signified that the breach of accounting rules in corporate South Korea might be widespread.

As for the case of Royal Ahold, the verdict came three years after the company went to the brink of bankruptcy in February 2003. Ahold operates grocery stores around the world, including the Stop & Shop and Giant chains. In their resignation letters, the disgraced executives reported that the company's earnings reports from 1999 to 2002 were not reliable. Ahold shares plunged by two-thirds of their value overnight. Moreover, the company was eventually found to have overstated earnings by more than 1 billion euros from 1999 to 2002, mostly by inflating sales from its U.S. Foodservice Inc. subsidiary.

While the above examples might be rare exemptions to the legions of South Korean and Dutch firms that prepare their accounting books accurately, the pressure to meet expectations is enormous. Zeckhauser et al. suggest that firms are more likely to post small increases more frequently than they post small declines. The implication is that "when corporations are in danger of posting slightly negative earnings comparisons, they will locate enough discretionary items to show marginally improved results." The authors also suggest that corporations might regard financial reporting as a technique to prop up stock prices, rather than the means to disseminate objective information. The temptation to enhance value might then become a dangerous obsession. As such, some companies might occasionally prop up values by obtaining lower-cost capital and creating higher earnings expectations than it could by preparing its financial statements strictly according to accepted principles. A second method is for the company to downplay contingent liabilities that threaten the firm's value.

All told, this is why analysts should be vigilant and thoroughly understand financial statements.

Sources: Adapted from "Asian Spreads Widen as SK Probe Bites," *Euroweek,* March 17, 2003, p. 1; "Hyundai Merchant Marine Co.: Regulators Disclose Violations in Accounting at Shipping Firm," *Wall Street Journal,* December 17, 2004, p. 1; Investment Chronology SK Corporation, Sovereign Global Investment, retrieved on May 13, 2006, www.sov.com/2_0en.asp?cid=52; updated http://www. sovereignglobal.com/2_0en.asp?cid=7, last accessed on June 12, 2008. "Ex-Ahold Executives Fined in Netherlands Fraud Case," *New York Times,* May 23, 2006, p. C5; Martin S. Fridson, *Financial Statement Analysis*, 2d ed. (New York: John Wiley & Sons, 1996), p. 6; Richard Zeckhauser, Jayendu Patel, Francois Degeorge, and John Pratt, "Reported and Predicted Earnings: An Empirical Investigation Using Prospect Theory," Project for David Dreman Foundation, 1994.

Figure 11.1   **Implementing the Strategic Plan: Using Financial Performance Measures**

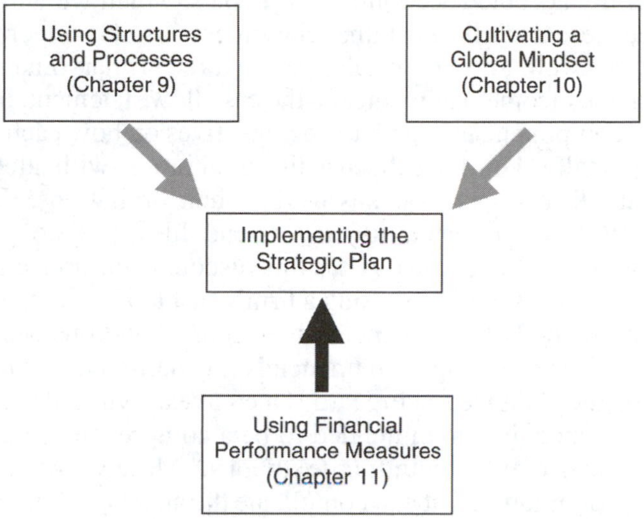

financial accountant, is to follow the prescribed procedures for calculating the necessary standard financial ratios and obtaining detailed information to ensure that one company's finances can be adequately compared to those of other companies. The second approach is that of a financial analyst, who is more concerned with pursuing accurate financial information and constructing patterns, particularly those that are congealed in common financial statements. For this type of analyst, genuine analysis starts after all standard analysis has been completed. A superior analyst adds value by raising questions that are not apparent from standard analysis.

In our view, there is a third possible role that derives from the second, that is, an analyst who is concerned about the sustainability of the firm's business model. In this regard, financial analysis represents yet another context for evaluating the quality of strategic implementation. Within this perspective, financial analysis is used as a form of management control, that is, in examining whether the firm has implemented its strategy adequately based on how its financial and operating performance compares against pre-established goals and standards. When conducted properly, financial analysis is used to assess the sustainability of a firm's strategy and can provide important insights about its competitive advantages, and whether its industry is protected by entry barriers. Specifically, the issue is whether the resources and assets owned by the firm are adequate in generating more value in ways that meet the requirements of the firm's future strategies and activities. It is this third perspective that we adopt in this chapter. Financial analysis is a necessary complement to our two previous chapters, which positioned strategic implementation as a "fit" between structures and processes (Chapter 9), and premised on the need to develop and cultivate a global mindset (Chapter 10). Viewing strategic implementation from the perspective of financial performance and control provides the third prism for evaluating the quality of strategic implementation (see Figure 11.1).

This chapter is organized as follows. First, we introduce the key premises and conventions used in the preparation of financial statements as espoused by the U.S. generally accepted accounting principles, which we will define later in this chapter. Since these underlie most financial statements, it is important to understand these conventions well. Second, we discuss the three primary financial statements: the balance sheet, the income statement, and the cash flow statement. In addition to describing their main components, we provide perspectives on how each can be used and interpreted strategically. Third, we discuss financial ratios, with attention to their use of "clues" into the firm's operations, as well as their limitations. Fourth, we discuss problems with ROE (return on equity) and extend this discussion to the logic underlying EVA (economic value added). After this discourse on financial analysis, we discuss how these can be used for assessing a firm's sustainability, using both traditional and more recent methods from financial management and business strategy. We conclude the chapter by presenting both financial and qualitative performance metrics, such as the use of the Balanced Scorecard. One caveat: while the chapter focuses on financial performance, it is not intended to be a comprehensive treatise as one would expect from finance and accounting textbooks.[9] Moreover, this chapter does not cover the effects of inflation that can complicate the analysis of financial statements. Our choice of topics was based on their relevance to the tasks of managerial control and the evaluation of strategic implementation. If necessary, we strongly encourage a review of the specifics of financial and accounting transactions, reporting, and procedures from relevant textbooks while reading this chapter.

THE FINANCIAL STATEMENTS: ACCOUNTING CONVENTIONS

If individuals want to know more about a company, particularly about its current health and prospects for the future, there is no better source of information than the company's financial statements. It has been often said, "Accounting is the language of business."[10] This is neither flippant nor patronizing toward the accounting profession. Indeed, a company's financial statements are particularly valuable and have been used as an analytical tool, a management report card, an early warning sign, a basis for prediction, and a measure of accountability and performance evaluation. For these reasons, financial statements are indispensable for developing an accurate assessment of a firm's performance and its prospects for sustaining it in the future.

Even so, financial accounting is not an exact science, a belief that is widely shared by accounting professionals themselves. While some statement transactions are measured with a high degree of accuracy (e.g., cash on deposit), others, such as goodwill, are not. Moreover, as we shall see, there are contestable issues dealing with the concept of valuation based on financial statements. Therefore, it behooves managers to bring in their judgment based on information that is not a part of the financial statements in order to ascertain how much these statements faithfully represent economic events and activities affecting the company.

Partly in response to these concerns, the accounting profession has developed a confluence of conventions, rules, guidelines, and procedures, collectively called the **generally accepted accounting principles (GAAP)**.[11] These principles govern accounting practice and they continue to evolve in response to changing business conditions. The goal of

GAAP is to ensure that financial statements clearly reflect the economic condition and performance of the company. The U.S. GAAP has decreed that financial statements should have the following qualitative characteristics, which are important to the needs of managers and professional analysts in their decision-making functions:[12]

- *Relevance*. Relevance helps users form a more accurate prediction and assessment of the future. This allows users to understand how past economic events might have affected their business.

- *Timeliness*. The information provided is relatively current and capable of influencing decisions.

- *Reliability*. This means that information provided is reasonably free of errors and bias, and that it faithfully represents what it purports to represent. Reliable financial information should be factual, truthful, and unbiased. Reliability can be further validated using three additional characteristics: (a) *verifiability,* that is, independent measures should get similar results when using the same accounting measurement methods; (b) *representational faithfulness,* that is, the degree to which the accounting actually represents the underlying economic event; and (c) *neutrality,* that is, information cannot be selected to favor one set of interested parties over another.

- *Comparability*. Unless financial information is measured and reported in a similar manner across companies, comparison across firms for purposes of evaluation is meaningless. Comparison allows analysts to identify the underlying economic similarities and differences among diverse companies that might be obscured by different accounting methods or disclosure practices.

- *Consistency*. This relates to the same accounting methods that are used to describe similar events from period to period. Consistency allows analysts to identify trends and turning points in the economic conditions and performance of a company over time.

In evaluating whether financial reports are complete, understandable, and helpful, accountants use two additional conventions: *materiality* and *conservatism*.[13] **Materiality** refers to the question of whether financial statements contain omissions or misstatements that can alter the judgment of a reasonable person. Such misstatements can result in material harm. The convention of materiality ensures that such consequences are taken into consideration. Accounting, by and large, is a conservative profession. **Conservatism** in accounting "strives to ensure that business risks and uncertainties are adequately reflected in financial reports."[14] Its extreme form is the traditional conservative adage, "anticipate no profit, but anticipate all losses." Financial reporting is focused on the accurate representation of transactions, not high-risk speculation. While there are a number of financial statements used by managers, three are particularly important and are discussed next.

THE BALANCE SHEET

For many years the balance sheet was the primary financial statement reported to external users.[15] It was designed for creditors, who require information about the resources available to pay debts, and claims to these resources. The **balance sheet** reports on the balances of the assets, liability, and owners' equity accounts at a particular date. Thus, it is often referred to as a "snapshot," revealing a firm's financial position at one point in time. It provides a good description of any company's financial situation because it reveals the cost of resources available to an organization at a particular time and date and a statement of the sources of financing used to acquire these resources. The relationship, *assets = liabilities + owners' equity*, is the fundamental balance sheet equation. Recall that resources are an integral part of a firm's business model (Chapter 3). The balance sheet has strategic importance because any firm needs resources in order to deploy its strategy, and, in a fundamental way, the balance sheet is a statement of a company's resources. Since we will be illustrating the case of Wal-Mart throughout this chapter, with a comparison of its performance in terms of a ten-year period; its 1990 and 2000 balance sheets are provided in Exhibit 11.1 for reference. A typical balance sheet can be classified into eight primary categories:[16]

- **Current assets** are cash or other resources that management expects to convert to cash or consume during the next fiscal year. Some current assets are liquid assets. Liquid assets are resources that can be converted to cash in a relatively short period. In addition to cash, current assets include (a) accounts receivables for which a company is expected to receive cash during the next fiscal year (typically within one year), (b) inventory a company expects to sell during the next fiscal year, and (c) resources a company expects to consume during the next fiscal year, such as supplies and prepaid insurance.

- **Current liabilities** refer to claims against assets that must be satisfied in one year, or within one operating cycle, whichever is longer. Current liabilities include (a) accounts payable (AP) and notes payable (NP), (b) the current portion of long-term debt, (c) accrued liabilities, and (d) deferred taxes. Accounts payable are short-term obligations arising from credit extended by the suppliers for the purchase of goods and services. Notes payable are short-term obligations in the form of promissory notes to financial institutions. For retail firms, the use of trade credit (AP), rather than bank borrowing (NP), can be a longer-term strategic decision as well as a shorter-term cash management decision.[17]

- **Long-term investments** occur when one company purchases the stock or bonds of another company. Companies often invest in other companies to share in their earnings, or to obtain access to resources, management skills, technology, and markets available to other companies.

- **Property, plant, and equipment** refers to long-lived, tangible, fixed or plant assets that are used in a company's operations. Unlike inventory, these assets are not intended for resale. Thus, U.S. GAAP requires fixed assets, other than land, to be depreciated over their estimated useful lives.

- **Other long-term assets** include noncurrent receivables, fixed assets held for sale, prepaid transactions that are not expected to be consumed within the next fiscal year, and long-term legal rights such as patents, trademarks, and copyrights. Note

Exhibit 11.1

Wal-Mart's 1990 and 2000 Balance Sheets (Excerpt) (amounts in US$ millions)

	January 31	
	1990	2000
ASSETS		
Current Assets:		
Cash and equivalents	$13	$1,856
Receivables	$156	$1,341
Inventory	$4,428	$19,793
Other	$116	$1,366
TOTAL CURRENT ASSETS	$4,713	$24,356
Productive Assets:		
Property, plant, & equipment	$4,402	$45,348
Accumulated depreciation	($972)	($9,379)
Net productive assets	$3,430	$35,969
Other Assets	$55	$10,024
TOTAL ASSETS	$8,198	$70,349
LIABILITIES AND SHAREHOLDERS' EQUITY		
Current Liabilities:		
Accounts payable	$1,827	$13,105
Current debt due	$24	$2,085
Other	$995	$10,613
TOTAL CURRENT LIABILITIES	$2,846	$25,803
Long-term Liabilities:		
Long-term debt	$185	$13,672
Long-term lease obligations	$1,987	$3,002
Deferred income taxes and other	$115	$759
Minority interest	$0	$1,279
TOTAL LONG-TERM LIABILITIES	$1,387	$18,712
Shareholders' Equity:		
Common stock	$237	$1,160
Retained earnings	$3,728	$25,129
Other equity adjustments	$0	($455)
TOTAL SHAREHOLDERS' EQUITY	$3,965	$25,834
Total liabilities and shareholders' equity	$8,198	$70,349

that long-term legal rights from the ownership of patents, copyrights, trademarks, and similar items are considered to be intangible assets, in contrast to tangible assets such as plant and equipment. Amortization is the process of systematically allocating an amount over a period of time.

- **Liabilities**. A balance sheet separates liabilities into current and long-term categories. **Current liabilities** are those obligations that management expects to fulfill during the next fiscal period. **Long-term liabilities** are those obligations that are not classified as current liabilities.
- **Working capital** is the amount of current assets minus the amount of current liabilities. It is commonly used to measure a company's liquidity (having sufficient liquid capital to cover current obligations). We will say more about this later in the chapter.

- **Stockholders' equity**. The stockholders' equity accounts on the balance sheet are the ending balances reported for those accounts on the statement of equity. These normally include the cumulative amount of contributed capital and retained earnings created by the corporation since its inception.

While the balance sheet is a remarkable invention (courtesy of monks, incidentally), it has two fundamental shortcomings.[18] First, even when it purports to have the values of all assets employed by the firm, these values prove elusive in practice. Second, many items can be construed as having value, but not all of them can be assigned a value and placed in the balance sheet. Central to the value problem is how to represent a "fair market value," perhaps more dramatically reflected in the difficulties experienced by the courts in attempting to value the assets of bankrupt companies.[19] The accounting profession has resolved this in part by adopting a conservative approach using historical costs as the basis of its system. Thus, the purchase of an asset is recorded at the time of purchase, which preserves its **historical** or **book value**. The cost of acquiring or constructing an asset at its historical value has the advantage of being objective and verifiable. Thus, if a company purchases an asset worth $1 million in 1980, this transaction provides an objective measure of its value, which is then recorded as such in the company's balance sheet. A second problem of the balance sheet is that an asset is only recognized when it is involved in a transaction. Unless it is part of a transaction, it is not recorded (such as an informal agreement for one company to provide funds to another in case of an emergency). While critics decry this, arguing that valuation should be made on the basis of its **fair market value**, that is, market or economic value, there are some questions as to whether this represents a valid point of comparison. We will say more about this value problem when we discuss the use of ROE (return on equity) and EVA (economic value added). Suffice it to say, the use of historical cost (or book value) serves the purpose of facilitating comparisons, particularly when analysts know a priori that these valuations are conservative. It is hardly the best approach, but at least the method is defensible. Even so, it is necessary to look beyond this financial statement to determine an appropriate value of assets when making a determination of the company's future earnings. This is addressed in the final sections of this chapter.

THE INCOME STATEMENT

The **income statement** was developed for corporate investors, who need information about a firm's earnings, specifically in evaluating management decisions that affect dividends and stock values.[20] An income statement (also called an earnings statement or a profit and loss) reports an organization's revenues and expenses for a fiscal period. The income statement measures the amount of goods and services provided to customers, and the resources consumed in the provision of these goods and services. Typically information is based on the operations for a fiscal period, such as a month, a quarter, or a fiscal year. Operating results are assessed on an **accrual basis**. This generally means that sales are recognized as soon as the effort required to generate

Exhibit 11.2

Wal-Mart's 1990 and 2000 Income Statement (Excerpt)
(Amounts in US$ millions except per share data)

	January 31	
	1990	2000
Net Sales	$25,985	$166,809
Cost and Expenses:		
Cost of Sales	$20,070	$129,664
Operating Expenses	$4,070	$27,040
Interest Expense	$138	$1,022
Other Expenses (Income)	0	$368
Total Costs & Expenses	$24,278	$158,904
Income Before Income Taxes (EBIT)	$1,707	$8,715
Provision for Income Taxes:		
Current Position	$609	$3,476
Deferred Position	$23	($138)
Total Provision	$632	$3,338
Net income	$1,075	$5,377
Dividends	($124)	($890)
Adjustments to Retained Earnings	0	($99)
Retained Earnings, Beginning Balance	$2,777	$20,741
Retained Earnings, Ending Balance	$3,728	$25,129

the sale is substantially complete and there is a reasonable certainty that the payment will be received. In other words, the accrual concept means that transactions are recognized and recorded at the time of transaction, not necessarily when payment is made or received. Revenues indicate the sales price of goods and services sold during the period, and the timing of the receipt of cash is a mere technicality. Because income statements do not indicate that cash was actually received, net income is *not* cash flow. Since the statement is developed over a period of time, it is occasionally referred to as a "flow" statement, in contrast to the balance sheet, which is a snapshot in time. Wal-Mart's 1990 and 2000 income statements are presented in Exhibit 11.2. The three categories of any income statement include the following:[21]

- **Gross profits** are the difference between the selling price of goods and services against the cost of goods and services sold. For manufacturing companies, the cost of goods sold is the product cost (materials, labor). For service companies, the cost of services is the cost of materials, labor, and other resources consumed directly in producing services sold during a period. Unlike product costs, these are not placed into inventory, but rather treated as an expense in the period in which the services are provided.
- **Operating expenses** are the cost of resources consumed as part of operating activities during a fiscal period that are not directly associated with specific goods and services. Most operating expenses are period costs because they are recognized in the fiscal period in which they occur. It is also acknowledged that operating expenses are under the control of designated managers.

- **Nonoperating items**, such as other revenues and costs, may occur that are not directly related to the company's primary operating activities. These are reported separately. Interest expenses are often listed here.

Analysis of the income statement typically consists of two tasks: first, the analyst has to determine the accuracy of the stated revenues, expenses, and earnings; and, second, the analyst has to determine whether the performance underlying the income statement is favorable, unfavorable, or neutral.[22] The income statement is strategic because it affords a consideration of earnings after all expenses are deducted, or what might be termed the "bottom line." In a fundamental way, it represents the efficiency with which the company generates earnings from its operations: an income of $10 out of gross sales of $1,000 is quite different from an income of $50 from the same revenue base ($1,000). The personal challenge to improve a firm's net profit is akin to an athlete's motivation to break a world record.[23] Analysis is like the stopwatch that evaluates how well (or how badly) a company is performing compared to its competitors. Consequently, it provides the basis for a comparative assessment using the financial ratios that are discussed in the next section. Moreover, by segregating operational from nonoperational revenue and costs, it highlights the performance of a firm's primary and secondary activities, thereby providing the basis for evaluating managers involved in these different activities.

The Cash Flow Statement

The purpose of the **statement of cash flow** is to identify the primary activities of a fiscal period that resulted in cash inflows and cash outflows.[24] Typically this would describe the cash flow results of financing, investing, and operating activities for the company.[25] It would explain changes in a company's cash balance. Wal-Mart's 1990 and 2000 cash flow statements are presented in Exhibit 11.3.

- **Operating activities** are transactions involving the acquisition or production of goods and services and the sale and distribution of these goods and services to customers. In the income statement, operating activities are measured on an accrual basis. In the cash flow statement, these activities are measured on a cash basis. Current assets and liabilities normally result from the operating activities of the firm, such as buying and selling merchandise. Therefore, cash flows associated with working capital items, such as the purchase of inventory, supplies, or prepaid insurance and payment of wages, are part of the operating activities section of the statement of cash flows. Nonoperating items such as the interest received or paid are included as operating activities on the cash flow statement because interest revenue and interest appear on the income statement.
- **Investing activities** are acquisitions or disposals of long-term assets during a fiscal period. Note that depreciation and amortization are not cash flow statements. Cash flow occurs when fixed or intangible assets are purchased or sold, not when these assets are depreciated or amortized (although these appear in operating activities as recurring items).

Exhibit 11.3

Wal-Mart's 1990 and 2000 Cash Flow Statement (Excerpt)
(Amounts in US$ millions)

	January 31	
	1990	2000
Cash Flows from operations:		
Net income	$1,076	$5,377
Adjustments to reconcile net income to other items		
Net cash provided by operating activities	$867	$8,194
Cash flows from investments	($894)	($16,846)
Cash flows from financing	$27	$8,629
Net increase in cash	$0.24	($23)
Cash and cash equivalents at the beginning of the year	$13	$1,879
Cash and cash equivalents at the end of the year	$13	$1,856
Supplemental disclosure:		
Income tax paid	$551	$2,780
Interest paid	$137	$849
Capital lease obligations incurred	$104	$378

- **Financing activities** are transactions between a company and its owners or between a company and its long-term creditors. The financing activities section reports only the cash flow effects of transactions associated with borrowing or repaying debt and investments by owners. Cash flows result when debt is issued or repaid and when stock is issued or repurchased. Payment of dividends is also a financing activity.

The cash flow statement is strategic because it presents, perhaps in a rather restrictive sense, the most realistic portrayal of the company's financial flexibility, that is, the amount of cash at hand. An individual might own a lot of assets and earn a huge amount of income, but, without cash, this individual is not liquid and has more limited options. In contrast, firms with a significant amount of what is called "free" cash flow, notably Microsoft and Google, have plenty of options for growth and investment that will not apply to a cash-strapped firm.[26] For many entrepreneurs and managers, cash flow is the most important of the three financial statements. It is not surprising that a cash flow statement is particularly useful when analyzing a troubled company, or when assessing cash needs for companies at different stages of the life cycle.[27] Taken altogether, the three financial statements represent the economic events that have changed the financial condition of the company from the beginning to the end of the fiscal period. While more analysis is clearly needed to ascertain the quality of strategic implementation, the relationships between these statements provide the first source for assessing the financial health and condition of the company.

STRATEGIC OBJECTIVES AND PERFORMANCE MEASURES

Given the vast range of strategic goals, objectives, and activities across multiple markets, there is a correspondingly broad array of financial performance measures and metrics for which to assess them. Central to such assessments are **"value-added" measures**, that is, the incremental or additional increase in quantity above a predetermined baseline.[28] While profit might not be an end in itself, it validates a firm's successful strategy and business model. With a sound business model, it is expected that value will be created and that superior financial performance will follow. By value (or value added), we mean the difference between the value of a firm's output and the associated costs of producing it. This is the core meaning of profit: the surplus of revenues over costs available for distribution to owners. Three representative "value-added" measures are:

- **EVA** (economic value added) and **MVA** (market value added) measure and ensure the financial health of an organization. Thus, these are oriented at measuring the profitability of a company with specific consideration of the firm's cost of capital. Accordingly, these are used primarily by financial analysts, investors, and creditors.
- **CVA** (customer value added) measures the value that customers and prospective customers ("prospects") perceive in a firm's products and services relative to competition. This is used primarily by marketing analysts.
- **PVA** (people value added) measures the value gained from enabling employees to be the most productive resources they can be. While this measure is relatively new, it is increasingly used by human resource management (HRM) managers, especially in assessing training programs.[29]

Within each of these categories, there are a number of specific performance measures that correspond to measures of financial profitability, marketing-related consumer satisfaction, and people-related efficiencies (see Exhibit 11.4). The three areas are relevant to strategic implementation because they relate directly to a firm's business model. We will be discussing these in more detail in this chapter. Suffice it to say that evaluating the effectiveness of goals and strategies in terms of financial measures constitutes one central feature of organizational control and strategic implementation.

ASSESSING FINANCIAL HEALTH THROUGH FINANCIAL RATIOS

Historically, the customary method of assessing a firm's financial health is through financial ratios constructed from financial statements, notably the income statement and the balance sheet. For perspective, it is unreasonable to expect that such simple calculations can lead to a comprehensive picture of an organization.[30] Some students are so bombarded about the limitations of ratio analysis that they became fearful about using it, and when they do, their presentations are laced with profuse qualifications and apologies. Perhaps taken in isolation, ratios might not reveal much. However, when used in tandem with in-depth interviews and other pieces of information and knowledge about the company and its industry, financial ratios can provide insightful clues about a company's operations and performance. After using them in practice, we have realized that if used with care and imagination, they can be very informative.

Exhibit 11.4

Standard Performance Measures

Performance type	Standard measure	Definition	Implications for strategy
Financial	Net income	Difference between total sales and total expenses	Higher-than-average profits comprise the core measure of a firm's success.
	Operating income	Revenue less cost of goods sold and direct operating expenses	This is particularly relevant to a strategist in that only operating revenue and costs are considered.
	Return	Profit as a percentage of sales/investment/assets/equity	Standard measure of profitability.
	EVA	Economic value added; value over and above the cost of invested capital	Measures value creation or destruction in incorporating the cost of capital.
Market	Revenue	Total sales; quantity sold × price	A standard marketing measure; can be used to assess pricing strategy.
	Market share	Percentage of total market share	Used to assess the effectiveness of a market strategy.
	Relative market share	Company sales divided by sales of largest competitor	Used to assess market dominance.
Human development	People value added	Quantitative and qualitative measures of employees' performance, growth of skills and knowledge	The structure of a company's recruitment, selection, training and development, and reward systems is central to a culture that values customers.

Three conditions of financial health are distinguished: *profitability, turnover/efficiency, and liquidity/financial leverage.* To illustrate these ratios, we take the case of Wal-Mart, currently the world's largest company. Our illustrations of some of Wal-Mart's financial ratios are taken from the strategic profit model, an earlier work by Penn State University professor Stephen F. Jablonsky and Villanova University professor Noah P. Barsky (See Box 11.2, p. 474).[31] For perspective, Wal-Mart's business model is presented in Exhibit 11.5.

PROFITABILITY

Profitability is a standard of how well a firm is earning and using its profits. The most popular measure is the return on equity (ROE), defined as:

$$Return\ on\ Equity = \frac{Net\ Income}{Shareholders'\ equity}$$

ROE is the measure of the efficiency in which the company used the owners' capital.[32] It is a measure of the percentage return to owners on their investment. It is used to

---

Box 11.2

Jablonsky and Barsky's Strategic Profit Model

Analyzing financial information for purposes of evaluating previous and current operating performance and improving future profitability is a key managerial function. Even so, managers are flooded with financial information, oftentimes laded with intensive technical information that makes the task difficult. It is not unusual to see footnotes, qualifications, and accounting rules and regulations that have more pages than a company annual report.

The strategic profit model is the first of four approaches presented in this book that provide valuable insights into the sustainability of any firm's strategy. Professors Stephen Jablonsky and Noah Barsky have developed a simplified and accessible framework to help managers relate business strategy to shareholder accountability using the firm's financial statements. While Wal-Mart's financial statements are used to illustrate their framework, the authors have also analyzed Dell computers, Pfizer, Inc., and Cisco Systems.

The strategic profit model is structured in two principal sections: financial statement analysis and market valuation and business strategy. The first part covers margin management, asset management, return on assets, financial management, comprehensive management, and long-term investment and financing. The second part includes market valuation decisions, such as market performance measures, the analysis of long-term debt, and common stocks. Some distinctive features of the strategic profit model include:

- the emphasis on the need for managers to properly share and communicate financial information with one another
- a focus on linking financial analysis directly to operational performance and business strategy
- an attention to operational control in analyzing changes in performance across different financial areas (margins, assets, returns, financing) over time with implications for business strategy

Taken altogether, the strategic profit model synthesizes traditional financial ratios and places them in context where managers can link these ratios to business strategy in a comprehensive manner. While we have illustrated some of these applications in this chapter, an interested analyst should read the entire strategic profit model (source listed below).

Source: Adapted from Stephen F. Jablonsky and Noah P. Barsky, *The Manager's Guide to Financial Statement Analysis,* 2nd ed. (New York: John Wiley & Sons, Inc., 2001).

---

compare a firm's performance against its own (historical analysis), that of its competitors, and the industry standard. It also gives shareholders the ability to compare it against alternative investments. For these reasons, it is perhaps the most popular of the financial ratios. Wal-Mart's information is presented below:

	ROE	**Net Income**	**Equity**
1990	27.1%	$1.075B	$3.965B
2000	20.8%	$5.377B	$25.834B

Jablonsky/Barsky's Analysis: If management had been able to maintain a 27.1 percent ROE in 2000, Wal-Mart would have generated an additional $1.624B in net income on shareholders' equity of $25.834 billion.[33]

Typically, we compare a company's ROE against its major competitors (for Wal-Mart, see Exhibit 11.6).[34] Viewing such, we can determine that Wal-Mart (21.6%) did not lead the pack; in fact, it falls short of Gap (58.8%) and Dollar General (23.6%), although it surpasses the industry average (17.8%) and other competitors. This might

Exhibit 11.5

Wal-Mart's Business Model and Preliminary Analysis

Business model components	Present	Defining elements
Strategy	Wal-Mart provides branded products at low cost across specific target markets.	Wal-Mart aggressively pursued scale economies in purchasing by leveraging its 50 percent market share position.
Resources	Wal-Mart focuses on large discount stores in small rural towns, creating lower operating costs, avoiding direct competition, and building entry barriers.	Wal-Mart also created a dedicated and committed staff through profit sharing, incentive bonus, and discount stock purchase plans. Wal-Mart also excelled in its management and information system for which important information was collected.
Customer interfaces	Distribution centers operates 24 hours per day to serve customers.	Wal-Mart's strategy was to guarantee "everyday low prices" as a way to pull in customers.
Value partnerships	While not entirely beneficial to all parties, Wal-Mart aggressively promotes captive loyalty by ensuring large sales to its suppliers.	Need to establish marketing presence in targeted markets.

Exhibit 11.6

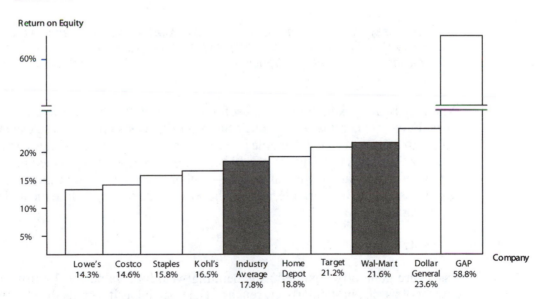

Source: Adapted from Stephen F. Jablonsky and Noah P. Barsky, *The Manager's Guide to Financial Statement Analysis* (New York: John Wiley, 2001), p. 14.

be good or bad, depending on the reasons underlying this pattern, one of which is disclosed with further analysis.

A related measure of profitability is return on assets (ROA), defined as:

$$Return\ on\ assets = \frac{Net\ Income}{Assets}$$

ROA is essentially a measure of the efficiency with which a company allocates and manages its resources. It is different from ROE in that it measures profit as a percentage of the money provided by *both* owners and creditors, instead of only profit provided by the owners.[35] In essence, it is interpreted as the return on the total assets under management control.

> *Jablonsky/Barsky's Analysis: In 1990, Wal-Mart earned 13.1 cents in profit for every $1.00 in total assets. In 2000, Wal-Mart earned 7.6 cents. Had Wal-Mart maintained its 1990 ROA, it would have generated an additional $3.869 billion in net income.[36]*

Another method of assessing profitability is return on sales (ROS), or the profit margin. This measures the fraction of each dollar of sales that becomes profit after expenses are deducted. Thus, it is useful in analyzing the company's pricing strategy and its ability to control operating strategy.[37]

$$Profit\ margin = \frac{Revenue - Costs}{Sales}$$

> *Jablonsky/Barsky's Analysis: In 1990, Wal-Mart earned 4.1 cents in profit for every $1.00 in net sales. In 2000, Wal-Mart earned 3.2 cents. The 0.9 cents decline in profit margin translates into $1.501 billion of net income (0.9 × $166,809).[38]*

When analyzing profitability, it is useful to differentiate between fixed and variable costs. **Fixed costs** remain constant, while **variable costs** change as sales vary. Firms with high fixed costs are vulnerable in recessionary periods because they cannot reduce fixed costs as sales fall. Unfortunately, these costs are not distinguished in the income statement. Fortunately, we can assume—rather reasonably—that most expenses in cost of goods sold are variable, as with the costs of marketing, while most of the other operating costs are fixed.[39]

TURNOVER/EFFICIENCY

Assets are generally regarded as generating wealth or value for the firm. Thus, the control of assets, particularly current assets, is crucial as it signals the ability of management to control costs.[40] This is reflected in **turnover/efficiency ratios**. Specifically, if sales decline rapidly, or if customers delay in their payment, or if a critical item fails to arrive, the company's current assets can rise very quickly. Unlike fixed assets, current assets can become a source of cash during a business downturn. As sales decline, a company's investment in accounts receivables and inventory should fall as well, freeing cash for use. However, the company's current assets will increase during a business upswing since the company will require loans for operations. It is useful to analyze the turnover of each type of asset on a company's balance sheet individually. Thus, turnover ratios provide clues on how well management is able to control its assets. Phrased differently, financial performance improves when asset turnover increases.

Inventory Turnover

Inventory turnover is expressed as:

$$\text{Inventory Turnover} = \frac{\text{Cost of goods sold}}{\text{Ending inventory}}$$

An inventory turnover of 4.0 means that items in a company's inventory turn over 4 times per year on the average. Phrased differently, a typical item sits in inventory almost 3 months before being sold (12 months/4 times). A similar formulation emphasizes the use of inventory over a specific time period, not simply the ending inventory. Accordingly, this formulation of inventory turnover is:

$$\frac{\text{Cost of goods sold}}{\text{Average inventory}}$$

In 1990, Wal-Mart's inventory turnover was 4.53; in 2000, it was 6.55. In 1990, a typical item would sit in inventory for about 2.65 months; in 2000, it was 1.83 months. Per Jablonsky/Barsky's analysis, Wal-Mart keeps prices low to generate higher gross margin. Higher inventory turnover generates more sales. Inventory management is one of Wal-Mart's many strengths.[41]

Collection Period

Collection period refers to the company's management of accounts receivable. It is defined as: *accounts receivable/credit sales per day.* If this amount is fifty days, for example, this generally means that the company has fifty days worth of credit sales tied up in accounts receivable.

In the case of Wal-Mart, the company generates a high level of cash but it does not allow the money to stay in banks for long. In 1990, it had 0.2 days net sales tied up in cash and equivalents; in 2000, it had 4.1 days net sales tied up in cash and equivalents.[42]

Payables Period

Payables period refers to the collection period applied to accounts payable. Thus, it is a control ratio for liability, and defined as: *accounts payable/credit purchases per day.*[43] It represents how long a company's suppliers will wait on average to receive payment.

> *In 1990, Wal-Mart's accounts payable represented 25.7 days' net sales; in 2000, the number of days associated with accounts payable was 28.7. Per Jablonsky and Barsky's analysis, Wal-Mart pays its accounts in less than a month, which is consistent with its overall strategy of building good relations with its suppliers.*[44]

Fixed Asset Turnover

Fixed asset turnover reflects the capital intensity of the business, and is defined as: *sales/net property, plant, and equipment.*[45] It states how much of a company's book value of property and equipment is accounted for in sales. In a modified treatment, accumulated depreciation is deducted from property, plant, and equipment to arrive at net productive assets, which represents assets that need to be recovered through future business operations.[46] In the case of Wal-Mart, its productive asset turnover ratios are as follows:

> *In 1990, Wal-Mart's fixed asset turnover was 7.58 (or $7.58 sales for every $1.00 invested in net productive assets); in 2000, it was 4.64 (or $4.64 sales for every $1.00 invested in net productive assets). Per Jablonsky and Barsky's analysis, this is a differential of $2.64 less in net sales over the ten-year period. This reflects a larger investment in property, plant, and equipment.*[47]

LIQUIDITY/FINANCIAL LEVERAGE

Liquidity/Financial leverage refers to the basic indebtedness of a company, or how much of its overall capital is accounted for by debt.[48] The most common measure of financial leverage is to compare the book value of a company's liabilities or debt to the book value of its assets or equity. Accordingly, two forms are generally used depending on whether the appropriate reference point is assets (total indebtedness) or equity (restricted only to shareholders).

$$\frac{Debt}{Assets} = \frac{Total\ liabilities}{Total\ assets}$$

This states that the money to pay off debt comes from creditors of one type or another.

$$\frac{Debt}{Equity} = \frac{Total\ liabilities}{Shareholders'\ equity}$$

This refers to the amount creditors supply the company for every dollar supplied by shareholders.

Jablonsky/Barsky Analysis: In 1990, Wal-Mart utilized $2.07 in total equity for every $1.00 of shareholders' equity; in 2000, it utilized $2.72. Relative to 1990, the increase in financial leverage had a positive impact on the 2000 ROE level.[49]

Closely related to financial leverage is the concept of liquidity. As noted, one determinant of a company's debt capacity is the liquidity of its assets.[50] An asset is liquid if it can be easily converted into cash; a liability is liquid if it must be repaid in the near future. Two common ratios are used, the current ratio and a more restricted form, the acid test ratio or quick ratio.

$$Current\ ratio = \frac{Current\ assets}{Current\ liabilities}$$

This compares the assets that will turn into cash within a year to the liabilities that must be paid within the year.

$$Acid\ test = \frac{Current\ assets - Inventory}{Current\ liabilities}$$

Also called the quick ratio, it is more conservative. It reduces the amount of assets by the value of the company's inventory based on the premise that inventory cannot be as readily converted into cash.[51]

In 1990, Wal-Mart's current ratio was 1.66; in 2000, it was 0.94. This indicates that Wal-Mart's indebtedness has increased over this time period. In 1990, Wal-Mart's acid test ratio was 0.10; in 2000, it was 0.18.

ANALYSIS BY DISAGGREGATION: THE DUPONT FORMULA

The preceding section introduced financial ratios as a way to gain insights about a company's operating and financial performance. Disaggregation can be applied in equity analysis, specifically through the DuPont formula, an idea credited to Donaldson Brown, who developed it while at E.I. du Pont de Nemours, then applied it

Exhibit 11.7

The DuPont Formula Applied, Selected Companies, 2006

Companies	Return on Equity		Profit Margins		Asset Turnover		Financial Leverage
Bank of America Corporation	15.62	=	18.06	×	0.08	×	10.79
Exxon Mobil Corp.	34.70	=	10.46	×	1.72	×	1.92
Google, Inc.	18.06	=	29.02	×	0.57	×	1.08
Nike, Inc.	23.73	=	9.97	×	1.52	×	1.57
Nordstrom, Inc.	26.34	=	7.14	×	1.57	×	2.35
Southwest Airlines Co.	7.74	=	5.49	×	0.68	×	2.09

Source: Adapted from Robert Higgins, *Analysis for Financial Management*, 5th ed. (New York: Irwin/McGraw, 1998), p. 40.

during the 1920s as vice president of finance at General Motors. The DuPont formula is defined as follows:

$$Return\ on\ equity\ (ROE) = \frac{Net\ Income}{Sales} \quad \frac{Sales}{Assets} \quad \frac{Assets}{Equity}$$

Note that ROE is now disaggregated into three components: profit margin, asset turnover, and financial leverage.[52] For managers, the analysis is useful in that it provides three distinct levers for controlling ROE and managing performance: (a) the earnings that can be generated out of each dollar of sales (profit margin); (b) the sales generated from each dollar of assets employed (asset turnover); and (c) the amount of equity used to finance the assets (financial leverage). Exhibit 11.7 shows such disaggregation for a selected group of companies.

These ratios have been discussed in the preceding section. We now turn our attention to how each can improve company performance in the context of the DuPont formula. The profit margin measures the fraction of each dollar of sales that becomes profits after expenses. It is significant for operating managers because it reflects the soundness of the company's pricing strategy (see Chapter 5) and its ability to control operating costs (i.e., costs that are generally part of operations and are considered to be under the control of managers). Therefore, improving the profit margin is one path to improving ROE. Asset turnover is an efficiency measure; it measures how much a company's assets generate sales. Higher asset turnover likewise improves ROE. Note that the two ratios tend to vary inversely.[53] Companies with high profit margins (e.g., Nordstrom) tend to have low asset turnover, and vice versa (e.g., Wal-Mart). Should a company add value to a product, it can command a higher profit margin in terms of higher prices (i.e., the differentiation strategy). But, adding value also entails spending more, or utilizing more assets, thereby lowering the asset turnover ratio. The third lever relates to financial leverage. A company is financially leveraged when it uses more debt relative to equity to finance its operations. Unlike the first two levers, however, financial leverage is not something that is necessarily sought for, but should be used with proper consideration of the cost of debt financing (more will be said in our discussion of EVA).[54] Suffice it to say this analysis provides specific paths on how ROE can be improved.

USING MARKETING RATIOS

Thus far, we have focused on the financial side of the company's transactions. Scholars in marketing have likewise used a number of ratios to assist in their assessment of marketing strategies, more specifically market share.[55] The prime source is Profit Impact of Marketing Strategy (PIMS), a database of the market profiles and business results of major American and European companies. The PIMS project was started by Sidney Schoeffler, who, while working with other senior managers at General Electric in the 1960s, wanted to know why some of their business units were more profitable than others. The study identified several strategic variables that determine firm profitability, with the most important being market share, product quality, investment intensity, and service quality.

On the basis of this study, market share has assumed prominence in marketing and business strategy. Two particular ratios are notable here:

$$Market\ Share = \frac{Sales}{Total\ Industry\ Sales}$$

This measures how a company stacks up against the overall industry. A composite is also used to determine the concentration of an industry (see Chapter 2).

$$Relative\ Market\ Share = \frac{Sales}{Sales\ of\ Largest\ Competitor}$$

This is a more restrictive measure of how a company's sales compare against that of its largest competitor.

Such analysis can disclose important information about a company's dominance or lack thereof (see Exhibit 11.8). Dominance provides a company with more options and opportunities to improve performance than less dominant firms. Among the most important findings from the PIMS research is the link between profitability and relative market share: the higher the market share, the higher the ROE.[56] According to the PIMS study, a firm with market dominance is able to improve its profitability through economies of scale, better negotiating power with suppliers, the ability to sell in high volumes, occasionally at lower prices, possible first-mover advantages in stocking new products, better access to advertising, and better options for expansion.[57]

Exhibit 11.8

Measures of Marketing Dominance: Rules of Thumb

Relative Market Share	Competitive Characteristic	Rule-of-Thumb Guidelines
4.0× or greater	Dominant	Extremely strong. Positioned to capitalize on scale and scope economies.
1.5× to 3.9×	Clear leadership	Very strong position. Good latitude for imposing core strategy, particularly if entry barriers are strong.
1.0× to 1.49×	Narrow leadership	Strong position. Need to check position and rivals carefully. Entry barriers might be untenable.
0.7× to 0.99×	Strong follower	Fairly strong. Some competitive advantage, although precarious. Need to be attentive to follower's guidelines.
0.3× to 0.69×	Follower	Moderate position. Need to be attentive to follower's guidelines. Be operationally efficient.
Less than 0.3×	Marginal player	Weak position. Need to be operationally efficient. Need to improve competitive position quickly.

Source: Adapted from Richard Koch, *The Financial Times Guide to Strategy* (London: Pittman Publishing, 1995), p. 31.

> *Wal-Mart's dominance is well established, but a comparison with its largest competitor, Target Stores, indicated the depth of such dominance. For perspective, in 2002, Target's overall sales were $40 billion, while Wal-Mart's were $218 billion. Thus: Wal-Mart's Relative Market Share = $218 divided by $40 = 5.45 times. Per Exhibit 11.8, this indicates an extremely strong dominant position in the United States.*

REVISITING THE VALUE PROBLEM: ROE VERSUS EVA

Despite the popularity of ROE, it has a number of significant limitations.[58] First, ROE is backward looking and focused on a single period. One example is when a company spends money on a new product that leads to a decrease in ROE. Because it includes only one year's earnings, it fails to capture the full impact on long-term, multiperiod decisions. Second, ROE does not reflect the risks undertaken by the company. That is, two companies might have similar ROEs, say 20 percent, but one company might have attained this through more debt than the other, thereby incurring a higher risk. ROE ignores risks in only looking at the returns. Third, ROE measures the book value of shareholders' equity, not its market value. The market value of equity is more significant to shareholders because it is current and measures the realizable worth of the shares.

Analysts have attempted to circumvent these difficulties by refining the ratios, or proposing new ones altogether. A refinement made to avoid distorting the effects of leverage on ROE and ROA is the return on invested capital, or the return on net assets (RONA), defined as follows:[59]

$$RONA = \frac{EBIT\,(1-Tax\ rate)}{Interest\ Bearing\ Debt + Equity}$$

While accounts payable are the source of cash, they are excluded because they carry no explicit cost.[60] Thus, RONA is the rate of return earned on the total invested capital regardless of whether it is debt or equity. Another proposal to circumvent the value problem is simply to substitute the book value of equity with its market value, or use the **market/book ratio,** defined as:

$$\frac{Market}{Book\ Value} = \frac{Market\ Value\ of\ Common\ Stock}{Shareholders'\ Equity}$$

This is another way of examining the relationship between management's performance and the market assessment of that performance.

Jablonsky/Barsky's Analysis: Between 1990 and 2000, Wal-Mart's common stock traded, on average, at 5.8 times its reported shareholders' equity. Wal-Mart's performance in this regard outperformed the Standard and Poor (S&P) 500 index and the S & P retail composite index.[61]

Another ratio used is the **price/earnings ratio** (P/E), defined as:

$$\frac{P}{E} = \frac{Price\ per\ share}{Earnings\ per\ share}$$

Jablonsky/Barsky's Analysis: Wal-Mart's average P/E ratio of 26.4 between 1990 and 2000 means that the market value of Wal-Mart's common stock has traded at 26.4 times its reported earnings. This is another way of examining management performance and the market assessment of this performance.[62]

These formulations might have resolved the value problem for economists, but they raise additional ones for accountants, if not for practitioners. Stock price (price per share) tends to be very sensitive to investors' expectations about the future.[63] The higher the stock price, the lower will be the earnings potential, thereby invalidating it as a performance measure. The use of P/E multiples involves investors' speculations about the future, and such can be easily trumped by extraneous events, such as terrorism, war, and so on.

It is not surprising that academicians who favor market values (mostly economists) and practitioners are constantly in disagreement over which measures to employ.[64] For some academicians, the stock price represents the value of the owners' equity in the firm, and because the goal of management is to maximize shareholders' equity, then stock price is the appropriate measure. Practitioners acknowledge this argument but do not see it working in practice. One difficulty is that of specifying precisely how operating decisions affect stock prices. Moreover, there is a difficult evaluation decision. Should managers be measured by stock prices? Since this figure is tempered by numerous factors, including many that are not in the control of managers, implementing this for performance appraisal and bonuses can be problematic. One promising effort to redress this problem is EVA, or *economic value added,* discussed in the next section.

Economic Value Added (EVA) and Market Value Added (MVA)

In late 1993, *Fortune* magazine ran a cover story, "The Real Key to Creating Wealth," that touted the use of **EVA** (economic value added), devised by Stern Stewart & Co., as the "hottest financial idea and getting hotter."[65] The formula for calculating EVA is as follows:

EVA = Net Operating Profit After Taxes (NOPAT) – (Capital × Cost of Capital)

What makes EVA particularly compelling for its supporters is its inclusion of the company's cost of capital, thereby incorporating risk into the analysis. The central message is that investment creates value for its owners only when the returns exceed its cost of capital. Phrased differently, EVA is earnings minus the cost of capital, or the opportunity cost of the capital invested. This interpretation suggests that earnings should be compared against the minimum rate of return expected by shareholders and lenders at comparable risk. EVA is popular because it can be calculated and used not just at the corporate level, but also at the level of business units and individual projects as well. Bennett Stewart, senior partner at consulting firm Stern Stewart & Co., which has trademarked the acronym, states: "EVA is a practical method of estimating the economic profit that is earned, as opposed to the accounting profit." He continues, "It's really a finance tool for nonfinance executives. Finance execs don't need EVA."[66] EVA's overall appeal is that it integrates three crucial management functions: capital budgeting, performance appraisal, and incentive management.[67] Consultants at Stern, Stewart & Co. have even developed a clever method of distributing a manager's bonus over several periods that places middle managers at risk as though they were the owners. This helps discourage myopic, single-period decision making. An interesting application of EVA as a proxy for prices and other related prices in a monopolistic firm without clear benchmarks is provided in our case-in-point at the end of this chapter. A closely related measure is MVA, or **market value added**. This measures the amount of wealth a company has created since its inception. MVA itself is the stock market's assessment of the net present value (NPV) of EVA.[68]

> In terms of EVA and MVA, Wal-Mart is rated among the very top in the country, second only to General Electric, as reported by Stern, Stewart & Co. In 2003, Wal-Mart's MVA was $21,340,000, and its EVA was $2,928,000. The report continues: "Wal-Mart's EVA is higher than Microsoft's, which means that the market is projecting different rates of growth for these companies. . . . Wal-Mart has stupendous growth prospects but the lowest return on capital, so it has significant growth at lower margins."[69]

Despite the appeal and popularity of EVA and MVA, they are limited in application by methods and assumptions required for their computation. For one, there are many ways to calculate cost of capital, ranging from the very basic to the very obtuse and mathematically complex (see a simplified example of Exhibit 11.9). There are also several adjustments in accounting needed to employ the formula. Stern, Stewart & Co., along with a host of other consultants, have capitalized on this opportunity by selling EVA computations for a fee. On occasion, EVA figures have also been published by *Fortune* magazine. A simple procedure for estimating EVA, suggested by Gene Johnson, marketing professor at University of Rhode Island, is provided in Exhibit 11.10.[70] EVA is particularly important for strategic analysis because it provides a score—a clear determination as to whether a company has created wealth for itself and shareholders, or destroyed wealth. Without the inclusion of cost of capital, it is literally impossible to do this. In this regard, it is seen as a superior measure to traditional ROE, despite its limitations. While EVA contributions approximate or equal its NPV (net present value) at the end of the project period, Stern and Stewarts' contributions relate to the use of EVA as an operational control.[71] When using NPV to calculate the value of a project over ten years, for example, one anticipates that cash flows materialize as expected. With EVA, however, one can evaluate NPV on a year-to-year basis and make adjustments to either stay on course, abandon, or reward managers on an annual basis. Thus, EVA provides an excellent method for connecting the short run and the long run. Even EVA, or a single measure, by itself is not likely to provide the full details of the ability of a firm to sustain its performance over time without seriously depleting its resources. Accordingly, a presentation of tests for sustainability is our next topic.

TESTING THE SUSTAINABILITY OF A BUSINESS STRATEGY

In previous chapters, we proposed that the central tenet of strategy lies in establishing a sustainable competitive advantage. We proposed some tests to assess whether resources that are inextricably related to a strategy are duplicable, durable, and imitatable. Within financial analysis, this same question is used to determine whether a company's historical growth rate is likely to continue. Particularly crucial in this analysis is whether growth can be sustained by factors beyond additions to earnings

Exhibit 11.9

Calculating the Cost of Capital

Calculating the cost of capital (opportunity) can be a tedious task. Nevertheless, a simple explanation that underlies the logic of this measure is presented below. Let us take the case of Bay View Corporation along with the following set of assumptions.

Bay View	Liabilities and Owners' Equity	Opportunity Cost of Capital
Debt	$500	10%
Equity	$1,000	20%

Creditors expect to earn 10 percent and shareholders expect to earn at least 20 percent on their investment.

How much money should Bay View earn annually on existing assets to meet the expectations of creditors?

Creditors expect 10 percent, or (.10)($500), or $50.00. Because interest payments are tax-deductible, the effective after-tax cost to the company in a 50% tax bracket would be (.50)($50.00), or $25.00.

How much money should Bay View earn annually on existing assets to meet the expectations of shareholders?

Shareholders expect 20 percent, or (.20)($1,000), or $200.00.

What is the rate of return the company must then earn in order to meet the expectations of both creditors and shareholders?

Since the total investment is $1,500, viz. ($500 + $1,000), the required rate of return is:

$$\frac{\$250}{\$1,500} = 16.6\%$$

In symbols, the amount of money Bay View must earn is:

$$(1-t)K(d)D + K(e)\ E$$

where $K(d)$ is the cost of debt and $K(e)$ is the expected return on equity. The cost of capital, $K(w)$ is hence:

$$\frac{(1-t)\ K(d)\ D + K(e)\ E}{D + E}$$

Source: Adapted from Robert Higgins, *Analysis for Financial Management*, 5th ed. (New York: Irwin/McGraw, 1998), pp. 277–278. Example and figures have been changed.

per share.[72] In terms of the DuPont formula, growth can arise from numerous sources, whether more earnings, more turnover, or higher financial leverage. Aggressive investments might boost asset turnover, but eventually assets will reach the level of diminishing returns. Return on sales is also limited in that overly high figures will

Exhibit 11.10

Calculating EVA: A Flow Diagram

EVA can be computed in two ways:

1. Earnings minus opportunity costs (standard method)

2. Investment at the beginning of the period multiplied by the difference between the rate of return on investment and the rate of return that is required on investments of identical risks (or the "spread").

    a.   Operating revenue less operating expenses = operating income
    b.   Operating income less income taxes = net operating profit after taxes
    c.   Total assets less liabilities and deferred credits = invested capital
    d.   Net operating profit after taxes / invested capital = return on invested capital
    e.   Return on invested capital less cost of capital = spread
    f.   Spread multiplied by invested capital = economic value added

simply attract unwanted entrants. Even leverage has a limit in that lenders will not continue to provide funds beyond a certain point at which financial risk begins to increase. Therefore, it is only through additions to retained earnings, which provide the engine for more income for which future strategic and operational activities can be financed, that growth can be sustained.

To encourage investors to keep their investment in the company, the firm occasionally distributes some income to these investors in the form of dividends.[73] What is retained as a portion of its earnings is what can be channeled for future growth. The higher the portion retained, the more book value is accumulated per share and the higher the Earnings Per Share (EPS) growth rate. In this context, a company's sustainable growth rate is the growth rate in equity.[74] Designating $g*$ to represent the sustainable growth rate, we establish that:

$$g^* = \frac{Change\ in\ equity}{Beginning-of-period\ equity}$$

Assuming that the firm issues no equity, the numerator in the above equation equals (R) times earnings, where (R) is the **firm's retention rate**, defined as the proportion of earnings that is reinvested in the business:[75]

$$g^* = \frac{(R)(Earnings)}{Equity}$$

Earlier, we already established that earnings/equity is ROE, thus:

$g^* = (R)$ ROE, or using the DuPont formula,
$g^* = PRAT$, where P is the profit margin, A is the asset turnover, and T is the assets-to-equity ratio.

By this line of reasoning, a **sustainable growth rate** is defined as follows:

Sustainable growth = (return on equity) × (income reinvestment rate), where
Income reinvestment rate is equal to (1 − dividend payout ratio).

Another perspective for assessing sustainability is to conduct a similar analysis, but with *cash flow* as the critical variable.[76] The excess of cash flow over cash is the amount available for the owners to reinvest back into the business model. Thus, the value of a business or a firm is the present value of its future free cash flow discounted at its cost of capital. This improves on the preceding method, which is limited to a particular time period. The focus on cash flow discounted over time represents a broader picture of a firm's sustainability (see Box 11.3).[77]

Using the logic suggested by University of Michigan's strategy professor Professor Allan Afuah, we can analyze Wal-Mart's position in 2000 to illustrate this application.[78] Wal-Mart's market valuation was $212.67 billion and its profits were $5.34 billion. The free cash flow that Wal-Mart has to generate every year in perpetuity would be: $C_f = (\$212.67$ billion x $r_k)$. Assuming that investors seek a 15% return, then Wal-Mart will have to generate ($212.67 x .15) = $31.90 billion a year to infinity. The strategic implication is that this figure will have to be examined against all future events and contingencies facing Wal-Mart. The underlying logic by Afuah is that the required free cash flow of $31.90 billion is significantly larger than the profit of $5.34, prompting the need to closely examine Wal-Mart's business model to see whether it can increase its profits further to maintain its advantage. This is not unreasonable in that Wal-Mart already faces a host of challenges, including many community reprisals whenever the company moves to a specific location. It is also presumptuous to expect that Wal-Mart's financing based on any cost of capital can last forever. This approach suggests that, while we can use and interpret cash flow as a baseline, we need to examine other facets of the business model to justify this valuation. In short, the use of cash flow analysis extends our evaluation of a firm's strategy beyond traditional ratio analysis and the disaggregated DuPont model, but there is the need to incorporate qualitative factors as well.

At heart, sustainability issues focus on how much a firm can grow without adverse effects on its current or available resource base. Not surprisingly, the attention is focused on earnings and/or cash flow as the critical components of growth, correcting for dividends given to claim holders. In this context, resources are limited in terms of their anticipated level of productivity. But what if resources can exceed these limits? The question is the subject of a more refined procedure suggested by two other prominent financial experts in the next section.

Box 11.3

Cash Flow Analysis, Sustainability, and Market Valuation

The second approach to evaluating the sustainability of a firm's strategy is based on an analysis of its discounted cash flows. Firms typically raise money by borrowing, as reflected in short- and long-term debt, and/or by issuing common stock. Unlike the cost of debt where there is a concrete interest rate, there is generally no market rate of interest associated with common stock. The current convention for calculating the firm's cost of (equity) capital involves the estimation of three variables:

- The risk-free rate, r_f, that can be estimated conservatively with the interest rate on U.S. treasury bills. Because treasury bills represent a minimum risk associated with the use of money, they have become the standard of comparison.
- The market risk premium, r_m, or the uncertainty related to earning the return on any common stock. This can be approximated by the historical returns earned by equity investors over and above the rate of return on treasury bonds.
- The firm's premium, β $(r_m - r_f)$, associated with a specific common stock relative to the overall stock market. The term β, or beta, is a statistical measure of the volatility of the market rates of return on a specific stock relative to the average rate of return of the overall market. Generally, a beta that is greater than 1 suggests more volatility; contrariwise, a beta of less than 1 suggests lower volatility.

The firm's specific cost of equity capital is equal to the sum of the risk-free rate and the premium for investing in the firm (i.e., the firm's premium). Using the firm's cost of capital, analysts are able to estimate the present value of a firm's projected stream of cash flows. In addition, analysts, such as professors Jablonsky and Barsky, have extended this analysis further in comparing this rate against the inflation rate, the interest rate on ten-year treasury bonds, and the cost of capital for the economy to arrive at much deeper understanding of a firm's (in their case, that of Wal-Mart) market valuation and financial condition. Moreover, by analyzing the *equity spread*, defined as (ROE − cost of capital), analysts can evaluate both the firm's actual performance along with market's expectations of the firm, as reflected in the cost of capital, consistent with the logic proposed by EVA proponents.

Cash flow analysis can also be framed to test for underlying assumptions about a firm's growth, market valuation, and sustainability. University of Michigan's management professor Allan Afuah's approach starts off with a representation of a firm and its future value as a series of present and future discounted cash flows:

$$V = C_0 = \frac{C_1}{(1+r_k)} + \frac{C_2}{(1+r_k)^2} + \frac{C_3}{(1+r_k)^3} \ldots \frac{C_n}{(1+r_k)^n}$$

$$= \sum_{t=0}^{t=n} \frac{C_t}{(1+r_k)^t}$$

C_0 is cash flow at time 0, C_t is the free cash flow at time t. The firm's cost of capital, r_k, or the expected rate of return that could be earned by investing money in another asset with comparable risk.

While this is a reasonable approximation, it is more difficult to project events and figures further ahead in the future because of greater uncertainty, as is generally presumed in forecasting methods. In view of this uncertainty, a widely accepted assumption is that the free cash flows generated by the firm will reach a constant amount (an annuity) after n years, at which case the above equation reduces to:

$$V = \frac{C_f}{r_k(1+r_k)^n}$$

(continued)

Box 11.3 *(continued)*

Assuming that the constant free cash flows start in the present year, then $n = 0$, and the equation is further reduced to:

$$V = \frac{C_f}{r_k}$$

A further assumption is that today's free cash flows, C_0, will grow at a constant rate of g forever. Accordingly, the value (V) becomes:

$$V = \frac{C_0(1 + g)}{(r_k - g)} \quad \text{or} \quad \frac{C_1}{(r_k - g)}$$

This application of cash flow can be extended to assess the strategic implications of high valuations. Professor Afuah takes the case of Cisco Systems that had a market valuation of $453.88 billion on March 14, 2000. Its profits in 1999 were $2.10 billion. Was Cisco Systems overvalued by market analysts? To understand this, one notes that the free cash flow that Cisco has to generate every year forever, for its $453.88 billion to be right is: $Cf = \$453.88 \times r_k$ billion. If we assume that investors seek a 15% return, then Cisco will have to generate ($453.88 billion $\times$ .15) = $68.08 billion a year to infinity. Since cash flows are less than profits, Cisco's profits have to be even more. What is it about Cisco's business model that would make one believe that it can ramp its profits from $2 billion to more than $68 billion each year to maintain such advantage?

Source: Adapted from Stephen F. Jablonsky and Noah P. Barsky, *The Manager's Guide to Financial Statement Analysis*, 2d ed. (New York: John Wiley & Sons, Inc., 2001), pp. 164–87; and Allan Afuah, *Business Models: A Strategic Management Approach* (New York: McGraw-Hill, 2004), pp. 212–13. We included an additional final equation for clarification.

RELATING VALUATION TO STRATEGY

For Bruce Greenwald, a business strategy and finance professor at the Columbia Business School, and Judd Kahn, the chief operating officer of Hummingbird Management, financial analyses argue that standard financial analysis (as depicted above) typically ignore a direct assessment of strategic issues.[79] These analyses are generally built around future estimates of cash flows but exclude the competitive conditions that affect firms. As a consequence, this analysis limits the quality of information and judgment when assessing the sustainability of the firm in a broader strategic context. Moreover, while the use of net present value (NPV) looks good in theory, the focus on NPV alone can undermine the consideration of the competitive environment in the future, and whether competitive advantages can exist. Specifically, Greenwald and Kahn argue that NPV has three major shortcomings:

- It does not segregate reliable information about current cash flows from less reliable information. Estimates of cash flows five to ten years out when assessing the value of the project tend to be speculative.

- It makes assumptions about future projects (i.e., sales and profit margins) that are, in fact, difficult to determine even for current products. As we have seen earlier, one remedy is to simplify the analyses with specific assumptions. Even so, small shifts in these variables can change the directionality of the analysis significantly.
- It discards much information that is relevant to the calculation of the economic value of a firm. There are two parts to any valuation: *resources* and *cash flows*. NPV focuses almost exclusively on cash flows but ignores the estimate of the assets or resources that are needed to create and sustain these cash flows.

The approach developed by Bruce Greenwald and Judd Kahn is directed at a strategic approach to valuation and incorporates the company's competitive position into the valuation. The process involves the consideration of three elements—*assets, current earning power,* and *growth*—in determining the value of investment. Three steps are employed in this analysis.[80]

First Cut: Assets

Asset valuation is the first step in determining the value of the company but some adjustments are necessary. The first important judgment is whether the industry in which the company operates will be economically viable in the future. If the industry is not viable and with no need to replace the assets currently in use, then industry-specific plant, property, and equipment (PPE) might only be worth scrap value and their value should be realized upon liquidation. If, however, the industry is growing, then some assets need to be replaced and should be valued at reproduction cost: that is, the cost of reproducing its economic function as efficiently as possible. Intangibles like customer relationships, organizational development, workforce acquisition and training, and product portfolios should be included as part of reproduction cost. Occasionally the cost for competitors to enter the business is also considered.

Second Cut: Current Earnings Power Value

After assessing assets and liabilities in the above manner, the second step involves the determination of current earnings power value (EPV) or the annual distributable cash flow of the company discounted to the present at the cost of capital (i.e., the present value of these flows). Greenwald and Kahn suggest specific adjustments that should be made with respect to the company's current net cash flow:

- Use operating earnings, Earnings Before Interest and Tax (EBIT), before interest and taxes, instead of net earnings to eliminate the effect of financial leverage (how much debt is carried by the firm as a percentage of assets).
- Incorporate "nonrecurring items." In practice, these are more frequent than otherwise reported. Furthermore, they tend to be overwhelmingly negative, oftentimes done to cram in all losses in past and anticipated years.
- Adjust current earnings to account for any cyclical variation.
- Account for accounting depreciation that might differ from economic depreciation.

The earning power value (EPV) is then computed by dividing EP (annual distributable cash flow) by the firm's cost of capital.

THIRD CUT: PUTTING ASSETS AND EARNINGS TOGETHER—FRANCHISE VALUE

Following the above two steps, three scenarios are possible: (1) EPV exceeds asset value; (2) they are essentially equal; or (3) asset value exceeds EPV. The difference is called **franchise value**, or the excess return earned by the firm with competitive advantages. For businesses operating without competitive advantages, and in industries not protected by entry barriers, the reproduction costs of the net assets and the EPV should be equal. If EPV is higher, then other companies will enter, and this additional competition will eliminate any surplus earnings power. If, however, a business has a sustainable advantage, then EPV will be higher than the asset value, because no new companies can enter to compete away the extra earnings. Using the data in a strategic framework, situations in which growth is bad, good, or neutral, can be analyzed.

- In bad growth, i.e., when asset value exceeds EPV, more growth will simply destroy value and make matters worse. That is, if managers do a poor job using current resources, they are not likely to improve with additional resources.
- In neutral growth, i.e., when asset value equals EPV, there is no gain or loss in value. This situation suggests the absence of competitive advantages.
- In growth situations, i.e., when EPV exceeds asset value, this suggests the condition of a business with a sustainable competitive advantage. Because it will be very difficult for new entrants to enter and compete away the extra earnings, competitive advantage can be sustained as the company grows. Earnings will grow faster than the additional assets necessary to sustain it.

This examination of the productive use of resources highlights the factor that makes growth valuable, that is, when sustainable competitive advantages exist. The goal of a business should be good growth, where benefits exceed the costs. This method provides yet another perspective in which to assess the financial health and operating performance of a company. It complements more traditional approaches in accounting and sustainability analysis by presenting a more incisive view of resources as income-generating variables, as opposed to static entities. The logic underlying this method lies in its ability to describe three growth "scenarios" for a firm. An analyst is able to relate these scenarios against the competitive advantages of the firm. Without competitive advantages, however, investments will revert back to the cost of capital. Thus, this method provides a more accurate representation of a manager's options, and, ultimately, some validation of its corporate strategies (see Box 11.4).

Even so, as the world grows even more complex, however, there is the question of whether any test for sustainability can be adequately captured by a number of financial variables, and the extent to which qualitative judgment is necessary. This question is addressed in the next section about the balanced scorecard. Already, some thoughtful scholars have begun to question the appropriateness of standard financial assumptions and conventions, and have proposed new measures and processes (see Box 11.5).

Box 11.4

An Application of Value Investing

Greenwald and Kahn's approach to value investing provides the timely reminder that not all economic growth is necessarily good, and that analysts need to evaluate the underlying conditions in which growth can also be good, neutral, or bad. In cases where the growth of a firm is good, there is compelling evidence that entry into the business will be very difficult, and that the firm can sustain its strategy. Applying this approach to valuation is extensive and can be tedious. To make this application more transparent, Greenwald and his colleagues have illustrated their approach using Intel Corporation, arguably one of the most successful firms in business history. The Intel case provides a detailed explanation of the three fundamental steps of value investing, the rationale and logic for various adjustments, and the conclusions about Intel's franchise. Even so, we strongly recommend a full reading of the case (see source below).

For perspective, three sources of intrinsic value are identified: the reproduction cost of the company's assets; the current earnings power of the franchise; and the value of its earnings growth within the franchise.

Step 1: Reproduction Cost of Intel's Assets. This valuation compares the price of Intel's shares to their book value per share. The objective is to estimate how much a competitor would spend to get into the business and compete directly with Intel.

Key Considerations: Did not adopt the most conservative net-to-net approach; instead, a comparison of the price of Intel's shares against the book value per share was used for this application.

Key Adjustments: Adjusted for bad debt allowances and collections; added LIFO reserve; adjusted for inventory; discounted deferred taxes to present value; adjusted property, plant, and equipment (net) values; and related goodwill to product portfolio and R & D; adjusted marketing, general, and administrative expenses.

Step 2: Computation of Earnings Power Value. This second step focuses on earnings rather than assets.

Key Considerations: Focused on how Intel would continue to grow (i.e., its current intrinsic value on the basis of its earning power).

Key Adjustments: Adjusted earnings for special charges, such as write-offs, provisions for layoffs, plant closings; evaluation of the stability of the memory versus the microprocessor markets; added some of R & D back to earnings; adjustments for depreciation, amortization, and maintenance capital expenditures.

Estimation of Appropriate Discount Rate: Evaluated Intel's earnings against future variability; adjusted for cash-debt (reduced debt and added back excess cash) to arrive at adjusted EPV.

Step 3: Evaluating Intel's Growth and Sustainability. This third step compares EPV against reproduction costs.

Key Considerations: If EPV exceeded reproduction costs of the assets, Intel should enjoy sustained competitive advantage. Intel's competitive position was also assessed in terms of its ascendancy into a premier brand leader (captive loyalty) and the existence of economies of scale (its ability to create a significant cost advantage).

Conclusions: After 1987, Intel enjoyed a significant and increasing competitive advantage using this valuation approach. From 1988 to 1991, Intel's EPV surpassed its asset value by an average of 25 percent per year. This difference was the value of Intel's franchise at the time. Intel's ability to sustain this advantage would depend on captive customers (differentiation) and from economies of scale in research and development (an advantage that can discourage entrants). Subsequent analysis indicated that Intel's growth for the designated time period could be accommodated within the franchise, establishing a margin of safety.

Source: Adapted from Bruce C. Greenwald, Judd Kahn, Paul D. Sonkin, and Michael van Biema, *Value Investing: From Graham to Buffett and Beyond* (Hoboken, NJ: John Wiley & Sons, Inc., 2001), pp. 107–137.

Box 11.5

Toward a Management of Means?

Despite the seeming bedrock of accounting and financial conventions, these have not escaped the scrutiny of their relevance and efficacy in managerial practice. In 1987, accounting professors Tom Johnson and Robert Kaplan sounded the alarm with the publication of *Relevance Lost.* They argued that the accounting profession had lost its way in becoming a pawn of number crunching and manipulations, with a misplaced focus on keeping the scorecard, as opposed to the actual process of creating profitability. This criticism led to activity-based accounting (ABC), which became integrated within the core of the accounting profession.

Johnson's experience with Toyota and Swedish manufacturer Scania prompted another call for possible reform. Undisputedly, Toyota is the leading automobile manufacturer in the world. Though not as well known, Scania has been the most profitable maker of large trucks in the world. In collaboration with Anders Bröms, Scania's co-founder and managing director, Johnson explained their success as their practice called "management by means," a departure from "management by results" that has dominated the thinking and practice of large industrial-age firms for decades. They discovered a complex web of local control that is fundamentally different from the traditional system of centralized control in typical manufacturing.

Local control finds its metaphor in biology, where a "cut in one's finger triggers coagulants that are generated locally and that flow immediately to the cut." Similarly, at Toyota, MIT professor Peter Senge argues that "each person's actions in the complex process of stamping, welding, painting, and assembly are coordinated completely by what goes on directly around them, paced by the urgency of meeting the needs of the customer."

To this end, Johnson and Bröms eschew the traditional mechanistic view of the world, one that dominates and guides traditional "management by results" thinking in favor of an organic living system that nurtures aspiration and awareness, as opposed to needs and goals. In lieu of preconceived accounting targets, Toyota and Scania are governed by three precepts: self-organization, interdependence, and diversity. By following precepts that emulate living systems, even a lean and profitable company can organize new ways to lessen waste and reduce instability.

Source: Adapted from Peter Senge's Foreword in H. Thomas Johnson and Anders Bröms, *Profit Beyond Measure: Extraordinary Results Through Attention to Work and People* (New York: The Free Press, 2000).

TOWARD A BALANCED SCORECARD

Good strategy is all about creating value. A highly promising method of linking financial performance to a company's business model is through *balanced scorecards.* Introduced by Robert Kaplan, professor at the Harvard Business School, and David Norton, a co-founder and president of Balanced Scorecard Collaborative, Inc., based in Boston, Massachusetts, the **balanced scorecard** methodology provides a systematic framework for balancing shareholder and strategic goals, a diagnostic for setting management priorities, and a basis for performance appraisal at all levels of the organization.[81] They describe the innovation of the balanced scorecard as follows:

> The balanced scorecard retains traditional financial measures. But financial measures tell the story of past events, an adequate story for industrial age companies for which investments in long-term capabilities and customer relationships were not critical for success. These financial measures are inadequate, however, for guiding and evaluating the journey that information age companies must make to create future value through investment in customers, suppliers, employees, processes, technology, and innovation.[82]

The performance metrics combine the following answers to four basic questions:

1. *How do we look to shareholders?* This financial perspective provides a basis for evaluating whether the organization can meet and sustain its financial performance.
   - Example of metrics for a for-profit organization: EVA, return on investment, cash flow, growth of earnings, market share, relative market share, and sustainability indices.
   - Example of metrics for a hypothetical MBA program: Graduation rate, placement statistics, starting salaries, and before-and-after salary differentials.
2. *How do customers see us?* This customer perspective provides the basis for evaluating the value of the organization on items that matter the most to the targeted market.
   - Example of metrics for a for-profit organization: Product/service quality, cost, defects and failure rates, and service management.
   - Example of metrics for a hypothetical MBA program: Exit assessment surveys, student rankings, focus groups, and participation in fund-raising.
3. *What must we excel in?* This internal business perspective provides the basis for business processes that significantly affect consumer satisfaction.
   - Example of metrics for a for-profit organization: Cycle time, quality, productivity, employee skills, core competencies, and critical technologies.
   - Example of metrics for a hypothetical MBA program: Recruitment, program visibility, curricular innovations, faculty research and training, service support, student experiences within and outside the classroom, internal ratings, placement service, a collaborative culture.
4. *Can we continue to improve and create value?* This innovation and learning perspective is a measure of how an organization can continue to reinvent itself to meet the demands of its fast-changing external environment.
   - Example of metrics for a for-profit organization: New product development, specific improvement goals, and continuous improvement over time.
   - Example of metrics for a hypothetical MBA program: Continuous reassessment of competencies, internal and external benchmarking, a focus on critical trends in program content and delivery, and partnerships with other external organizations.

By balancing the requirements of strategy and finance, the scorecard methodology permits us to evaluate the strategy of the firm, its broader business model, and how value for shareholders is created over time. What financial analysis (including sustainability analysis) lacks, the balanced scorecard informs. Specifically, the balanced scorecard provides a more comprehensive platform, one that includes both financial and nonfinancial items, in which to assess strategy. However, it can likewise be argued that the advantage of having financial figures, such as EVA, is that they present the end score—something that is not as evident in a process-driven methodology such as the balanced scorecard. These only suggest that both kinds, if not many other variations, of assessments are needed to evaluate a complex phenomenon such as the organization's strategy. An example of a balanced scorecard is provided in Exhibit 11.11.

Exhibit 11.11   **An Illustration of the Balanced Scorecard**

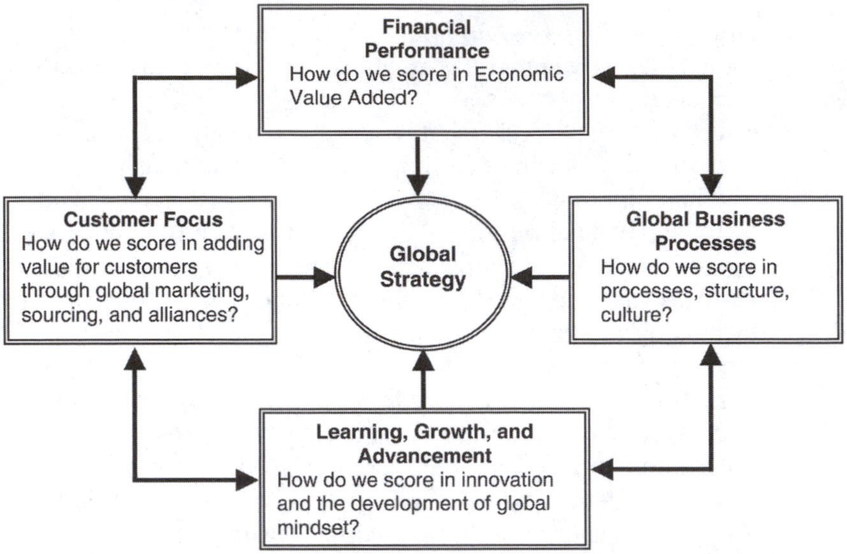

Source: Adapted from Robert Kaplan and D.P. Norton, "The Balanced Scorecard: Measures That Drive Profitability," *Harvard Business Review* (January–February 1992).

FINANCIAL REPORTING IN THE CONTEXT OF INTERNATIONAL OPERATIONS

Our discussion of financial analysis and reporting has assumed a largely generic context, one that applies largely to the United States. As firms escalate their international activities in their quest for global presence and dominance, the need to reconcile different variations of financial reporting and analysis will become even more compelling.[83] Strategic analysis cannot be successful until reliable financial information that reflects international investments and shifts in resources is obtained in a timely manner. This task, of course, comes along with the need to resolve differences in currencies and accounting rules as financial statements of foreign and domestic units of a firm are combined into consolidated statements. One complication is that accounting standards and measurement rules vary from one country to another. For example, Ericsson uses Swedish GAAP, Wal-Mart uses U.S. GAAP, and Nokia prepares its statements using International Accounting Standards (IAS). Thus, Wal-Mart's reported profit levels might not be comparable to those calculated by Swedish or IAS rules since income recognition rules and guidelines are different.[84]

Other complications include the following: First, in some countries, there is a conformity between the accounting methods used in shareholders' financial statements and the rules used in computing taxable income.[85] Thus, the legislative branch of the government sets acceptable standards and guidelines. In other countries, the accounting profession sets accounting principles, and these financial rules differ from taxation rules. Second, in the United States, the Securities and Exchange Commission (SEC) allows foreign businesses to list their securities on a U.S. stock exchange as long as proper procedures are followed.[86] Foreign firms that do so must follow a procedure that translates foreign GAAP financial statements into U.S. GAAP. However, the financial reporting requirements for foreign companies listed on the London Stock Exchange permit greater flexibility than those that currently exist in the United States.[87] Given these differences, with more evolving over time, firms with increased international operations are encouraged to be more watchful and mindful of how financial information is developed, configured, and transmitted across borders.

To conclude, financial statements are an extremely important source of information about a company's financial health, its operating performance, and to some extent, its success in implementing its strategy. Even so, to echo our cautionary note in the beginning of the chapter, financial statements should be "sniffed" but not "swallowed." In this chapter, we have presented the use of the financial statements as they relate to the strategic and operating activities of the firm. We have also presented the traditional and more contemporary approaches to sustainability assessment and the valuation of a firm's business model. If there is a good reason why managers believe that implementation is difficult, perhaps even more demanding than strategy formulation, it is because implementation is multifaceted. It involves people, processes, structures, a mindset, and control. This chapter highlights the role of financial analysis that is not as detailed, nor as emphasized in business strategy courses. Strategic implementation, as a multifaceted phenomenon, means that there are a number of things that can go wrong. However, strategies, when properly implemented, create the differential and enduring advantage for firms.

SUMMARY

1. The two traditional roles of financial analysis are: to calculate and obtain financial information for purposes of comparison, and to analyze underlying patterns that might not be disclosed by the statements themselves. A third possible role is to analyze the financial statements with the end in view of assessing the sustainability of a firm's business strategy.

2. The accounting profession has developed formal guidelines and conventions under the auspices of GAAP. Within GAAP, five key characteristics underlie the preparation and use of financial statements: relevance, timeliness, reliability, comparability, and consistency.

3. The balance sheet is designed to meet the needs of creditors who want information about the resources available to pay debt and claims to these resources. A typical balance sheet can be classified into eight primary categories. The limitations of the balance sheet are that measuring value is elusive in practice, and that an asset is only recognized when it is involved in a transaction.

4. The income statement is designed to meet the needs of corporate investors who want information about a firm's earnings, as a guide to evaluating dividends and stock value. Per the accrual concept, revenues are not necessarily cash at hand. A typical income statement consists of three primary categories.

5. The cash flow statement describes the primary activities within a time period for which cash flows and inflows were recorded. It is strategic because it presents a realistic picture of the firm's financial flexibility.

6. For purposes of analysis, there are three "value-added" measures: economic value added (EVA), customer value added (CVA), and people value added (PVA). These are used primarily by financial analysts, marketing analysts, and HR managers respectively.

7. Three types of financial ratios can be distinguished for use in analyses: profitability, turnover/efficiency, and liquidity/financial leverage. The chapter illustrates these three using Wal-Mart as an example.

8. Additional analysis can be employed using methods of disaggregation. Among the most popular is the DuPont formula, which disaggregates return on equity (ROE) into three components: profit margin, return on assets, and leverage. Through disaggregation, an analyst is able to discern specific areas in which to improve the overall profitability of the firm.

9. Marketing analysts employ two principal ratios: market share and relative market share. Both are measures of dominance. A dominant firm can improve margins significantly due to scale and scope economies.

10. Despite the popularity of ROE, it has three limitations: first, it fails to capture the full impact of long-term, multiyear decisions; second, it does not reflect the risks undertaken by the company; and third, it measures the book value of shareholders' equity and thus is very conservative. Some ways of addressing these limitations are to use the return on net assets (RONA) and to compute the ratio of market/book value.

11. The value problem concerns the appropriate financial information to use for assessing the value of a firm and the sustainability of its current operations. While academicians prefer market measures, such as stock price, practitioners are wedded to ROE. Both have advantages and disadvantages.

12. The emergence of EVA and MVA was heralded as circumventing the inherent limitations of ROE because both incorporate the firm's cost of capital. The logic underlying both measures is that a firm only creates value when its earnings exceed the cost of capital invested to generate that profit.

13. Analysts concerned with assessing the sustainability of a firm's operations typically define sustainable growth as the firm's earnings multiplied by its retention rate. The logic is that a firm occasionally gives out dividends that should be recognized before it reinvests back into current operations. Thus, the value of the firm is the present value of its future free cash flows.

14. More recent treatises call into question the failure of the net present value (NPV) method to incorporate business policy issues, such as the competitive advantages of a firm, and the underlying conditions of its business environment. Therefore, in a revised formulation, the value of assets are modified into reproducible and nonreproducible categories and compared against annual distributable cash flow of the company (EPV). Depending on whether the two are equal, or when one exceeds the other, scenarios underlying good, bad, and neutral growth are

identified. Under conditions of bad growth, further investment will only hurt the firm. A good growth scenario suggests that sustainable advantages are present, and that the firm's industry is protected by entry barriers.

15. The balanced scorecard is a comprehensive method that retains the financial measures, but enhances the analysis with qualitative judgment. Such considerations include the interests of shareholders, customers, business processes, and organizational learning.

16. In international transactions, complications include different methods in preparing shareholders financial statements and the rules used in computing taxable income. It becomes important to study other countries' GAAP to account for differences and to ensure a proper comparison.

KEY TERMS

Generally accepted accounting principles (GAAP)
Materiality
Conservatism
Balance sheet
Current assets
Current liabilities
Long-term investments
Property, plant, and equipment
Other long-term assets
Liabilities
Current liabilities
Long-term liabilities
Working capital
Stockholders' equity
Historical or book value
Fair market value
Income statement
Accrual basis
Gross profit
Operating expenses
Nonoperating items
Statement of cash flow
Operating activities
Investing activities

Financing activities
"Value-added" measures
EVA (economic value added)
MVA (market value added)
CVA (customer value added)
PVA (people value added)
Profitability
ROE
ROA
Fixed costs
Variable costs
Turnover/efficiency ratios
Inventory turnover
Collection period
Payables period
Fixed asset turnover
Financial leverage
Market/book ratio
Price/earnings ratio
EVA
Market value added
Firm's retention rate
Sustainable growth rate
Franchise value
Balanced scorecard

DISCUSSION QUESTIONS

1. How do financial analyses inform strategic implementation? How does this discussion complement the two previous chapters (organizational structures/processes and the development of a corporate global mindset)?
2. Discuss the differences between financial and behavioral control. How do these differences relate to EVA, CVA, and PVA?
3. In which way does the advantage of the cash flow statement correspond to the shortcomings of the income statement?
4. How is EVA an improvement over ROI, ROE, or EPS?
5. Why should you be interested in EVA? MVA?
6. Discuss the advantages and disadvantages of the two different methods for analyzing sustainability presented in this chapter.
7. Is financial evaluation and control appropriate for a firm that is oriented toward innovation (Chapter 8)? Are control and creativity compatible?
8. Check the most recent *Fortune* magazine for its yearly rankings of the Most Admired Companies. How much of the ranking is influenced by financial analyses, particularly financial profitability? To what extent is an analysis of a firm's sustainability included? Why or why not?
9. Consider the following information for Bay View Corporation that manufactures customized vitamins.

Income Statement	2000 (in thousands)	2005 (in thousands)
Revenue	$6,000	$8,000
Cost of Goods Sold*	-$3,000	-$2,500
Sales and Administration*	-$1,200	-$2,000
EBIT	$1,800	$3,500
Interest	-$300	-$420
Taxable Income	$1,500	$3,080
Taxes @ 40%	-$600	-$1,232
Net Income	$900	$1,848

* Includes depreciation of $400.

Position Statement	2000	2005
Assets		
Current assets	$2,000	$2,200
Fixed Assets	$3,400	$4,800
Total	$5,400	$7,000
Liabilities & Equity		
Current liabilities	$1,000	$1,000
Long-term debt (12%)	$2,500	$3,500
Common (Par & Surplus)	$1,000	$1,000
Retained Earnings	$900	$1,500
Total	$5,400	$7,000

9A. Compute the following for 2000 and 2005: (a) ROE, (b) ROA, (c) EVA, (d) Relative Market Share. Largest competitor is Ryaid Corporation with revenues of $5,500 in 2000 and $7,800 in 2005.

9B. The company president has informed you that it wants to pursue a focused differentiation strategy. Based on your calculations and analysis, would you recommend this strategy? Why or why not? Please substantiate your answer.

CASE-IN-POINT. BENCHMARKING TO ECONOMIC VALUE ADDED: THE CASE OF AIRWAYS CORPORATION OF NEW ZEALAND LIMITED
BY LLOYD M. AUSTIN[88]

INTRODUCTION

This case examines the development of the benchmarking and pricing policies of a partially privatized air traffic and navigation services company, Airways Corporation of New Zealand (ACNZ). A major motivation is to examine the reaction of the corporation to the threat of price controls and the adoption of the economic value added (or EVA[89]) methodology to benchmark financial performance and manage its monopolistic profits. The development of the corporation's pricing policies also used EVA profits as the original plan aimed to earn only the cost of capital by limiting earnings to a self-imposed level of zero economic surpluses. That is, the planned EVA was set to zero to provide a benchmark to limit earnings and control pricing and wealth creation related to monopoly-owned assets and investments.

ACNZ was established on April 1, 1987, as a result of the New Zealand government's corporatization program for state trading organizations. ACNZ took over the commercial, regulatory, and security functions as well as the assets and liabilities of the Civil Aviation Division of the Ministry of Transport. The corporation has two shareholders, the ministers of finance and state-owned enterprises, and is thus a 100 percent state-owned enterprise (SOE) with two main sets of activities:

1. To provide air navigation and related services for New Zealand. The corporation has a monopoly on these activities, which in 2003 constituted 88 percent of its revenues and 95 percent of its operating assets.
2. The remaining balance of its revenues and operating assets are provided by "other services" for which there are competitors, namely consulting services, aviation publishing, corporate property, and corporate treasury activities.

Under the State Owned Enterprises Act 1985, the boards of SOEs have autonomy on operational matters, including the use of resources, pricing, and marketing. Section 4 of the act requires that SOEs including ACNZ have to be managed as if they were privately owned. The SOE Act of 1985 prevents the government from guaranteeing or underwriting the obligations of ACNZ in any way. The corporation is expected to pay a dividend.

When setting up ACNZ it was realized that the company was largely a natural monopoly.[90] However, it was government policy not to impose price controls on any SOEs, including ACNZ. To deter abuse of its monopoly position, the Commerce Act of 1985 provided for so-called reserve regulation, the imposition of price controls on the SOEs if monopoly pricing was proved. This threat of regulation and market pressure from the airlines was considered sufficient to curb excessive pricing of the corporation's services.

Air Navigation Service Privatization

To appreciate the development of ACNZ, its evolution should be put into the context of the growth and changes in air navigation service (ANS) operations in the rest of the world. ACNZ was one of the first and is among the most successful of the ANS partial privatizations to date. The model adopted was the first of three recognized privatization modes for ANS operations,[91] that is, sale to a private entity that is wholly owned by the government.[92] This model was also later adopted by Australia (in 1995) and other ANS providers. The second model involves the setting up of a nonprofit entity (often a trust) managed by a "stakeholders board," as established by ANS services in Canada. These first two approaches are usually considered to be partial privatizations. The third approach involves full privatization by selling a government department to a "for-profit" commercial entity, as in the UK. There have also been a number of (mainly) partial ANS privatizations, centered in Europe and some other areas. The privatizations and partial privatizations usually discussed in the regulation/privatization literature are those in Australia, Canada, and the UK.

ANS operations in Australia were partially privatized in 1995 when the Civil Aviation Authority split into two separate government bodies, the Civil Aviation Safety Authority and Airservices Australia (AA), the latter taking responsibility for air traffic control activities. AA is similar to ACNZ in that it was set up as a government business enterprise, or GBE,[93] a company wholly owned by the Australian government and governed by a board of directors appointed by the minister for transport and regional services. The company is run on commercial lines and is expected to earn a profit, section 13 of the Air Services Act 1995 providing the "need to earn a reasonable rate of return on AA's assets." Apart from some price capping for a limited range of activities, there are no specific price controls imposed, though the pricing of many of the remaining activities is subject to price surveillance by the Australian Competition and Consumer Commission (ACCC), which assesses any proposed price increases.

The position is different in Canada, where Nav Canada was incorporated in 1995 as a nonprofit, nonshare capital corporation under the Canada Corporations Act in 1995. The company has no equity and raises its operating funds on the bond market. Government has no investment in the company and does not directly subsidize it. Its four members, representing its key stakeholders, incorporated the company: the Federal Government, its employees' union, the Air Transport Association of Canada, and the Canadian Business Aircraft Association. These members nominate ten directors to the board that is responsible for the performance of Nav Canada. The costs of providing ANS were initially aided by a special tax, but the Civil Air Navigation Services Commercialization Act stipulates that the company is only permitted to collect revenues to cover its costs, plus reasonable and prudent financial reserves. Thus Nav Canada operates on a near break-even basis. Any surpluses that may arise are refunded to customers in the form of reduced user fees.

In the UK, the National Air Transport Service (NATS) was established in 1962 as a government department reporting to the Ministry of Aviation and Secretary of State for Air. In 1972 the Civil Aviation Authority (CAA) was formed with NATS reporting to its chairman and the chief of air staff. NATS became partially privatized in 1996 when it became a wholly owned subsidiary of the CAA. Monopoly en-route services are charged on a cost recovery basis, under the terms of the Eurocontrol Multilateral Agreement. Charges are adjusted annually to recover costs that include the repayment of interest on borrowings, but not a return on equity funds. Most of the partially competitive "target sector" activities (airports, oceanic and other activities) are charged at cost plus a predetermined percentage return on capital.

In 2000, following government plans to separate it from the CAA, NATS became a "public-private partnership," that is, a government-private enterprise partnership. This arrangement took NATS out of the public sector borrowing requirement that eased borrowing and excluded such liabilities from the public debt. It also established transparency between NATS and the CAA. An airline consortium consisting of seven airlines[94] owns 46 percent of NATS. Employees own 5 percent and the government holds the remaining 49 percent stake.

As noted, a number of ANS operations in Europe and other areas have been (mainly) partially privatized, but with a larger number still operating through government departments. In Asia, most ANS are still controlled by non-corporatized government agencies with some exceptions, like Thailand. There has been little privatization of ANS in the United States, although there is currently a large amount of discussion on the topic. Many of the preliminary legislative changes allowing privatization have been made.

AIRWAYS CORPORATION BENCHMARKING CRITERIA

A large part of the costs of ACNZ are fixed in nature and the corporation initially followed a price-averaging policy, which became an issue with its customers after the big increase in ANS transactions after 1992. Profits, both EVA and conventional, increased (see Table 11.1), as did the likelihood of regulation in the form of price controls under the Commerce Act. ACNZ needed an approach to pricing its services to reduce this risk and also to compare its financial and operating activities with other firms in the same industry.

The company developed a form of benchmarking for these pricing, performance, and regulatory issues. In this connection, Penman points out the need for benchmarks to analyze a firm's financial performance: "Benchmarks are established by reference to other firms (usually in the same industry) or to the same firm's past history. Comparison to another firm is called cross-sectional analysis. Comparison to a firm's own history is called time-series analysis."[95]

For ACNZ, the choice of benchmarks was limited. Being one of the first partially commercialized ANS authorities, it was difficult to make meaningful cross-sectional comparisons with other operators who were still largely government departments, or the few recent privatizations with their divergent pricing regimes, ranging from no major controls to break-even charging. Direct comparisons with earlier ACNZ results were not relevant, as commercial accrual accounting principles had not been used before partial privatization. Under these conditions, the company adopted a policy of benchmarking its accounting profit to an "economic" measure of performance and in 1994 changed its objectives to "provide an appropriate return on the shareholders' investment in the monopoly air traffic services business by achieving its economic cost of capital . . . and to maximise returns from the related [services] businesses."[96]

This change would provide an indication of the company's economic performance and would ensure that its pricing policy did not lead to the imposition of price controls under the Commerce Act.[97]

ECONOMIC VALUE ADDED

These objectives of measuring economic performance and preventing exploitative monopoly pricing were operationalized and measured by the adoption of supplementary financial statements using the EVA methodology, starting in the year ending June 30, 1995. Specifically, the goal in these supplementary statements was to achieve an EVA result equal to zero over time. The stated rationale for targeting EVA to zero was to provide:

> An objective means of balancing the demands of the shareholder to be "as profitable as comparable businesses" against the demands of customers who require safe, efficient and cost effective air navigation services. When EVA equals zero the corporation produces a return that fairly compensates the shareholders for the nature of risks it bears from investing in Airways.[98]

Table 11.1

Comparison of EVA, Conventional Profit (Profit), and Operating Cash Flows (CFO) (in $000)

Year	NOPAT*	Capital charge	EVA	Profit (loss)	CFO	Dividends paid
2003	10,225	7,703	2,522	7,116	16,564	6,000
2002	9,593	7,019	2,754	7,504	19,150	8,000
2001	8,846	6,866	1,980	4,579	20,837	5,000
2000	7,379	5,989	1,390	8,749	17,235	6,000
1999	3,512	7,030	(3,518)	7,445	14,383	1,500
1998	6,478	8,077	(1,599)	(1,317)	16,483	3,800
1997	4,056	9,138	(5,082)	(137)	16,581	6,000
1996	3,997	9,140	(5,143)	848	12,979	11,175

*Net Operating Profit After Tax.

This adoption of EVA to provide limitations on earnings and wealth creation for monopoly-owned assets and investments was a unique application of the EVA methodology, which normally provides criteria for the maximization of wealth. ACNZ produced the EVA information as additional supplements to the conventional financial reports. Table 11.1 compares the EVA measures with the conventional profit and cash flow information for the period 1995–2003. In each of these years the conventional accounting profit exceeded the EVA measure. In loss periods the accounting loss was less than the corresponding EVA deficit. Both EVA and the conventional accounting profit are accrual measures. The cash from operating activities (CFO) is free from accounting accruals and was always positive in the period under consideration and well able to support the dividend payments shown.

THE EVA METHODOLOGY

EVA calculates a form of "economic profit" that indicates whether the firm has covered all its expenses, including the economic cost of supplying equity funds, as the latter are excluded in the conventional measure of profit. If the dollar value of the weighted cost of capital is split into its two constituent costs (debt and equity), the general format can be shown as Table 11.2.

Alternatively, EVA can be expressed as: NOPAT – (WACC × capital employed), where the WACC (weighted average cost of capital) is expressed as a percentage cost, specifically the average of the costs of both the debt and equity in proportion to the funds used. The NOPAT (net operating profits after taxes) excludes all financing costs and requires adjustments to the conventional accounting profit[99] for items like:

- reserves and provisions, which are reversed because they obscure the timing of actual cash receipts and payments;
- the deferred tax provision, which is adjusted to reflect the tax actually paid;

Table 11.2

The General Format of the EVA Profit and Loss Account

Net operating profit after tax (NOPAT)		xxxxxx
Less weighted average cost of capital (WACC):		
Cost of debt	xxxxx	
Cost of equity	xxxxx	xxxxxx
Equals economic value added		xxxxxx

- extraordinary items, that is NOPAT is calculated on a normalized basis;
- interest income and expense, which are added back to arrive at the NOPAT;
- imputed interest expenses on operating leases which are included in income: the operating leases are capitalized like finance leases (similarly, research and development expenses are capitalized and form part of the operating assets); and
- taxation, which is adjusted to exclude financing effects.

In calculating WACC, the interest cost comprises the expense actually paid during the period and a treasury gain or loss, which is the difference between the opportunity cost of interest included in the cost of capital and the actual interest paid. The equity cost is the imputed charge for the equity funds employed, as these costs would not appear in the conventional accounting profit and loss account. Specifically, the cost of capital is calculated using the capital asset pricing model, the form of which used by ACNZ is:

Cost of capital = risk free return after tax + business risk premium = (insert eq here)

$$R_f \times (1-T_d) + B_u \times R_m$$

where

R_f = the risk-free rate, being the rate on five-year government securities
T_d = the corporate tax rate, that is, 33 percent
B_u = the asset beta, representing an assessment of the risk attached to the operating assets of the business. Successive annual reports state that "Airways monopoly activity is considered a low risk" and asset betas are low, ranging between 0.30 and 0.32 in the years 1995–2003.
R_m = the market risk premium. ACNZ used 8 percent for years up to 2000 and 9 percent for subsequent years.

ACNZ takes the view that the cost of capital is derived from the risks associated with the operations (assets) of the business and is not affected by the financial gearing of the company. In the model used, the cost of equity funds will rise with the increased use of debt funds, but the weighted cost of capital remains constant. When calculated, the WACC is applied to the assets, which generate the profits. This "operating capital" is made up of fixed assets and current assets less short-term debt. The assets are adjusted to include such items as capitalized operating leases and research and development expenses. The adjusted assets are considered to be carried at their "economic" values. Normally this is not the market value of the assets, which is a better base on which to calculate the capital charge.[100] For ACNZ, the nature of the assets means that the difference between the economic value and market values of the assets is minimal.

The resultant EVA, that is NOPAT less the capital charge, is an economic profit in the sense that it allows for the recovery of the full cost of financing. Table 11.3 shows the average operating capital and the cost of capital in both percentage and dollar terms for the years 1995–2003. The operating capital fell for the period until 2000 as technological developments reduced the cost of replacing and expanding the corporation's productive capacity. After 2000 rapid expansion has raised the level of assets.

EQUIVALENCE OF EVA AND NET PRESENT VALUES

Because ACNZ adopted EVA as a benchmark to manage the firm's value and to control its pricing policy, the legitimacy of the approach as a determinant of the firm's value needs to be established. Most accepted valuation methodologies use the techniques of net present value (NPV), which discounts the future benefits to be generated by the firm and compares the result with the present value of the assets. In practical terms, the calculation of EVA is similar to the flows prepared for a NPV exercise, that is, the annual flows are calculated before financing costs. The action of discounting effectively adjusts for the cost of funds. A positive result indicates that the present value of the future benefits exceed the costs of the assets generating the benefits. Thus the correct use of EVA for benchmarking and planning has the same effect on the value of the firm as discounted cash flow valuation using the net present value (NPV) approach. Maximizing the present value of EVA should maximize the value of the firm in the same way as maximizing NPV. The equivalence of the two methodologies is important because they both lead to the same value for the firm.[101] An expanded explanation of the equivalence of the two approaches is included in the appendix. If the firm's policy was to maximize the present value of future economic value added, this would be equivalent to maximizing the firm's value by accepting projects with the highest (risk adjusted) net present values.[102] Likewise, if a firm (as in this study) adopted a policy of achieving zero net present values for its existing and future projects, this could be paralleled by an appropriate present value of economic value added policy. The advantage of the EVA approach is that the adjustments necessary are more transparent as they are seen in the EVA financial statements.

THE USE OF EVA IN ACNZ ACCOUNTS

In the EVA financial statements of ACNZ, the funds of the corporation are divided between operating capital, which finances operating assets (see Table 11.3), which in turn generate the NOPAT, and nonoperating capital, which consists of work in progress

Table 11.3

Operating Capital and Cost of Capital, 1995–2003

Year	Averaging operating capital ($ million)	Weighted average cost of capital (%)	Weighted average cost of capital ($ million)
1995	121.41	8.07	7.70
1996	115.59	7.91	7.70
1997	104.76	8.72	9.14
1998	97.26	8.30	8.08
1999	91.30	7.70	7.03
2000	86.54	6.92	7.99
2001	95.96	7.16	6.87
2002	102.37	6.86	7.02
2003	111.55	6.91	7.70

and other assets. The weighted average cost of the funds relating to operating capital is deducted from the NOPAT. As noted, this charge covers the imputed costs of the equity and debt used to finance the operating capital. Any surplus after this financing charge is economic profit or EVA.

Before commencing the supplementary EVA accounts in 1995, a series of calculations was made to derive the annual EVA for the seven years starting in 1988 and ending in 1994. The idea was to show the surplus monopoly profits accumulated in the period before the adoption of EVA accounting in 1995. Table 11.4 shows this series, which ended with a $6.6 million accumulated EVA reserve in 1994.

From 1995 onward that part of the annual EVA generated by monopoly assets was added to the EVA reserve and a deficit EVA for the year was deducted. The intention was to reduce this reserve to zero in succeeding years by transferring planned annual deficit EVA to the reserve. The deficits arose from the reduced revenues charged for the corporation's monopoly activities by way of discounts and reduced prices for services. Clearly it is hard to adjust the prices and services to obtain a smooth change to the reserve balance. This difficulty was recognized:

> It is not practical to achieve EVA = 0 on an annual basis due to the difficulty in accurately forecasting the volume and mix of aircraft movements on which to generate the appropriate level of revenue. Airways' objective is therefore to achieve EVA = 0 over a three-year period.[103]

In contrast to the attempt to eliminate surplus EVA from monopoly activities, that part of annual EVA generated by the nonmonopolistic competitive "other business" is transferred to equity and is available for distribution. The intention is to maximize this part of EVA. The general format of the EVA profit and loss account shown earlier can be expanded as shown in Table 11.5.

Table 11.3 shows the total charge on operating capital.[104] Only this charge is offset against the NOPAT. Table 11.6 shows the monopoly portions of successive annual EVA, which were offset against the EVA reserve. The EVA reserve was kept separate from the other equity items until 1999 and is not disclosed after that date.

Table 11.4

Cumulative EVA 1998–1994, Calculated to Provide the EVA Reserve Account Balance

	1994	1993	1992	1991	1990	1989	1988
Air traffic services	11.1	14.6	8.5	3.8	6.0	(4.6)	20.6
Other business	2.7	3.3	(2.2)	(2.1)	(1.5)	0.4	0.6
NOPAT	13.8	17.9	6.3	1.7	4.5	(4.2)	21.2
Less cost of capital	10.1	11.0	10.1	5.6	5.3	4.9	7.6
Annual EVA	3.7	6.9	(3.8)	(3.9)	(0.8)	(9.1)	13.6
Cumulative EVA	6.6	2.9	(4.0)	(0.2)	3.7	4.5	13.6
Made up of:	5.3	4.4	0.8	2.4	4.2	3.5	13.0
Air traffic services	1.3	(1.5)	(4.8)	(2.6)	(0.5)	1.0	0.6
Other business	6.6	2.9	(4.00	(0.2)	3.7	4.5	13.6

Table 11.5

The Expanded General Format of the EVA Profit and Loss Account

Net operating profit after tax	xxxx
Less weighted average cost of capital	xxxx
Economic value added	xxxx
Transferred:	
Monopoly portion to EVA reserve	(xxxx)
Non-monopoly portion to general equity	(xxxx)
Balance	Nil

DISCUSSION

The extent to which in the absence of suitable external comparators the internal benchmarking the financial performance to EVA was successful is in part illustrated by how well ACNZ attained its objectives of avoiding price controls and achieving financial stability. Certainly, price controls have been avoided. This contrasts with other former government operations in New Zealand that have been privatized, for example airports and port companies, both groups of which have been strongly threatened with price controls. Others, like electricity distributors, have been subjected to price regulation. The role of EVA in managing prices of services and profits is measured by the changes in the balance of the EVA reserve account, which is shown in Table 11.6.

The movement of the reserve followed the desired direction, that is, it fell in the period 1995–1999. In 1998–2000 the reserve has had negative balances. On this criterion ACNZ has achieved its goal of controlling prices and returning to its customers the surplus monopoly EVA balances accumulated up to 1995. The EVA reserve balance was reduced from $9,194,000 to $557,000 in the three-year period 1995–1997 and from $730,000 to $58,000 in the period 1998–2000. After this period the reserve is no longer disclosed. Thus, the pricing policy of ACNZ was adjusted to earn an economic profit sufficient to ensure its survival without facing charges of overpricing.

When the accumulated EVA reserve was effectively returned to its customers,

Table 11.6

Opening and Closing Balances of the EVA Reserve Account, 1995–2000 ($000)

	Opening balance of EVA reserve	EVA from monopoly ANS services	Charge on EVA reserve[a]	Closing balance of EVA reserve
2000	(2,126)	2,068	—	(58)
1999	(730)	(1,396)	—	(2,126)
1998	557	(1,491)	204	(730)
1997	4,836	(4,817)	538	557
1996	9,194	(4,908)	550	4,836
1995	6,314	2,256	624	9,194

Note: In 1999 the EVA reserve was transferred to the general equity account and is no longer disclosed. The figures for 2000 have been derived from the financial statements.

[a]The charge on the EVA reserve is made because the EVA reserve is part of the equity funds financing the assets.

ACNZ dropped the "zero EVA" policy but continued to use its EVA results as a benchmark for pricing services. In 2001 a "partnership plan" was started, one of the main provisions of which was a framework for consulting with customers on pricing policy and providing rebates if the corporation's EVA is positive. Over 2 percent of gross revenues for the years 2001–2003 have been rebated.

The success of the pricing and financial policies of ACNZ has been recognized by the International Air Transport Association (IATA). ACNZ was one of three (out of 180) air navigation service providers to win the 2003 IATA Eagle Award. The awards are given to ANS providers who, apart from following the policies on charges established by the International Civil Aviation Organization (ICAO), have good performance records and make measurable efforts to contain costs and pass on the savings to customers. The citation speech lauded ACNZ as "one of the best [ANS providers] in the world." ACNZ was also named the 1993 New Zealand Services Exporter of the Year for its success in international markets. The corporation increased its annual foreign exchange earnings from $6 million in 2000 to $12 million in 2002 and 2003.

After withdrawing the EVA = 0 policy ACNZ adopted a policy of producing, generating positive EVA from its monopoly activities, similar to its nonmonopoly activities, which were never subject to a minimization constraint. This change in policy is contingent on the requirement to provide rebates when EVA is positive. In the 1998 Annual Report the performance objectives include a goal to "provide a return to the shareholder that is not less than the cost of equity capital."[105] The 2000 annual report refers to generating "impressive returns" for the shareholders and comments on achieving sizeable increases in EVA.

There are a number of reasons for this change in emphasis. First, aerodrome services were deregulated in 1997 and in response, location-specific pricing was introduced that same year. The deregulation introduced the possibility of competition in the supply of ANS services, though none has yet emerged.

Second, full privatization was possible. The 1999 Annual Report states: "governments will increasingly choose to exit the business of providing ANS and new, private sector investors will be entering the industry."[106]

A move toward full privatization would mean that retaining a policy of minimal EVA could lower the potential sale value of the corporation. A potential buyer would ignore the restriction, but a valuation using past profits as an input would be made more difficult and uncertain. Current government policy means that full privatization is not an issue in the immediate future.

Third, as ACNZ has become a mature successful operator, the constraints of the original SOE model have become more apparent. The government shareholder needs the dividends from the SOE, but has been concerned by the overly commercial activities that generate the corporation's income. Without major legislative changes it would appear difficult to change the statement of corporate intent to reconcile the need to be as commercially efficient as possible and to be socially responsible. One witness at a UK House of Commons Select Committee stated that the New Zealand SOE model "was never designed to last as long as this. It is creaking a wee bit. It asks a lot of ministers . . . it was not seen necessarily as a structure that would last ten or eleven years."[107]

As ACNZ develops it appears necessary to either become increasingly attached to government policy or become more independent, that is fully privatized.

In addition, there are a number of technical and measurement issues that impact on the validity of the EVA results obtained. First, the calculation of EVA includes the measurement of the assets in place at their economic value, but this is affected by prior accounting choices. Some authorities, for example De Villiers, suggest using the current value of the assets, and Bacidore and co-authors propose that the market values of the assets will substantially reduce the level of error.[108] Airways Corporation restates its operating assets to economic value in its EVA supplementary accounts. The difference between economic and market values is small and any distortions arising from differing asset values are not significant.

Second, there are difficulties in the calculation of the cost of capital. The selection of the asset beta (ranging 0.30–0.32) in each year of operation is not explained in the calculations used by ACNZ. Further, the cost of capital in most discounted cash-flow valuations assumes that the market values of debt and equity are used for weighting purposes. If future expansion assumes that the market mix of funds will be used, then EVA should be calculated using market values to determine the weighted average cost of capital. The EVA calculations appear to have been adjusted for market values in the ACNZ financial statements. There are some conceptual difficulties in this area and these issues are discussed by De Villiers and Dodd and Chen.[109] However, it is probable that, given ACNZ's relatively straightforward calculations of the cost of capital, the significance of errors from this source is also minimal.

CONCLUSION

The adoption of EVA as a method of benchmarking performance and controlling monopoly earnings has been a successful strategy for ACNZ. The initial approach focused on an EVA reserve in which excess monopoly profits were transferred to a reserve and managed. The reserve was eventually exhausted.

Changes in the environment in which Airways Corporation operates, with possible competition in its previous monopoly activities, shareholder demands (the government) for larger dividends, and possible future privatization have led to a change from minimizing EVA to using EVA as a general guide to pricing and other policies. This "economic income" approach differs from the conventional control mechanisms of direct price control or limitations on the return on assets. This does not detract from the use of the approach as a valid way of establishing prices and controlling monopoly profits for firms like ACNZ, with a clearly defined asset base, uncomplicated sources of funding, and reasonably predictable revenue streams.

CASE DISCUSSION QUESTIONS

1. Why is the adoption of economic value added (EVA) income appropriate as a benchmark for setting pricing and other policies for a state-owned enterprise in the absence of normal benchmarking mechanisms?
2. Please explain the following statement: "By earning zero economic value added profits the enterprise earns its cost of capital and escapes claims of monopolistic pricing and possible regulation."
3. The case provides evidence that the enterprise was successful in avoiding charges of monopolistic pricing and subsequent regulation by linking pricing and other policies to its economic results. To what extent can the success of benchmarking using economic value added be generalized for other firms and environments?
4. The case was used to illustrate the objective of minimizing economic income, rather than the traditional goal of maximizing income. What are some limitations of this approach?

APPENDIX TO THE ACNZ CASE

This appendix provides a guide to the equivalence of EVA and the widely accepted net present value (NPV) approach to the valuation of the corporation.[110] Evidence of the equivalence of the two approaches provides credibility to any attempts to use EVA as a determinant of pricing and valuation policies.

Assume that a project (or group of assets) has a life of n years with zero salvage value at the end of the project's life. The NPV equation can be written:[111]

$$NPVj = \sum_{t=1}^{t=n} \frac{ROC\,(Initial\,Investment)}{(1+WACC)^t} - \sum_{t=1}^{t=n} \frac{WACC\,(Initial\,Investment)}{(1+WACC)^t}$$

$$NPVj = \sum_{t=1}^{t=n} \frac{ROC\,(initial\,investment)}{(1+WACC)^t} - \sum_{t=1}^{t=n} \frac{WACC\,(initial\,investment)}{(1+WACC)^t}$$

Where ROC = return on capital and WACC = the weighted average cost of capital. ROC = EBIT($1-t$)/initial investment.

Where EBIT = earnings before interest and tax. Multiplying by the expression ($1-t$), (where t = the tax rate) gives the after-tax earnings before interest.

EBIT is adjusted to exclude the "capital" charges of lease payments and excludes any items like R&D, which produce benefits in the future.

As EVA = (ROC − WACC) (initial investment), this expression can be substituted into the above equation to reconfigure the NPV equation as follows:

$$NPVj = \sum_{t=1}^{t=n} \frac{(ROC - WACC)\,(Initial\ Investment)}{(1+WACC)^t} = \sum_{t=1}^{t=n} \frac{EVA}{(1+WACC)^t}$$

EVA assumes that the present value of depreciation covers (equals) the present value of the initial investment, that is, depreciation is treated as a return on capital.

Alternatively, the value of the firm (V) can be written as: V = value of assets in place + value of future growth; or V = (investment in existing assets + NPV assets in place) + NPV of all future projects; or V = (1 + NPV assets in place) + $\Sigma\ i = 1\ i = N\ NVPi$.

In EVA terms this is expressed as: V = capital invested + PV of EVA from existing projects + PV of EVA from future projects.

NOTES FOR CHAPTER 11

1. Patrick M. Reilly, "Woolworth Investigates 'Irregularities,' Will Restate Fiscal-Year Interim Results," *Wall Street Journal*, March 31, 1994, p. A3; Stephanie Strom, "Woolworth's Treasurer Blew Whistle," *New York Times*, May 20, 1994.

2. Reilly, "Woolworth Investigates 'Irregularities.'"

3. Timothy O'Brien and Laura Bird, "Woolworth's Board Is Said to Force Resignation of Chief Executive Lavin," *Wall Street Journal*, October 3, 1994, p. B4.

4. Reilly, "Woolworth Investigates 'Irregularities,'" and Reilly, "Woolworth Restates Quarterly Results for Latest Year but Maintains Dividend," *Wall Street Journal*, April 14, 1994, p. A3.

5. Reilly, "Woolworth Investigates 'Irregularities.'"

6. Reilly, "Woolworth Restates Quarterly Results."

7. O'Brien and Bird, "Woolworth's Board Is Said to Force Resignation of Chief Executive Lavin."

8. Martin S. Fridson, *Financial Statement Analysis: A Practitioner's Guide* (New York: John Wiley & Sons, 1996), pp. 3–4.

9. See Lawrence Revsine, Daniel W. Collins, and W. Bruce Johnson, *Financial Reporting and Analysis* (Upper Saddle River, NJ: Prentice Hall, 2001); Robert C. Higgins, *Analysis for Financial Management*, 5th ed. (New York: McGraw-Hill, 1998); and Fridson, *Financial Statement Analysis*.

10. See Roman L. Weil, *Accounting: The Language of Business*, 10th ed. (Glen Ridge, NJ: Thomas Horton & Daughters, 1999).

11. See "Qualitative Characteristics of Accounting Information," *Statement of Financial Accounting Concepts No. 2* (Stamford, CT: FASB, 1980).

12. In view of the highly technical nature of the information, this section is excerpted from Revsine, Collins, and Johnson, *Financial Reporting and Analysis*, pp. 15–16, with permission.

13. Ibid., p. 16.

14. Ibid., p. 16. A technical definition of "conservatism" is suggested in Ross L. Watts, "Conservatism

in Accounting—Part I: Explanations and Implications" (May 16, 2003), Simon School of Business Working Paper No. FR 03-16, Social Science Research Network, Massachusetts Institute of Technology. Conservatism is defined as the differential verifiability required for recognition of profits versus losses. Its extreme form is the traditional conservative adage: "anticipate no profit, but anticipate all losses." We thank Professor John O'Shaughnessy for pointing this out.

15. Excerpted with permission from Robert Ingram and Bruce Baldwin, *Financial Accounting*, 3d ed. (Cincinnati, OH: South-Western Publishing Company, 1998), p. 172.

16. In view of the technical language and for precision, we have excerpted these eight categories from Ingram and Baldwin, *Financial Accounting*, pp. 181–85, with permission.

17. We are grateful to Professor Joe Messina for pointing this out.

18. Fridson, *Financial Statement Analysis: A Practitioner's Guide*, p. 29.

19. The "fair market value problem" is widely recognized by accountants, as well as GAAP conventions. This section draws heavily from Robert C. Higgins, *Analysis for Financial Management,* pp. 21–27; also see page 318 on the requirements of a "fair market value."

20. The definition and intended audiences are excerpted with permission from Robert Ingram and Bruce Baldwin, *Financial Accounting* (Cincinnati, OH: Southwestern Publishing Company, 1998), p. 172.

21. In view of the technical language and for precision, we have excerpted these three categories from Ingram and Baldwin, *Financial Accounting*, pp. 175–77, with permission.

22. Fridson, *Financial Statement Analysis*, p. 68.

23. Analogy is from ibid.

24. Excerpted with permission from Ingram and Baldwin, *Financial Accounting*, p. 172.

25. In view of the technical language and for precision, we have excerpted these three categories from Ingram and Baldwin, *Financial Accounting*, pp. 184–85, with permission.

26. Free cash flow can be estimated as cash flow less capital expenditures. This is regarded as cash resources available at the discretion of management. Although its calculation is not as straightforward, it has also been called "organic growth," or the basis for a firm's future growth.

27. See Fridson, *Financial Statement Analysis*, pp. 110–11, for an excellent example as to why cash flow, not reported income, is a better basis for evaluating the downside of leveraged buyouts.

28. We are using "value added" in a broader context in this section. It is not to be confused with the accepted definition that it is the difference between a firm's output and its inputs.

29. Based on a lecture by Professor Gene Johnson, University of Rhode Island, MDRG Training Seminars, 1999–2000. He particularly recommended the use of PVA (People Value Added).

30. Because financial ratios are relatively simple, their use is occasionally discouraged. While we acknowledge the limitations of this analysis, we think that they are useful in depicting patterns when done in tandem with other information. Also, see Higgins, *Analysis for Financial Management*, p. 59 and pp. 61–62 on how to use financial ratios.

31. An excellent analysis of Wal-Mart is developed by Stephen F. Jablonsky and Noah P. Barsky, *The Manager's Guide to Financial Statement Analysis* (New York: John Wiley & Sons, 2001). The authors present one of the most comprehensive analyses of Wal-Mart's financial performance in developing their strategic profit model. We encourage readers to read the book in order to appreciate the power of their analysis. We use their analysis of Wal-Mart's financial ratios in this chapter in specified passages of this chapter.

32. To retain the technical meaning of the ratios discussed in this section, we have occasionally excerpted or closely paraphrased them based on Higgins, *Analysis for Financial Management*, pp. 38–60.

33. Jablonsky and Barsky, *The Manager's Guide to Financial Statement Analysis*, pp. 13–14.

34. This analysis is from Jablonsky and Barsky, *The Manager's Guide to Financial Statement Analysis*, p. 14.

35. Partly paraphrased from Higgins, *Analysis for Financial Management*, p. 41.

36. This analysis is from Jablonsky and Barsky, *The Manager's Guide to Financial Statement Analysis*, p. 21.

37. Partly paraphrased from Higgins, *Analysis for Financial Management*, p. 40.

38. This analysis is from Jablonsky and Barsky, *The Manager's Guide to Financial Statement Analysis*, p. 22.

39. Higgins, *Analysis for Financial Management*, pp. 41–42.

40. Ibid., pp. 42–43.

41. See Jablonsky and Barsky, *The Manager's Guide to Financial Statement Analysis*, pp. 49–50.

42. Ibid., p. 47.

43. See Higgins, *Analysis for Financial Management*, p. 45.

44. This analysis is from Jablonsky and Barsky, *The Manager's Guide to Financial Statement Analysis*, p. 76.

45. See Higgins, *Analysis for Financial Management*, p. 46.

46. We note that for many manufacturing firms with large amounts of fixed assets, the depreciation expense, which is usually also large, is recorded as part of cost of goods sold. Depreciation expense is usually not shown as a line item on the income statement, but it is part of cost of goods sold and revealed in a footnote. One can also find depreciation expense in the statement of cash flows as part of operating inflows. We thank Professor Messina for this note.

47. This analysis is from Jablonsky and Barsky, *The Manager's Guide to Financial Statement Analysis*, p. 54.

48. See Higgins, *Analysis for Financial Management*, pp. 46–47.

49. This analysis is from Jablonsky and Barsky, *The Manager's Guide to Financial Statement Analysis*, p. 72.

50. Paraphrased slightly from Higgins, *Analysis for Financial Management*, p. 51.

51. Paraphrased slightly from ibid., p. 53.

52. This section draws largely from ibid., pp. 38–39.

53. Paraphrased slightly from ibid., p. 40. This entire section is based on Higgins' analysis.

54. Ibid., pp. 46–47.

55. R. D. Buzzell and B. T. Gale, *The PIMS Principles: Linking Strategy to Performance* (New York: Free Press, 1987).

56. Ibid.

57. Ibid.

58. Higgins, *Analysis for Financial Management*, pp. 53–55.

59. Ibid., p. 54.

60. Ibid. In the RONA equation, the interest on accounts payable is not included. Any interest that is not tax deductible usually plays no role in valuation calculations, per the Modigliani and Miller valuation approach. Because RONA is one of the performance or valuation-related equations, accounts payable interest is typically not included. However, when evaluating strategic decisions such as long-run capital structure, specifically trade credit for retail businesses, accounts payable balances are sometimes included in leverage ratio considerations. We thank Professor Joe Messina for pointing this out.

61. This analysis is drawn from Jablonsky and Barsky, *The Manager's Guide to Financial Statement Analysis*, p. 81.

62. Ibid., p. 141.

63. See Higgins, *Analysis for Financial Management*, p. 57.

64. Ibid.

65. Shawn Tully, "The Real Key to Creating Wealth," *Fortune*, September 20, 1993, p. 38. For a historical background of EVA, see Joel M. Stern and John Shiely, *The EVA Challenge: Implementing Value-Added Change in an Organization* (New York: John Wiley & Sons, 2001).

66. Stephen Taub, "MVPs of MVA: Which Companies Created the Most Wealth for Shareholders Last Year? Enter MVA—or Market Value Added," *CFO Magazine*, July 1, 2003.

67. This analysis is drawn largely from Higgins, *Analysis for Financial Management*, p. 301. He extends the discussion of EVA from a measure to a management tool, such as discouraging myopic

tendencies and making middle managers operate as if they were owners, at which case, they assume the risk.

68. Market value added was also advanced by Stern Stewart & Co. It is the difference between the market value of the company and investment in it over the years. The following passage clarifies its specific computation: "To determine market value, equity is taken at the market price on the date the calculation was made, and debt at the book value. The total investment in the company since day one is then calculated—interest bearing debt and equity, including retained earnings. Present market value is then compared with total investment . . . If the latter is greater than the former, the company has created wealth. If not, it has destroyed wealth . . . Recently, MVA has also been called Management Value Added because it is the value added to net assets for which management is held accountable." Excerpted from Stern and Shiely, *The EVA Challenge: Implementing Value-Added Change in an Organization,* p. 16.

69. Stephen Taub, "MVPs of MVA: Which Companies Created the Most Wealth for Shareholders Last Year? Enter MVA—or Market Value Added," *CFO Magazine.*

70. The diagram builds on an alternative method of calculating EVA, one that is acknowledged in standard finance textbooks. We are also grateful to Professor Emeritus George Racette, University of Oregon, for his notes in this regard.

71. Taub, "MVPs of MVA". See Higgins, *Analysis for Financial Management*, p. 299, which relates EVA to investment analysis.

72. Fridson, *Financial Statement Analysis*, p. 235.

73. This statement oversimplifies the dividend-distribution decision a bit. Current thinking in finance is that dividends are more accurately explained as a function of the corporate life cycle, as well as signals from management to investors. Specifically, during the startup phase, a firm is expected to have a small cash flow to justify dividend payouts. During the high-growth phase, all cash flows are reinvested back into the business in order to support growth that is in accordance with the best interests of stockholders. When firms reach maturity, however, the need for internal funds subsides and firms are then considered to be safe enough to warrant substantial levels of debt financing. The commencement of a cash dividend is usually a signal that a firm has reached a degree of maturity and profitability, and that long-term growth will be slower. Once a cash dividend begins, it is usually good practice to follow a nondecreasing pattern, that is, it does not have to increase each year, but should not be decreased. We thank Professor Messina for this note.

74. This section draws on an analysis provided by Higgins, *Analysis for Financial Management*, pp. 119–123. Professor Messina points out, however, that this equation assumes an all-equity firm. While conclusions are the same, the exact formula is: $g^* = [R + (R - Rd)D/E](1 - T)b$, where R = rate of return on assets, Rd = interest rate of firm's debt, D/E is the firm's debt/equity ratio, T = corporate income tax rate, and b = fraction of net income reinvested in assets, $(1 - b)$ = dividend payout ratio. Thus, If $D/E = 0$ and $T = 0$, then $g = Rb$. However, the conclusion is the same. If b goes up then g goes up. If b goes down then g goes down.

75. Sustainable growth rates using historical book values are not particularly useful. Some analysts have substituted expected future rates of return for historical book values.

76. See Allan Afuah, *Business Models: A Strategic Management Approach* (New York: McGraw-Hill, 2004), pp. 212–213.

77. Professor Afuah's analysis is far more descriptive than the one presented in this book. For a detailed account of how the value of a firm is represented by cash flows, including various simplifications that incorporate the Capital Asset Pricing Method (CAPM), see pp. 212–213. Other aspects of the CAPM are detailed in Eugene F. Brigham and Philip Daves, *Intermediate Financial Management,* 8th ed. (Mason, OH: Thomson/South-Western, 2004). For related criticisms of NPV, see Bruce Greenwald, Paul Sonkin and Michael von Biema, *Value Investing: From Graham to Buffett and Beyond* (New York: John Wiley & Sons, Inc., 2004), pp. 32–33. Professor Joe Messina suggests that we specify how cash flows and the discount rate are defined. In this Wal-Mart example, we have assumed an all-equity firm. In such a case, the surrogate for *Rf* depends on the purpose of the evaluation. For example,

if we are evaluating a mutual fund's month-to-month performance over a particular period we usually use the 30-day T-Bill rate; however, when valuing a common stock, a longer-term Treasury security is used. For stocks in today's market, people will usually use the 10-year Treasury bond because it is the longest-term risk-free bond being actively traded. When the 30-year bonds are resumed, then practitioners may change to something longer. If the firm is not levered then the WACC = Re and the CAPM equation provide the correct estimate of the WACC. For a firm in the mature phase of its life cycle, with no indication of decline or termination over the foreseeable future, then the present value formula of the future after tax cash flow simplifies to $V = Co (1 + g)/(R - g)$ (Wal-Mart is probably fine unless its growth rate is abnormally high). Where Co is the most recent after-tax cash flow, $R =$ WACC, g = expected average annual growth rate in cash flows. If $g = 0$, then the value $V = Co/R$ (approximating firms in stagnant industries).

78. Based on the approach recommended by Afuah, *Business Models: A Strategic Management Approach*, pp. 212–213. We used Wal-Mart's figures provided by Professor Afuah on page 214.

79. This entire section draws heavily on the work of Bruce Greenwald and Judd Kahn, *Competition Demystified* (New York: Penguin, 2006), p. 322. We appreciate the guidance by Professor Greenwald in facilitating the inclusion of his work. In a correspondence with Professor Greenwald, he has discussed some important qualifications to his model, which he is addressing in a revision.

80. See Greenwald, Sonkin, and von Biema, *Value Investing: From Graham to Buffett and Beyond*, where an application of this model to the Intel Corporation, is presented. The case study (pp. 107–137) is particularly recommended for students who like to see an extended application, including the adjustments for determining reproduction costs and the EPV that are discussed in this section.

81. Robert Kaplan and D.P. Norton, "The Balanced Scorecard: Measures That Drive Profitability," *Harvard Business Review* (January/February 1992).

82. Ibid., p. 1.

83. This entire section is cited largely from Revsine, Collins, and Johnson, *Financial Reporting and Analysis*, pp. 22–23.

84. Ibid., p. 22.

85. Ibid., p. 23.

86. Ibid.

87. Ibid.

88. This case was prepared by Lloyd M. Austin, Department of Accounting and Finance, University of Auckland, Auckland, New Zealand. Mr. Austin kindly granted the authors permission to include this case.

89. The term "economic value added" is registered to Stern Stewart, a U.S. consulting firm, and EVA is a registered trademark of Stern Stewart.

90. House of Commons, "UK House of Commons Select Committee on Environment, Transport and Regional Affairs Minutes of Evidence," January 28, 1998.

91. Elliott Sclar and the HDR Management Consulting Group, "Pitfalls of Air Traffic Control Privatization." Report for the National Air Traffic Controllers Association, February 2003.

92. When the organization of ACNZ was being developed, consideration was given to alternatives such as an "airline club" form of ownership, whereby the users of the ANS services to be supplied would control the organization. The potential dominance of a few major airlines mitigated against this format.

93. In 1997, Airservices' status was amended to that of a commercial authority.

94. The shareholders in NATs are British Airways, BMI British Midland, Virgin Atlantic, Britannia, Monarch, EasyJet, and Airtours.

95. S. Penman, *Financial Statement Analysis and Security Valuation*, 2d ed. (New York: McGraw-Hill/Irwin, 2004).

96. Airways Corporation of New Zealand, *Airways Corporation of New Zealand Annual Reports*, 1994, available at: www.airways.co.nz.

97. Benchmarking performance to periodic income is used in other areas; for example, management

bonus schemes are often linked to "the financial statements [which] are used . . . as the benchmark for the firm's performance"; see G. White, A. Sondhi, and D. Fried, *The Analysis and Use of Financial Statements*, 3d ed. (New York: Wiley, 2003), p. 174.

98. Airways Corporation of New Zealand, *Airways Corporation of New Zealand Annual Reports*, 1995, available at: www.airways.co.nz.

99. In fact, Stern Stewart's EVA calculation requires over 250 adjustments to normal accounting statements. Only a small number of these adjustments were relevant for ACNZ and most companies find "no more than 15 are of material significance"; see J. Bacidore, J. Boquist, T. Milbourn, and A. Thakor, "The Search for the Best Financial Performance Measure," *Financial Analysts Journal* 53, no. 3 (1997): 11–20.

100. Bacidore et al., "The Search for the Best Financial Performance Measure."

101. "The mathematical equivalence is achieved because the EVA formula is a modified version of a standard DCF formula within a mathematical construct in which all the adjustment in the EVA formula to the DCF must result net to zero. The result of this construct is that it does not matter what beginning capital base is used in an EVA valuation—the result value will always be zero." See M. Storrie and D. Sinclair, "Is EVA™ Equivalent to DCF?" *CPS Accair Global Review* 3, no. 5 (1997): 5–6.

102. In a few circumstances, maximizing EVA may lower the firm's value, if the higher EVA increases risk and lowers the present value of the future benefits. Similarly, if the increase in the year-to-year EVA has been achieved by decreasing future year's EVA, total firm value may fall.

103. Airways Corporation of New Zealand, *Airways Corporation of New Zealand Annual Reports*, 1997, p. 19, available at: www.airways.co.nz.

104. The corporation's balance date was March 31 up to the year ending March 31, 1992. The balance date was changed to June 30 in the 1993 year.

105. Airways Corporation of New Zealand, *Airways Corporation of New Zealand Annual Reports*, 1998, p. 18, available at: www.airways.co.nz.

106. Airways Corporation of New Zealand, *Airways Corporation of New Zealand Annual Reports*, 1999, p. 17, available at: www.airways.co.nz.

107. HOC, "UK House of Commons Select Committee on Environment, Transport and Regional Affairs Minutes of Evidence."

108. J. de Villiers, "The Distortions in Economic Value Added Caused by Inflation," *Journal of Economics and Business* 49, no. 3 (1997): 285–300; Bacidore et al., "The Search for the Best Financial Performance Measure."

109. de Villiers, "The Distortions in Economic Value Added"; J. Dodd and S. Chen, "EVA: A New Panacea?" *Business and Economic Review* 42 (1996): 26–28.

110. The appendix to the case is from *Benchmarking: An International Journal* 12, no. 2 (2005): 138–150.

111. This explanation follows A. Damodaran, *Damodaran on Valuation: Security Analysis for Investment and Corporate Finance* (New York: John Wiley & Sons, 1994); and Storrie and Sinclair, "Is EVA™ Equivalent to DCF?"

PART I: THE GLOBAL CONTEXT

1. Global Strategic Management: An Overview

PART II: EXTERNAL / INTERNAL ANALYSIS

2. Analyzing the External Environment
3. Formulating Strategy and Developing a Business Model

PART III: STRATEGIC CHOICE AND POSITIONING

4. Positioning Strategic Choices in a Global Context

PART IV: LEVERAGING COMPETITIVE ADVANTAGE

5. Leveraging Advantage Through Global Marketing
6. Leveraging Advantage Through Global Sourcing
7. Leveraging Competitive Advantage Through Strategic Alliances
8. Leveraging Advantage Through Innovation

PART V: IMPLEMENTING THE STRATEGIC PLAN

9. Implementing Strategy Using Structures and Processes
10. Implementing Strategy by Cultivating a Global Mindset
11. Implementing Strategy Using Financial Performance Measures

PART VI: INTEGRATION

12. Integration and Emerging Issues in Global Strategic Management

12 Integration and Emerging Issues in Global Strategic Management

> *If you don't know where you are going, any road will take you there. . . .*
> —Lewis Carroll, English author and recreational mathematician (1832–1898)

> *Now,* here, *you see, it takes all the running you can do, to keep in the same place. . . .*
> —Red Queen to Alice, in Lewis Carroll's Through the Looking Glass

CHAPTER OUTLINE

- Objectives
- A Case Study: Can Strategy Save Argosis?
- Reviewing the Global Strategic Management (GSM) Framework
- Exploring Future Trends and Directions

LEARNING OBJECTIVES

- To review and apply global strategic management to Argosis.
- To understand future trends and directions as a global managers.

OBJECTIVES

The objectives of this final chapter are twofold: first, we offer an opportunity to integrate the concepts, tools, and frameworks provided in this book in terms of a case study; and, second, we explore some emerging trends and developments in strategic thinking and global management as they affect our framework for global strategic management. Why a case study? While the format for a case study was inspired elsewhere, the facts and events are based partly on the experiences of various organizations that we have worked with over the past years.[1] The case weaves various frameworks and analytical tools developed in our different chapters into an integrated learning experience. To the second point, it is customary for readers to expect discussion of emerging trends, and to assess how these relate to the framework we developed throughout this book. This section affords another occasion to weave together seemingly disparate themes to build a case that these are part of an integral whole of challenges and opportunities for the international manager.

A CASE STUDY: CAN STRATEGY SAVE ARGOSIS?

Note: Our fictional Sarah Hughes might be you in the distant future. As you read this case, place yourself in Sarah's shoes and see if you can follow her analysis.

Sarah Hughes had just settled into her new office, small by the usual standards, but highly functional. It was a tough recruiting season. For a while, she feared that the continuing outsourcing of jobs to Asia might drastically limit her job prospects, but she was wrong, and delightfully so. Global Strategy Associates, a newcomer in strategy consultancy services, offered her a nice job, a superb salary plus additional incentives, perks, and benefits, her own office in Palo Alto, and even her own parking space.

Even so, Sarah's thoughts were focused on a written assignment that she needed to submit in less than forty-eight hours. As she prepared her report, she reflected on events over the past three months that had led to this assignment.

THE ASSIGNMENT

Her new boss, Tegan, who had approached her on a warm and sunny morning, came straight to the point. "We hired you because you had superb training at your university and this project suits you well. Another consultant wanted the assignment, but I thought of you ever since you showed me your project for a global strategy class."

Realizing Tegan's high expectations, Sarah's anxiety began to rise. Nevertheless, she knew that with excellent work, she could leverage this project toward an early promotion. "So what is this assignment?" she inquired.

"Well, Argosis, a repeat client, has a problem. The immediate concern is that sales are up, profits hardly go up, and ROI [return on investment] keeps slipping. The firm also wants to develop a global presence, but does not know how to do it. It seems like a straightforward case. But you should go and talk to the firm yourself for the details. The CEO's name is Phil."

THE FIRST VISIT

Argosis was a relatively new startup in the last five years, but already one with a growing reputation for its innovativeness. The firm pioneered a technological breakthrough—the ability to provide customized and personalized vitamins and dietary supplements to customers. At its core was a tremendous increase in variety and customization for customers at relatively affordable prices—**mass customization**.[2] Much of its current success is based on prior breakthroughs in genomic research and nanotechnology (see Box 12.1). Based on these breakthroughs, mass customization for personalized medicine with extensions to dietary supplements had come a long way. To illustrate, in the past, an individual with needs for vitamins A, E, C, D, and zinc, for example, had to rely on standard "one size fits all" multivitamins—products

Box 12.1

Personalized Medicine: A Dream Realized

Argosis's breakthrough in customized dietary supplements is an example of recent successes in personalized medicine thanks to nanotechnology. Personalized medicine provides the capability of specifically tailoring or customizing treatments for individual to patients. Advances in personalized medicine are the result of a better understanding of genomics (the sequencing of the DNA of a set of chromosomes), to the point that a precise drug and dosage can be formulated and administered to meet each patient's individual needs (also see Box 9.2, "How New Strategies Can Change Implementation in the Pharmaceutical Industry"). This would not have been possible without nanotechnology, the new science of anything that can be done at the so-called nanoscale—between 1 and 100 nanometers. A nanometer is a billionth of a meter; a human hair is about 80,000 nanometers wide. With nanotechnology, doctors and scientists will improve their ability to test a patient and formulate a precise dosage based on specific genome patterns (see Chapter 2).

Genomics has its advantages in drug development. It promotes a greater understanding of the human genome, making it is easier to identify those in high-risk categories for certain diseases, and to produce drugs that pinpoint those diseases. For example, Herceptin, a breast cancer drug produced by Genentech, is prescribed for a patient who tests positive for HER2, an unusual gene that can contribute to breast cancer.

Personalized drugs that are developed from nanotechnological applications will be more critical in the United States as the population ages. It is reported that seniors take more than three times the amount compared to others in different age strata. But the application is not confined to pharmaceutical drugs. Within the neutraceutical industry, there are recent reports of the discovery of immune activity at a molecular weight range that are smaller than currently achieved levels. Far from being science fiction, nanotechnology and personalized medicine have the potential to produce revolutionary changes in health care.

Source: Adapted from "Personalized Medicine and Nanotechnology: Trying to Bring Dreams to Market," Knowledge@Wharton (March 7, 2006).

with predetermined amounts of vitamins and dietary supplements. With Argosis' new technology, however, this individual's experience would be entirely different. Depending on the results of a medical checkup, a nutritional test, and a deep knowledge of genomics, Argosis could create this individual's *own* customized supplements based on his/her *own* nutritional needs and profile, not the standard ones from Costco, GNC, or any "over-the-counter" nutritional store. To accentuate this differentiation, the individual's products would even have *his/her* name on it. Moreover, because the vitamins were in powder form (patent approved) that had a smaller molecular size (patent approved), they would be 80 percent more effective than multivitamins in tablet form. When the company placed its IPO a number of years ago, its stock soared and the three founders became instant multi-millionaires. Up to this day, the medical and herbal communities continue to be proponents of this revolutionary product.

But the first meeting between Sarah and Phil was an anxious one. Phil, the CEO, repeated the facts that Tegan had told Sarah earlier: rising sales, declining profits in recent years, falling ROI in recent years. He explained that he was a hands-on manager who had never much time for "all the strategy stuff," but he wanted advice on what might be wrong, and whether it could be fixed. "If I can't explain to Toronto [head office] what's wrong and how to fix it, I'm history," he said. Deep down, Sarah realized that if she could not help him, she might be a casualty herself.

Thinking back to the first steps in any analysis, Sarah recalled that her instructor had advised students to understand the firm's business model and its industry environment. When Sarah mentioned this to Phil, he simply said, "Aw shucks . . . that is typical *consultantese*." Even so, he was willing to try it out. With a gust of confidence, Sarah asked: "Phil, it would help if I knew your mission, product scope, strategy, resources and skills, and your relations with consumers and partners. And that is just the beginning. . . ."

INDUSTRY ANALYSIS AND EXTERNAL ENVIRONMENTAL ASSESSMENT

Phil suggested another meeting with Sarah at a local Starbucks, one close to the newly remodeled Stanford Memorial Stadium at Palo Alto. Sarah then recalled the Starbucks case discussed in one of her classes. If only the real world were this easy, she thought. Compared to Starbucks, Argosis appeared to be quite daunting.

Phil had staggered in with a couple of spreadsheets, barely in control of a café mocha in his other hand. "Wow, I thought for a while that you were full of academic baggage," he started, "but as soon as I did this, I am beginning to understand why you asked for it."

"To begin with, our company mission is simple," he said: "A premier choice for personalized health care products and services." And, he added, "because our firm offers a unique service, we can offer a higher price for our product." As he looked at Sarah for approval, she was already thinking, Argosis had a differentiation strategy. Sarah mused that Michael Porter's framework might actually work after all. Argosis's business model, as described by Phil, is provided in Exhibit 12.1. Argosis's value proposition was likewise developed in order to highlight its distinctiveness from its competitors (see Exhibit 12.2). While Sarah's reaction was favorable at the time, some elements still troubled her. *Are these elements of the business model consistent? Mutually supportive? Sustainable? Why? Why not?*

THE SWOT WORKSHOP

At this juncture, Sarah decided to meet other members of Argosis by conducting an internal SWOT (strengths-weaknesses-threats-opportunities) workshop. She remembered her professor saying that the process of conducting the session could be as valuable as the results themselves. At the time, she did not fully comprehend what he meant.

At a monthly outdoor luncheon on a beautiful afternoon, employees of Argosis, dressed informally in their Friday gear, had congregated outside the company's Palo Alto headquarters. The upbeat *mariachi* band enhanced the festive atmosphere and added to the celebratory occasion. Phil introduced Sarah to much applause. "Boy," she said, "this is one high-spirited, motivated, and enthusiastic group."

Exhibit 12.1

Argosis's Business Model

Core Strategy	Resources	Customers	Partnerships
Mission: "A premier choice for personalized health care products and services."	Assets: Palo Alto (marketing); Toronto (headquarters); Canada/India/Taiwan (manufacturing bases)	Marketing is currently confined to networks ("word-of-mouth")	Doctors: They like the product and recommend it over traditional "over-the-counter" products.
Scope: Currently, the United States and Canada. Plans for Europe and selected parts of Asia are under way.	Competencies: Very strong R&D Firm employs 70 nutritionists, 5 doctors, 5 lobbyists, and 100 product manufacturing specialists	Trial customers were linked to company's doctors and nutritionists. Test results are electronically transmitted to manufacturing for customized parameters.	Herbal communities: Very strong support. Hailed as the rising star in the industry.
Advantage: First mover, pioneer in the area. Good patents. Perceived to be superior to traditional product forms.	Process: Patented manufacturing process that is used in Canada. Asia is a second source for manufacturing.	Marketing utilizes a network covering one million customers, with incentives for repeat purchases.	
Broad differentiation	Patented processes/great human resources	Network marketing	"Complementors"

Exhibit 12.2

Value Proposition, Product Benefits, and End-User Price

Value proposition	Increase the amount of vitamins the body absorbs without having to swallow a pill each day. Customized for each individual.
Product benefits	Increases the amount of vitamins absorbed into the body by up to 65 percent, while providing constant transmission and a comfortable delivery system.
End-user price	$56.00 per bottle (two-month supply)

As expected, the workshop involving about 300 employees (30 percent) was a frank and open discussion. At one point, Phil even offered to leave in order for the comments to be candid, but the group prevailed on him to stay. Sarah was quite impressed by this level of trust. The resulting SWOT report is shown in Exhibit 12.3.

INDUSTRY ANALYSIS: WEEKS 3–4

Sarah had asked Phil to provide her with information for an industry analysis. Not wanting to completely rely on one source (Phil), she decided to call on a number of industry experts (doctors, nutritionists, health care experts, market distribution companies, etc.). Based on all these, Sarah was able to construct a preliminary analysis (see Exhibit 12.4).

Exhibit 12.3

Report from the SWOT Workshop

Strengths	Weaknesses	Opportunities	Threats
• Location (Palo Alto)	• Lack of consumer awareness	• Large market (est. $1.3 trillion)	• Larger and ruthless competitors at low end
• Employees	• Small company size	• Technological expertise and demand in the health care community	• Convergence to low-cost products and services
• Partnerships with medical and herbal communities	• Weak distribution system	• A growing bio-tech and life sciences sector	• Financial vulnerability
• Patents	• Financial vulnerability	• "Complementors"	• Future reactions by pharmaceuticals in case Argosis becomes too big
• Efficient manufacturing base	• High dependence on debt funding		
• Strong morale			
• Product innovator			
• Brand image			

After reviewing her analysis again, Sarah felt taxed. Gosh, Argosis has a strong differentiation position in a rather attractive industry, she concluded. But if so, why is the firm underperforming? Where is the pressure coming from? Which competitive force could unravel the industry? Could low-cost producers and high-end differentiators, such as Argosis, continue to coexist?

MARKET ANALYSIS: WEEKS 5–8

"Hey, what about my project?" Phil asked. "I have to be in a headquarters' meeting in a month, maybe two. And I am paying your firm a bundle of money for advice." He had been calling twice a week. Sarah was beginning to feel even more stressed.

Sarah decided to be even more aggressive: "Phil, I will need your financial statements soon . . . and I will need your staff to assist in obtaining marketing information."

"No problem," he replied. "For marketing information, just contact Tracy, our marketing manager."

"You look a little young to be a consultant," Tracy had started to tease her. Although bothered by this comment, Sarah decided to ignore it. "Yes, young and a bit anxious. I need you to define your market segments, telephone numbers to call, possible e-mail addresses, and possible focus group sites. We need these to validate your business model. Also, please ask Phil about any plans for the company relating to overseas expansion." Tracy stopped her patronizing tone from that time on and Sarah was relieved, sensing a momentary victory. Still, she was curious: *What would the market results indicate?*

For the next month, Sarah put her marketing research skills to task. With some staff help from Global Strategy Associates, she was able to obtain responses from

Exhibit 12.4

Preliminary Industry Analysis

Competitive Forces	Relative Importance (Distribution of 100 pts.)	Competitive Impact (Unfavorable impact = 1 Favorable impact = 5)	Assessment of Global Strategy Comparative Position
Competitive rivalry	20	4	Favorable (It's a growth industry. Health care ranks among the top 2 concerns. Industry can accommodate cheap and expensive products.)
Competitor entry	25	3	Medium threat (When patents expire in 7 years, it will be a free-for-all. Cost of entry not very high.)
Substitutes	25	4	Favorable (Many substitutes for the health care products—i.e., eat well, exercise, etc.—but they are not strong.)
Supplier power	10	5	Very favorable (Compounds are widely available.)
Buyer power	20	3	Medium threat (Thus far, buyers rely on the industry for health care. Many use pharmaceutical and herbal products.)
Competitive Attractiveness Index = 3.25. This a weighted average of relative importance and relative impact.			Conclusion: Strong growth and the relative lack of rivalry make the industry attractive.

3,054 persons through a website questionnaire. In addition, she conducted three focus groups, with her office staff contributing information from another three focus groups. With guidance and help from her old class notes, Sarah prepared the analysis shown in Exhibit 12.5.

She started to review the results again. Argosis's share was about 11 percent in a growing market. Not bad, she concluded, but could this be improved? Upon further analysis, however, she also noted that the key factors that determined market share—awareness, availability, attractiveness, and pricing—turned out to be significantly *inhibiting* Argosis's growth. *Why was this so? What could be done about it?*

To supplement her analysis, Sarah decided to compare Argosis against two other competitors—NASAD, the leader in tablet-form vitamins, with retail channels in places like Costcom, and Symbiosis, also a multivitamin provider but not customized to individual clients. Symbiosis offered multivitamins in liquid form to be mixed with water or milk. By then Sarah had received an analysis by an independent group on a competitive positioning for Argosis. She was particularly interested in where Argosis resided in the competitive matrix (see Exhibit 12.6), its level of customer satisfaction (Exhibit 12.7), and where current and future threats might be. She reviewed this analysis yet another time.

Reflecting on this material, Sarah was confident that that low end (NASAD) and high end (Argosis) provided value to different market segments, consistent with the industry analysis. However, she was a bit surprised by the differential separating Argosis and Symbiosis because she had initially surmised that the two had similar business models. The analysis prompted other questions: *How long could the low- and*

Exhibit 12.5 **Market Share Index**

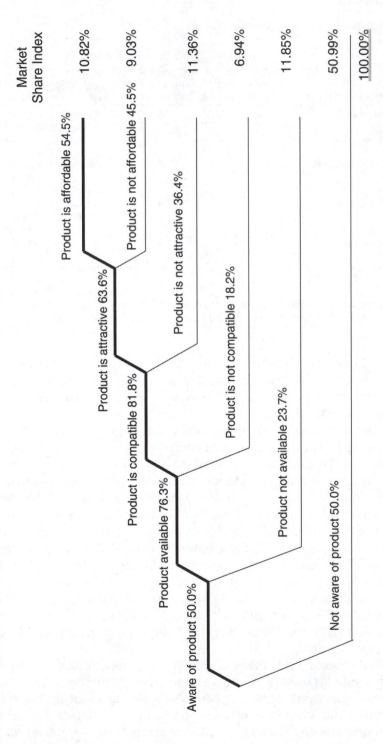

	Market Share Index
Product is affordable 54.5%	10.82%
Product is not affordable 45.5%	9.03%
Product is not attractive 36.4%	11.36%
Product is not compatible 18.2%	6.94%
Product not available 23.7%	11.85%
Not aware of product 50.0%	50.99%
	100.00%

Product is attractive 63.6%

Product is compatible 81.8%

Product available 76.3%

Aware of product 50.0%

Source: Format adapted from Roger J. Best, *Market-Based Management: Strategies for Growing Customer Value and Profitability* (Upper Saddle River, NJ: Prentice Hall, 1997), p. 243. Data based on a supervised student project (D. Chen, L. Henriksen, V. Lai, F. Stutedja, and D. Sutiono), 2000.

Exhibit 12.6 **Competitive Positioning for Argosis**

Competitive Advantage

	Differentiation	Cost

	Differentiation	Cost
Broad	GNC Costcom	America Marketing Renewal
Narrow	NASAD Genesis-Japan	Argosis, Symbiosis, GGSI

Competitive parameters (left axis label)

Exhibit 12.7

Customer Satisfaction Requirements

Customer Satisfaction Requirements	Importance of Requirement[a]	Competitors' Performance[b]		
		Argosis	NASAD	Symbiosis
Functional quality/effectiveness	9	8	5	7
Ease of use	9	6	9	6
Technical support	8	8	4	7
Affordability	8	6	10	7
After-sales service	8	6	5	6
FDA support	8	5	8	4
Research database	7	9	5	8
Availability	7	6	9	5
Consumer referrals and feedback	7	7	8	8

Note: 710 = maximum score, a performance rating of 10 on each factor. The maximum score will vary with the number of factors and the importance assigned to each performance factor.

[a]Importance of requirements rated from 1 (very unimportant) to 10 (very important)
[b]Manufacturer performance rated from 0 (disastrous) to 10 (outstanding)
CSI (Argosis—Customized powder) = 67.6
CSI (NASAD—Traditional tablets) = 70
CSI (Symbiosis—Milk/lactase medium) = 64

high-end segments continue to coexist? If convergence occurred, what direction would it take—the high or the low end? And, finally, it was clear to Sarah that whatever actions Argosis took would be bound to impact Symbiosis. What type of competitive retaliation should Argosis expect?

Sarah then decided to call her former professor for advice. After the salutations, she summarized her preliminary analysis and asked his opinion. In his usual Socratic fashion, her professor appeared nonchalant: "What is the primary issue?" Sarah thought hard and managed a response: "I think the firm's positioning problem is that potential customers are not aware of the products. Not being aware, these customers do not realize the benefits of the customized product. Even if they did, the higher price should not even be an issue because the cost-conscious segment will continue to buy tablets from Costco. With these two separate markets that are not overlapping, Argosis's market position should be secure."

Her professor responded: "Yes, but don't you realize that by building awareness for Argosis, you might also build awareness and add publicity to Symbiosis and other future competitors, maybe unwittingly? In effect, will you not be building awareness for Argosis's competition as well?" Before they could resolve the issue, however, her professor had to end the conversation.

Sarah was a bit stumped. Maybe it would have been better had she not talked to him, since he had only introduced more complications. But she decided to take that evening off. She played her favorite Miles Davis CD, *Sketches of Spain,* uncorked a bottle of red wine, and relaxed in her new Jacuzzi.

FINANCIALS: WEEKS 9–10

Sarah remembered another of Phil's early-morning calls. "Hey, what's up? It has been a while since I heard from you, and I am beginning to get worried. I called your boss, who told me that you were deep into my project, and that you would have very good recommendations. Anyway, I brought you the financials that you requested."

As she mulled through the financials (Exhibit 12.8), Phil called again. "Can you drop by tomorrow?" he asked. "I have a few suggestions to make . . . and I will treat you to Venezia on University Avenue." She was anxious about what Phil had to say.

With spring approaching, people had begun to congregate around shopping centers, ready to spend money obtained from President Bush's tax cuts. Phil appeared nervous. "Hey, I have to fly to Toronto in a few days to present a turn-around strategy, if you can call it that, for Argosis. Your boss has told me that you have this thing just about wrapped up. You should—since I paid your firm a bundle for your services.

"Anyway, I have done some thinking on my own. This strategy stuff you introduced me to is rather good. Maybe I will finally go for my MBA. But, that is something that we can discuss later. I think that Argosis needs a more aggressive marketing plan. If we sell more and make potential buyers aware of our products, we can reverse that flat pattern of income and improve ROI. I have a preliminary budget for you (Exhibit 12.9). Think about it and tell me if this can be used this in your final report."

Sarah had asked about international opportunities. Phil responded: "As you know, we already have manufacturing operations in Canada and Guangzhou, but maybe we should market our products there as well. The Chinese, in particular, should like it. They are so group-oriented and into herbal medicine. Hell, let's be frank. Eastern

Exhibit 12.8

Financial Statistics for Argosis (in U.S. dollars)

	Year 1	Year 2	Year 3	Year 4	Year 5
Income:					
Sales revenue	1,811,537	2,264,422	2,830,527	3,038,159	3,312,088
Cost of Goods Sold	62,615	62,544	68,305	75,382	80,022
Gross profit	1,748,922	2,201,878	2,762,222	2,962,777	3,232,066
Expenses:					
Rent	18,000	18,252	18,508	18,767	19,029
Employees	501,000	508,014	515,126	522,338	550,000
Utilities	18,000	18,252	18,508	18,767	19,029
Office supplies	6,000	6,084	6,169	6,256	6,343
Phone	12,000	12,168	12,338	12,511	12,686
Internet T3	26,964	27,341	27,724	28,112	28,506
Hosting	31,680	32,124	32,573	33,029	39,492
Marketing	120,000	127,680	133,011	152,099	187,200
Commissions	88,650	97,515	135,067	220,000	300,706
TOTAL EXPENSES	822,294	847,430	899,024	1,011,879	1,162,991
Earnings Before Income Taxes:	926,628	1,354,448	1,932,825	1,950,898	2,069,075
Depreciation	12,088	15,080	19,080	23,080	27,080
Income tax	430,034	498,696	688,948	712,014	753,118
NET INCOME	484,506	840,672	1,155,170	1,215,804	1,288,877
Percent increase/decrease	—	73.50	37.41	5.24	6.01

Exhibit 12.9

Marketing Costs (in U.S. dollars)

	Year 1	Year 2	Year 3
Sales force:			
Network commissions	90,000.00	94,500.00	99,225.00
Network incentives	80,000.00	84,000.00	88,200.00
Customer service reps	36,000.00	37,800.00	39,690.00
Brochures	10,000.00	10,300.00	10,506.00
Trade shows	7,500.00	7,875.00	8,268.75
Advertisements	30,000.00	31,500.00	33,075.00
TOTAL	258,500.00	271,975.00	286,164.75

Source: Marketing costs are obtained from a supervised student project.

medicine is their turf and our products fit into the Chinese cultural context. Now let's stop talking business and eat."

The food was delicious but the ambience made Sarah feel more edgy: With Phil's high expectations, could she deliver the results that could save Argosis?

After reviewing the conversation with Phil, Sarah became engrossed with her analysis thus far and reflected on how she should write the report (see Exhibit 12.10). She needed a good framework to build a case for Argosis going global, that is, assuming it *should* even go global at all. Upon returning to her office, Sarah received another call from Phil. He was quite upbeat and suggested a short meeting at the Hong Kong

Exhibit 12.10

Argosis's Performance Indicators and Phil's Comments

Performance Indicators	Argosis	Phil's Comments
Patterns of sales, income, and ROI	Sales growth is steady, but income and ROI are off in recent years	"Can't figure out what is wrong beyond maybe controlling costs."
Market share	About 11.0%	"Is this consistent with the size of our market niche?"
Relative market share (Argosis sales/sales of largest competitor)	.66 (low)	"We can be dominated by low-end firms, but we also hold a strong position in high-end differentiated offerings."
Return on assets	1.1	"Should this not be higher given our network marketing?"
Return on investment	15–18%, but slipping in recent years	"What on earth is going wrong?"
Debt/equity	1.88	"But that was the result of rising capitalization in recent years."
Price/earnings multiple	4.00	"Someone likes us."

Flower Lounge in Millbrae the following week. The best *dim sum*, he said. She was hoping that her progress on the project could be as good.

With other increasing work, the week passed by quickly. Soon enough, Sarah was meeting once again with Phil at the Hong Kong Flower Lounge. With the second cart of *dim sum* specialties whisked by their table, Phil got down to business. He had mulled over the financials and had come to the sobering conclusion that his costs were rising too quickly. "Maybe I should use suppliers from abroad," he opined. He provided Sarah with a list of prospective suppliers that had been compiled by another consultant (Exhibit 12.11). "As you can see," he continued, "I have options, plenty of them . . . but I can't get through how to process this stuff." All he wanted was to bring costs down.

But deep down, Sarah was aware of other complicating issues. The manufacturing process combined high and low tech: the nanotechnology and genomic formulae were proprietary and comprised the high-tech sector, but the actual mixing of ingredients was standard and could be done in any factory. Global sourcing had become more intricate. In previous years, suppliers had functioned merely to provide supplies, much like Original Equipment Manufacturer (OEM). However, with time and opportunities to learn, suppliers had begun to delve into actual design. Partly because of this, the Japanese, for example, had opted to keep many activities, particularly design, in-house, much like Toyota. In time, Phil's suppliers could become his future foes.

Complicating this decision was Phil's insistence that the choice of his global suppliers had to be linked with his future marketing plans. Phil wanted to source in a country where he could later market his products. When Sarah started to explain how this could complicate things, he interjected, "Hey, Nike has been addressing this in recent years, shifting away considerations of cost in one country while marketing in another. Why can't this also work for me?"

There was much to think about but not much time. Sarah's presentation to Argosis was scheduled in two weeks. The company expected a solution to its immediate

Exhibit 12.11

Argosis' Prospective Suppliers

Country	Description
Hong Kong	A textile company in Hong Kong that has heavily engaged in adopting nanotechnology in fabric and garment finishing expressed an interest in Argosis. This company has over ten years' experience in nanotechnology. Given the trend of losing textile manufacturing to China, this company is looking for opportunities for diversification.
Singapore	The prospective supplier in Singapore is a company that does advanced thin-film coating using nanotechnology. The coating is usually applied to computer hard disks or computer readers. The company has its own patents in this specific type of technology and has its own research team to branch into genotechnology.
Taiwan	A very resourceful computer hardware manufacturer approached Argosis. It used to be an original equipment manufacturer (OEM) firm and later developed its own brand. The brand has been quite successful in many countries, particularly in Asia, but not in North America. This company has moved all its manufacturing facilities to China. Only research and development is carried out in Taiwan.
Japan	A natural food supplement producer finds Argosis' area a promising one for diversification. This company is a small family business. It has a wide variety of products, all grown out of its own R&D. Even though there are plenty of imitations of their products, the company managed to make a profit every year for the past ten years.
Brazil	A company that grows genetically modified crops in Brazil is offering their expertise to Argosis. This company has over a decade of experience in food production and has benefited from the efforts put forth by the government-sponsored Argentinean-Brazilian Biotechnology Centre.
Spain	The most successful Spanish Internet company approached Argosis. The owner of this company is a Spanish entrepreneur who had worked in a Palo Alto–based software company for seven years before opening her own company in Spain, which now has offices in Madrid and Barcelona. Like many Spanish firms that are outsourcing partners of U.S. companies, this firm positions itself as low-cost and high-productivity.
Philippines	The country's only biotech company is very interested in becoming a source supplier. It has several joint ventures with biotechnology firms around the world. While the company will be dependent on these partners for any technical expertise, it has been reliable from all published reports. Moreover, the Philippines is highly regarded because it is one of the largest markets in the world in terms of alternative medicine.

problem. It would want to know how it could leverage any of its advantages abroad. Sarah was still wrestling with whether global sourcing could significantly reduce costs, not to mention the need to obviate complications from cross-cultural management. As she began to write an outline of her presentation, it promised to be a long and arduous two weeks . . .

REVIEWING THE GLOBAL STRATEGIC MANAGEMENT (GSM) FRAMEWORK

As the Argosis case illustrates, strategy is both a process and a discovery. It is also a deliberate application of stepwise problem solving, using both heuristics and analysis.

Exhibit 12.12

The Global Strategic Management Process: Key Issues and Managerial Questions

The Global Strategic Management Process	Key Issues	Managerial Questions
1. Assessing the external environment	Broad evaluation of world trends, particularly globalization, technological advances, and worldwide service imperatives.	Know/assess how globalization, technology, and service requirements affect your business.
2. Industry analysis/ globalization potential	Refinement of external environmental assessment. Delineates factors that affect industry profitability and the pace of industry globalization.	Is my industry attractive or not, and why? What is the pace of globalization in my industry?
3. Business model	Defines value-creating elements of a firm's strategy, resources, customer interfaces, and value partnerships.	How strong is my business model as formulated? Is the source of competitive advantage sustainable and compelling?
4. International growth trajectories	Juxtaposes the pace of globalization against the firm's ability to exploit advantages internationally.	Where is my company positioned?
5. Leveraging competitive advantages abroad	Provides four paths to such leverage: markets, costs, reach, and transformation.	How can we use a few, or a combination, of these four paths to leverage any competitive advantage?
6. Implementing strategy	Provides three ways of achieving effective implementation: structures/processes; a global mindset; and through financial control and sustainability assessment.	What is our implementation plan? How appropriate are our underlying structures and processes? Are we prepared to go abroad based on our mindset? Do our financials justify current activities and future plans?

In the preceding case, we have attempted to provide a sampling of such a voyage. As with most ongoing cases, we decided not to provide any final answer, but we will use the context of the case to integrate the subject matter of this book and to reinforce the logic of the frameworks and analytical tools provided as defining structure of GSM.

The application of the GSM framework should flow like a story with a strong logical thread linking all the parts, much like a roadmap. It should outline where a business is, its desired destination, and the types of resources, conditions, and obstacles it will face in its quest to reach this destination. By way of a commentary, we will discuss the underlying logic of global strategic management using a roadmap as our guiding metaphor (see Exhibit 12.12). Specifically the roadway is organized in terms of six major imperatives that comprise sound strategic analysis.

1. Assessing the Environment Is a First Useful Step

Most strategists conceded that assessing the external environment is the first step in this process. Some thoughtful critics have argued that a firm should focus on its resources and strengths, more so than its external environment, because the former constitute the "drivers" of firm activities, strategies, and performance (i.e., the resource-based view of the firm). There is no question that resources and capabilities are important, if not crucial. Even so, this choice should not be considered as an "either-or" proposition, but simply a matter of different starting points.[3]

For firms seeking to extend operations internationally, there is no substitute for analyzing the external environment, specifically the effects and the pace of globalization. Globalization is such a pervasive force shaping current events in world society, politics, and economy that not knowing its effects can prove ill-advised and highly risky. The three major trends advanced in this book—globalization, technological advances, and the emergence of a service sector—are so intertwined that a deep understanding of all three and how they are linked provides the first roadmap in designing a firm's strategy.

The case of Argosis will not be atypical in years to come. The firm is a microcosm that fuses new drivers of our contemporary world: technologies (nanotechnology), globalization (fast diffusion of application), and service orientation (personalized service to knowledgeable people). When all three are operative, these effects can be very compelling.

2. Industry Analysis and Globalization Potential Provide Specific Links Between the External Environment and the Strategies and Performance of Firms

Some thoughtful critics, along with a chorus of students, have suggested that an assessment of the external environment can be unduly complicated.[4] There are too many data and analytics, too overwhelming to process.

Industry analysis is a useful method for parsing this analysis to its basic roots (although many still claim that even the five forces model is too complicated). Many users have found that the model makes explicit linkages and assumptions that might otherwise be obscured in the analysis of the external environment. Industry analysis boils down to the question: *Why do some industries consistently outperform others, and why?* When analyzed in tandem with a firm's business model, this question suggests an additional one: *Why do some firms succeed in an otherwise unattractive industry, and why do others fail in an otherwise attractive one?*

Applied to the case of Argosis, the relevant issue is the firm's underperformance in the context of a relatively attractive industry. This suggests that Argosis is not correctly positioned, or that perhaps the dynamics of this otherwise attractive industry have yet to fully unfold.

George Yip's globalization drivers, as well as Adam Brandenburger's addition of complementors (e.g., value net) add further refinement to industry analysis. Yip's globalization framework is very useful as a basis for positioning global strategies and growth trajectories.[5] The application of the value net, in particular, highlights the role of cooperation in the context of competition, but in a manner that avoids the escalation of competitive moves.

3. THE FIRM'S BUSINESS MODEL IS INDISPENSABLE FOR ANY TYPE OF PLANNING

A business model is at the heart of this strategy, as it provides clear options of what should be done next. We have encountered many forms of business models and have argued that they tend to be confused with strategy. For many managers, a business model simply tells them "how a firm makes money."

Of the various business models, Gary Hamel's formulation (Chapter 3) is particularly useful because of its comprehensiveness.[6] The business model should state a firm's strategy and source of competitive advantage unambiguously. The inability to define a firm's source of competitive advantage is too often a reflection of the fact that it does not really have one, or has one that is inadequately formulated. But a business model goes beyond strategy: it also consists of the firm's resources, as well as its value proposition with customers and alliance partners. More important, it has the capacity of highlighting how value is created through each of these components, as well as their linkages.

Returning to the case of Argosis, its strategy is product and service differentiation, one that is not too surprising given the nature of personalized dietary supplements. Yet after an assessment of how its resources, customers, and partners support its differentiation strategy, the question is: *Does its differentiation strategy go far enough?* On occasion, a firm will pride itself in some aspect of differentiation, but might de-emphasize whether it is truly consequential for consumers. In the case of Argosis, there is some indication that this is the case.

4. PLAN THE INTERNATIONAL GROWTH TRAJECTORY

For those firms seeking to operate internationally, the first three steps are not enough—an international growth strategy must also be planned and implemented. However, firms are in varying stages of development as far as their business models are concerned, and they also tend to face different industries in different phases of growth. Clearly, there is no "one-size-fits-all" strategy. Worse still, forging ahead with any strategy can be fatal: a firm can overinvest when it does not need to, or it can underinvest when it needs to invest more.

The juxtaposition of globalization potential (Yip's model) and a firm's business model (its ability to exploit international markets) provides a framework for thinking through this decision. For some, this appears obvious: a firm that is unprepared for global competition should stay at home, at least until it marshals sufficient strength and resources. Even so, beyond this initial case, things can be murky. What happens if the pace of globalization is slow, fast, or its ability to exploit international markets is stronger, or less strong? The framework depicting possible resolution by way of multilocal core formula, incremental, and global strategies should provide first approximations of a growth trajectory, not necessarily the final one. Why? Because the firm can develop ways to further leverage its competitive advantage.

For Argosis, the issue of international growth is largely an embryonic one. It already sources its products from Canada. Yet cost considerations impel it to closely consider two markets that provide points of leverage for both sourcing and marketing: the Philippines and China. For Argosis, two refinements in its business model are the extent to which it can leverage domestic advantages abroad, and where to do this.

5. Leveraging Advantages Through Marketing, Sourcing, Partnerships, and Innovation

As indicated, firms are hardly static: they can develop ways to further leverage their competitive advantages abroad. This book builds on the logic of reach (marketing), costs (sourcing), partnerships (alliances), and transformation (innovation). The logic of reach follows the triadic marketing decision: *where to market, how to market,* and *when to market.* The logic of reach incorporates research on location, know-how and timing, and pioneer versus follower advantages. The logic of sourcing follows extensions to supply chain management and more recent outsourcing benefits. It addresses the impact of globalization and technology, specifically where both physical and virtual supply chains can reduce costs, even when market demand is so constrained. The logic of partnerships is closely associated with the benefits of strategic alliances. Simply phrased, no one firm is capable of going it alone in today's global environment. Finally, the logic of transformation is related to a firm's capacity to innovate, or develop a successful innovative climate. Properly implemented, these can all confer significant competitive advantages on any firm.

Despite the merits of these directions, research suggests that firms do *not* perform these activities well. Specifically, in the case of many U.S. firms, they are reluctant to market abroad, or do so in an inconsistent manner. They are also at the embryonic stage of global sourcing, although the spate of outsourcing is bound to bring in anticipated returns in the future. Strategic partnerships fail as often as they succeed, and firms lack a meaningful process of strategic innovation. To the extent possible, we combed prescriptions and frameworks from seasoned practitioners to help guide these processes in the desired destinations.

In the case of Argosis, they are faced with these options, but the operative concept is that of purposeful focus: *where should managerial attention be directed?* Argosis faces several options for leveraging the firm's strengths, but needs to be cognizant that in choosing one, it cannot compromise another. Some readers will argue—correctly—that the firm might need to focus on strengthening elements of its business model first.

6. Adopt Varied Perspectives of Implementation

This cannot be stated forcefully enough: without a good implementation plan, the most well-intended strategy (or business model, by extension) is bound to fail. Most seasoned executives will reinforce this belief. Surprisingly, books give short shrift to this important implementation phase. Implementing strategy is difficult enough in a domestic setting; on an international plane, it's daunting. One person who has addressed this in depth is Jay Galbraith, whose work we featured prominently in

Chapter 9. He has spent several decades examining how structures and processes are designed and used to support the requirements of strategy.[7] Clearly, proper structures and processes are indispensable for purposes of implementing strategy. In an international context, another imperative for good implementation comes by way of the "softer" side of management, that is, developing and cultivating a global mindset. In our work with firms, managers, and students, the biggest enemy is ethnocentrism, and this is not confined to any one culture. The antidote to ethnocentrism is the use of cultural dilemmas to reveal one's inner biases and predispositions, not so much eliminating ethnocentrism (we doubt it), as reducing it.

Another perspective is borne from understanding and analyzing financial statements. The strategic perspective goes beyond the statements, financial ratios, and ROEs to issues relating to sustainability, valuation, and resuscitating resources. Financial analyses will reveal much about the quality of strategic implementation, much as one can glean from analyzing structures, processes, and the global mindset.

This is perhaps at the heart of the Argosis case. It appears that the corporate culture is sound, and structures and processes, while embryonic, are designed in the right direction. However, the financials do not support Argosis's claim to sustained differentiation. Phrased differently, profit margins might not be sufficient to support rising operational costs. It is at this juncture where one has to reverse directions and reexamine the paths toward exploiting competitive advantage: better sourcing, larger markets, creative partnerships, and renewed transformation. It also brings into focus the underlying assumptions about Argosis's business model: *Is its core structure sufficient to prepare it for future competition?*

In closing this case study, it is best to return to the six summary points in this section. The roadmap begins with a broad view of external environmental opportunities. For each opportunity, now honed to specificity through industry analysis, requirements of success are set. Through a close examination of a firm's business model, one is able to examine conditions that enhance or limit performance, and that influence the direction of its international growth trajectory. Taken collectively, these provide cues for what firms can do to improve their business models and to leverage competitive advantages internationally. Each aspect of any strategy and decision can then be scrutinized in terms of strategic implementation, financial analysis and control, and broader performance issues. All six imperatives are, in turn, tempered by emerging trends and developments that we discuss in the next section.

EXPLORING FUTURE TRENDS AND DIRECTIONS

An oft-cited saying goes, "May you live in interesting times." If this was meant as a challenge, there is no better time than the present, as managers are constantly beset with change and uncertainty: accelerating technological advances, the new world order with the worldwide collapse of communism and the Cold War, global financial contagion, volatile currency and commodity fluctuations, the pervasive threat of worldwide terrorism and the growing instability of particular regions, the continuing economic and political integration within the European Union, and the emergence of China and India as potential economic powers, along with the recession of the

Exhibit 12.13

The Global Strategic Management Process and Selected Future Trends and Developments

The Global Strategic Management Process	Selected Future Trends and Developments
1. Assessing the external environment	• The coming demographic divide: the "graying" developed versus the "young" developing economies • Technological discontinuities: stem cell research, nanotechnology, and radio frequency identification (RFID) • Poverty: Who will attend to 40% of the rest of the world?
2. Industry analysis/globalization potential	• Continued blurring of industry boundaries: will the concept of an industry even be meaningful? • The pace of globalization: who will be future winners and losers?
3. Business model	• Sustainable competitive advantage versus hypercompetition • Firms versus strategic platforms
4. International growth trajectories	• Convergence versus diversity
5. Leveraging competitive advantages abroad	• New sources of competitive advantage: functional differentiation versus structural form
6. Implementing strategy	• The emerging network structure: the need for social capital and relational skills • Improving the measurement of global services • Corporate governance reforms and natural environmental issues

Japanese economy for more than a decade. At the industry and business levels, there portend the opportunities of nanotechnology, new science, and cell research. Moreover, spirited calls for corporate governance reform are manifested in the Sarbanes-Oxley and related reform imperatives. Lurking in the shadows is the uncertainty surrounding the response by developed countries to the problems of worldwide poverty and sustainability issues that relate to global warming and the environment. Some specific trends and developments that are directly relevant to our global strategic management framework are discussed next and provided in Exhibit 12.13.

TRENDS IN THE EXTERNAL ENVIRONMENT

It is the external environment that provides business opportunities for the firm, but also reveals current and future threats. While a reader will find the context of this environment to be constantly shifting and in flux, some trends are notable and will occupy the attention of managers for years to come. These relate to demographics, continuous technological advances, and the unattended problems about world poverty.

Trend 1. The Coming Demographic Divide: The "Graying" Developed Versus the "Young" Developing Economies

Among external environmental trends, changing demographics will influence our assumptions about human resources. The most significant trend is the aging of the baby boomers, which has far-reaching implications for business and society. The most immediate effect is the reduction in the labor force, which can reduce economic growth. Based on assumptions provided by the U.S. Bureau of Labor Statistics, baby boomers will start retiring by 2010. If so, annual labor force growth is expected to slow from 1.2 to 0.6 percent. It will continue to decelerate to 0.2 percent between 2015 and 2020, before recovering to 0.3 percent between 2020 and 2030.[8] Specifically, the prime-age workforce, those between the ages of 25 and 54, has been growing far more slowly than the total labor force, and yet this segment is considered to be among the best contributors to economic growth. In contrast, those under the age of 25 are still learning on the job and are much less productive.[9]

If such trends are ominous for the economic growth potential in the United States, this pattern of an aging working population is worse in other countries.[10] It is argued that, in order to maintain a stable population, a country must produce a birthrate of 2.1 children per female. Yet the European Union (EU) has a birthrate of only 1.8. In Japan, it is worse, at 0.8. According to United Nations estimates, during the two decades from 2005 to 2025, the working-age population in the European Union and in Japan will decline, and such a decline will even accelerate faster in the following twenty-five years. China presents a brighter future: the work force is expected to grow through 2025, although thereafter, its growth will turn negative. All in all, the growth of the U.S. population, including positive net migration, is just above the replacement level, but Europe and Japan both have birthrates below replacement.[11]

While it is early to forecast specific impacts on these countries, managers need to be aware of these impending demographic trends.[12] One such unknown is the future pattern of immigration, specifically any movement of skilled workers from the developing to the developed economies. Another is how long baby boomers can be expected to keep working, much as there is discussion of the retirement age increasing to age seventy years and beyond. A third unknown is how demographics will be affected by the wave of offshore outsourcing (Chapter 6). A prescient manager can start adjusting to this trend, instead of having to react to it when options are severely constrained.

Trend 2. Technological Discontinuities: Toward "Sense-and-Response" Modalities

A major theme of this book is the pervasiveness of new technological changes and advances. In Chapter 2, we reviewed some of the major technologies whose development is under way. In this section, we highlight two technologies that are particularly salient: sense-and-response and radio frequency identification (RFID). The third, nanotechnology, was featured in the opening vignette of Chapter 2, and in the integrating case in this chapter. The fusion of biology and technology has led to models of the enterprise that are adaptive, interconnected, and continually evolving—the **sense-and-response** trend that has begun to shape management thinking; these technologies are highly promising.[13]

Another technology in the making is RFID. This involves a reader that transmits a low-power radio frequency signal through its antenna, along with a transponder, or a tag, which receives the signal via its own antenna and processes the exchange of information. Because it can be transmitted through a variety of circumstances such as snow, fog, ice, and other settings where vision is otherwise impaired, RFID technology is remarkably resilient. Users now include retailers, consumer product makers, software companies, security systems providers, and transportation services.[14]

What is noteworthy about these two applications (as well as nanotechnology) is that they amplify the integration of sense-and-respond modalities within the business models of organizations. The current buzz in strategic thinking is about *business ecology*. Strategies are increasingly based on models of biology, ecology, and "complexity theories." Yet underlying these concepts are continuous advances in technology that have shaped our thinking about competitive advantage, or about competition in general. When successfully integrated, sense-and-respond modalities will transform business models that are otherwise passive and reactionary into ones that are continuously learning and proactive.[15]

Trend 3. Poverty: Who Will Attend to 40 Percent of the Rest of the World?

Most, if not all, strategy books (including this one) focus on tools and frameworks for the developed, and, to some extent, the developing world. Conspicuously absent is the poverty-stricken part of the world, or close to 40 percent of the world's population.[16] The World Bank classifies economies as "low income," "middle income" (subdivided into lower, middle, and upper), and "high income" based on gross national income (GNI) per capita. The conventional interpretation is that not all economies in a group are necessarily experiencing similar development; in fact, there are inequalities within a particular economy (e.g., the poor, middle, and affluent individuals in the United States). Even so, based on the World Bank classification, roughly 1.1 billion people are considered to be living in the lowest economic condition of "low income," or "extreme poverty." Slightly above them are the 1.6 billion who are deemed "lower middle income," followed by the 2.5 billion who are "middle-to-upper income" and the 1 billion who live in the "high-income" economy.[17]

While a large part of the world has seen great economic growth and development, sub-Saharan Africa continues to be afflicted by extreme poverty, political strife, unstable political regimes, and debilitating diseases. Almost 50 percent of the population survive by earning under $1 a day, or about $271 a year—the highest rate of extreme poverty in the world. More than 24.4 million people have been rampaged by HIV/AIDS and more than 17 million have died from the pandemic.[18] Almost all (93 percent) of the extreme poor live in three regions: sub-Saharan Africa, South Asia, and East Asia. The situation is getting worse in Africa, but it has improved in East Asia due to a higher literacy rate, lower infant mortality, lower total fertility rate, better irrigation, and more financial aid.[19]

Jeffrey Sachs, director of the Earth Institute at Columbia University and special advisor to the United Nations' Millennium Development Goals Project, explains how the inability of the poor to secure means to improve themselves leads to the **poverty trap**.[20] This depicts how rigidities arising from demographic, economic, sociocultural, and rural-urban factors prevent the extreme poor from pulling themselves out of poverty on their own. Because the above factors are interconnected, they create a self-reinforcing mechanism. Consequently, the extreme poor are "trapped" and become increasingly dependent on others to break away from this destitute situation. The poverty trap, as defined by Sachs, is as much an emotional issue, as it is an economic one. Sadly, this plight of the extreme poor has prompted the observation that they are "too poor to live."

Addressing the problems faced in Africa and the rest of the world is a daunting task. Providing outright financial aid has not proven to be the solution.[21] Nor does a transfer of wealth necessarily cause differences from one region to another. While there has been a general increase in the world's income, some parts of the world have not been able to take part in this increased prosperity. One perspective is offered by Peruvian economist Hernando de Soto, author of *The Mystery of Capitalism: Why Capitalism Triumphs in the West and Fails Everywhere Else.*[22] De Soto argues that what has limited the poor (i.e., moderate poverty) is their lack of property rights. Without such rights, it is virtually impossible to secure loans, get collateral, build capital, or even obtain a proper identification. This lack of property rights leads to what he calls "dead capital." Contrary to the perception that the poor have no assets, De Soto has estimated that the property value alone amounts to $9.3 trillion. In this context, the principal problem is that the poor, without legal property rights, have no means of significantly improving their lot, even if they are entrepreneurial. While De Soto's research does not fully solve the problems of the extreme poor, he offers valuable insights about opportunities for alleviating the plight of the poor.

TRENDS IN INDUSTRY ANALYSIS AND GLOBALIZATION POTENTIAL

The dynamics of change in globalization and technology continue to redefine industries. An industry can become more distinct, but other related ones might divide or co-evolve. Thus, industry dynamics will be a subject for analysts and strategies, as what will be crucial is how firms are able to identify these changes and respond to them in ways that create and sustain value.

Trend 4. Continued Blurring of Industry Boundaries: Will the Concept of an Industry Even Be Meaningful?

Michael Porter's five forces framework has long been a staple in analyzing industries. It is powerful in terms of describing forces that can lead to rivalry becoming ferocious and an industry becoming unattractive. Even so, the validity and utility of this framework rests on the clear demarcation of industry boundaries, and the fact that such boundaries endure over time.

Technological advancements, globalization, and deregulation have caused formerly distinct industries to blur and intersect. Consider computing power. For a long time, the distinctions between a supercomputer, mini-supercomputer, mainframe, PC, and laptop were clear and distinct. However, with advances in semiconductor design (see Moore's law, Chapter 8), these boundaries have begun to blur and converge. Similarly, the markets for media, communications, and computing are converging.

The increasing convergence of telecommunications and information technologies has produced novel combinations of service offerings: telephone networks are increasingly used to transmit data, television provides viewers access to the World Wide Web, and hand-held devices, such as cell phones, are now equipped to download movies and television programs.[23] Multimedia applications afford opportunities for hybrid services that combine voice, data, text, and/or images. For example, electronic encyclopedias combine text, video, sound, movies, and links.

Beyond new applications and service offerings, the blurring of industry boundaries has challenged old business models. Blurring industry boundaries have also given rise to entirely new industries. Nokia's latest smart phones have computerlike applications, such as e-mail, Web browsing, and music downloading.[24] In terms of Porter's five forces framework, with the continuing blurring of industries, the determination of industry attractiveness will not be as straightforward as with single industries. The profitability of these industries in flux will be a function of how the industries co-evolve, and the economics of value creation will depend on network linkages and externalities (Chapter 9).

Contemporary approaches to external analysis focus on the permeability of industry boundaries, often eschewing the very notion of an "industry classification." C.K. Prahalad notes that the traditional view of competition is based on assumptions that industry boundaries are clear and that industries have distinctive characteristics. He argues, "there is absolutely no way, in the evolving marketplace, that you can know exactly who are the suppliers, customers, competitors, and collaborators."[25]

Trend 5. The Pace of Globalization: Who Will Be Future Winners and Losers?

The application of George Yip's industry globalization framework yields industries that are fast becoming globalized, as opposed to others that are not. In Chapter 1, we presented research findings that indicated how globalization affects different countries in different ways, producing winners and losers both between countries and within them. The obvious winners are countries that benefit from globalization by becoming part of the world economic system. However, research also shows that the digital divide between the rich and the poor has become more accentuated—the gains accruing to those that have become part of the world economy far outstrip the losses or incremental gains by the poor that are excluded from this economy.

In a 2001 World Bank Study, economists Paul Collier and David Dollar identified the winners and the losers in globalization, the characteristics that differentiated these two groups, and the consequences of this growing divide.[26] The winners included: India, Bangladesh, Brazil, Malaysia, Hungary, Uganda, Vietnam, and Mexico. These countries (a total of 24 with 3 billion people) were able to double their ratio of trade-to-income over the last two decades, raise the average number of years of schooling and life expectancy to levels comparable to the developed countries by 1960, and reduce the number of people living in dire poverty.

This profile is a stark contrast to the losers in globalization, estimated at about 2 billion people in 2001, many of them from Africa and the former Soviet Union. These countries, also burdened with significantly high populations, experienced shrinking income and rising poverty. Many of these countries actually traded more twenty years ago than they did in 2001. For the most part, these countries have been excluded from international trade and are in danger of becoming marginal to the world economy.[27]

There are far-reaching implications arising from this growing divide between the rich and the poor. Analyst David Wells sees migration patterns as one important consequence of this growing divide.[28] In comparison with previous waves of migration (i.e., from 1870 to 1914) the current migration pattern is distinguished by the *quality*, and not the volume, of immigrants. For example, he notes that Asians (mostly Indians) accounted for as much as 40 percent of the Silicon Valley entrepreneurial ventures during the dot.com boom of the 1990s.

Another implication is the need to explore new and creative ways for addressing the solution to world poverty and the growing divide between the rich and the poor. One such example is the work of Sixto K. Roxas, an economist from the Philippines, who has developed a bold program based on an ideology oriented at building community stakeholder wealth and welfare.[29] This ideology is supported by a variety of new community valuation metrics (socio-accounting, use of the ecological footprint) and organizational processes (community brokering) aimed at building self-sustaining and empowered communities in relation to their respective habitats. He sees communities, defined broadly as families, villages, and towns, as arising naturally from their integration and balance with the natural environment. For Roxas, the dominant logic of classifying regions and communities into sectors (e.g., a sugar town, a logging establishment, mining villages and so on) disintegrates these natural connections. In addition, Roxas sees world poverty and environmental degradation to be inextricably related; as apocalyptic twins, one cannot be separated from the other. Stronger communities are not simply better off economically; they are more likely to be better stewards of the natural environment they belong to than business corporations that can leave at their discretion.

TRENDS IN BUSINESS MODELS

Sustaining competitive advantage and firm performance are central concepts underlying strategy. Yet the core meaning of competition is also evolving. Intense competition has led to hypercompetitive behaviors. Moreover, the sheer size of many multinationals brings into focus their role and accountability in the new world order.

Trend 6. Sustainable Competitive Advantage versus Hypercompetition

Traditional theories of strategy have been used to explain the growth and dominance of market leaders such as IBM, DEC, General Motors, and Sears Roebuck. For the most part, these firms built their advantage on the basis of economies of scale and scope. Once considered unassailable, however, these firms have ceded ground to Microsoft, Toyota, and Wal-Mart. As such, the weathered strategy rulebook on how to manage, which is premised on a firm's ability to sustain its competitive edge, is now challenged by new theories of strategy that allege that competitive advantages can no longer be sustained, at least for a long time. The traditional theories fall short in describing the "new rules" of the new competitive environment, and how to compete in it.

Richard D'Aveni takes on the challenge in explaining why traditional sources of advantage no longer provide long-term security.[30] One does not have to look beyond the experiences of IBM and General Motors, household names in computers and automobiles that were once viewed as unassailable in global competition. Both companies had economies of scale, massive advertising budgets, excellent distribution systems, cutting-edge R&D, deep cash pockets, and power over buyers and supplies. Yet, both fell prey to industries, both companies appeared inertial, unable to exploit major opportunities. Former Hewlett-Packard CEO Lewis Platt says that, "The only mistake they [the above companies] made is, they did whatever it was that made them leaders a little too long."

Porter and his colleagues stress the pursuit of a sustainable competitive advantage. Consider strategy guru Pankaj Ghemawat, who argued that: "The distinction between contestable and sustainable advantage is a matter of degree. Sustainability is greatest when based on several kinds of advantages rather than one, when the advantage is large and when few environmental threats to it existed."[31] D'Aveni argues that strategy is also the creative destruction of the opponents' advantage. He views hypercompetition as particularly pervasive, extending from high-technology industries to more mundane ones like hot sauce and cat food. His work raises the question as to whether the quest for stability (sustainable competitive advantage) and continuity will continue to the bases of strategy, or whether the focus should shift to disruption and discontinuity.

Trend 7. Firms versus Strategic Platforms

As his sequel, D'Aveni has presented counterrevolutionary strategies and tactics that any industry leader or established company can use to defend itself against revolutionaries, disrupters, or hypercompetitors.[32] His premise is that rule makers still rule, and that making the "rules-of-the-game" is the key imperative. In fundamental ways, he compares the modern multinational with its size and market prowess to a sovereign country. As much as these megacorporations compete and cooperate for power and turf just like countries do, managers need to be cognizant of this and manage the process accordingly. In contrast to hypercompetition, the position for resource-rich firms is to create stability and orderly change and to be the first to define the playing field.

D'Aveni provides a detailed account of powerhouses like Disney, Microsoft, and Procter & Gamble that achieved preeminence by reconceptualizing their product portfolios as "spheres of influence."[33] By restructuring portfolios around a core geographic/product market, spheres enable any company to "influence the behavior and positioning of rivals, pool resources with other firms to create competitive cooperatives, restrict the scope of competitive activity (as NBC contained ABC), and stabilize an entire industry's global power system." Nevertheless, D'Aveni cautions that spheres of influence keep growing until companies become overstretched (much like the Roman Empire in its later stages). Because companies do not necessarily have the resources to do a good job in all parts of the sphere, they become vulnerable to strikes from so many competitors. D'Aveni's theme raises the role of mega-corporations in the future: to what extent will they hold themselves accountable when some, if not many, are larger and more powerful than many sovereign nations.

TRENDS ON INTERNATIONAL GROWTH TRAJECTORIES AND COMPETITIVE ADVANTAGE

The quest for global presence and dominance involves careful deliberation about how a firm should expand, that is, its international growth trajectory. The current debate focuses on whether the path is oriented toward convergence or whether it will assume diverse patterns.

Trend 8: Convergence versus Diversity

Defining international growth strategies and learning trajectories is hardly a new issue. Scholars in the past have attended to how multinational corporations have evolved over time, with attention to how differences might be manifested in the experiences of American, European, and Asian firms.[34] Growth strategies are intertwined with issues related to locating a firm's business activities and how to coordinate and control them.

The consideration of global location issues has centered on replicability, scalability, and learning. On one hand, a firm can duplicate an activity in many foreign locations, or it can keep core activities in-house, while transferring others abroad. Learning compromises two paths: the first is how much a firm can diffuse its activities by building scale and scope abroad; the second relates to how much a firm learns from the local environment, or the process of localization. Current discussions of this subject have focused on transplanting a firm's DNA, or its core business strategy, practices, and beliefs. This entails clarifying the firm's core competencies; identifying the most effective mechanisms for transferring these strategies, practices, and beliefs; and identifying the processes to embed them in any new subsidiary. To the extent that a firm successfully implements this, convergence with its overall business model is attained.

However, the process of transplanting a firm's DNA is hardly seamless. Walt Disney's much awaited entry into Paris in the 1990s was met with considerable resistance from French applicants, employees, and labor leaders (see Chapter 3). What was not disclosed in the case was that the company was forced to rethink its dress code, its ban on facial hair and colored stockings, as well as its standards for neat physical appearance. Even a strong company such as Wal-Mart has had to adjust to pressures regarding local labor laws and zoning requirements. Starbucks was compelled to offer different food item menus in Asia to accommodate local tastes (see Chapter 1). The need for local adaptation will continue to pressure firms to adjust their strategies and adopt some divergence in their otherwise core beliefs and practices.

The issue relating to convergence and divergence will only become more salient as firms attempt to achieve greater standardization and convergence through scale and scope, while local markets invigorate latent tastes and demands. This mirrors the broader debate between proponents and opponents of globalization. Taken altogether, the international growth strategies and learning trajectories will continue to be influenced and tempered by considerations of replicability and local adaptation.

Trend 9. New Sources of Competitive Advantage: Cost/Differentiation versus Structural Form

Mainstream theories of strategy focus primarily on cost and differentiation as the sources of competitive advantage. Cast in terms of a firm's international strategies, outsourcing is positioned as lowering a firm's overall costs while improving its capacity for differentiation by attending to its core competencies.

In an informative study about patterns of outsourcing, the MIT Industrial Performance Center Globalization Team, headed by political science professor Suzanne Berger, reexamined standard ideas about globalization, specifically the convergence of work activities and even firm strategies.[35] Using a bottom-up analysis of the actual experiences of 500 companies in North America, Berger's team found that firms enacted different solutions to the same economic challenges.

For example, Dell Computers, which focuses its organization on distribution, has outsourced nearly all of its components overseas. It is as profitable as Samsung, which has taken a different approach by making everything under its roof—a classic case of vertical integration. While American apparel retailers have outsourced all their production, the fastest growing retailer in rich countries, Zara, a Spanish company, makes more than half of its clothing in Spain, which enables it to turn around products in rapid time. Even so, the decision to outsource is influenced by the local context and previous experience. For example, some Japanese electronics firms retained design capabilities in Japan, having been a victim of bad experiences with Koreans and Taiwanese in the past. And because of the high costs of building new wafer plants, some U.S., Japanese, and European electronics tended to outsource to various fabless firms (i.e., firms performing design, sales, and marketing, but not manufacturing). Berger's research indicates that there are different approaches taken by firms to respond to globalization, and that there is no primary or overriding strategy.

To the extent that this pattern holds, there are implications for thinking about competitive advantage in a global setting. Whereas in traditional strategy, such advantages were conferred on firms with cost and quality advantages, in the global environment, such advantages become congealed in patterns of outsourcing. Dell Computers cannot sustain its low-cost advantage without outsourcing, much in the manner Zara has solidified its differentiation strategy using in-house design combined with the speed of delivery afforded by information technology. The MIT study reveals more complicated patterns, such as the Japanese preference for sourcing to suppliers that are themselves quite integrated. In their case studies, there are a number of firms that decided to in-source some activities that were previously outsourced. With the ever-changing economics of outsourcing, future sources of competitive advantages might reside more in modularity and the architecture of a firm's internal and external value chain, rather than simple execution of cost and differentiation strategies.

TRENDS IN IMPLEMENTING GLOBAL STRATEGIES

Implementation is a highly complex process even for the most seasoned manager. The process is bound to be even more complicated with growing network structures, the need to create better measures for service productivity, and escalating calls for corporate reform, better ethics, and a concern for the natural environment.

Trend 10. The Emerging Network Structure: The Need for Social Capital and Relational Skills

In Chapter 10, we proposed the emergence of the new network organizational form. Two factors have accelerated this trend: first, the lowered costs of communications and the increased value of information have led to new organizational forms; and the second relates to the emerging modular form of internal organization.[36]

Working within a network structure entails the development of different types of skills. One such skill, explored in Chapter 10, is that possessed by **central connectors**: "people who, by virtue of their relationships with people in different organizations, serve as boundary spanners (moving information and context from one group to another) or bottlenecks (impeding the flow of information and context)."[37] In Malcolm Gladwell's *Tipping Point*, central connectors are significant in influencing a transition of an innovative idea from its embryonic form into a fad or a trend, or from its inception to "crossing the chasm."

Two other valuable assets are worth noting. First is **social capital**, defined as actual and potential resources that are linked to networks.[38] Thus, it is an informal norm that promotes cooperation between two or more individuals, all the way up to a complex and culturally embedded network such as *guangxi*. Because social capital must lead to cooperation in groups, it is related to traditional virtues like honesty, keeping commitments, performing duties reliably, reciprocating in kind, and the like.[39]

Another set of skills are relational and have to do with the ability to understand, motivate, and communicate with other people. **Relational skills** refer to the ability to relate, access, and to understand another person's mindset. These skills are primarily interpersonal but the ability to empathize with others is crucial. To the extent that network-centric forms of organizations and alliances become more prevalent, managers will need social and relational skills to complement their strategic, managerial, and human resources competencies.

Trend 11. Improving the Measurement of Global Services

At the peak of the Internet-centric and IT applications during the early 1990s, optimism was dented by Robert Solow, the Nobel laureate economist, who said: "we see computers everywhere except in the productivity statistics." Popularly known as the "**productivity paradox**," Solow's oft-cited remark has been used to describe the difficulty in measuring service productivity.[40] The difficulty in measuring service productivity has confounded academicians, policymakers, managers, and consultants. In contrast to a manufacturing business that can raise productivity by reducing costs in production and distribution, improving service productivity is trickier for a number of reasons.[41] First, there is too much variation in their customers and service activities. Second, differences in experience, skills, and training of individuals confound measurement. Third, unlike manufacturing, where the value of the product can be determined at the final stage of the manufacturing process, service transactions are characterized by the mutual participation of producers and consumers in a process characterized as "co-production."[42]

Taken altogether, measuring service productivity is a daunting task. With significant increases in the service sector across the world, the task of measuring services cannot be ignored just because of its difficulties. Yet top executives face resistance from managers and frontline personnel who consider services to be personalized, unpredictable, and uncontrollable.[43]

Although some variance in services is inescapable, a promising procedure is properly accounting for differences in the size and type of customers they serve and in the service agreements they reach.[44] This can provide the basis for comparing performance across different service environments.

Peter K. Mills, University of Oregon management professor and an expert on service organizations, sees the issue of service productivity as going beyond measurement issues to encompass the "right" organizational structures that can enhance the process of "co-production."[45] According to Mills, the fundamental problem is that, even when distinctions between services and manufacturing are recognized, the underlying assumptions on how to manage and organize service organizations remain keyed to the logic of manufacturing industries, impeding the development of the requisite marketing and management skills for service firms. Based on the kinds of relationships established between service-providers and the customers they serve, Mills has proposed radically different structures (internal service delivery, flexiform, ecological, ecological-interactive) that are more appropriate for different types of services (maintenance-interactive, technical-interactive, process-interactive, and personal-interactive). For Mills, therefore, the measurement of services can only be realized if and when proper organizational structures are designed and implemented for service firms. Because manufacturing carries a specific logic of development, it is insidiously organized to fit a particular pattern of management and measurement that precludes a deep understanding of service productivity. To this end, reversing manufacturing-centric thinking is the key to arriving at a better understanding and valuation of service transactions. Developing a more accurate measurement of service productivity and the "right" organizational structures will be a continuing challenge in the emerging knowledge-based, service economy.

Trend 12. Toward Corporate Governance, Corporate Ethics, and Environmental Sustainability

In the wake of various financial scandals (see Chapter 11), concerns about excessive executive compensation, and the growing alarm over the power of corporations, there have been increasing calls for reform within the corporate governance structures in many countries. Corporate scandals have damaged the reputations of Adelphia, Enron, Arthur Anderson, WorldCom, and Tyco. On average, CEO pay has risen by 279 percent from 1990 to 2002, far more than the 166 percent rise in Standard & Poor's 500-Stock Index over the same period.[46] Boards have also been criticized for controlling the process of selecting future directors and for allowing excessive executive compensation.

Over the past decade, but more accentuated in recent years, the topic of corporate governance has come to the fore. **Corporate governance**, broadly defined, refers to the relationship between three groups (investors/shareholders, top management, board of directors) in determining the direction and performance of the corporation.[47] In the past, Americans have tried to balance the power of corporations with government oversight. Even so, four shifts have led to the modern form and power of corporate structure and enterprise: a vested legal personality; the incorporation of limited liability for investors;[48] the transferability of investors' interests; and the control by professional managers acting as "agents" for stockholders.[49] By the 1890s, economists developed the theory of a business enterprise into a rigorous mathematical model, and with the ensuing standardization of managerial accounting and its extension into systematic corporate budgeting, the current corporate structure has evolved into a powerful and pervasive force in today's world.[50] In view of such power, it is widely recognized today that government oversight alone is inefficient without broad-based systems of accountability, transparency, and self-policing. The advent of NGOs and the growing visibility of antiglobalists (Chapter 1) are considered to be countervailing checks on excessive corporate power. Moreover, large stockholders and institutional investors, such as pension fund holder CalPERS, have become fierce advocates for corporate governance reforms.[51]

Specific calls for reform entail structural changes, such as having more outsiders on the board, and breaking down the function of the CEO, that is, separating the role of the CEO as chief executive of the company and also chairman of the board. One-third of U.S. firms already split these functions. Of the *Fortune* 500 companies surveyed, 70 percent favor this move.[52] The U.S. Securities and Exchange Commission (SEC) is also proposing new rules to make it easier for shareholders to nominate candidates to the board and to have nominees' names appear on corporate proxy ballots, particularly when the company has demonstrated governance problems.[53] Perhaps the more salient manifestation of this need for reform is seen in the passage of the **Sarbanes-Oxley Act of 2002**. This act requires all companies to file periodic reports with the SEC on matters dealing with accounting oversight, auditor interdependence, disclosure, analysts' conflicts of interest, accountability for fraud, and attorney's responsibilities. Sarbanes-Oxley also led to the creation of the Public Company Accounting Oversight Board to oversee the audits of public companies.

Closely related to corporate reform are issues on corporate ethics and, to a much lesser extent, one pertaining to the sustainability of the natural environment, although the latter are expected to intensify in the near future. Greggory Cates, the founder of San Francisco–based Global Citizen, with operations in South Africa, envisions his firm as a catalyst offering products and services that are consistent with the needs of a local market but also incorporating new technologies that are environmentally friendly. Specifically, one product is a Mosquito Fish that is a solar powered 500 gallon recirculating fish tank. It converts mosquitoes/insects to fish feed in order to reduce the vector for malaria while producing a protein food source in the form of fish, specifically tilapia. Another product is a portable solar/battery-powered structure that contains a dry-composting toilet, lighting, and ventilation. It meets the requirements of the American Disabilities Act but is small enough to be shipped fully assembled through normal logistical and distribution systems around the world. Other proposals call for an entirely new set of measurements that take into account the effects of the natural environment (see Box 12.2).[54]

In two heralded publications, *The Ecology of Commerce and Natural Capitalism*, environmentalist Paul Hawken and his colleagues have offered a new and revolutionary blueprint for rethinking about the natural environment, sustainability issues, and the role of business.[55] Hawken argues that businesses should be accountable for the full costs of the products produced—a reversal of the dominant logic in which environment and pollution are treated as "externalities" or spillover that are passed on to some third party. Thus, prices set by companies do not reflect the costs borne by the natural environment or the communities that suffer from pollution. One proposal for companies is not to use hazardous chemicals and ingredients, but instead use products that are biodegradable, or that can be broken down into natural materials after they are disposed. By selling by-products instead of merely dumping them, companies would not only improve their environmental record and enhance their reputations, but, as Hawken illustrates with his case studies, this practice would improve their productivity as well.

Hawken and his colleagues, Amory Lovins and L. Hunter Lovins, also support **green taxes**, or taxes and incentives designed to support ecologically sustainable activities. For example, a carbon tax could be imposed on the use of fossil fuel, or on effluents, and polluting materials. Conceivably, a green tax could reduce corporate and individual taxes as well. Green taxes could raise the awareness of environmental issues and enable consumers to make better choices in their purchase and use of certain products.

Overall, Hawken and his colleagues have put forward a bold agenda for combining sustainability issues with managerial capitalism. They have proposed four general principles that can improve resource productivity but not necessarily reversing the goal and the pursuit of profits. **Natural capitalism** is defined as "enabling countries, companies, and communities to operate by behaving as if all forms of capital were valued."[56] The full set of capital consists of four types: *financial* (monetary), *manufactured* (machines, tools, and infrastructure), *human* (labor, intelligence, cultural, and organization), and *natural* (resources, living systems, and ecosystems). One intriguing proposal is the application of **biomimicry**, a principle that every waste product (i.e., input) can be redesigned and reversed in ways for which it can be reused in other processes (i.e., output). Biomimicry has since been formulated as a new science that "studies nature's models and then imitates or takes inspiration from these designs and processes to solve human problems."[57] The power of biomimicry is based on its use of an ecological standard, or what we know has worked for thousands, if not millions of years, such as the ability of spiders to construct waterproof fibers that are five times stronger than steel, or shatterproof ceramics that are made from mother-of-pearl.[58]

More so than before, modern corporations will face challenges that transcend their objectives of maximizing shareholders' welfare. In this fast-changing globalizing world, there are challenges associated with intense competition, growing consumer

Box 12.2

Tyranny of Measures for Well-Being

With increasing concern for the natural environment, new measures of well-being have been proposed. These proposals are in response to criticisms that gross national product (GNP) and gross domestic product (GDP) do not reflect issues concerning the natural environment, and, for that matter, overall general happiness. Underlying these new measures is the belief that material well-being is simply one component of human well-being. It does not ensure that one is at peace with the environment and in harmony with others.

Consider the following proposals:

- *Green Gross Domestic Product* (Green GDP) is an index of economic growth that factors in environmental consequences of economic growth. The measure received wide attention in 1984, when China's Wen Jiabo announced that it would replace the GDP index in personnel decisions of China's Communist Party. Even so, it is fraught with methodological problems, specifically in its attempt at monetization of the loss of biodiversity or the impact of climate change caused by carbon dioxide emissions.
- The *Ecological Footprint* measures the cost to the natural world in acres to sustain a given population over the course of a year. According to the *2005 Footprint of Nations* report, for example, humanity's footprint is 57 acres per person, while the Earth's biological capacity is just 41 acres per person. By comparing a population's footprint with the earth's biological capacity, this measure indicates whether or not that population is living within its ecological means. If a population's footprint exceeds its biological capacity, that population is engaging in unsustainable ecological overshoot.
- *Gross National Happiness* (GNH) has been suggested by Bhutan's King Jigme Singye Wangchuck as a measure that balances economic growth with preserving cultural traditions, protecting the environment, and maintaining a responsive government. This proposal spurred about 400 people from more than a dozen countries to gather and consider new ways of defining growth and prosperity.

Other measures on a smaller scale are being developed in many countries. In Great Britain, an "index of well-being" will be developed to take into account not only income, but mental illness, civility, access to parks, and crime rates. Another strategy is to track trends that affect a community's well-being in order to arrive at some summary of sustainable development indicators. One example is Sustainable Seattle, which started in 1980 and monitors more than a hundred factors that affect the quality and sustainability of human life in King County, the administrative area that includes Seattle. Even with all these initiatives, many are of the firm belief that extant measures like GNP will never be replaced. However, the quest for more meaningful and complete measures is likely to continue.

Sources: Adapted from Andrew C. Revkin, "A New Measure of Well-Being from a Happy Kingdom," *The New York Times* (October 4, 2005); *Wikipedia,* s.v. "Green Gross Domestic Product"; Richard Douthwaite, *Short Circuit: Strengthening Local Economies for Security in an Unstable World* (Devon, U.K.: Resurgence, 1996). The passage on the Ecological footprint is excerpted from the UF Office of Sustainability, Report published by Redefining Progress, December 13, 2005, https://sustainability.ufl.edu/forum/messageview.aspx.

demands, and the need for transformation and innovation. However, from a societal perspective, the development and implementation of a firm's global strategy will also need to take into account the unrelenting pace of the move toward more accountable and transparent corporate governance, a deeper adherence to corporate ethics, and a more proactive approach to dealing with environmental issues.

SUMMARY

1. The case "Can Strategy Save Argosis?" is designed to help the reader integrate the different parts of this book into a total, compelling argument. The case is woven from real-life experiences with a number of different companies. While it does not represent a case of a single firm, it is inspired by real events.

2. The choice to assess the external environment, or to delve into a firm's resources and competencies, is a choice of starting points. Ultimately, both are essential in any analysis.

3. While complicated, the five forces framework is useful in parsing the analysis of economic and competitive behavior in terms of its basic roots. Of the five forces, entry barriers and differentiation have received the strongest empirical support.

4. A business model should state a firm's strategy and source of competitive advantage, hopefully unambiguously. The inability to define a firm's competitive advantage is too often a reflection that it does not have one, or has one that is developed inadequately.

5. International growth trajectories are options. There is no "one-size-fits-all" strategy. Forging ahead with any strategy can be fatal: a firm can overinvest when it does not need to, or it can underinvest when it needs to do more.

6. Published research suggests that firms do *not* perform leveraging activities well. Specifically, many U.S. firms are reluctant to market abroad, or do so in an inconsistent manner. They are also at the infancy stages of global sourcing, although the spate of outsourcing is bound to bring in anticipated returns in the future. Strategic partnerships fail as often as they succeed, and firms lack a meaningful process of strategic innovation.

7. Without a good implementation plan, the most well-intended strategy (or business model, by extension) is bound to fail. In an international context, another imperative for good implementation comes by way of the "softer" side of management, that is, developing and cultivating a global mindset. In our many encounters with firms, managers, and students, the biggest enemy is ethnocentrism, and this is not confined to any one culture.

8. Among external environmental trends, changing demography presents insights about how we will need to modify our assumptions about human resources. The most significant trend is the aging of the baby boomers, which has far-reaching implications for business and society.

9. A major theme of this book is the pervasiveness of new technological changes and advances. Stem cell research, RFID, and nanotechnology hold potential as they epitomize the "sense-and-response" trend that has begun to shape management thinking.

10. Most, if not all, strategy books (including this one) focus on tools and frameworks for the developed, and, to some extent, the developing world. Conspicuously absent is the poverty-stricken part of the world, comprising close to 40 percent of the world's population. Emerging studies (Hernando de Soto; Muhammad Yunus) challenge traditional belief that this segment is so impoverished that it cannot help itself.

11. Beyond new applications and service offerings, the blurring of industry boundaries has challenged old sensibilities and institutions. Blurring industry boundaries also gives rise to entirely new industries.

12. Globalization affects different countries in different ways, producing winners and losers, both between countries and within them. The most obvious winners are countries that benefit from globalization by becoming part of the world economic system. Research also shows that the digital divide between the rich and the poor has become more accentuated.

13. Globalization, new technologies, new global competitors, and other trends have eroded the traditional sources of advantage. Future competition may depend on platforms and spheres of interest. In an age of hypercompetition, firms have to be prepared and resilient in terms of their strategies and resources.

14. Current discussions of this subject have focused on transplanting a firm's DNA, or its core business strategy, practices, and beliefs. This entails clarifying the firm's core competencies; identifying the most effective mechanisms for transferring these strategies, practices, and beliefs; and identifying the processes to embed them in any new subsidiary. However, the process of transplanting a firm's DNA is hardly seamless. Firms have to be patient and persevering.

15. Whereas in traditional strategy, advantages were conferred on firms with cost and quality advantages, in the global environment such advantages are congealed in patterns of sourcing and outsourcing.

16. Future trends depict organizations and individuals making the shift to understanding how social networks shape our lives and our work, and learning how to identify, assess, and manage these networks. Social and relational skills are needed.

17. Measuring and monitoring service performance (and its variance) is a fundamental prerequisite for identifying efficiencies and best practices and for spreading them throughout the organization. Although some variance in services is inescapable, much of what executives consider unmanageable can be controlled with significant adjustments.

18. Among the key challenges faced by today's managers are the unrelenting pace of more accountable and transparent corporate governance, a deeper adherence to corporate ethics, and a more proactive approach to dealing with environmental issues.

KEY TERMS

Mass customization
Sense-and-response
Poverty trap
Central connectors
Social capital
Relational skills

Productivity paradox
Corporate governance
Sarbanes-Oxley Act of 2002
Green taxes
Natural capitalism
Biomimicry

DISCUSSION QUESTIONS

1. Discuss how changes in demographic patterns are likely to influence the activities of multinational firms.

2. How are technological changes going to affect the sources of competitive advantages in the future?

3. If a firm does not, or refuses to, become involved in poverty-stricken nations, what types of signals does it send?

4. In what ways are multinationals developing new networks? Give an example of a network firm that has arisen recently in the current environment. Discuss how individuals within this firm will need to acquire or develop social and relational skills.

5. Do you think that international growth trajectories will be more convergent or more divergent in the future? What arguments are being advanced by the proponents of these different views?

NOTES FOR CHAPTER 12

1. The format of this case study was adapted from Richard Koch, *The Financial Times Guide to Strategy* (London: Pitman Publishing, 1995), pp. 16–73.

2. For more about mass customization, see B. Joseph Pine II, *Mass Customization: The New Frontier in Business Competition* (Boston: Harvard Business School Press, 1993).

3. See review of the theory by Birger Wernerfelt, "The Resource-based View of the Firm: Ten Years After," *Strategic Management Journal* 16, no. 3 (1995): 171–174.

4. See, for example, Bruce Greenwald and Judd Kahn, *Competition Demystified* (New York: Penguin Books, 2005), pp. 4–5.

5. See Adam M. Brandenburger and Barry J. Nalebuff, *Co-Opetition* (New York: Doubleday, 1996), pp. 16–17; and George S. Yip, *Total Global Strategy* (Englewood Cliffs, NJ: Prentice Hall, 1992), pp. 28–63.

6. Gary Hamel, *Leading the Revolution* (Boston: Harvard Business School Press, 2000), pp. 74–119.

7. Jay Galbraith and Daniel Nathanson, *Strategy Implementation: The Role of Structure and Process* (St. Paul, MN: West Publishing, 1978); also see Jay Galbraith and R. Kazanjian, *Strategy Implementation: The Role of Structure and Process*, 2nd ed. (St. Paul, MN: West Publishing Company, 1986).

8. The statistics from the Bureau of Labor Statistics are cited in *Trends Magazine*, August 2005. A publication offered by AudioTech, Willowbrook, IL: pp. 18–27. See March 2000, "Current Population Survey," U.S. Census Bureau, www.census.gov/prod/2000pibs/tp63.pdf.

9. See Diane Lim Rogers, Eric Toder, and Landon Jones, "Economic Consequences of an Aging Population," at the Urban Institute website: www.urban.org/urlprint.cfm?ID=7247.

10. Statistics are drawn from *Trends Magazine*, August 2005, p. 19.

11. Statistics and analysis are drawn from *Trends Magazine*, September 2007, pp. 5–6.

12. *Trends Magazine*, August 2005. A publication offered by AudioTech, Willowbrook, IL: pp. 19–20.

13. See Christopher Meyer and Stan Davis, *It's Alive: The Coming Convergence of Information, Biology, and Business* (New York: Cap Gemini Ernest & Young, 2003).

14. *Trends Magazine*, August 2005. A publication offered by AudioTech, Willowbrook, IL: pp. 19–20.

15. Meyer and Davis, *It's Alive: The Coming Convergence of Information, Biology, and Business*.

16. In a provocative book, *The 86% Solution*, it is argued that most global businesses focus on selling to the wealthiest 14 percent of the world's population: the developed world. However, the rapid development of the other 86 percent of the world population with a per capita gross national product (GNP) of less than $10,000 has created a land of opportunity, but will require different market strate-

gies. See Vijay Mahajan and Kamini Banga, *The 86% Solution: How to Succeed in the Biggest Market Opportunity of the 21st Century* (Upper Saddle River, NJ: Wharton School Publishing, 2006).

17. These statistics are provided by Jeffrey D. Sachs, *The End of Poverty* (New York: The Penguin Press, 2005), pp. 18–19. Similar statistics are provided in C.K. Prahalad, *The Fortune at the Bottom of the Pyramid: Eradicating Poverty through Profits* (Upper Saddle River, NJ: Pearson Education, 2005), p. 4. While figures provided by the World Bank are not exact, some even contentious, they depict a stable pattern of income distribution in different parts of the world.

18. See http://library.thinkquest.org/05aug/00282/over_world.htm and see http://english.peopledaily.com.cn/200302/17/eng20030217_111773.shtml.

19. See Sachs, *The End of Poverty*, p. 70.

20. Ibid., pp. 56–66.

21. William Easterly, *The White Man's Burden: Why the West's Efforts to Aid the Rest Have Done So Much Ill and So Little Good* (New York: Penguin Press, 2006), p. 11.

22. Hernando de Soto, *The Mystery of Capital: Why Capitalism Triumphs in the West and Fails Everywhere Else* (New York: Basic Books, 2000).

23. See http://www.ntia.docgov/ntiahome/congress/reauthtestimony51199htm, p. 5.

24. "Nokia Bows Deeply to Operators," GSM Mobile Operations programs (February 14, 2005), http://www.mobilemonday.net/news/nokia-bows-deeply-to-operators. Examples from Michael Dorland, *Cultural Industries in Canada: Problems, Policies, and Prospects* (Toronto: James Lorimer & Company Publishers, Ltd., 1996), p. 285.

25. C.K. Prahalad, "Strategies for Growth," in Rowan Gibson (ed.), *Rethinking the Future* (London: Nicholas Brealey Publishing, 1977), p. 66.

26. Paul Collier and David Dollar, *Globalization, Growth, and Poverty: A World Bank Policy Research Report* (Washington, D.C.: The International Bank for Reconstruction and Development/The World Bank, 2002): 1–7.

27. Ibid.

28. David H. Wells, "Beyond Stereotypes: Globalization's Winners and Losers," *APF Reporter 21*, no. 2, http://www.aliciapatterson.org/APF2102/Wells/Wells.html.

29. Sixto K. Roxas, "Giving the Earth Charter a Local Habitation and a Name in the Philippines." In *The Earth Charter in Action*, ed. P.B. Corcoran, M. Vilela, & A. Roerink (Amsterdam: Royal Tropical Institute, 2006). Available at www.earthcharterinaction.org.

30. Richard D'Aveni, *Hypercompetition* (New York: Free Press, 1995).

31. Pankaj Ghemawat, *Commitment* (New York: Free Press, 1991), p. 122.

32. Richard D'Aveni with Robert Gunther and Joni Cole, *Strategic Supremacy: How Industry Leaders Create Growth, Wealth, and Power through Spheres of Influence* (New York: Free Press, 2001).

33. Ibid., front flap; pp. 7–8; 72–74.

34. Christopher A. Bartlett and Sumantra Ghoshal, *Managing Across Borders: The Transnational Solution*, 2d ed. (Boston: Harvard Business School Press, 1998).

35. Suzanne Berger, *How We Compete: What Companies Around the World Are Doing to Make It in Today's Global Economy* (New York: Currency, 2005). The examples of Zara and American, Japanese, and European electronics firms are taken from her analysis on pages 168–170.

36. See Paul DiMaggio, ed., *The Twenty-First Century Firm: Changing Economic Organization in International Perspective* (Princeton, NJ: Princeton University Press, 2001); and Lowell L. Bryan and Claudia L. Joyce, *Mobilizing Minds: Creating Wealth From Talent in the 21st Century Organization* (New York: McGraw-Hill, 2007).

37. Definition from Patricia Anklam, Review of Robert L. Cross, A. Parker, and Rob Cross, *The Hidden Power of Social Networks* (Boston: Harvard Business School Press, 2004). Review submitted on May 12, 2004. In Amazon's Customer Reviews, http://www.amazon.com./reviews/product/1591392705/ref=sr_1_1_cm_cr_acr_img?%5Fencoding=UTF8&showviewpoints=1, accessed March 17, 2006. Malcolm Gladwell, *The Tipping Point: How Little Things Can Make a Big Difference* (New York: Little, Brown, 2002), pp. 30, 38.

38. Definition adapted from Pierre Bourdieu, "The Forms of Capital," in J.G. Richardson (ed.), *Handbook of Theory and Research for the Sociology of Education* (New York: Greenwood Press, 1986), pp. 241–58. For a comprehensive treatment of social capital, see Nan Lin, *Social Capital: A Theory of Social Structure and Action* (Cambridge, UK: Cambridge University Press, 2001). An extension of how micro-informal links (based on social capital) can facilitate cooperation between various subsidiaries,

see Mike Peng and Y. Luo, "Managerial Ties and Firm Performance in a Transition Economy: The Nature of a Micro-Macro Link," *Academy of Management Journal*, 43, no. 3 (2000): 486–501.

39. Francis Fukuyama, "Social Capital and Civil Society." Paper, *IMF Conference on Second Generation Reforms* (October 1, 1999). http://www.imf.org/external/pubs/ft/seminar/1999/reforms/fukuyama.htm.

40. The productivity paradox was identified in early 1986 when economist Stephen Roach demonstrated that the huge increase in organizational expenditures on IT (computers, peripheral devices, software, and related services) between 1975 and 1985 was accompanied by virtually no gains in organizational productivity. "Within weeks, *Fortune* magazine's cover story was about 'The Puny Payoff' from computers, and the rest of the business trade press soon followed. Nobel Prize–winning economist Robert Solow quipped, 'We see computers everywhere except in the productivity statistics'." See full article by John L. King, "IT Responsible for Most Productivity Gains," *Computing Research News* 15, no. 4 (September 2003): 1, 6.

41. Eric Harmon, Scott C. Hensel, and Timothy E. Lukes, "Measuring Performance in Services," *McKinsey Quarterly* (March 22, 2006).

42. The first two reasons are drawn from ibid. The issue of co-production is the core subject of Peter Mills, *Managing Service Industries: Organizational Practices in a Post-Industrial Economy* (New York: Ballinger, Harper & Row, 1986).

43. Harmon, Hensel, and Lukes, "Measuring Performance in Services."

44. Ibid.

45. Peter K. Mills, "Getting Organizational Structures Right in Services." Working Paper, Lundquist College of Business, University of Oregon, Eugene, Oregon.

46. Sarah Anderson, John Cavanagh, Chris Hartman, and Scott Klinger, "Executive Excess 2003: CEOs Win, Workers and Taxpayers Lose." Tenth Annual CEO Compensation Survey, Institute for Policy Studies and United for a Fair Economy, August 26, 2003.

47. See Robert A.G. Monks and Nell Minow, *Corporate Governance*, 3d ed. (New York: Blackwell, 2004), p. 2.

48. Robert C. Clark, *Corporate Law* (Boston: Little, Brown & Co., 1986), p. 2.

49. Adolph Berle and Gardiner Means, *The Modern Corporation and Private Property* (New Brunswick, NJ: Transaction Publishers, 2007). Originally published by Harcourt, Brace & World., Inc. in 1932.

50. Sixto K. Roxas, *Jueteng Gate: The Parable of a Nation in Crisis* (Manila, Philippines: Bancom Foundation, 2000), p. 85.

51. J. Light, J. Lorsch, J. Sailor, and K. Pick, "California PERS (B)," Harvard Business School, 9–201–091 (February 5, 2001). Also personal communication with Ted White, director of Corporate Governance, PERS, November 4, 2003.

52. See Anderson et al., "Executive Excess 2003."

53. Stephen Labaton, "Market Place: S.E.C. to Revise Election Rules for Directors," *New York Times*, October 1, 2003.

54. Personal communication, Greggory Cates, October 2006. Stephan Crawford, Director of the United States Commercial Service, San Francisco, U.S. Department of Commerce, is also quite involved in clean tech for applications in international countries. A good overview of clean technology is provided by Ron Pernick and Clint Wilder, *The Clean Tech Revolution* (New York: HarperCollins, 2007). Also see William McDonough and Michael Braungart, *Cradle to Cradle: Remaking the Way We Make Things* (New York: North Point Press, 2002).

55. Paul Hawken, *The Ecology of Commerce* (New York: HarperBusiness, 1993); Paul Hawken, Amory Lovins, and L. Hunter Lovins, *Natural Capitalism: Creating the Next Industrial Revolution* (New York: Little, Brown, 1999). Section is based partly on Erika Mitchell's review at amazon.com (December 11, 2004).

56. Hawken, Lovins, and Lovins, *Natural Capitalism: Creating the Next Industrial Revolution*, p. 13.

57. Janine M. Benyus, *Biomimicry: Innovation Inspired by Nature* (New York: Harper Perennial Books, 2002), p. 1.

58. Ibid., pp. 97, 129–139.

Name Index

Page numbers in italic refer to boxed text and exhibits.

Adams, John W., 460
Adler, Selig, 460
Aldrich, Douglas, 114
Applegate, Lynda, *391–392*
Arndt, Michael, *380–381*
Arnst, Catherine, *380–381*
Arroyo, Gloria, *192*
Artzt, Edwin, 31
Aumann, Robert, *121*
Austin, Lloyd M., 501–512
Axelrod, Robert, *121, 126*

Balfour, Frederik, *249*
Ballmer, Steve, 363
Barger, Ken, *437*
Barney, J. B., *106*
Barsky, Noah P., 473–474, *474, 475,* 476–477, 479, 483, *490*
Barta, Patrick, *251*
Barthelémy, Jerome, *247*
Bartlett, Christopher, 28, *162*
Batra, Eavi, *14–15*
Batson, Daniel, *378*
BCC Monitoring Asia Pacific, 210
Beamish, P. W., *281, 287*
Beinhocker, Eric, 442–443
Berger, Suzanne, 547
Berner, Robert, *328, 340*
Bernstein, Aaron, *249,* 264
Berryman, Michael, 353
Best, Roger J., *68,* 103, *105,* 208, *208,* 214, *528*
Bezos, Jeffery P., 342
Bhagwati, Jagdish, *14–15*
Bird, Allan, *428*
Birmingham Post, 210
Bleeke, Joe, *287*

Bloch, Serge, *344–345*
Bond, Michael, 424
Bond, Michael Harris, *438*
Borel, Emile, *121*
Boston Consulting Group, *340*
Bove, Jose, 11
Boyce, Jose, 11
Boyett, Jimmie T., *11, 199–200*
Boyett, Joseph H., *11, 199–200*
Brady, Diane, *328, 340*
Brandenburger, Adam, 69–70, *70, 121*
Breen, Bill, 351–356
Bremner, Brian, *251*
Brilloff, Abraham, 459
Brin, Sergey, 312
Bröms, Anders, *494*
Brown, Donaldson, 479–480
Brown, John Seely, 330
Brown, Juanita, *10*
Bruce, Gordon, 354–355
Bryan, Lowell, *11*
Burrows, Peter, 313
Byung-Chull, Lee, 166

Cannon, John H., 460
Capell, Kerry, *380–381*
Carey, John, *380–381*
Carlyle, Thomas, 94
Carroll, Glenn, *100*
Carroll, Lewis, 521
Carter, Jimmy, 47
Catalanello, Ralph, 119, *391–392*
Cates, Greggory, 550
Cavanagh, John, *14–15*
Chandler, Alfred, 380–382
Chesbrough, Henry, 333, 343
Chidambaram, P., *251*
Child, John, 372

Chopra, Anil, 222–223
Chow, David, 263–265
Christensen, Clayton, 207, 334–335
Chung, Kook Hyun, 353
Cohen, Betty, *345*
Collier, Paul, 543
Collins, David, *106*
Contractor, F., *281*
Courtney, Hugh, 122–123, *122*

Darley, John, *378*
Darwin, Charles, *100,* 346
D'Aveni, Richard, 117, 119, 545–546
De Gues, Arie P., 119
De la Rosa, Rafael, *162*
De Soto, Hernando, 542
Deal, Terrence E., *377*
Dean, Mark, *345*
Degeorge, Francois, *462*
Dell, Michael, 70, 231
Dickel, Karl, 87
Dicken, Peter, *10*
Dimancescu, Dan, *391–392*
Disney, Walt, 132–133
Dixit, Avinash, *121*
Dobson, Paul, 61, 63, 65, 92
Dollar, David, 543
Dornila, Amando, *192*
Douthwaite, Richard, *552*
Doz, Yves, 286
Duerr, Edwin, 303–307
Duerr, Mitsuko, 303–307
Dunning, John, 24–25, 30–31, 150
Dymsza, William, 283
Dyson, Esther, *245*

Eastman, George, 95
The Economist, 53
Edison, Thomas, 188
Edwards, Graeme, 143
EIU ViewsWire, *53*
Engardio, Pete, *249, 251*
Engle, Allen D., *398*
Ernst, David, *287*
Estrada, Joseph, *192*

Fackler, Martin, 177–181
Falvey, David, *345*
Far Eastern Economic Review, 55
Farrell, Diana, *251*

Fiorina, Carly, 289
Fitzmaurice, Donald, 48–49
Flood, Brian, 460
Ford, Henry, 20, 321
Forero, Juan, *12*
Fortune, 58–59
Foster, Dick, 442
Foster, Jane, *11*
Fowler, Geoffrey, 39
Franko, L. G., *281*
Freeman, John, *100*
Freidheim, Cyrus, *278,* 299, *300*
Freitag, Markus, *329*
French, Hilary, 9
Fridson, Martin S., *462*
Friedman, Thomas L., *10,* 13, *17,* 23–25
Fukuda, Tamio, 353
Fukuyama, Francis, 417

Galagan, Patricia A., *429*
Galbraith, Jay R., 367–368, *370,* 382, *383, 385,* 386,
 537–538
Gandhi, Mahatma, 416
Garg, Rachna, 220
Gates, Bill, 241
Geranmayeh, Ali, *391–392*
Ghemawat, Pankaj, *121,* 172–173, 545
Ghoshal, Sumatra, 28, 155–156
Gilheany, Steve, *318*
Gladwell, Malcolm, 337, 548
Glick, W., *287*
Govindarajan, Vijay, 29, *207,* 338–339, 434,
 435, 436
Graham, William, 437
Grant, Robert, 56, 64, 65, 106, 115
Greene, Jay, *249*
Greenwald, Bruce, *125,* 490–491, *493*
Greider, William, *14–15*
Greiner, Larry, 382
Gretzky, Wayne, 101–102, 185
Grow, Brian, *249*
Guillen, Mauro, 27
Gupta, Anil K., 29, *207,* 434, *435, 436*

Hagel, John III, 114, 330
Halal, W., *391–392*
Hall, Edward T., 421–422, 437, 440
Hamel, Gary, 30, 98, *106, 294, 295,* 339, 536
Hamm, Steve, *249*
Hampden-Turner, Charles, *425,* 442

Hannah, Michael, *100*
Harrigan, K., *281*
Harsanyi, John, *121*
Hart, Sir Liddell, 99
Hart, Stuart L., 209
Harvey, Michael G., *397*
Hawken, Paul, 551
Helander, Nina, 114
Heskett, James, 376
Hewlett, William, 459
Higgins, Robert, *486*
Hill, Charles, 290
Hines, Peter, *391–392*
Hivornen, Paulina, 114
Hoff, Marcian E. "Ted," *345*
Hofstede, Geert, 282, 419, 424, *426,* 437, 444
Holzmüller, Hartmut, *438*
Hori, Shigeyuki, 345
Hrebiniak, Lawrence G., 43, 367, *367*
Hu Jintao, 266
Huber, G., *287*
Huff, Ted, 318
Hume, David, 18

Iger, Robert, 342
Illia, Tony, *152–153*
Immelt, Jeff, 341
Intelligence Brief, *53*
International Monetary Fund (IMF), *148*

Jablonsky, Stephen F., 473–474, *474, 475,* 476–477,
    479, 483, *490*
Jaikishan, Priya, 222
Jiang Zemin, 266
Jobs, Steve P., 312–314, 343, 352
Johnson, Gene, 485
Johnson, H. Thomas, *494*
Joyce, William, 43
Jun, Fu, 264

Kadish, Ronald T., *344*
Kahn, Judd, *125,* 490–491, *493*
Kallasvuo, Olli-Pekka, 364–365
Kamprad, Ingvar, 226
Kaplan, Robert, 494, *494*
Kaplan, Sarah, 442
Kawai, Roichi, 167
Kay, Alan, 3
Keeley, Larry, *344*
Keen, Peter, 373, 376, *391–392*

Keller, Thomas, 351
Kelley, David, 342
Kelley, Tom, 341, 345, *346*
Kennedy, Allan A., *377*
Key, Alan, 3
Kilby, Jack, 87
Killing, J. P., *281*
Kim, Ryan, *118*
Kim, W. Chan, 117, *118*
Kingston-McCloughry, E.J., 28
Kirkpatrick, David, *344–345*
Kittering, Charles, 5
Kiuchi, Masao, 179
Klein, David, *391–392*
Kleinfeld, Klaus, 373
Kleisterlee, Gerard, 410–412
Knowledge@Wharton, *523*
Kogut, Bruce, 154
Kotler, Philip, *216,* 327
Kotter, John, 376
Kripalani, Manjeet, *249*
Kroc, Ray, 211
Kublanov, Eugene, 225

Lafley, Alan G., 339, 341
LaFraniere, Sharon, *25*
Laitamakki, Jukka, 450
Lane, H., *287*
Larsen, Chris, 159–161, 204
Larsen, Ralph S., 363
Lavin, William K., 460–461
Lawrence, Paul, 381
Lay, Kenneth, 461
Lazaridis, Mike, *344*
Lee, Kun Hee, 352–353
Lee, Miri, 356
Lee, Sangyeon, 356
Lei, D., *287*
Lelic, Simon, *425*
Levin, Bruce, 94
Levitt, Theodore, 28, 72
Lewis, David, 13, *17*
Li Peng, 266
Lorange, P., *281*
Lorenzo, Frank, 120
Lorsch, Jay, 381–382
Louie, Gilman, 204–205
Lovins, Amory, 551
Lovins, L. Hunter, 551
Loyalka, Priti, 220

Luce, R. Duncan, *121*
Lyons, John, *152–153*

Machiavelli, Niccolo, 271
Machicado, Jorge, 240–241
Mahoney, J., *106*
Maiani, Luciano, *344*
Mander, Jerry, *14–15*
Mankin, Michael, 293
Mann, Robert, 87
Marn, Michael V., *216*
Marr, Merissa, *343*
Masanell, Ramon Casadesus, *69*
Mason, Richard, 87
Mattu, Sasha, *69*
Mauborgne, Renee, 117, *118*
Maxmin, James, 317, 324, *325*
Mazur, Jay, *13*
McAfee, John, 331
McAfee, R. Preston, 81
Medley, Patrick, 221
Mendenhall, Mark E., *398*
Metcalfe, Bob, 319
Meyer, John, 37
Miho, James, 354–355
Miles, Raymond, 299, *370*
Mill, John Stuart, 416
Mills, Peter K., 549
Mintzberg, Henry, *100*
Mitchell, Will, *292*
Mockler, Robert, 87
Mohn, Robert., 206
Monczka, Robert M., 233, *234, 243, 245*
Montgomery, Cynthia, *106*
Moore, Geoffrey A., 335–337, *336,* 346–347, *347*
Moore, Gordon, 89, 317
Moore, Karl, 13, *17*
Morgonstein, Oskar, *121*

Nader, Ralph, *14–15*
Nadler, David, 286, *370*
Naito, Yoshinobu, 180
Nakagone, Yuka, 180
Nalebuff, Barry, 69–70, *70, 121*
Narang, Sonia, *118*
Nash, John, *121*
Nathanson, Daniel, *370,* 382
Neal, Annamarie, 404–409
Needle, David, *205*
Neeleman, David, 442

Newcomb, Theodore M., 417
Newman, Richard G., *232*
Nike Corporation, *115*
Nisbett, Richard, 417
Norton, David, 494
Novicevic, Milorad M., *397*
Noyce, Robert, 87

O'Connell, Jamie, *162*
Ohmae, Kenichi, *10,* 110
Ollila, Jorma, 364
Omidyar, Pierre, 110–111, 312
Oppenhiem, Jeremy, *11*
O'Reilly, Charles, *377*

Pacek, Nenad, 188
Palmeri, Christopher, *346*
Pandian, J.R., *106*
Park, Seung Ho, 277, *278, 281, 282, 287*
Parker, Barbara, *10*
Patel, Jayendu, *462*
Paul, Herbert, 431–434
Peterlaf, M.A., *106*
Peters, T., *370*
Pfeffer, Jeffrey, *247*
Phillips, J.R., *370*
Platt, Lewis, 117, *545*
Polanyi, Karl, 440
Polanyi, Michael, 253
Political Risk Ratings, *193*
Pontin, Jason, *344–345*
Porter, Michael E., 56, *57,* 67, 85, *100,* 116–117, 119, 150, 153–154, *155, 281,* 524, 542
Poundstone, William, *121*
Pourdehnad, John, *391–392*
Powers, Richard L., *398*
Prahalad, C.K., 30, *106,* 109, 209, 543
Pratt, John, *462*
Prystay, Chris, 220–223
Pyke, David, 230, 232

Quinn, James Brian, *100, 101*

Raiffa, Howard, *121*
Rajesh, K.K., 223
Rall, William, *11*
Ramaswamy, Venkat, 109
Rangan, Srinivasa U., 274
Redding, John, 119, *391–392*
Reich, Robert, 293

Revkin, Andrew C., *552*
Rhinesmith, Stephen H., 430–431, *431, 432*
Ricardo, David, 18
Rich, Nick, *391–392*
Richards, John, 63, 92
Robert, Michael, *377*
Roberts, Dexter, *210, 251*
Roegner, Eric V., *216*
Rogers, Will, 143
Rosen, Robert, *11*
Rosensweig, Jeffrey A., *11*
Rowe, Alan, 87
Rowling, J.K., 337
Roxas, Sixto K., 544
Royal, Ahold, *462*
Ruefli, Timothy, 443, *457*
Rugman, Alan, 27
Russo, Michael, *281*
Ryan, Elizabeth, 404–409

Sawyer, R. Keith, *344*
Schaefer, George, 101
Schilling, Thomas, *121*
Schoeffler, Sidney, 481
Schrager, James, 272
Schubert, Siri, *329*
Schultz, Howard, 38
Selten, Reinhard, *121*
Sen, Tai Chik, 112
Senge, Peter, *494*
Seok, Na Hong, 166
Serapio, Manuel, *248, 256,* 404–409
Singer, Marc, 114
Sinkovics, Rudolf, *438*
Skilling, Jeffrey, 461
Slocum, J., *287*
Smith, Adam, 18–20, 246
Snow, Charles, 299
So, Sherman, 263–266
Solow, Robert, 548
Sonkin, Paul D., *493*
Soota, Ashok, 450–455
Soros, George, *14–15*
Sparks, Jac D., *292*
Speier, Cheri, *397*
Spencer, Herbert, *100*
Spencer, Richard, *237*
Stanat, Ruth, *199–200*
Starkey, Kenneth, 63, 92
Stata, Ray, 119

Stedham, Yvonne, *398*
Steers, Richard M., *372*
Stephens, Robertson, 204
Stevens, Michael J., 428, *456*
Stewart, Bennett, 484
Stiglitz, Joseph E., *14–15*
Stuckey, J.A., *281*
Sun, Xiaolun, *147, 148*
Symonds, William C., *203*

Tae-won, Chey, *462*
Taiwan Headlines, 237
Talley, John, *345*
Tan, Chieko, 180
Tata, Ratan, 102
Taylor, Frederick, 20
Thompson, James, 254–255, *296*
Thorniley, Daniel, 188
Tonelson, Alan, *14–15*
Tovin, Hal, *344*
Trent, Robert J., 233, *234, 243, 245*
Trimble, Chris, 338–339
Trompenaars, Fons, *420, 422, 425,* 442, 444
Tushman, Michael L., 286, *370, 377*
Tzu, Sun, 271

Ungson, Gerardo R., *281, 282, 287,* 303–307
United Nations Conference on Trade and Development (UNCTAD), *147*
Upin, Eric, 204
Usery, W.J., 305

Van Biema, Michael, *493*
Vasella, Daniel, *345*
Vashistha, Atul, *238*
Vashistha, Avinash, *238*
Von Neumann, John, *121*

Walker, Marcus, *251*
Walton, Sam, 102
Waterman, Robert, Jr., *370*
Weber, Joseph, *346*
Weintraub, Arlene, *380–381*
Welch, Jack, 102, 250, 252, 342
Wells, David, 544
Wen Jiabao, 266
West, Chris, *199–200*
Whittington, Richard, *100, 101*
Wiggins, Robert, 443
Williams, Chris, *53*

Wilson, Charles E., 317
Wolf, Martin, *10, 14–15*
Wong, Yim-Yu, 303–307
World Trade Organization, *21, 22, 23*
Wylie, Ian, 410–412
Wynett, Craig, *344*

Yip, George S., 71, *71,* 78, *79,* 154, 159, 213, 433,
    535–536, 543
Yoffie, David, *69*

Yoshino, Michael, 274
Young, Charles T., 460–461

Zambrano, Loranzo, *151*
Zawada, Craig C., *216*
Zeckhauser, Richard, *462*
Zeilstra, Sara, 204
Zhu Rongji, 266
Zimmerman, Ann, 177–181
Zuboff, Shoshana, 317, 324, *325*

Subject Index

Italic page references indicate tables, charts and boxed text.

AAA Triangle, 173
Accounts payable (AP), 466
Accounts receivable, 477
Accrual basis, 468–469
Accrued liabilities, 466
Achievement-oriented culture, 423
Action plan, 112–113, *112*
Activism, 111–112
Adaptation, 173
Adverse selection, 248
Africa, 25, *25*
Age of firm, 286
Age of Wintelism, 69, *69*
Aggregation, 173
Air Products and Chemicals, 232
Airways Corporation of New Zealand (ACNZ)
    Limited, 501–512, *505, 506, 508, 509, 510*
Alibaba.com, 111
Alliances. *See specific type*
Amazon, 24, 98–99
Annheuser-Busch Companies, 102
Antiglobalization movement, 9–13, *13*
Antitrust, 80–81
Apple Computer, 313–314, 343
Aravind Eye Care System, 330
Arbitrage, 173
Argosis case study of global strategic management
  assignment, 522
  business model, 525, *525*
  external environmental assessment, 524
  financial analysis (weeks 9–10), 530–533, *531, 532, 533*
  first visit, 522–524
  industry analysis
    weeks 1–2, 524, *527*
    weeks 3–4, 525–526, *528*

Argosis case study of global strategic management
  (continued)
  market analysis (weeks 5–8), 526–527, *526, 528, 529,* 530
  mass customization, 522, *523*
  overview, 35, 522
  SWOT workshop, 524–525, *526*
Ascription-oriented culture, 423
Asea AB of Sweden, 389, 434
Asian financial crisis (1997), 11–12, 26, 405
Asian lifestyles, 54, *55*
Assets, 466–467, 476, 491
AT&T, 81, 196, 288

Baby Bells, 81
Balance, 379
Balance sheet, 465–468, *467*
Balanced Scorecard, 464, 493, 495, *496*
Bargaining power
  of buyers, 65–66
  of suppliers, 65–66
Barnes & Noble, 98–99
BBC Brown Boveri Ltd., 389, 434
BCG (Boston Consulting Group), 74
Bell Laboratories, 331
Benchmarking, 501–512, *505, 506, 508, 509, 510*
Bernstein Investment Research and Management, 264
Biomimicry, 551
Birkenstock, 329
Book value, 468
Borrowing good ideas, 338–339
Brands, top 100, *213*
Breadth and scope of firms, 285
British Airways, 279
Building persona, 342
Bumper mission statements, 103, *104*
Business model
  Argosis case study of global strategic management, 525, *525*

Business model *(continued)*
  bumper mission statements and, 103, *104*
  capabilities, 106
  changes in, 24
  competencies, 106–107, *108*
  competitive advantage, 115–117, 119, *120*
  competitive dynamics
    defining, 119–121
    extending structure of game, 126–128
    game theory, 120–121, *121*
    sequential games, 120–124, *122*
    simultaneous games, 120–121, 124–126, *125*
  components of, 98–99, 101–103
  customer interfaces, 108–113
  developing, 130–132
  Eastman Kodak Co., 94–97
  future trends and directions, 544–546
  overview, 33, 128–129
  resource-based theory and, 106, *106*
  strategy and, 97–98, *98*
  value partnership, 113–115, *115*
  value propositions, 103, 105–106, *105*
Buyers, bargaining power of, 66–67

CalPers, 111–112, 550
Capabilities, 106
Capital intensity, 384, 386
Capital investment, 384, 386
Cash flow analysis, 488, *489–490*
Cash flow statement, 470–471, *471*
Category Renewal Zone, 346
Caterpillar, 122–123, *122*, 153, 166–169, *168*, 348
CEMEX, 150, *151–152*
CENCOR (calibrate, explore, create, organize, and
    realize), 341
Central connectors, 548
Centric approaches, 393–395, *394*
Chaebols, 12, *462*
Charles Schwab, 78
Chesbrough, Henry, 333, 343
China, 52, 76, 111, 197, 209, *210–211*, 212, *251*, 292,
    328–329, 389
Chrysler, 231
Cirque du Soleil, *118*, 330
Cisco, 113
Clayton Act (1914), 80
Closed innovation, 333–334
Co-creation, 322, 324
Co-production, 322
Coca-Cola, 62, 127, 201, 203, 212
Cold War, 24

Collaborative membrane, 293, *294*
Collection period, 477
Collectivism, 422, 424, 426
Common customer needs and tastes, 72
Communication skills, 240–241, 244
Comparability, 465
Comparative advantage theory of, 18
Competencies, 106–107, *108,* 250, 252, 314–315,
    444–445, *445, 446*
Competency-based approach, 396–398, *398*
Competency cube, 397–398, *398*
Competition
  direct versus indirect, 283–284
  essence of, 99, 101–103
  uncertainty and, 97
Competitive advantage. *See also* Global marketing;
    Global sourcing; Innovation; Strategic alliances
  business model, 115–117, 119, *120*
  cost advantage versus, 116, *116*
  defining, 115–116
  differentiation advantage versus, 116, *116*
  future trends and directions, 546–547
  new sources of, 547–548
  sources of, 115–117, 119, 157–158, *158*
  sustainable, 544–545
  transferable, 78
  treatments on, contemporary, 119, *120*
Competitive dynamics
  defining, 119–121
  extending structure of game, 126–128
  game theory, 120–121, *121*
  sequential games, 120–124, *122*
  simultaneous games, 120–121, 124–126, *125*
Competitive globalization drivers, 77–78
Competitive intensity, 291
Competitive risks, 157
Competitors
  from different continents, 77
  foreign direct investment and, 152
  globalization of, 30
  government-owned, 76
  response patterns, 216–217
Complementarity, 281
Complementary bandwagon effects, 320
Complementary overlap, 284
Complementors, 67, 69–70
Complex systems, 346
Concentration, 99
Conflict resolution, 298–299
Congruency/fit design principle, 365–366, 376–379,
    403

Connectivity, 26
Connectors, 337, 548
Conservatism, 465
Consistency, 378, 465
Consortium, 280
Consumer Intimacy Zone, 346, 348
Consumer satisfaction index (CSI), 105
Consumers, globalization of, 368
Contemporary sources of advantage, 117, 119
Contingency, 378
Contingency frameworks, 298
Continuous innovation, 334–335
Controls, 298–299
Convergence, 427, 546–547
Convergence theory, 427
Core competencies, 107, 250, 314–315
Core-formula strategy, 166
Corporate culture
  components of, 376
  consensus and, 376
  creating strong, 160–163
  defining, 419
  as design variable, 376, *377*
  innovation and, 342–343, *344–345,* 345
  intensity and, 376
  strategic alliances and, 289–290
Corporate ethics, 550–552, *552*
Corporate governance, 550
Corporate reform, 549–550
Cost advantage, 116, *116*
Cost of capital calculation, 485, *486*
Cost globalization drivers, 73–75
Country-centered strategy, 161
Country costs, differences in, 75
Creative organization, development of, 328, *328*
Creativity. *See* Innovation
Credit sales per day, 477
Cross-border alliances, 279, *287*
Cross-border coordination, 384, 386
Cross-cultural differences, 282–283
Cross-cultural recovery, 443
Cross-cultural skills, building, *425,* 439–443
Cross-ownership, 196–197
Cross-vergence theory, 428
Cultural diversity, 450–455, 546–547
Cultural fit, 290
Cultural recovery system, developing, 441–442
Cultural relativism, *425*
Culture. *See also* Corporate culture; Global mindset
  achievement-oriented, 423
  ascription-oriented, 423

Culture *(continued)*
  collective, 422, 424, 426
  convergence theory and, 427
  cross-vergence theory and, 428
  defining, 419
  diffuse, 423
  divergence theory and, 427–428
  emerging global, *428*
  emotional, 422
  environment and, 423–424
  feminine, 427
  globalization and, 26, 427–428
  individualistic, 422, 424, 426
  long-term orientation, 427
  management and
    dimensions of culture, 424, *425,* 426–427, *426*
    extension to management practices, 422–424
    overview, 419–421, *420*
    silent language, 421–422
  masculine, 427
  model of, 420, *420*
  national, 419
  neutral, 422
  particularistic, 422
  power distance and, 424
  professional, 419
  short-term orientation, 427
  specific, 423
  time and, 423
  uncertainty avoidance and, 424
  universalistic, 422
Current assets, 466
Current earnings power value, 491–492
Current liabilities, 466–467
Customer Initiatives Action Plan, 112–113, *112*
Customer value, 187
Customers
  foreign direct investment and, 152
  global, 72
  globalization of, 30
  government-owned, 76
  interfaces, 108–113
  needs and tastes of, common, 72
CVA (customer value added), 472
Cyworld, 111

DaimlerChrysler, 272
Deep support economies, 323–324
Defense Advanced Research Projects Agency, 343
Deferred taxes, 466

Dell Computers, 62, 70, 78–79, 113, 169–174, *170, 171,* 231, 547
Demographic divide, 539–540
Demographics, 53–54, 540
Dependency spiral, 293
Differentiation, 64, 373, 536, 547–548
Differentiation advantage, 116, *116*
Diffuse culture, 423
Digitally based economy
　business and, 324–327
　defining, 316–317
　drivers of
　　co-creation, 322
　　co-production, 322
　　enterprise logic, 322–324
　　individual consumption, 321–322
　　Metcalf's law, 319–321, *320*
　　Moore's law, 317–319, *318,* 321
　　new technologies, 317–318
　　overview, 317, *325*
　　personalized experience, 322
　innovation in
　　disruptive versus continuous, 334–335
　　open versus closed, 333–334
　　overview, 331–333, *332*
　　Technology Adoption Life Cycle, 335–337, *336*
　trends leading to emergence of global, 50–51
Digitally based technologies, 7–8
Direct competition, 283–284
Disaggregation, 479
Disruptive innovation, 334–335
Distinctive competence, 107, *108*
Distributed economies, 323–324
Distribution channels, 63–64
Divergence theory, 427–428. *See also* Diversity
Diversity, 450–455, 546–547
Domestic purchasing, 228–229, 234
Dunning's electic paradigm, 149–151, 157
DuPont formula, 479–481, *480*
Dutch India Company, 18
Dynamic competencies, 252

E-LOAN, 159–163, *161,* 169, 204
Earnings Per Share (EPS) growth rate, 487
Earnings statement, 468–470, *469*
Earth-moving equipment (EME), 166–169, 348
East India Company, 18
Eastman Kodak Co., 94–97, 99
eBay, 24, 111, 204
EBIT (earnings before interest), 491
Eclectic paradigm, 149–151, 157

Eclectic Theory of International Production, 149–151, 157
Ecological Footprint, *552*
Economic trends, 24, 52–53
Economies of scale, 62, 152–153
Efficiency, 379
Efficiency imperative, 29
E.I. du Pont de Nemours, 479
Eli Lilly, 333–334
Emotional culture, 422
Emotional intelligence, 431
Enron Company, 461
Enterprise logic, 322–324
Entry to target markets
　modes, 194–198, *199–200*
　strategy, 219
　timing, 198, 201, *201, 202, 203*
Environment and culture, 423–424
Environmental sustainability, 549–552
EPV (earnings power value), 491–492
Equity joint ventures, 275–276
Equity sharing arrangements, 275–276
Ericsson, 496
Ethnocentric approach, 393–394, *394*
Ethnocentrism, 436–439, *438,* 449–450
European Union, 76, 540
EVA (economic value added), 368, 472, *473,* 482–485, 505–509, *506*
Evolutionary school of strategy, *100*
Experimentation, 111
Export department, 387
Exports, 77, 194
External environment
　antitrust and, 80–81
　Argosis case study of global strategic management, 524
　bargaining power
　　of buyers, 66–67
　　of suppliers, 65–66
　changing, 49–50
　complementors, 67, 69–70
　future trends and directions, 539–542
　globalization potential analysis, 71–80
　implications, 81–82
　industry analysis, 56–57, *58–59,* 60–65, *68*
　macroenvironmental analysis, 50–56
　nanotechnology and, 47–49
　overview, 33, 82–83

Fair market value, 468
Federal Trade Commission (FTC), 80

Femininity, 427
Financial analyses
  Argosis case study on global strategic management, 530–533, *531, 532, 533*
  strategic implementation and, 461, *462,* 463–464, *463*
Financial irregularities, 461, *462*
Financial leverage, 478–479
Financial performance measures
  Balanced Scorecard, 464, 493, 495, *496*
  conservatism and, 465
  DuPont formula, 479–481, *480*
  EVA, 484–485
  financial analyses and, 461, *462,* 463–464, *463*
  financial ratios
    overview, 472–473
    profitability, 473–474, *475*
    turnover/efficiency, 473, 476–479
  financial statements
    balance sheet, 465–468, *467*
    cash flow statement, 470–471, *471*
    generally accepted accounting principles and, 464–465
    income statement, 468–470, *469*
    materiality and, 465
    overview, 464–465
  in international operations context, 496–497
  market value added, 484–485
  marketing ratios, 481–482, *482*
  overview, 35, 497–499
  strategic implementation, 463, *463*
  strategic objectives and, 471–472
  sustainability of business strategy, 485–488, *489–490*
  using, 463, *463*
  valuation and strategy, 490–492
  value problem, 482–484
  Woolworth, 460–461
Financial ratios
  overview, 472–473
  profitability, 473–474, *474, 475*
  turnover/efficiency, 476–479
Financial statements
  balance sheet, 465–469, *467*
  cash flow statement, 470–471, *471*
  conservatism and, 465
  generally accepted accounting principles and, 464–465
  income statement, 468–470, *469*
  materiality and, 465
  overview, 464–465
Financing activities, 471

Firms. *See also* Corporate culture; *specific name*
  ability to exploit the market, 207–208
  retention rate, 487–488
  strategic platforms versus, 545–546
First Industrial Revolution, 19
First-mover advantages, 198, *199–200,* 201, *201, 202,* 203–205, *203, 205*
First phase of globalization (1450–1800), 16, *17,* 18
Five Forces model of competition
  bargaining power
    buyers, 66–67
    suppliers, 65–66
  blurring of industries and, 543
  intensity of rivalry, 60–62
  overview, 56–57, *57,* 60
  threat of new entrants, 62–64
  threat of substitutes, 64–65
Fixed asset turnover, 478
Fixed costs, 384, 386, 476
Flatteners, 24
Florists Transworld Delivery, Inc. (FTD), 195
Ford Motor Company, 113
Foreign direct investment (FDI)
  competitors and, 152
  customers and, 152
  defining, 144–145
  flows, 146, *147*
  historical perspective
    liberalized investment environment, 146, *147,* 148–149, *148*
    overview, 146
    reasons for, 149–153
  horizontal, 146
  vertical, 146
Forgetting old ideas, 338
Formal structure, 372–373
Franchise value, 492, *494*
Franchising, 195
Fraport AG, *192*
Freitag bags, 329, *329*
Fuji Xerox, 271–272, 298
Functional alliances, 275
Fungibility, 253

Game theory, 120–121, *121*
General Agreement on Trade and Tariffs (GATT), 23
General Electric (GE), 29–30, 241, 250, 252, 341, 481
General Motors (GM), 62, 117, 279, 303–307, 338
Generally accepted accounting principles (GAAP), 464–466, 496–497
Generic strategies, 117, *117*

Genomics, *523*
Geocentric approach, *394,* 395
Geography of Thought (Nisbett), 417
Geopolitical uncertainty, 368–369
Germany, 373
Gillette, *203*
Global business units (GBUs), 173
Global channels, 72–73
Global Citizen, 550–551
Global complexity, 368
Global customers, 72
Global industries, 145, 153–155, *155*
Global marketing
　analytical framework
　　overview, 208–209
　　pricing, 214–217
　　targeted market, adapting products and services to,
　　　211–214
　components of market share and, *208*
　customer value and, 187
　Microsoft, 185–186
　need for, 186–187, *187*
　orientation, developing, 187–188
　overview, 217–218
　pricing, 214–217
　production versus marketing orientation and, 188, *189*
　strategy, developing
　　how to enter, 194–198, *199–200*
　　overview, 188–189
　　risk analysis, 189–193, *192, 193*
　　when to enter, 198, 201, *201, 202, 203*
Global mindset
　assessment methodology, 444–445, *445,* 446
　cross-cultural skills, developing, *425,* 439–443
　cultivating, 438–439
　culture and managerial behavior
　　cultural dimensions, 424, *425,* 426–427, *426*
　　extension to management practice, 422–424
　　overview, 419–421, *420*
　　silent language, 421–422
　defining, 418, 429–430
　emerging, *428*
　ethnocentrism, 436–439, *438*
　Geography of Thought and, 417
　Govindarajan and Gupta's perspective, 434–436,
　　435, 436
　imperative for, 429, *430*
　management traits and, 429–431, *429, 430, 432, 435,*
　　436
　overview, 34–35, 447–448
　Paul's perspective, 431–434

Global mindset *(continued)*
　Rhinesmith's perspective, 430–431
　strategic implementation and, 417–419, *418*
　synthesizing frameworks, 427–428
Global perspective, 110
Global position, 212
Global scale economies, 73–74
Global sourcing. *See also* Outsourcing
　benefits of, 242–244, *245*
　defining, 227
　development levels, 233–235
　from domestic purchasing to, 228–229
　IKEA, 226–227
　implementation guidelines, 241–242
　leveraging strategic advantage and, 227, *228*
　management and, 241
　organizations, 242, *243*
　to outsourcing, 245–246
　overview, 34, 260–261
　partners for, locating, 235–236, *238*
　reasons for, 227–228
　success factors, key, 236–241
　Taiwan and, *237*
　types of
　　evaluating, 232, *232*
　　hybrid network sourcing, 232–233
　　multiple suppliers sourcing, 229–230
　　single sourcing, 230–232
Global strategic management (GSM). *See also* Argosis
　　case study of global strategic management
　adopting, 6–7
　defining, 6
　framework, 30–35, *31,* 533–538
　future trends and directions
　　business models, 544–546
　　external environment, 539–542
　　industry analysis, 542–544
　　international growth trajectories and competitive
　　　advantage, 546–547
　　overview, 438–439, *539*
　　strategic implementation, 548–552, *552*
　generic strategies, 33
　overview, 33, 521, 553–554
　phases of planning and analysis, 32–33
　process, 534, *534,* 539, *539*
　reviewing framework, 533–538
Global strategy. *See also* Strategy
　framework for, 155–158, *156, 158*
　future trends and directions, 548–552
　for global industries, 155, *155*
　Kingston-McCloughry's use of, 28

Global strategy *(continued)*
  for multidomestic industries, 155, *155*
Global System Mobile Communication (GSM), 107
Global webs, 24
Globalization
  antitrust and, 80–81
  arguments, core, 27–28
  competitive landscape and, changing, 5–7
  of competitors, 30
  connectivity and, 26
  of consumers, 368
  culture and, 26, 427–428
  of customers, 30
  dark side of, 9–13, *13*
  debate, 13, *14–15*
  defining, 7, 9, *10*
  digitally based technologies and, 7–8
  as dynamic process, 27, 37–40
  economic side of, 26
  evidence of, 9, *11*
  historical context
    first phase (1450–1800), 16, *17,* 18
    origin of trade, 16
    overview, 13, 16
    second phase (1800–1931), *17,* 18–20
    third phase (1970–2000), *17,* 20–23, *21, 22, 23*
    2000s, *17, 22,* 23–26, *23*
  imperatives of, 28–30
  Internet and, 80
  knowledge-based services and, 8
  management and
    challenges for, 7–9
    implications for, 26–28
  opponents of, 9–13, *13*
  overview, 35–36
  pace of, 26, 543–544
  political side of, 26
  potential, analyzing
    competitive globalization drivers, 77–78
    cost globalization drivers, 73–75
    future directions and trends, 542–544
    government globalization drivers, 75–77
    market globalization drivers, 72–73
    overview, 71–72, *79*
  scenarios
    favorable, 4
    overview, 3–5
    unfavorable, 4–5
  services and, 78–80
  spatial connectedness and, 24
  technological side of, 26

Globalized competition, 77–78
Goldman Sachs, 180
Good Samaritan parable, *378*
Google, 24, 368, 471
Government appropriation, 191–193
Government globalization drivers, 75–77
Green gross domestic product (Green GDP), *552*
Green taxes, 551
Gross national happiness (GNH), *552*
Gross profits, 469, 476
Growth imperative, 29
Guanxi, 254

Haier, 441
Hewlett-Packard (HP), 117, 289
Hindustan Lever Ltd. (HLL), 209
Historical value, 468
Hollander Sweetener Company (HSC), 127
Honda, 257
Horizontal direct investment, 146
Huawei, 263–266
Human resource management (HRM)
  centric approaches, 393–395, *394*
  competency-based approach, 396–398
  defining, 390
  global, role of, 404–409
  inpatriates and, 397, *397*
  PVA and, 472
  reorientation of, 393
  strategic implementation and, 365, 390, 392–398
  system-based approach, 395–396
  traditional perspective, 393
Hybrid network sourcing, 232–233
Hypercompetition, 117, 119, 544–545
Hyundai Merchant Marine, *462*
Hyundai Motor Company, 196, 212

IBM-Cisco alliance, 276
Idiosyncratic task, 253
IFPI (International Federation of the Phonographic
    Industry), 190
IKEA, 29, 72–73, 226–227
Imports, 77
Income statement, 468–470, *469*
Increasing returns, 319
Incremental strategy, 169
Index of well-being, *552*
India, 52, *251,* 330
Indirect competition, 283–284
Individual consumption, 321–322
Individualism, 422, 424, 426

Individuals and strategic implementation, 371–372
Industry analysis
  Argosis case study of global strategic management
    weeks 1–2, 524, *527*
    weeks 3–4, 525–526, *528*
  complete, 67, *68*
  external environment, 56–57, *58–59,* 60–65, *68*
  Five Forces model of competition
    bargaining power of buyers, 66–67
    bargaining power of suppliers, 65–66
    intensity of rivalry, 60–62
    overview, 56–57, *57,* 60
    threat of new entrants, 62–64
    threat of substitutes, 64–65
  future trends and directions, 542–544
  industry structure, 60
  profitability, 57, *58–59*
Industry boundaries, blurring of, 542–543
Industry dynamics, understanding, 85–87
Industry globalization drivers
  competitive, 77–78
  cost, 73–75
  government, 75–77
  market, 72–73
  overview, 71, *79*
  understanding, 27
Industry structure, 60
Information Age, 109–110
InnoCentive, 333–334
Innovation. *See also* Digitally based economy;
    Technology
  Apple Computers, 313–314
  closed, 333–334
  continuous, 334–335
  corporate culture and, 342–343, *344–345,* 345
  corporate leaders' thoughts on, *344*
  creative organization and, development of, 328, *328*
  defining, 327
  disruptive, 334–335
  lab, successful, 345, *346*
  in life cycle, 346–348
  managing, 342, *343*
  market-based, 327–328
  myths, 338, *340*
  open, 333–334
  overview, 34, 348–349
  people-centric roles for
    building persona, 342
    learning persona, 341–342
    organizing persona, 342
  product, 328–329

Innovation *(continued)*
  reasons for, 314–315, *315*
  S-shaped curve, 331, 335–336, *336*
  Samsung, 351–356
  services, 329–330
  strategic
    at all stages of life cycle, 346–348, *347*
    borrowing good ideas, 338–339
    corporate culture, building corporate, 342–343,
      344–345, 346
    defining, 338
    forgetting old ideas, 338
    institutionalizing activities that generate, 341–342
    learning new ideas, 339
    leveraging, 314–315, *315*
    overview, 338
    renewal of organization, 339, 341
    transformation of organization, 339, 341
  top companies (2005), 338, *340*
  types, 327–331
  zones, 346–348
Inpatriates, 397, *397*
Integrating purchasing, 235
Intellectual intelligence, 431
Intellectual property rights, 190
Intelligence, 431
Intensity of rivalry, 60–62
Interconnectedness, 254–255
Interdependence, 77, 255
Internal consistency, 378
Internal environment. *See* Business model
Internalization, 388–389
Internalization-specific advantages, 149–150
International Accounting Standards (IAS), 496
International Business Machines (IBM), 117, 146, 333
International development. *See* Levels of
    internationalization
International groups and divisions, 388
International growth trajectories, 546–547
International marketing. *See* Strategic positioning
International product life cycle, 153
International purchasing, 234
International Warehouse and Distribution Solutions
    (IWDS), 404–409
Internationalization, level of, 290–291
Internet, 80
Inventory turnover, 477
Investing activities, 470, *494*
Investments, 466

Japan, 236, 437, 440, 547

JetBlue Airways, 442
Joint-stock charted company, 18
Joint venture (JV), 196–197, 275–276, *281, 282,*
    284–285, 302–303. *See also* Strategic alliances
Jollibee, 162–163, *162,* 388
Just-in-time (JIT) management, 230–231

Kaizen system, 343
Kenya Airways, 52, *53*
Kinney, 460
Kiva.org, *118*
Knowledge-based economy, 316–317. *See also*
    Digitally based economy
Knowledge-based services, 8
Knowledge imperative, 29–30
Komatsu Ltd., 77, 122–123, *122,* 153, 166–169, *168,*
    348
Korn/Ferry International, *430*

Lead countries, 73, 277
Learning dynamics, 342
Learning experience effects, 63
Learning new ideas, 339
Learning persona, 341–342
Less developed countries (LDCs), 168
Levels of internationalization
    defining, 290–291
    internalization, 388–389
    international groups and divisions, 388
    local export mode, 386–387
    overview, 384–386
    partnering mode, 387
    transnational form, 389–390
Levi's, 72
Li & Fung, 230
Liabilities, 466–467
Liberalism, 19
Licensing, 195
Life cycle of product, 153
Liquidity of firm, 467
Liquidity/leverage ratios, 473
Location-specific advantages, 150
Locked-in market, 326
Logistical alliances, 275
Logitech, 208–209
London Stock Exchange, 497
Long-term assets, 467–468
Long-term debt, 466
Long-term investments, 466
Long-term liabilities, 467

Machicado, Jorge, 240–241
Macro-organizational risks, 157
Macroenvironmental analysis
    demographics, 53–54
    economic trends, 52–53
    overview, 50–51
    political/legal environment, 51–52
    sociocultural environment, 54, *55,* 56
    technological environment, 54
Make-or-buy decision, 246–249, 251
Management. *See also* Global strategic management;
    Human resource management (HRM); Strategic
    alliances
    cross-cultural skills, building, *425,* 439–443
    culture and
        dimensions of culture, 424, *425,* 426–427, *426*
        extension to management practices, 422–424
        overview, 419–421, *420*
        silent language, 421–422
    ethnocentrism and, 436–439, *438*
    global mindset traits and, 429–431, *429, 430, 432,*
        435, 436
    global sourcing and, 241
    globalization and
        challenges for, 7–9
        implications for, 26–28
    of innovation, 342, *343*
    intelligence of, 431
    just-in-time, 230–231
    of means, *493*
    traits, present and future, *429,* 539
Market analysis, 526–527, *526, 528, 529,* 530
Market-based innovation, 327–328
Market/book ratios, 483
Market globalization drivers, 72–73. *See also* Global
    marketing
Market niches, 117, *118*
Market share, 481
Market valuation, 488, *489–490*
Marketing to masses, 209, *210–211*
Marketing orientation, 188, *189*
Marketing ratios, 481–482, *482*
Marketing regulations, 76
Mary Kay Cosmetics, 204
Masculinity, 427
Mass customization, 522, *523*
Materiality, 465
Matsushita, 102, 154, 434
McDonald's, 11, 74, 204, 211–212
McKinsey and Company, 114
McKinsey Global Institute (MGI), 246

Measurability, 254
Mercantilism, 18
Mercedes-Benz, 29, 102
Metcalf's law, 319–321, *320*
Microsoft, 81, 185–186, 190, 241, 471
Migrations, 257–258, *259*
Miller Brewer Company, 102
Mindset, 418. *See also* Global mindset
MindTree Consulting, 450–455
Ministry of International Trade and Industry (MITI),
    236
MIT Industrial Performance Center Globalization
    Team, 547
Mixed/matrix structures, 389
Mobile ESPN, *118*
Model T, 20, 321
Moore's law, 317–319, *318,* 321
Moral hazard, 248
Motorola, 345
Multidomestic industries, 145, 153–155, *155*
Multilocal strategy, 154
Multinationals, 12, 28, 150, *151–152,* 368
Multiple suppliers sourcing, 229–230
Mutual interdependence, 255
MVA (market value added), 472, 484–485

Nanotechnology, 47–49
Napster, 111
National alliances, *287*
National culture, 419
Natural capitalism, 551
Negotiation skills, 240–241
Nenita dolls, 143–144
Netflix, *344*
Netscape, 24
Network effects, 319
Networking, 110–111
Neutral culture, 422
Neutrality, 465
New and emerging organizational structures, 390,
    391–392
New entrants, threat of, 62–64
New technologies, 317–318
New United Motor Manufacturing (NUMMI), 279,
    303–307
New York Times, 338–339
Newcomb, Theodore M., 417
Nike Corporation, 72, 79, 102, 115, *115,* 188, 369,
    433
95:95:95: rule, 454
Nokia, 113, 329, 364–366, 496, 543

Noncomplementary overlap, 284
Noncore activities, 245
Noncore competencies, 250
Nonoperating items, 470
Nontechnological joint ventures, 284–285
North Atlantic Treaty Organization (NATO), 211
Notes payable (NP), 466
NPV (net present value), 490–491, 507
Nukak-Makú, 11, *12*
Nutraceutical products, *118*
Nutrasweet, 127

Online micro-financing, *118*
Open innovation, 333–334
Open-source movement, 24
Operating activities, 470
Operating expenses, 469
Operational Excellence Zone, 346
Organization for Economic Cooperation and
    Development (OECD), 12
Organizational age, 286
Organizational fit, 289–290
Organizational size of firms, 285
Organizational structures, basic, 373, *374–375*
Organizing persona, 342
"Out-of-the-box" thinking, 343, *344–345*
Outsourcing
    activities for, 245
    decision, examining, 255, 257–260
    defining, 245
    framework for analysis of, 252–255
    global sourcing to, 245–246
    hidden costs of, *247*
    from "make-or-buy" to strategic transformation,
        246–249, 251
    perspectives on, *246*
    reasons for, *248*
    role playing, 263
    stages of, *249*
    subcontracting and, 248–249
Outsourcing Index, 255, *256*
Overlap, complementary versus noncomplementary,
    284
Overseas Private Investment Corporation (OPIC), 192
Owner's equity, 466
Ownership-specific advantages, 149

Parallel dependence relationships, 295–296
Particularism, 422
Partnering and partnerships, 382. *See also* Strategic
    alliances

Payables period, 478
Peet's Coffee, 124–126, *125*
Pepsi, 62, 127, 201, 203
Peripheral activities, 245
Personalized experience, 322
Personalized medicine, 522, *523*
PEST (political-economic-social-technological)
    analysis, 50, 56, *56*, 81, 84
Pharmaceutical industry, 379, *380–381*
Philips, 154, 410–412
Piatco, *192*
Pixar-Disney partnership, 114, 276
Plan of action, 101
Plant, property, and equipment (PPE), 466, 491
Political/legal environment, 51–52
Political risks, 157
Polycentric approach, 394–395, *394*
Pooled interdependence, 255
Positioning, 212
Poverty, 437–438, 541–542
Poverty trap, 541–542
Power distance, 424
Price/earning ratios, 483
Pricing, 209, 211, 214–217
Pricing collaborations, 275
Prisoner's Dilemma, 123–126, *124*
Process innovation, 330–331
Processes, 373, 376
Processual school of strategy, *100–101*
Procter & Gamble (P&G), 73, 153, 157, 173, 217, 339,
    341, 385, 388, 433
Product
  awareness, 208–209
  development costs, 75
  diversification, 160
  innovation, 328–329, *344*
  positioning, 209, 211
  pricing, 209, 211
  service alliances, 275
Product Leadership Zone, 346
Production orientation, 188, *189*
Productivity paradox, 548
Professional culture, 419
Profit Impact of Marketing Strategy (PIMS),
    481
Profit and loss report, 468–470, *469*
Profits, 469, 473–474, *474*, 476
Promotional alliances, 275
Prosper.com, 204
Purchasing, 228–229, 234–235, 238–239
PVA (people value added), 472, *473*

Quantum, 196
QWERTY format, 326

Radio frequency identification (RFID), 540–541
Rational/classical school of strategy, *100*
Regulatory policies, 64, 76, 80–81
Relational skills, 548
Relationship-based enterprise, 299
Relative market share, 481
Relevance, 465
Reliability, 465
Renewal of organization, 339, 341
Representational faithfulness, 465
Research and development alliances, 275
Resource-based theory, 106, *106*
Resource risks, 157
Reverse auction, 233
Risk analysis, political/economic, 189–193, *192, 193*
Rivalry, 60–62, 283
ROA (return on assets), 476
ROE (return on equity), 464, 473–474, *475*, 476,
    480–484
Role playing of outsourcing, 263
RONA (return on net assets), 482–483
Royal Ahold, *462*

S-shaped innovation curve, 331, 335–336, *336*
Salomon Brothers, 112
Samsung, 73, 107, 212, 351–356
Sarbanes-Oxley Act (2002), 550
Scania, *493*
Scientific management, 20
Scope economies, 292
Second phase of globalization (1800–1931), *17*, 18–20
Securities and Exchange Commission (SEC), 497
Segmentation, 99
SEMATECH, 280
Semiconductor industry, 87–90
Sense-and-response trend, 540–541
Sequential games, 120–124, *122*
Sequential interdependence, 255
Sequential process, 331
Serial dependence relationships, 295
Service recovery, 441–442
Services, 78–80
Sherman Act (1890), 80
Silent language, 421–422
"Silo" thinking, 433
Simultaneous games, 120–121, 124–126, *125*
Single sourcing, 230–232
Six Sigma, 341

SK Global, *462*
Social capital, 548
Sociocultural environment, 54, *55, 56*
Sourcing partners, 235–236, *238*
South Korea, 11–12, 53, 111, *462*
Southwest Airlines, 255
Spatial connectedness, 24
Specialization, 253–254
Specific culture, 423
Spider web chart, 444, *446*
Stage-of-growth design principle, 366, 380–382
Standard enterprise logic, 323
Standardization, 213–214
Starbucks Corporation, 29, 37–40, 124–126, *125*
Statement of cash flow, 470–471, *471*
Stern, Stewart & Co., 484–485
Stickiness factor, 337
Stockholders' equity, 468
Strategic alliances
  benefits of, 276–277
  building, 241
  corporate culture and, 289–290
  DaimlerChrysler, 272
  defining, 273–276
  dependence and, 295–296, *296*
  emerging, 299–300
  failure of, causes
    cross-cultural differences, 282–283
    organizational structures and processes, 285–286
    overview, 282–283
    rivalry, 283–285
  Fuji Xerox, 271–272
  as global sourcing success factor, 241
  learning trajectories, 292–293
  lessons, 272–273
  leveraging, *274*
  management
    appropriate processes over course of alliance, 291–292
    competitive intensity, 291
    controls and mechanisms, designing, 297–299, *300*
    cultural fit, 290
    internationalization, 290–291
    learning trajectories, 292–293
    organizational fit, 289–290
    partner selection, 286–288
    scope of economies, 292
    strategic fit, 288–289
    transparency, fostering, 293–296, *295*
    trust, building, 297
  in new competitive landscape, 277, *278, 279*–280

Strategic alliances *(continued)*
  overview, 34, 300–301
  reasons for, 273
  risks of, 280, *281*
  values and goals, 291–292, *292*
Strategic choices, 144
Strategic fit, 288–289
Strategic focus, 117, *118*
Strategic implementation
  applying, 365, *366*
  design principles
    changing, 384, *385*
    congruency/fit, 376–379, 403
    organizational framework, 382–384; *383*
    stage-of-growth, 380–382
  design variables
    culture, 376, *377*
    formal structure, 372–373
    individuals, 371–372
    overview, 369, *370, 379*
    processes, 373, 376
    strategy, 369, *370,* 371
    tasks, 369, *370,* 371
  failure of, 367–368, *367*
  financial analysis in, 461, *462, 463*–464, *463*
  financial performance measures, 463, *463*
  geopolitical uncertainty and, 368–369
  global complexity and, 368
  global mindset and, 417–419, *418*
  global organization, designing
    internalization level, 388–389
    international groups and divisions level, 388
    local/export mode level, 386–387
    new and emerging organization structures, 390, *391–392*
    overview, 384–386
    partnering mode level, 387
    transnational form level, 389–390
  globalization of consumers and, 368
  human resource management and, 365, 390, 392–398
  importance of, 367–368
  new organizational structures, 390, *391–392*
  Nokia, 364–366
  organizational structure and, *374–375*
  overview, 34, 398–401
  pharmaceutical industry and, 379, *380–381*
  principles, 368–369
  reasons for, 365–366
Strategic importance of the market, 207
Strategic innovation. *See* Innovation

Strategic learning, 119
Strategic objectives, 156, 471–472
Strategic outsourcing. *See* Outsourcing
Strategic perspective, 7
Strategic platforms versus firms, 545–546
Strategic positioning. *See also* Foreign direct
    investment (FDI)
  in global context
    Dell Computers, 169–174, *170, 171*
    E-LOAN, 159–163, *161*
    Komatsu Ltd., 166–169, *168*
    overview, *145,* 158–159
    Wal-Mart, 163–166, *164, 165*
  global and multidomestic industries, 153–155, *155*
  importance of, 144–146
  industry analysis, 177
  Nenita dolls, 143–144
  overview, 33–34, 174–175
Strategic profit model, 473, *474*
Strategic transformation, 250, 252
Strategy. *See also* Global strategy; Strategic
    implementation
  business model and, 97–98, *98*
  core-formula, 166
  country-centered, 161
  defining, 98–103, 368–369, *370, 371*
  entry to target markets, 219
  generic, 117, *117*
  incremental, 169
  low-cost producer, 160
  metaschools of, 99, *100–101*
  multilocal, 154
  plan of action and, 101
  sustainability of business, 485–488, *489–490*
Subcontracting, 248–249
Substitutes, threat of, 64–65
Sun Microsystems, 241
Suppliers, 65–66, 244
Supply chain processes and practices, 238–239
Sustainability of business strategy, 485–488,
    489–490
Sustainable gap, 103
Sustainable growth rate, 488
Sustaining technologies, 334
Swedish GAAP, 496
Switching costs, 61, 63
SWOT (strengths-weaknesses-opportunities-threats),
    107, *108,* 524–525, *526*
System-based approach, 395–396
Systemic school of strategy, *101*
Systems engineering, 20

Tacit knowledge, 297–298
Tacit specialization, 253–254
Tae Kuk, 355–356
Tae-won, Chey, *462*
Taiwan, 236, *237*
Targeted markets, 211–214. *See also* Entry to target
    markets
Tasks and strategic implementation, 369, *370, 371*
Tata International, 276
Tata Motors Ltd., 102
Technological environment, 54
Technological joint ventures, 284–285
Technology. *See also* Digitally based economy;
    Innovation
  adoption life cycle, 335–337, *336,* 346–348, *347*
  Africa and, *25*
  digitally based, 7–8
  discontinuities, 540–541
  disruptive, 334–335
  exchanging information, 297–298
  fast-changing, 75
  Information Age, 109–110
  Internet, 80
  nanotechnology, 47–49
    new, 317
  product innovation and, *344*
  semiconductor industry, 87–90
  standards, compatible, 76
  sustaining, 334
Technology Adoption Life Cycle, 335–337, *336,*
    346–348, *347*
Teijin Limited, 343
Theorization, 298
Theory of comparative advantage, 18
Third phase of globalization (1970–2000), *17,* 20–23,
    21, 22, 23
Thought experiment, 37
Threat of new entrants, 62–64
Threat of substitutes, 64–65
Time and culture, 423
Timeliness, 465
Tipping tendencies, 337
Total Quality Management (TQM), 272
TOWS (threats-opportunities-weaknesses-strengths),
    107
Toyota Motor Corp., 97, 279, 303–307, 330–331, 343,
    345, *493*
Trade barriers, 150, 152
Trade, origins of, 16
Trade policies, 75–76
Transactional economics, 323

Transferable marketing, 73
Transformation of organization, 339, 341
Transformation, strategic, 250, 252
Transnational organization, 28, 389–390
Transparency, fostering, 293–297, *295*
Transportation costs, 150
Triobriand Islanders, 440
Trompenaars, Fons, 422–424, 442
Trust, building, 297
Turnkey projects, 194–196
Turnover/efficiency ratios, 473, 476–479

Uncertainty avoidance, 424
Unilever, 220–223, 233
Universalism, 422
Upin, Eric, 204
U.S. Department of Justice, 80
U.S. GAAP, 464–466, 496–497

Valuation, 490–492
Value added, 108–109, 472
Value investing, *494*
Value net, 69, *70*
Value partnership, 113–115, *115*

Value problem, 482–484
Value proposition, 103, 105–106, *105,* 524, *525*
Value realization, 323
Variable costs, 476
Verifiability, 465
Vertical foreign direct investment, 146
Volkswagen, 62, 240
Volume operations, 346

Wal-Mart, 29, 72, 74, 102–103, 163–166, *164, 165,* 177–181, 466, *467,* 469–470, *469, 471,* 473–474, *475,* 476–488, *482,* 496, 546
Walt Disney Company, 107, 132–137, 342, 546
Wholly owned operation, 197
Wiggins, Robert, 443
Wintel, 69, *69*
Woolworth, 460–461
Working capital, 467
World Bank, 541
World Bank Study (2001), 543

Yahoo, 24

Zara, 547

About the Authors

Gerardo R. Ungson is the Y.F. Chang Endowed Chair and Professor of International Business, San Francisco State University. He has taught at the University of Oregon and Pennsylvania State University, and was a visiting professor at the Amos Tuck School of Business, Dartmouth College; the University of California–Berkeley; the International University of Japan; and Nijenrode, Netherlands School of Business. His current research covers strategic alliances, global strategies, and the community empowerment in developing countries. He has published numerous journal articles and has coauthored five books: *Decision Making: An Interdisciplinary Inquiry* (with Daniel Braunstein), *Managing Effective Organizations* (with Richard Steers and Richard Mowday), *Chaebol: Korea's New Industrial Might* (with Richard Steers and Y.K. Kim), *Korean Enterprise: The Quest for Globalization* (with Richard Steers and Seung Ho Park), and *Engines for Prosperity: New Templates for the Information Age* (with John Trudel). He has served on the editorial review board of the *Academy of Management Review,* and serves on the editorial board of *Journal of High Technology.* He is the recipient of numerous teaching excellence awards, and is on the faculty of executive management programs in Asia and in Europe. He received his B.S. from Atenco de Manila University and his M.B.A. and Ph.D. from Pennsylvania State University in 1978.

Yim-Yu Wong is Professor of International Business at the College of Business, San Francisco State University. She has taught at Indiana State University and has been visiting professor at the China MBA program of the Hong Kong Polytechnic University, the MBA program at Huazhong University of Science and Technology, and Group Ecole Superieure de Commerce de Tours. She has published articles in *Business Horizons, Management and Organization Review, Asia Pacific Journal of Management, Business Forum, Multinational Business Reviews, S.A.M. Advanced Management Journal,* and *Business and the Contemporary World.* Her research areas include global strategy, strategic management planning, diversification and firm performances, cultural impacts in the workplace, knowledge transfer, and business management and strategies in China. She holds a Ph.D. from the University of Nebraska–Lincoln.